LOCAL AREA NETWORKS

A BUSINESS-ORIENTED APPROACH

Second Edition

JAMES E. GOLDMAN
PHILLIP T. RAWLES

Purdue University

John Wiley & Sons, Inc.

New York • Chichester • Weinheim • Brisbane • Singapore • Toronto

ACQUISITIONS EDITOR	Beth Lang Golub
ASSISTANT EDITOR	Samantha Alducin
MARKETING MANAGER	Jessica Garcia
SENIOR PRODUCTION EDITOR	Patricia McFadden
DESIGN DIRECTOR	Madelyn Lesure
ILLUSTRATOR	Curtis A. Snyder
PRODUCTION MANAGEMENT	Hermitage Publishing Services

This book was set in 10/12 Palatino by Hermitage Publishing Services and printed and bound by R. R. Donnelley & Sons. The cover was printed by Phoenix Color.

This book is printed on acid-free paper. ⊗

ISBN 0-471-33047-7

Printed in the United States of America

10 9 8 7 6 5 4 3

James E. Goldman: To Susan, Eric, and Grant

Phillip T. Rawles: To Cheri

PREFACE

▪ THE NEED FOR THIS BOOK

The field of information systems has undergone a major paradigm shift from mainframe-oriented, hierarchical information systems architectures to distributed, LAN-based client-server information systems architectures. However, this transition is far from complete as information systems architectures continue to evolve to include seamless integration with world wide web and Internet technologies, as well as more transparent interoperability with legacy or mainframe systems. Today's resultant information systems architecture is comprised of a complicated array of interacting technologies combining elements of client-server, web-based, Internet, intranet, legacy applications, and database management systems. However, the Local Area Network is the key building block to all of these interacting technologies.

Designing, implementing, and managing Local Area Networks require sophisticated business-oriented analysis, design, and problem-solving skills. Furthermore, the collaborative computing and multimedia applications that are likely to be executed on these information systems are highly dependent on properly designed networks for successful delivery of interactive content. The interdependency of application and network development for successful deployment of distributed information systems is all too often overlooked by information systems professionals.

In order to effectively design today's highly integrated, distributed local area networks, a comprehensive systems engineering approach that incorporates business analysis, application development, database systems integration, distributed network design, and structured technology analysis is required. Such a business-first, technology-last, top-down model was introduced in *Applied Data Communications: A Business-Oriented Approach* by James E. Goldman of Purdue University.

Analyzing and designing Local Area Networks was introduced in the first edition of *Local Area Networks*. Unlike many of the currently available books and texts on Local Area Networks that seem to be either too broadly focused and conceptual or too narrowly focused and technical, this text struck a balance between the two extremes while offering the reader a structured approach to local area network analysis and design from initial business considerations through final technology choices.

■ NEW TO THE SECOND EDITION

The authors have tried to improve upon the first edition without losing any of the previously mentioned positive attributes of that text. Among the changes to be found in the second edition are the following:

- More emphasis on organizing the entire text according to the OSI 7 layer model

- All new case studies in every chapter.

- Created a dedicated LAN protocol chapter (Chapter 4) before going into network operating system specifics in Chapters 5 through 8

- Increased the technical depth as well as breadth of coverage throughout the text

- Added a dedicated chapter on Network Design using TCP/IP (Chapter 12)

- Expanded coverage of network security architecture design (Chapter 16)

- Created a new chapter on Middleware (Chapter 9)

- Background chapters on client and server hardware and software have been included on a supplementary CD. These chapters are from *Client Server Information Systems: A Business Oriented Approach* (1999, John Wiley & Sons)

■ DESCRIPTION

Local Area Networks: A Business-Oriented Approach, Second Edition provides a thorough explanation of the analysis, design, integration, and technology choices involved with deploying effective local area networks and Internetworks.

The text is flexibly organized to cater to a variety of course orientations. The general organization and key features of the text will be as follows:

- The text is divided into four major sections to maximize flexible use by a wide variety of course orientations:

  Part 1: Local Area Network Infrastructure

  Part 2: Local Area Network Software

  Part 3: Local Area Network Connectivity

  Part 4: Local Area Network Administration

- There are sixteen chapters of manageable length that allow instructors to pick and choose chapters as appropriate for course content, focus, length, and intended audience.

- It is written in a logical, problem-solving style applauded by both students and faculty from academia and industry.

- The text material is organized into overall architecture or models. By providing students with the "big picture" first, the text assists students in understanding how particular individual topics relate to other topics and to the overall scheme of things.

- The text stresses analytical questioning and problem solving skills as being key to successful design of client-server information systems.

- The text provides working models into which students can organize their problem solving approach. These models are reinforced and used throughout the text. Examples include:

  Top Down Model

  TCP/IP Model

  OSI Model

- Business cases reprinted from professional periodicals are included in each chapter. Questions guide students toward development of analytical skills and business-oriented client-server information systems design capabilities.

- The text equips students with real world skills. In a fashion similar to Professor Goldman's previous texts, *Local Area Networks: A Business-Oriented Approach* teaches students how to *do* LAN design rather than merely read about it.

■ APPROACH

The text follows the top down model used in Professor Goldman's previous textbooks, examining the many options, standards, interfaces, implications, advantages, and disadvantages in each of the top down model's five layers:

     Business

     Application

     Data

     Network

     Technology

Concept roadmaps are located throughout the text stressing the relationship between chapters and to an overall LAN architecture, as well as between topics within chapters. Each chapter begins with an outline of new concepts introduced, previous concepts reinforced, and the learning objectives for that chapter. Section and paragraph headings help students to organize and identify key concepts introduced in each chapter. End of chapter material includes: chapter summaries, key term listings, abundant review questions, as well as activities and problems for active student learning. As previously mentioned, business cases from professional periodicals are reprinted at the close of each chapter with associated analysis questions to be answered by students or used as the basis for classroom discussion. A liberal use of clear, concise diagrams adds to the usability of the text and the understanding of the students.

▨ TARGET AUDIENCES/COURSES

Due to the modular nature of this text, a variety of audiences/courses could be well served. Among the courses as potential adoptees of this text are the following:

- An introductory level course on local area networks. The practical nature of the text would make this book appealing as well as its broad coverage and architectural orientation. Advanced sections of the text could be easily avoided.

- A junior level course on LAN design and implementation in either a lecture only or lab/lecture format. Such a course would be part of a concentration in data communications and networking or telecommunications.

- As client/server information systems have taken on strategic importance to businesses, and local area networks are no longer just departmental computing solutions, the text may also have appeal in those M.B.A. programs offering a concentration in M.I.S. The managerial perspective sections and business cases would have particular appeal to this potential audience.

▨ SPECIAL FEATURES

Although some of these features have been mentioned previously, they are repeated here to stress the unique nature of this text as a purveyor of practical, business-oriented local area network analysis skills and problem solving abilities rather than a mere collection of concepts and facts.

- A modular approach allows flexible use of text to fit instructor and course needs.

- Real business case studies stressing the business impact of client/server architectures integrated with web, Internet, and legacy application technologies assist students in sharpening their analysis and problem solving skills. Directed questions accompanying each case stimulate classroom discussion as well.

- "In Sharper Focus" sections highlight more detailed, more advanced, or background information for concepts introduced within a chapter. These sections can be included or excluded at the instructor's discretion.

- "Managerial Perspective" sections take a "bottom-line" approach to client server information systems analysis and design. The potential impact of management decisions in a variety of situations are highlighted in these sections which may be of particular interest to M.B.A. audiences.

- Applied Problem Solving sections of chapters focusing on the use of analytical models for Applied Problem Solving activities are highlighted for the benefit of both instructors and students. By stressing problem solving activities, students can be assured of learning how to *do* local area network analysis and design.

- Emphasizing the practical nature of the text, instances of practical advice or warnings are highlighted in order to call the reader's attention to important but often overlooked information.

- The OSI (Open Systems Interconnection) Model is used throughout the text as an analysis tool for student problem solving and design opportunities.

▦ SUPPLEMENTS

The CD-based *Instructor's Resource Guide* will contain thorough answers to all review questions featured at the end of each chapter in the text. In addition, solutions to case study questions will be provided. An abundant selection of additional questions in a variety of formats will be provided for each chapter. Finally, all illustrations in PowerPoint 97 format will be provided on the CD in order to expedite the production of transparencies and class notes to accompany the text.

ABOUT THE AUTHORS

JAMES E. GOLDMAN

James E. Goldman is currently Professor of Computer Information Systems and Assistant Department Head for Telecommunications and Networking in the nationally prominent Department of Computer Technology at Purdue University. An award winning teacher, Professor Goldman is the only faculty member in the history of the School of Technology to win all three school-level teaching awards: The James G. Dwyer Outstanding Teacher Award, the School of Technology Outstanding Non-Tenured Faculty Award, and the School of Technology Tenured Faculty Award, as well as the Purdue University Charles B. Murphy Award for Outstanding Undergraduate Teaching.

Professor Goldman is the author of *Applied Data Communications: A Business Oriented Approach* (third edition under development), a first-of-its-kind text that took a process-oriented, business-first, problem-solving approach to data communications education. This text has been adopted around the world at all levels of higher and professional educational institutions. *Client/Server Information Systems: A Business Oriented Approach* was published in 1998 with fellow Purdue professors Phil Rawles and Julie Mariga. Professor Goldman is Executive Vice President of Dynamic Systems (*www.dssg.com*), a technology solutions provider to Fortune 100 global corporations, and is a MCSE (Microsoft Certified Systems Engineer).

PHILLIP T. RAWLES

Phillip T. Rawles is an Assistant Professor of Computer Information Systems and Technology at Purdue University in West Lafayette, Indiana. Professor Rawles' primary areas of interest are network systems administration, enterprise network management, and network simulation and optimization. In three semesters at Purdue, Professor Rawles has developed or significantly re-developed courses in local area networking, systems administration, and enterprise network management.

Professor Rawles is a contributing author to *High-Performance Networking Unleashed* (1997, SAMS, IN.) and is co-author of *Client/Server Information Systems: A Business Oriented Approach* (1999, John Wiley & Sons, NY) Professor Rawles maintains an active consulting practice, is a MCSE (Microsoft Certified Systems Engineer), and holds Master of Technology and Bachelor of Computer Integrated Manufacturing Technology degrees from Purdue University.

ACKNOWLEDGMENTS

We are indebted to a number of people whose efforts were crucial in the development of this book.

For the outstanding quality illustrations which appear in the book as well as for his unwavering support, we'd like to thank Curt Snyder, our wonderful and talented illustrator.

For their collaborative efforts in turning a manuscript into a professional published book, we'd like to thank the following professionals at John Wiley & Sons: Beth Golub, Acquisitions Editor, Samantha Alducin, Assistant Editor, Madelyn Lesure, Design Director, Patricia McFadden, Senior Production Editor, and the Staff at Hermitage Publishing Services.

Reviewers

A special debt of gratitude is owed to the professionals who were kind enough to review the manuscript of this book prior to publication. It is through your effort that an accurate text of high quality can be produced.

Russell Albright, City University, WA
Ray J. Blankenship, Marshal University
Gregory B. Brewster, DePaul University
Gerald C. Canfield, University of Maryland, Baltimore County
Lauren Eder, Rider University
Coomaraswamy Gopinath, Suffolk Community College
Thomas Gorecki, Charles County Community College
Russell Jones, Arkansas State University
Robert E. Morris, DeVry Institute of Technology, GA
Sharon W. Tabor, Boise State University
Jeffrey M. Whitmer, Indiana University

CONTENTS

CHAPTER 14   REMOTE ACCESS AND WIRELESS NETWORKING   **639**

LOCAL AREA NETWORK INFRASTRUCTURE

Part 1 of the text provides vital background information that forms the foundation for much of the remainder of the book. In Chapter 1, Local Area Networks: A Business Perspective, the reader is introduced to the what, how, and why of local area networking. In addition, key challenges and solutions to effective LAN analysis, design, and implementation are introduced.

Chapter 2, Local Area Network Architectures, more deeply explores the underlying local area network architectures that allow hardware and software technologies to transparently interact. In this chapter, the components of a network architecture will first be explored, followed by comparative evaluations of the numerous network architectures either currently available or emerging into the networking marketplace.

Local Area Network Hardware, Chapter 3, focuses on the hardware technology including wiring centers, network interface cards, and media that must be employed to implement a given network architecture.

Having covered the alternatives for LAN connectivity on OSI Model Layers 1 and 2 in the first three chapters, Chapter 4 introduces the communications protocols that work on OSI Model layers 3 thru 7. Once the generalized behavior of networking protocols is understood from this chapter, the second part of the text introduces the differences between specific network operating system implementations.

CHAPTER 1

LOCAL AREA NETWORKS: A BUSINESS PERSPECTIVE

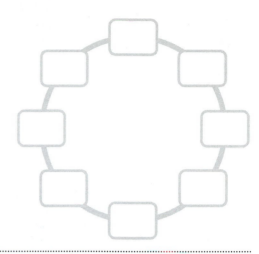

Concepts Introduced

Local Area Networks	Top-Down Model
OSI 7 Layer Model	Network Interface Cards
Internet Suite of Protocols Model	Network Operating Systems
I-P-O Model	Protocols and Compatibility
Business-Oriented LAN Analysis	Logical Network Design

OBJECTIVES

After mastering the material in this chapter you should:

1. Understand what a Local Area Network is

2. Understand how hardware and software technology are combined to implement a LAN

3. Understand the business needs and functional requirements fulfilled by a LAN

4. Understand the key business driven characteristics of a LAN

5. Understand the use of the top-down model in business-oriented LAN analysis

6. Understand the use of the OSI model and other models in LAN connectivity analysis

■ WHAT IS A LOCAL AREA NETWORK?

A **Local Area Network (LAN)** is a combination of hardware and software technology that allows computers to share a variety of resources such as:

- printers and other peripheral devices

- data

- application programs

- storage devices

LANs also allow messages to be sent between attached computers thereby enabling users to work together electronically in a process often referred to as collaborative computing. The local nature of a local area network is a relative rather than absolute concept. There is no hard and fast rule or definition as to the geographic limitations of a network that qualifies to be called a local area network. In general, LANs are confined to an area no larger than a single building or a small group of buildings.

LANs can be extended by connecting to other similar or dissimilar LANs, to remote users, or to mainframe computers. This process is generally referred to as LAN connectivity and is covered in-depth in Part Three of the text. LANs of a particular company can be connected to the LANs of trading partners such as vendors and customers. These trading partners may be located in the same town or around the globe. Arrangements linking these trading partners are commonly referred to as enterprise networks. These enterprise networks are created by combining LANs with a variety of Wide Area Network (WAN) services, including the Internet.

Strictly speaking, the computers themselves are not part of the LAN. In other words, a single user could be productive on a stand-alone personal computer (PC). However, in order to share information, resources, or messages with other users and their computers, a LAN must be implemented to connect these computers. The LAN is the combination of technology that allows computers and their users to interact. Figure 1-1 provides a conceptual illustration of a LAN.

▦ HOW IS A LOCAL AREA NETWORK IMPLEMENTED?

Whereas most of the remainder of the text is dedicated to answering the previous question, the purpose of this section is merely to introduce, in a highly conceptual manner, how a simple LAN is implemented. Complex LAN interconnectivity, LAN remote access, and LAN to Mainframe connectivity are purposefully ignored in this discussion.

To begin with, appropriate networking hardware and software must be added to every computer or shared peripheral device that is to communicate via the local area network. Some type of network media must physically connect the various networked computers and peripheral devices. The various connected computers and peripheral devices will share this media to converse with each other. As a result, LANs are sometimes more specifically referred to as **shared media LANs** or media-sharing LANs. Figure 1-2

BEFORE:

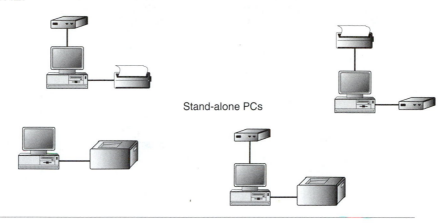

Stand-alone PCs

AFTER:

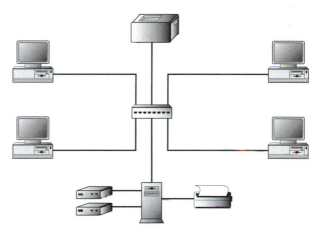

The same PCs with the addition of a Local Area Network (LAN.) A LAN is a combination of hardware and software technology which enables communication and resource sharing among attached computers.

Figure 1-1   What Is a Local Area Network?

provides a highly conceptual view of how a shared media local area network might be implemented

Don't be fooled by the apparent simplicity of Figure 1-2. All of the illustrated networking hardware and software must be compatible not only with the computer or peripheral device in which it is installed, but also with the hardware and software that comprises the LAN itself, and the networking hardware and software installed on all other computers and peripheral

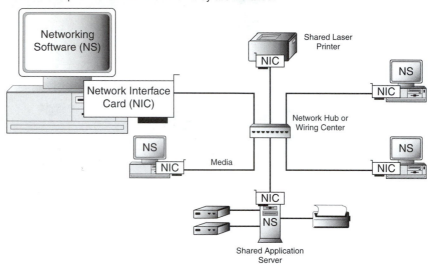

Figure 1-2   How Is a Local Area Network Implemented?

devices attached to the LAN. Compatibility refers to the ability of hardware and software, manufactured by various vendors, to work together successfully without intervention by the end user. In other words, the combination of compatible hardware and software technology is transparent to the end user. Users realize that they are receiving the information they need to do their job effectively. Compatibility among networking hardware and software technology is one of the key challenges to successful LAN analysis and design.

Networking Hardware

Among the types of possible networking hardware employed in implementing a LAN are:

- Network interface cards that must be installed in every linked computer and peripheral device

- Some type of network hub, switch, or wiring center into which the networked devices can be physically linked

Most LAN-connected PCs require specialized network interface cards (NICs). Rather than using NICs, zero-slot LANs use existing serial or parallel ports of personal computers and peripheral devices for communication.

Given the relative slow speeds of the serial and parallel ports as compared to most NICs, Zero-Slot LANs are usually limited to two to four users. Many computers, especially laptops, are now equipped with built-in infrared transmission ports that enable them to transfer data to other similarly equipped computers without the need for additional wires or cables.

The **network interface card** (or adapter) is appropriately named. Its job is to provide a transparent interface between the shared media of the LAN and the computer into which it is physically installed. The NIC takes messages which the computer directs it to send to other LAN attached computers or devices and formats those messages in a manner appropriate for transport over the LAN. Conversely, messages arriving from the LAN are reformatted into a form understandable by the local computer. In order to assure compatibility, all hardware and software technology interacting on the LAN must adhere to the same agreed upon message format.

Most LANs now use some type of **hub,** also sometimes known as a LAN switch, wiring hub, or wiring center. The reasons why most LANs use hubs or switches as well as descriptions of LANs that don't use hubs will be explained further in Chapter 2, "Local Area Network Architectures." The hub provides a connecting point through which all attached devices are able to converse with one another. Hubs must be compatible with both the attached media and the NICs which are installed in client PCs.

Networking Software

Among the types of possible networking software employed in implementing a LAN are:

- Software that allows personal computers which are physically attached to the LAN to share networked resources such as printers, data, and applications

- Software that runs on shared network devices such as printers, data storage devices, and application servers which allow them to be shared by multiple LAN-attached users

A stand-alone (not LAN-attached) PC requires software in order to operate. Commonly referred to as the operating system, this software interfaces between application programs such as a word processing program, and the client hardware (CPU, memory, disk drive).

The software that runs on personal computers and allows them to log into a LAN and converse with other LAN-attached devices is sometimes referred to as client software or client network software. A **client** PC is a computer that a user logs into in order to access LAN-attached resources and services. A LAN-attached client PC is sometimes characterized as a service requester. The client network software must be compatible with the network software running on all LAN-attached clients and servers. This compatibility is most easily assured by having both the clients and the servers install the same **network operating system** software. Examples of popular network operating systems are NetWare and Windows NT, now renamed Windows 2000. Local Area Network software will be discussed extensively in Part Two of the text.

Servers such as application servers and print servers are usually dedicated computers accessed only through LAN connections. Although a client could be considered a service requester, servers are characterized as service providers. It would stand to reason that the server's job of trying to fulfill the requests of multiple LAN-attached clients quickly and efficiently is more complicated than a single LAN-attached client making a single request for a service. Therefore, the server version of a particular network operating system is more complex, expensive, and larger than the client version of the same network operating system. Client and server versions of network operating systems are purchased separately. Client licenses are usually purchased in groups (5-user, 25-user, 100-user), whereas most server licenses are purchased individually.

Compatibility is again an issue, because any network operating system must be compatible with the operating system and hardware of the client or server on which it is installed. Additionally, the network operating system software must be able to successfully communicate with the installed network interface card. The specifics of network operating system/network interface card compatibility will be discussed further in Chapter 3, "Local Area Network Hardware." Compatibility issues and analysis in general will be discussed later in this chapter in the section entitled "Introduction to Protocols and Compatibility."

Networking Media

Network media can vary widely depending on required transmission speed and a variety of other factors such as network interface card type, security needs, as well as the physical characteristics of the environment in which the media is to be deployed. Even the air can serve as a LAN media as evidenced by the many wireless LAN alternatives currently available.

LAN media must be installed carefully and according to industry standard specifications. Something as innocent as pulling a cable tie too tightly can wreak havoc on high-speed LAN performance. LAN media must be compatible with network interface cards and hubs or wiring centers. LAN media alternatives and selection criteria will be reviewed in Chapter 2.

Figure 1-3 offers a visual guide to further information on the elements of a LAN discussed in the previous section. Chapters that are more specifically related to client and server hardware and software as opposed to local area network technology are now included on the accompanying CD and are designated as "CD Chapters" in Figure 1-3.

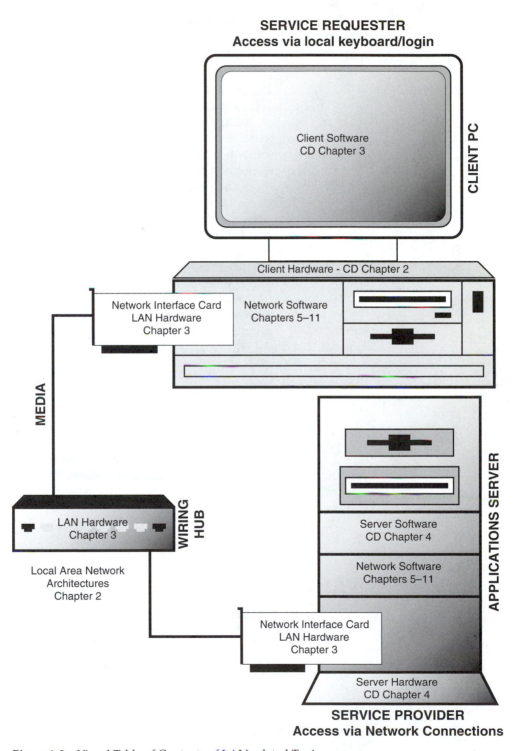

Figure 1-3   Visual Table of Contents of LAN-related Topics

■ WHY ARE LOCAL AREA NETWORKS IMPLEMENTED?

Business Needs—The Underlying Motivation

Business needs as articulated by management are not inherently local area networking business needs, nor do they necessarily imply local area networks as a business solution. Only by analyzing business activities and asking business analysis questions will it be determined whether or not a local area networking solution is appropriate.

Business needs or perspectives provide the motivation for further business network analysis and design. A clear understanding of management's perspectives before beginning any technical analysis will make it easier to sell eventual proposals to management after having completed technical analysis, assured that this proposal will meet management's business objectives. These business needs and perspectives provide the network analyst with a frame of reference within which to conduct research and evaluate options. Figure 1-4 lists a few typical business needs and perspectives that may lead to Local Area Networking solutions.

The previously listed high-level business needs and perspectives are representative examples, typical of the kinds of upper-level management priorities that are often articulated. There are many other possible business needs or perspectives which could have been listed. Business needs and perspectives are dynamic, changing in response to shifting economic and competitive climates, and management teams and philosophies.

In order to make this exercise in business-oriented LAN analysis and design most effective, add business needs and perspectives that management has articulated to you. Management's business needs and perspectives should be clearly documented and understood before beginning network analysis and design. These same needs and perspectives should be referred to on a continual basis as a means of testing the feasibility of various technical networking options.

Although all business needs and perspectives will not necessarily be solved by implementing local area networks, it can be unequivocally stated

---

- Recognition of information as a corporate asset to be leveraged to competitive advantage

---

- Increased data accessibility for faster business decision making

---

- Improved customer service

- Save money, reduce expenses, increase profitability

- Increase productivity

Figure 1-4 Business Needs and Perspectives That May Lead to Local Area Networking Solutions

that local area networks should only be implemented if they meet stated business needs. Furthermore, the analysis and design methodology that leads up to LAN implementation should be of a structured nature and should be documentable in order to justify final conclusions and recommendations. The business needs and perspectives listed in Figure 1-4 will be used as a basis for further business-oriented LAN analysis and design later in this chapter.

Strategic Role of Local Area Networks

As the strategic importance of information as a corporate asset to be leveraged for competitive advantage becomes clearer to senior business management, the key role played by local area networks to deliver that precious information to the right user at the right place and time has become equally clear. Many networking organizations within corporations write a strategic vision statement that clearly and concisely describes the role of the network to the overall organization. An example of such a vision statement might be: "In order to meet the critical business needs of Company X, the information network must be continuously available, reliable, and secure in its mission to deliver the right information to the right user at the right place and time."

Key Business-Driven Characteristics of Local Area Networks

How can such a vision statement be translated into more concrete terms or measurable objectives? Key elements of the network strategy that would support such a lofty vision statement can be identified. Objectives or evaluation criteria for each of these business-driven network characteristics can then be established. Some possible business-driven strategic characteristics of Local Area Networks and the later chapters in which these issues are explained further are listed in Figure 1-5.

Strategic LAN Characteristic	Follow-up Chapter
Availability/Reliability/Fault tolerance/Redundancy	Chapter 15
Responsiveness/Performance	Chapter 15
Connectivity	Chapters 4, 5
Interoperability	Chapters 9, 13
Management	Chapter 15
Security	Chapter 16
Directory Services	Chapter 9, 10

Figure 1-5   Strategic LAN Characteristics

The Importance of Effective LAN Analysis and Design

Given that LANs are implemented to solve real-world business needs as articulated by senior management and that recommended solutions must be both justifiable and documentable, it is essential that LAN analysis and design be conducted in a structured, effective manner. As will be seen in the following section, because of the number of possible different pieces of hardware and software technology manufactured by different vendors that may have to interoperate, effective LAN analysis and design can be an overwhelming task. From a business perspective, senior management wants assurance that money invested in technology will have the desired business impact.

Managerial Perspective

Chief Executive Officers seek business solutions, not technical solutions, and are concerned with ensuring that information technology spending practices are properly aligned with strategic business objectives. Furthermore, senior business executives realize that the most expensive technology is not always the best at delivering business solutions and that, in fact, less expensive technology is often sufficient. Perhaps most important, CEOs are concerned with the inevitable, constant, accelerating rate of technological change. Dealing with this technological change by having a well-defined, strategic technology plan and infrastructure closely aligned with business strategic plans is the best way to prevent technological obsolescence from determining business outcomes.

Many networking organizations now take the time to create formal documents that articulate how the company's business mission is aligned with a clearly articulated network architecture plan. Such a document assures senior management that the network organization is strategically aligned with the corporate business mission while also providing written documentation of acceptable processes and technology to be used by any employee involved with the corporate network infrastructure.

Mapping business strategic plans to technological strategic plans is the purpose of LAN analysis and design. By first understanding the challenges to effective LAN analysis and design, the proposed solutions and resultant methodology should be more meaningful. In the remainder of the chapter, challenges and solutions to effective LAN analysis and design are explained followed by an example of how to get started with business-oriented LAN analysis and design.

■ CHALLENGES AND SOLUTIONS TO EFFECTIVE LAN ANALYSIS, DESIGN, AND IMPLEMENTATION

Challenge: Information Technology Investment vs. Productivity Gains, Ensuring Implemented Technology Meets Business Needs

In the past decade, more than $1 trillion has been invested by business in information technology. Despite this massive investment, carefully conducted research indicates that there has been little if any increase in productivity as a direct result of this investment. In 1990, Paul Strassman wrote in *Business Value of Computers* that there was no relationship between expenses for computers and business profitability. This dilemma, in which investments in technology have no relationship to traditional measurements of productivity such as return on investment, is known as the **productivity paradox.** Erik Brynjolfsson of MIT concluded that the problem lies in the measurements that have been used to gauge the impact of technology investment. In other words, the real return on investment from information technology is not in the incremental cost savings incurred by computerizing manual tasks previously done by humans. Rather, successful information technology investment must be more closely linked to business strategy and organizational structure. More profitable technology investments are achieved by computerizing new tasks and business processes that deliver higher value to the customer, such as better designs, faster delivery, higher quality, greater customization, or better customer service. Clearly, something is wrong with an analysis and design process which recommends technology implementations that fail to meet strategic business objectives.

What are the characteristics required of a business first–technology last analysis and design process with the potential to overcome the productivity paradox?

Solution: The Top-Down Approach

In order to overcome the productivity paradox, a structured methodology must be followed to ensure that the implemented network meets the communications needs of the intended business, organization, or individual.

One such structured methodology is known as the top-down approach. Such an approach can be graphically illustrated in a **top-down model** as shown in Figure 1-6. Using a top-down approach as illustrated in the top-down model is relatively straightforward. Insisting that a top-down approach to network analysis and design is undertaken should ensure that the network design implemented will meet the business needs and objectives that motivated the design in the first place.

This top-down approach requires network analysts to understand business constraints and objectives as well as information systems applications and the data on which those applications run, before considering data communications and networking options.

Notice where the Network Layer occurs in the top-down model. It is no accident that Data Communications and Networking form the foundation of today's sophisticated information systems. A properly designed network supports flexible delivery of data to distributed application programs, allowing businesses to respond quickly to customer needs and rapidly changing market conditions.

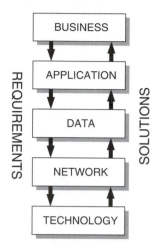

Figure 1-6   The Top-Down Model

■ THE TOP-DOWN MODEL

How does the proper use of the top-down model ensure effective, business-oriented LAN analysis and design? Figure 1-7 lists the analysis processes associated with each layer of the top-down model. One must start with the *business* level objectives. What is the company (organization, individual) trying to accomplish by installing this network? Without a clear understanding of business level objectives it is virtually impossible to configure and implement a successful network. In many cases, firms take this opportunity to critically reexamine their business processes in an analysis methodology known as **business process reengineering** (BPR). In what is perhaps the most famous book on BPR, *Reengineering the Corporation: A Manifesto for Business Revolution* by Michael Hammer and James Champy, the authors state that "Business reengineering means starting all over, starting from scratch. Business reengineering means putting aside much of the received wisdom of two hundred years of industrial management. It means forgetting how work was done in the age of the mass market and deciding how it can best be done now. In business reengineering, old job titles and old organizational arrangements—departments, divisions, groups, and so on—cease to matter. They are artifacts of another age."

Once business level objectives are understood, one must understand the *applications* that will be running on the computer systems attached to these networks. After all, the applications will be generating the traffic that will travel over the implemented network.

Once applications are understood and have been documented, the data which those applications generate must be examined. In this case, the term *data* is used in a general sense as today's networks are likely to transport a variety of payloads including voice, video, image, and fax in addition to true

Top-Down Model Layer	Associated Analysis Processes
Business Layer	• Strategic business planning • Business process reengineering • Identify major business functions • Identify business processes • Identify business opportunities
Applications Layer	• Applications development • Systems analysis and design • Identify information needs • Relate information needs to business processes and opportunities
Data Layer	• Database analysis and design • Data modeling • Data distribution analysis • Client/server architecture design • Distributed database design • Relate data collection and distribution to information and business needs
Network Layer	• Network analysis and design • Logical network design (what) • Network implementation planning • Network management and performance monitoring • Relate logical network design to data collection and distribution design
Technology Layer	• Technology analysis grids • Hardware-software-media technology analysis • Physical network design (how) • Physical network implementation • Relate physical network design to logical network design

Figure 1-7   Analysis Processes of the Top-Down Model

data. Data traffic analysis must determine not only the amount of data to be transported, but also must determine important characteristics about the nature of that data.

Once data traffic analysis has been completed, the following should be known:

1. Physical locations of data   (Where?)

2. Data characteristics and compatibility issues (What?)

3. Amount of data generated and transported   (How much?)

Given these requirements as determined by the upper layers of the top-down model, the next job is to determine the requirements of the *network* that will possess the capability to deliver this data in a timely, cost-effective manner. These network performance criteria could be referred to as *what* the implemented network must do in order to meet the business objectives outlined at the outset of this top-down analysis. These requirements are also sometimes referred to as the **logical network design.**

The *technology* layer analysis, in contrast, will determine *how* various hardware and software components will be combined to build a functional network that will meet predetermined business objectives. The delineation of required technology is often referred to as the **physical network design.**

Overall, the relationship between the layers of the top-down model could be described as follows: Analysis at upper layers produces requirements that are passed down to lower layers, while solutions meeting these requirements are passed back to upper layers. If this relationship among layers holds true throughout the business-oriented network analysis, then the implemented technology (bottom layer) should meet the initially outlined business objectives (top layer). Hence, the name, the Top-Down Approach.

Challenge: Analysis of Complex LAN Connectivity and Compatibility Issues

Assuming that the proper use of the top-down model will ensure that implemented technical solutions will meet stated business requirements, the more technical challenges of LAN analysis and design must be addressed.

Introduction to Protocols and Compatibility

In previous discussions of how LANs are implemented, the term **compatibility** was introduced and explained. Solving incompatibility problems is at the very heart of successful LAN implementation. Compatibility can be thought of as successfully bridging the gap or communicating between two or more technology components, whether hardware or software. This logical gap between components is commonly referred to as an **interface.**

Interfaces may be physical (hardware to hardware) in nature. For example:

- Cables physically connecting to serial ports on a computer

- A network interface card physically plugging into the expansion bus inside a computer

Interfaces may also be logical or software-oriented (software to software) as well. For example:

- An Internet Browser client software (NetScape) communicating with the client PC's operating system (Windows 95)

- A client-based data query tool (Microsoft Excel) gathering data from a large database management system (Oracle)

Finally, interfaces may cross the hardware to software boundary. For example:

- A network operating system specific piece of software known as a driver which interfaces to an installed network interface card (NIC)

- A piece of operating system software known as a kernel which interfaces to a computer's CPU chip

The reason that these various interfaces are able to be bridged successfully, thereby supporting compatibility between components, is due to **protocols.** Protocols are nothing more than rules for how communicating hardware and software components bridge interfaces or talk to one another. Protocols may be proprietary (used exclusively by one or more vendors) or open (used freely by all interested parties). Protocols may be officially sanctioned by international standards-making bodies such as the ISO, or may be purely market driven (de facto protocols). Figure 1-8 illustrates the relationship between interfaces, protocols, and compatibility.

For every potential hardware to hardware, software to software, and hardware to software interface imaginable, there is likely to be one or more possible protocols supported. The sum of all of the protocols employed in a particular computer is sometimes referred to as that computer's **protocol stack.** Successfully determining which protocols must be supported in which instances for the multitude of interfaces possible in a complicated LAN design is likely to be the difference between success or failure in a LAN implementation.

How can a network analyst possibly keep track of all potential interfaces and their associated protocols between all LAN-attached devices? What is needed is a framework in which to organize the various potential interfaces and protocols in such complicated internetwork designs. More than one such framework, otherwise known as communications architectures, exists. Two of the most popular communications architectures are the 7-layer OSI model and the 4-layer Internet suite of protocols model.

Solution: The OSI Model

Determining which technology and protocols to employ to meet the requirements determined in the logical network design, yielded from the network layer of the top-down model, requires a structured methodology of its own. Fortunately, a framework for organizing networking technology and proto-

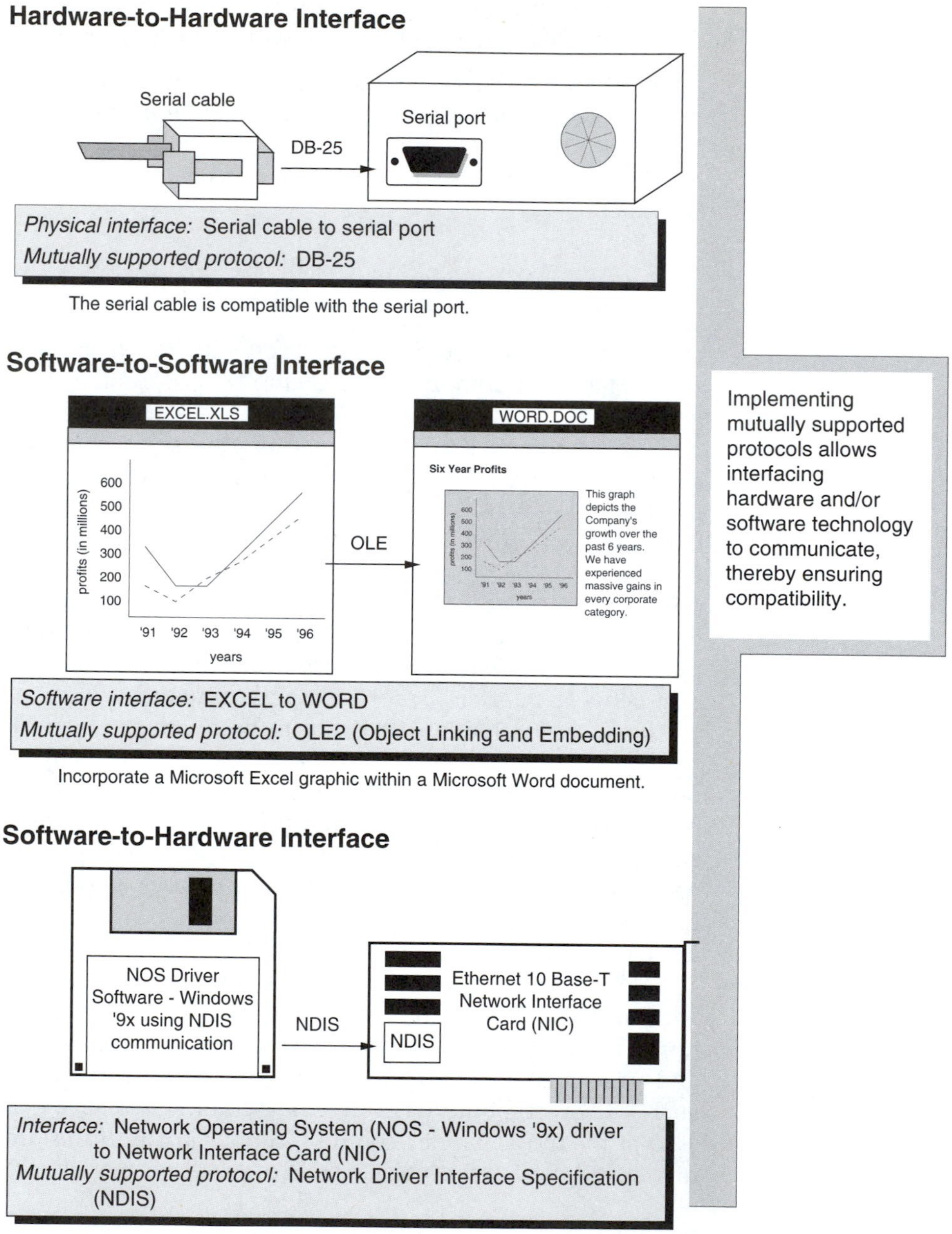

Hardware-to-Hardware Interface

Serial cable

Serial port

DB-25

Physical interface: Serial cable to serial port
Mutually supported protocol: DB-25

The serial cable is compatible with the serial port.

Software-to-Software Interface

EXCEL.XLS

WORD.DOC

profits (in millions)

600
500
400
300
200
100

'91 '92 '93 '94 '95 '96
years

OLE

Six Year Profits

This graph depicts the Company's growth over the past 6 years. We have experienced massive gains in every corporate category.

'91 '92 '93 '94 '95 '96
years

Software interface: EXCEL to WORD
Mutually supported protocol: OLE2 (Object Linking and Embedding)

Incorporate a Microsoft Excel graphic within a Microsoft Word document.

Software-to-Hardware Interface

NOS Driver Software - Windows '9x using NDIS communication

NDIS

NDIS

Ethernet 10 Base-T Network Interface Card (NIC)

Interface: Network Operating System (NOS - Windows '9x) driver to Network Interface Card (NIC)
Mutually supported protocol: Network Driver Interface Specification (NDIS)

Implementing mutually supported protocols allows interfacing hardware and/or software technology to communicate, thereby ensuring compatibility.

Figure 1-8 Interfaces, Protocols, and Compatibility

col solutions has been developed by the International Standards Organization (ISO) and is known as the Open Systems Interconnection (OSI) model. The **OSI model** is illustrated in Figure 1-9.

The OSI model divides the communication between any two networked computing devices into seven layers or categories. Network analysts literally talk in terms of the OSI model. When troubleshooting LAN problems, inevitably the savvy network analyst starts with the physical layer (layer 1) and ensures that protocols and interfaces at each layer are operational before moving up the OSI model. The OSI model allows data communications technology developers as well as standards developers to talk about the interconnection of two networks or computers in common terms without dealing in proprietary vendor jargon.

These "common terms" are the result of the layered architecture of the seven layer OSI model. The architecture breaks the task of two computers communicating to each other into separate but interrelated tasks, each represented by its own layer. As can be seen in Figure 1-9, the top layer (layer 7) represents the services required by the application program running on each

OSI Model Layer	Functionality	Automobile Assembly Line
7: **Application**	User application programs interact and receive services	Dealer-installed options: options desired by users are added at the dealership
6: **Presentation**	Ensures reliable session transmission between applications; takes care of differences in data representation	Painting and finish work: the vehicle is painted and trim is applied
5: **Session**	Enables two applications to communicate across the network	Interior: seats and dashboard are added to passenger compartment
4: **Transport**	Ensures reliable transmission from end to end, usually across multiple nodes	Electrical: electrical system and compartments are added
3: **Network**	Sets up the pathways or end-to-end connections, usually across a long distance, or multiple nodes	Body: passenger compartment and fenders are attached to the chassis
2: **Data Link**	Puts messages together, attaches proper headers to be sent out or received, ensures messages are delivered between two points	Engine/drive train: engine and transmission components provide the vehicle with propulsion
1: **Physical**	Concerned with transmitting bits of data over a physical medium	Chassis/frame: steel is fabricated to form the chassis on which all other components will travel

Figure 1-9   The OSI Model

computer and is therefore aptly named the application layer. The bottom layer (layer 1) is concerned with the actual physical connection of the two computers or networks and is therefore named the physical layer. The remaining layers (2 through 6) may not be as obvious but, nonetheless, represent a sufficiently distinct logical group of functions required to connect two computers, as to justify a separate layer. As will be seen later in the text, some of the layers are divided into sublayers.

To use the OSI model, a network analyst lists the known protocols for each computing device or network node in the proper layer of its own seven-layer OSI model. The collection of these known protocols in their proper layers in known as the protocol stack of the network node. For example, the physical media employed such as unshielded twisted pair, coaxial cable, or fiber-optic cable would be entered as a layer 1 protocol, whereas Ethernet or Token Ring network architectures might be entered as a layer 2 protocol. Technically speaking, the electrical and mechanical specifications of the selected media type are the actual layer 1 protocols. The media itself is sometimes referred to as layer ∅.

The OSI model allows network analysts to produce an accurate inventory of the protocols present on any given network node. This protocol profile represents a unique personality of each network node and gives the network analyst some insight into what **protocol conversion,** if any, may be necessary in order to get any two network nodes to communicate successfully. Ultimately, the OSI model provides a structured methodology for determining what hardware and software technology will be required in the physical network design in order to meet the requirements of the logical network design.

Perhaps the best analogy for the OSI reference model which illustrates its architectural or framework purpose, is that of a blueprint for a large office building or skyscraper. The various subcontractors on the job may only be concerned with the "layer" of the plans that outlines their specific job specifications. However, each specific subcontractor needs to be able to depend on the work of the "lower" layers' subcontractors just as the subcontractors of the "upper" layers depend on these subcontractors performing their function to specification.

Similarly, each layer of the OSI model operates independently of all other layers, while depending on neighboring layers to perform according to specification while cooperating in the attainment of the overall task of communication between two computers or networks.

The OSI model is neither a protocol nor group of protocols. It is a standardized, empty framework into which protocols can be listed in order to perform effective LAN analysis and design. As will be seen later in the text, however, the ISO has also produced a set of OSI protocols that correspond to some of the layers of the OSI model. It is important to differentiate between the OSI model and OSI protocols.

The OSI model will be used throughout the remainder of the text as the protocol stacks of various network operating systems are analyzed, and in the analysis and design of advanced LAN connectivity alternatives.

Solution: The Internet Suite of Protocols Model

Although the OSI model is perhaps more famous than any OSI protocol, just the opposite could be said for a model and associated protocols known as the **Internet suite of protocols model.** Also known as the TCP/IP protocol suite, or TCP/IP architecture, this communications architecture takes its name from **TCP/IP (Transmission control protocol/Internet protocol),** the de facto standard protocols for open systems internetworking. As can be seen in Figure 1-10, TCP and IP are just two of the protocols associated with this model.

Like the OSI model, the TCP/IP model is a layered communications architecture in which upper layers use the functionality offered by the protocols of the lower layers. Each layer's protocols are able to operate independently from the protocols of other layers. For example, protocols on a given layer can be updated or modified without having to change all other protocols in all other layers. A recent example is the new version of IP known as IPng (IP next generation), or IPv6 (IP version 6) which was developed in response to a pending shortage of IP addresses. This proposed change is possible without the need to change all other protocols in the TCP/IP communication architecture. The exact mechanics of how TCP/IP and related protocols work will be explored in greater depth in Chapter 8, "Unix, TCP/IP, and NFS."

Figure 1-10 compares the four-layer Internet suite of protocols model with the seven-layer OSI model. Either communications architecture could be used to analyze and design communications between networks. In the case of the Internet suite of protocols model, the full functionality of internetwork communications is divided into four layers rather than seven. Some network analysts consider the Internet suite of protocols model simpler and more practical than the OSI model.

Solution: The I-P-O Model

Once the protocols are determined for two or more computers or networks that wish to communicate, the next step is to determine the type of technology required to deliver the identified internetworking functionality and protocols.

In order to understand the basic function of any piece of networking equipment, one need only understand the differences between the characteristics of the data that came IN and the data that went OUT. Those differences identified were PROCESSed by the data communications equipment being analyzed.

This Input-Processing-Output or **I-P-O Model** is another key model used throughout the textbook in order to analyze a wide variety of networking equipment and opportunities. The I-P-O model provides a framework in which to focus on the difference between the data that came into a particular

Layer	OSI	INTERNET	Data Format	Protocols
7	Application	Application	Messages or Streams	TELNET FTP TFTP SMTP SNMP CMOT MIB
6	Presentation			
5	Session			
4	Transport	Transport or Host-Host	Transport Protocol Packets	TCP UDP
3	Network	Internet	IP Diagrams	IP
2	Data Link	Network Access	Frames	
1	Physical			

Figure 1-10   Internet Suite of Protocols vs. OSI

networked device (I) and the data that came out of that same device (O). By defining this difference, the processing (P) performed by the device is documented.

Although at first glance the I-P-O model may seem overly simplistic, it is another valuable model that can assist network analysts in organizing thoughts, documenting requirements, and articulating needs.

▪ GETTING STARTED WITH BUSINESS-ORIENTED LAN ANALYSIS AND DESIGN

Figure 1-4 lists examples of high-level business perspectives and needs that might lead to local area network solutions. Following is an example of how high-level business needs and perspectives can serve as a starting point for business-oriented LAN analysis and design. In compliance with the top-down model as an overall guide to LAN analysis and design, investigation of application, data, network and technology issues must occur in addition to this business-layer analysis. While the business-layer issues will be further analyzed here, the remaining layers of the top-down model will be more thoroughly investigated and analyzed throughout the remainder of the text.

Business Activities Should Support Business Needs

The business activities listed in Figure 1-11 are more precisely the information systems or networking-related business activities identified as possibly supporting the expressed business needs and perspectives. Obviously, the term *business activities* could be more broadly defined to include sales, inventory control, marketing, research and development, accounting, payroll, and such. If business activities in these other areas were listed, they should still fulfill one or more of the identified business needs.

In order to ensure consistency within the top-down business model and compliance of business activities with stated business needs, a grid such as that in Figure 1-11 can be employed. For each network-related activity that must be supported in the eventual network design, check off which strategic

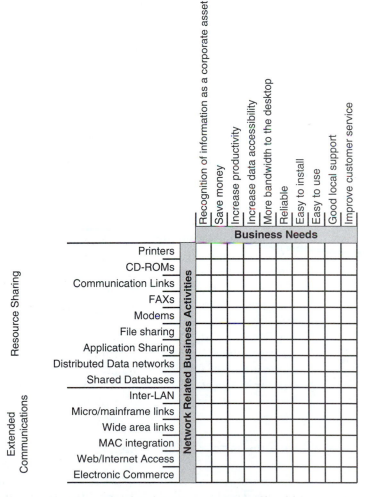

Figure 1-11   Network-related Business Activities Should Support Business Needs

business perspective is being satisfied. Any proposed network activities that do not support a strategic business need or perspective should be reevaluated. Modify the grid as necessary, substituting your own business needs and/or activities, and evaluating accordingly.

The reason for the assurance at this point that possible network-related business activities fulfill specific, stated business needs is to avoid seeking technical local area networking options or features that either do not support or, even worse, contradict stated overall business needs. As stated earlier in the chapter, senior management is seeking business solutions, not technology solutions.

Once the initial merit of the business activities has been assured by completing an evaluation grid (see Figure 1-11), substantially more detailed data regarding these network-related business activities must be gathered before proceeding with the investigation of technical options through application, data, network and technology layer analysis.

Role of the Network Analyst as a Business/Technology Intermediary

These information systems-related business activities are often expressed by nontechnical business management people either directly or through interviews. It is important to understand that these listed activities are general in nature rather than technically specific. Don't expect business management to be able to articulate technical specifications.

Armed with these general business needs, the network analyst prepares a series of business analysis questions to learn more about the information system-related business activities in order to ensure that the eventual networking proposal will adequately support the required business activities.

Subsequent analysis by the network analyst of available technology through interaction with vendors and technical specialists creates a role as intermediary for the network analyst. On the one hand, the network analyst must be able to understand the business needs and activities of an organization, while at the same time understanding the technical specifications of the networking hardware and software that will ideally meet the organization's business needs.

Furthermore, the successful network analyst must be able to handle constant change. Change is constantly occurring not just in technology, but also in the architectural design of networks and information systems required to deliver business solutions. Technical skills must be constantly updated in response to the demands of the job market.

Business Analysis Questions Dig Deeper

Possible business analysis questions for Local Area Networking solutions are listed in Figure 1-12. Notice that these questions "dig deeper" into the more general previously listed business activities. These questions would be directed toward end users and business management and are centered around **what** the network must eventually do, rather than **how** it will do it. The how questions will be more technical in nature and will be dealt with further down this trip through the top-down model.

The list of business analysis questions in Figure 1-12 is not meant to be exhaustive or all-encompassing. The questions listed are a direct result of the business activities and needs from the top-down model used in this chapter as

	Current	2-3 Years	5 Years
User Issues How many users? What are their business activities? What is the budgeted cost/user? Comprehensive cost of ownership? What are the security needs? (password protection levels, supervisor privileges) What are the support issues?			
Local Communication Required speed?			

Resource Sharing
How many CD-ROMs, printers, modems, and FAXs
    are to be shared?
What is the greatest distance from the server to each
    service?			

File Sharing Is printer/queue management required? How many simultaneous users?			
Application Sharing What is the number and type of required applications? Are E-mail services required?			
Distributed Data Access Where will shared data files be stored?			
LAN Management/Administration Will training be required to manage the network? How easy is the network to use?			

Extended Communication
How many MACs will be part of the network?
How many mini/mainframe connections are needed?
    (and what type, IBM, DEC, UNIX based?)
Will this be an Inter-LAN network? (LAN-LAN
    concerns. Which NOS? Must other protocols be
    considered? Are the connections local or remote
    (long-distance)?)
What are the needs for electronic commerce?
What are the needs for access to/from the
    Internet/World Wide Web?			

Figure 1-12   LAN Business Analysis Questions

an example. Add, modify, or delete questions from this list as necessary. Two important things to remember about any list of business analysis questions are:

1. The questions should dig deeper into the required information systems-related business activities.

2. The answers to these questions should provide sufficient insight as to enable the investigation of possible technical solutions.

Each of the categories of business analysis questions is explained briefly below.

User Issues   User satisfaction is the key to any successful network implementation. In order to satisfy users, their needs must be thoroughly understood. Beyond the obvious questions of "How many users must the network support?" are the more insightful questions dealing with specific business activities of individual users.

1. Do users require large file transfers at certain times of day?

2. Do users process many short transactions throughout the day?

3. Are there certain activities that must be done at certain times of day or within a certain amount of elapsed time?

4. How fast must files be transferred between employees?

These questions are important in order to establish the amount of network communication required by individual users. Required levels of security should also be addressed.

1. Are payroll files going to be accessed via the network?

2. Who should have access to these files and what security measures will ensure authorized access?

3. What is the overall technical ability of the users?

4. Will technical staff need to be hired?

5. Can support be obtained locally from an outside organization?

Budget Reality   The most comprehensive, well-documented, and researched networking proposal is of little value if its costs are beyond the means of the funding organization or business. Initial research into possible networking solutions is often followed by the publication of feasibility option reports that outline possible network designs of varying price ranges. Senior management then dictates which options deserve further study based on financial availability.

In some cases, senior management may have an approximate project budget in mind that could be shared with network analysts. This acceptable financial range, sometimes expressed as budgeted cost per user, serves as a frame of reference for analysts as technical options are explored. In this sense, budgetary constraints are just another overall, high-level business need or perspective that helps to shape eventual networking proposals.

Local Communication   Because these are business analysis questions and not technical analysis questions, users really can't be asked how fast their network connections must be. Bits per second or megabits per second have little or no meaning for most users. If users have business activities such as CAD/CAM (Computer Aided Design/Computer Aided Manufacturing) or other 3-D modeling or graphics software that will be accessing the network, the network analyst should be aware that these are large consumers of network bandwidth.

Bandwidth requirements analysis as well as the bandwidth offered by various networking alternatives will be explored later in the text. It is sufficient at this point to document those information system-related business activities that may be large consumers of networking bandwidth.

Resource Sharing   The resource sharing business analysis questions for LANs are similar to the business analysis questions for peripheral/printer sharing devices outlined previously. It is important to identify which resources and how many are to be shared: printers, modems, faxes, cd-roms; and the preferred locations of these shared resources. The required distance between shared resources and users can have a bearing on acceptable technical options.

File Sharing and Application Sharing   In many cases, network versions of software packages may cost less than multiple individual licenses of the same software package for individual personal computers. The network analyst is trying at this point to compile a listing of all applications programs that will be shared by users. Not all PC-based software packages are available in network versions and not all PC-based software packages allow simultaneous access by multiple users.

1. Which programs or software packages will users need to perform their jobs?

2. Which programs are they currently using?

3. Which new products must be purchased?

Once a list of required shared application programs has been completed, it is important to investigate both the availability and capability of the network versions of these programs in order to ensure satisfied, productive users and the successful attainment of business needs.

Distributed Data Access   Although users cannot be expected to be database analysts, sufficient questions must be asked in order to determine which data are to be shared by whom, and where these users are located. This process is known as data distribution analysis. The major objective of data distribution analysis is to determine the best location on the network for the storage of various data files. That best location is usually the one closest to the greatest number of the most active users of that data.

Some data files that are typically shared, especially in regionalized or multi-location companies, include customer files, employee files, and inventory files. Distributed data access is even more of a concern when the users sharing the data are beyond the reach of a LAN and must share the data via wide area networking solutions. A good starting point for the network analyst might be to ask: Has anyone done a comparison of the business forms that are used in the various regional and branch offices to determine which data need to be sent across the network?

Extended Communications   The ability of certain local area networking solutions to communicate beyond the local area network remains a key differentiating factor among local area networking alternatives. Users should be able to articulate connectivity requirements beyond the LAN. The accomplishment of these requirements is the job of the network analyst.

Some possible examples of extended communications might include communications to another LAN. In this case, the network analyst must investigate all of the technical specifications of this target LAN in order to determine compatibility with the local LAN. An example of such a compatibility issue would be the need to connect an Apple MAC network to a PC-based network. The target LAN may be local (within the same building) or remote (across town or around the world). LAN to LAN connection is known as internetworking and will be studied in depth in Chapter 13.

The explosive growth of mobile computing has led to a tremendous need for users to be able to access corporate information systems from home, automobiles, hotels, and even airplanes. Remote computing will be explored in depth in Chapter 14.

Other examples of extended communications may be the necessity for LAN users to gain access to minicomputers or mainframes, either locally or remotely. Again, users are only asked *what* they need connections to, and *where* those connections must occur; it is the network analyst's job to figure out *how* to make those connections function.

LAN Management and Administration   Another key differentiating factor among LAN alternatives is the level of sophistication required to manage and administer the network. If the LAN requires a full-time, highly trained manager, then that manager's salary should be considered as part of the purchase cost as well as the operational cost of the proposed LAN.

Second, the users may have requirements for certain management or administration features that must be present. Examples might be user-ID creation or management, or control of access to files or user directories.

Practical Advice and Information

ACCURATE AND COMPLETE BUDGETS ARE A MUST

Detailed and accurate cost projection is a very important skill for network analysts. Management does not appreciate surprises of a financial nature due to unanticipated costs.

In order to ensure that all necessary costs have been determined, it is essential to identify all user needs (the cost generators). Thorough user needs identification is the goal of the business analysis questions phase of the top-down model.

Anticipated Growth Is Key   User needs are not always immediate in nature. These needs can vary dramatically over time. In order to design networking solutions that will not become obsolete in the near future, it is essential to gain a sense of what the anticipated growth in user demands might be. Imagine the chagrin of the network analyst who must explain to management that the network which was installed last year cannot be expanded and must be replaced due to unanticipated growth of network demand.

One method of gaining the necessary insight into future networking requirements (illustrated in Figure 1-12), is to ask users the same set of business analysis questions with projected time horizons of two to three years and five years. Incredible as it may seem, five years is about the maximum projected lifetime for a given network architecture or design. Of course, there are exceptions. End users may not have the necessary information or knowledge to make these projections. Management can be very helpful in the area of projected growth and informational needs, especially if the company has engaged in any sort of formalized strategic planning methodology.

The Logical Network Design

At this point, a network analyst should have a fairly clear picture of the business networking requirements identified through the use of the top-down model. Because technology-specific issues have not been covered as yet, only the logical or functional aspects of network design have been discussed. All of the numerous architecture, topology, hardware, and software considerations will be explored in the remaining chapters of the text.

As each area of new technology alternatives is discussed, that technology which meets logical network design requirements will be investigated further for possible inclusion in a physical network design. The physical network design is a map of the actual hardware and software technology that gets implemented and through which the data physically flow.

As physical network design alternatives are explored in the remainder of the text, the business requirements analyzed and determined in this chapter will be referenced less frequently. If the overall philosophy of the top-down model has been adhered to, the now complete logical network design should ensure achievement of the agreed-upon business layer requirements.

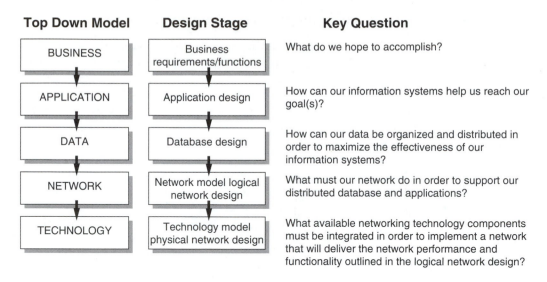

Figure 1-13 Physical and Logical Network Designs Support Business Requirements

It should follow then, as Figure 1-13 illustrates, that as long as the physical network design (Technology layer) supports the logical network design (Network layer), then the final implemented network should support the strategic business requirements—the ultimate goal of the top-down approach to LAN analysis and design.

SUMMARY

Perhaps the most significant conclusion that should be drawn from this chapter is that networking analysis in general, and local area network analysis in particular, must yield business solutions, not technology solutions. Given a knowledge of what a LAN is and how a LAN is implemented, the challenge of the network analyst is to produce a documentable, justifiable network design capable of delivering stated business objectives. The key to success in this endeavor is the use of a structured methodology for LAN analysis and design. That structured methodology

must ensure that technology investments will yield desired productivity increases or other business objectives. In addition, the analysis and design methodology must have some way to deal with the myriad of possibilities for the combinations of hardware and software protocols yielding compatibility between communicating computers or networks. The use of standardized models would seem to be essential to a successful outcome of the LAN analysis and design process. Adhering to the structure and associated approach of the top-down model should assure that the implemented physical network design will support strategic business objectives. In order to apply some structure to the analysis of complex internetwork communication, either the OSI model or the Internet suite of protocols model (TCP/IP model) should offer a suitable framework for verifiable analysis and design.

KEY TERMS

business process
client
compatibility
hub
I-P-O model
interface
Internet suite of protocols
LAN
local area network

logical network design
network interface card
network operating system
NIC
OSI model
physical network design
productivity paradox
protocol conversion
protocol stack

protocols
queue management
reengineering
servers
shared media LANs
TCP/IP
top-down model

REVIEW QUESTIONS

1. What is a local area network?
2. What are the advantages of a local area network as opposed to a group of stand-alone PCs?
3. What are the potential disadvantages or negative aspects of a local area network?
4. How would a business know when it needed a LAN?
5. What are the most popular business uses of a LAN?
6. What is the difference between file transfer and file sharing?
7. What types of hardware and software technology are required to support file sharing?
8. What resources other than printers are LAN-attached computers likely to want to share?
9. What is meant by the term *media-sharing LAN?*
10. Are all LANs media-sharing LANs? Explain.
11. Simply speaking, what hardware and software technology components are required to implement a LAN?
12. What is the function of a network interface card?
13. What is the function of a hub or wiring center?

14. In simple terms, what is the difference between an operating system and a network operating system?
15. What other technology must a NIC be able to interface with in a compatible fashion?
16. What other technology must a hub be able to interface with in a compatible fashion?
17. What is the function of a client PC operating system?
18. What is the function of a client PC network operating system?
19. How do client and server versions of the same network operating system differ?
20. What is the difference in terms of usage and function between client and server PCs?
21. What other technology must network media be able to interface with in a compatible fashion?
22. Why is it important for a network analyst to understand management's business needs and perspectives?
23. What are some examples of management business needs and perspectives?
24. Give examples of the potential impact of management's business needs and perspectives on network analysis and design.

25. What is the importance of a structured, documentable methodology for network analysis and design?
26. What are some typical business views of technology held by senior management?
27. What is the productivity paradox?
28. What is the top-down model and why is it important?
29. What is business process reengineering and what is its relationship to the top-down model?
30. What is the overall relationship between the layers of the top-down model?
31. If the top-down model is used as intended, what can be assumed about implemented systems?
32. What is the difference between logical and physical network design?
33. Why is it important to allow logical and physical network designs to vary independently?
34. What is the relationship between the terms *interface, protocols,* and *compatibility*?
35. What is meant by the term *protocol stack* in terms of its importance to internetwork design?
36. Differentiate between the following protocol-related terms: *open, proprietary, de facto.*
37. Describe the importance of the OSI model.
38. What is the relationship between the layers of the OSI model?
39. What is the difference between the OSI model and OSI protocols?
40. Compare and contrast the OSI model with the Internet suite of protocols model.
41. Describe the types of skills (technical, personal, business) required of a successful network analyst.
42. Describe the impact of the accelerating rate of technological change in the networking field on networking personnel.

ACTIVITIES

1. Prepare a chart outlining advantages, disadvantages, and current pricing in terms of cost per user for various LANs and LAN alternatives.
2. Interview a network administrator, a network analyst, a network technician, and a director of M.I.S. Compare and contrast their perspectives on business vs. technical orientation of their responsibilities.
3. Investigate and report on the possible ways in which Macs can communicate with DOS or Windows-based PCs.
4. Prepare a chart outlining the level of training and technical expertise required to implement and manage various LANs and LAN alternatives.
5. Interview senior nontechnical business administrators from a variety of companies and report on their views of the impact of technology on their operations.
6. Investigate and prepare a paper or presentation on the productivity paradox.
7. Find a description of an implemented network in a professional periodical. Place pertinent facts from the article in the appropriate layers of the top-down model. Examine your results. What questions do you have?
8. Prepare a paper on a variety of companies that have attempted business process reengineering. Has there been a variable rate of success in these efforts? Is there a right way and a wrong way to do BPR?
9. Prepare a chart with examples including employed protocols for each of the following types of interfaces: hardware/hardware, software/software, hardware/software.
10. Prepare a chart listing as many protocols as possible and categorize them as: open, proprietary, officially sanctioned, or de facto.
11. Fill in a copy of the OSI model with as many OSI protocols as you can find. In another OSI model, list alternatives to the OSI protocols.
12. Interview networking personnel as to how they use the OSI model or Internet suite of protocols model. Explain your results.
13. Prepare a chart listing the types of skills required of successful network analysts and the intended source of those skills.

CASE STUDY

Managing the Tightest Ship in the Shipping Biz

For UPS—a company that has built its reputation on speedy package delivery—spending three months to distribute software within its own network was unacceptable.

It used to take that long, but now UPS can deliver software to thousands of its PCs and servers in three to five business days.

To achieve this acceleration, Atlanta-based UPS last year installed a software distribution application from Tivoli as part of a management framework that includes software for remotely controlling and monitoring systems.

UPS has made its move at a time when so-called "framework" management software from vendors such as Tivoli and Computer Associates is coming under increasing fire for being expensive and difficult to implement. Part of the reason UPS went with the software is that the company found that the software had a function UPS could benefit from: software distribution.

Previously, UPS would update software across its 1,200 sites via a huge sneakernet, says Glen Barry, project leader of the Tivoli implementation at UPS.

"We would create more than 1,000 upgrade CDs, send them to regional tech support,

and dispatch support people to each site," he says.

The support people would install the in-house software on Windows NT machines at each of the sites. The software helps UPS track the packages it ships around the country.

Now software is distributed and installed electronically from a central data center over a frame relay network to locations throughout the U.S. The company has performed more than 30,000 distributions since last August.

While UPS won't say how much it is saving by using the Tivoli software, Barry says, "We're happy with our return on investment."

The implementation isn't perfect, however. UPS still needs to upgrade to the latest version of Tivoli Enterprise to get two critical functions, Barry says. One is the ability to distribute software to AS/400s. The other is a much leaner management agent that takes up only 250K bytes on end stations.

FRAMEWORK VS. FUNCTION

The software distribution function fits into the Tivoli Enterprise framework, which unites many network and systems management features under a common umbrella.

Industry analysts say this approach is starting to lose favor because hundreds of management software startups are rushing into the market to provide individual functions at a lower cost.

"Most of the innovation these days is in the point tools," says John McConnell, president of McConnell Associates in Boulder, Colo. He adds that many users can get value from loosely coupled systems from different vendors.

"We framework vendors kind of do ourselves a disservice in leading with the framework rather than leading with the solution," acknowledges Leo Cole, director of network management at Tivoli. Deploying and monitoring software are functions that users can derive real value from—and that should be the focus.

"The fact that there may be a framework [to those functions], you shouldn't care about," Cole says. "When you're doing an ROI analysis, do it on a function basis."

GIVING UPS A BOOST

Other functions in the framework that UPS uses include monitoring servers at its many sites. Systems managers are able to keep an eye on performance problems and available disk space, Barry says. Once the managers understand and correct any problems occurring at one site, they can propagate corrections to other sites, ensuring that the problems don't crop up there, as well.

Barry says going with Tivoli also helped UPS because the company has many different kinds of systems to manage—including mainframes, IBM AS/400 mid-range computers, Unix boxes, NT servers and OS/2 desktops. With Tivoli software, UPS can monitor and manage all these disparate systems using the same tools.

UPS' technical support staff also uses Tivoli's remote control software to take over computers remotely via the network and fix any problems.

"The frameworks tend to have value for large organizations, rather than small ones," McConnell says. A large company such as UPS can benefit from the tools being consolidated in one place.

As for the criticism that framework-based management software is difficult to implement, Barry says his implementation went off without a hitch. However, UPS went through a methodical process of testing that started in June 1997. Implementation began in January 1998, and deployment wasn't completed until August 1998.

But with the framework in place, UPS is hoping it can easily plug in new applications. Barry says UPS will extend its use of Tivoli software next year with the vendor's new Cross-Site product. Cross-Site lets users send data securely through a firewall over an open network such as the Internet. While Cross-Site is intended for use between businesses that are partners in a supply chain, UPS plans to use it to send updates of salesforce automation software to its sales executives on the road.

Based on the success with Tivoli so far, UPS plans to implement Tivoli software for its entire worldwide operation by 2004.

Source: Jeff Caruso, "Managing the Tightest Ship in the Shipping Biz," *Network World,* vol. 16, no. 19 (May 10, 1999), p. 51. Copyright Network World. Reprinted with permission.

BUSINESS CASE STUDY QUESTIONS

Activities

1. Complete a top-down model for this case by gleaning facts from the case and placing them in the proper layer of the top-down model. After having completed the top-down model, analyze and detail those instances where requirements were clearly passed down from upper layers to lower layers of the model and where solutions to those requirements were passed up from lower layers to upper layers of the model.

2. Detail any questions about the case that may occur to you for which answers are not clearly stated in the article.

Business

1. What was the business motivation or problem that initiated the search for the implemented solution?

2. What was the productivity impact of the implemented solution?

3. Why do you think UPS won't say how much it is saving by using their Tivoli investment?

4. How long did the deployment of the software take?

5. How many locations are currently being managed by the Tivoli framework?

6. By when does UPS anticipate having Tivoli deployed over their worldwide network?

Application

1. How did UPS conduct software distribution prior to purchasing the Tivoli software?

2. What business function did the application software that was being upgraded serve?

3. What is the problem with the framework approach to enterprise network management software?

4. What is the alternative to the all-inclusive but expensive frameworks?
5. What are some new applications that UPS is intending to use the Tivoli framework for?

Data

1. What key functionalities are not being currently met, thereby forcing UPS to upgrade?
2. What are point products?
3. What are some of the other functions in the framework used by UPS?

Network

1. What type of network is used for the electronic software distribution?
2. What operating system was the software installed on?

3. What are some of the different types of computing platforms used by UPS?
4. Can they all be monitored from a single application?

Technology

1. What was the key function of the network management framework that UPS was most interested in?
2. What was the traditional negative opinion about enterprise network management frameworks?
3. Did UPS agree or disagree with this traditional view? Why or why not?

CHAPTER 2

LOCAL AREA NETWORK ARCHITECTURES

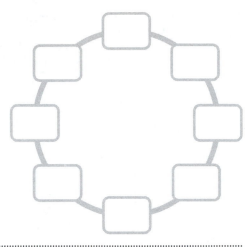

Concepts Reinforced

OSI Model   Top-Down Model
Hardware/Software Compatibility   Protocols and Standards
Local Area Networks

Concepts Introduced

Access Methodologies   Network Architectures
Physical Topologies   High-Speed Network
IEEE 802 Standards   Architectures
Logical Topologies

OBJECTIVES

After mastering the material in this chapter you should:

1. Understand how access methodologies, logical topologies, and physical topologies combine to form alternative network architectures

2. Understand the similarities, differences, advantages, and disadvantages to current network architectures such as Ethernet, Token Ring, and FDDI

3. Understand the similarities, differences, advantages, and disadvantages of emerging high-speed network architectures such as 100BaseT, 100VG-AnyLAN, isoEthernet, and Gigabit Ethernet

4. Understand the value of the OSI model in the analysis of network architecture alternatives

5. Understand how proper LAN analysis can help determine which network architecture is most appropriate in any given situation

▓ INTRODUCTION

Chapter 1 answered several key questions, at least on an introductory level:

- What is a local area network?

- How is a local area network implemented?

- Why are local area networks implemented?

Armed with a basic understanding of the what, how, and why of local area networks, this chapter explores in depth the underlying local area network architectures that allow hardware and software technologies to transparently interact. Clients and servers are able to communicate and share information thanks to the combined components of the local area network that links them. These local area network components are able to offer transparent network transmission services to clients and services due to their adherence to standards and protocols. One of the key distinguishing characteristics of a particular local area network is the network architecture adhered to by a particular LAN. In this chapter, the components of a network architecture will be first explored, followed by comparative evaluations of the numerous network architectures either currently available or emerging into the networking marketplace.

The OSI model, first introduced in Chapter 1, will be explained in more detail as a means by which to organize comparative information regarding alternative network architectures and computer-to-computer communications.

▓ THE OSI MODEL REVISITED

Overall Structure and Characteristics

The **OSI Model** consists of a hierarchy of seven layers that loosely group the functional requirements for communication between two computing devices regardless of the software, hardware, or geographical differences between those computing devices. The power of the OSI model, officially known as ISO Standard 7489, lies in its openness and flexibility. It can be used to organize and define protocols involved in communicating between two computing devices in the same room as effectively as two devices across the world from each other.

Each layer in the OSI model relies on lower layers to perform more elementary functions and to offer total transparency to the intricacies of those functions. At the same time, each layer provides incrementally more sophisticated transparent service to upper layers. In theory, if this transparency model is supported, changes in the protocols of one layer should not require changes in protocols of other layers. A **protocol** is a set of rules that govern communication between hardware and/or software components.

Physical Layer

The **physical layer,** also known as layer 1, is responsible for the establishment, maintenance, and termination of physical connections between communicating devices. These connections are sometimes referred to as **point-to-point data links.** The physical layer transmits and receives a stream of bits. There is no data recognition at the physical layer.

Specifically, the physical layer operation is controlled by protocols that define the electrical, mechanical, and procedural specifications for data transmission. The RS232-C specification for serial transmission is an example of a physical layer protocol. Strictly speaking, the physical layer does not define the specifications for connectors and cables, which are sometimes referred to as belonging to layer 0.

Data-Link Layer

The **data-link layer** is responsible for providing protocols that deliver reliability to upper layers for the point-to-point connections established by the physical layer protocols. The data-link layer is of particular interest to the study of local area networks because this is the layer in which network architecture standards are defined. These standards are debated and established by the **IEEE (Institute of Electrical and Electronic Engineers) 802 committee** and will be introduced and explained later in this chapter. The number 802 is derived from the date of the committee's formation in 1980 (80) in the month of February (2).

The data-link layer provides the required reliability to the physical layer transmission by organizing the bit stream into structured **frames,** which add addressing and error-checking information. Additional information added to the front of data is called a **header,** whereas information added to the back of data is called a **trailer.** Data-link layer protocols provide error detection, notification, and recovery.

The data-link layer frames are built within the **network interface card** installed in a computer according to the predetermined frame layout particular to the network architecture of the installed network interface card. Network interface cards are given a unique address in a format determined by their network architecture. These addresses are usually assigned and preprogrammed by the NIC manufacturer. The network interface card provides the connection to the LAN, transferring any data frames that are addressed to it from the connected network media to the computer's memory for processing.

The first two layers of the OSI model, physical and data-link, are manifested as hardware (media and NICs, respectively), whereas the remaining layers of the OSI model are all installed as software protocols.

Sub-Layers

In order to allow the OSI model to more closely adhere to the protocol structure and operation of a local area network, the IEEE 802 committee split the data-link layer into two sub-layers.

Media Access Control   The **media access control** or **MAC sub-layer** interfaces with the physical layer and is represented by protocols that define how the shared local area network media is to be accessed by the many connected computers. As will be explained more fully later is this chapter, Token Ring (IEEE 802.5) and Ethernet (IEEE 802.3) networks use different media access methodologies and are therefore assigned different IEEE 802 protocol numbers. Unique addresses assigned to NICs at the time of manufacture are commonly referred to as MAC addresses or MAC layer addresses.

Logical Link Control   The upper sub-layer of the data-link layer that interfaces to the network layer is known as the **logical link control** or **LLC sub-layer** and is represented by a single IEEE 802 protocol (IEEE 802.2). The LLC sub-layer also interfaces transparently to the MAC sublayer protocol beneath it. The advantage to splitting the data-link layer into two sub-layers and to having a single, common LLC protocol is that it offers transparency to the upper layers (network and above) while allowing the MAC sub-layer protocol to vary independently. In terms of technology, the splitting of the sub-layers and the single LLC protocol allows a given network operating system to run equally well over a variety of different network architectures as embodied in network interface cards.

Network Layer

The **network layer** protocols are responsible for the establishment, maintenance, and termination of **end-to-end network links.** Network layer protocols are required when computers that are not physically connected to the same LAN must communicate. Network layer protocols are responsible for providing network layer (end-to-end) addressing schemes and for enabling inter-network routing of network layer data **packets.** The term *packets* is usually associated with network layer protocols, whereas the term *frames* is usually associated with data-link layer protocols. Unfortunately, not all networking professionals or texts adhere to this generally accepted convention. Addressing schemes and routing will be thoroughly reviewed in the remainder of the text.

Network layer protocols are part of a particular network operating system's protocol stack. Different networking operating systems may use different network layer protocols. Many network operating systems have the ability to use more than one network layer protocol. This capability is especially important to heterogeneous, multi-platform, multi-vendor client/server computing environments.

Transport Layer

Just as the data-link layer was responsible for providing reliability for the physical layer, the **transport layer** protocols are responsible for providing reliability for the end-to-end network layer connections. Transport layer protocols provide end-to-end error recovery and flow control. Transport layer protocols also provide mechanisms for sequentially organizing multiple network layer packets into a coherent **message.**

Transport layer protocols are also supplied by a given network operating system and are most often closely linked with a particular network layer protocol. For example, NetWare uses IPX/SPX in which IPX (Internet Packet Exchange) is the network layer protocol and SPX (Sequenced Packet Exchange) is the transport layer protocol. Another popular transport/network protocol duo is TCP/IP in which TCP (Transmission Control Protocol), the transport layer protocol, provides reliability services for IP (Internet Protocol), the network layer protocol.

Session Layer

The **session layer** protocols are responsible for establishing, maintaining, and terminating sessions between user application programs. Sessions are interactive dialogues between networked computers and are of particular importance to distributed computing applications in a client/server environment. As the area of distributed computing is in an evolutionary state, the session layer protocols may be supplied by the distributed application, the network operating system, or a specialized piece of additional software designed to render differences between computing platforms transparent, known as middleware. RPC, or remote procedure call protocol, is one example of a session layer protocol.

Presentation Layer

The **presentation-layer** protocols provide an interface between user applications and various presentation-related services required by those applications. For example, data encryption/decryption protocols are considered presentation-layer protocols as are protocols that translate between encoding schemes such as ASCII to EBCDIC. A common misconception is that graphical user interfaces such as Windows and Presentation Manager are presentation-layer protocols. This is not true. Presentation-layer protocols are dealing with network communications, whereas Windows and/or Presentation Manager are installed on end-user computers.

Application Layer

The **application layer,** layer 7 of the OSI model is also open to misinterpretation. Application-layer protocols do not include end-user application programs. Rather, they include utilities and network-based services that support end-user application programs. Some people include network operating systems in this category. Strictly speaking, the best examples of application-layer protocols are the OSI protocols X.400 and X.500. X.400 is an open systems protocol that offers interoperability between different e-mail programs and X.500 offers e-mail directory synchronization among different e-mail systems. DNS, Domain Name Service, which is an Internet protocol that resolves a computer's common or domain name to a specific IP address, is also considered an application-layer protocol.

Figure 2-1 offers a conceptual view of the OSI model and summarizes many of the previous comments.

Encapsulation/De-encapsulation

The previous discussion highlighted the roles of the various OSI model layer protocols in a communication session between two networked computers. How the various protocol layers actually interact with each other to enable an end-to-end communication session is highlighted in Figure 2-2.

As illustrated in Figure 2-2, a data message emerges from a client front end program and proceeds down the protocol stack of the network operating system installed in the client PC in a process known as **encapsulation.** Each successive layer of the OSI model adds a header according to the syntax of the protocol which occupies that layer. In the case of the data-link layer, both a header and trailer are added. The bit stream is finally passed along the shared media that connects the two computing devices. This is an important point. Although the OSI model may seem to imply that given layers in a protocol stack talk directly to each other on different computers, the fact is that the computers are only physically connected by the media, and that is the only layer which talks directly between computers.

When the full bit stream arrives at the destination server, the reverse process of encapsulation, **de-encapsulation,** takes place. In this manner, each successive layer of the OSI model removes headers and/or trailers and processes the data that were passed to it from the corresponding layer protocol on the source client. Once the server has processed the client's request for data in the server back-end engine application, the whole process is reversed and the requested data will be encapsulated by the server's protocol stack, transmitted over the communications media, and de-encapsulated by the

LAYER	USER APPLICATION			DATA FORMAT	ENABLING TECHNOLOGY	
7 APPLICATION	Provides common services to user applications. ➡ X.400 E-MAIL interoperability specification ➡ X.500 E-MAIL directory synchronization specification ➡ Strictly speaking, does **not** include user applications	Higher layer protocols - independant of underlying communications network	Node-to-node sessions			SOFTWARE
6 PRESENTATION	Provides presentation services for network communications. ➡ Encryption ➡ Code translation (ASCII to EBCDIC) ➡ Text compression *Not* to be confused with ➡ Graphical User Interfaces(GUIs)					
5 SESSION	Establishes, maintains, terminates node-to-node interactive sessions.			sessions Interactive, real-time dialogue between 2 user nodes	Distributed applications, middleware, or network operating systems.	
4 TRANSPORT	Assures reliability of end-to-end network connections.		End-to-end user network connection.	messages Asembles packets into messages.	Network Operating Systems	
3 NETWORK	Establishes, maintains, and terminates end-to-end network connections.	Network		packets Embedded within frames.	Network Operating Systems.	
HARDWARE/SOFTWARE INTERFACE					**NIC DRIVERS**	
2 DATA LINK	Logical Link control sub-layer. Media access control sub-layer.	Specified by 802.X protocols. ➡Assures reliability of point-to-point data links.	Communications / Point-to-point data link	frames Recognizable as data.	Network Interface Cards.	HARDWARE
1 PHYSICAL	Establishes, maintains, and terminates point-to-point data links.			bits Unrecognizable as data	Media	

Figure 2-1   OSI Model—A Conceptual View

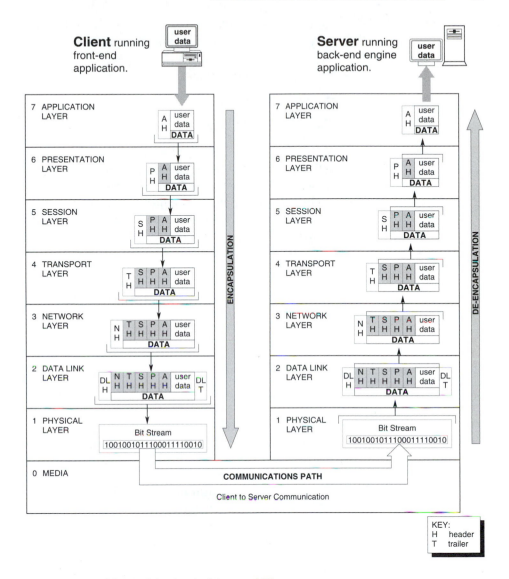

Figure 2-2   OSI Model—An Architectural View

client PC's protocol stack before being ultimately delivered to the client front-end application which requested the data in the first place.

■ THE LOCAL AREA NETWORK ARCHITECTURE MODEL

Although not all network architectures are standardized by the IEEE or some other standards-making organization, all network architectures are made up of the same logical components. In order to accurately describe a given network architecture, one needs to know the following:

- access methodology
- logical topology
- physical topology

As numerous network architectures are evaluated later in the chapter, these three major components will be discussed in each case. The only other variable added to the network architecture of choice is the particular media over which a given network architecture can operate. As will be seen, most network architectures are able to operate over a variety of media types. Although networking vocabulary is by no means standardized, the previously mentioned combinations of variables can be summarized in the following manner:

- Network Architecture = access methodology + logical topology + physical topology
- Network Configuration = network architecture + media choice

Access Methodology

Realizing that more than one user is likely to be sending requests onto the shared local area network media at any one time, the need for some way to control which users get to put their messages onto the network and when should be obvious. If the media is to be shared by numerous PC users, there must be some way to control access by multiple users to that media. These media-sharing methods are properly known as **access methodologies.** Sharing the media is an important concept to Local Area Networks, which are sometimes referred to as **Media Sharing LANs.**

Logically speaking, there are really only two philosophies for controlling access to a shared media. An analogy of access to a crowded freeway can provide a vivid illustration of access methodology choices.

CSMA/CD   One philosophy says, "Let's just let everyone onto the media whenever they want and if two users access the media at the exact same split second, we'll work it out somehow." Or … in the analogy…" Who needs stoplights! If we have a few collisions, we'll work it out later!"

The access methodology based on this model is known as **Carrier Sense Multiple Access with Collision Detection,** or **CSMA/CD** for short. A clearer understanding of how this access methodology works can be achieved if the name of this access methodology is examined one phrase at a time.

Carrier Sense: the PC wishing to put data onto the shared media listens to the network to see if any other users are "on the line" by trying to sense a neutral electrical signal known as a carrier. If no transmission is sensed, then "Multiple Access" allows anyone onto the media without further permission required. Finally, if two user PCs should both sense a free line and access the media at the same instant, a collision occurs and "Collision Detection" lets the user PCs know that their data were not delivered and controls retransmission in such a way as to avoid further data collisions. Another possible factor leading to data collisions is the **propagation delay,** which is the time it takes a signal from a source PC to reach a destination PC. Because of this propagation delay, it is possible for a workstation to sense that there is no signal on the shared media, when in fact another distant workstation has transmitted a signal that has not yet reached the carrier sensing PC.

In the event of a collision, the station that first detects a collision sends out a special jamming signal to all attached workstations. Each workstation, or more precisely the network interface card in the workstation, is preset to wait a random amount of time before retransmitting, thus reducing the likelihood of reoccurring collisions. If successive collisions continue to occur, the random time-out interval is doubled.

CSMA/CD is obviously most efficient with relatively little contention for network resources. The ability to allow user PCs to access the network easily without excessive permission requesting and granting reduces overhead and increases performance at lower network usage rates. As usage increases, however, the increased number of data collisions and retransmissions can negatively effect overall network performance.

Token Passing   The second philosophy of access methodology is much more controlling. It says, "Don't you dare access the media until it's your turn. You must first ask permission, and only if I give you the magic token may you put your data onto the shared media." The highway analogy would be the controlled access ramps to freeways in which a driver must wait at a stoplight and somehow immediately get to 60 mph in order to merge with the traffic.

Token Passing ensures that each PC User has 100% of the network channel available for its data requests and transfers by insisting that no PC accesses the network without first possessing a specific packet (24 bits) of data known as a **token.** The token is generated in the first place by a designated PC known as the **active monitor** and passed among PCs until one PC would like to access the network.

At that point, the requesting PC seizes the token, changes the token status from free to busy, puts its data frame onto the network, and doesn't release the token until it is assured that its data were delivered successfully. Successful delivery of the data frame is confirmed by the destination workstation setting **frame status flags** to indicate successful receipt of the frame and continuing to forward the original frame around the ring to the sending PC. Upon receipt of the original frame with frame status flags set to "destination address recognized, frame copied successfully," the sending PC resets the token status from busy to free and releases it. After the sending PC releases the token, it is passed along to the next PC, which may either grab the free token or pass it along.

16 Mbps Token Ring network architectures use a modified form of token-passing access methodology in which the token is set to free and released as soon as the transmission of the data frame is completed rather than waiting for the transmitted data frame to return first. This is known as the **early token release mechanism.** The software and protocols that actually handle the token passing and token regeneration (in the case of a lost token) are usually located in the chips on the network adapter card. Figure 2-3 illustrates a simple token-passing access methodology LAN.

Token passing's overhead of waiting for the token before transmitting inhibits overall performance at lower network usage rates. However, because all PC users on a token-passing access control network are well behaved and always have the magic token before accessing the network, there are, by definition, no collisions, making token passing a more efficient access methodology at higher network utilization rates.

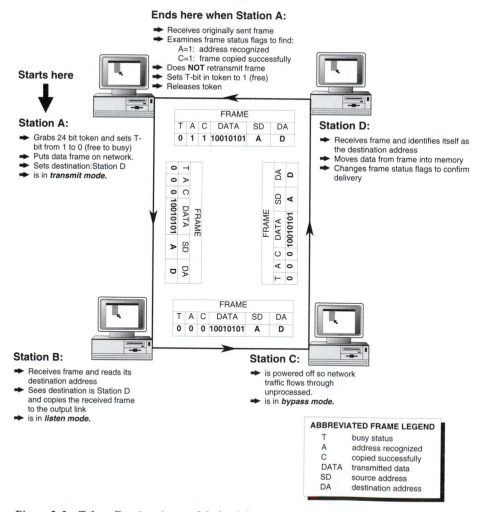

Figure 2-3   Token-Passing Access Methodology

Logical Topology

Once a data message is onto a shared LAN media which is connected to numerous workstations, the next thing to be determined is how that message will be passed from workstation to workstation until it ultimately reaches its intended destination workstation. The particular message-passing methodology employed is more properly known as a network architecture's **logical topology.** An analogy used to describe logical topologies has to do with the best way to put out a fire in a PC user's wastebasket.

Sequential   The first logical topology or method of delivering data is known as **sequential.** In a sequential logical topology, also known as a **ring** logical topology, data are passed from one PC (or node) to another. Each node examines the destination address of the data packet to determine if this particular packet is meant for it. If the data were not meant to be delivered at this node, the data are passed along to the next node in the logical ring.

This is the bucket brigade logical topology method of putting out a fire in a PC user's wastebasket. A bucket of water is filled by one PC user and passed to the neighboring PC user. That user determines if his/her wastebasket is on fire. If it is, the user douses the flames with the bucket of water. Otherwise, the user passes the bucket along to the next user in the logical ring.

Broadcast   The second logical topology or method of delivering data is known as **broadcast.** In a broadcast logical topology, a data message is sent simultaneously to all nodes on the network. Each node decides individually if the data message was directed toward it. If not, the message is simply ignored. There is no need to pass the message along to a neighboring node; they've already gotten the same message.

This is the sprinkler system logical topology method of putting out a fire in a PC user's wastebasket. Rather than worry about passing a bucket of water around a logical ring until it finally reaches the engulfed wastebasket, the water is broadcast over the entire network, thereby notifying the wastebasket on fire that the water was meant for it.

To summarize, in order to appreciate the key difference between sequential and broadcast logical topologies, focus on the role or responsibility of the intermediate workstations to which a destination message is not actually addressed. In the case of sequential logical topology, the non-recipient workstation has a job to do. It must continue to pass the message along to its next sequential neighbor. In the case of a broadcast logical topology, however, the non-recipient workstation has no further responsibilities.

Physical Topology

Finally, the clients and servers must be physically connected to each other according to some configuration and be linked by the shared media of choice. The physical layout of this configuration can have a significant impact on LAN performance and reliability and is known as a network architecture's **physical topology.**

Bus   The **bus** topology is a linear arrangement with terminators on either end and devices connected to the "bus" via connectors and/or transceivers. The purpose of the terminator is to close off the ends of the bus topology, thereby completing the electrical circuit and allowing the data signals to flow. A bus topology without properly matched terminators will not work. The weak link in the bus physical topology is that a break or loose connection anywhere along the entire bus will bring the whole network down.

Ring   The **ring** topology suffers from a similar Achilles' heel. Each PC connected via a ring topology is actually an active part of the ring, passing data packets in a sequential pattern around the ring. If one of the PCs dies, or a network adapter card malfunctions, the "sequence" is broken, the token is lost, and the network is down. In addition, any cable breaks bring down the entire network.

Star   The **star** physical topology avoids these two aforementioned potential pitfalls by employing some type of central management device. Depending on the network architecture and sophistication of the device, it may be called a hub, a wiring center, a concentrator, a MAU (Multiple Access Unit), a repeater, or a switching hub. All of these devices will be studied later in the text. By isolating each PC or node on its own leg or segment of the network, any node or cable failure only affects that leg, whereas the remainder of the network continues to function normally.

Because all network data in a star topology are going through this one central location, it makes a marvelous spot to add system monitoring, security or management capabilities. Conversely, since all network data are going through this one central location, it makes a marvelous networking no-no known as a **single point of failure.** The good news is: any node can be lost and the network will be fine. The bad news is: lose the hub and the whole network goes down.

As we will see shortly in the study of hubs, vendors have risen to the occasion, offering such reliability extras as redundant power supplies, dual buses, and "hot swappable" interface cards. Figure 2-4 highlights the differences between these physical topologies.

■ NETWORK ARCHITECTURES

Ethernet

Origins   The invention of **Ethernet** is generally credited to Robert Metcalfe who went on to become the founder of 3COM Corporation. Although

Bus topology

Star topology

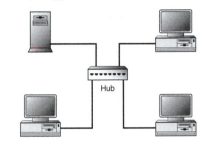

Ring topology

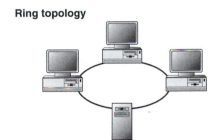

Figure 2-4   LAN Physical Topology Choices

strictly speaking, Ethernet and **IEEE 802.3** are conflicting standards, the term *Ethernet* is commonly used to refer to any IEEE 802.3 compliant network. Differences between the two standards will be outlined shortly.

Functionality

- Access Methodology: CSMA/CD

- Logical Topology: Broadcast

- Physical Topology: Traditionally—Bus; Currently—Most often Star

Standards   The first Ethernet standard was developed by Digital, Intel, and Xerox Corporation in 1981, and was known as DIX 1.0, sometimes referred to as Ethernet I. This standard was superseded in 1982 by DIX 2.0, the current Ethernet standard, also known as Ethernet II. The frame layouts for **Ethernet II** and IEEE 802.3 are illustrated in Figure 2-5.

As illustrated in Figure 2-5, both Ethernet II and IEEE 802.3 frames can vary from 64 to 1518 octets in length.

Ethernet II   The Ethernet II frame layout consists of the following fields:

- The Ethernet II frame starts with a preamble of eight octets. The purpose of the preamble is to alert and synchronize the Ethernet network interface card to the incoming data.

- The destination and source addresses are each six octets long and are also known as MAC layer addresses. These addresses are permanently burned into the ROM (Read Only Memory) of the Ethernet II network interface card at the time of manufacture. The first three octets of the address identify the manufacturer of the network interface card and are assigned by the IEEE. The last three octets are assigned by the manufacturer producing unique MAC layer addresses for all Ethernet network interface cards.

- The type field identifies which network protocols are embedded within the data field. For example, if the data field contained Network IPX/SPX protocols, the type field would have a value of 8137 (hexadecimal) and if the data field contained TCP/IP protocols, the type field would contain a value of 0800 (hexadecimal). These type values are assigned by the IEEE. The type field is important in order to enable multiple protocols to be handled by a single network interface card which enables multiple protocol stacks to be loaded in a

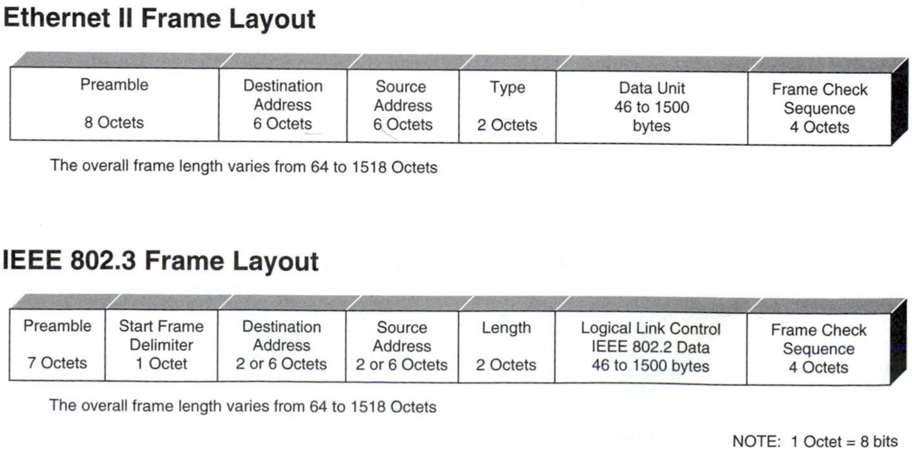

Ethernet II Frame Layout

Preamble 8 Octets	Destination Address 6 Octets	Source Address 6 Octets	Type 2 Octets	Data Unit 46 to 1500 bytes	Frame Check Sequence 4 Octets

The overall frame length varies from 64 to 1518 Octets

IEEE 802.3 Frame Layout

Preamble 7 Octets	Start Frame Delimiter 1 Octet	Destination Address 2 or 6 Octets	Source Address 2 or 6 Octets	Length 2 Octets	Logical Link Control IEEE 802.2 Data 46 to 1500 bytes	Frame Check Sequence 4 Octets

The overall frame length varies from 64 to 1518 Octets

NOTE: 1 Octet = 8 bits

Figure 2-5   Ethernet and IEEE 802.3 Standards

given client or server. Once the network interface card identifies which protocol is embedded within the data field, it can forward that data field to the proper protocol stack for further processing. Multiple protocol stacks allow communication between clients and servers of different network operating systems, which is essential to transparent distributed computing.

- The data unit field contains all of the encapsulated upper layer (network through application) protocols and can vary in length from 46 to 1500 bytes. The 46-byte minimum data field length combines with the 18 octets of fixed overhead of all of the other fields to produce the minimum frame size of 64 octets.

- The **frame check sequence (FCS)** is an error-detection mechanism generated by the transmitting Ethernet network interface card. A 32-bit **cyclical redundancy check (CRC)** is generated over the address, type, and data fields. The receiving Ethernet network interface card regenerates this same CRC on the address, type, and data fields in the received frame and compares the regenerated CRC to the transmitted CRC. If they match, the frame was received error free; 32-bit CRCs have the ability to detect error bursts of up to 31 bits with 100% accuracy.

IEEE 802.3   The IEEE 802.3 frame layout is similar to the Ethernet II frame layout. Highlights of the IEEE 802.3 frame layout are as follows:

- The 7 octet preamble plus the 1 octet starting frame delimiter perform the same basic function as the 8 octet Ethernet II preamble.

- Address fields are defined and assigned in a similar fashion to Ethernet II frames

- The 2 octet length field in the IEEE 802.3 frame takes the place of the type field in the Ethernet frame. The length field indicates the length of the variable length **LLC** (**Logical Link Control** – IEEE 802.2) data field which contains all upper-layer embedded protocols.

- The type of embedded upper-layer protocols is designated by a field within the LLC data unit and is explained more fully in the "In Sharper Focus" section below.

- The frame check sequence is identical to that used in the Ethernet II frame.

IEEE 802.2 AND ETHERNET SNAP

In Sharper Focus

In order for an IEEE 802.3 compliant network interface card to be able to determine the type of protocols embedded within the data field of an IEEE

802.3 frame, it must refer to the header of the **IEEE 802.2** Logical Link Control (LLC) data unit. Figure 2-6 illustrates the fields contained in the IEEE 802.2 data unit.

IEEE 802.3 frame layout
IEEE 802.2 LLC data unit layout

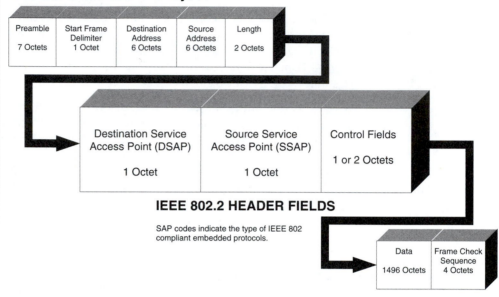

IEEE 802.3 frame layout
IEEE 802.2 LLC data unit layout with SNAP

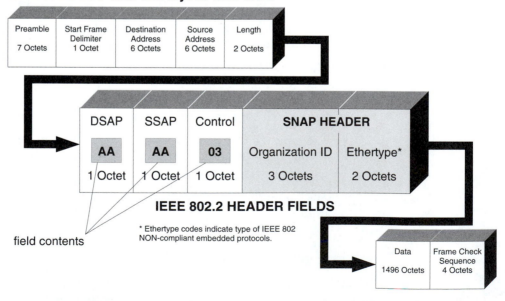

Figure 2-6   IEEE 802.2 and Ethernet SNAP

More specifically, the types of protocols embedded within the data unit are identified within the destination and source service access point fields (**DSAP** and **SSAP**). These fields are analogous to the type field in the Ethernet frame. SAP codes that identify a particular protocol are issued by the IEEE to those companies that register their IEEE-compliant protocols. For example, a SAP code of E0 identifies a Novell protocol and a SAP code of 06 identifies a TCP/IP protocol. NetWare frames adhering to this standard are referred to as NetWare 802.2 (802.3 plus 802.2)

In some cases, however, rendering network protocols to be IEEE 802 compliant was not an easy task. In order to ease the transition to IEEE 802 compliance, an alternative method of identifying the embedded upper-layer protocols was developed, known as **SNAP** or **Sub-Network Access Protocol.** Any protocol can use SNAP with IEEE 802.2 and appear to be an IEEE 802 compliant protocol. In some cases, network operating systems vendors such as NetWare used SNAP until modifications were made to bring protocols into compliance with IEEE standards. Now that NetWare is IEEE 802 compliant and has a designated SAP code, NetWare users can choose a NetWare 802.2 frame layout.

In the case of Ethernet SNAP, a single SAP code of AA in both the DSAP and SSAP, and a Control code of 03 are always used to identify all noncompliant protocols. In order to differentiate which particular noncompliant protocol is embedded, any packet with AA in the DSAP and SSAP fields also has a 5 octet SNAP header known as a **protocol discriminator** following the Control field as illustrated in Figure 2-6. The first three octets of the protocol discriminator are called the Organization ID and indicate to which company the embedded noncompliant protocol belongs, whereas the last two octets are called the EtherType field, which indicates which particular protocol is embedded. All zeros in the Organization ID field indicate that it is a generic Ethernet frame, not unique to any particular company. Examples of EtherType values include:

- 08-00 for TCP/IP
- 81-37 for NetWare

NetWare frames adhering to this specification are known as NetWare 802.2 SNAP (802.3 plus 802.2 plus SNAP).

Media Related Ethernet Standards   Ethernet can run over numerous media types. Various media alternatives and their electrical and transmission characteristics will be explored in the next chapter. The unshielded twisted pair media employed in an Ethernet standard known as **10BaseT** sells for as little as 6 cents per foot. The "10" in 10BaseT refers to 10Mbps capacity. The "Base" refers to **baseband transmission,** meaning that the entire bandwidth of the media is devoted to one data channel. The "T" stands for Twisted Pair, the media of choice. Another important distinction of 10BaseT is that it specifies the use of a star topology with all Ethernet LAN segments connected to a centralized wiring hub. Other Ethernet standards and associated media are listed in Figure 2-7.

Application   The potential for collisions and retransmission on an Ethernet network thanks to its CSMA/CD access methodology has already been mentioned. In some cases, Ethernet networks with between 100 and 200 users barely use the 10 Mbps capacity of the network. However, the nature of the data transmitted is the key to determining potential network capacity problems. Character-based transmissions, such as typical data entry, in which a few characters at a time are typed and sent over the network are much less likely to cause network capacity problems than the transfer of GUI, or graphical user interface screen oriented transmission such as Windows Based Applications. CAD/CAM images are even more bandwidth intensive.

Simultaneous requests for full screen Windows based transfers by 30 or more workstations on a single Ethernet LAN segment can cause collision and network capacity problems on an Ethernet network. As with any data communication problem, there are always solutions or workarounds to these problems. The point in relaying these examples is to provide some assurance that although Ethernet is not unlimited in its network capacity, in most cases, it provides more than enough bandwidth.

Standard	Popular Name	Speed	Media	Maximum Segment Length
10Base5	Frozen yellow garden hose	10 Mbps	Thick coaxial cable (RG-11) (.405 in. diameter)	500 meters
10Base2	ThinNet, CheaperNet	10 Mbps	Thin coaxial cable (RG-58)	185 meters
10BaseT	10BaseT, twisted pair Ethernet	10 Mbps	Unshielded twisted pair	100 meters
10BaseF	Fiber Ethernet FOIRL (Fiber-Optic Inter Repeater Link)	10 Mbps	Multimode fiber optic cable	Described by IEEE 802.1j-1993 standard (1000 meters)
1Base5	StarLAN	1 Mbps	Unshielded twisted pair	500 meters
10BaseT	StarLAN10	10 Mbps	Unshielded twisted pair	100 meters

Figure 2-7   Ethernet Media-specific Standards

Token Ring

Origins   The credit for the first Token Ring network architecture has been attributed to Olaf Soderblum, who proposed such a network in 1969. IBM has been the driving force behind the standardization and adoption of Token Ring with a prototype in IBM's lab in Zurich, Switzerland, serving as a model for the eventual **IEEE 802.5** standard.

Functionality

- Access Methodology: Token Passing

- Logical Topology: Sequential

- Physical Topology: Traditionally—Ring; Currently—Most often Star

Standards   Unlike IEEE 802.3 Ethernet networks that have a speed of 10 Mbps specified as part of the IEEE standard, the IEEE 802.5 Token Ring standard does not include a speed specification. IBM, the leading advocate of the Token Ring network architecture, has specified Token Ring network architectures that operate at 4 Mbps and 16 Mbps.

As mentioned earlier in the discussion of the token passing access methodology, the token is actually a 24-bit formatted data packet and is illustrated in Figure 2-8 along with the IEEE 802.5 Token Ring MAC sub-layer frame layout.

The IEEE 802.5 token frame layout consists of the following fields:

- The starting delimiter field alerts the Token Ring network interface card installed in a workstation that a Token Ring frame is approaching. Notice that both the token frame and the MAC sub-layer frame both start with the starting delimiter.

- Once the Access Control field is received, the workstation can distinguish between tokens and MAC sub-layer frames. If the token bit within the Access Control field (see Figure 2-8) is set to 0, then the received frame represents a free token, in which case the access control field would be immediately followed by an ending delimiter. The workstation is welcome to receive the full token frame and change the token bit from 0 to 1 to indicate a busy token. The received starting delimiter field plus the access control field with the T (Token) bit now set to 1 form the first two fields of an IEEE 802.5 MAC sub-layer data frame, allowing the sending workstation to just append address information, data, and the remaining fields in the data frame layout and transmit this frame onto the ring.

- If the token bit on the received frame was set to 1, then the next field is the frame control field which indicates whether this frame contains data or is a special network management frame.

IEEE 802.5 Token Frame Layout

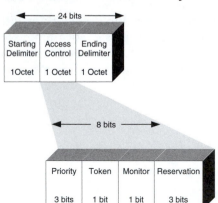

IEEE 802.5 MAC Sub-Layer Frame Layout

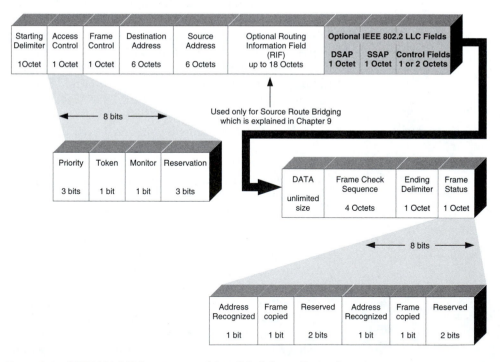

Figure 2-8   IEEE 802.5 Token Ring and MAC Sub-layer Frame Layout

- Following the frame control field are the destination and source address fields. The receiving network interface card would read the destination address to determine if it was the frame's intended recipient. If it was, then the workstation will read the rest of the frame into memory. If not, then the NIC will simply pass the rest of the bits of the frame along the ring without transferring them to the workstation's memory. No snooping allowed.

- The routing information field is used with devices known as source routing bridges which are able to link together multiple Token Ring LANs. Source route bridging and other LAN-to-LAN connectivity options will be discussed in Chapter 14.

- The IEEE 802.2 header fields are used in an identical manner as they are used with IEEE 802.3 Ethernet MAC sub-layer frames. Similarly, IEEE 802.2 SNAP is also supported within the IEEE 802.5 MAC sub-layer frame.

- The data field contains data in the form of embedded upper-level protocols if this is a data frame, and network management information if this is a network management frame as indicated by the frame control field. The data field does not have a fixed maximum length as in the case of Ethernet but is effectively controlled by a timing limit as to how long any workstation can hold onto a token. The timing limit of 10 ms (milliseconds) imposes a practical limit on the size of the data field in a 4 Mbps Token Ring network to about 4500 bytes and on a 16 Mbps Token Ring network to about 16,000 to 18,000 bytes. Token Ring timing issues are explained further in an "In Sharper Focus" section later in this chapter.

- The Frame Check Sequence uses a 32-bit cyclical redundancy check in an identical manner to IEEE 802.3.

- The ending delimiter can not only let the workstation know that the end of the frame has arrived but can also let the workstation know if this was an intermediate frame with more related data to follow immediately behind. The ending delimiter can also indicate if another station has found an error in a frame and has indicated that it should be ignored and returned around the ring to the source address workstation for removal from the ring.

- The Frame Status field serves an important role in letting the sending workstation know whether or not the frame was successfully delivered. If the destination workstation recognized its address, then the A (Address Recognized) bits are set to 1 and if the frame was successfully copied into the destination workstation's memory, then the C (Frame Copied) bits are set to 1. There are two sets of A and C bits for redundancy in order to help eliminate errors. To be more specific, since the A and C bits are set by the destination station after the frame has been received, they are not covered by the Frame Check Sequence error detection mechanism.

One workstation on every Token Ring LAN is designated as the active monitor and acts as a kind of caretaker of the Token Ring network architecture. Being the active monitor requires no special hardware or software and all other workstations are designated standby monitors. Among the tasks that can be performed by the active monitor are the following:

- Removes frames from the ring which have not been removed by their sending workstations.

- Regenerates lost or damaged tokens

- Provides a special 24-bit buffer if the physical ring is so small that it does not have enough delay or latency to hold the 24-bit token. For more information, see the "In Sharper Focus" entitled "Token Ring and Timing."

- Controls the master clock

- Makes sure that there is only one designated active monitor on this ring.

Application   IBM's Token Ring network architecture, adhering to the IEEE 802.5 standard, utilizes a star configuration, sequential message delivery, and a token-passing access methodology scheme.

Remembering that the sequential logical topology is equivalent to passing messages from neighbor to neighbor around a ring, the Token Ring network architecture is sometimes referred to as **Logical Ring, Physical Star.**

The Token Ring's use of the token passing access methodology furnishes one of the key positive attributes of this network architecture. The guarantee of no data collisions with assured data delivery afforded by the token-passing access methodology is a key selling point in some environments where immediate, guaranteed delivery is essential.

The second attribute in Token Ring's favor is the backing of a computer company of the magnitude of IBM. For those businesses facing integration of PCs with existing IBM mainframes and minicomputers, IBM's Token Ring network architecture offers assurance of the possibility of such an integration.

Although Token Ring is IBM's PC networking architecture, it is neither a closed system nor a monopoly. Third-party suppliers offer choices in the network adapter card and wiring hub (Multiple Access Unit) markets while numerous network operating systems run over the Token Ring architecture. Competition encourages research and development of new technology and can eventually drive prices down. Price is an important point about Token Ring. Network adapter cards for a Token Ring network tend to cost between one and one-half to two times as much as Ethernet network adapter cards.

ADDRESS BIT-ORDER REVERSAL

One small but significant difference between Ethernet and Token Ring networks is known as **address bit order reversal.** As illustrated in Figure 2-9,

In Sharper Focus

Original Data Stream of 6 bytes

6 BYTES					
11110101	00110111	10111011	10000110	01110010	01010110

IEEE 802.3 Transmission

DESTINATION ADDRESS CONSISTING OF 6 BYTES					
BYTE 0	BYTE 1	BYTE 2	BYTE 3	BYTE 4	BYTE 5
1 1 1 1 0 1 0 1	0 0 1 1 0 1 1 1	1 0 1 1 1 0 1 1	1 0 0 0 0 1 1 0	0 1 1 1 0 0 1 0	0 1 0 1 0 1 1 0
bit 7 bit 6 bit 5 bit 4 bit 3 bit 2 bit 1 bit 0	bit 7 bit 6 bit 5 bit 4 bit 3 bit 2 bit 1 bit 0	bit 7 bit 6 bit 5 bit 4 bit 3 bit 2 bit 1 bit 0	bit 7 bit 6 bit 5 bit 4 bit 3 bit 2 bit 1 bit 0	bit 7 bit 6 bit 5 bit 4 bit 3 bit 2 bit 1 bit 0	bit 7 bit 6 bit 5 bit 4 bit 3 bit 2 bit 1 bit 0

Note that in the IEEE 802.3 transmission the least significant bit (BIT 0) is transmitted last.

IEEE 802.5 Transmission

DESTINATION ADDRESS CONSISTING OF 6 BYTES					
BYTE 0	BYTE 1	BYTE 2	BYTE 3	BYTE 4	BYTE 5
1 0 1 0 1 1 1 1	1 1 1 0 1 1 0 0	1 1 0 1 1 1 0 1	0 1 1 0 0 0 0 1	0 1 0 0 1 1 1 0	0 1 1 0 1 0 1 0
bit 0 bit 1 bit 2 bit 3 bit 4 bit 5 bit 6 bit 7	bit 0 bit 1 bit 2 bit 3 bit 4 bit 5 bit 6 bit 7	bit 0 bit 1 bit 2 bit 3 bit 4 bit 5 bit 6 bit 7	bit 0 bit 1 bit 2 bit 3 bit 4 bit 5 bit 6 bit 7	bit 0 bit 1 bit 2 bit 3 bit 4 bit 5 bit 6 bit 7	bit 0 bit 1 bit 2 bit 3 bit 4 bit 5 bit 6 bit 7

Note that in the IEEE 802.5 transmission the least significant bit (BIT 0) is transmitted first.

Figure 2-9   Address Bit-Order Reversal in Ethernet and Token Ring

both Ethernet and Token Ring refer to the first (left-most) octet of the address as Byte 0. Also, both Ethernet and Token Ring believe that bit 0 on byte 0, referred to as the **least significant bit,** should be transmitted first. However, in the case of IEEE 802.3, the least significant bit is the right-most bit of the byte and in the case of IEEE 802.5, the least significant bit is the left-most bit of the byte. This bit order reversal is especially troublesome for translating bridges which must translate between Token Ring and Ethernet frames.

In Sharper Focus

TOKEN RING AND TIMING

In order for the Token Ring network architecture to operate correctly, the 24-bit token must circulate continuously even if no workstations are in need of transmitting data. Therefore, the entire Token Ring network must possess enough delay or latency to hold the entire 24-bit token. This latency or required delay can be computed by dividing the length of the token (24 bits) by the ring's transmission speed (4 Mbps) yielding a required latency of 6 microseconds. The next question is how far can an electrical signal travel in 6 microseconds? The answer to that question will depend on the media through which the signal is traveling, with different media possessing different propagation velocities. For example, unshielded twisted pair has a propagation velocity of .59 times the speed of light, denoted as "c." The speed of light is equal to 300,000,000 meters/sec. Finally, the minimum ring size to introduce the required 6 microseconds of delay can be calculated as follows:

$$
\begin{aligned}
\text{Minimum Ring Size} &= \text{Required Latency} \times \text{propagation velocity of media} \\
&= 0.000006 \text{ seconds} \times .59 \times 300,000,000 \text{ meters/second} \\
&= 1062 \text{ meters} \\
&= 1.062 \text{ kilometers}
\end{aligned}
$$

According to this calculation the minimum size of a Token Ring network, even for three or four workstations would have to be more than a kilometer in length. This is obviously not practical. As mentioned earlier, the active monitor station adds a 24-bit delay buffer to the ring to ensure that regardless of the physical size of the ring, the token will be able to continually circulate.

Managerial Perspective

TOKEN RING OR ETHERNET?

Discussions as to the relative merits of Token Ring or Ethernet network architectures were once conducted with all the fervor of a religious war. There seems to be less argument now as estimates put the ratio of Ethernet networks to Token Ring networks at about 3 to 1. This is not to say that Ethernet is a better network architecture. The significant advantage in terms of Ethernet market share probably has more to do with the affordability and availability of Ethernet vs. Token Ring hardware. Ethernet cards sell from $20 to $150, whereas Token Ring cards sell from $219 to $475. A 16-port 10 Mbps Ethernet hub sells for as little as $120, whereas the equivalent Token Ring MAU (Multistation Access Unit) sells for $750.

In terms of performance, the fact is that Ethernet works just fine in most installations. Although Ethernet is said to offer 10 Mbps, when collisions and overhead are taken into consideration, actual throughputs of 6 Mbps are more the norm. There is no argument that Token Ring's deterministic access methodology eliminates collisions at higher traffic levels. However, due to the overhead associated with the token management, performance at lower traffic levels can suffer. Research performed on 16 Mbps Token Ring, which features the early token release mechanism, has shown conflicting results. Some studies show that network performance is not significantly greater than 10 Mbps, whereas others show nearly a full 16 Mbps throughput. If one considers cost/Mbps of throughput rather than just pure equipment cost differences, Token Ring begins to look more favorable.

At one time, Token Ring network architectures were more easily integrated with minicomputer and mainframe environments. This is no longer true since the mainframe/minicomputer world has evolved to embrace open systems, TCP/IP, and Ethernet.

In conclusion, the biggest difference between Token Ring and Ethernet continues to be the initial expense of the Token Ring hardware and the overwhelming market share of Ethernet. Performance is not significantly different and interoperability between the two network architectures is possible, although challenges do exist. Ethernet/Token Ring bridges provide transparent interoperability between the two network architectures and will be detailed in Chapter 13.

In Sharper Focus

ARCNET

ARCNet (Attached Resources Computer Network) was a popular local area network architecture that was originally developed by Datapoint, Inc. It offered 2.5 Mbps transmission speed and used a token-passing access methodology, a broadcast logical topology, and a star physical topology over RG-62 coaxial cable. Since RG-62 is the same cable used to connect IBM 3270 terminals to cluster controllers, ARCNet was often installed in downsized IBM installations where the cable could be reused. ARCNet was never standardized by the IEEE and has been largely replaced by Ethernet and Token Ring network architectures.

FDDI

Origins   **Fiber Distributed Data Interface (FDDI)** is a 100 Mbps network architecture that was first specified in 1984 by the ANSI (American National Standards Institute) subcommittee entitled X3T9.5. It is important to note that FDDI is not an IEEE standard. However, FDDI does support IEEE 802.2 Logical Link Control protocols offering it transparent interoperability to IEEE compliant upper-layer protocols (layers 3–7).

Functionality

- Access Methodology: Modified Token Passing

- Logical Topology: Sequential

- Physical Topology: Dual Counter-Rotating Rings

Built-in Reliability and Longer Distance   FDDI (Fiber Distributed Data Interface) supplies not only a great deal (100 Mbps) of bandwidth, but also a high degree of reliability and security while adhering to standards-based protocols not associated with or promoted by any particular vendor.

FDDI's reliability comes not only from the fiber itself, which is immune to both **EMI** (Electro Magnetic Interference) and **RFI** (Radio Frequency Interference), but an additional degree of reliability is achieved through the design of the physical topology of FDDI.

FDDI's physical topology is comprised of not one, but two, separate rings around which data move simultaneously in opposite directions. One ring is the primary data ring, whereas the other is a secondary or backup data ring to be used only in the case of the failure of the primary ring or an attached workstation. Although both rings are attached to a single hub or concentrator, a single point of failure remains in the hub while achieving redundancy in the network media. Figure 2-10 illustrates some of the key features of the FDDI network architecture and technology, while Figure 2-11 more specifically illustrates the self-healing capabilities of the dual counter-rotating rings network architecture of FDDI.

In addition to speed and reliability, distance is another key feature of an FDDI LAN. Up to 500 nodes at 2 km apart can be linked to an FDDI network. The total media can stretch for a total circumference of up to 200 km (125 miles) if repeaters are used at least every 2 km. This increased distance capability makes FDDI an excellent choice as a high-speed backbone network for campus environments.

Another positive attribute of FDDI, illustrated in Figure 2-10, is its ability to interoperate easily with IEEE 802.3 10 Mbps Ethernet networks. In this

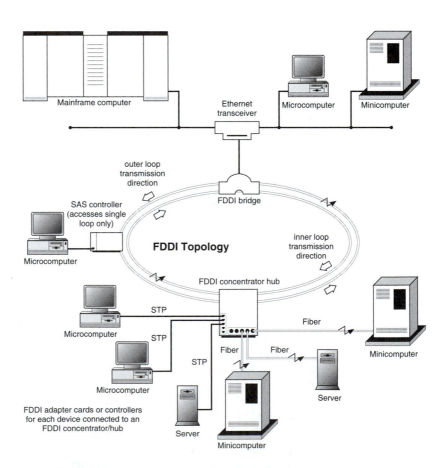

Figure 2-10   FDDI Network Architecture and Technology

Dual-Attached Workstations in ***Normal Operation***

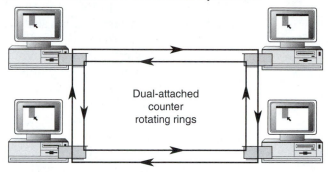

Self healed after ***Link Failure***

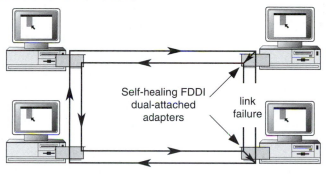

Self-healed after ***Station Failure***

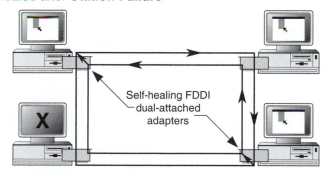

Figure 2-11   FDDI's Self-healing Ability

way, a business does not have to scrap its entire existing network in order to upgrade a piece of it to 100 Mbps FDDI. An FDDI to Ethernet bridge is the specific technology employed in such a setup.

The technology involved with FDDI network architectures is similar in function to that of other network architectures and is illustrated in Figure 2-10. PCs, workstations, minicomputers, or mainframes that wish to access the FDDI LAN must be equipped with either internal FDDI network adapter cards or external FDDI controllers.

One way that some network managers cut down on FDDI's cost while still benefiting from the 100 Mbps bandwidth is to connect only to one of FDDI's two fiber rings. This type of connection is sometimes called **SAS,** or **Single Attachment Stations,** as opposed to **DAS,** or **Dual Attachment Stations,** in which both FDDI rings are accessed. Obviously, if a device is attached to only one FDDI ring, it forgoes the reliability afforded by the redundant secondary data ring.

At the heart of the FDDI LAN is the FDDI Concentrator or Hub. The design of these hubs is often modular, with backbone connections to both FDDI rings, management modules, and device attachment modules in various media varieties available for customized design and ease of installation. In reality, most FDDI traffic is directed through routers with inserted FDDI modules rather than dedicated FDDI hubs or concentrators. Routers will be discussed further in Chapter 13.

Another key piece of FDDI technology is the FDDI to Ethernet bridge, which allows 10 Mbps Ethernet LANs to interface with the 100 Mbps FDDI LANs. The Ethernet LANs are often department-based based networks, whereas the FDDI is more likely to be a campus-wide backbone. Bridges may be able to connect either a single Ethernet or several Ethernets to the FDDI LAN.

Standards FDDI uses a modified token-passing access methodology. The word *modified* is used here because it is different from the IEEE 802.5 Token Ring type token-passing in at least two key respects.

- First, because of the great potential distances on an FDDI LAN, it was impractical to turn "free" tokens into "busy" tokens and let a single station monopolize that token until it had received confirmation of successful delivery of its data. Instead, unlike Token Ring, which just flipped the T bit in the access control byte from 0 to 1 and appended a data frame, FDDI physically removes the token from the ring and transmits a full data frame. Upon completion of transmission, it immediately releases a new token. Recall that Token Ring waited until the transmitted frame returned before releasing the token. Collisions are still avoided, since only one station can have the free token at a time, and stations cannot put data messages onto the network without a token.

- A second token passing modification in FDDI is that numerous messages may be sent by a single PC before relinquishing the token as opposed to the "one message per token per customer" philosophy of the IEEE 802.5 token-passing access methodology. Frames transmitted in a continuous stream are known as **synchronous frames** and are prioritized according to a methodology known as **synchronous bandwidth allocation** or **SBA,** which assigns fixed amounts of bandwidth to given stations. While synchronous frames are being transmitted, any unused network capacity can still be used by other workstations transmitting **asynchronous frames.**

Figure 2-12 illustrates both a FDDI token layout and a FDDI data frame layout.

An alternative to fiber-based FDDI is to run FDDI over copper wiring, either shielded or unshielded twisted pair, as used in Ethernet and Token Ring installations. Cost savings of UTP over fiber amount to about 33%. Because running a fiber-based architecture over copper sounds a little strange, this variation of FDDI has been dubbed **CDDI** or **Copper Distributed Data Interface.** Although it will still support 100 Mbps, distance is limited to 100 meters per segment as compared with the 2 km per segment of Fiber-Based FDDI. The official ANSI standard for CDDI is known as **TP-PMD** (Twisted Pair-Physical Media Dependent). The pinouts or wiring pattern for TP-PMD are not the same as 10BaseT Ethernet over twisted pair pinouts. CDDI has been largely forgotten with the introduction of 100 Mbps Ethernet alternatives, explained later in this chapter.

Application

In order to understand FDDI and CDDI, it is necessary to first understand why 10 Mbps Ethernet and 16 Mbps Token Ring may not contain sufficient bandwidth for the bandwidth-hungry applications of the not-too-distant future. The major bandwidth drivers fall into two major categories:

FDDI Token Layout

Preamble	Starting Delimiter	Frame Control	Ending Delimiter
8 Octets	1 Octet	1 Octet	1 Octet

FDDI Data Frame Structure

Preamble	Starting Delimiter	Frame Control	Destination Address	Source Address	DATA up to	Frame Check Sequence	Ending Delimiter	Frame Status
8 Octets	1 Octet	1 Octet	6 Octets	6 Octets	4500 Octets	4 Octets (32 bit CRC)	.5 Octet (4 Bits)	1.5 Octets (12 Bits)

Figure 2-12   FDDI Token and Data Frame Layouts

1. Network Architecture Trends

2. Network Application Trends

As more and more users become attached to LANs, the demand for overall network bandwidth increases. LANs are increasing both in size and overall complexity. Internetworking of LANs of various protocols via bridges and routers creates more overall LAN traffic. FDDI is frequently used as a high-speed backbone network architecture servicing multiple lower-speed network segments, each of which supports multiple workstations, although even higher-speed network architectures are being introduced into the network bandwidth hierarchy.

Network applications are driving the demand for increased bandwidth as well. Distributed computing, data distribution, and client/server computing all rely on a network architecture foundation of high bandwidth and high reliability. Imaging, multimedia, and data/voice integration all require high amounts of bandwidth in order to transport and display these various data formats in "real" time.

In other words, if full-motion video is to be transported across the LAN as part of a multimedia program, there should be sufficient bandwidth available on that LAN for the video to run at full speed and not in slow motion. Similarly, digitized voice transmission should sound "normal" when transported across a LAN of sufficient bandwidth.

The uses of the FDDI or other high-speed network architectures seem to fall into three categories. Although FDDI may fulfill any of the listed roles, with the proliferation of relatively inexpensive 100 Mbps Ethernet network interface cards, hubs, and switches, FDDI has been largely relegated to a campus backbone role.:

1. Campus backbone—Not necessarily implying a college campus, this implementation is used for connecting LANs located throughout a series of closely situated buildings. Remember that the total ring circumference can equal 200 km and multiple FDDI LANs are always a possibility. Building backbones would fall into this category as well, with perhaps a 100 Mbps FDDI building backbone going between floors connecting numerous 10 Mbps Ethernet LANs located on the various floors via routers. High-bandwidth devices such as servers can be connected to the FDDI backbone via concentrators. Multiple concentrators attaching multiple devices to the FDDI rings as illustrated in Figure 2-13 is known as a **dual ring of trees.** In some cases, a given server may be connected to more than one FDDI concentrator to provide redundant connections and increased fault tolerance. Dual connecting servers in this manner is known as **dual homing.**

2. High Bandwidth Workgroups—The second application category is when the FDDI LAN is used as a truly local area network, connect-

Backbone

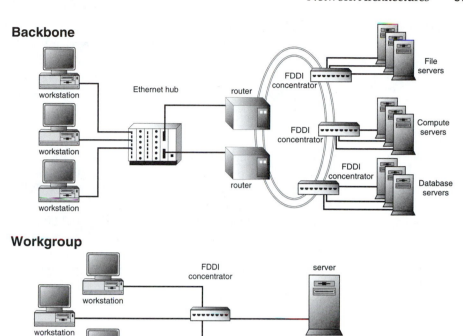

Workgroup

Sub-workgroup

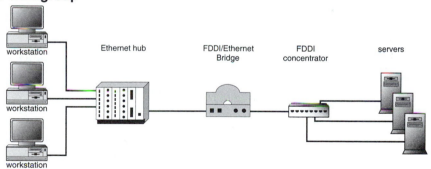

Figure 2-13   Alternative Applications of the FDDI Network Architecture

ing a few (fewer than 20) PCs or Workstations that require high bandwidth communication with each other. Multimedia workstations, engineering workstations, or CAD/CAM workstations are good examples of high bandwidth workstations. As "Power Users" turn increasingly toward high-bandwidth Graphical User Interfaces (GUI), this constituency's bandwidth requirements will rise as well.

3. High Bandwidth Sub-WorkGroup Connections—In some cases, only two or three devices, perhaps servers, need high bandwidth

requirements. As distributing computing and data distribution increase as part of the downsizing and applications rightsizing trends sweeping the information systems industry, an increasing demand for high-speed server to server data transfer will be seen. Figure 2-13 illustrates alternative applications of the FDDI network architecture.

After all of these positive things are said about FDDI, surely there must be something negative about this LAN network architecture. Chief among the negatives is price, although how long price will be a negative remains to be seen. As with any other shared media network architecture, in order for a PC to access an FDDI LAN, it must be equipped with an FDDI network adapter card. These cards range from $800 to $1,000, with the "lower" priced FDDI network adapter cards able to attach to and use only one of the two FDDI data rings. Compare these prices with the average Ethernet Card at $25 to $200 and the average Token Ring card at approximately twice that price.

As FDDI gains in popularity and competition increases in the FDDI technology market, prices will undoubtedly fall, although it is doubtful that they will ever reach Ethernet price levels. The fiber media itself is seen as a negative factor by some as well. Although fiber is lightweight and can be packed more densely than copper wire, it is made of glass and can break. Also, connecting, terminating, and splicing fiber-optic cables require special tools and training. These obstacles can be overcome and, at least in some cases, the "fear of fiber" may be nothing more than the fear of the unknown.

Managerial Perspective

FDDI'S FUTURE

Occasionally in the field of data communications and networking, one technology is eclipsed or replaced by a newer technology that might be cheaper, easier to work with, or both. This may be the fate of FDDI. At one time, FDDI was the only network architecture alternative to turn to when Ethernet and Token Ring could no longer meet demands for bandwidth capacity. As will be seen in the next section, today there are numerous alternative high-speed network architectures that are able to exceed FDDI in terms of price, performance, and ease of use. That is not to say that FDDI is dead, but as will be seen in the next section, the handwriting may be on the wall.

■ HIGH-SPEED NETWORK ARCHITECTURES

100BaseT

100BaseT represents a family of Fast Ethernet standards offering 100 Mbps performance and adhering to the CSMA/CD access methodology. The details of the operation of 100BaseT are in the **IEEE 802.3u** standard. The three media-specific physical layer standards of 100BaseT are as follows:

- **100BaseTX**—this is the most common of the three standards and the one for which the most technology is available. It specifies 100 Mbps performance over two pair of Category 5 UTP (Unshielded Twisted Pair) or two pair of Type 1 STP (Shielded Twisted Pair).

- **100BaseT4**—physical layer standard for 100 Mbps transmission over four pair of Category 3, 4, or 5 UTP.

- **100BaseFX**—physical layer standard for 100 Mbps transmission over duplex multimode fiber-optic cable.

Network Architecture   100BaseT standards use the same IEEE802.3 MAC sub-layer frame layout and yet transmit it at 10 times faster than 10BaseT. Obviously, there must be a trade-off somewhere. The trade-off comes in the maximum network diameter:

- 10BaseT's maximum network diameter is 2,500 meters with up to four repeaters/hubs between any two end nodes

- 100BaseT's maximum network diameter is 210 meters with up to only two repeaters/hubs between end nodes

100BaseT is implemented as a shared-media LAN network architecture that links 100BaseT workstations via 100BaseT hubs and repeaters.

In Sharper Focus

TIMING ISSUES AND 100BaseT NETWORK DIAMETER

Collisions are a fact of life with any CSMA/CD-based network architecture. The time required for a given workstation to detect a collision is known as **slot time** and is measured in bits. When collisions occur, the transmitting station must be notified of the collision so that the affected frame can be retransmitted. However, this collision notification and retransmission must occur before the slot time has expired. The slot time for both 10BaseT and 100BaseT is 512 bits or 64 bytes.

The speed of 100BaseT is obviously 10 times as fast as 10BaseT. In order to be certain that collision notifications are received by 100BaseT network-attached-workstations before their constant slot time expires, the maximum network diameter must be reduced proportionately to the increase in network speed. As a result, the maximum network diameter shrinks from 2,500 meters to 210 meters.

Technology   Most of the 100BaseT NICs are called **10/100 NICs,** which means that they are able to support either 10BaseT or 100BaseT, but not simultaneously. These cards cost slightly more than quality 10BaseT only cards, allowing network managers to buy 100BaseT capability, which can be enabled later when the requisite 100BaseT hubs are installed.

The 10BaseT and 100BaseT networks can only interoperate with the help of internetworking devices such as 10/100 bridges and routers. These types of technology will be discussed in more depth in Chapter 13.

Some Ethernet switches (discussed in Chapter 3) have the capability to support 100BaseT connections and to auto-sense, or distinguish between, 10BaseT and 100BaseT traffic. Figure 2-14 illustrates a representative 100BaseT installation.

100VG-AnyLAN

100VG-AnyLAN is a 100 Mbps alternative to 100BaseT, which replaces the CSMA/CD access methodology with **Demand Priority Access** or **DPA,** otherwise known as **Demand Priority Protocol** or **DPP.** Details of the 100VG-AnyLAN network architecture are contained in the proposed **IEEE 802.12** standard. The "AnyLAN" part of this network architectures name refers to its ability to deliver standard IEEE 802.3 or IEEE 802.5 MAC layer frames. However, both of these frame types cannot be delivered simultaneously by the same 100VG-AnyLAN network.

IEEE 802.3 and IEEE 802.5 Support   100VG-AnyLAN's ability to support IEEE 802.3 and IEEE 802.5 frame types and networks more specifically means:

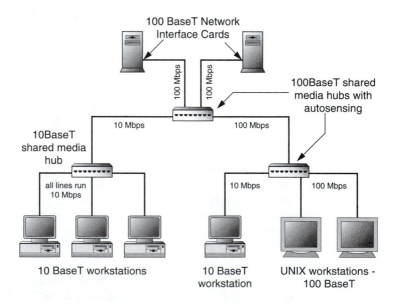

Figure 2-14   100BaseT Network Architecture Implementation

- If current cabling for existing 10BaseT or Token Ring LANs meets the respective cabling specifications for those LANs, then 100VG-Any-LAN will run over the existing LAN cabling without changes to network design or cabling.

- Current network operating systems and application programs need not be modified in order to operate with the upgraded 100VG-Any-LAN network interface cards.

- 10BaseT and Token Ring LANs can communicate with 100VG-Any-LANs by linking the respective LANs with internetworking devices such as bridges and routers.

Figure 2-15 illustrates the integration of IEEE 802.3, IEEE 802.5, and 100VG-AnyLAN network architectures.

Network Architecture   100VG-AnyLAN is able to match 100BaseT's speed performance and offer the following network architecture characteristics:

- Supports a network diameter of up to 2,500 meters between any two end nodes. This is the same as 10BaseT and more than 10 times the maximum diameter of 100BaseT.

- Supports up to four hubs/repeaters between any two end nodes while 100BaseT supports up to two.

Obviously, 100VG-AnyLAN cannot offer these gains in network architecture as compared to 100BaseT without some sort of trade-off.

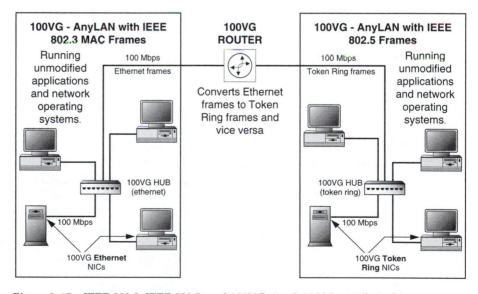

Figure 2-15   IEEE 802.3, IEEE 802.5, and 100VG-AnyLAN Network Architectures

The major difference is in the cabling requirements. Whereas 10BaseT and 100BaseT only require two pair of UTP to operate, 100VG-AnyLAN requires four pair of either Category 3, 4, or 5 UTP using a signaling methodology known as quartet signaling or channeling. Cabling standards have also been defined for two pair of Type 1 shielded twisted pair, as well as single mode and multimode fiber-optic cable.

Demand Priority Access   Perhaps the most unique aspect of the 100VG-AnyLAN network architecture is the Demand Priority Access access methodology, also known as DPMA (Demand Priority Media Access). This unique access methodology eliminated the collisions and retransmissions that are characteristic of Ethernet and the token rotation delays of Token Ring. Key points of this access methodology are as follows:

- Specialized 100VG-AnyLAN hubs control all access to the network

- Using a **round robin polling scheme,** the hubs scan each port in sequence to see if the attached workstations have any traffic to transmit. The round robin polling scheme is distributed through a hierarchical arrangement of cascaded hubs.

- Ports can be designated as high priority, thereby giving priority delivery status to time-sensitive types of traffic such as video or voice that require guaranteed delivery times for smooth presentation. This makes 100VG-AnyLAN especially well suited for multimedia traffic.

- These high and low priorities can be assigned by application programs as well as ports.

- High-priority ports cannot permanently monopolize the entire network. Once lower-priority ports have been timed out for 250–300 ms (milliseconds), they are boosted to high priority.

In Sharper Focus

CASCADING HUBS AND THE ROUND ROBIN POLLING SCHEME

As illustrated in Figure 2-16, the central hub, also known as the controlling hub or the root hub, controls the access to the network, whereas all lower-level hubs maintain communication with attached workstations and maintain address tables identifying which workstations are attached to which ports. When a workstation requests permission of its locally attached hub to load a message onto the network, that request for permission is passed up through the hierarchy of hubs until it reaches the designated controlling hub. The permission granted in response to this request to transmit onto the network is passed down through the hub hierarchy to the initially requesting workstation. Remember, a maximum of only four hubs or repeaters can lie between any two end nodes or workstations.

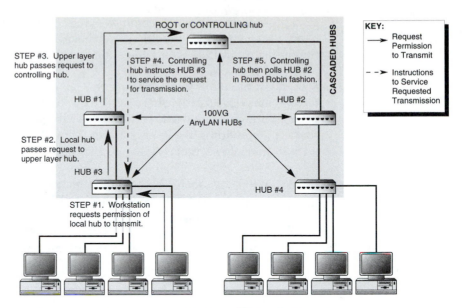

Figure 2-16   Cascading Hubs and the Round Robin Polling Scheme

Technology   The implementation of a 100VG-AnyLAN requires compliant NICs, driver software, and hubs. 100VG-AnyLAN NICs cost between $260 and $315, whereas hubs cost about $230 per port. For ease of migration most 10/100 Ethernet 100VG-AnyLAN NICs are available for less than $300. It is important to determine whether this 100VG-AnyLAN technology will be transporting Ethernet frames or Token Ring frames. Specific NICs and hubs must be purchased for each of the two transported frame types, with Ethernet 100VG-AnyLAN technology being more readily available than Token Ring 100VG-AnyLAN technology. The indisputable fact is that regardless of comparative technical merits, 100BaseT has won the Fast Ethernet network architecture battle and investment in 100VG-AnyLAN technology should be carefully scrutinized.

Isochronous Ethernet

Although the ability to transport time-sensitive traffic such as voice, video, or multimedia is one of the advantages of 100VG-AnyLAN, other network architectures such as **Isochronous Ethernet,** also known as **Iso-Ethernet,** can also effectively transport such traffic, although not at 100 Mbps performance. Details of the Iso-Ethernet network architecture are contained in the **IEEE 802.9a** standard, which is officially known as Isochronous Ethernet Integrated Services. The term **isochronous** refers to any signaling system in which all connections or circuits are synchronized using a single common clocking reference. This common clocking mechanism allows such systems to offer guaranteed delivery times, which are very important to streaming or time-sensitive traffic such as voice and video.

Network Architecture   One unique feature of the Iso-Ethernet network architecture is its close relationship with **ISDN (Integrated Services Digital Network)** wide area network services. Iso-Ethernet offers a combination of services by dividing the overall 16.144 Mbps bandwidth delivered to each workstation into several service-specific channels:

- A 10 Mbps ISDN **P channel** is reserved for Ethernet traffic and is completely compatible with 10BaseT Ethernet. In fact, this P channel can be used by 10Base T NICs, allowing network managers to selectively or gradually migrate to Iso-Ethernet offering the multimedia capabilities to only those workstations that require it.

- A 6.144 Mbps ISDN **C channel** is reserved for streaming time-sensitive traffic such as multimedia applications.

The 6.144 Mbps C channel is in fact further subdivided into:

- 96 64 Kbps ISDN **B channels,** which carry the actual multimedia traffic. Applications are able to aggregate these B channels as needed up to the 6.144 Mbps limit.

- 1 64 Kbps ISDN **D channel** which is used for management tasks such as call control and signaling.

The 6.144 Mbps C channel which carries the multimedia traffic uses the same 8 KHz clocking signal as the commercial ISDN WAN services offered by long-distance carriers, enabling a transparent interface between the Iso-Ethernet LAN and WAN segments. This "same clocking signal" is the derivation of the term *Iso* (same as) *chronous* (timing).

Network diameter of an Iso-Ethernet network is limited to 100 meters from the most distant LAN workstation to the WAN interface. Iso-Ethernet runs over two pair of Category 3 or 5 Unshielded Twisted Pair, allowing it to operate over existing network wiring in many cases.

Iso-Ethernet networks operate in three different service modes:

1. 10BaseT Mode—Uses only the 10 Mbps P channel for Ethernet traffic.

2. Multi-service Mode—Uses both the 10 Mbps P channel for Ethernet and the 6.144 Mbps C channel for video/multimedia.

3. All Isochronous Mode—Uses all 16.144 Mbps (248×64 Kbps channels) for streaming protocols. This amount of isochronous bandwidth will support real-time video or voice distribution.

Figure 2-17 illustrates an implemented Iso-Ethernet architecture including WAN links, transparent interoperability with 10BaseT workstations, and simultaneous transmission of Ethernet and multimedia traffic. Figure 2-18 illustrates the breakdown of the 16.144 Mbps Iso-Ethernet bandwidth.

Technology Iso-Ethernet hubs are known as **Attachment Units (AU)** and cost between $400 and $500 per port, whereas Iso-Ethernet NICs cost between $200 and $300 each. Most Iso-Ethernet Attachment Units include an integrated WAN port, which is configured to be linked to commercial ISDN services available from long-distance carriers. A workstation with an Iso-Ethernet NIC installed is properly referred to as **Integrated Services Terminal Equipment (ISTE).** In order to transmit isochronous traffic, 10BaseT NICs and hubs must be replaced. However, all 10BaseT NICs and hubs do not have to be replaced at the same time.

High-Speed Token Ring—HSTR

A 100 Mbps Token Ring network architecture, otherwise known as **high-speed token ring (HSTR),** has been approved by an organization known as the High-Speed Token Ring Alliance. One of the interesting characteristics of

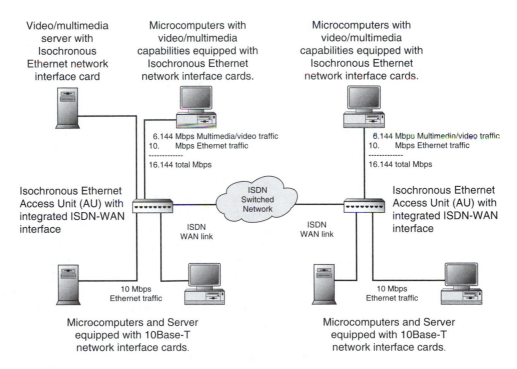

Figure 2-17   Isochronous Ethernet Network Architecture

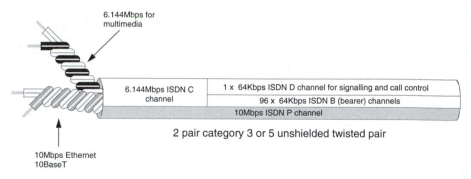

6.144Mbps for
multimedia

6.144Mbps ISDN C
channel

1 x 64Kbps ISDN D channel for signalling and call control

96 x 64Kbps ISDN B (bearer) channels

10Mbps ISDN P channel

2 pair category 3 or 5 unshielded twisted pair

10Mbps Ethernet
10BaseT

Figure 2-18   Isochronous Ethernet Bandwidth Profile

the 100 Mbps standard is that it supports a standard for virtual LANs (Chapter 3) known as IEEE 802.1q that will allow Ethernet frames to be encapsulated within Token Ring frames, an important characteristic in those organizations that must support both network architectures. Although 100 Mbps Token Ring NICs, switches, and router modules may be available, remember that compatible driver software must be available to allow any network operating system to be able to communicate with these devices. To date, high speed token ring has generated little interest in comparison to 100 Mbps Ethernet alternatives.

**In Sharper
Focus**

FULL DUPLEX NETWORK ARCHITECTURES

Switched LAN architectures, which will be studied more thoroughly in the next chapter, depend on specialized LAN wiring centers known as switches and are able to provide dedicated point-to-point links between communicating clients and servers. In the case of Ethernet switches, for example, since the point-to-point link between two communicating PCs is dedicated, there can be no data collisions and there is no longer a need for an access methodology such as CSMA/CD, since no other workstations are contending for this dedicated bandwidth connection. As a result, communication between the two computers that serve as the end points of this switched dedicated connection could both send and receive data to and from each other simultaneously. This switch dependent capability is known as **Full Duplex Ethernet** and requires specialized full duplex Ethernet NICs, NIC drivers, and full duplex Ethernet switches. Many Ethernet switches allow certain ports, such as those attached to servers, to be set for Full Duplex Ethernet. In such an implementation, only the servers attached to Full Duplex switch ports would require Full Duplex NICs. In theory, full duplex Ethernet should allow twice the normal Ethernet performance speed by offering a dedicated 10 Mpbs communication channel in each direction for a total available bandwidth of 20 Mbps.

In practice, the throughput, or actual data transferred, on full duplex Ethernet connections is not nearly 20 Mbps. Chief among the reasons for this is that the amount of network transmission is a product of application program design. Most distributed application programs tend to exhibit short requests for services from clients to servers followed by large transfers of data from the server back to the client. However, this does not mean that the technology lacks the ability to deliver higher performance. Controlled tests involving high bandwidth applications have produced throughput of 20 Mbps. As a result, the most likely implementation scenarios for Full Duplex Ethernet is in switch-to-switch connections and switch-to-server connections.

Because the full duplex NIC installed in the computer is both sending and receiving data simultaneously, a multithreaded operating system and network operating system are required to take full advantage of this technology. Examples of such multithreaded operating systems and network operating systems are Windows NT, OS/2, NetWare 3.11 and 4.1, as well as most varieties of UNIX. Full duplex Ethernet has gathered sufficient interest from the networking technology vendor and user communities to warrant the formation of the **IEEE 802.3x** committee to propose standards for full duplex Ethernet. Full duplex technology is also either under development or available in Full Duplex Fast Ethernet (200 Mbps), Full Duplex Token Ring (32 Mbps), and Full Duplex FDDI (200 Mbps) varieties.

Gigabit Ethernet

Network Architecture   **Gigabit Ethernet,** also known as 1000Base-X, is an upgrade to Fast Ethernet that was standardized as the **IEEE 802.3z** standard by the IEEE on June 25, 1998. The standard defined the following configurations:

- **1000Base-SX:** Uses short wavelength (850 nanometers) laser fiber-optic media, primarily used for horizontal building cabling on a given floor

- **1000Base-LX:** Uses long wavelength (1300 nanometers) laser fiber-optic media, primarily used for high-speed campus backbone applications

- **1000Base-CX:** Uses copper twinaxial cable and transceivers for distances of only 25 meters, used primarily to link servers within a data center or high-speed network devices within a wiring closet

- **1000Base-TX:** Expected to be ratified in 1999, this standard would allow gigabit ethernet to travel over four pair of Category 5 unshielded twisted pair at a distance of 100 meters

Specifics of the gigabit Ethernet standard are listed in Figure 2–19. It should be pointed out that the maximum recommended distance over FDDI-style multimode fiber-optic cable is only 220 meters.

Standard	Fiber Type	Fiber Diameter	Bandwidth	Range
1000Base-SX	Multimode	62.5 microns	160	2 m to 220 m
1000Base-SX	Multimode	62.5 microns	200	2 m to 275 m
1000Base-SX	Multimode	50.0 microns	400	2 m to 500 m
1000Base-SX	Multimode	50.0 microns	500	2 m to 550 m
1000Base-LX	Multimode	62.5 microns	500	2 m to 550 m
1000Base-LX	Multimode	50.0 microns	400	2 m to 550 m
1000Base-LX	Multimode	50.0 microns	500	2 m to 550 m
1000Base-LX	Single mode	9 microns	N/A	2 m to 5 km or more

Figure 2-19   Gigabit Ethernet Fiber Dependent Configurations

Technology   Most gigabit Ethernet switches and network interface cards only support either the 1000Base-SX or 1000Base-LX standards. Among vendors of gigabit Ethernet switches and NICs are familiar names such as Cabletron, Lucent, Cisco, Hewlett-Packard, and Bay as well as new names such as Foundry, Extreme Networks, and Packet Engines. As with any relatively new technology, multi-vendor interoperability is a major concern as subtleties of implementation of the gigabit Ethernet standard are ironed out. Also, beware of switches that merely introduce gigabit Ethernet interfaces without upgrading the bandwidth of the aggregate switch backplane. Appropriately sized switches should have backplane capacity in the tens of gigabits per second, and tens of millions of packets per second.

Although most organizations will implement full-duplex gigabit Ethernet in a gigabit Ethernet switch-based configuration, the CSMA/CD MAC protocol was retained for backward compatibility with 10Base T and 100Base T half-duplex shared-media Ethernet implementations. In addition, the minimum and maximum Ethernet frame size has not changed. However, to maintain the required slot time (see the In Sharper Focus section earlier in this chapter, "Timing Issues and 100Base T Network Diameter") given the tenfold increase in speed over Fast Ethernet would have reduced maximum cable lengths to only 10 meters. As a solution, gigabit Ethernet increases the slot size, but not the minimum frame size, from 64 bytes to 512 bytes in a process called carrier extension.

Fibre Channel

While gigabit Ethernet runs at 1000 Mbps (or 1 G-bps), an alternative network architecture known as **fibre channel** (ANSI standard X3T9.3) has been defined to run at speeds of 133 Mbps to 1.062 Gbps over optical fiber and copper cables. Support for speeds up to 4.268 Gbps are expected in the future. Fibre channel is often used to connect high-performance storage devices and RAID subsystems to computers. Fibre channel switches and NICs are also available.

LAN-Based ATM

ATM (Asynchronous Transfer Mode) is a switched network technology that has been defined at speeds ranging from 25 Mbps to several gigabits per second. Network interface cards are available for both workstations and servers. However, in order for ATM-based computers to communicate with non–ATM-based computers, a process known as LAN emulation must be implemented. LAN emulation and other ATM-based network architectures fall into the realm of enterprise networking and will be described in more detail in Chapter 3. Moreover, in order for applications to take full advantage of ATM's speed and features, they must be "ATM aware." Although desktop ATM has been implemented in such industries as animation and stock trading, many of the previously mentioned high-speed network architectures are more likely to be implemented for local area networks. With that said, however, ATM is a fairly popular choice for high-speed backbone networks.

Applied Problem Solving

NETWORK ARCHITECTURES IN A NUTSHELL

Many of the shared media network architectures reviewed in this chapter are ideal in certain situations. There is no one "best" network architecture. In addition to all of the shared media network architectures reviewed in this chapter, another entire category of network architectures known as switched network architectures will be reviewed in the next chapter. In order to decide which network architecture is best in any given situation, a top-down approach should be taken:

What types of applications are required to meet business objectives?
- Multimedia?
- Collaborative or distributed computing?
- Large or frequent distributed database lookups?
- Specialized applications such as CAD/CAM, medical imaging, or video editing?
- Internet or IP-based Telephony?

What are the bandwidth and network delivery requirements of the data which is produced by these applications?
- High bandwidth needs?
- Guaranteed delivery times for time sensitive or streaming traffic?
- Large database downloads or replications?

- Additional bandwidth is not always the answer. Application or processing latency can vary independently of the amount of bandwidth. Understand bottlenecks thoroughly before designing your network.

What is the cost threshold for upgrading to a high-speed network architecture?
- FDDI NICs traditionally cost about $1,000 each and offer 100 Mbps
- 10/100BaseT NICs cost as little as $75 each and offer 100 Mbps. At these prices, perhaps a company doesn't even need a high-bandwidth or time-sensitive application in order to justify upgrading to a high-speed network architecture. Even traditional applications will be transported much more quickly.

Which upgrade philosophy is preferred?
- Replace all NICs, hubs, and possibly cabling?
- Replace hubs and NICs in a gradual manner?
- Replace just the hubs and leave the NICs and cabling alone? This option is available only with switched network architectures, which will be studied in the next chapter.

When considering an upgrade to a particular high-speed network architecture, these are just some of the issues that may require attention:
- New NICs
- New NIC drivers can be a real problem. What is the source of these drivers? As will be explained later in the text, drivers must be compatible with a particular NIC and the network operating system and operating system of the computer in which the NIC is installed.
- Proper cabling to meet new cable specifications
- New hubs
- Management software
- New distance limitations
- New rules for cascading hubs or maximum number of repeaters between two end nodes
- Availability of internetworking hardware such as bridges and routers which are compatible with this particular high-speed network architecture. Without such hardware, the network will not be able to be extended beyond the immediate local network.

SUMMARY

In order to properly analyze and design local area networks, it is absolutely essential to have a thorough understanding of the OSI model and its constituent layers. Of particular interest is the data link layer that serves as the home of the IEEE LAN standards and is subdivided into the MAC and LLC sub-layers for that purpose. The processes of encapsulation and de-encapsulation as OSI model processes are the basis of understanding communication between two computing devices. The importance of protocol compatibility to network communications can be modeled using the OSI model as an open framework for protocol compatibility design.

The local area network architecture model distills all network architectures into three basic components: access methodology, logical topology, and physical topology. Network architectures applied to a variety of media alternatives are known as network configurations. Key access methodologies are CSMA/CD and token passing, whereas logical topologies are either broadcast or sequential and physical topologies are most often star, but bus and ring are also possible.

Two of the most popular network architectures are Ethernet (IEEE 802.3) and Token Ring (IEEE 802.5). Comparisons between the two are no longer as intense as they might have been given Ethernet's market dominance and significant price advantage. The most popular current implementation of Ethernet is 10BaseT, which uses unshielded twisted pair as media.

FDDI is the most stable traditional high-speed network architecture offering 100 Mbps performance over dual counter-rotating rings of fiber-optic cable. The dual counter-rotating network architecture affords FDDI exceptional fault tolerance, redundancy, and reliability.

More recent high-speed network architectures have been proposed. 100BaseT is a CSMA/CD-based 100 Mps network architecture that operates over the two pair of twisted pair but is limited to a network diameter of only 210 meters. 100VG-AnyLAN is compatible with both IEEE 802.3 Ethernet and IEEE 802.5 Token Ring, but requires four pair of unshielded twisted pair in order to operate and is championed primarily by a single vendor—Hewlett-Packard. 100VG-AnyLAN uses Demand Priority Protocol as an access methodology allowing time-sensitive traffic such as voice, video, and multimedia to be delivered effectively. An alternate method of delivering multimedia traffic is Isochronous Ethernet, which is closely aligned with ISDN standards. Iso-Ethernet offers both a 10 Mps channel for Ethernet as well as a 6.144 Mbps channel for multimedia or time-sensitive traffic. Gigabit Ethernet, 1000BaseX, offers extremely high bandwidth over fiber-optic cable. Other high-speed architectures continue to be proposed and developed as the thirst for more bandwidth continues unabated.

No one network architecture can be considered the best in all situations. Top-Down analysis examining business, application, and data issues is required before determining which network architecture is most appropriate in each situation.

KEY TERMS

10/100 NICs
1000BaseSX
1000BaseLX
1000BaseCX
1000BaseTX
100BaseFX
100BaseT4
100BaseTX

10Base2
10Base5
10BaseF
10BaseT
1Base5
access methodologies
active monitor
address bit order reversal

applications layer
asynchronous frames
Attachment Units
AU
B channel
baseband transmission
broadcast
bus

C channel
Carrier Sense Multiple Access
   with Collision Detection
CDDI
Copper Distributed Data
   Interface
CRC
CSMA/CD
cyclical redundancy check
D channel
DAS
data-link layer
de-encapsulation
Demand Priority Access
Demand Priority Protocol
DPA
DPP
Dual Attachment Station
dual homing
dual ring of trees
early token release mechanism
EMI
encapsulation
end-to-end network links
Ethernet
Ethernet II
FDDI
Fiber Distributed Data Interface
frame check sequence
frame status flags
frames
full duplex Ethernet
gigabit Ethernet

header
high-speed Token Ring
HSTR
IEEE
IEEE 802.12
IEEE 802.2
IEEE 802.3
IEEE 802.3u
IEEE 802.3z
IEEE 802.5
IEEE 802.9a
Institute of Electrical and
   Electronic Engineers
Integrated Services Digital
   Network
Integrated Services Terminal
   Equipment
ISDN
Iso-Ethernet
isochronous
Isochronous Ethernet
ISTE
least significant bit
LLC
LLC sub-layer
logical link control
Logical Ring, Physical Star
logical topology
MAC sub-layer
media access control
media-sharing LANs
message
network interface card

network layer
OSI Model
P channel
packets
physical layer
physical topology
point-to-point data links
presentation layer
propagation delay
protocol
protocol discriminator
RFI
ring
round robin polling scheme
SAS
SBA
sequential
session layer
Single Attachment Station
single point of failure
slot time
SNAP
star
sub-network access protocol
synchronous bandwidth
   allocation
synchronous frames
token
token passing
TP-PMD
trailer
transport layer

REVIEW QUESTIONS

1. What is the importance of the OSI model to local area network analysis and design?
2. What is a protocol?
3. What is the relationship between protocols and the OSI model?
4. What is the overall purpose of the physical layer?
5. What are the major differences between a point-to-point link and an end-to-end link?
6. Why is the data link layer of particular interest to LAN network architectures?
7. Define the relationship between the two data-link layer sub-layers.
8. What does the introduction of data-link layer sub-layers offer in terms of increased interoperability options?
9. In general, what are the purposes of the header and trailer added to data-link layer frames?
10. Where are data-link layer frames built and why is this an appropriate place?

11. What is the relationship between the network layer and the data-link layer?

12. What is the relationship between the transport layer and the network layer?

13. Why is the session layer of more interest to client/server information systems?

14. Name at least two misconceptions as to the interpretation of layer functionality.

15. Briefly explain the purpose of encapsulation/de-encapsulation.

16. What are the three elements that make up any network architecture?

17. Compare and contrast CSMA/CD and token passing as access methodologies.

18. What are two different potential causes of collisions in Ethernet networks?

19. What does the early token release mechanism accomplish?

20. What actually is a token?

21. What is the difference between a logical and a physical topology?

22. Differentiate between the broadcast and sequential logical topologies.

23. Differentiate between the bus, star, and ring physical topologies.

24. Differentiate between Ethernet II and IEEE 802.3 Ethernet.

25. What is the relationship between IEEE 802.2 and IEEE 802.3?

26. Differentiate between IEEE 802.2 and Ethernet SNAP.

27. What is a protocol discriminator?

28. Differentiate between the various media-specific alternative configurations of Ethernet.

29. What are the unique characteristics of a Token Ring network architecture?

30. What is the role of the active monitor in a Token Ring network?

31. How are timing issues significant to Token Ring networks?

32. Differentiate between Ethernet and Token Ring in terms of performance at various traffic levels.

33. What advantages does FDDI offer over Ethernet and Token Ring?

34. Explain the self-healing powers of FDDI.

35. What are FDDI's primary negative attributes?

36. What are the three primary uses of the FDDI network architecture?

37. What are the advantages and disadvantages of CDDI as opposed to FDDI?

38. What is the advantage of dual homing?

39. Compare the advantages and disadvantages of 100BaseT and FDDI.

40. Describe the three standards defined for 100BaseT.

41. What is the advantage of buying 10/100 NICs?

42. Describe demand priority protocol.

43. How does demand priority protocol ensure that low priority traffic does not get permanently shut out of network access?

44. Compare the advantages and disadvantages of 100BaseT and 100VG-AnyLAN.

45. Compare the advantages and disadvantages of Isochronous Ethernet and 100VG-AnyLAN.

46. What are some unique attributes of Isochronous Ethernet when compared to other high-speed network architectures?

47. What does isochronous mean?

48. Describe the relationship between Isochronous Ethernet and ISDN.

49. What are the advantages and disadvantages of gigabit Ethernet?

50. What are the advantages and disadvantages of high-speed Token Ring?

ACTIVITIES

1. Prepare a presentation or bulletin board consisting of an empty OSI 7 layer model. As local area networks or network operating systems are encountered, place the protocols in the proper layers of the OSI model.

2. From the previous activity, determine which categories of protocols do not conform well to a particular layer of the OSI model.

3. Design an alternative network communications protocol model to the OSI model. Justify

why the new model is more effective than the OSI model.

4. Choose a particular protocol stack and outline the frame layouts for each protocol in each layer of the OSI model. Be sure to indicate relationships between protocols as to which protocols are encapsulated by which other protocols.

5. Investigate the IEEE 802.4 Token Bus standard. Report on its history, implementation, available technology, current status, and an explanation of this current status.

6. Survey the local area network implementations in your school or business. Report on the physical topologies found. Explain your results.

7. Investigate the daisy chain physical topology. Is it truly a unique physical topology or a variation of one of the three primary physical topologies?

8. Conduct a survey of Ethernet networks in your school or business. What is the media of choice in each installation? Why was each media chosen in each situation?

9. Survey schools or companies that have installed Token Ring networks. Report on the reasons for their choice and add your own analysis of the results.

10. Survey schools or businesses that employ FDDI network architectures. Gather information regarding motivation, installation date, satisfaction, problems, and the outcome of a similar decision on network architecture made today.

11. Investigate the availability and cost of technology for the three standards defined for 100BaseT. Analyze your results.

12. Investigate the availability and cost of technology for 100VG-AnyLAN varieties. Analyze your results.

13. Compare the availability and cost of 100BaseT technology and 100VG-AnyLAN technology. Analyze your results.

14. Investigate the cost and availability of Isochronous Ethernet technology. Analyze your results.

15. Investigate the gigabit Ethernet and high-speed Token Ring markets. Which market has more technology to offer? What are the statistics on market size for each technology? Analyze and present your results.

CASE STUDY

Goodbye Token Ring, Hello Ethernet

Making the move from token ring to Ethernet? If so, go as far as you can as fast as you can.

That's the advice from Equitable Life Assurance Society's IT staff, which recently finished moving the company's service organization from a shared 4/16M bit/sec token-ring environment to a switched 10/100M bit/sec Ethernet network.

The company had been considering moving away from its 800-user token-ring network for several years. The time seemed right when the company decided to upgrade its desktop and server platforms and consolidate its service organization at a new site here.

The migration project, which involved grouping three service centers into one,

has cost the company more than $1 million.

Given that the network can now speed traffic along five to 50 times faster, Equitable figures the project will pay off in increased productivity and the ability to support expanded workflow and imaging applications.

Because it was moving to a new site, Equitable ditched

most of its token-ring gear, some of which was 10 years old and fully depreciated.

"Token ring has been fading because Ethernet is simpler, has higher bandwidth and has been less expensive to deliver," says Charles Sokolski, managing director of IT operations and infrastructure at Equitable. And besides, "we had a clean slate," he says.

Equitable received vendor proposals for its new network by the summer of 1997 and picked Cisco as its primary network equipment supplier that fall. The key device in the Equitable network is the Catalyst 5500 switch, which can be used in wiring closets and to anchor backbone networks.

The Catalyst 5500 can also handle Ethernet and token-ring traffic.

By May 1998, Equitable was installing desktop machines in Charlotte, and the company was able to start up its new network during two weekends in July.

The Charlotte network consists of 45 NT, OS/2 and Unix servers, 10 Catalyst 5500s and a pair of Cisco 7513 routers. Currently, there are about 150 token-ring workstations on the network, which is home to more than 800 desktops servicing 650 users.

The company has experienced a few bugs translating between token-ring and Ethernet traffic, but no "show stoppers," Sokolski says.

Traffic is transported between the 5500s using Cisco's Inter Switch Link (ISL) tagging protocol, which encapsulates Ethernet and token-ring frames over Fast Ethernet. Frames can then be translated from Ethernet to token ring, or vice versa, by the 7513 routers.

"ISL is the key to a media-independent backbone—one that simultaneously supports both token-ring and Ethernet frames," says Frank Whitten, a Cisco product manager who worked on the Equitable project. "Since the technology is based on Ethernet, when Equitable is finished with its migration, it is left with an Ethernet backbone and uplinks."

Source: Marc Songini, "Goodbye Token Ring, Hello Ethernet," *Network World,* vol. 16, no. 3 (January 18, 1999), p. 17. Copyright Network World. Reprinted with permission.

BUSINESS CASE STUDY QUESTIONS

Activities

1. Complete a top-down model for this case by gleaning facts from the case and placing them in the proper layer of the top-down model. After having completed the top-down model, analyze and detail those instances where requirements were clearly passed down from upper layers to lower layers of the model and where solutions to those requirements were passed up from lower layers to upper layers of the model.
2. Detail any questions about the case that may occur to you for which answers are not clearly stated in the article.

Business

1. Why was this network migration performed at this particular time?
2. What was the cost of the network migration?
3. How could the network migration be cost justified?

Application

1. How many desktops are supported on the new network?

Data

1. What level of bandwidth is available both to the desktop and on the backbone?

Network

1. What network architectures did the Equitable move from and to?
2. What were the relative merits of the old and new network architectures?
3. How was the migration planned?
4. Are there any Token Ring workstations on the new network?

5. Is Token Ring to Ethernet frame conversion required?
6. How is the frame conversion handled?
7. Differentiate between the functionality offered by the different classes of switches and routers.

Technology

1. What type of switch is used in the network architecture?

2. What types of functionality does the chosen switch offer?
3. What different types of computing platforms and operating systems must be supported?

CHAPTER 3

LOCAL AREA NETWORK HARDWARE

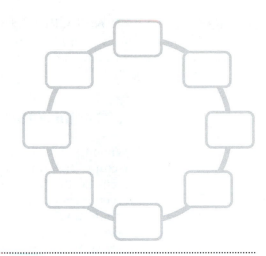

Concepts Reinforced

OSI Model	Physical Topologies
Network Architectures	High-Speed Network
IEEE 802 Standards	Architectures
Protocols and Standards	Hardware/Software Compatibility
Top-Down Model	

Concepts Introduced

LAN Technology Architecture	Switched LAN Architectures
Network Interface Card	Shared-Media LAN Wiring
Technology	Centers
Network Interface Card Drivers	LAN Switches
LAN Media Alternatives	Desktop ATM

OBJECTIVES

After mastering the material in this chapter you should:

1. Understand the interaction between the various hardware and software components of the local area network technology architecture

2. Understand the differences between switched LAN architectures and shared-media LAN architectures

3. Understand the importance of compatible network interface card drivers to overall network implementation

4. Understand the comparative differences between and proper application of available network interface cards

5. Understand the comparative differences between and the proper application of available hubs, MAUs, switching hubs, concentrators, and similar devices

87

6.   Understand the comparative differences between and the proper application of the various available types of LAN media

■ INTRODUCTION

While Chapter 2 reviewed the relative merits of the various network architectures that can be implemented to link clients and servers, Chapter 3 will focus on the hardware technology that must be employed to implement a given network architecture. The transition from shared-media network architectures to hardware-based switched network architectures is a development of major proportions of which informed network analysts must be aware. As applications demand more and more bandwidth, numerous alternatives exist for upgrading network capacity. Choosing the right upgrade path requires a thorough understanding of the local area network hardware described in this chapter.

In order to provide an appreciation for the interaction of all of the various LAN hardware components, this chapter begins by introducing the reader to the Local Area Network Technology architecture. In order to understand the role of LAN switches in network architectures, the differences between switched-based and shared-media LAN architectures are outlined prior to a detailed review of LAN hardware alternatives.

The issues, technology, and protocols involved with the management of LAN hardware are covered in Chapter 15, Local Area Network Management."

■ THE LOCAL AREA NETWORK TECHNOLOGY ARCHITECTURE

In general terms, any local area network, regardless of network architecture, requires the following components:

- A central wiring concentrator of some type which serves as a connection point for all attached local area network devices. Depending on the particular network architecture involved and the capabilities of the wiring center, this device can be known alternatively as a hub, MAU, CAU, concentrator, LAN switch, or a variety of other names

- Media such as shielded or unshielded twisted pair, coaxial cable, or fiber-optic cable must carry network traffic between attached devices and the wiring center of choice.

- **Network Interface Cards (NIC)** are installed either internally or externally to client and server computers in order to provide a connection to the local area network of choice.

- Finally, network interface card drivers are software programs that bridge the hardware/software interface between the network interface card and the computer's network operating system. Figure 3-1 summarizes the key components of the LAN technology architecture.

Implications of LAN Technology Choices

Within each of the major categories of LAN technology illustrated in Figure 3-1, numerous alternatives exist as to the specific make, model, and manufacturer of technology that may be chosen. It is important to note that choosing a particular technology in one LAN technology category may have significant implications or limitations on available technology choices in other LAN technology categories. It is important for a network analyst to fully understand the implications of a given technology decision prior to purchase. Figure 3-2 attempts to graphically portray some of the relationships and dependencies between technology choices in a variety of LAN technology categories.

PC Hardware

As can be seen in Figure 3-2, choices of PC hardware play an especially important role in the overall LAN technology architecture. A thorough knowledge of PC hardware is required in order to make intelligent choices of servers and workstations. Although a detailed discussion of PC architecture issues is beyond the scope of this text, readers are encouraged to see CD

Logical Diagram

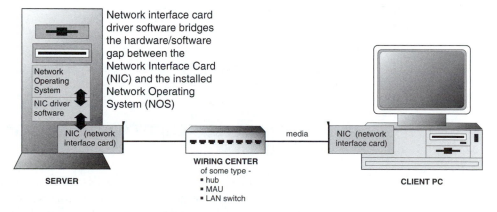

Figure 3-1   The Local Area Network Technology Architecture

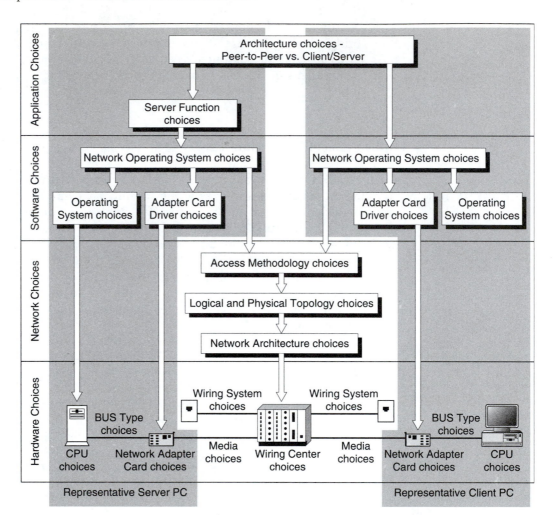

Figure 3-2 Implications of LAN Technology Choices

Chapter 2, Client Hardware; and CD Chapter 4, Server Hardware and Software on the accompanying CD entitled, Client/Server Information Systems Background Material.

▧ MEDIA-SHARING LAN ARCHITECTURES VS. SWITCHED LAN ARCHITECTURES

As client/server information systems and distributed computing applications have put increasing demands on the local area network infrastructure in terms of the amount of data traffic to be transferred, network architects and technology providers have responded with alternative solutions.

As mentioned in Chapter 2, one solution to the network bandwidth crunch is to offer higher-speed **shared-media network architectures** such as 100BaseT, 100VG-AnyLAN, Isochronous Ethernet, high-speed Token Ring, or gigabit Ethernet. Each of these alternatives possesses the same basic shared-media structure as Ethernet and Token Ring with the only difference being that the higher-speed alternatives offer more bandwidth for all attached workstations to share. Media-sharing network wiring centers such as hubs offer all attached workstations shared access to a single LAN segment. If the hub happens to be a 10BaseT Ethernet hub, then all attached workstations must share access to the single 10 Mbps LAN segment, while 100BaseT hubs offer shared access for all attached workstations to a single 100 Mbps LAN segment. The shared-media approach is the same in both cases, the only difference being the amount of available bandwidth to be shared.

Switched LAN architectures depend on wiring centers called LAN switches or switching hubs which offer all attached workstations access to a switching matrix that provides point-to-point, rather than shared, connections between any two ports. Each port on the LAN switch is effectively a dedicated LAN segment with dedicated bandwidth offered to attached devices. Each port on the LAN switch may be assigned to a single workstation or to an entire LAN segment linked by a media-sharing network architecture (non-switching) hub. Although shared-media LAN segments can link to a LAN switch to take advantage of its dedicated connections and guaranteed bandwidth, there is no shared media or shared bandwidth within the switched LAN architecture itself. The limiting factor in a switch-based LAN architecture is the number of simultaneous point-to-point connections which a given switch can support. Figure 3-3 contrasts the differences in wiring center functionality between media-sharing and switch-based LAN architectures.

Managerial Perspective

ADVANTAGES OF SWITCHED LAN ARCHITECTURES

It is important to note that switched LAN architectures implementations only change the wiring center technology and, as a result, the manner in which workstations are able to set up point-to-point communications to each other. In other words, network interface cards, network interface card drivers, and media do not change. For this reason, installing a LAN switch is often the first and easiest alternative chosen when network bandwidth demands exceed current supply. In order to go from an Ethernet shared-media architecture to an Ethernet switch-based architecture, it is only necessary to replace the shared-media hub with an Ethernet LAN switch. In order to migrate from a Token Ring shared-media environment to Token Ring switch-based architecture, it is only necessary to replace the shared media MAUs (Multistation Access Units) with a Token Ring LAN switch.

Shared Media LAN Architecture

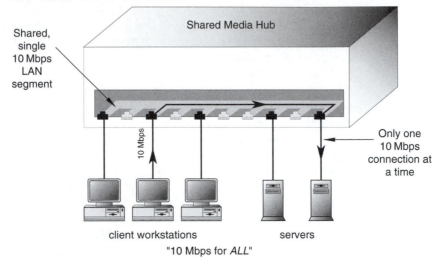

Switch-Based LAN Architecture

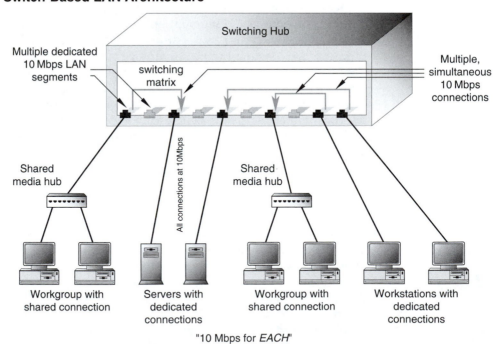

Figure 3-3 Switched LAN Architectures vs. Media-sharing LAN Architectures Wiring Center Functionality

LAN SWITCH TRAFFIC ANALYSIS

It is important to analyze the traffic patterns between attached clients and servers before swapping out hubs and installing switches. In order to minimize the inter-switch traffic that represents a potential bottleneck, the following is suggested:

- It is important to have those workstations and servers that communicate most often with each other use the same switch since switches differ in their cascadability and in the speed of the inter-switch communications connection.

- Another benefit of analyzing traffic patterns before installing the switch is to identify those users and workstations that must have a dedicated switch port and those that can reside on a shared LAN segment attached to a switched port.

Following are a few general guidelines for switch port allocation:

- Servers and UNIX workstations should ideally have their own switch port

- Distributed computing power users with frequent queries to servers should be able to be connected to switch ports via shared LAN segments of up to eight users

- Casual or light traffic users accessing only e-mail and terminal, character-based programs can be connected to switch ports via shared LAN segments of 50 or more users.

- The ability of LAN switches to support multi-workstation LAN segments on a single switch port may vary among switches.

- The number of workstation addresses that can be supported by a given switch port may vary as well.

Furthermore, swapping a shared-media hub for a LAN switch will not necessarily improve all network traffic situations. If a server only has one 10 Mbps network interface card installed with which it must service all client requests, a LAN switch will not improve the network performance. In fact, due to the latency introduced by the switch to set up switched connections, the performance may actually degrade. The power of a LAN switch is its ability to support simultaneous connections between any combination of clients and servers. It is but one part of a solution to network performance bottlenecks that can be effectively implemented only after a thorough network traffic analysis has been conducted.

Implementation Scenarios for Switched LAN Architectures

Depending on switch capacity and installed components, LAN switches can be implemented to fulfill a variety of different roles.

- **Stand-alone Workgroup/Departmental LAN switches** offer dedicated connections to all attached client and server computers via individual switch ports. Such an implementation is appropriate for multimedia or videoconferencing workstations and servers. In some cases, such as a distributed computing environment, dedicated ports are only necessary for servers, while client workstations share a switch port via a cascaded media-sharing hub. This variation is sometimes referred to as a **server front-end LAN switch.**

- **Backbone-attached Workgroup/Departmental LAN switches** offer all of the local switching capabilities of the stand-alone workgroup/departmental LAN switch plus switched access to higher-speed backbone networks. This higher-speed backbone connection may be to a higher-capacity backbone switch or may be to a higher-speed shared-media device such as a backbone router.

- **Backbone/Data Center Switches** offer high-capacity, fault-tolerant, switching capacity with traffic management capabilities. These high-end switches are really a self-contained backbone network that is sometimes referred to as a **collapsed backbone network.** These backbone switches most often offer switched connectivity to other workgroup switches, media-sharing hubs, and corporate servers which must be accessed by multiple departments/workgroups. They are often modular in design, allowing different types of switching modules such as Ethernet, Token Ring, Fast Ethernet, and ATM (Asynchronous Transfer Mode) to share access to a high-capacity switching matrix or backplane.

Figure 3-4 highlights the differences between these switched-LAN architecture implementation scenarios.

■ NETWORK INTERFACE CARDS

Functionality

Network adapter cards, also known as Network Interface Cards or NIC, are the physical link between a client or server PC and the shared media of the network. Providing this interface between the network and the PC or workstation requires that the network adapter card have the ability to adhere to the access methodology (CSMA/CD or Token Passing) of the network architecture (Ethernet, Fast Ethernet, Token Ring, FDDI/CDDI, ATM, etc.) to which it is attached. These software rules implemented by the network adapter card, which control the access to the shared network media, are known as Media Access Control (MAC) protocols and are represented on the MAC sub-layer of the Data-Link Layer (Layer 2) of the OSI 7 layer reference model.

Stand-Alone Workgroup/Departmental LAN Switches

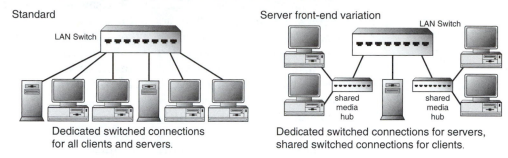

Standard

LAN Switch

Dedicated switched connections
for all clients and servers.

Server front-end variation

LAN Switch

shared
media
hub

shared
media
hub

Dedicated switched connections for servers,
shared switched connections for clients.

Backbone-Attached Workgroup/Departmental LAN Switches

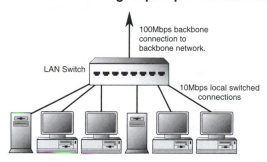

100Mbps backbone
connection to
backbone network.

LAN Switch

10Mbps local switched
connections

Backbone/Data Center Switches

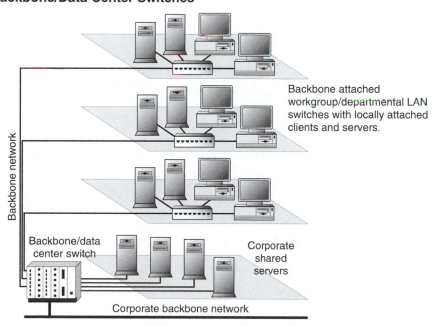

Backbone attached
workgroup/departmental LAN
switches with locally attached
clients and servers.

Backbone network

Backbone/data
center switch

Corporate
shared
servers

Corporate backbone network

Figure 3-4   Implementation Scenarios for Switched LAN Architectures

Since these are MAC Layer interface cards and are therefore the keepers of the MAC Layer interface protocol, it's fair to say that it is the adapter cards themselves which determine network architecture and its constituent protocols more than any other component. Take an Ethernet adapter card out of the expansion slot of a PC and replace it with a Token Ring adapter card and you have a Token Ring workstation. In this same scenario, the media may not even need to be changed since Ethernet, Token Ring, and FDDI/CDDI often work over the same media.

A network adapter card is a bit like a mediator or translator. On one side it has the demands of the client or server PC in which it is installed for network-based services, whereas on the other side it has the network architecture with its rules for accessing the shared network media or LAN switch. The network adapter card's job is to get the PC all of the network services it desires while adhering to the rules (MAC Layer Protocols) of the network architecture.

Technology Analysis

Listed below are some of the key differences in adapter design and available features:

- Bus Type
  - ISA (8 or 16 bit)
  - EISA (16 or 32 bit)
  - MCA
  - NuBus (Apple)
  - PCI
  - PCMCIA
  - SBus (Sun)

- On-Board Processor Capabilities

- Amount of On-Board memory

- Data Transfer Techniques
  - Bus Mastering DMA
  - DMA
  - Shared Memory
  - Programmed I/O

- Media Interfaces

- System Memory Requirements

- Internal Adapters vs. External Adapters

- Network Drivers Included

- Network Architecture(s) Supported

**Applied
Problem
Solving**

NETWORK INTERFACE CARD TECHNOLOGY ANALYSIS GRID

Many of these features are listed in Figure 3-5, the Network Interface Card Technology Analysis Grid. A technology analysis grid is a structured analysis tool for mapping functional networking requirements as identified by the logical network design of the networking layer in the top-down model to the technical capabilities and characteristics of available technology. In this manner, technology can be comparatively evaluated in an objective fashion. Recalling the basic premise of the top-down model, assuming that each lower layer offers solutions that meet the requirements of the immediate

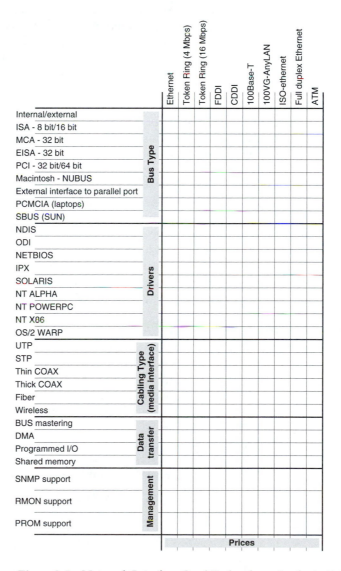

Figure 3-5   Network Interface Card Technology Analysis Grid

upper layer, then the chosen technology incorporated in the physical network design should meet the original business goals and objectives as identified in the business layer.

As a practical example, whereas servers will need to transfer large quantities of data more quickly than client PCs, technology analysis should be performed in order to purchase more powerful, faster NICs for servers than for clients in order to minimize potential bottlenecks.

Bus Type The bus into which a network adapter card is attached allows many different types of add-in cards to be attached to this data transfer pipeline leading to the CPU and RAM memory. The expansion bus in a PC is a lot like a straight line of empty parking spaces waiting to be filled by PC expansion cards of one type or another. These expansion cards draw electricity from and transfer data to/from other system components such as the CPU or memory through the expansion bus. NICs are manufactured to physically interface to a particular type of bus.

The PCI bus offers its own clocking signal and low CPU utilization and seems to be the bus of choice for high-performance NICs. PCI bus compatible NICs are now available for a variety of network architectures, with some taking advantage of the PCI bus's ability to cascade buses by delivering four network interface ports on a single network interface card. Some PCI-based cards also have full-duplex capabilities. Such high-capacity cards are most appropriate for servers with high data transfer demands.

Sbus is the type of bus included in Unix workstations (SPARCstations) from Sun Microsystems.

The important choice related to bus architecture is that a network adapter card is chosen that not only "fits," or is compatible with, the installed bus, but more important, takes full advantage of whatever data transfer capability that given bus may afford.

Data Transfer Method The key job of the network adapter is to transfer data between the local PC and the shared network media. Ideally, this should be done as quickly as possible with a minimum of interruption of the PC's main CPU. Two hardware related network adapter characteristics that can have a bearing on data transfer efficiency are the amount of on-board memory and the processing power of the on-board CPU contained on the network adapter card. Figure 3-6 summarizes four network adapter card-to-PC memory data transfer techniques:

- Programmed I/O (Input/Output)
- DMA (Direct Memory Access)
- Shared Memory
- Bus Mastering DMA

Network adapter cards may support more than one of these techniques. Some of these data transfer techniques are only possible with the more

Programmed I/O

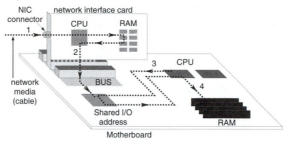

Steps
1. Data enters network interface card through the network media and connector.
2. Adapter card CPU loads network data into a specific I/O address on the motherboard.
3. Main CPU checks I/O area for data
4. If data exists, it is transferred to main memory, RAM, by main CPU.

Keynote
The motherboard's CPU has the ultimate responsibility of data transfer into RAM.

DMA (Direct Memory Access)

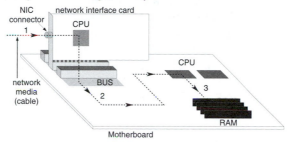

Steps
1. Data enters network interface card through the network media and connector.
2. Adapter card CPU interrupts the motherboard CPU.
3. Main CPU stops other processing and transfers the data to RAM.

Keynote
The motherboard's CPU has the ultimate responsibility of data transfer into RAM.

Shared Memory

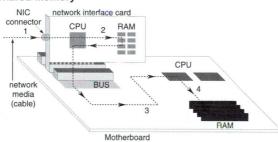

Steps
1. Data enters network interface card through the network media and connector.
2. Adapter card CPU stores data on its RAM.
3. Adapter card CPU interrupts the motherboard CPU.
4. Main CPU stops other processing and transfers data into RAM.

Keynote
The motherboard's CPU has the ultimate responsibility of data transfer into RAM.

Bus Mastering DMA

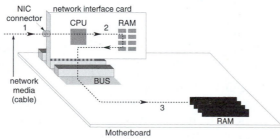

Steps
1. Data enters network interface card through the network media and connector.
2. Adapter card CPU temporarily stores data on its RAM.
3. Adapter card CPU sends data directly t motherboard RAM when network transmission completes (it does NOT interrupt the main CPU.)

Keynote
The adapter card's CPU has the ultimate responsibility of data transfer into RAM.

Figure 3-6   Network Interface Cards Data Transfer Methods

sophisticated buses such as EISA, MCA, or PCI; with certain network architectures; or with a certain level of CPU power.

Remembering that one of the objectives of network-to-PC data transfer was to minimize the number of interruptions of the system CPU, it can be seen in Figure 3-6 that only the **Bus Mastering DMA** (Direct Memory Access) data transfer technique leaves the system CPU alone to process other applications. In Bus Mastering DMA, the CPU on the network adapter card manages the movement of data directly into the PC's RAM memory without interruption of the system CPU by taking control of the PC's expansion bus. PCI bus-based NICs also exhibit low utilization of the main CPU thanks to the intelligence of the PCI bus itself.

Bus Mastering DMA as a feature on adapter cards requires the expansion bus in the PC to support being "mastered" by the CPU on the network adapter card. Some buses are more sophisticated (MCA, EISA, and PCI) in bus mastering by maintaining more control and management over how the mastering of the expansion bus by the network adapter card CPU is handled. Also, the CPU and operating system must have the capability to relinquish control of the expansion bus in order for bus mastering network adapter cards to function correctly.

Basic NIC Configuration

Once NICs have been physically installed inside a computer, they must be properly configured in order to interact successfully with that computer. The role of the NIC driver software will be explained later in this chapter. However, there are some other key configuration issues more related to the physical or hardware interaction of the NIC and the computer into which it has been installed. Among these parameters to be familiar with are the following:

- **IRQ - Interrupt request**—The network interface card, like every other hardware device in the computer, must interrupt and request resources such as CPU cycles and memory from the CPU itself. It must be assigned an IRQ or interrupt request number so that the CPU knows that it is the NIC requesting these services. The key issue regarding IRQ assignments is that the IRQ must not be used by any other device and must be supported by the NIC. IRQ 3 or 5 are typically used for NICs. Some NICs are able to use different IRQs and some are not. Typical IRQ assignments are listed in Figure 3-7.

- **Base I/O Port Address**—This address defines a memory location through which the data will flow between the network interface card and the CPU. It is somewhat analogous to a mailbox through which messages are transferred into and out of. All NICs need an available base I/O address as part of their configuration.

- **Base Memory Address**—Not to be confused with Base I/O address, some NICs require a base memory address to indicate the starting

IRQ Number	Typical Use - Note: PCI bus IRQ settings may vary
0	Reserved-CPU tick counter
1	Reserved-keyboard controller
2	Reserved-cascade controller
3	Usually COM2 and COM4
4	Usually COM1 and COM3
5	Usually LPT2 or sound card
6	Floppy Disk Controller
7	LPT1
8	Reserved-real-time clock
9	Reserved-slave controller
10	Usually available
11	Usually available
12	Usually available
13	Co-processor error
14	Non-SCSI fixed disk
15	Usually available

Figure 3-7   Typical IRQ Assignments

location in the computer's memory that can be used by the NIC as a buffer memory. Not all NICs need to use the computer's memory and therefore would not need a base memory address.

Media Interfaces   A network adapter card must worry about hardware compatibility in two directions. First, the card must be compatible with the expansion bus into which it will be inserted. Second, it must be compatible with the chosen media of a particular network architecture implementation. Supported media types are dependent on standards defined for a particular network architecture. All NICs do not support all media types. In addition to the type of media, the physical connector that must interface between the NIC and the media can differ.

Several network adapter cards come with interfaces for more than one media type with "jumpers" or switches enabling one media type or another. Ethernet adapter cards with interfaces for both 10BaseT (**RJ45** or 8 pin Telco plug) and thin coax connections known as a **BNC connector,** or with both thick and thin coax connections are quite common. Thick coax connectors are 15 pin interfaces (DB-15) also called **AUI** connectors. AUI connectors allow Ethernet NICs to be attached to thin or thick coax Ethernet backbone networks via **transceivers** (transmitter/receivers) and AUI or transceiver cables. Figure 3-8 illustrates the three common Ethernet media interfaces and connection of an Ethernet NIC to an Ethernet backbone network via transceivers.

All of the discussion thus far regarding installation of network adapter cards has assumed that the adapters are internal or connected directly to the system expansion bus. Alternatively, network adapters can be connected externally to a PC via the PC's parallel port. This market has grown considerably with the proliferation of laptop or notebook computers lacking internal expansion capability. In these cases, **external adapters,** as small as a pack of cigarettes, are interfaced between the PC's parallel port and the network media. External adapters cannot draw electricity from the expansion bus like internal adapters and therefore require a power source of their own, such as an AC adapter in most cases. Some external adapters are able to draw power from the keyboard jack on the notebook computer, eliminating the need for bulky and inconvenient AC adapters.

In a good example of the Principle of Shifting Bottlenecks, although NICs can transfer data at rates of several Mbps, throughput on existing parallel ports hovers around 130 Kbps, whereas a newer **High Performance Parallel Port,** also known as **EPP** or **Enhanced Parallel Port,** delivers a throughput of up to 2 Mbps. Remember that the parallel port is a component

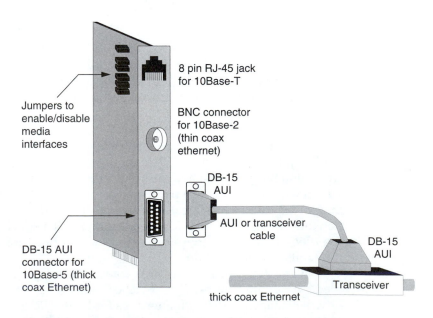

Figure 3-8   Ethernet Media Interfaces

of the laptop PC, not the external adapter. An alternative to parallel port external adapters is **PCMCIA adapters.** Fast Ethernet PCMCIA adapters operating at 100 Mbps are readily available. Although parallel port adapters for laptop computers are still available, they have been largely replaced by PCMCIA adapters, which are explained in the next section.

PCMCIA STANDARDS

PCMCIA is actually a series of specifications that represent the physical and functional/electrical standards for technology adhering to these specs. Figure 3-8 summarizes the physical specifications and Figure 3-9 summarizes the functional/electrical specifications for the PCMCIA standard.

Types I through III all must support the standard PCMCIA 68 pin interface and the 85.6 × 54 mm credit card size dimensions. Certain vendors are producing disk drives that are 16 mm thick, and calling them PCMCIA Type IV. These standards are strictly proprietary since the PCMCIA Forum has not approved a Type IV specification.

The introduction of PCMCIA technology has not been without its trials and tribulations. Prior to the introduction of the V2.1 specification, incompatibility problems were very common. The Card Services and Socket Services provided a layer of transparency and compatibility between the notebook computer's hardware, the PCMCIA card, and the notebook computer's operating system software. Technical aspects of Card Services and Socket Services will be covered in the discussion of driver software, later in this chapter.

Version 2.1 minimized, although did not eliminate, many of the incompatibility problems associated with previous versions of the PCMCIA standard.

Version 3.0 of the PCMCIA standards vastly improves the throughput of the specification by increasing the bus width to 32 bits and the clock speed to as high as 33 MHz. This new standard, commonly known as CardBus, also adds bus-mastering capability in order to increase the efficiency of moving data from the card to the computer's system memory. CardBus adds multi-function capabilities for cards so that a single card

PCMCIA Card/Slot Type	Maximum Thickness	Typical Use
Type I	3.3 mm	Memory Cards
Type II	5.5 mm	Modems, Network Interface Cards
Type III	10.5 mm	Disk Drives

Figure 3-8   PCMCIA Physical Specifications

PCMCIA Spec. Version	Bus Width	Clock Speed	Comments
1.0	8 bits	up to 6 MHz	Used for memory cards. No I/O functions or software drivers defined
2.0	8–16 bits	up to 6 MHz	Introduced I/O but left software drivers up to card manufacturers
2.1	8–16 bits	up to 6 MHz	Introduced card services and socket services
PC Card (3.0)	32 bits	20–33 MHz	Up to 80 Mbps throughput

Figure 3-9   PCMCIA Functional/Electrical Specifications

might include a fax/modem, an Ethernet network interface card, and 4 MB of cache memory. In the interest of improving battery life on notebook computers, the CardBus standard also outlined operations at 3.3 volts rather than 5 volts. As part of the CardBus standard the name of the cards themselves was changed to PC Card rather than the much maligned PCMCIA

The future looks bright for CardBus. PC Card slots are now being included on desktop computers as well as notebooks in order to allow users to make the most of their investments in peripherals. Vendors are finding new uses such as dial-in servers for the PC Card. However, the reality of the situation is that today there is no guarantee that a particular PCMCIA card will work well, if at all, with a particular computer.

Network Interface Card Trends

Among the trends in Network Interface Cards which are either emerging or under development are the following:

- Dual Speed Cards—Some 10/100 Ethernet cards feature autosensing which can automatically determine whether traffic is being transmitted and received at 10 or 100 Mbps through a single media interface connector. Others, especially 100VG-AnyLAN 10/100 cards, have two separate media interface connectors, one for 10 Mbps Ethernet and one for 100VG-AnyLAN. 10/100 cards are important as a means to ease migration from a 10 Mbps network architecture to a 100 Mbps network architecture.

- Integrated or On-board NICs—Some computer manufacturers such as Hewlett-Packard now include an Ethernet NIC right on the PCs motherboard, thereby saving a slot on the expansion bus.

- Multi-port NICs—The cascading ability, otherwise known as the mezzanine architecture of the PCI bus has allowed multi-port NICs to be manufactured on a single card. In this manner, servers with high traffic demands can have up to four links to the network while using only a single expansion slot.

- On-NIC Virus Protection and Security—As security and virus protection have become more important issues, focus had shifted to the NIC as the entry point for network communications. Some NICs now offer either encryption, virus protection, or both as means of protection against network infiltration.

- Integrated Repeater Modules—Some NICs have incorporated integrated repeater modules which allow up to seven additional devices to be cascaded from the NIC and attached to the network via a single 10BaseT hub port.

- Full-Duplex Mode—Some Ethernet NICs have full duplex capability. Recall that implementation of full duplex Ethernet is dependent on the Full Duplex Ethernet NIC being directly connected to a port on a full duplex Ethernet switch.

- Performance Improvements—Several manufacturers of Ethernet NICs have implemented **packet overlapping** or **fast-packet forwarding** technology in order to improve overall NIC performance by as much as 50%. Traditionally, Ethernet NICs only forwarded one packet at a time from the CPU bus, through the buffer memory on the NIC, to the network media. With packet overlapping technology, the next packet of information is immediately forwarded as soon as its start of frame is detected rather than waiting for the previous frame to be totally onto the network media before beginning transmission of the next packet.

■ NETWORK INTERFACE CARD DRIVERS

Role of Adapter Card Drivers

Ensuring that a purchased network interface card interfaces successfully to both the bus of the CPU as well as the chosen media of the network architecture, will assure hardware connectivity. Full interoperability however, depends on compatibility between the NIC and the network operating installed in a given computer and is delivered by **network interface card drivers.** Any driver software must be compatible with the hardware card itself, which is why many adapter card manufacturers ship numerous drivers from which to choose with their adapter cards. A given network adapter card may also be required to be compatible with a number of different network operating systems. The network operating systems use the adapter card drivers to communicate with the adapter cards and the network beyond. Without the proper adapter card drivers, there can be no communication out through the adapter card and, as a result, there is no network.

Driver Availability

Initially, drivers were written for specific combinations of a particular adapter card and a particular version of an operating system or network operating system. It was to an adapter card vendor's advantage to ship drivers for as many operating systems and network operating systems as possible. Examples of drivers typically included might be:

- LANtastic
- LANManager
- LANServer
- Pathworks
- PowerLAN
- NetWare Version 2.X, NetWare Version 3.X, NetWare 4.X for DOS and OS/2
- Vines
- Windows
- OS/2
- Windows NT
- UNIX (many varieties)

This is obviously a fairly long list and drivers may well have to be rewritten for each new version of an operating system or network operating system. Drivers written for specific adapter card/network operating system combinations are known as **monolithic drivers.** Network interface card drivers were also supplied by network operating system vendors. In these cases, the competition centered around which network operating system vendor could include drivers for the largest number of network interface cards. As the number of possible combinations of network interface cards and network operating systems continued to increase, network interface card vendors and network operating system vendors found themselves spending ever-increasing amounts of time and money on driver development.

A more generic approach to the problem was for adapter card manufacturers to supply drivers that could interact successfully with either NetBIOS or TCP/IP. The reasoning in this case is that most network operating systems, in turn, communicate with either NETBIOS (PC environment) or TCP/IP (UNIX environment). These drivers were generally successful except for the occasional incompatibilities among NETBIOS versions, so long as a given operating system supported NETBIOS or TCP/IP. Also, specifically written, monolithic drivers were more efficient and better performing in most cases.

Another approach is for network adapter card manufacturers to emulate the adapter interface specifications of market-leading network interface cards for which drivers are most commonly available. The NE2000 adapter card, originally manufactured by Eagle Technologies and since purchased by Novell, is often emulated by other manufacturers that subsequently claim that their adapters are NE2000 compliant.

Multiprotocol Network Interface Card Drivers

Novell was the first network operating system to attempt to eliminate the need for specially written drivers for every possible adapter card/network operating system combination. By allowing adapter card vendors to develop one file called IPX.COM which was linked with a Novell file called IPX.OBJ through a process known as WSGEN, unique drivers could be more easily created and updated. However, even these "bound" drivers were still monolithic in the sense that only a single protocol stack, Novell's IPX/SPX, could communicate with the installed network adapter card. Thus, an industry initiative was undertaken that would develop driver software which would accomplish two major objectives:

1. Adapter card specific drivers should be developed independently from network operating system specific protocol stack drivers, and the two drivers should be bound together to form a unique driver combination.

2. Driver management software should allow for installation of both multiple network adapter cards and multiple protocol stacks per adapter card.

This initiative was undertaken by two independent industry coalitions:

- Microsoft and 3Com, a major adapter card manufacturer, developed **NDIS (Network Driver Interface Specification).**

- Novell, producers of NetWare, and Apple joined forces to develop **ODI (Open Data-Link Interface).** Most adapter cards are now shipped with both NDIS and ODI drivers.

The significant operational difference offered by these two driver specifications is that they are able to support multiple protocol stacks over a single adapter card. For example, a network adapter card with an ODI driver installed could support communications to both a NetWare server via IPX protocols as well as to a UNIX host via TCP/IP protocols. Layer 3, 4, and 5 Communications protocols will be introduced in Chapters 4, whereas network operating systems and their protocol stacks will be detailed in Part Two.

NDIS

NDIS is a driver specification that offers standard commands for communications between NDIS-compliant network operating system protocol stacks (NDIS Protocol Driver) and NDIS-compliant network adapter card drivers (NDIS MAC Drivers). In addition NDIS specifies a **binding** operation which is managed by a separate program known as the **Protocol Manager.** (PROTMAN.DOS in DOS-based systems.) As will be seen, the Protocol Manager program does much more than just supervise the binding of protocol drivers to MAC drivers. NDIS also specifies standard commands for communication between the Protocol Manager program and either protocol or MAC drivers.

Protocol Drivers and MAC Drivers that adhere to the NDIS specification work as follows:

1. When a DOS-based computer is first booted or powered up, a configuration file known as CONFIG.SYS is executed. One line in this file specifies that the Protocol Manager program (PROTMAN.DOS) should be initiated.

2. The first job of the Program Manager is to access a text file known as PROTOCOL.INI which contains:
   - Set-up information about protocol drivers and MAC drivers
   - Binding statements that link particular protocol drivers to particular MAC drivers

3. Having read PROTOCOL.INI and parsed its contents into usable form, the Protocol Manager program loads the PROTOCOL.INI information into a memory resident image.

4. As new protocol drivers or MAC drivers are loaded, they
   - Ask the Protocol Manager program for the location of the memory resident image of PROTOCOL.INI
   - Look in PROTOCOL.INI for set-up information about the MAC driver or protocol driver with which they wish to bind
   - Identify themselves to the Protocol Manager program which adds their information to the PROTOCOL.INI file.

5. Binding takes place when the Protocol Manager program oversees the exchange of characteristic tables between protocol drivers and MAC drivers.

In Sharper Focus

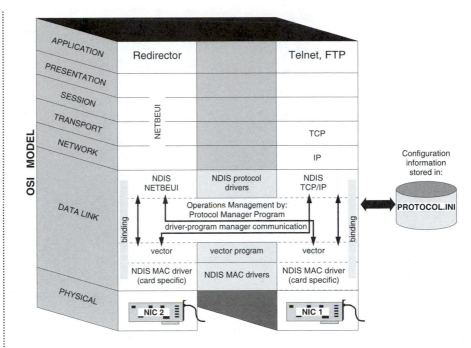

Figure 3-11   Network Device Interface Specification (NDIS) Architecture

6. Once bound and operating, packets of a particular protocol are forwarded from the adapter card to the proper protocol stack by a layer of software known as the **vector.**

Figure 3-11 illustrates many of the concepts and components of the NDIS specification.

ODI

Like NDIS, ODI allows users to load several protocol stacks simultaneously for operation with a single network adapter card and supports independent development with subsequent linking of protocol drivers and adapter drivers. In ODI, users enter configuration information regarding network adapter settings and protocol driver information into a file named NET.CFG. Operations of ODI are similar to the basic functionality of NDIS and are orchestrated by a program known as LSL.COM where **LSL** stands for **Link Support Layer.** Network interface card drivers are referred to as **Multi-Link Interface Drivers** or **MLID** in an ODI-compliant environment. Figure 3-12 illustrates the basic architecture of an ODI-compliant environment.

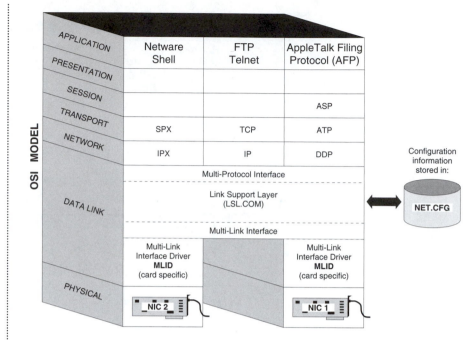

Figure 3-12   Open Data-Link Interface (ODI) Architecture

PCMCIA Drivers

When network interface cards are PCMCIA-based, two levels of driver software are required:

1. Drivers to interface to operating systems and network operating systems such as NDIS 2.0 for DOS and OS/2 and ODI for DOS and OS/2. Occasionally, NetWare specific drivers may also be available with certain PC Cards.

2. Drivers to interface the PCMCIA controller to the PCMCIA card and to the aforementioned client software drivers.

As previously noted, with the introduction of PCMCIA Specification Version 3.0, the term *PCMCIA* has been replaced by the terms *PC Card* and *CardBus.*

Compatibility problems and lack of standardized driver software were common occurrences with PCMCIA-based network interface cards prior to the release of PCMCIA version 2.1 with its **Card and Socket Services** driver specification. **CSS** enables the following capabilities and is supposed to be relatively self-configuring:

*   hot swappable devices allowing PCMCIA cards to be removed and inserted while the notebook computer is powered up

- automatic PCMCIA card configuration

- multiple PCMCIA card management

- standby mode

- I/O conflict management

CSS is split into two logical sub-layers:

1. The **Card services** sub-layer is hardware independent and interfaces to the client operating system or network operating system driver software. Card services deliver error messages, and enable resource management and configuration.

2. The **Socket services** sub-layer is written specifically for the type of PCMCIA controller included in a notebook computer. Among the common varieties of controllers are Intel, Cirrus Logic, Databook, Vandem, Toshiba, VLSI, and Ricoh. Socket services are more hardware oriented and provide information concerning insertion and removal of cards from available slots.

If compatible CSS drivers are not available for a particular PC Card/Controller combination, or if the amount of memory CSS drivers require is unacceptable, then lower-level drivers known as **direct enablers** must be configured and installed. Direct enablers, like the socket services of CSS are controller specific and must be configured for each PC Card/Controller combination, unlike the Card and Socket Services drivers which allow multiple cards to be swapped in and out of a given PCMCIA slot without the need for reconfiguration. Direct enabler drivers are often supplied on diskette along with CSS drivers by the PCMCIA card vendors.

Practical Advice and Information

It is in an adapter card manufacturer's best interests to include as many drivers as possible with their adapter cards in order to ensure that they will work with as many network operating systems as possible. However, before purchasing any adapter card be sure that proven software drivers compatible with the installed or chosen network operating system(s) are included with the purchase of the adapter cards.

Remember that drivers for various cards are often supplied with the installed networking operating system as well. One of these drivers may be more efficient in terms of operation or required memory than another.

SHARED-MEDIA LAN WIRING CENTERS

The most common network physical topology employed today is the star topology, and the heart of the star topology is the wiring center. A wiring center may be alternatively known as a hub, a concentrator, a repeater, a MAU (Multistation Access Unit), or a variety of other terms. In this section, wiring center functionality, technology, management, and analysis will be examined for shared-media network architectures; LAN switches and switching hubs appropriate for switch-based network architectures will be covered in the next section.

Wiring Center Categories

In terms of network architectures supported, Token Ring wiring centers are known as **MAUs (Multistation Access Unit)** while wiring centers for all other network architectures are known as **hubs.** All hubs, or MAUs, are basically just multiport digital signal repeaters. They do not make logical decisions based on the addresses or content of messages; they merely repeat all digital data received among connected ports. In terms of the OSI model, repeaters or hubs are Layer 1 or Physical layer devices dealing only with bit streams.

In terms of functionality and features, wiring centers can be separated into three broad categories:

1. **Stand-alone hubs** are fully configured hubs offering a limited number (12 or fewer) ports of a particular type of network architecture (Ethernet, Token Ring) and media. They are fully configured and include their own power supply but are not generally expandable, do not include management software, and are the least expensive of the three wiring center categories.

2. **Stackable hubs** add expandability and manageability to the basic capabilities of the stand-alone hub. Stackable hubs can be linked together, or cascaded, to form one larger virtual hub of a single type of network architecture and media. Given the larger number of ports, management software becomes essential. Most stackable hubs offer some type of local management software as well as links to enterprise management software platforms such as HP Open-View, Sun's SunNet Manager, IBM NetView, Novell's ManageWise, and Microsoft SMS.

3. **Enterprise hubs,** also known as **Modular Concentrators,** differ from stackable hubs in both physical design and offered functionality. Rather than being fully functional self-contained units, enterprise hubs are modular by design, offering a chassis-based architecture to which a variety of different modules can be inserted. In some cases, these modules can be inserted and/or removed while the hub remains powered-up, a capability known as **hot-swappable.** Among the possible modules supported by enterprise hubs are:
    *   Ethernet, Fast Ethernet, Gigabit Ethernet, Token Ring, and FDDI port modules in a variety of port densities and media choices
    *   Management modules

- Router modules
- Bridge modules
- WAN link modules
- Multiple power supplies for redundant power

These broad category definitions and labels are not standards and are not universally adhered to by manufacturers. Signaling standards defined as part of the IEEE or ANSI LAN standards allow hubs and NICs of different vendors to interoperate successfully in most cases. Figure 3-13 illustrates some of the physical differences between the three major categories of hubs, whereas Figure 3-14 differentiates between the functionality of the major categories of wiring centers.

Stand-alone hubs

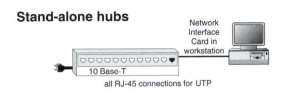

Network Interface Card in workstation

10 Base-T

all RJ-45 connections for UTP

→ Fixed number of ports
→ Single network architecture
→ Not expandable
→ Single media type

Stackable hubs

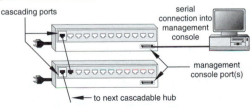

cascading ports

serial connection into management console

management console port(s)

to next cascadable hub

→ Each hub has a fixed number of ports
→ Hubs are cascadable
→ Single network architecture and media
→ Provides management software and link to network management console

Enterprise hubs

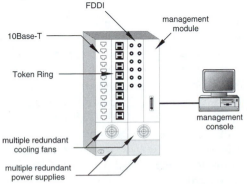

FDDI

management module

10Base-T

Token Ring

management console

multiple redundant cooling fans

multiple redundant power supplies

→ Modular chassis-based design
→ Supports multiple network architectures and media types
→ Integrated management module
→ May include internetworking or WAN modules

Figure 3-13   Major Categories of Hubs

	Multiport digital signal repeater	Network Architectures					Stand-alone	Cascadable	Modular chassis-based	Includes internetworking modules (bridges and routers)	Includes WAN links	Includes network management
		Ethernet	Token Ring	FDDI	100Base-T	100VG-AnyLAN						
Repeaters	●	●	●	●			●					
Stand-alone hubs	●	●		●	●	●	●					
Stackable hubs	●	●		●	●	●		●			●	●
MAUs stand-alone	●		●				●					
MAUs stackable	●		●					●			●	●
Enterprise hubs	●	●	●	●	●	●		●	●	●	●	

Figure 3-14   Wiring Center Functional Comparison

Repeaters

A repeater, as its name would imply, merely "repeats" each bit of digital data that it receives. This repeating action actually "cleans up" the digital signals by retiming and regenerating them before passing these repeated data from one attached device or LAN segment to the next. Repeaters can only link devices or LAN segments of similar network architectures.

Hubs

Hubs are a subset of repeaters that allow attachment of single devices rather than LAN segments to each hub port. The terms *hub* and *concentrator* or "intelligent concentrator" are often used interchangeably. Distinctions can be made between these broad classes of wiring centers, although there is nothing to stop manufacturers from using the terms as they wish.

A hub is often the term reserved for describing a stand-alone device with a fixed number of ports which offers features beyond that of a simple repeater. The type of media connections and network architecture offered by the hub is determined at the time of manufacture as well. For example, a 10BaseT Ethernet hub will offer a fixed number of RJ-45 twisted pair connections for an Ethernet network. Additional types of media or network architectures are not usually supported.

Stackable Hubs

Hubs may also be cascadable or stackable via **cascading ports** which may be specialized ports on the hub or may be switch configurable "normal" ports allowing repeated data to flow out of a cascading port to the next hub rather than the normal inbound-only port traffic flow. In general, cascading ports are proprietary in nature, thereby making it impossible to cascade hubs of different vendors together. Specialized hub-to-hub cascading cables may also be required and the maximum allowable distance between stacked hubs may vary as well. Stackable hubs also vary as to stackability, with the number of stackable hubs ranging from 4 to 20 and the total number of stacked ports ranging from 48 to 768. Cost per port can range from $35 to $147 with most per port costs in the $60 to $70 range.

MAUs

A MAU or Multistation Access Unit is IBM's name for a Token Ring Hub. A MAU is manufactured with a fixed number of ports, and connections for unshielded or shielded twisted pair. IBM uses special connectors for Token Ring over shielded twisted pair (STP) connections to a MAU known as Type 1 connectors. Some MAUs support RJ-45 connectors rather than the more bulky and difficult to work with Type 1 connectors. MAUs typically have eight ports with two additional ports labeled RI (Ring In) and RO (Ring Out). These specialized cascading ports allow multiple MAUs to be linked in single logical ring. MAUs may also be cascaded to each other via fiber-optic cable as opposed to shielded twisted pair.

MAU's offer varying degrees of management capability. **Active management MAUs** are able to send alerts to management consoles regarding malfunctioning Token Ring adapters and can also forcibly remove these misbehaving adapters from the ring. Removing malfunctioning nodes is especially critical in Token Ring LANs due to the possibility of one of the malfunctioning nodes becoming disabled while holding onto the token. Although such an event would be at the very least inconvenient, it would not be catastrophic since the active monitor workstation is capable of regenerating a new token.

Enterprise Hubs

The terms *concentrator, intelligent concentrator, smart hub,* or *enterprise hub* are often reserved for a device characterized by its flexibility and expandability. A concentrator starts with a fairly empty, boxlike device often called a chassis. This chassis contains one or more redundant power supplies and a "built-in" network backbone. This backbone might be Ethernet, Token

Ring, FDDI, Appletalk, 100BaseT, 100VG-AnyLAN, or some combination of the above. Into this "backplane," individual cards or modules are inserted.

For instance, an 8 or 16 port twisted pair Ethernet module could be purchased and slid into place in the concentrator chassis. A network management module supporting the SNMP (Simple Network Management Protocol) network management protocol could then be purchased and slid into the chassis next to the previously installed 10BaseT Port module. In this "mix and match" scenario, additional cards could be added for connection of PCs with Token Ring adapters, PCs or workstations with FDDI adapters, or "dumb" asynchronous terminals. These modules are most often hot-swappable, allowing modules to be added or removed without shutting down the entire enterprise hub. Obviously, the capacity of these enterprise hubs is equally as important as the flexibility afforded by the modular design. In fact, several hundred ports of varying network architectures are often supported by enterprise hubs.

This "network in a box" is now ready for workstations to be hooked up to it through twisted pair connections to the media interfaces on the network interface cards of the PCs or workstations. Allowing different media types to be intermixed in the concentrator was one of its first major selling points. Remember that Ethernet can run over UTP, STP, Thick and Thin Coax as well as Fiber.

Additional modules available for some concentrators may allow data traffic from this "network in box" to travel to other local LANs via bridge or router add-on modules. Bridges and routers will be discussed later in the text. These combination concentrators are sometimes called Internetworking Hubs. Communication to remote LANs or workstations may be available through the addition of other specialized cards, or modules, designed to provide access to Wide Area Network services purchased from common carriers such as the phone company. Whereas all local network traffic travels through this single enterprise hub, it is also an ideal location for security modules to be added for either encryption or authorization functionality.

Backplane design within enterprise hubs is proprietary and, as a result, the modules for enterprise hubs are not interoperable. Therefore, it is important to ensure that the enterprise hub to be purchased has available all required types of modules in terms of network architecture, media type, management, internetworking, WAN interfaces, or security. Vendors' promised delivery dates for required modules are often unreliable.

Hub Management

Because all local area network traffic must pass through the hub, it becomes an ideal place for installation of management software to both monitor and manage network traffic. As previously stated, stand-alone hubs are rarely manufactured with management software. In the case of stackable and enterprise hubs, two layers of management software are most often involved:

1. First, **local hub management software** is usually supplied by the hub vendor and runs over either DOS or Windows. This software allows monitoring and management of the hub from a locally attached management console.

2. Second, since these hubs are just a small part of a vast array of networking devices that might have to be managed on an enterprise basis, most hubs are also capable of sharing management information with **enterprise network management systems** such as HP Open View, IBM NetView, Sun SunNet Manager, Novell ManageWise, or Microsoft SMS (System Management Server).

Although Chapter 15 will cover network management in more detail, a brief explanation here as to how this hub management information is fed to the Enterprise Network Management system is appropriate.

Network management information transfer between multivendor network devices and enterprise network management systems must be characterized by standards-based communication. The standards that govern this network management communication are part of the TCP/IP family of protocols more correctly known as the Internet Suite of Protocols. Specifically, network management information is formatted according to the **SNMP** or **Simple Network Management Protocol.** The types of information to be gathered and stored have also been defined as **MIBs** or **Management Information Bases.** There are actually numerous MIBs defined with the most often used one for network monitoring and management known as the **RMON (Remote Monitoring) MIB.** Network statistics and information is gathered in the first place and packetized in SNMP format by specialized software known as **agents** which reside within the monitored network device and are supplied by the network device's manufacturer. Enterprise network management systems such as HP Openview are able to interpret, consolidate, and display information and alarms from a variety of different networking equipment manufactured by a variety of different vendors, thanks to standards-based communication protocols. Figure 3-15 illustrates the relationship of the various aspects of the standards-based network management communications protocols.

Practical Advice and Information

Some hub management issues are particular to stackable and/or enterprise hubs. For example:

*   Many stackable hubs offer network management capabilities as an optional hardware or software upgrade. It is important to fully

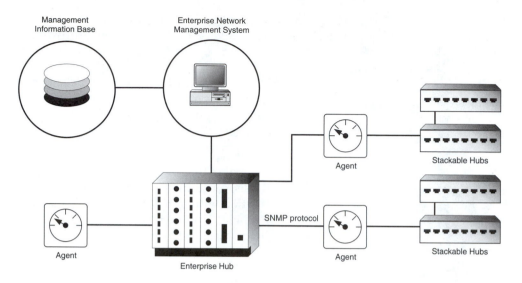

Figure 3-15 Standards-Based Network Management Communications Protocols

understand the ease with which this upgrade can be accomplished and whether or not the hubs must be powered off while doing so.

- The network management traffic may exit the hub via a separate serial port or travel along a separate bus within the hub so as not to diminish the amount of bandwidth available for data. These options are sometimes referred to as out-of-band management connections.

- The entire stack of hubs should be viewed, monitored, and managed by the network management software as a single, virtual hub.

- The local hub management software should be simple, easy to use, and preferably Windows-based with the capability to talk to enterprise network management system platforms should that need arise.

- If possible, management modules or upgrades should be included with the original purchase in order to avoid potential upgrade hassles. Buying management modules at purchase time is often more economical than buying upgrades later, thanks to vendor discount packages.

- An issue particular to Token Ring modules included in enterprise hubs is that the management software should be able to dynamically assign ports located on the same physical module onto different logical rings in order to optimize network performance.

**Applied
Problem
Solving**

WIRING CENTERS TECHNOLOGY ANALYSIS

Some of the major technical features to be used for comparative analysis are listed in Figure 3-16. Before purchasing a wiring center of any type, consider the implications of the various possible features listed in the Wiring Center Technology Analysis.

Wiring Center Characteristic	Implications/Options
Expandability	Most stand-alone hubs are neither expandable nor cascadable. Stackable hubs are cascadable and enterprise hubs are expandable by adding more LAN modules. Enterprise hubs vary in the number of open slots from approximately 5 to 20. Total backplane capacity (speed) is important because this is the shared network media that must be shared by all attached modules.
Network Architectures	Options: Ethernet, Token Ring, FDDI, Appletalk, 100Base-T, 100VG-AnyLAN. Not all enterprise hubs have all types of network architecture modules available.
Media	Options: UTP, STP, thin coax, thick coax, fiber-optic cable. Modules also differ according to supported media. Remember that a NIC is on the other end of the connection to the hub module. Is this hub module media type and connector compatible with installed NICs?
Macintosh Communications	Can an Apple Macintosh be linked to the hub?
Terminal Communications	Can "dumb" asynchronous terminals be connected directly to the hub? What is the physical connector and serial transmission specification? (DB-25?, RS-232?)
Internetworking	Are bridging and or routing modules available that can redirect traffic from module to module? Across different types of network architecture modules? Across which different network architecture modules will traffic need to be bridged?
Wide Area Networking	Is this hub connected to other hubs remotely through the use of carrier-based data services? If so, which WAN services are supported? Options: Frame Relay, ISDN, Switched 56K, Digital leased lines from 9.6 Kbps to 1.544 Mbps (T-1)

(continued)

Wiring Center Characteristic	Implications/Options
Management	Is a local hub management program available? Are SNMP management protocols supported? Can individual ports be managed? Is monitoring software included? What security services are available? Can ports be remotely enabled/disabled? Can the hub be controlled by a port attached workstation or only by a special management console? Can the hub be controlled remotely? via modem? Are management statistics and alarms graphically displayed? How are alarm thresholds set? How are faults managed? Can port access be limited by day and/or time? What operating systems can the management software run on? Options: DOS, OS/2, Windows, Windows NT, UNIX, Mac, etc. Can a map of the network be displayed? Which enterprise network management systems are supported? Options: HP Open View, IBM NetView, Sun SunNet Manager, Novell ManageWise.
Reliability	Is an integrated UPS included? Are power supplies redundant? Are modules hot-swappable? Are cooling fans redundant? Which components are capable of being replaced by the user?

Figure 3-16 Wiring Centers Technology Analysis

▓ LAN SWITCHES

The "network in a box" or "backbone in a box" offered by concentrators and hubs shrinks the length of the network backbone but doesn't change the architectural characteristics of a particular network backbone. For instance, in an Ethernet concentrator, multiple workstations may access the built-in Ethernet backbone via a variety of media, but the basic rules of Ethernet such as CSMA/CD access methodology at 10 Mbps still control performance on this "Ethernet in a box." Only one workstation at a time can broadcast its message onto the shared 10 Mbps backbone.

Switch Classification

Supported Network Architectures A **Switching hub,** or **LAN switch,** seeks to overcome this "one-at-a-time" broadcast scheme which can potentially lead to data collisions, retransmissions, and reduced throughput between high-bandwidth-demanding devices such as engineering workstations or server-to-server communications. By adding the basic design of a data PBX to the modular designed concentrator, numerous manufacturers have delivered "switched" Ethernet connections at 10 Mbps to multiple users simultaneously through a process known as parallel networking.

The Ethernet switch is actually able to create connections, or switch, between any two attached Ethernet devices on a packet-by-packet basis in as little as 40 milliseconds. The "one-at-time" broadcast limitation previously associated with Ethernet is overcome with an Ethernet switch. Figure 3-3 illustrated the basic functionality of an Ethernet switch. Ethernet is not the only network architecture for which LAN switches are available. Either stand-alone versions or slide-in modules for enterprise switches are also available for Token Ring, FDDI, and Fast Ethernet.

In addition, many high-end LAN switches also support **ATM (Asynchronous Transfer Mode)** which is a type of switching that allows not only the previously mentioned LAN network architectures to be switched extremely quickly but can also switch voice, video, and image traffic equally well. In fact ATM can switch any type of digital information over LANs or WANs with equal ease and speeds that are currently in the gigabit/second range.

Super-Switches or Mega-Switches support multiple different LAN architectures, ATM, as well as interface to WAN services.

Functional Differences   Switches can vary in ways other than just the types of network architecture frames that are switched. Significant functional differences between switches can have a dramatic effect on switch performance. The first major functional difference involves how the network architecture frames are processed before they are switched to their destination:

- **Cut-Through Switches** read only the address information in the MAC layer header before beginning processing. After reading the destination address, the switch consults an address lookup table in order to determine which port on the switch this frame should be forwarded to. Once the address lookup is completed, the point-to-point connection is created and the frame is immediately forwarded. Cut-through switching is very fast. However, because the Frame Check Sequence on the forwarded frame was not checked, bad frames are forwarded. As a result, the receiving station must send a request for retransmission followed by the sending station retransmitting the original frame, leading to overall traffic increases.

- **Store-and-Forward Switches** read the entire frame into a shared memory area in the switch. The contents of the transmitted Frame Check Sequence field is read and compared to the locally recalculated Frame Check Sequence. If the results match, the switch consults the address lookup table, builds the appropriate point-to-point connection, and forwards the frame. As a result, store-and-forward switching is slower than cut-through switching but does not forward bad frames.

- **Error-Free Cut-Through Switches** read both the addresses and Frame Check Sequences for every frame. Frames are forwarded immediately to destinations nodes in an identical fashion to cut-through switches. However, should bad frames be forwarded, the error-free cut-through switch is able to reconfigure those individual ports producing the bad frames to use store-and-forward switching. As errors diminish, to preset thresholds, the port is set back to cut-through switching for higher performance throughput.

SWITCH TECHNOLOGY ISSUES

Practical Advice and Information

Switch Flow Control   Switches are often employed to make switched connections between multiple network architectures. A common role of LAN switches is to provide switched connections between 10 Mbps and 100 Mbps network architectures. However, when servers on high-speed (100 Mbps) switched connections blast high-bandwidth data traffic back to clients on shared 10 Mbps port connections, data traffic can get backed up and data frames can be lost once buffers designed to hold overflow data become filled.

Switch vendors have attempted to respond to this situation in a variety of ways. Some switches include so-called deep buffers which allow more overflow traffic to be buffered before it is discarded. However, the dilemma with this approach is that memory is expensive and it is difficult to determine how much buffer memory is enough while still keeping switch costs reasonable.

A second approach involves implementing a feedback mechanism known as **backpressure.** In the case of Ethernet switches, backpressure prevents lost frames during overload conditions by sending out false collision detection signals in order to get transmitting clients and servers to time-out long enough to give the switch a chance to forward buffered data. It is somewhat ironic that the CSMA/CD access methodology which the switch sought to overcome is being used to improve switch performance. The difficulty with backpressure mechanisms in the case of multiple device LAN segments being linked to a single switch port is that the false collision detection signal stops all traffic on the connected LAN segment, even peer-to-peer traffic, which could have been delivered directly without the use of the switch. One possible solution to this shortcoming is to only enable backpressure on those switch ports that are connected to single devices such as servers.

Switch Management   Another major issue to be faced by network managers before jumping blindly onto the LAN switch bandwagon is the matter of how to monitor and manage switched-LAN connections. Unlike shared-media LAN management tools that are able to access all network traffic from a single interface to the shared-media hub, switched architecture management tools must be able to monitor numerous point-to-point dedicated connections simultaneously. In a switched-LAN architecture, each port is the equivalent of a dedicated LAN that must be individually monitored and managed. Switch vendors currently offer three basic approaches to the switch management dilemma:

1. **Port mirroring** copies information from a particular switch port to an attached LAN analyzer. The difficulty with this approach is that it only allows one port to be monitored at a time.

2. **Roving port mirroring** creates a roving RMON (Remote Monitoring) probe that gathers statistics at regular intervals on multiple switch ports. The shortcoming with this approach remains that at any single point in time, only one port is being monitored.

3. **Simultaneous RMON View** allows all network traffic to be monitored simultaneously. Such a monitoring scheme is only possible on those switches that incorporate a shared memory multi-gigabit bus as opposed to a switching matrix internal architecture. Furthermore, unless this monitoring software is executed on a separate CPU, switch performance is likely to degrade.

There is little doubt that properly deployed LAN switches can greatly improve network performance. However, management tools for LAN switches continue to evolve and network managers should be wary of introducing technology into an enterprise network whose impact cannot be accurately monitored and managed.

Applied Problem Solving

LAN SWITCH TECHNOLOGY ANALYSIS

Some of the important analysis issues surrounding LAN switch selection are highlighted in Figure 3-17.

LAN Switch Characteristic	Implications/Options
Switching Architecture	Options include cut-through, store-and-forward, and error-free store-and-forward.
Token Ring Switches	Some Token Ring switches also employ store-and-forward switching with buffering on the outbound port so that the outbound port has time to wait until the token reaches that switch port when multiple Token Ring devices are attached to a single switch port. Token Ring switches are also able to reduce NetBIOS and Source route bridging broadcast traffic by filtering. Some Token Ring switches also support full duplex Token Ring networking, also known as DTR (Dedicated Token Ring), IEEE 802.5r.

(continued)

LAN Switch Characteristic	Implications/Options
Network Architectures	Switches may support one or more of the following: Ethernet, Token Ring, FDDI, Fast Ethernet, Gigabit Ethernet, and ATM. Network architectures may be available in a variety of different media types.
Port Configuration	Switches can vary in both the number of MAC addresses allowed per port as well as the total number of MAC addresses supported for the entire switch. Some switches only allow single devices to be attached to each LAN switch port. How easily can devices be assigned/reassigned to switch ports? Can devices that are physically attached to different switch ports be assigned to the same virtual LAN?
Full Duplex	Some switches allow some ports to be enabled for full duplex operation. Full duplex switch ports will only communicate with full-duplex NICs, whereas "normal" switch ports will communicate with existing NICs.
Switch-to-Switch Connection	Some switches use Ethernet or Token Ring switched ports, whereas others use higher-speed architectures such as FDDI or ATM. These inter-switch connections are sometimes referred to as the Fat Pipe.
Internetworking	In addition to merely establishing switched connections and forwarding traffic, some switches also have the ability to examine the addressing information contained within the data frames and perform bridging and routing functions. Token Ring switches may or may not perform source route bridging which is specific to the Token Ring architecture. Some routing models can also examine embedded protocols and make routing and filtering decisions based on that criteria.
Management	Does the switch support both SNMP and the RMON or SMON MIB? Does the switch contain a management port and management software? Which type of RMON probe is supported? Is a separate CPU provided for processing system monitoring software? Does the local management software support Enterprise Network Management software such as HP Openview, IBM NetView, Sun SunNet Manager? Is a port provided to which a protocol analyzer can be attached?

Figure 3-17   LAN Switch Technology Analysis

ATM for the LAN

ATM (Asynchronous Transfer Mode) is a connection-oriented switched transmission methodology that holds great promise for becoming a single solution for the transmission of data, voice, and video over both local and wide area networks. The word *promise* in the previous sentence is significant. Any technology that sounds as if it is the ultimate solution to the world's transmission needs would obviously require an enormous amount of standards-making and interoperability planning efforts. Such is the case with ATM.

One of the characteristics of ATM that affords it the capability of delivering a variety of traffic over both local and wide area networks is the fixed-length 53-byte cells into which all traffic is segmented. This uniform length allows timed, dependable delivery for streaming traffic such as voice and video, while simplifying troubleshooting, administration, setup, and design. Standards-making activities are divided into two major efforts:

1. **UNI** or **User-Network Interface** defines standards for interoperability between end-user equipment and ATM equipment and networks. These standards are well defined and most equipment is widely available.

2. **NNI** or **Network-Network Interface** defines interoperability standards between various vendors' ATM equipment and network services. These standards are not as well defined as UNI.

As a result, single vendor solutions are currently the safest bet for network managers requiring ATM's speed and flexibility. ATM cabling/speed specifications for which technology is currently available are listed in Figure 3-18.

Costs for ATM technology vary widely and should decrease significantly with increased demand. Following are some typical cost ranges:

- 25 Mbps adapter cards: $400–$1,500 each

- 100 Mbps and 155 Mbps adapter cards: $1,200–$3,000 each

- Per port cost on ATM hubs/switches: $1,000–$5,000 each

ATM Speed	Cabling Type
25 Mbps	STP, UTP3 or better
100 Mbps	UTP5
155 Mbps	Single and Multimode Fiber-Optic Cable and UTP5
622 Mbps	Single and Multimode Fiber-Optic Cable

Figure 3-18   Available ATM Speed/Cabling Specifications

As is the case with any high-speed network architecture, migration strategies from existing network architectures to ATM are of critical importance. Two basic migration approaches have been defined:

1. **IP over ATM,** otherwise known as **Classical IP,** adapts the TCP/IP protocol stack to employ ATM services as a native transport protocol directly. This is an IP specific proposal and is not an option for LANs using other protocol stacks such as NetWare's IPX/SPX.

2. **LAN Emulation** provides a translation layer that allows ATM to emulate existing Ethernet and Token Ring LANs and allows all current upper-layer LAN protocols to be transported by the ATM services in an unmodified fashion. With LAN emulation, ATM networks become nothing more than a transparent, high-speed delivery service. LAN emulation is most often implemented by the ATM vendor by the installation of an **address resolution server** that provides translation between the ATM addressing scheme and the addressing scheme which is native to a particular emulated LAN.

Figure 3-19 illustrates a typical ATM implementation featuring an ATM local workgroup, connection of legacy LANs to a local ATM network, the local ATM switched network itself acting as a local high-speed backbone, and access to wide area ATM services which may be either a private network or purchased from an ATM WAN service provider.

■ LAN MEDIA ALTERNATIVES

Although a variety of wire and fiber media alternatives are reviewed in this section, wireless alternatives for LAN media are explored in the Chapter 14, "Remote Access and Wireless Networking."

Not Twisted Pair

The type of phone wire installed in most homes consists of a tan plastic jacket containing four untwisted wires—red, yellow, green, and black—and is also known as **4 conductor station wire** or **RYGB.** This type of wire is not suitable for data transmission and is not the unshielded twisted pair (UTP) that is so often mentioned.

Another popular type of phone wiring is referred to as **flat gray modular** wiring, also known as gray satin or silver satin. Inside this flat gray jacket are either four, six, or eight wires which get crimped into either RJ-11 (4 wire), RJ-12 (6 wire), or RJ-45 plugs (8 wire) using a specialized crimping tool. Premises phone wiring as well as phones; crimp tools, RJ-11 plugs, and flat gray modular wire are attainable at most hardware or department stores.

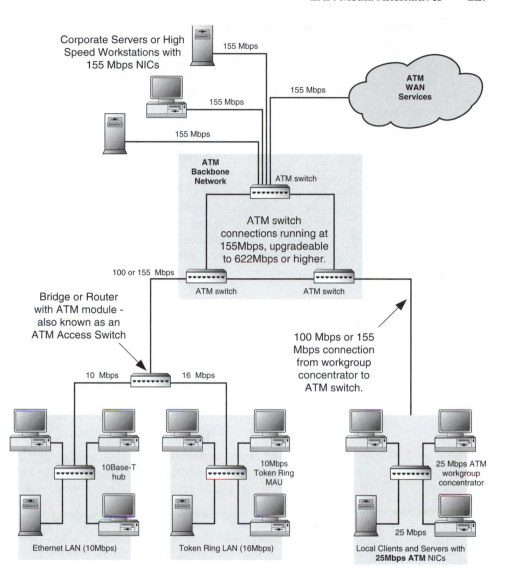

Figure 3-19   ATM Implementation

Flat gray modular wire is not the same as twisted pair and is only suitable for carrying data over short distances. For instance, this type of cable is often used between a PC or workstation and a nearby RJ-11 jack for access to premises wiring systems or LAN backbones. Modular adapters with RJ-11 input jacks mounted within RS-232 hoods are available to quickly construct data cables of various pin-out configurations without having to crimp RS-232 pins on individual conductors.

Unshielded Twisted Pair

Twisted pair wiring consists of one or more pairs of insulated copper wire that are twisted at varying lengths, from 2 to 12 twists per foot, to reduce interference both between pairs and from outside sources such as electric motors and fluorescent lights. Interference can cause data errors and necessitate retransmission. These individually twisted pairs are then grouped together and covered with a plastic or vinyl covering or jacket. No additional shielding is added before the pairs are wrapped in the plastic covering. Thus, the completed product is known as **unshielded twisted pair** or **UTP.** The most common numbers of twisted copper wire pairs combined to form the unshielded twisted pair cables are 2, 3, 4, and 25.

All UTPs are not created equal. One of the common appeals of UTP is that it is often already installed in modern buildings for the purpose of carrying voice conversations through the voice PBX. Frequently, when the twisted pair wiring for the voice PBX was installed, extra pairs were wired to each office location. This leads some people to conclude that they don't need to invest in any new wiring to carry data transmission throughout their buildings; they can just use the existing extra pairs of unshielded twisted pair wiring. The problem is that there are five different categories of UTP as specified by **EIA/TIA 568** (Electronics Industry Association/Telecommunications Industry Association). In addition to specifying UTP specifications, EIA/TIA 568 also specifies:

- The topology, cable types, and connector types to be used in EIA/TIA 568 compliant wiring schemes

- The minimum performance specifications for cabling, connectors, and components such as wall plates, punch-down blocks, and patch panels to be used in an EIA/TIA 568 compliant installation

Although Category 1 UTP, otherwise known as voice-grade, need only carry voice conversations with reasonable clarity, Categories 3–5 (data-grade) cable must meet certain predefined electrical characteristics that ensure transmission quality and speed. Before assuming that the UTP in a building is suitable for data transmission, have its transmission characteristics tested, and ensure that these characteristics meet listed data-grade UTP specifications. Figure 3-20 summarizes the specifications for Categories 1–5 UTP.

Wire thickness is measured by gauge and represented with the unit **AWG** (American Wire Gauge). The higher the gauge number, the thinner the wire. UTP wiring of different categories must meet specifications for resistance to different forces that interfere with signal strength. Two of the more common sources of interference or loss of signal strength are as follows:

UTP Category	Specifications/Applications
Category 1 UTP	22 or 24 AWG. Not recommended for data.
Category 2 UTP	22 or 24 AWG. Only suitable for data transmission of less than 1 Mbps.
Category 3 UTP	24 AWG. Very common in existing installations. Most often used for voice-only installations. Suitable for data up to, but not including, 16 Mbps. As a result, it can be used reliably for 4 Mbps Token Ring and 10 Mbps Ethernet. Tested for attenuation and near-end crosstalk up to 16 MHz.
Category 4 UTP	22 or 24 AWG. Tested for attenuation and near-end crosstalk up to 20 MHz. Not widely used in favor of Category 5 UTP.
Category 5 UTP	22 or 24 AWG. Tested for attenuation and near-end crosstalk to 100 MHz. Capable of transmitting up to 100 Mbps when strictly installed to EIA/TIA 568 specifications. Currently the most commonly installed category of UTP.

Figure 3-20   Unshielded Twisted Pair Specifications

1. **Attenuation** is the decrease in the power of signal over a distance in a particular type of wire or media.

2. **Near-End Crosstalk (NExT)** is signal interference caused by a strong signal on one pair (transmitting) overpowering a weaker signal on an adjacent pair (receiving). Near End Crosstalk and Attenuation to Crosstalk Ratio (ACR) are both measured in dB or decibels. A decibel is a logarithmic rather than linear measurement of the ratio between two powers, often a data signal and some type of noise or interference.

Practical Advice and Information

BEYOND CAT 5

Enhanced Category 5 UTP (EC5), otherwise known as **Category 5+** or **CAT5e,** offers enhanced performance over CAT5 UTP due to the following improvements in electrical specifications:

- Attenuation to Crosstalk ratio of 10 dB at 155 MHz

- A minimum 400% improvement in capacitance, or ability of a wire to store an electrical charge

- A 250% improvement in frequency

Level	Highest Test Frequency	Required Frequency in MHz for Attenuation to Crosstalk Ratio (ACR) at 10dB (Powersum Bandwidth)
5	200 MHz	80 MHz
6	350 MHz	100 MHz
7	400 MHz	160 MHz

Figure 3-21   UTP Level 5, 6, and 7 Performance Specifications

- A 35% improvement in resistance

- An average of 5% improvement in attenuation

- An average of a 6 dB improvement in NEXT

Although no official Category 6 cable has become standardized, media vendors are attempting to develop cable that is capable of carrying data at frequencies of up to 600 MHz. Some such attempts are not truly unshielded twisted pair but rather are FTP or foil-twisted pair cable that is more closely related to shielded twisted pair. Buyers must be wary of so-called Category 6 cable by focusing on whether or not the cable is truly UTP and whether or not it is a specified EIA/TIA standard.

Anixter, a major cabling manufacturer, has proposed a Levels '97 program to define performance characteristics for cabling tested beyond the 100 MHz required for CAT 5. Since higher-speed network architectures such as Fast Ethernet and Gigabit Ethernet require four pair of UTP to be transmitting power simultaneously, it was determined that crosstalk should be measured by taking into account the crosstalk influence from all pairs in the cable, whether 4-pair or 25-pair rather than just crosstalk between adjacent pairs, or pair-to-pair, as had been required for CAT5 certification. This type of crosstalk test is called **Powersum Crosstalk.** Key performance specifications for Level 5, 6, and 7 are detailed in Figure 3-21.

COMMON UTP INSTALLATION MISTAKES

Practical Advice and Information

As mentioned in the Category 5 UTP definition in Figure 3-20, strict adherence to EIA/TIA 568 installation standards is essential for successful transmission at 100 Mbps over UTP Category 5. Because a less-than-perfect installation will probably transport 10 Mbps traffic without any problem, noncompliant installations may not surface until upgrades to 100 Mbps network architectures are attempted. Among the most common installation mistakes are the following:

- Untwisting the UTP wire more than the maximum 13 mm in order to secure the UTP to wall plates or punch-down blocks

- Exceeding the maximum bend radius specified for UTP. By over-bending the wire, cross-talk between stretched pairs of wires can be increased.

- Bundling the groups of UTP together too tightly with cable ties. By excessively pinching the UTP together, cross-talk between pairs is increased.

STP—Shielded Twisted Pair

Data transmission characteristics, and therefore the data transmission speed, can be improved by adding **shielding** both around each individual pair as well as around the entire group of twisted pairs. This shielding may be a metallic foil or copper braid. The function of the shield is rather simple. It "shields" the individual twisted pairs as well as the entire cable from either EMI (Electromagnetic Interference) or RFI (Radio Frequency Interference). Installation of shielded twisted pair can be tricky.

Remember that the shielding is metal and is therefore a conductor. Often, the shielding is terminated in a drain wire, which must be properly grounded. The bottom line is that improperly installed Shielded Twisted Pair Wiring can actually increase rather than decrease interference and data transmission problems. STP was commonly specified for Token Ring installations. However, recent specifications for CDDI, Fast Ethernet, ATM and other high-speed network architectures are using Category 5 UTP rather than STP.

Coaxial Cable

Coaxial cable, more commonly known as coax or cable TV cable, has specialized insulators and shielding separating two conductors, allowing reliable, high-speed data transmission over relatively long distances. Figure 3-22 illustrates a cross-section of a typical coaxial cable. Coax comes in various thicknesses and has been historically used in Ethernet network architectures. In some cases, these network architecture specifications include required characteristics of the (physical layer) coaxial cable over which the (data-link layer) MAC layer protocol is transmitted.

Ethernet 10Base5 specifies coaxial cable known as Thick Coax or more affectionately known as "frozen yellow garden hose," giving a hint as to how easy this medium is to work with.

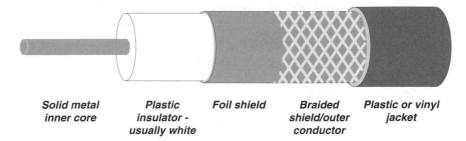

Solid metal inner core **Plastic insulator - usually white** **Foil shield** **Braided shield/outer conductor** **Plastic or vinyl jacket**

Figure 3-22 Coax Cable: Cross-Section

Fiber-Optic Cable

Coax was at one time the media of choice for reliable, high-speed data transmission. But times and technology change, and people now often turn to fiber-optic cable when seeking reliable, high bandwidth media for data transmission beyond the capabilities of Category 5 UTP. Price is still a factor, however, as one can see from Figure 3-24. Fiber-optic cable is still the most expensive media option available. This expensive media delivers high bandwidth in the range of several Gigabytes (billions of characters) per second over distances of several kilometers.

Fiber-optic cable is also one of the most secure of all media since it is relatively untappable, transmitting only pulses of light, unlike all of the aforementioned media that transmit varying levels of electrical pulses. Whereas fiber-optic is really a thin fiber of glass rather than copper, this media is immune to electromagnetic interference contributing to its high bandwidth and data transmission capabilities. Another important thing to remember is that it is glass and thus requires careful handling. Fiber-optic cable made of plastic is under development but does not deliver nearly the speed and bandwidth of the glass fiber cable. Fiber-optic cable comes is a number of varieties. Figure 3-23 illustrates a cross-section of a fiber-optic cable.

Light Transmission Modes   Once a pulse of light enters the core of the fiber-optic cable, it will behave differently depending on the physical characteristics of the core and cladding of the fiber-optic cable. In a **Multimode** or **Multimode Step Index** fiber-optic cable, the rays of light will bounce off the cladding at different angles and continue down the core while others will be absorbed in the cladding. These multiple rays at varying angles cause distortion and limit the overall transmission capabilities of the fiber. This type of fiber-optic cable is capable of high bandwidth (200 Mbps) transmission but usually over distances of less than 1 km.

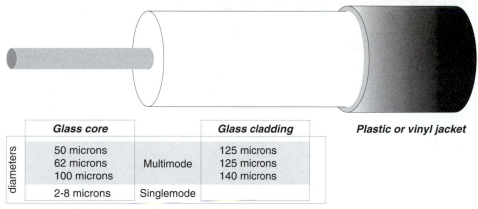

	Glass core		Glass cladding
diameters	50 microns 62 microns 100 microns	Multimode	125 microns 125 microns 140 microns
	2-8 microns	Singlemode	

Note: A micron is a millionth of a meter

Figure 3-23   Fiber-Optic Cable: Cross Section

By gradually decreasing a characteristic of the core known as the refractive index from the center to the outer edge, reflected rays are focused along the core more efficiently yielding higher bandwidth (3 GBps) over several kilometers. This type of fiber-optic cable is known as **Multimode Graded Index Fiber.**

The third type of fiber-optic cable seeks to focus the rays of light even farther so that only a single wavelength can pass through at a time, in a fiber type known as **Single Mode.** Without numerous reflections of rays at multiple angles, distortion is eliminated and bandwidth is maximized. Single mode is the most expensive fiber-optic cable, but it can be used over the longest distances.

Core Thickness   The thickness of fiber-optic cable's core and cladding is measured in microns (millionths of an inch). The three major core thicknesses are 50, 62, and 100 microns with their associated claddings being 125, 125, and 140 microns, respectively. The increasing core thicknesses generally allow transmission over longer distances but at a greater expense.

Light Source Wavelength   The wavelength of the light that is pulsed onto the fiber-optic cable is measured in nanometers (nm) with the optimal light transmitting wavelengths coming in three distinct windows of 820 nm, 1310 nm, 1500 nm. Windows of 820 nm and 1310 nm are most often used for local and campus-wide networking such as FDDI, whereas 1310 nm and 1500 nm are used by carriers to deliver high-bandwidth fiber-based service over long distances. The higher-frequency light-emitting sources carry a higher pricetag.

LAN MEDIA TECHNOLOGY ANALYSIS

Media Type	Also Called	Bandwidth	Distance Limits	Connectors	Comments/Applications	Token Ring	Ethernet	FDDI	CDDI	Fast Ethernet	ATM	Price ($)
4-wire phone station wire	Quad RYGB	3 Kbps	200 feet	RJ-11 jacks	4 insulated wired- red,green, yellow, black. Home phone wiring. Voice Applications							0.09/foot
Flat gray modular	Flat satin, telephone cable, silver satin	14.4 Kbps	10-20 feet	RJ-11 or RJ-45 plugs	Comes with 4,6,8 conductors. Used for short data cables using modular (mod-tap) adapters	■	■		■	■	■	0.09- 0.18/foot
Unshielded twisted pair	UTP	100 Mbps	100 feet	RJ-45	5 Designated categories. Twists prevent interference, increase bandwidth. Voice grade usually not suitable for data	■	■		■	■	■	0.10/foot
Shielded twisted pair	STP	16 Mbps	100 feet	RJ-45 or IBM data connectors	Shielding reduces interference but complicates installation	■	■		■	■	■	0.42/foot
Coax- thick	Frozen yellow garden hose	10 Mbps	500 feet	AUI (attachment unit interface)	Original Ethernet cabling		■					1.10 foot
Coax-thin	RG-58, thinnet, cheapernet	10 Mbps	200 feet	BNC connector	Looks like cable TV cable. Easier to work with than thick coax.		■					0.32/foot
Coax-thin	RG-62	2.5 Mbps	200 feet	BNC or IBM data connector	Similar to RG-58 (thinnet) but different electrical characteristics make these cables NOT interchangeable	■						0.32/foot
Fiber-optic cable	Fiber Glass	several Gbps	several kilometers	SI or SMA 905 or SMA 906	Difficult to install but technology is improving. High bandwidth, long distance, virtually error free, high security	■	■	■			■	1.00/foot

(Architectures column group: Token Ring, Ethernet, FDDI, CDDI, Fast Ethernet, ATM)

Figure 3-24 LAN Media Technology Analysis

■ LAN ENCODING SCHEMES

Regardless of network architecture, all computers attached to a LAN communicate with each other by representing humanly readable characters and symbols in machine readable format. The process of transforming humanly readable characters into machine readable code is known as **character encoding.**

Using a particular encoding scheme, characters are turned into a series of ones and zeros. Why ones and zeros? The one and zero are used as symbols to represent two discrete states, much like a light switch being on or off. These discrete states can be easily represented electrically by discrete voltages of electricity. In turn, these discrete voltages of electricity representing coded characters can then be easily transmitted, received, and examined by data communications equipment.

The individual 1's and 0's that constitute a given character are known as **bits.** The series (usually 8) of bits representing the entire encoded letter is known as a **byte.** These 1's and 0's, or digits, represented by discrete voltages of electricity are in **digital** format and are known as digital data. Now that the humanly readable character is in machine readable form, it (these bits) can now be transmitted over the shared LAN media. If the shared LAN media is copper based, the ones and zeros will be represented by discrete levels of electrical voltages. If the shared LAN media is fiber-optic cable, then the ones and zeros will be represented by discrete levels of light or optical energy.

Characters can be encoded according to a variety of protocols or standards. A few of the currently popular encoding standards are described in the following paragraphs.

ASCII

American Standard Code for Information Interchange (ASCII) is one standardized method for encoding humanly readable characters. ASCII uses a series of seven bits to represent 128 ($2^7 = 128$) different characters including upper- and lowercase letters, numerals, punctuation and symbols, and specialized control characters. Figure 3-25 is an ASCII table.

EBCDIC

Extended Binary Coded Decimal Interchange Code (EBCDIC) is an 8bit code capable of representing 256 different characters, numerals, and control characters ($2^8 = 256$). EBCDIC is the primary coding method used in IBM mainframe applications. Figure 3-26 is an EBCDIC table.

USING ASCII AND EBCDIC TABLES

Practical Advice and Information

Using ASCII or EBCDIC tables to interpret character encoding is relatively straightforward. The tables are arranged according to groups of bits otherwise known as bit patterns. The bit patterns are divided into groups. In the case of ASCII, bits 6 through 4 are known as the most significant bits (MSB), while bits 3 through 0 are known as the least significant bits (LSB). In the

<table>
<tr><td rowspan="3">MSB</td><td>Bit 6</td><td>0</td><td>0</td><td>0</td><td>0</td><td>1</td><td>1</td><td>1</td><td>1</td></tr>
<tr><td>Bit 5</td><td>0</td><td>0</td><td>1</td><td>1</td><td>0</td><td>0</td><td>1</td><td>1</td></tr>
<tr><td>Bit 4</td><td>0</td><td>1</td><td>0</td><td>1</td><td>0</td><td>1</td><td>0</td><td>1</td></tr>
</table>

Bit 0	Bit 1	Bit 2	Bit 3								
0	0	0	0	NUL	DLE	SP	0	@	P		p
1	0	0	0	SOH	DC1	!	1	A	Q	a	q
0	1	0	0	STX	DC2		2	B	R	b	r
1	1	0	0	ETX	DC3	#	3	C	S	c	s
0	0	1	0	EOT	DC4	$	4	D	T	d	t
1	0	1	0	ENQ	NAK	%	5	E	U	e	u
0	1	1	0	ACK	SYN	&	6	F	V	f	v
1	1	1	0	BEL	ETB		7	G	W	g	w
0	0	0	1	BS	CAN	(	8	H	X	h	x
1	0	0	1	HT	EM	)	9	I	Y	i	y
0	1	0	1	LF	SUB	*	:	J	Z	j	z
1	1	0	1	VT	ESC	+	;	K	[	k	{
0	0	1	1	FF	FS	,	<	L	\	l		
1	0	1	1	CR	GS		=	M	]	m	}
0	1	1	1	SO	RS	.	>	N	^	n	~
1	1	1	1	SI	US		?	O	-	o	DEL

Figure 3-25   ASCII Table

<table>
<tr><td rowspan="3">MSB</td><td>Bit 6</td><td>0</td><td>0</td><td>0</td><td>0</td><td>1</td><td>1</td><td>1</td><td>1</td></tr>
<tr><td>Bit 5</td><td>0</td><td>0</td><td>1</td><td>1</td><td>0</td><td>0</td><td>1</td><td>1</td></tr>
<tr><td>Bit 4</td><td>0</td><td>1</td><td>0</td><td>1</td><td>0</td><td>1</td><td>0</td><td>1</td></tr>
</table>

Bit 0	Bit 1	Bit 2	Bit 3								
0	0	0	0	NUL	DLE	SP	0	@	P		p
1	0	0	0	SOH	DC1	!	1	A	Q	a	q
0	1	0	0	STX	DC2		2	B	R	b	r
1	1	0	0	ETX	DC3	#	3	C	S	c	s
0	0	1	0	EOT	DC4	$	4	D	T	d	t
1	0	1	0	ENQ	NAK	%	5	E	U	e	u
0	1	1	0	ACK	SYN	&	6	F	V	f	v
1	1	1	0	BEL	ETB		7	G	W	g	w
0	0	0	1	BS	CAN	(	8	H	X	h	x
1	0	0	1	HT	EM	)	9	I	Y	i	y
0	1	0	1	LF	SUB	*	:	J	Z	j	z
1	1	0	1	VT	ESC	+	;	K	[	k	{
0	0	1	1	FF	FS	,	<	L	\	l		
1	0	1	1	CR	GS		=	M	]	m	}
0	1	1	1	SO	RS	.	>	N	^	n	~
1	1	1	1	SI	US		?	O	-	o	DEL

Figure 3-26   EBCDIC Table

Humanly Readable	ASCII	EBCDIC
A	1000001	11000001
x	1111000	10100111
5	0110101	11110101
LF (line feed)	0001010	00100101

Figure 3-27   Humanly Readable, ASCII, and EBCDIC Coding

case of EBCDIC, bits 0 through 3 are known as the MSB and bits 4 through 7 are known as the LSB.

In order to find the bit pattern of a particular character, one needs to combine the bit patterns that intersect in the table at the character in question, remembering that most significant bits always precede least significant bits. In the case of ASCII, this means that bits are arranged from bit 6 to bit 0, while EBCDIC is arranged from bit 0 to bit 7. As an example, representative characters, numerals, and control characters and their bit patterns are highlighted with shading in the ASCII and EBCDIC tables and are displayed in Figure 3-27 in humanly readable, ASCII, and EBCDIC formats.

Line Encoding

Two of the more popular methodologies in which ones and zeros are actually represented by discrete levels of voltages are **manchester encoding** and **differential manchester encoding.** Both of these encoding schemes allow sufficient transitions between positive and negative voltages in order to ensure the required signal timing and reliability. Time slots in which a given signal voltage is sampled are known as bit times. As illustrated in Figure 3-28, transitions between positive and negative voltages occur during these bit times. In the case of manchester encoding, a transition from negative to positive within a bit time represents a binary one, while a transition from positive to negative voltages within a given bit time slot represents a binary zero. Differential manchester encoding takes into account the additional factor of the *difference* between the voltage level at the beginning of the current bit time and the voltage level at the end of the previous bit time. If these two voltage levels are the same, a one is represented. If the voltage level at the beginning of a given bit time is the opposite of the voltage at the end of the previous bit time, a zero is being represented in that bit time. Figure 3-28 illustrates the difference between manchester encoding and differential manchester encoding.

Manchester Encoding

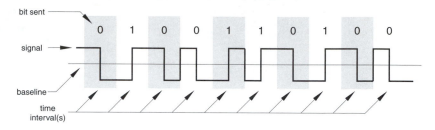

Differential Manchester Encoding

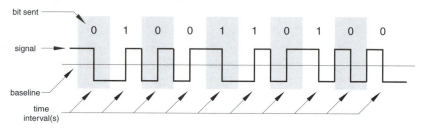

Figure 3-28   Manchester Encoding vs. Differential Manchester Encoding

SUMMARY

The hardware required to implement any local area network architecture falls into a relatively few broad categories: network interface cards, media, and wiring centers. Linking this hardware to the network operating system and operating system software is the network interface card driver. Advances in wiring center technology have enabled an entirely new, switch-based LAN architecture. LAN switches are extremely popular as an upgrade strategy for bandwidth-hungry networks since they do not require any changes to network interface cards, drivers, or media. However, pre-upgrade traffic analysis is prudent as inter-switch bottlenecks can actually degrade, rather than improve, performance.

PCI-based network interface cards are emerging as the high-performance NIC of choice, thanks largely to PCI's own clock, CPU, and mezzanine architecture. The key operational characteristics of network interface card drivers are the ability to support multiple protocol stacks on a single network adapter card and the need to avoid having to write monolithic drivers for every possible network interface card/network operating system combination. NDIS and ODI are the two most popular multiprotocol NIC drivers.

Shared-media wiring centers include stand-alone hubs, stackable hubs, enterprise hubs, and MAUs. These shared-media hubs merely collapse the shared-media LAN backbone into a single enclosure, while maintaining the one-at-a-time access methodologies. Hub management is especially important as numbers of users grow into the 100's. Hub management software should be able to tie into Enterprise network management software.

LAN switches offer multiple simultaneous connections to attached workstations as opposed to the one-at-a-time access schemes of the shared-media hubs. However, LAN switches are a relatively new technology and have their definite drawbacks. For one, when high-speed ports transfer large amounts of data to shared lower-speed ports, data overflow and lost data can occur. Second, management of switched connections that may last

for only fractions of a second is not nearly as straightforward as managing a shared-media hub. Each of these challenges is being addressed by LAN switch vendors.

LAN media can differ significantly in cost, supported speeds, ease of use, and network architectures supported. Although fiber-optic cable was at one time considered to be the only media suitable for speeds of 100 Mbps and greater, Category 5 Unshielded Twisted Pair seems to be a common media option for high-speed network standards. New advanced testing techniques have been developed to ensure that UTP will be capable of transmitting high-speed network architectures such as gigabit Ethernet.

KEY TERMS

4 conductor station wire
ACR
active management MAUs
address resolution server
agents
asynchronous transfer mode
ATM
attenuation
attenuation to crosstalk ratio
AWG
backbone-attached LAN switch
backbone/data center switch
backpressure
base I/O address
base memory address
binding
bus mastering DMA
card and socket services
card services
cascading ports
CAT 5
classical IP
collapsed backbone network
CSS
cut-through switches
differential manchester
  encoding

direct enablers
EIA/TIA 568
Enhanced CAT5
enterprise hubs
enterprise network
  management systems
error-free cut-through switches
fast packet forwarding
flat gray modular
full-duplex Ethernet
hot swappable
hubs
IEEE 802.3x
Interrupt request
IRQ
IP over ATM
LAN emulation
LAN switch
link support layer
local hub management software
LSL
management information base
manchester encoding
MAU
MIB
MLID
modular concentrators

monolithic drivers
multi-link interface drivers
multimode
multimode graded index
multimode step index
multistation access unit
NDIS
near-end crosstalk
network device interface
  specification
network interface card drivers
network interface cards
network-network interface
NExT
NICs
NNI
ODI
open data-link interface
packet overlapping
port mirroring
powersum crosstalk
protocol manager
remote monitoring
RMON
roving port mirroring
RYGB
server front-end LAN switch

shared-media network
   architecture
shielding
simple network management
   protocol
simultaneous RMON view
single mode
SNMP

socket services
stackable hubs
stand-alone hubs
stand-alone LAN switches
store-and-forward switches
switched LAN network
   architecture
switching hub

UNI
unshielded twisted pair
user-network interface
UTP
vector
zero slot LANs

REVIEW QUESTIONS

1. List the broad functions and interrelationships of each of the major categories of technology cited in the LAN Technology Architecture.
2. Differentiate between a shared-media network architecture and a switch-based network architecture in terms of advantages and disadvantages of each.
3. What are some of the potential drawbacks or cautions to upgrading to a LAN switch?
4. Differentiate between the three major implementation scenarios for LAN switches in terms of delivered functionality and corresponding required switch technology.
5. Describe the advantages and disadvantages of a collapsed backbone network.
6. What are the advantages and disadvantages of full duplex network architectures?
7. What do full duplex architectures require, in terms of both hardware and software, beyond normal switch-based LAN architectures?
8. What applications are full duplex network architectures especially well suited for?
9. What is the meaning of the sentence "The NIC is the keeper of the MAC layer protocol"?
10. What unique advantages can PCI bus NICs offer?
11. Which NIC data transfer method is most efficient and why?
12. Why is it not safe to assume that a bus mastering DMA NIC will work on any computer?
13. What is the disadvantage of using external adapters on notebook or laptop computers?
14. What is the functional role of a network interface card driver?
15. What are the disadvantages of monolithic drivers?
16. What are the two major advantages of multi-protocol network adapter card drivers?
17. Compare and contrast NDIS and ODI in terms of architecture and functionality.
18. What is the significance of binding in a NDIS environment?
19. Which files and programs are involved in a binding operation?
20. How are protocols actually directed to the proper protocol stack in a NDIS environment?
21. What are the differences between PCMCIA Card Services and Socket Services?
22. What are the differences between PCMCIA CSS and direct enablers?
23. Differentiate among the three major categories of hubs in terms of delivered functionality and required technology features.
24. What important advantages does an active management MAU offer?
25. Why can't modules from one vendor's enterprise hub be used in another vendor's enterprise hub even though both modules support the same network architecture?
26. What are the differences between the two levels of management software that hubs should support?
27. How is it possible for an enterprise network management system to compile statistics from networking equipment manufactured by a variety of different vendors?
28. What are the major functional differences between how LAN switches process and forward packets? What are the advantages and disadvantages of each method?
29. In what types of LAN switch implementations is backpressure likely to be an issue?

30. Why is traffic monitoring and management more of a challenge in LAN switches than in shared-media hubs?

31. Differentiate among the three major LAN switch traffic monitoring and management techniques.

32. What are the advantages and disadvantages of assigning multiple workstations per switch port?

33. What switching issues are unique to Token Ring switches?

34. What roles can ATM play in a local area network?

35. How can "legacy LANs" be integrated into an ATM network?

36. What are the unique capabilities of ATM which account for all of the interest in this technology?

37. What is LAN emulation and why is it important?

38. Why is twisted pair twisted?

39. What is the importance of EIA/TIA 568?

40. What is the most common category of UTP installed today and why?

41. Why is UTP Category 5 favored over shielded twisted pair, coax, and fiber-optic cable for many high-speed network architectures?

42. Why is shielded twisted pair considered trickier to install than UTP?

43. What is the difference between powersum crosstalk and pair-to-pair crosstalk?

44. How are Levels 5, 6, and 7 different from Category 5?

45. Why are testing and certification specifications required beyond CAT 5?

ACTIVITIES

1. Research the relative market sizes of hubs vs. LAN switches over the past three years. Interpret your results.

2. Find actual LAN switch implementations and analyze and compare the various implementation scenarios. What function is the LAN switch serving in each case? Are there implementation categories beyond those listed in Chapter 3? Were examples found of each scenario listed?

3. Find actual implementations of full duplex network architectures and report on the applications served by this technology. Is traffic level measured in this application? If so, report on the findings.

4. Research the network interface card market and report on those features or functions offered by the most advanced NICs.

5. Locate a computer that uses NDIS drivers. Print out the CONFIG.SYS and PROTOCOL.INI files. Trace the binding operation between MAC drivers and protocol drivers.

6. Locate a computer that uses ODI drivers. Print out the CONFIG.SYS and the NET.CFG files. Determine how multiple protocol stacks can be assigned to a single NIC.

7. Research data communications catalogs, buyers' guides, and product literature for the latest information on PCMCIA adapters. Report on the latest trends and capabilities. Are multiple functions, such as modems and NICs, being included on a single card?

8. Research data communications catalogs, buyers' guides, and product literature for the latest information on hubs. Pay special attention to the availability of management features, especially ties to enterprise management systems.

9. Research the topic of the RMON MIB. Which standards-making organization is responsible for the definition? What types of information are collected in the RMON MIB? What are RMON probes and how do they function?

10. Research data communications catalogs, buyers' guides, and product literature for the latest information on LAN switches. Pay special attention to how the switches handle flow control issues and report on the alternative methods.

11. Research data communications catalogs, buyers' guides, and product literature for the latest information on LAN switches. Pay special attention to how the switches handle monitor-

ing and management of LAN switch traffic and report on the alternative methods.

12. Research data communications catalogs, buyers' guides, and product literature for the latest information on ATM technology for the LAN. What is the availability and cost range for ATM NICs of various speeds? Which vendors seem to have the most complete "single-vendor solutions"?

13. Prepare a display including electrical specifications of the various types of LAN media

cited in Chapter 3. Detail network architectures and maximum transmission speeds to which each media type is assigned.

14. Research the pros and cons and advantages and disadvantages of gigabit Ethernet vs. ATM. What does each architecture do well and not so well? What are the best uses of each? Is either one better in all cases? Present your results in a research paper or panel discussion.

CASE STUDY

Users Get Bad to the Backbone with Gigabit Ethernet

It is the ultimate in bursty traffic: more than 100 servers containing tens of thousands of Web sites doing a daily backup to a storage array.

It used to take up to 16 hours each day for the process to trickle through the Fast Ethernet pipes at HiWay Technologies, a Web site hosting firm. With plans to expand to up to 2,000 servers, the provider needed something faster.

The company had an idea: build a separate infrastructure, identical to the existing one, dedicated to performing daily data backups. This plan would have required a second network card in every server to hook into a second Fast Ethernet backbone. HiWay also considered installing Fibre Channel, but

that also would have required a separate network.

Instead, HiWay decided to replace the Fast Ethernet backbone network with Gigabit Ethernet and send backup traffic over the same lines as other data. The company didn't have to install additional cards in its servers, and at $120,000, this approach cost one-third as much as setting up a separate network, says David Hartman, manager of network systems at HiWay.

Last June, the company installed a Gigabit Ethernet backbone anchored by a pair of Foundry Networks' BigIron 4000 switches. A handful of Foundry FastIron switches link to the backbone and connect the servers through their 24 Fast Ethernet ports.

Because these connections don't use Gigabit Ethernet, HiWay didn't have to upgrade the cards in the servers.

It now takes four to six hours to back up the company's 125 servers. That's still too long, Hartman says, but the bottleneck isn't the network.

The problem is the server that manages backups, a Silicon Graphics Origin 2000 machine connected to the backbone via a Gigabit Ethernet card. "We got rid of the network problem and pushed it to the CPU on the Origin 2000," Hartman says.

The server moves at a speed of only about 300M bit/sec, and Hartman is looking for Silicon Graphics to get that rate increased to about 750M bit/sec by tweaking the network card and improving the speed of its server. Hartman's goal is to back up all the servers in just a couple of hours.

Backups are really the only reason HiWay chose Gigabit Ethernet. Without the bursts caused by the high-volume backups, less than 10% of the backbone is used, Hartman says. Because the company hosts Web sites, most of the traffic is outbound to the Internet.

"The traffic in and out of the Internet doesn't warrant Gigabit Ethernet," Hartman says. At peak times, the traffic level reaches only about 70M bit/sec through HiWay's three T-3 lines to ISPs. But installing Gigabit Ethernet gives the company some headroom for at least the next three years, Hartman estimates.

Right now, HiWay doesn't use any of the Layer 3 functions of its BigIron switches. But one reason the company chose Foundry equipment is that it supports Open Shortest Path First (OSPF) routing. OSPF is a routing protocol that can adapt quickly to network changes.

Today, HiWay manually sets up static routes to its servers via the Cisco 7505 routers it uses to connect to the Internet. But that will change. Using OSPF, the servers will be automatically discovered, reducing the administrative burden of manually defining them, Hartman says. This will be critical as the company adds hundreds of new servers.

HiWay also plans to use Virtual Router Redundancy Protocol, a standard that defines how a backup router can automatically take over when another router fails. This way, if HiWay loses one of its two Layer 3 switches, the second can pick up the slack.

But the company hasn't had much trouble with outages. In fact, of the switches it uses, only one port on one of the switches has failed.

"That's unbelievable as far as I'm concerned," Hartman says.

Source: Jeff Caruso, "Users Get Bad to the Backbone with Gigabit Ethernet," *Network World,* vol. 15, no. 49 (December 7, 1998), p. 22

BUSINESS CASE STUDY QUESTIONS

Activities

1. Complete a top-down model for this case by gleaning facts from the case and placing them in the proper layer of the top-down model. After having completed the top-down model, analyze and detail those instances where requirements were clearly passed down from upper layers to lower layers of the model and where solutions to those requirements were passed up from lower layers to upper layers of the model.
2. Detail any questions about the case that may occur to you for which answers are not clearly stated in the article.

Business

1. What is the key business activity of the organization profiled in this article?

2. What was the importance of the network to the achievement of this organization's business mission?
3. What was the cost of the implemented upgrade in comparison to other upgrade strategies?

Application

1. What was the business application driving the need for changes in the network?
2. How many servers were included in expansion plans?

Data

1. How much data were being backed up over the network?
2. What is a storage array and how does it differ from alternative storage architectures?

Network

1. What were the original and new network architectures?
2. What was the impact of the new architecture in terms of performance?
3. What were some of the alternative architectures considered for potential upgrades?
4. Explain how multiple network architectures were able to interact successfully in this article.
5. What percentage of the bandwidth is used at times other than when the critical application is running?
6. Do you feel that the upgrade is cost-justified? Explain your answer.
7. What type of network connections does this company have to the Internet?
8. Which layer 3 protocols or routing protocols are mentioned in the article?
9. Why would this company not need layer 3 protocol or OSPF functionality?
10. How is this company currently maintaining routing tables?
11. What advantage would OSPF offer this company?
12. What is Virtual Router Redundancy Protocol? Is it an open or proprietary standard?

Technology

1. Detail the technology actually implemented.
2. Why were these particular technologies chosen?
3. How does this case illustrate the principle of shifting bottlenecks?
4. What must be done to further improve performance?

CHAPTER 4

NETWORK LAYER COMMUNICATIONS PROTOCOLS

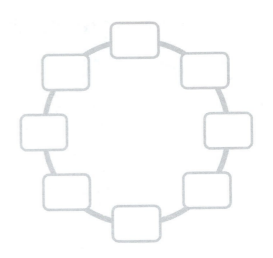

Concepts Reinforced

OSI Network Reference Model	Protocol Encapsulation

Concepts Introduced

Network Addressing	Address Resolution
Routing	Packet Fragmentation
IPX	IPv4
IPv6	AppleTalk

OBJECTIVES

After mastering the material in this chapter you should:

1. Understand the concept of protocol encapsulation
2. Understand address resolution and its role in the delivery of data
3. Differentiate between packets and frames
4. Understand the role of the network layer of the OSI Network Reference Model
5. Understand the IPX addressing and routing
6. Understand IPv4 addressing and routing
7. Understand IPv6 addressing and routing
8. Understand the various methods of transitioning to IPv6
9. Understand AppleTalk DDP addressing and routing

■ INTRODUCTION

Local area network communications protocols can be thought of as the language of computer networks: They provide the language and grammatical rules that define communication. Just as humans have to agree on common languages to communicate, local area networks must agree on common protocols to communicate.

In this chapter, the general concepts of LAN communications protocols will be developed and specific protocol implementations will be discussed. This chapter focuses on protocols that operate at the third layer of the OSI model, which control communication between nodes on interconnected networks.

■ LAYER 3—THE NETWORK LAYER

The third layer of the OSI Network Reference Model is the network layer. The network layer is primarily concerned with providing a means for nodes to communicate with other nodes on different network segments. As explained in Chapter 2, the data-link layer provides a means for two nodes on a *common* network segment to communicate. Technologies such as Ethernet and Token Ring provide this intra-segment connectivity.

Network layer protocols expand the capabilities of the network by providing a means of delivering data (called packets) between network segments. A network layer protocol provides a means of addressing a node on the interconnected network and a means of delivering data across the network to destination nodes. The process of determining the best path to the destination node and delivering the data is known as routing. Network layer addresses can be categorized in terms of these two basic functions: addressing and routing.

In Sharper Focus

FRAMES AND PACKETS

It is important to note the difference in the terminology used to describe the data being transmitted at each of these layers of the OSI Network Reference Model. The data link layer (layer 2) transmits *frames* of data. The network layer (layer 3) transmits *packets* of data.

In Sharper Focus

NETWORKS AND SEGMENTS

A constant source of confusion is the use of multiple terms to describe network architectures. Different sources commonly use different terms to mean the same thing. Regardless of terminology, there are two key levels of networking: single segments where every node receives every packet, and multi-segment networks where some inter-networking device forwards packets between network segments.

Single network segments are commonly referred to as segments, sub-networks, or subnets. Interconnected segments are commonly referred to as networks or inter-networks. Don't let these varying terms confuse you: if every node sees every frame of data on the LAN, it's a segment. If more than one segment is used, it's an inter-network.

While this chapter focuses on the network layer of the OSI Network Reference Model, each protocol discussed is part of an overall protocol family that integrates protocols from layers 3 through 7 of the OSI model. These associated protocols will be discussed in more detail in subsequent chapters.

Network Layer Addressing

The role of network layer addresses is to provide a means to uniquely identify a node on the inter-network. The network layer address is used in the routing process to deliver a packet of data to the correct network segment for delivery. In this manner, network addresses are used for "end-to-end" or "inter-segment" communication.

There are two basic components to a network layer address: a network segment address and a node address. The **network segment address** identifies on which network segment the destination node is located. This address is used by the routing process to determine the destination network segment and deliver the packet to that segment. Once the packet has arrived at the correct network segment, the **node address** is resolved to a physical address and passed to the data-link layer for delivery. The relationship between address components and their purpose is illustrated in Figure 4-1.

Collectively, these two parts identify a node on the inter-network. The segment address must be unique to the inter-network to ensure that the packet is delivered to the correct network segment. Similarly, a node address must be unique *within a network segment*. As shown in Figure 4-2, it is possible to use the same node address on multiple segments. There is no chance

Address Component	Layer	Purpose
Network Segment Address	Network	Used by routers to forward data to the correct network segment.
Node Address	Network	Identify a node within a network segment. Resolved to physical address for actual data delivery.
Physical Address	Data Link	Used to deliver data to the destination node.

Figure 4-1   Network Address Components

for confusion between the nodes, because the packet will be routed to the network segment of the correct node based on the segment address.

Network layer addresses are assigned on a per-NIC basis. It is possible for a single device to contain more than one NIC. In this case, each NIC will have its own network layer address (segment address + node address). Devices that contain more than one NIC are said to be **multi-homed.**

There are several reasons to multi-home a device, including performance, reliability, and stability. However, the primary reason a device is multi-homed is to allow it to forward packets from one network segment to another. By definition a device that performs packet forwarding is known as a **router.** In Figure 4-2, the devices in the center of the diagram that connect to two network segments are functioning as routers, forwarding packets as needed from one segment to another

Network Layer vs. Data-Link Layer Addressing   As previously mentioned, the network layer is primarily responsible for addressing nodes uniquely on an inter-network and providing a means of delivering data across network segments. The responsibility of moving data within a network segment is that of the data-link layer. As described in Chapter 2, the data-link layer uses the physical address (also known as the MAC addresses for Ethernet and Token Ring technologies) of the NIC to deliver data rather than the network layer node address.

For the network and data-link layers to successfully interact to deliver data, a direct, one-to-one mapping must be made between the network layer address and the data-link layer physical address. Although the exact method used to make this mapping varies between the various network layer proto-

Physical Topology

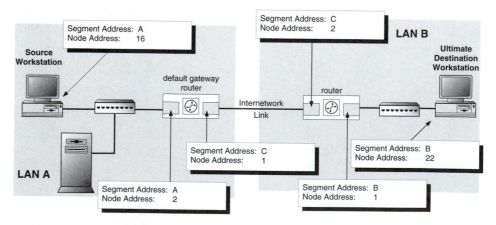

Figure 4-2   Node Addressing

cols, every network layer protocol has a standardized method for mapping its node address to the physical address associated with the NIC. The process of determining the physical layer address of a NIC from the network layer address is known as **address resolution.**

Each NIC has a data-link layer physical address and an associated network address. The network layer address is used by upper-layer protocols to denote with which node they wish to communicate. The network layer is also used to transport (route) data through the network to the destination network segment. Once the data arrive at the destination network segment, the network layer address is resolved to a physical address and delivered to the destination node (NIC) by the data-link layer.

The process of delivering data to a destination node is analogous to the method used to deliver a letter to a person's house. The zip code (network segment address) is used to route the mail to the correct postal route. The mail carrier for that route then looks at the street address (node address) to determine the final destination of the letter. The carrier then resolves the street address to a physical mailbox location (physical address) for delivery. This relationship is shown in Figure 4-3.

Protocol Encapsulation/De-encapsulation   While different layer 3 protocols use different techniques for addressing and packet construction, a layer 3 packet will always contain at least three sections: source network address, destination network address, and data. The source and destination addresses are used in the routing process and the data are the reason the packet was sent. Packet construction will be detailed in subsequent sections for the most commonly used network layer protocols.

Packets are sent through the network by encapsulating them in data-link layer frames. As illustrated in Figure 4-4, a packet of data from the network layer is placed in the data section of a data-link layer frame. Known as **encapsulation,** this process adds both a header and trailer to the packet. The bit stream is finally passed along the shared media that connects the two computing devices. When the full bit stream arrives at the destination server, the reverse process of encapsulation, **de-encapsulation,** takes place. In this manner, the destination data-link layer strips the layer 2 header and trailer and passes the packet to network layer for processing.

Network Data Delivery	Mail Delivery
Network Segment Address	Zip Code
Node Address	Street Address
Physical Address	Physical Mailbox Location

Figure 4-3   Network Data Delivery versus Mail Delivery

LAYER 3 *PACKET*

LAYER 2 *FRAME*

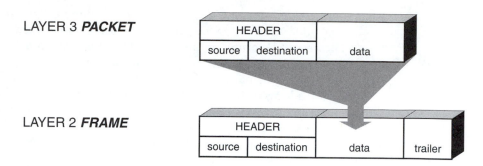

Figure 4-4   Protocol Encapsulation

Fragmentation   Every protocol has a maximum overall packet (or frame) length. This length is the maximum size of a packet (or frame) including the header and data. The maximum size of a packet or frame of data is known as the **Maximum Transmission Unit** (MTU).

In the event that a higher-level packet will not fit into a lower layer's available payload area, the higher-level packet is broken into two or more packet fragments. These packet fragments are sent across the network and reassembled into a single packet before being sent back up the protocol stack on the destination node. **Fragmentation** allows large quantities of data to be sent across the network in smaller, more manageable "chunks" of data.

Data fragmentation is required between the application layer and the network layer for large quantities of application layer data (such as a 10 MB file) to be sent across a network. However, data fragmentation between the network layer and the data-link layer represents additional overhead and should be avoided if possible. Fragmenting network layer packets is required when the underlying layer 2 frame's data payload is not capable of transporting the entire layer 3 packet. Such fragmentation requires that the layer 3 packet be broken into multiple layer 2 frames of data that are sent across the physical network and reassembled at the layer 2 destination node.

The impact of network layer packet fragmentation is illustrated in Figure 4-5. When the source creates a packet that is larger than the underlying layer 2 transport protocols, each router on path between the source and destination must break the packet into multiple fragments, then send each fragment across the layer 2 link to the next router. Each frame that contains a fragment of the packet must also contain a copy of the packet's header to ensure that the packet is properly reassembled.

The next router must collect the fragments, reassemble them into the original network layer packet, and repeat the process for the next hop. Such repeated packet fragmentation and reassembly place a large processing burden on routers, effectively reducing their overall routing capacity.

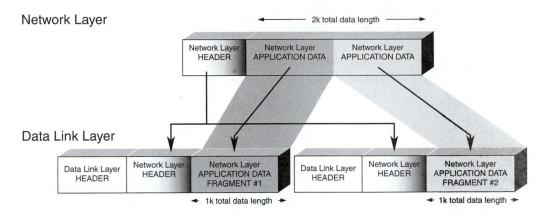

Figure 4-5   Layer 3 Packet Fragmentation

Compare Figure 4-5 with Figure 4-6. Figure 4-6 represents the same network, but the layer 3 packet size has been set equal to or lower than the underlying layer 2 frame data payload. In Figure 4-6, each router merely has to package each network layer packet into a single layer 2 frame and send it along the route to its destination. Packet fragmentation is currently one of the key capacity limitations on most routed networks, especially when the network includes WAN links that potentially use much smaller frame sizes than LAN links.

Routing

Routing is the process of moving data across network segments toward its final destination. Routers receive frames of data, de-encapsulate the layer 3 packet, examine the network layer packet header, determine the next hop of

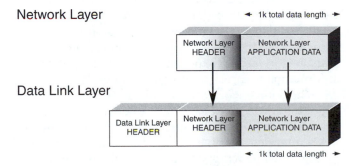

Figure 4-6   Layer 3 Packet Fragmentation Eliminated

the packet, package the packet into a new data frame, and transmit the new frame.

Going back to the mail example in the previous section, the routing process is analogous to the method used by the post office to deliver a letter. Someone places a sheet of paper (data) in an envelope (packet), addresses it, places it in their mailbox, and raises the flag (transmits the packet). The mail carrier picks up the letter and places it in a mail bag (data frame) and takes it to the post office (default gateway). At the post office, the letter is taken out of the mail bag (data frame), and the zip code (network segment address) is used by the post office to determine where to send the letter (routing). After the next hop is determined, the letter is placed into a new mail bag (data frame) for transmission to the destination post office (router on the destination network segment). This process continues until the letter reaches the post office that services the destination zip code (router to the destination segment).

At the destination post office, the letter is removed from the mail bag and placed into the mail bag of a mail carrier who services the destination street address. The mail carrier then places the mail in the mailbox of the destination street address for final delivery to the recipient.

Routing Is Address Processing   Although routing will be explained in detail in Chapter 13, it is important to understand some basic routing concepts in order to appreciate routing protocol functionality. Perhaps the most important thing to understand about routing is that it is nothing more than address processing performed when messages need to travel beyond the local LAN. By keeping track of the following address-related issues, the entire routing process can be largely demystified. As illustrated in Figure 4-7, the only thing that changes throughout the routing process is that the source and destination physical addresses are changed during each hop on the way to the destination node. For this example, network layer addresses are given in the format Letter:Number where letter is the segment address and number is the node address.

The first logical step in the routing process is for the source workstation to fill in the source address field in the network layer header with its own network layer address and the destination address field in the network layer header with the network layer address of the ultimate destination workstation. Because the destination workstation is not on the local LAN, the packet must be forwarded to the local gateway, or router, which will have sufficient information to forward this packet properly.

The source workstation looks in its network layer configuration information in order to determine the network layer address of its default gateway. The default gateway is the only way out for packets off of the local LAN. In order to deliver this packet to the router for further processing, the packet must be wrapped in a data-link layer frame such as Ethernet, Token Ring, or FDDI. Addresses that are included in the data-link layer header are

Physical Topology

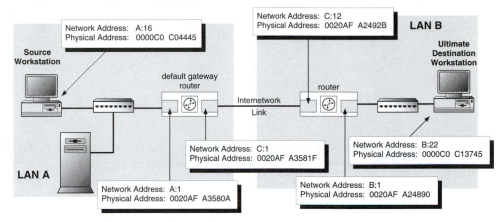

Address Processing

From source workstation to default gateway router found on LAN A:

Data-Link		Network	
source 0000C0 C04445	destination 0020AF A3580A	source A:16	destination B:22

From LAN A router to next hop router towards ultimate destination as noted in routing table:

Data-Link		Network	
source 0020AF A3581F	destination 0020AF A2492B	source A:16	destination B:22

From LAN B router to locally attached ultimate destination workstation:

Data-Link		Network	
source 0020AF A24890	destination 0000C0 C13745	source A:16	destination B:22

Figure 4-7   Routing Is Address Processing

known as physical addresses. Although the source workstation has the network address of the default router in its network configuration file, it does not know the physical address of that router. The source workstation determines the physical address of the router through address resolution.

Once the source workstation determines the physical address, it encapsulates the network layer packet in a data-link layer frame. The physical address associated with its own NIC is placed in the source address field of the data-link layer frame and the physical address of the default gateway is placed in the destination address of the data-link layer frame.

The default gateway or local router receives the data-link layer frame explicitly addressed to it and examines the ultimate destination address held in the packet. The router then consults its routing tables to see if it has an entry for a known path to the ultimate destination workstation. That known path may be via another router, or the ultimate destination workstation may be part of a different LAN connected to this same router through a different NIC. In either case, the packet and its addresses are not modified but are instead re-encapsulated in a fresh data-link layer frame with the physical layer destination address of either the ultimate destination workstation, or of the next router along the path to that workstation. The source address field on the fresh data-link layer frame is filled in with the physical address of the default router which has just completed processing the packet.

Routing Protocols   In the previous example it was assumed that each router intuitively knew where to send a packet to get it to its destination. However, when a router is initially started, it only knows about the interfaces connected to it or **static routes** that have been configured by an administrator. In order for a network to dynamically build comprehensive routing tables that automatically add new routes and remove old ones, a routing protocol must be used. Routing protocols provide routers a means of automatically exchanging routing tables to ensure that each router knows where to route packets for a given destination.

While routing protocols will be discussed in detail in Chapter 13, a brief introduction is necessary to understand the routing capabilities of the various network layer protocols discussed in this chapter. The two major categories of routing protocol algorithms are distance vector and link state. Distance vector protocols broadcast their entire routing table periodically. In this manner, changes to the network routing tables slowly make their way through the network. A router using a distance vector algorithm knows nothing about the makeup of the network beyond the next hop to the destination, merely that by sending a packet of data to the next hop, it should eventually arrive at the destination.

Link state protocols transmit a more complete picture of the network between routers. Through the use of link state packets (LSP), each router learns the structure of the entire network. In this manner, the link state algorithm can make better routing decisions. Link state routing reacts more quickly to changes in the routing structure than distance vector routing while using less bandwidth to maintain routing tables. Implementation and maintenance consideration for routing protocols will be discussed in Chapter 13.

■   LAYER 4—THE TRANSPORT LAYER

The fourth layer of the OSI Network Reference Model is the transport layer. Also known as the host-to-host layer, the transport layer is primarily concerned with creating, maintaining, and tearing down end-to-end network connections. When an application needs to send data to a remote network node, the transport layer is responsible for determining the correct network layer address and initiating the connection to the remote node. The transport layer also performs error control and correction and flow control for host-to-host connections. This includes ensuring that all packets arrive at the destination node without errors caused by dropped packets, duplicate packets, packets arriving out of order, or packets corrupted in transmission.

The transport layer can be thought of as being responsible for creating a communication channel between two nodes on an internetwork. While the network layer actually transports the packets between the two nodes, the transport layer ensures that the packets flow as a data stream rather than as a series of independent packets. From the perspective of higher-level protocols, the connection is a pipeline directly to the other node, independent of the routers and network links that must be traversed. For this reason the transport and all higher levels are collectively known as end-to-end layers.

Unlike network layer protocols that are **connectionless** in nature, transport layer protocols are usually **connection-oriented** and therefore provide reliable data transmission. Each packet is assigned a sequence number that uniquely identifies it in the data flowing through the connection. By referencing the sequence numbers, the destination node can ensure that packets are arriving in the proper order and that no packets have been dropped. The destination node must then respond to each packet with either an acknowledgment (ACK) of correct receipt or a negative acknowledgment (NAK) to indicate an error condition.

As illustrated in Figure 4-8, the destination node acknowledges the correct receipt of each packet by sending an ACK back to the sender that includes the sequence number of the packet. If a packet fails the error check upon receipt, the destination node responds with a NAK for the sequence number. If a packet arrives out of order, the destination node examines the sequence number, realizes it is not the correct next packet, and responds with a NAK for the missing sequence number. The sending node also keeps track of the time since a packet was sent. If the destination node doesn't respond with an ACK within a preset time period, the sending node assumes that packet was dropped and re-sends that packet with the original sequence number. This is referred to as a packet time-out or a time-out error.

Data sent via a connection-oriented transport layer protocol will either arrive at the destination safely or the sending application will be alerted that the transmission failed. Because of their reliability, most data streams make use of connection-oriented transport protocols. However, a connection-oriented protocol adds overhead to the communication process. A connection must be built between the two nodes before any data are transmitted. The process of building a connection can require that multiple packets of data be exchanged between the two nodes. Each packet that is sent via the connection requires an ACK packet in response. At the end of the communication, the transport layer must also exchange packets to tear down the connection.

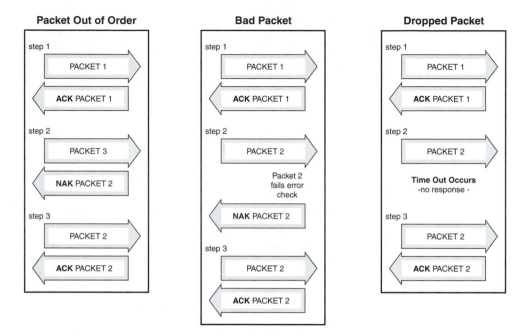

Figure 4-8   Connection Oriented Error Correction

In Sharper Focus

CONNECTIONLESS OR CONNECTION-ORIENTED?

Although connection-oriented protocols require more overhead than connectionless protocols, they provide an assurance that the data will accurately reach the destination. This reliability is important for most data streams since the data they carry is important or they would not have been sent in the first place. It would certainly make sense for a bank to use a connection-oriented protocol to carry financial transaction data—you wouldn't want any packets to be dropped without notice and error correction!

However, there are cases in which the use of a connection-oriented protocol may not be required. For messages that can be contained in a single packet, the overhead of establishing and tearing down a connection and processing ACKs can add more overhead than the message is worth. An example of a non-urgent, single packet message is a routing protocol packet. Because routing protocol packets are routinely sent between routers, dropping a single packet is not a catastrophic event. It makes more sense to risk an occasional dropped packet than to add the overhead associated with a connection-oriented protocol for this application.

Another common application for connectionless protocols is streaming media. Streaming multimedia application layer protocols that can carry audio and video data across data networks are now commonplace. For these protocols to provide clear sound and pictures, it is important that every packet be accurately delivered to the destination. It is inevitable that packets will be dropped from the media stream at some point regardless of the protocol used; the issue is what to do when a packet is dropped. Is it worth the additional overhead of a connection-oriented protocol to re-send dropped packets or is it better to simply miss an occasional second of the stream?

LAYER 5—THE SESSION LAYER

The fifth layer of the OSI Network Reference Model is the session layer. The session layer is responsible for establishing, maintaining, and terminating logical sessions between applications. In the event of session failure, the session layer is responsible for reestablishing the session.

The session layer builds upon the functionality of the transport layer by adding a mechanism to differentiate between applications at each end of a connection. It ensures that a packet gets to the correct application on the remote node after it crosses the connection. If there are two different communications sessions running between two nodes (such as a Telnet session and a WWW session), the session layer identifies the packets for each session and keeps them separated.

Session layer protocols identify sessions through the use of **ports** and **sockets.** Although these terms have slightly different meanings depending on the protocol, they represent the "address" of an application on a node. Each application on a node is assigned a unique port number. Most session layer protocols make use of fixed port numbers for commonly used services, which greatly simplifies the establishment of sessions between these services. Other application protocols may use a range of ports that are dynamically assigned. Regardless of the manner in which port numbers are assigned, no two applications can concurrently use the same port. To ensure that a packet is delivered to the correct address on the correct destination node, both the network layer address and port number must be specified.

Going back to the letter-addressing example used earlier in this chapter, the port or socket number is analogous to the person's name on the letter. The network layer is concerned only with getting the letter to the correct mailbox. It's the responsibility of the session layer to get the letter to the correct person in the house (application).

Although the functionality of the session layer is distinct from that of the transport layer, most protocol suites merge transport and session layer functionality into a single protocol.

LAYERS 6 AND 7—THE PRESENTATION AND APPLICATION LAYERS

The sixth layer of the OSI Network Reference Model is the presentation layer. The presentation layer is responsible for formatting data for transmission across the network. The presentation layer performs encryption and compaction of data and converts between data communication codes as required.

The seventh layer of the OSI Network Reference Model is the application layer. The application layer is responsible for providing data transmission services to user applications. The application layer provides these services via an Application Programming Interface (API). Any application that makes calls to the API can use the services of the application layer and its underlying layers for data communication. Presentation layer functionality is closely related to application layer functionality and both are commonly integrated into a single protocol. For the remainder of this chapter, the presentation and application layers will be grouped as upper-layer protocols.

Each protocol suite takes significant liberties in the assignment of functionality to protocols above the network layer. In practical terms it is impossible to match single end-to-end protocols with a specific layer of the OSI Network Reference Model. However, the protocols of a particular protocol suite collectively provide the complete functionality as described in the OSI model.

LOCAL AREA NETWORK PROTOCOLS

There are many different network layer protocols currently in use. IPX, IP, and AppleTalk are the three most commonly used protocols for local and wide area network traffic. The remainder of this chapter will discuss these protocols in depth and illustrate the key implementation and maintenance considerations for each.

NETWARE (IPX/SPX) PROTOCOL SUITE

The IPX/SPX protocol suite was originally developed by Novell for its NetWare network operating system. IPX/SPX has also found its way to Microsoft operating systems and is commonly used to support network computer games due to its ease of configuration.

Network Layer Protocol—IPX

Internet Packet Exchange (IPX) was developed for and is still most commonly used in NetWare environments. Although the I in IPX stands for internet, don't confuse it with **The Internet** (capital I). The Internet uses IP rather than IPX as its network layer protocol.

IPX, like most network layer protocols, serves as a basic delivery mechanism for upper-layer protocols such as SPX, RIP, SAP, and NCP. This delivery mechanism is accomplished through encapsulation whereby upper-layer protocols are encapsulated within properly addressed IPX "envelopes." Network layer protocols are generally characterized as:

- **Connectionless**—implying individual, fully addressed packets, or datagrams, are free to negotiate their way through the network in search of their final destination.

- **Unreliable**—implying that the network layer does not require error checking and acknowledgment of error-free receipt by the destination host.

The entire IPX packet is, in turn, encapsulated within a data-link layer frame, which corresponds to the installed network interface card. For example, if the workstation in question has a Token Ring card, the entire IPX packet will be inserted into the data field of the Token Ring frame. If an Ethernet card is present, the encapsulation of the IPX packet will be into the data field of the designated type of Ethernet frame.

IPX is a fairly small, easily configured protocol primarily designed to support local area network configurations. IPX is supported by many operating systems including Novell NetWare and Microsoft Windows. While IPX was once the default network layer protocol for both NetWare and Windows networking, it has seen its usage decline with the explosion of the IP based Internet.

Addressing   Addressing in IPX is straightforward and relatively easy. The segment address and node address are kept separate and are automatically determined by most nodes on the network.

Network Segment Address   IPX uses a 32-bit segment address that is usually displayed in hexadecimal (base 16). This gives an available IPX address space ranging from 0000 0000 to FFFF FFFF, which correspond to 4.29 billion different network segments. Segment addresses are hierarchical in nature, allowing easier routing within IPX networks.

Assignment of segment address to IPX network nodes is a two-part sequence. Routers are assigned a segment address by a network administrator. In addition to physical routers, any Novell NetWare servers running IPX also serve as an IPX router, even if they contain only one NIC.

Once the routers are properly configured they will broadcast the IPX segment address to the remaining nodes on the network as part of the normal routing protocol update process. Segment addresses are sent in RIP (Routing Information Protocol) packets that are sent every 60 seconds by all IPX routers. Upon receiving an initial RIP packet, network nodes that are not IPX routers read the segment address and configure themselves accordingly. This process is illustrated in Figure 4-9.

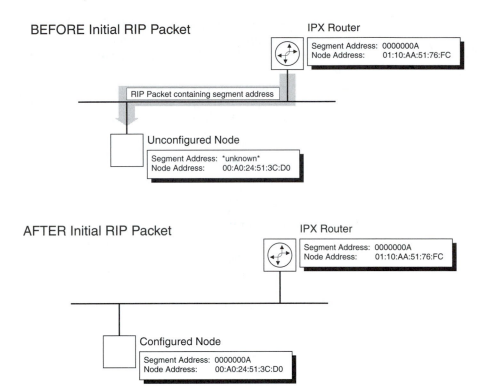

Figure 4-9   IPX Segment Address Assignment

The process of broadcasting network addresses makes the initial setup of IPX extremely easy. The only configuration required is to set the segment address on any IPX routers on the segment; the remaining nodes will be automatically configured. However, it is critical that each router on a network segment be assigned the same network address. If a single router is mis-configured it will broadcast incorrect address information to any unconfigured nodes on the network segment, resulting in a large collection of nodes that cannot communicate with any correctly configured nodes on the network. This is the most common mistake made in IPX network configuration.

Node Address   As mentioned earlier in this chapter, a network layer node address is associated with a NIC card and must correlate with the underlying NIC's physical address (the MAC address for Ethernet and Token Ring NICs). To keep configuration of IPX networks as simple as possible, the designers of the IPX protocol simply use the NIC's MAC address as the IPX node address.

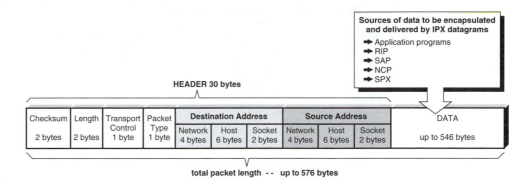

Figure 4-10 IPX Packet Layout

MAC addresses are six bytes long and are usually reported as six sets of two hexadecimal numbers (such as 00-A0-24-51-3C-D0). Since MAC addresses are by design unique (no two NICs can have the same MAC address), each node address on an IPX segment is therefore unique. In addition to eliminating the need to configure each node on an IPX network, this design also eliminates the need to resolve IPX layer 3 node addresses to physical addresses: The node address *is* the physical address.

Socket Address In addition to the required segment and node address, IPX also provides a **socket** address. Technically a transport layer function, the socket address indicates which process on the destination node is to process the packet. IPX supports up to 50 sockets per computer. Upper-layer protocols to which IPX transfers data frequently via encapsulation, such as NCP, SAP, RIP, and NetBIOS, have reserved socket numbers. Sockets will be discussed in more detail in Chapter 5. Together the segment address, node address, and socket address make up a complete IPX address. Sockets will be discussed in more detail in Chapter 12.

Packet Construction IPX packets can carry a payload of up to 546 bytes of encapsulated data. Packet delivery is controlled with a 30-byte packet header consisting of multiple fields used to deliver packets to their destination. The packet layout for IPX is shown in Figure 4-10, and a detailed description of the fields and their roles is presented in Figure 4-11.

IPX LIMITATIONS

In Sharper Focus

Every network layer protocol is limited by its construction and the information carried in its header fields. In the case of IPX, the key limitations are the overall packet length and the transport control limit.

IPX Packet Fields	Function/Importance
Checksum	Not used by IPX. No error checking in IPX, hence its "unreliable" characterization. IPX depends on upper-layer protocols such as SPX for error checking and proper sequencing of messages and file transfers which span multiple IPX packets.
Length	Length of the entire IPX packet in bytes.
Transport Control	Also known as a hop-counter or "time-to-live" timer. Ensures that free-floating datagrams do not meander infinitely around the network occupying unnecessary bandwidth. Every time a router processes the IPX packet, this counter is incremented by 1. When this field reaches 16, the packet is deleted to avoid further aimless wandering. This is one of the reasons why IPX packets may never reach their intended destination.
Packet Type	As illustrated in Figure 4–10, the data field of an IPX packet may contain a variety of different upper-layer protocols each of which needs to be processed in its own unique way. By identifying the embedded upper-layer protocol in the header's Packet Type field, the upper-layer protocols can be properly processed.
Addressing	Both source and destination addresses are comprised of three segments: • Network Segment Address • Host (Computer) Address • Socket Address
Data	As previously described and illustrated in Figure 4-10, upper-layer protocols are encapsulated within the data field.

Figure 4-11   IPX Header Fields

Due to its relatively small size of 576 bytes, IPX loses some efficiency in a common Ethernet-based local area network. As described in Chapter 3, Ethernet frames have a payload capacity of 1508 bytes. However, since only a single layer 3 packet can be encapsulated in one Ethernet frame, IPX cannot make full use of Ethernet's capacity, resulting in extra overhead. This can be easily understood by taking a look at a message consisting of 1152 bytes. Although this message could theoretically fit into a single Ethernet frame, it must be broken into two IPX packets, each of which will require separate Ethernet frames, resulting in increased overhead.

The other key limitation of IPX is the hard-coded maximum transport control value of 16. This limitation directly affects maximum network diameter because it is not possible to pass an IPX packet across more than 15 routers. Even if a large IPX network is designed to require only 14 hops on the longest run, it is still possible to drop packets if one of the links along the shortest run fails and the backup run requires more than 15 hops.

IPX Routing Protocols   IPX supports two basic routing protocols: RIP and NLSP.

RIP   NetWare's **Routing Information Protocol (RIP)** is a router-to-router protocol used to keep routers on a NetWare network synchronized and up-to-date. RIP information is delivered to routers via IPX packets. Figure 4-12 illustrates the fields of information included in a RIP packet.

As can be seen in Figure 4-12, the RIP packet can request or report on multiple reachable networks in a single RIP packet. In other words, a RIP packet can transport multiple routing table entries in a single packet. Although there is only one operation field per RIP packet, the network number, number of router hops, and number of tick fields are repeated as often as necessary up to the length limit of the RIP packet. This group of three fields (network number, number of router hops, number of ticks) that represent a routing table entry for a single network is sometimes referred to as a **tuple.** The role of each field in the RIP packet layout is detailed in Figure 4-13.

In terms of generated network traffic, one of the undesirable qualities of RIP is that every router broadcasts its entire routing table every 60 seconds to all other routers to which it is directly attached. As will be seen, this short-coming has been dealt with in NetWare 4.1. One very desirable quality of NetWare's RIP protocol is that routing table entries to particular networks can be updated and replaced if faster delivery routes are discovered based on the contents of the number of tick fields. The contents of routing tables and routing logic will be reviewed in-depth in Chapter 12.

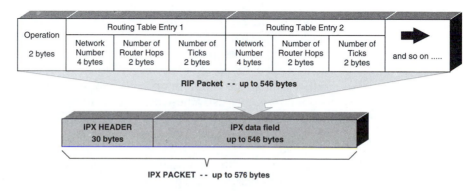

Figure 4-12   RIP Packet Layout

RIP Packet Fields	Function/Importance
Operation	This field indicates whether this RIP packet is a request for routing information on a particular network or if it is a response supplying routing information. A request is indicated by a hexadecimal 01 and response is indicated by a hexadecimal 02. This operation field applies to the entire RIP packet.
Network Number	This is the assigned address number of the network for which routing information is being either requested or supplied.
Number of Router Hops	This field indicates how many routers the packet must pass through in order to reach the desired destination network. Each additional router represents one additional hop.
Number of Ticks	This field indicates the length of time it will take for a given packet to reach its desired destination network. In this case, time is measured in ticks, which are roughly equal to one-eighteenth of a second. This field was added because the route with the smallest number of router hops may not be the fastest depending on the traffic characteristics of the circuits linking the routers.

Figure 4-13 RIP Field Descriptions

NLSP NLSP or **NetWare Link Services Protocol** is introduced in NetWare 4.1 in an effort to overcome the inefficiencies introduced by RIP. When dealing strictly with local area networks and their megabit-per-second bandwidths, protocols such as RIP, which broadcast every 60 seconds, are nothing more than a slight nuisance. However, when expensive, limited bandwidth WAN links are involved, chatty protocols such as RIP become intolerable.

To be specific, the major problem with RIP is that all RIP-based IPX routers broadcast their entire routing table every 60 seconds whether or not anything has changed since the last broadcast. In contrast, NLSP only broadcasts as changes occur, or every two hours at a minimum. Real-world implementations of NLSP have reported 15 to 20 times (not %) reduction in WAN traffic with Novell claiming up to 40-fold decreases in router-to-router traffic as possible. Obviously, these data traffic reductions are only possible if both communicating routers support NLSP. Novell's multi-protocol router currently supports NLSP, but other vendors' routers need to be carefully reviewed.

Another limitation of RIP was its maximum of 16 hops before the RIP packet was discarded. This 16-hop limit effectively limited the physical size of the inter-network linking IPX LANs. NLSP has also addressed this shortcoming by increasing the maximum hop count to 128. NLSP is inter-operable or backward compatible with RIP, allowing gradual migration by network segment to the more efficient NLSP. This feature is especially important to large inter-networks manned by typically small networking staffs.

NLSP is known as a link-state routing protocol, whereas RIP is known as a distance vector routing protocol. Although the full differentiation between these two categories of routing protocols will be explored in Chapter 12, suffice to say at this point that link-state protocols are more efficient in their updates of routing tables and more intelligent in their routing directions recommendations for data packets than distance vector protocols.

Transport/Session Layer Protocols

Although IPX is technically a network layer protocol it also provides session layer addressing via sockets. An application layer protocol can directly address a remote application using only IPX as long as it specifies the socket number of the application on the destination node. For simple communication between two nodes such as exchanging routing information, IPX may be the only protocol required. Applications that require a reliable network transport mechanism require the use of SPX.

SPX **Sequenced Packet Exchange (SPX)** is a transport/session layer protocol that can be used with IPX to provide reliable communication. The key characteristics of SPX are:

- **Connection-oriented**—implying that specific paths known as **virtual circuits** are explored and determined prior to the first packet being sent. Once the virtual circuit is established directly from the source host or node to destination node, then all packets bound for that address follow each other in sequence down the same physical path. Virtual circuits are especially important when the source host and destination host reside on different networks.

- **Reliable**—implying that SPX requires error checking and acknowledgment in order to ensure reliable receipt of transmitted packets. Because transfer of a single file may be broken up across multiple IPX packets, SPX adds sequence numbers to ensure that all pieces are received and that they are reconstructed in the proper order. In order to ensure that packets are not lost accidentally due to hosts or routers suffering from buffer overflow, SPX also has mechanisms to institute flow control.

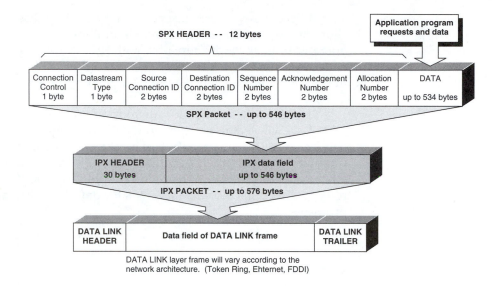

Figure 4-14 SPX Packet Layout and Encapsulation

SPX provides reliability by adding sequence numbers and acknowledgments to IPX. Figure 4-14 illustrates an SPX packet including the fields in the SPX header and shows the relationship between SPX and IPX. As can be seen, SPX is encapsulated within IPX and therefore depends on IPX for delivery to the destination workstation via the local network interface card. The role of each field in the SPX packet layout is detailed in Figure 4-15.

Upper-Layer Protocols

SAP The **Service Advertising Protocol (SAP)** is used by network servers to advertise the services they provide. Servers broadcast this information every 60 seconds. Networked servers receiving SAP broadcasts store that information for future reference. Local workstations requiring a particular service are able to query their local server, which consults its list to provide the latest information as to the closest availability of any network service. SAP uses IPX packets as its means of delivering its service advertising requests or responses throughout the network. Figure 4-16 illustrates a physical representation of the uses of SAP, whereas Figure 4-17 illustrates the header fields of a SAP packet.

In a manner similar to RIP, information regarding multiple servers can be either requested or supplied within a single SAP packet. Although only one operation type field per SAP packet is permitted, the remaining six fields can be repeated up to seven times in a single SAP packet. The role of each field in the SAP packet layout is detailed in Figure 4-18.

SPX Packet Fields	Function/Importance
Connection Control	Different 1 byte flags inserted into this field assist with the overall flow control and reliability for which SPX is responsible. Examples include: end of message flags and acknowledgment request flags.
Datastream Type	This 1 byte field allows upper-layer protocols to offer hints as to the protocols or information contained within the SPX data field so that it might be processed more efficiently. This field is analogous to including an Attention: line on the outside of an envelope. It allows that envelope to be properly routed for processing without having to examine the contents (data) contained within the envelope.
Connection IDs	Source and Destination Connection IDs are used to identify communication sessions between two communicating processes. A connection ID is another layer in the hierarchical addressing scheme introduced in IPX. Just as multiple socket IDs were possible for each host ID, multiple connection IDs can be associated with each socket ID.
Sequence Number	As the name implies, this field is used to ensure the proper sequencing of packets in multi-packet file transfers.
Acknowledgment Number	This field is incremented by the destination host as it receives sequenced packets. When the next packet is received, it will be error checked and the acknowledgment will be sent to the source workstation with this number included.
Allocation Number	This number is used in the implementation of the flow control mechanism. It is used to inform the source workstation of the number of buffers that the destination workstation can afford to allocate to SPX connections.

Figure 4-15 SPX Header Fields

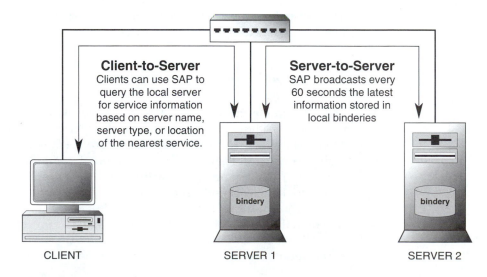

Figure 4-16 Uses of SAP

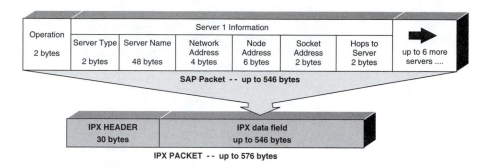

Figure 4-17 SAP Packet Layout and Encapsulation

■ THE INTERNET SUITE OF PROTOCOLS: OVERALL ARCHITECTURE AND FUNCTIONALITY

TCP/IP (Transmission Control Protocol/Internet Protocol) is the term generally used to refer to an entire suite of protocols used to provide communication on a variety of layers between widely distributed different types of computers. Strictly speaking, TCP and IP are just two of the protocols contained within the family of protocols more properly known as the **Internet Suite of Protocols.** TCP/IP was developed during the 1970s and widely deployed during the 1980s under the auspices of **DARPA** or Defense Advanced Research Projects Agency in order to meet the Department of Defense's need to have a wide variety of different computers be able to interoperate and communicate. TCP/IP became widely available to universities and research agencies and has become the de facto standard for communication between heterogeneous networked computers.

Overall Architecture

TCP/IP and the entire family of related protocols are organized into a protocol model. Although not identical to the OSI 7 layer model, the TCP/IP Model is no less effective at organizing protocols required to establish and maintain communications between different computers. Figure 4-19 illustrates the TCP/IP model, its constituent protocols, and its relationship to the OSI Model Network Reference Model.

As illustrated in Figure 4-19, the OSI model and TCP/IP model are functionally equivalent, although not identical, up through the transport layer. While the OSI model continues on with the session, presentation, and applications layers, the TCP/IP model has only the application layer

SAP Packet Fields	Function/Importance
Operation Type	This field defines whether this SAP packet contains a request for service information or a broadcast of existing or changed information. Only one operation type is allowed for each SAP packet.
Server Type	This field identifies the particular type of service offered by a server. One server can offer multiple different services. The valid service types are defined by Novell and are identified by unique hexadecimal values in this field. Following are a few of the defined service types and their hex values:

Service Type	Hex Value
File server	4
Job server	5
Gateway	6
Print server	7
Archive server	9
SNA Gateway	21
Remote Bridge Server	24
TCP/IP Gateway	27
NetWare Access Server	98

SAP Packet Fields	Function/Importance
Server Name	This field identifies the server or host offering the type of service identified in the service type field.
Network Address	This is the address of the network on which the server resides.
Node Address	This is the address of the server itself.
Socket Address	This is the socket address on this particular server to which requests for this particular type of service must be addressed.
Hops to Server	This field indicates how far from the local server this particular service is located. This field is used on queries from workstations desiring the nearest available service of a particular type.

Figure 4-18   SAP Header Fields

remaining with utilities such as Telnet (terminal emulation) and FTP (file transfer protocol) as examples of application layer protocols.

Individual Protocols: Architecture and Functionality   Figure 4-20 illustrates the placement of many of the TCP/IP family of protocols into their respective layers of the TCP/IP model. Each of these protocols, as well as several

Layer	OSI	INTERNET	Data Format	Protocols
7	Application	Application	Messages or Streams	TELNET FTP TFTP SMTP SNMP CMOT MIB
6	Presentation	Application	Messages or Streams	TELNET FTP TFTP SMTP SNMP CMOT MIB
5	Session			
4	Transport	Transport or Host-Host	Transport Protocol Packets	TCP UDP
3	Network	Internet	IP Diagrams	IP
2	Data Link	Network Access	Frames	
1	Physical	Network Access	Frames	

Figure 4-19   The TCP/IP Model

others, will be explained in detail. Many protocols involved with network management, routing, and remote access do not logically fit into any of the layers of the TCP/IP model and therefore are not listed. The same lack of a proper layer into which to place such protocols is also true in the OSI model as well.

IP Version 4

The most commonly used network layer protocol is IP, or the **Internet Protocol.** As its name would indicate, IP is the protocol used on the World Wide Internet. All World Wide Web browsing, e-mail exchanging, and media streaming on the Internet is carried by IP.

The Internet Protocol was the first packet-switched protocol. Originally developed to allow communication on the ARPAnet, IP has continually evolved and remains the most important layer 3 protocol currently in use. The version of IP most currently used is version four or IPv4. As IP continues to gain acceptance and the size and traffic levels on the Internet continue to grow, IPv4 is hitting its limits. To resolve these issues, the Internet Engineer-

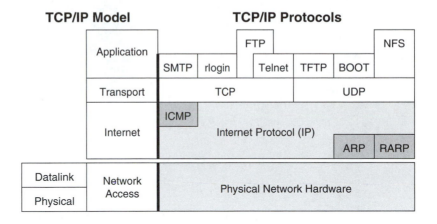

Figure 4-20 TCP/IP Family of Protocols

ing Task Force (the standard-bearers for IP) has created an updated version of IP: IPv6, also known as **IPng** (for Next Generation).

Both IPv4 and IPv6 will be discussed in this chapter, together with a brief description of how to transition between the two versions. Additional details on IP network design and implementation can be found in Chapter 12.

IP Addressing   Rather than breaking the segment and node portions of the network layer address into separate units as was done in IPX, IP combines the two into a single hierarchical IP address. While the hierarchical nature of IP addresses makes routing of IP packets easier, it makes understanding IP addressing somewhat confusing.

IPv4 addresses are 32 bits long and are represented as a sequence of four **octets.** Each octet is a decimal representation of an eight-bit section of the overall IP address. As shown in Figure 4-21, each eight-bit section of the overall IP address is converted to its decimal value and separated by a "." This is commonly referred to as a dotted decimal approach to representing IP addresses. Although people commonly refer to sections of an IP-based network by the IP address, it's important to remember that the binary value determines how the address is parsed and utilized.

Subnet Masks   An IP address contains both a segment address and a node address for a node ran together. The first X bits represent the segment address and the remaining 32-X bits represent the node address. However, as illustrated in Figure 4-22, there is no way of knowing exactly how many bits are used for each by merely looking at the IP address.

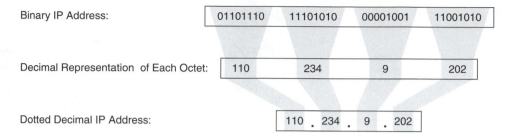

Figure 4-21 IP Address Construction

The separation of an IP address into its segment and node address components is accomplished via a **subnet mask.** A subnet mask is a 32-bit binary sequence that divides the IP address by using a 1 to indicate that the corresponding position in the IP address is part of the segment address and by using a 0 to indicate that the corresponding portion in the IP address is part of the node address. Because the segment address is the first x bits and the node address is the remaining bits, a subnet mask will always consist of x ones followed by 32-x zeros. The effect of using varying subnet masks on an IP address is shown in Figure 4-23. Just like IP addresses, subnet masks are usually referred to in dotted decimal format.

Once an IP address has been divided into a segment address and a range of node addresses through the application of a subnet mask, the resulting IP addresses may be assigned to the nodes on the network segment. However, there are two reserved addresses that may not be assigned to a node: the address that corresponds to all ones in the node section and the address that

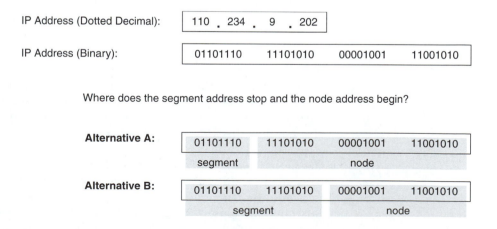

Figure 4-22 IP Segment Address vs. Node Address

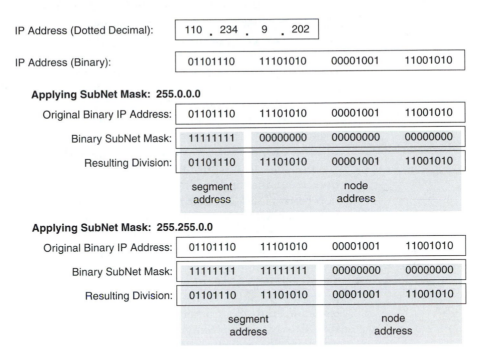

Figure 4-23 Use of Subnet Masks

corresponds to all zeros in the node section. All ones in the node section of the IP address is the broadcast address for the network segment. This address is used to send a single message to every node on the network segment. All zeros in the node section of the IP address is the address of the network segment itself. This address is used by routers to refer to the network in their routing tables. For a class "C" network these addresses correspond to x.x.x.255 and x.x.x.0, respectively.

IP Address Classes   An IP address can be broken anywhere into a segment address and a node address as long as both the segment address and node address consist of at least two bits. However, to make IP addresses easier to work with, it's customary to divide them at the octet boundaries. IP addresses divided this way are known as **classfull** addresses. In Figure 4-23, subnet mask B represents a **classfull** address. IP addresses that are not broken on octet boundaries are known as **classless** addresses. The remainder of this chapter will use classfull addressing. Classless addressing is discussed further in Chapter 12.

Classfull addresses are broken apart on octet boundaries. Therefore, there are three basic classes of addresses. As illustrated in Figure 4-24, these classes are known as class A, B, or C networks. To distinguish between classes, the first few bits of each segment address are used to denote the address class of the segment.

In addition to these basic address classes, there are two additional classes—class D and class E—that can be used for IPv4 addressing. Class D addresses are reserved for multicast systems such as routers, whereas Class E addresses are reserved for future use.

The assignment of address classes and network ID ranges to a particular organization wishing to connect to the Internet is the responsibility of the Internet Corporation for Assigned Names and Numbers (ICANN). ICANN ensures that all organizations using the Internet for network communications have unique IP addresses for all of their workstations. If an organization has no intention of ever accessing the Internet, it may not be necessary to register with ICANN for an IP address class and range of valid network IDs. Even in this case, however, all workstations on all communicating networks must have IP addresses unique within the internal corporate network.

Subnetworking   One of the strengths of the IP protocol is its ability to support network **subnetworking.** In many cases, a given organization may be issued a single class B network ID address with its associated 65,534 host IDs. This may seem like more than enough addresses until one considers that most organizations are distributed across multiple, geographically

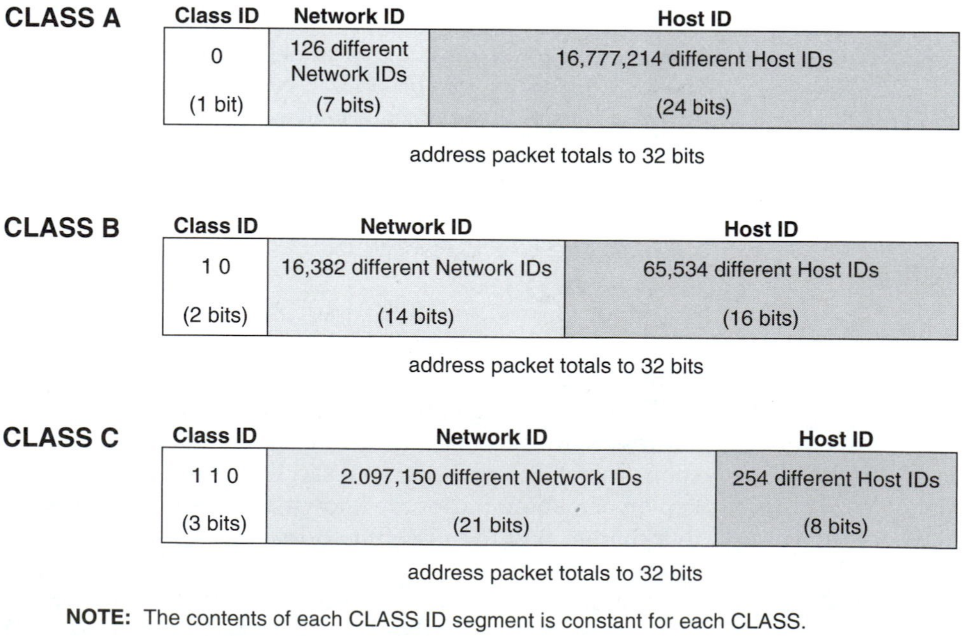

CLASS A

Class ID	Network ID	Host ID
0	126 different Network IDs	16,777,214 different Host IDs
(1 bit)	(7 bits)	(24 bits)

address packet totals to 32 bits

CLASS B

Class ID	Network ID	Host ID
1 0	16,382 different Network IDs	65,534 different Host IDs
(2 bits)	(14 bits)	(16 bits)

address packet totals to 32 bits

CLASS C

Class ID	Network ID	Host ID
1 1 0	2.097,150 different Network IDs	254 different Host IDs
(3 bits)	(21 bits)	(8 bits)

address packet totals to 32 bits

NOTE: The contents of each CLASS ID segment is constant for each CLASS.

Figure 4-24   IPv4 Address Classes

distributed locations. Internetworking devices known as routers must be employed to ensure that information which must travel from one corporate location to another is properly routed. The difficulty with this scenario is that the networks connected to the routers must all have unique segment addresses so that the router can distinguish one destination network from another. As previously stated, however, the organization in question was only issued a single segment address by ICANN.

The solution to the preceding dilemma is subnetworking. By applying a 32-bit subnet mask to a Class B IP address, a portion of the bits that comprise the host ID can be reserved for denoting subnetworks, with the remaining bits being reserved for host IDs per subnetwork. If the first eight bits of the host ID were reserved for subnetwork addresses and the final eight bits of the host ID were reserved for hosts per subnetwork, this would allow the same class B address to yield 254 subnetworks with 254 hosts each as opposed to one network with 65,534 hosts. Figure 4-25 provides examples of subnet masks. The overall effect of subnetworking is to create multiple network segments within the address space given by the IAB.

Subnetworking allows multiple network segments to be created within a single IP network address space. By creating such subnetworks, routing is also easily extended. From the perspective of a node outside the network, all nodes on any of the subnetworks appear to be on the original single network. Therefore these nodes simply route the packets to the gateway router for the network regardless of the actual destination subnetwork. The gateway router is configured to understand the subnetworking method used and routes the packets across the subnetworks to their intended destination. This process is illustrated in Figure 4-26 where the gateway router accepts all packets destined for the 10.x.x.x network and routes them based on class B subnetworking where the third octet has been made part of the network address rather than part of the node address.

	Binary Subnet Mask	Decimal Subnet Mask	Number of Subnetworks	Number of Hosts per Subnetwork
Default Class B Subnet Mask	11111111 11111111 00000000 00000000	255.255.0.0	1	65,534
Alternative Subnet Mask Used to Subnet Class B Network	11111111 11111111 11111111 00000000	255.255.255.0	254	254

Figure 4-25   IPv4 Subnetworking

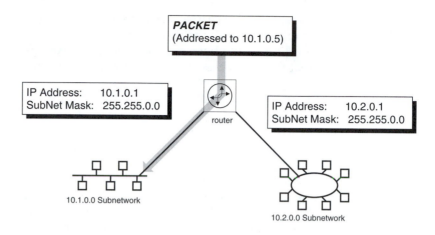

Figure 4-26 Routing with Subnetworking

Special Addresses Within a network segment there are two special addresses: the **broadcast address** and the network address. The broadcast address consists of a node address of all ones. All nodes on the network segment receive any packet addressed to the broadcast address. The network address consists of a node address of all zeros. The network address is used by routers to refer to the network segment itself, rather than any particular node on the segment.

Default Gateway (Router) For IP networks that consist of a single network segment, the specification of an IP address and a segment mask is adequate to ensure proper packet delivery. However, most IP networks have multiple segments; in fact, support for multiple segments is one of the key reasons to use IP in the first place.

For IP networks that consist of multiple network segments, each node must also be configured with a **default gateway** address. The default gateway address represents a router that should be used to route packets on remote network segments. The default router must reside on the same network segment as the node: if the node cannot talk to remote segments without a default gateway, how could it talk to a default gateway on a remote segment?

Although any valid address within a network segment can be declared the default router, it is common to use either the largest valid node address or the smallest valid node address. As mentioned earlier in this chapter, all zeros in the node section of the IP address denote the address of the network segment itself and all ones in the node section of the IP address denote the broadcast address for the network segment. Therefore, the default router is usually set at either all zeros with a one in the least significant bit or all ones with a zero in the least significant bit. For a class "C" network segment this would correspond to either x.x.x.1 or x.x.x.254, respectively. Regardless of which approach is taken, it is best to be consistent in terms of default gateway address across the inter-network. If x.x.x1 is the default router on one segment, it should be the default router on *all* segments.

IP to Data-Link Address Resolution   Unlike IPX, an IP node address has no direct relationship with its associated NIC's data-link (MAC) address. Therefore a mechanism to resolve IP addresses to data-link addresses is required to deliver packets within a local area network. This process is analogous to the use of directory assistance services in order to find a desired phone number. There are two protocols that resolve between IP addresses and data-link addresses: ARP and RARP.

ARP or **Address Resolution Protocol** (RFC 826) is used if an IP address of workstation is known but a data-link layer address for the same workstation is required. Each node on the network uses ARP to determine the data-link address for each destination.

RARP or **Reverse Address Resolution Protocol** is used if the data-link layer address of the workstation is known but the IP address of the same workstation is required. RARP is most commonly used to provide configuration information to nodes at boot time.

ARP and RARP are broadcast protocols. The requests for addresses are broadcast to an entire IP network segment. It should be obvious that this could represent a significant traffic burden. Routers do not rebroadcast ARP or RARP packets and thereby act as a filter to prevent infinite propagation of ARP/RARP broadcasts. Responses to ARP and RARP requests are sent directly to the requesting workstation rather than being broadcast to all attached workstations. The ARP response is sent by the workstation whose IP address is found in the destination address field of the broadcast ARP packets. To reduce the overhead required by ARP requests, ARP responses are stored in an ARP cache so that it will not be necessary to re-broadcast for the same address.

Packet Construction   IP packets have a minimum length of 576 bytes and a maximum length of 64K bytes. Depending on the underlying layer 2 protocol(s) used to deliver the packet, an IP packet may be broken into smaller packet fragments as described earlier in this chapter. As shown in Figure 4-27, the IP header can be either 20 or 24 bytes long resulting in an effective data payload of 552 to 65516 bytes. Packets are sent with the bits transmitted in **network byte order** (from left to right). The IPv4 packet layout is illustrated in Figure 4-27 and a detailed description of each field in the IP header is presented in Figure 4-28.

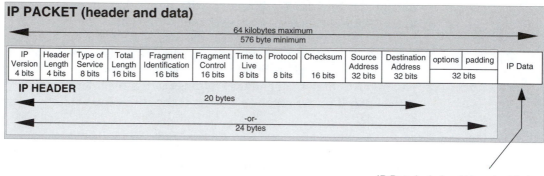

Figure 4-27   IPv4 Packet Layout

IP Support Protocols   Although IP is by definition an unreliable transport mechanism, it does have a mechanism to deliver error and status message via the Internet Control Message Protocol. To make it easier to remember IP addresses, the DNS system resolves hierarchical alphanumeric names to and from IP addresses.

ICMP—Internet Control Message Protocol   The **Internet Control Message Protocol (ICMP)** delivers a variety of error status and control messages related to the ability of IP to deliver its encapsulated payloads. ICMP uses IP as a transport mechanism and is able to deliver a variety of error and control messages through the use of type and code fields as illustrated in Figure 4-29. ICMP carries 13 different message types as detailed in Figure 4-30.

The most common use of ICMP from the user's perspective is checking for network connectivity between two nodes. The ping application is used to generate and process ICMP echo/reply packets, commonly referred to as "ping" packets. The process of checking for connectivity in this manner is commonly referred to as "pinging" the address.

IP Routing Protocols   There are two basic non-proprietary routing protocols used to maintain IP routing tables: RIP and OSPF

RIP—Routing Information Protocol   Having gained a basic understanding of how routing works, the importance of router-to-router communication for establishment, maintenance, and updates of routing tables should be obvious. One such router-to-router protocol associated with TCP/IP is **RIP** or **Routing Information Protocol.** A routing table in a router serviced by RIP contains multiple records as illustrated in Figure 4-31.

IP Packet Field	Function/Importance
IP Version	It is important for computers and internetwork devices processing this IP packet to know the version of IP with which it was written in order to preclude any potential cross-version incompatibility problems.
Header Length	The header can be either 5 or 6 32-bit words (20 or 24 bytes) depending on whether or not the options field is activated.
Type of Service	The flags in this field can be used to indicate eight levels of precedence as well as different types of service for low delay, high throughput, or high reliability. Unless routers are able to read this field and respond accordingly, they are of no use.
Total Length	This is the total length of the IP packet including the header and the IP data.
Fragment Identification	This is a 16-bit integer ID of a fragment. IP packets must be fragmented as dictated by the limitations of lower layer (data-link) network architectures.
Fragment Control (Flags and Offset)	Fragment flags (3 bits) are used to indicate the last fragment of an original datagram as well as if a datagram should not be fragmented. Fragment offset (13 bits) indicates the relative position of this fragment in the original IP datagram.
Time to Live	This field is a simple hop counter that is decremented every time this IP packet is handled by a router. When the Time to Live counter reaches 0, the packet is discarded so that it does not wander around the network for an infinite amount of time monopolizing bandwidth. The counter can be initialized as high as 255 but is more typically set to 32 or 16.
Protocol	This is an important field, since it indicates which protocol is embedded with the IP data area. By reading this field, the IP software is able to forward the IP data to the proper transport layer protocol stack for further processing. Typical values and their corresponding protocols are as follows: 17 – UPD 6 – TCP 1 – ICMP 8 – EGP 89 – OSPF
Checksum	This field is more correctly known as the IP Header Checksum, since it only provides error detection for the IP header. Reliability checks for the IP data are provided by upper-layer protocols.
Source Address	32 bit IP address of source computer
Destination Address	32 bit IP address of ultimate destination computer
Options	Used for diagnostics purposes, these fields are sometimes set by other TCP/IP family utilities such as Ping or Trace Route. Security and source routing options can also be set using this field. These features must be supported by all workstations and routers in a given network in order to be implemented fully and effectively.
Padding	Depending on how many options are selected, padding of zeros may need to be added in order to bring the IP header to the full 6×32 bit word (24 byte) length.

Figure 4-28   IP Header Fields

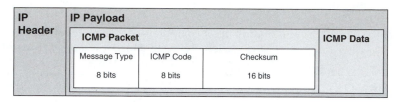

Figure 4-29   ICMP Protocol Layout

RIP broadcasts its routing tables to all directly connected routers every 30 seconds. Those directly connected routers then propagate the new routing table information to the routers directly connected to them. This pattern continues, and after about 7 minutes (30 sec. intervals × 15 hop max.), all routing tables have been updated and, for the moment, are synchronized. However, the delay that occurs while all of the routers are propagating their routing tables, known as **slow convergence,** could allow certain routers to assume that failed links to certain networks are still viable. In order to reduce the convergence time, the following optional approaches have been added to RIP:

- **Split horizon** and **reverse poison** prevent routers from wasting time broadcasting routing table changes back to the routers that just supplied them with the same changes in the first place.

- **Triggered updates** allow routers to immediately broadcast routing table updates regarding failed links rather than having to wait for the next 30 sec. periodic update.

However, it should be pointed out that even with these improvements, RIP is still not as efficient as other routing protocols that will be explored shortly. Figure 4-32 illustrates the layout of the RIP protocol, and field descriptions are given in Figure 4-33.

OSPF—Open Shortest Path First   Router-to-router protocols, such as RIP, which only consider the distance between networks in hops as a determination of the best internetwork path are known as **distance vector protocols.** A more sophisticated category of routing protocols known as **link state protocols** takes into account other factors regarding internetwork paths such as link capacity, delay, throughput, reliability, or cost.

OSPF or **Open Shortest Path First** (RFC 1247) is an example of a link state protocol that was developed to overcome some of RIP's shortcomings such as the 15 hop limit and full routing table broadcasts every 30 seconds. OSPF uses IP for connectionless transport. Detailed explanations of OSPF are provided in Chapter 13.

Limitations of IPv4   Although IPv4 is the most commonly used network layer protocol, there are some key limitations that affect its usage.

ICMP Type	Name	Explanation/Use
0	Echo Reply	This is the ICMP message expected from a workstation which has been "pinged" by an ICMP Type 8 message.
3	Destination unreachable	This message would be returned by a router to the source workstation or router along with a code indicating a more specific reason why the destination was unreachable. In this case unreachable means that the network identified in the IP address could not be found. Possible reason codes include: 0 – Network unreachable 1 – Host unreachable 2 – Protocol unreachable 3 – Port unreachable 4 – Fragmentation needed but the "Do not fragment" bit is set 5 – Source route failed
4	Source quench	This is how IP's version of flow control is implemented. The source quench message is a request from a computer or router to a source of IP datagrams to slow down the flow of IP datagrams in order to avoid data loss.
5	Redirect a route	Also known as route change request, this ICMP message is used only by routers when they receive an IP packet that they believe could be handled more quickly or efficiently by a different router. In that case, the originating workstation or router is notified of the new suggested route, and the original message is also forwarded to the preferred router in order to expedite the delivery of the original IP packet.
8	Echo request to a remote station	This is the ICMP message sent out by the Ping utility. ICMP message type 0 is the expected return from a successful Ping.
11	Time exceeded for datagram	This message is usually sent from routers to originating workstations if the Time to Live field (TTL) in the IP header has been decremented to 0. This can be caused if a hop count has been exceeded or if a network failure has occurred causing an IP packet to be processed by more routers than usual.
12	Parameter problem with a datagram	This message is fairly serious since it indicates that a parameter within the IP header could not be understood. Luckily, the message includes an indication of where the parameter problem occurred in the IP header in order to more easily diagnose the problem.
13	TimeStamp request	This message is used to request the time of day from a networked host.
14	TimeStamp reply	This is the reply message type for message type 13 requests.
15	Information request	This message is used to request the network number of the network to which the requesting host is attached. The most likely scenario when a host wouldn't know the network to which it is attached is in remote access situations using SLIP or PPP.
16	Information reply	This is the ICMP message type used to reply to ICMP message type 15.
17	Address Mask request	This message type is used to request the subnetwork mask of the network to which a host is connected. It is likely to be used in the same situations as ICMP message type 15.
18	Address Mask reply	This is the ICMP message type used to reply to ICMP message type 17.

Figure 4-30   ICMP Message Types

Field	Description and Purpose
Address	IP address of the network which this record contains information about.
Gateway	IP address of the next hop router, or directly reachable router along the path to the network identified in the Address field. It is to these directly connected routers to which RIP broadcasts its routing table every 30 seconds. In larger networks, these routing table broadcasts can amount to a substantial quantity of network traffic.
Interface	The MAC layer address or port number of the physical interface on this router which is connected to the link that leads to the next hop gateway identified in the previous field.
Metric or Hop Count	Total number of hops, or intermediate routers, between this router and the destination network. RIP limits the number of intermediate hops between any two networks to 15, thereby limiting the physical size of RIP-supported networks. Hop counts of 16 are used to indicate that a network is unreachable.
Timer	Age of this entry. Two separate timers are used. One is usually set to 180 seconds when an entry is first updated and counts down until the 0 when the entry is marked for deletion. Remember that entries are normally updated every 30 seconds. The second timer controls when the entry is actually physically deleted from the table.

Figure 4-31 Routing Table Fields

As the number of nodes on the Internet grows, the 32-bit address space provided by IPv4 is running out. Although it provides almost 4.3 billion addresses, the hierarchical nature of IP addressing greatly limits the efficiency with which IP addresses can be used. Consider, for example, the class C address range 192.168.1.x. This network segment takes up 254 addresses regardless of how many nodes are actually attached. Although this appears to be a waste of address spaces, the routing benefits of such a hierarchical addressing approach greatly outweigh the inefficiency of address utilization.

The second class of problems with IPv4 is that the design of the protocol results in increased processing at each router. This major problem is the result of several smaller problems. Fragmentation between the network layer and the data-link layer forces each router to carve an IP packet into

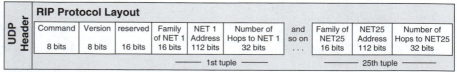

Figure 4-32 RIP Protocol Layout

RIP Packet Field	Function/Importance
Command	This field identifies if this RIP packet is an explicit request for routing information (1) or the associated response (2), as opposed to the default 30 sec. Interval broadcasts
Version	This field identifies the version of RIP supported in order to avoid possible incompatibilities due to RIP upgrade versions.
Family of Net 1	This field is used to identify the network layer protocol used in the network described in this routing table entry. RIP is able to build routing table entries for networks with network layer protocols other than IP. Net 1 refers to the first network entry in the routing table update being broadcast by RIP. RIP is limited to either 25 network entries per RIP packet or a maximum packet length of 512 bytes.
Net 1 Address	The network address of this network entry in the RIP routing table update. The address format will correspond to the network layer protocol identified in the Family of Net 1 field.
Number of Hops to Net 1	This field indicates the number of hops, or intermediate routers, between the router broadcasting this routing table update and Net 1.

Figure 4-33   RIP Header Fields

smaller sections and reassemble them at the next hop. This problem mainly manifests itself when local area networks are interconnected via wide area networks. LANs typically run over fast, relatively error-free data-link layer technologies such as Ethernet. With an available payload of 1508 bytes, it makes sense to set the IP packet size at 1500 bytes. However, if these packets are required to cross a WAN link, they will be carried on data-link layer technologies that typically can handle only a 576 byte payload, resulting in packet fragmentation and increased router workload.

In Sharper Focus

IMPROVING WINDOWS INTERNET ACCESS BY REDUCING FRAGMENTATION

The network functionality of the Microsoft Windows family of operating systems was primarily designed to connect clients to local servers. Because of this focus, the default maximum transmission unit for IPv4 is 1500 bytes. While this setting provides increased efficiency on Ethernet networks by reducing packet header overhead, it usually results in fragmented packets when accessing the Internet.

If the primary network connectivity issue for a computer is Internet access through a modem to an ISP, reducing the IP MTU to 576 can potentially increase Internet connectivity speed. By setting the MTU to 576, the ISP's gateway router no longer needs to fragment and reassemble every packet transmitted between the router and the remote node. Changes to the IP MTU can be made through the registry editor. Instructions are available at many locations on the Internet.

Another major router processing problem with IPv4 is the variable length IP packet header. As previously mentioned, the *options* and *padding* fields are optional; this forces each router to parse the packet header to determine where the packet header stops and the data begin, wasting router resources.

Other concerns with IPv4 include the need for new functionality that is not included in the current version of the protocol. With the advent of streaming media on the Internet, there is a strong need for multicasting to be supported under IP. **Multicasting** allows a single packet to be sent to multiple nodes (but not all nodes) on multiple network segments. In the current unicast model, if five nodes on one network need to receive the same packet of data, it must be sent five times—one packet addressed to each node. In a multicasting model only a single packet would have to be sent, thus reducing the load on the routers and reducing the bandwidth required to support the transmission.

The third class of problems with IPv4 involves the evolution of data networks. Data networks are currently being used to carry data types that the creators of IPv4 couldn't have expected. Sensitive final data, streaming media, Internet telephone calls, and other time-sensitive data were not considered when the protocol was originally developed. These new applications create another issue that cannot be easily resolved on IPv4: different packets have different levels of importance. Under IPv4 there is no way to indicate that a packet carrying payroll data is more important than a packet carrying a media stream of a basketball game. If a router becomes overloaded, it will drop whichever packet comes after the buffer is full. Ideally the router should make a decision to drop lower-priority packets from the buffer to allow higher-priority packers to reach their destinations. This ability is commonly known as **class of service.**

The final concern with IPv4 is that there are absolutely no security features. While data in the higher level protocols can be encrypted, the resulting ciphertext is readily available to anyone who wants to "listen" for it anywhere along the route to the destination. There is also no mechanism in IPv4 to prevent a node from pretending to be someone it's not. This process of deception, known as spoofing, presents a serious security threat to IP-based networks.

IP Version 6

To address the previously listed shortcomings of IPv4, the Internet Engineering Task Force has developed a new version of the Internet Protocol—IPv6, also known as IPng (Next Generation).

Addressing   IPv6 resolves the IPv4 address space problem by expanding IP addresses to 128 bits, an 8×10 to the 28th power improvement. Instead of the familiar dotted decimal notation, IPv6 addresses are represented in a manner similar to MAC addresses: as a series of six four-byte hexadecimal codes separated by colons. An example IPv6 address is: FF0E:0:0:A0B9:0:23. As can be seen in this example a section of all zeros is simply expressed as a single zero. Subnet masks are expressed in a similar manner. An example IPv6 subnet mask would be FFFF:FFFF:FFFF:0:0:0.

Other Improvements   Other improvements address the fragmentation problem. For those data streams that require multiple packets to be sent, an explorer packet is sent to the destination to determine the smallest underlying data-link layer payload on the route. The source node then uses this setting as the maximum transmission unit for that connection, thus effectively eliminating packet fragmentation and its resulting processor overhead.

To further reduce the processing load on routers IPv6 utilizes fixed length field headers. While the overall packet header for IPv6 is larger than IPv4 due to the increased length of the source and destination addresses, each header is constructed in exactly the same format, thus removing the requirement that routers parse each packet. Packet header error checking has been removed, since it is somewhat redundant: If a packet header has an error, it is doubtful whether it would reach its destination in the first place, so why bother to check for errors?

To address the need for classes of service, IPv6 numbers each data stream and labels it as either congestion controlled or non-congestion controlled. Congestion-controlled data streams can tolerate delays, while non–congestion- controlled data streams cannot tolerate delays. An example of a congestion-controlled data stream might be a file transfer, while an example of a non–congestion-controlled data stream might be an Internet telephone call. IPv6 also includes support for multicast addresses and a new unicast address method called anycast that streamlines routing through IPv6 networks along with traditional support for broadcast addresses.

Security has been addressed on two fronts: authentication and encryption. IPv6 packets can be set to authenticate their origin, which prevents another node from spoofing an IP address and fraudulently gaining access to sensitive data. IPv6 packets can also be encrypted at the network layer, thus eliminating the need for each higher-level protocol to implement its own encryption methodology.

Packet Construction   The IPv6 packet header is 40 bytes long. Although this is longer than the 20 to 24 bytes of IPv4, the fixed header structure and field lengths combine to increase routing performance. The packet layout of an IPv6 packet is shown in Figure 4-34. A detailed description of the IPv6 header fields is given in Figure 4-35.

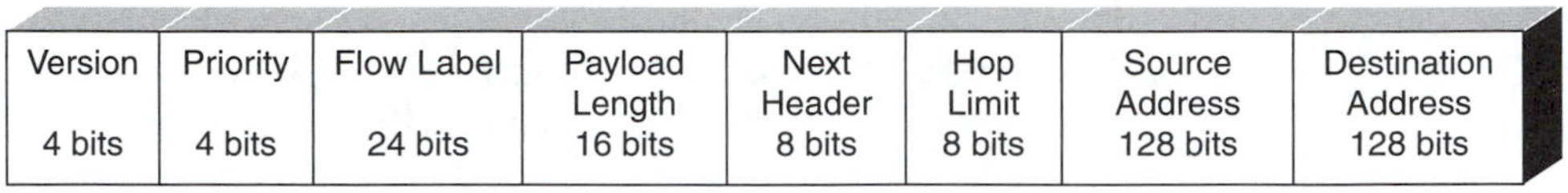

Version 4 bits	Priority 4 bits	Flow Label 24 bits	Payload Length 16 bits	Next Header 8 bits	Hop Limit 8 bits	Source Address 128 bits	Destination Address 128 bits

Figure 4-34 IPv6 Packet Layout

Transition from IPv4 to IPv6 Although there are compelling technical reasons to transition all IP-based networks to IPv6 as soon as possible, the actual transition itself is problematic at best. Consider a large corporate private network consisting of 5000 nodes in 17 cities spread across 6 time zones. It is simply not realistic to say that at midnight GMT on a certain date every node will change over to IPv6. The Internet exacerbates the problem with its constituent networks under the control of various organizations spread literally around the globe. What is needed is a mechanism to allow IPv4 and IPv6 to coexist for a period of time until the transition can be completed.

IPv6 provides three such mechanisms. A NIC can be bound to two IP addresses: one IPv4 and one IPv6. Such a dual addressed node would

IPv6 Header Field	Function/Importance
Version	It is important for computers and inter-network devices processing this IP packet to know the version of IP with which it was written in order to preclude any potential cross-version incompatibility problems.
Priority	Priority of the packet. This field indicates the class of service of the packet.
Flow Label	Uniquely identifies the stream of data relative to other streams between the same source and destination.
Payload Length	This field indicates the length of the data in the packet.
Next Header	This field indicates what type of header is contained in the payload of the IP packet. It tells the destination node what protocols are encapsulated in the packet.
Hop Limit	This field corresponds to the Time To Live counter in IPv4. It is a simple eight bit (up to 255) hop counter that prevents a packet from wandering around an IPv6 network forever.
Source Address	128 bit IP address of source computer
Destination Address	128 bit IP address of ultimate destination computer

Figure 4-35 IPv6 Header Fields

respond to either IP address as if it were the node's only address. A second approach is to tunnel IPv6 data across IPv4 network backbones. This approach works well for organizations that interconnect their data networks via the Internet. They can transition their internal networks to IPv6 then literally stuff the IPv6 packet into an IPv4 packet payload for delivery across the Internet where the IPv6 packet is removed and routed to its destination.

The third approach provides the most seamless solution to the problem by adding the ability to translate headers between IPv4 and IPv6 at the routers between IPv4 and IPv6 networks. In this manner, an IPv6 node can directly communicate with an IPv4 node. Ironically this solution increases the load on the routers until all the nodes have been converted to IPv6—exactly the opposite of what IPv6 is intended to do. However, it can be thought of as an investment to make the transition as straightforward as possible.

Transport Layer Protocols

As previously mentioned, Internet protocols implement OSI network model functionality in a slightly modified manner. As illustrated in Figure 4-19, Internet transport or host-to-host protocols implement both transport layer functionality and session layer addressing functionality. The remaining OSI session, presentation, and application layer functionality are implemented by Internet application layer protocols. This chapter will focus on Internet protocols through the transport layer. Application layer protocols will be covered in subsequent chapters on network operating systems.

UDP—User Datagram Protocol   The **User Datagram Protocol (UDP)** is used to provide unreliable, connectionless messaging services for applications. The main purpose of the header is to allow UDP to keep track of which applications it is sending a datagram to and from through the use of port addresses and to pass those messages along to IP for subsequent delivery. Because UDP does not provide reliable connection-oriented services, the UDP packet header is small. UDP uses only an 8-byte header as illustrated in Figure 4-36. A description of the UDP header fields is presented in Figure 4-37.

Due to the small size of UDP packet headers and the fact that they require no acknowledgments from the receiving node, UDP is the perfect transport/session layer protocol for delivering streaming media packets. The overhead associated with a connection-oriented protocol would greatly reduce the number of clients that a streaming media server could support when compared with the relatively efficient UDP protocol.

IP HEADER	IP DATA				
	UDP Header				**UDP Data**
20 or 24 bytes	Source Port 16bits	Destination Port 16 bits	Length 16 bits	Checksum 16 bits	Upper Layer Protocols and User Data
	8 bytes				

Figure 4-36   UDP Header Layout

TCP—Transmission Control Protocol   The majority of network traffic requires a more reliable connection than UDP offers. To provide connection-oriented, reliable data transmission the **Transmission Control Protocol (TCP)** is the transport/session layer protocol of choice. Reliability is ensured through the additional fields contained within the TCP header which offer flow control, acknowledgments of successful receipt of packets after error checking, retransmission of packets as required, and proper sequencing of packets.

The fact that TCP is considered connection-oriented implies that a point-to-point connection between source and destination computers must be established before transmission can begin and that the connection will be torn down after transmission has concluded. This is accomplished through the use of TCP flags. When an originating node needs to establish a connection with another node it sends a TCP packet containing a SYN flag and a sequence number to the destination. This sequence number is used as the starting point for the stream of TCP packets from the source to the destination.

When the destination node receives the initial SYN packet, it responds by sending an ACK of the SYN packet's sequence number with a SYN packet and sequence number to establish the return half of the connection. The originating node then sends an ACK to the destination node's SYN packet and the connection is established. Subsequent packets in each direction incre-

UDP Header Field	Function/Importance
Source Port	Port address of the application on the source node that sent the packet
Destination Port	Port address of the application on the destination node that is to receive the packet
Length	Overall length of the UDP datagram
Checksum	Checksum calculated on both the UDP header and data

Figure 4-37   UDP Header Fields

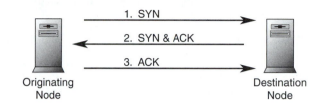

TCP Connection Creation

TCP Connection Tear-Down

Figure 4-38   Connection Creation and Tear Down

ment the sequence numbers. When communication is complete the originating node sends a FIN flag to the destination and tears down the connection. This process is illustrated in Figure 4-38.

The TCP header layout is illustrated in Figure 4-39 and the header fields are explained in Figure 4-40.

UDP and TCP Port Numbers   UDP and TCP provide session layer addressing through the use of **ports.** Ports are specific 16-bit addresses that are uniquely related to particular applications. Source port and destination port addresses are included in the UDP/TCP header. The unique port address of an application combined with the unique 32-bit IP address of the computer on which the application is executing is known as a **socket.** Some typical port numbers for popular TCP/IP applications are listed in Figure 4-41.

IP HEADER	IP DATA									
	TCP HEADER									**TCP DATA**
	Source Port 16 bits	Destination Port 16 bits	Sequence Number 32 bits	Acknowledgement Number 32 bits	Data Offset and Codes 16 bits	Window 16 bits	Checksum 16 bits	Urgent Pointer 16 bits	Options and Padding 32 bits	Upper Layer Protocols and User Data
20 or 24 bytes	24 bytes									

Figure 4-39   TCP Header Layout

TCP Header Field	Function/Importance
Source Port	The port address that uniquely identifies the particular application from which this packet is sent.
Destination Port	The port address that uniquely identifies the particular application to which this packet is addressed.
Sequence Number	The sequence number of the first octet of data in this segment. This allows TCP at the destination address to properly re-sequence the data stream if IP happens to deliver the segments out of order.
Acknowledgment Number	In order to meet its objective of ensuring reliable transmission, the transmitting computer must know the sequence number of the segment that was last successfully received by the receiving computer. The transmitted acknowledgment number is, in fact, the segment number of the last successfully received segment plus one. This lets the transmitting computer know which segment the receiving computer is waiting for. If the acknowledgment number does not increment before a preset retransmission timer expires, then the transmitting computer assumes that the repeated acknowledgment number's segment never arrived and that it must retransmit that segment.
Data Offset	The length of the TCP header in terms of the number of 32-bit words before the start of the TCP data. The entry in this field would be 5 (20 bytes) if options and padding are not enabled or 6 (24 bytes) if they are enabled.
Reserved	Set to all zeros.
Codes	Also known as flags, are used for connection setup, management, and termination. There are six possible codes: • SYN – Used to initially set up connections and to synchronize sequence numbers. • ACK – Indicates validity of acknowledgment number, especially important at connection setup time. • URG – Indicates validity of urgent pointer field. • PSH – The Push flag is used to cause TCP to flush data buffers immediately in order to push this packet directly to the application whose port number is indicated in the TCP header. • FIN – Used to terminate connections normally. • RST – Used to reset the connection, thereby forcing a connection termination.
Window	The window field is used by TCP as a means of a sort of flow control. The window value is sent from a destination node to a source node advertising how many bytes of free buffer space are available on the destination node for this connection. This number then becomes the limit as to how much data can be sent by the source before receiving an acknowledgment from the destination node.
Checksum	This is a calculated checksum on the TCP header and data that are transmitted to the destination node for error-detection purposes.
Urgent Pointer	Tells the destination where to look in the data field for an urgent message such as a break signal or some other type of interrupt.
Options and Padding	The only option typically set with TCP is a value for maximum segment size which lets the destination node know the largest acceptable segment length. Padding is used to extend the options field to a full 32-bit word, and is used only if options are set.

Figure 4-40   TCP Header Fields

TCP/IP Application	Port Number
HTTP	80
Telnet	23
FTP	21
SMTP	25
BootP client	68
BootP server	67
TFTP	69
Finger	79
NetBIOS session service	139
X.400	103
SNMP	161

Figure 4-41   Selected Port Numbers

Internet Support Protocols and Services

Although the following protocols and services are not required to make an IP-based network function, they offer services that greatly increase the usability and manageability of such networks.

Automatic IP Address Assignment   Each node on an IP-based network must have a unique IP address. Traditionally these addresses were statically assigned to each node through an interactive process. Although this is an effective manner to assign IP addresses, it does create some problems:

- Someone must serve as the central authority to ensure that each node has a unique IP address. From a practical perspective it makes sense to have the DNS administrator perform this task as they keep track of all IP addresses while managing the DNS tables.

- When a node is moved from one node to another it requires administrator intervention in assigning a new IP address.

To resolve these issues two services have been developed to automatically assign IP addresses to network nodes: BOOTP and DHCP. BOOTP, the boot protocol, is a static address assignment method. When a node is configured to use BOOTP it broadcasts a data-link layer frame to the network segment requesting an IP address. A BOOTP server on the network then looks up the physical (MAC) address of the requesting station in a table and replies with the correct IP address. Through the use of BOOTP relay agents the requirement that each network segment contain a BOOTP server can be eliminated. A BOOTP relay agent listens for BOOTP requests and forwards them to the server. The server looks up the IP information, then sends it to the relay agent who replies to the requesting node.

Although BOOTP was a step in the right direction for solving manual IP address assignment problems, it still requires a one-to-one mapping between nodes and IP addresses. This is especially a concern given the explosive growth of the Internet. With nodes connecting to the Internet on an occasional dial-in basis, it is extremely inefficient to assign each node a unique IP address, especially considering the fact that IPv4 address space is rapidly running out.

To resolve this issue, the **Dynamic Host Configuration Protocol (DHCP)** was developed. An extension of the original BOOTP protocol, the Dynamic Host Configuration Protocol allows special servers to dynamically assign TCP/IP addresses to nodes. A DHCP server references a database of available IP addresses and can dynamically assign available addresses to requesting clients. IP addresses issued by DHCP are leased, rather than being permanently assigned, and the length of time that IP addresses can be kept by DHCP clients is known as the **lease duration.** Dial-in users are typically assigned an IP address only for the duration of their call. In addition to dynamically assigning IP addresses, DHCP can statically assign addresses in a manner similar to BOOTP through the use of address reservations.

Use of DHCP for Servers

Practical Advice and Information

DHCP can greatly reduce IP addressing issues for network clients. Servers, on the other hand, should always be assigned permanent IP addresses to ensure that clients can locate them on the network. DHCP can still be used to assign IP addresses to servers, but DHCP reservations should be used to ensure each server maintains a consistent network address.

Domain Name System   IP addresses are used to uniquely identify nodes on an IP-based network. However, 32-bit IPv4 addresses are difficult for humans to memorize and work with, even in dotted decimal form. IPv6 promises to make this problem even worse with its 128-bit addresses. To make identifying node addresses easier for people, the **Domain Name System (DNS)** has been created. DNS provides the following key services:

- Uniquely identifies all hosts connected to the Internet by name

- Resolves, or translates, host names into IP addresses (and vice versa)

- Identifies which services are offered by each host such as gateway or mail transfer, and to which networks these services are offered

DNS is a hierarchical naming structure with the hierarchical layers being separated by dots such as "www.company.com". DNS addresses are listed in inverse order with the hostname being the first word and the domain name being the following words. In the www.company.com example, www is the hostname and company.com is the domain name. The last section of a domain name is called the top level domain. Top level domains are carefully managed to ensure that there is no confusion between DNS domains. To make DNS as intuitive as possible, consistent naming conventions need to be established. For nodes connected directly to the Internet, standard top level domains such as .edu for educational institutions, .com for commercial entities, and .gov for government agencies are issued. Private institutions not directly connecting to the Internet are welcome to establish their own naming schemes for use within their corporate networks.

DNS is physically implemented in a client/server architecture in which client-based DNS software known as the DNS or name **resolver** sends requests for DNS name resolution to a **DNS** (or name) **Server.** The address of the nearest (primary) DNS server, as well as at least one backup (secondary) DNS server, is entered into a configuration file when TCP/IP is installed on the local client. Networks that connect to the Internet must supply both a primary and backup DNS server in order to process name queries from Internet attached hosts. DNS is a hierarchical service in that if a given DNS server cannot resolve a name as requested, it will reply with the address of a DNS server of a higher authority which may have more available information. Alternatively, the local DNS server may contact the higher authority DNS server itself, thereby increasing its own knowledge while meeting the client request in a process known as **recursion.** The scope of coverage, or collection of domains, for which a given DNS server can resolve names is known as a DNS **zone.**

■ APPLETALK

The AppleTalk protocol family was originally developed by Apple Computer to provide connectivity among their Macintosh products introduced in 1984. The original implementation, known as LocalTalk, was designed as an inexpensive solution that connected Macintoshes via their serial ports. As the need for more bandwidth grew, AppleTalk Phase 2 was developed to run over Ethernet (EtherTalk) and Token Ring (TokenTalk) data-link technologies. AppleTalk Phase 2 utilizes IEEE 802.2 compliant data-link interfaces and has an improved address space compared to the original AppleTalk specification. All subsequent references to AppleTalk refer to AppleTalk Phase 2. Figure 4-42 shows the AppleTalk family of protocols and their mapping against the OSI Network Reference Model. This chapter focuses on the layer 2 and 3 capabilities of AppleTalk.

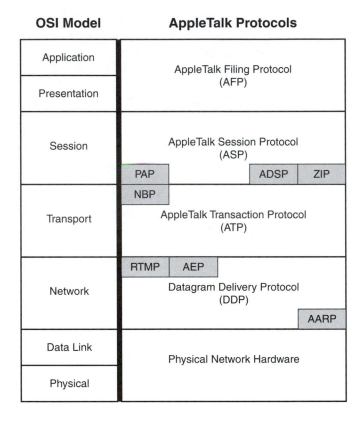

Figure 4-42   The AppleTalk Family of Protocols

DDP

The **Datagram Delivery Protocol (DDP)** is the network layer protocol for the AppleTalk protocol suite. DDP is a routable, connectionless, nonreliable protocol that is used to encapsulate all higher-level AppleTalk protocols.

Addressing   DDP addresses are composed of three parts: network address, node address, and socket address. The network (segment) address is 16 bits long. A network address of all ones (65535) is reserved by Apple Computer and is therefore illegal for normal use. The node address is eight bits long. A node address of all ones (255) is used as the broadcast address for the network segment. A node address of 0 specifies the local node. The socket address is eight bits long and identifies the process on the node that is responsible for the packet.

DDP addresses are resolved to data-link addresses via the AppleTalk Address Resolution Protocol (AARP). Similar to ARP on IP-based networks, AARP is a broadcast based protocol. When a node needs the data-link address for a DDP address, it broadcasts an AARP packet querying the destination DDP address. The node with the destination DDP address responds with its data-link address, which is then used to address the data-link layer frame to the destination. In addition to the base addressing functionality provided directly by DDP, AppleTalk makes extensive use of AppleTalk Zones to identify networks.

Packet Construction   There are two types of DDP packets: long packets and short packets. Part of the original AppleTalk specification, short packets were used exclusively for communication within a network segment and are no longer supported under AppleTalk Phase 2. The difference between short packets and long packets is the number of fields in the DDP header. A short DDP packet has only four header fields: destination socket, source socket, length, and DDP Type. A long DDP packet adds additional header fields required to transmit packets across an inter-network.

DDP long packets consist of 10 fields totaling 13 bytes. The maximum data payload for a DDP packet is 586 bytes, for a maximum transmission unit (MTU) of 599 bytes. The DDP packet header layout is shown in Figure 4-43 and a detailed description of each field in the DDP header is presented in Figure 4-44.

AppleTalk Routing Protocols   The protocol used to distribute routing information through DDP based networks is the **Routing Table Maintenance Protocol (RTMP).** RTMP is a distance vector routing protocol similar to RIP in IP-based networks. Routing information is regularly broadcast through the network, with old routes being removed by a routine aging process where table entries are deleted when they no longer are received via RTMP broadcasts. AppleTalk Phase 2 also includes support for split horizon routing. In split horizon routing RTMP transfers routing data only about directly attached networks. This helps reduce the overhead traffic associated with distance vector protocols.

Transport Layer Protocols

The **AppleTalk Transaction Protocol (ATP)** is a transport layer protocol that provides connection-oriented, reliable delivery of data across DDP-based networks. ATP uses a bitmap token to provide sequence numbers and han-

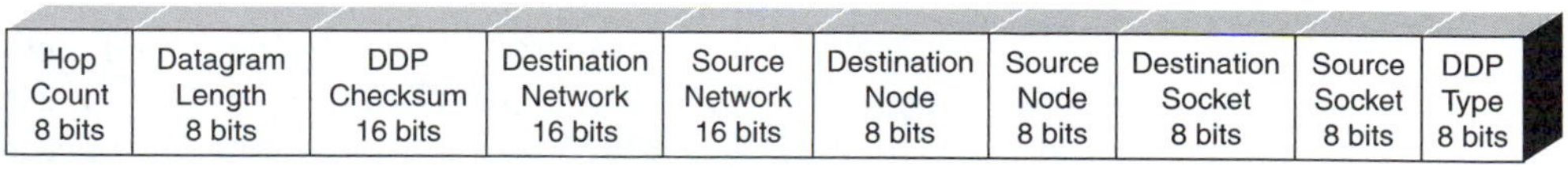

Hop Count 8 bits	Datagram Length 8 bits	DDP Checksum 16 bits	Destination Network 16 bits	Source Network 16 bits	Destination Node 8 bits	Source Node 8 bits	Destination Socket 8 bits	Source Socket 8 bits	DDP Type 8 bits

Figure 4-43   DDP Packet Layout

DDP Packet Field	Function/Importance
Hop Count	A simple hop counter designed to prevent packets from wandering about forever. After 16 hops the packet is discarded.
Datagram Length	Total length of the datagram including the header.
DDP Checksum	Checksum of the entire datagram beginning after the checksum field. A value of zero indicates that the checksum is not in use.
Destination Network	Destination network segment address.
Source Network	Source network segment address.
Destination Node ID	Destination node address.
Source Node ID	Source node address.
Destination Socket	Destination service socket address.
Source Socket	Source service socket address.
DDP Type	Destination network/node/socket in the format NNNN.nn (ss) where NNNN is the network number, nn is the node address, and ss is the socket address.

Figure 4-44   DDP Header Fields

dle acknowledgment and flow control. A series of reserved bytes are used by higher-level protocols for flow management.

Session Layer Protocols

The **AppleTalk Session Protocol (ASP)** manages sessions for higher-layer AppleTalk protocols. ASP issues a unique session identifier for each logical connection and continuously monitors the status of each connection. It maintains idle sessions by periodically exchanging keep-alive frames in order to verify session status.

The **AppleTalk Data Stream Protocol (ADSP)** provides a data channel for the hosts. It is a connection-oriented protocol that guarantees in-sequence data delivery with flow control. ADSP typically bypasses ASP and connects directly to DDP to deliver streaming data.

Other AppleTalk Protocols   Similar to IP-based ping (ICMP Echo/Reply packets), the **AppleTalk Echo Protocol (AEP)** provides an echo service for AppleTalk networks. Up to 585 bytes of data can be specified for an echo transaction.

The **AppleTalk Filing Protocol (AFP)** is the file sharing protocol of the AppleTalk network architecture. It provides application layer connectivity between clients and servers for file sharing. AFP provides a mechanism to support the dual data structure of Apple files. Apple files are comprised of two data structures or forks. The data fork holds the actual data and the resource fork contain information relevant to the operating system such as icons and drivers and applications required to access the file.

The **AppleTalk Name Binding Protocol (NBP)** manages the use of names on an AppleTalk network. NBP maintains a directory of names including those registered by hosts and bound to socket addresses. An AppleTalk host can perform a name lookup to find the node and socket address associated with the name.

The **Printer Access Protocol (PAP)** manages the virtual connections between servers and printers. PAP is used to convey connection status and coordinate data transfer.

The Apple Talk **Zone Information Protocol (ZIP)** manages the relationship between network numbers and zone names. AppleTalk networks primarily implement ZIP in routers that gather network number information by monitoring RTMP packets.

STAND ALONE TRANSPORT LAYER PROTOCOLS

NetBEUI (NBF)

NetBEUI Frame is a simple transport/session layer protocol that does not provide any network layer functionality. The lack of network layer addressing results in a non-routable protocol limited to use on networks consisting of a single network segment.

As the expansion of NetBEUI (NetBIOS Extended User Interface) implies, NetBEUI is an extended version of the original NetBIOS API used in Microsoft LAN Manager and OS/2 LAN Server. NetBEUI is a connection-oriented, reliable protocol that makes use of sequence numbers and acknowledgments to ensure correct data transmission. NBF improves on NetBEUI's data transfer performance in connection-oriented sessions by adopting an **adaptive sliding window protocol** which allows for more efficient data transfer. As will be seen, the word *window* in the name of this protocol is not related to the term *window* as in Windows NT.

NBF is able to adjust how many packets can be sent by the sending computer before an acknowledgment must be received. Ideally, the sending computer wants to send the maximum number of packets possible while avoiding the need to retransmit packets due to transmission errors. The number of packets allowed to be sent before the receipt of an acknowledgment determines the size of the **send window.** Should a negative acknowledgment be received, thereby necessitating a packet retransmission, the sending window will slide back to the packet that was received in error and retransmit it.

The second major improvement of NBF over NetBEUI has to do with **session limits.** Since NetBEUI is NetBIOS-based, it was forced to support the 254-session limit of NetBIOS. The source of this limit is a variable within NetBIOS known as the **local session number.** The local session number is a one byte (eight bit) field with a limit of only 256 possible entries (2 to the eighth = 256, less reserved numbers = 254). Because Windows NT servers using the NBF communications protocol could easily need to support more than 254 sessions, some way to overcome the 254-session limit had to be found. Although a detailed explanation of the mathematical algorithms behind the solution is beyond the scope of this chapter, the key to the solution is a two-dimensional matrix maintained by NBF which maps 254 logical session numbers against the network address of each computer with which it may establish a session. The end result of the maintenance and translation of the various matrices is that each client-to-server connection can support 254 sessions, rather than a grand total for all connections of 254 sessions.

USE OF NETBEUI

Practical Advice and Information

NetBEUI has two selling points: efficiency and ease of configuration. Because NetBEUI is not routable, there is no need to assign network addresses or to reserve space in the packet header to carry them. However, these points are overshadowed by the fact that NetBEUI is non-routable.

The only reason to use NetBEUI is connection with legacy equipment that requires its use. At this point, there is no reason to install a new NetBEUI-based network.

DLC

DLC or **Data Link Control** is a communication protocol traditionally reserved for communication with IBM mainframe computers. DLC is used by Microsoft SNA Gateway for Windows NT to allow transparent interoperability between Windows NT clients and IBM mainframe computers. By using a gateway server, the Windows NT clients do not require any hardware or software modifications in order to communicate with the IBM mainframe. DLC has also been adopted as a means to communicate between print servers and printers directly attached to the network through network interface cards such as Hewlett-Packard JetDirect cards.

Similar to NetBEUI, DLC is a transport-layer-only protocol that is non-routable and applicable only to single segment networks. DLC does adhere to the OSI model principle of independence of the functional layers by running equally well over Ethernet or Token Ring network interface cards and attached network architectures. In addition, DLC is also compatible with the IEEE 802.2 LLC (Logical Link Control) specification and frame layout.

NETWORK PRINTERS AND DLC

Practical Advice and Information

Although DLC is a viable protocol solution for network attached printers, only a single print server can attach to a DLC connected printer at a time. Combined with the requirement that the print server be physically located on the same network segment as the printer, this greatly limits network printing scalability.

If IP is in use on the network, a better solution to connect to network attached printers is the LPR protocol. Most network printer cards support this protocol that allows multiple servers to attach to a single printer. Because LPR is an application layer protocol that runs over IP, it allows print servers throughout the network to print to network attached printers.

■ WAN OR REMOTE ACCESS PROTOCOLS

While this chapter has focused on using local area network technologies such as Ethernet and Token-Ring to provide data link layer services, there are many applications where distance limitations preclude the use of these technologies. For wide area network applications where the network has to span a much larger geographic area there are two additional protocols that can be used in conjunction with a high speed serial link to provide data link layer services: SLIP and PPP.

SLIP

The **Serial Line Internet Protocol (SLIP)** is the older of the two serial WAN protocols. Originally designed as a wan transport for the Internet, SLIP only supports IP as a network layer protocol and is very limited in overall features. SLIP is a point-to-point solution that can establish IP connectivity between two computers over an asynchronous serial link. The asynchronous link can be a direct serial connection or can involve modems over either a dial-up line or leased line.

In terms of the OSI model, SLIP is really providing an alternative data-link layer protocol frame in which to embed IP packets. In a local area network environment, these IP packets would have been embedded in Ethernet, Token Ring, FDDI, or some other network architecture's data link layer frames. Unlike most LAN data-link layer protocols, SLIP does not provide any error detection mechanism. Figure 4-45 illustrates some of the characteristics of SLIP-based connections.

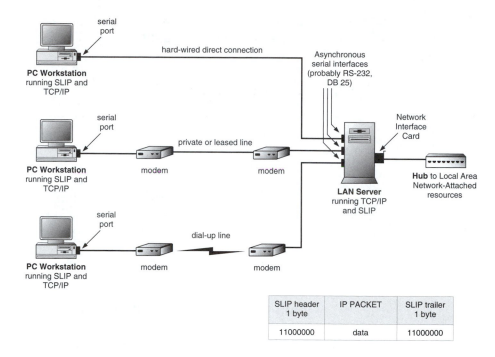

Figure 4-45   SLIP Connections

PPP

The **Point-to-Point Protocol (PPP)** is a WAN datalink layer protocol that seeks to overcome some of the shortcomings of SLIP. As the demand for remote access to enterprise networks has increased due to industry's increased interest in telecommuting, PPP has played an increasingly important role. Strictly speaking, PPP is actually a collection of protocols that has been extended over time by the issuance of additional RFCs (Request for Comments). Although the extendibility of PPP is a positive attribute, it is somewhat of a double-edged sword, as technology's claims of PPP compatibility must be carefully investigated to determine exactly which features of PPP are actually supported.

Perhaps the most important distinction between SLIP and PPP is that while SLIP is only able to transport IP packets, PPP is able to deliver multiple network layer protocols including IP, IPX, AppleTalk, and OSI protocols. To be more specific, PPP is able to support multiple network layer protocols simultaneously over a single WAN connection. PPP is able to establish these connections over a variety of WAN services including ISDN, Frame Relay, SONET, X.25, as well as synchronous and asynchronous serial links. Figure 4-46 illustrates potential PPP implementation scenarios and the PPP frame layout. The PPP header fields are shown in detail in Figure 4-47.

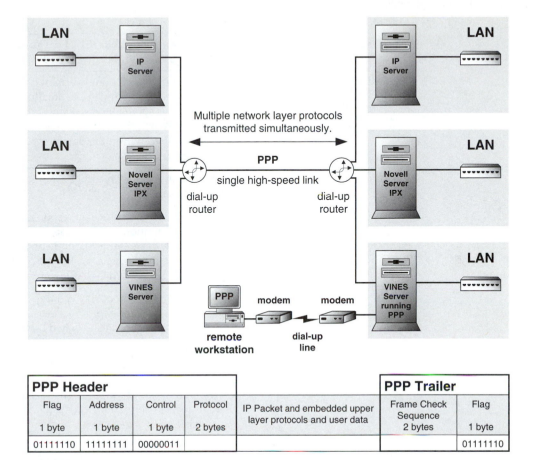

PPP Header					PPP Trailer	
Flag	Address	Control	Protocol	IP Packet and embedded upper layer protocols and user data	Frame Check Sequence	Flag
1 byte	1 byte	1 byte	2 bytes		2 bytes	1 byte
01111110	11111111	00000011				01111110

Figure 4-46   PPP Protocol Layout and Implementation Scenario

MLPPP

While PPP was an improvement over SLIP, **Multilink Point-to-Point Protocol (MLPPP)** improves on PPP by being able to support multiple simultaneous physical WAN links. Rather than replacing PPP, MLPPP is an additional protocol that sits between PPP and the network layer protocols to be transported. In addition to supporting more than one physical WAN link simultaneously, MLPPP can combine multiple channels from a variety of WAN services into a single logical link. Examples of such WAN services include multi-channel switched service like ISDN (Integrated Services Digital Network), as well as packet-switched services like Frame Relay, and cell-based services like ATM. PPP links are identified with a particular MLPPP group identifier during PPP connection setup.

By acting as a separate logical link combining a variety of WAN services between two points to deliver required bandwidth, MLPPP compliant

PPP Header Field	Function/Importance
Flags	A specific sequence of bits (01111110) is used to indicate both the beginning and end of the PPP frame.
Address	Since PPP only creates point-to-point connections, there is no need for addressing on the datalink layer. Therefore this field is set to all ones. Don't forget, the IP address is essential to successful delivery of this packet and is embedded within the data payload section of the PPP frame.
Protocol	There are three major protocol types required to support PPP connections:

LCP – Link Control Protocol is responsible for the creation and termination of the connection. It is able to negotiate with the distant PPP node on such issues as data encapsulation format, packet size, link quality, and authentication (PAP and CHAP).

IPCP – IP Control Protocol is in charge of negotiating with the remote IP node for IP addresses to be used once the connection has been established by LCP.

NCP – Network Control Protocol. Once LCP and IPCP have established the connection, NCP then transports the multiple different network layer protocols between the two end nodes of the connection. A different type of NCP protocol is defined for each network layer protocol transported. |
| **Frame Check Sequence** | This is the standard 16 bit frame check sequence used by the PPP protocol at either end of the connection to detect errors prior to passing embedded information on to the local node for further processing. |

Figure 4-47   PPP Header Fields

devices are also able to deliver "bandwidth on demand" for dial-up connections in a process referred to as **inverse multiplexing** or bonding. In inverse multiplexing a single connection is established for normal operation. When a burst of network traffic begins to erode performance, additional connections can be dynamically added to the connection to provide the required bandwidth. Once bandwidth requirements subside, these additional connections can be dropped. By using inverse multi-plexing, performance can be optimized while minimizing toll charges. This is a particularly important feature for unpredictable, bursty, LAN-to-LAN traffic. Figure 4-48 illustrates the relationship between PPP, MLPPP, network layer protocols, and WAN services.

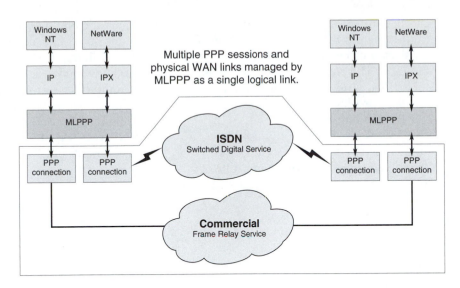

Figure 4-48   Multilink Point-to-Point Protocol

SUMMARY

The network layer of the OSI Network Reference Model is concerned with addressing and routing data packets between nodes on connected inter-networks. All data from higher-level protocols are encapsulated in network layer protocols for transmission across network segments.

Each node must be given a fully qualified network layer address consisting of both a network segment address and a node address. This fully qualified network layer address is resolved to an underlying NIC physical address when the layer 3 packet is encapsulated in a layer 2 frame for transmission at the Data-Link Layer of the OSI model.

The transport layer of the OSI Network Reference Model is concerned with the cre-ation, maintenance, and destruction of logical network connections between nodes. Typically connection-oriented packets sent across a transport layer connection are subject to error correction and flow control.

The session layer of the OSI Network Reference Model is concerned with addressing data streams to particular applications running on each node. These connections, know as sessions, are typically identified via ports and sockets.

There are three major network layer protocol suites currently in use: IPX/SPX, TCP/IP, and AppleTalk. IPX/SPX is the traditional network layer protocol for Novell NetWare systems and provides an easy to configure inter-network protocol.

TCP/IP is the protocol suite used to transmit data across the Internet. The TCP/IP suite consists of three major protocols: IP, TCP, and UDP. The current version of the IP protocol is IPv4. A newer version of the IP protocol (IPv6 or IPng) is currently being prepared for implementation.

AppleTalk is most commonly used in Apple Macintosh installations to support client/server computing applications. Other commonly used protocols for LAN applications include NetBEUI for inter-node communications on a single segment LAN and DLC for connection to LAN-attached printers.

To allow network access across serial lines, remote access protocols are used to provide data-link layer functionality. The two most commonly used remote access protocols are SLIP and PPP. SLIP is limited to carrying IP data, whereas PPP can carry many higher-level protocols.

KEY TERMS

address resolution
Address Resolution Protocol (ARP)
AppleTalk Data Stream Protocol (ADSP)
AppleTalk Echo Protocol (AEP)
AppleTalk Filing Protocol (AFP)
AppleTalk Name Binding Protocol (NBP)
AppleTalk Routing
AppleTalk Session Protocol (ASP)
AppleTalk Transaction Protocol (ATP)
AppleTalk Zone Information Protocol (ZIP)
Boot Protocol (BOOTP)
broadcast address
classfull
connectionless protocols
connection-oriented protocols
Data-Link Control protocol (DLC)
Datagram Delivery Protocol (DDP)
de-encapsulation
default gateway
distance vector protocol
Domain Name System (DNS)

Dynamic Host Control Protocol (DHCP)
encapsulation
fragmentation
host-to-host
Internet Control Message Protocol (ICMP)
Internet Packet Exchange (IPX)
Internet Protocol (IP)
inverse multiplexing
IP Next Generation (IPng)
link state protocol
Maximum Transmission Unit
multicasting
multi-homed
Multilink Point-to-Point Protocol (MLPPP)
NetBEUI Frame (NBF)
NetWare Link Services Protocol (NLSP)
network segment address
node address
octet
Open Shortest Path First (OSPF)
Point-to-Point Protocol (PPP)
Port
Printer Access Protocol (PAP)
Recursion
resolver

Reverse Address Resolution Protocol (RARP)
reverse poison
router
Routing Information Protocol (RIP)
Routing Table Maintenance Protocol (RTMP)
Sequenced Packet Exchange Protocol (SPX)
Serial Line Internet Protocol (SLIP)
Service Advertising Protocol (SAP)
slow convergence
socket
split horizon
subnet mask
subnetworking
Time To Live (TTL)
Transmission Control Protocol/Internet Protocol (TCP/IP)
triggered updates
tuple
virtual circuits
zone

REVIEW QUESTIONS

1. What are the two components of a network layer address?
2. Explain the concept of protocol encapsulation.
3. Explain the concept of address resolution.
4. What layer's address is used to deliver data across an inter-network (end-to-end delivery)?
5. What layer's address is used to deliver data to a NIC within a network segment (point-to-point delivery)?
6. What is meant by protocol fragmentation?
7. What is the implication of fragmentation between the network and data-link layers of the OSI Network Reference Model?
8. What does a router do?
9. What address does a router use to make routing decisions?
10. Why are routing protocols used?
11. What is the difference between a distance vector routing protocol and a link state routing protocol?
12. Explain the difference between connectionless and connection-oriented protocols.
13. Why are all connectionless protocols considered unreliable?
14. What is a session?
15. Explain the purpose of ports and sockets.
16. List the protocols in the IPX/SPX protocol suite. What is the primary purpose of each protocol?
17. How are IPX network segment addresses assigned to IPX routers?
18. How are IPX network segment addresses assigned to non-routing IPX nodes?
19. How are IPX node addresses assigned?
20. What is the address resolution process used to resolve physical addresses from IPX addresses?
21. What is a socket?
22. What is the MTU of an IPX packet?
23. What field in an IPX packet prevents a packet from wandering through an inter-network forever?
24. What is the distance vector routing protocol used with IPX?
25. What is the link state routing protocol used with IPX?

26. List the protocols in the TCP/IP protocol suite. What is the primary purpose of each protocol?
27. How is address resolution accomplished within the IP network layer protocol?
28. Explain the concept of subnetworking.
29. What are the first three bits of a class C IP address?
30. Break the IP address 192.168.101.4 (subnet mask 255.255.255.0) into its network segment and node address components.
31. What class of IP address is 172.16.1.254?
32. What is the broadcast address for the network that contains the node with IP address 192.168.5.68 (subnet mask 255.255.255.0)?
33. Given the Class A IP network address 10.x.x., how many subnetworks of how many nodes can be created by applying a subnet mask of 255.255.0.0?
34. What is the maximum and minimum MTU of IPv4?
35. What are the major problems associated with version four of the IP protocol?
36. What field in an IP header prevents a packet from wandering around an IP network infinitely?
37. What two fields are always present in a network layer packet header regardless of the protocol?
38. What is the purpose of ICMP?
39. Explain the purpose of the Domain Name System.
40. What is the distance vector routing protocol used with IP-based networks?
41. What is the link state protocol used with IP-based networks?
42. What is the purpose of the hop count (or metric) field in a routing table?
43. What is the difference between broadcasting and multicasting?
44. How does IPv6 solve the address space concerns of IPv4?
45. How does IPv6 solve the fragmentation issues associated with IPv4?
46. Does IPv6 implement class of service? How?
47. What new security features does IPv6 add?

48. List three strategies to transition from IPv4 to IPv6.
49. Explain the process of building a TCP connection. What flags are sent and why?
50. List the protocols in the AppleTalk protocol suite. What is the primary purpose of each protocol?
51. How is address resolution implemented in DDP?
52. How many bits are in a fully qualified DDP network layer address?
53. What is the routing protocol used in AppleTalk networks?
54. What is the network layer protocol used in AppleTalk networks?
55. When is NetBEUI a viable primary LAN protocol?
56. For what applications is DLC commonly used?
57. What network layer protocols are supported by the SLIP remote access protocol?
58. What network layer protocols are supported by the PPP remote access protocol?
59. What is the network layer protocol traditionally used with Novell NetWare?
60. What network layer protocol is used on the Internet?

ACTIVITIES

1. Prepare a chart that maps the protocols in the IPX/SPX protocol suite against the OSI Network Reference Model. Which protocols are connectionless and which are connection-oriented?
2. Prepare a chart that maps the protocols in the TCP/IP protocol suite against the OSI Network Reference Model. Which protocols are connectionless and which are connection-oriented?
3. Prepare a chart that maps the protocols in the AppleTalk protocol suite against the OSI Network Reference Model. Which protocols are connectionless and which are connection-oriented?
4. The TCP/IP protocol suite was the first packet-switched protocol suite. Research the history of TCP/IP and prepare a report explaining its evolution.
5. Research the capabilities of current operating systems to support IPv6.
6. Visit the network department of your school or company. Ask about the design of its data network. Prepare a chart that explains the network address scheme used.
7. Visit the network department of your school or company. Ask about its plans for implementing IPv6.
8. Visit the network department of your school or company. Prepare a report that describes the routing protocols used.
9. Are there other LAN protocols available than those discussed in this chapter? Research and prepare a paper on other LAN protocols.
10. Routers can translate between different network layer protocols. Research the capabilities of such a router to translate between IP and IPX.

CASE STUDY

ATM Answered the Call for Mentor Graphics

Mentor Graphics' network operations staff is faced with a unique situation: squeezing more out of its "old" ATM net.

The company installed a private ATM network two years ago to solve one major problem: File transfers by Mentor's software engineering staff consistently clogged the company's 56K bit/sec private-line network, preventing the sales force from accessing its interactive applications.

"The priority was: Make that stop," says Thomas Magee, Mentor's network operations manager.

Because the firm was an early adopter of ATM WAN technology, it had to take the hardware available at the time, and that resulted in an overbuilt net that is not only bullet-proof, but may be even bomb-proof, Magee says. If Mentor's backbone were built today, many of the 18 Nortel Networks ATM switches and 20 Nortel PBXs in the net could be replaced with smaller, less expensive models.

Rather than swap out the older, larger switches, Mentor made better use of the backbone's power and ability to support mixed voice and data nets.

Magee knows that at least $50,000 per month has been cut off voice expenses because the company recently directed all interoffice traffic over the private ATM net rather than the public phone network.

Also, an internal 800 number used to access a centralized voice mail system has been discontinued because most of the voice mail is handled by one PBX connected to the ATM net. On the voice side, the company recently upgraded its dumb key systems to PBXs in all offices to allow direct inward dialing so customers can more easily reach sales staff. The PBXs also support call detail recording that can better control phone costs.

The net boosts backbone bandwidth from 56K bit/sec to 1.5M bit/sec, and branch-office trunks from 56K bit/sec to 256K bit/sec. The increased bandwidth solved the logjam problem and has allowed room for ever-increasing data traffic over the net.

The ATM switches also allow for more efficient use of the net by diverting traffic around congested links. That redirection means more traffic can be added without buying larger private lines between sites.

The $3.2 million that Mentor spent on the initial overhaul included rebuilding its voice and data nets. But because features have been added that were not in the original network, it is impossible to quantify return on investment for the project, Magee says.

Source: Tim Greene, "ATM Answered the Call for Mentor Graphics," *Network World,* vol. 16, no. 2 (January 11, 1999), p. 21. Copyright (January 11, 1999), Network World.

BUSINESS CASE STUDY QUESTIONS

Activities

1. Complete a top-down model for this case by gleaning facts from the case and placing them in the proper layer of the top-down model.

After completing the top-down model, analyze and detail those instances where requirements were clearly passed down from upper layers to lower layers of the model and where solutions to those requirements were passed up from lower layers to upper layers of the model.

2. Detail any questions about the case that may occur to you for which answers are not clearly stated in the article.

Business

1. What was the primary reason that Mentor Graphics initially installed their ATM network?

2. How has Mentor Graphics managed to save at least $50,000 per month from their network?

3. It could be said that the majority of the case study violates the top-down model. Why?

Application

1. What business applications has Mentor Graphics added to their network since the initial roll-out?

2. What applications have been added to the ATM attached PBXs to improve customer service?

Data

1. What kind of data does the system carry?

Network

1. What types of locations are served by the network?

2. How much bandwidth is dedicated to each type of location?

Technology

1. What technology is used to provide the required bandwidth?

2. Who manufactured the equipment in the network?

LOCAL AREA NETWORK SOFTWARE

Part 2 of the text builds on the knowledge of LAN infrastructure and software gained in Part 1 by exploring the software components associated with LAN systems. These concepts are explored from network operating systems through LAN application software.

Chapter 5, "Local Area Network Operating Systems," introduces the reader to LAN-enabled operating systems in general. In this chapter, network operating system functionality is examined for both client and server network operating systems. This functionality is representative of current network operating systems in general rather than any particular product. This review of overall network operating system functionality will serve as a basis of comparison for the more detailed analysis of particular network operating systems offered in Chapters 6 through 8.

Chapter 6, "Novell NetWare," focuses on the NetWare network operating system from Novell using the framework developed in Chapter 5. Each major version of NetWare is covered in detail throughout the course of the chapter. Special attention is paid to the communications protocols that perform the bulk of the work in any network operating system. Remote access and interoperability with other network operating systems such as Windows are explored from both architectural and functional perspectives as well. Finally, issues and options surrounding the migration between NetWare versions are detailed.

Chapter 7, "Windows NT (2000)," reviews the Microsoft Windows NT and Windows 2000 family of network operating systems using the framework developed in Chapter 5. The overall purpose of the chapter is to introduce the reader to the important architectural and functional characteristics of Windows NT/2000. Special emphasis is placed on the issues surrounding the release of Windows 2000 and on migration issues.

Chapter 8, "UNIX," analyzes UNIX as a network operating system using the framework developed in Chapter 5. Although not distributed as a ready-to-run network operating system solution, a network operating system can be built using UNIX as a foundation. Combined with NFS to provide a network aware file system, UNIX can offer the majority of the functionality of commercially available single-product network operating systems.

Chapter 9, "Middleware," introduces the reader to Middleware. Middleware can be thought of as the "/" in client/server computing—the glue that holds the client and server applications together. Various categories of Middleware are introduced throughout the chapter and a detailed technical description of each is presented.

Chapter 10, "Client/Server Application Development and Integration," focuses on methods to develop network applications. Various categories of application development environments and methods of deploying the resulting applications throughout the network are introduced. While many of the discussed development environments can be used to develop stand-alone applications, emphasis is placed on the features required to develop and deploy client/server applications. Methods of integrating client/server applications with existing applications are also covered.

Chapter 11, "Local Area Network Applications Software," highlights several key LAN applications. LAN software is distinguished from other application software by its ability to communicate across the LAN between clients and servers, between two or more servers, and/or to enterprise management workstations. In other words, software that can be run on a stand-alone machine is by definition not LAN software. While most software is now "LAN aware" with optional features that only run in a LAN environment, the software discussed in this chapter can be run only on LAN-attached computers.

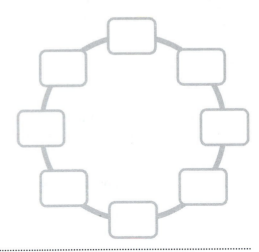

CHAPTER 5

LOCAL AREA NETWORK OPERATING SYSTEMS

Concepts Reinforced

OSI Model	Top-Down Model
Protocols and Standards	Hardware/Software Compatibility
Client/Server Technology Model	Network Architectures
LAN Software Architecture	

Concepts Introduced

Network Operating System Functionality	Functional Network Analysis
Peer-to-Peer Network Operating Systems	Client/Server Network Operating Systems
Network Technology Analysis	Network Operating Systems Architectures
Client Network Operating Systems	Server Network Operating Systems

OBJECTIVES

After mastering the material in this chapter you should:

1. Understand the compatibility issues involved with implementing LAN software

2. Understand the basics of network operating system functionality

3. Understand the important differences between peer-to-peer and client/server network operating systems architectures.

4. Understand the emerging role of the client network operating system and the universal client.

5. Understand how to analyze functional networking requirements and match those requirements to available technology.

■ INTRODUCTION

Network operating systems, like most other aspects of data communications, are undergoing tremendous change. As a result, before examining the operational characteristics of a particular network operating system, it is important to gain an overall perspective of network operating systems in general. In particular, network operating systems architectures are in a state of transition from closed environments in which only clients and servers running the same network operating system could interact, to open environments in which universal clients are able to interoperate with servers running any network operating system.

In this chapter network operating system functionality is examined for both client and server network operating systems. This functionality is representative of current network operating systems in general rather than any particular product. This review of overall network operating system functionality will serve as a basis of comparison for the more detailed analysis of particular network operating systems offered in Chapters 6 through 8.

■ NETWORK OPERATING SYSTEMS ARCHITECTURES

Traditional Differentiation: Peer-to-Peer vs. Client/Server

Traditionally, there were two major product categories of network operating systems:

- **Peer-to-peer network operating systems** also known as DOS-based LANs or Low-cost LANs, offered easy to install and use file and print services for workgroup and departmental networking needs.

- **Client/Server network operating systems** offered more powerful capabilities including the ability to support hundreds of users, and the ability to interact with other network operating systems via gateways. These client/server network operating systems were both considerably more expensive and considerably more complicated to install and administer than peer-to-peer network operating systems.

Peer-to-Peer   One of the early appeals of peer-to-peer network operating systems was their relatively minimal hardware requirements in terms of memory and disk space. In addition, the fact that they ran as a background application over the DOS operating system made them considerably less complicated to install and administer than client/server network operating systems. When printer sharing and file sharing for fewer than 50 users represented the major functional requirements of a network operating system, peer-to-peer network operating systems such as Artisoft's LANtastic and

Performance Technology's PowerLAN were popular choices in this technology category.

In most peer-to-peer LANs, individual workstations can be configured as a service requester (client), a service provider (server), or a combination of the two. The terms *client* and *server* in this case describe the workstation's functional role in the network. The installed network operating system is still considered a peer-to-peer network operating system, because all workstations in the network use the same networking software. Designed as a low-cost, workgroup solution, most peer-to-peer network operating systems lacked the ability to access servers of client/server network operating systems and suffered from exponential performance decreases as the number of users increased. As a result, traditional peer-to-peer network operating systems were characterized as lacking interoperability and scalability.

Client/Server   In contrast to the homogeneous peer-to-peer software environment, traditional client/server network operating systems require two distinct software products for client and server computers. The specialized client software required less memory, disk space, and was less expensive than the more complicated and expensive server software. NetWare 3.12 and Microsoft LANManager are examples of traditional client/server network operating systems. The client software was made to interact with the corresponding server software. As a result, although traditional client/server network operating systems overcame the scalability limitation of peer-to-peer network operating systems, they did not necessarily overcome the interoperability limitation. Functionally, client/server network operating systems offered faster, more reliable performance than peer-to-peer LANs as well as improved administration, scalability, and security. Figure 5-1 illustrates the key differences between traditional peer-to-peer and client/server network operating systems.

Current Differentiation: Client NOS vs. Server NOS

Functional Requirements of Today's Network Operating Systems   Although traditional peer-to-peer and client/server network operating systems successfully met the functional requirements for workgroup and departmental computing, since these departmental LANs needed to be integrated into a single, cohesive, interoperable, enterprise-wide information system, the limitations of these traditional NOS (network operating system) architectures became evident.

In order to understand the architectural specifications of today's network operating systems, it is first necessary to understand the functional requirements that these network operating systems must deliver. In taking a top-down approach to network operating system requirements analysis, one might ask, "What are users of an enterprise-wide information system demanding of a network operating system in terms of services?" The answer

Peer-to-Peer

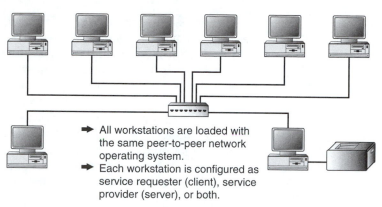

➡ All workstations are loaded with the same peer-to-peer network operating system.
➡ Each workstation is configured as service requester (client), service provider (server), or both.

Client/Server

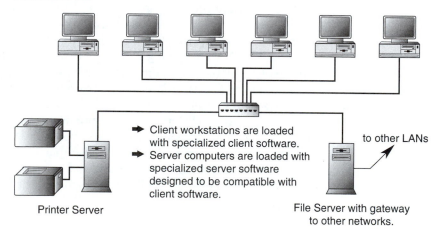

➡ Client workstations are loaded with specialized client software.
➡ Server computers are loaded with specialized server software designed to be compatible with client software.

to other LANs

Printer Server

File Server with gateway to other networks.

Figure 5-1 Peer-to-Peer vs. Client/Server Network Operating Systems

to this question lies in the application layer of the top-down model. Given that it is distributed applications which will enable enterprise-wide productivity and decision making, the underlying network operating systems must support these distributed applications by supplying the message services and global directory services required to execute these applications in an enterprise-wide, multiple server environment.

Figure 5-2 illustrates these functional requirements and contrasts them with the requirements traditionally demanded of client/server and peer-to-peer network operating systems.

As illustrated in Figure 5-2, the new or emerging demands being put on network operating systems are:

		All services delivered seamlessly across multiple server platforms regardless of installed network operating system		
Traditional Requirements		Emerging Requirements		
FILE SERVICES	PRINTER SERVICES	APPLICATION SERVICES	DIRECTORY SERVICES	INTEGRATION/MIGRATION SERVICES
		➡ Database back-end engines ➡ Messaging/communication back-end engines SUPPORT FOR: ➡ 32-bit symmetrical multiprocessing ➡ Preemptive multitasking ➡ Applications run in protected memory mode ➡ Multithreading	➡ Global directory or naming services ➡ All network objects defined in single location and shared by all applications ➡ Directory information is stored in replicated, distributed databases for reliability, redundancy, fault tolerance	➡ Allow multiple different client network operating systems to transparently interoperate with multiple different server network operating systems ➡ Provide easy-to-implement paths for upgrades to more-recent versions or migration to different network operating systems

Figure 5-2   Required Network Operating System Services: Traditional vs. Current

- **Application Services**
- **Directory Services**
- **Integration/Migration Services**

In order to successfully meet these functional requirements, network operating system architectures have shifted from integrated, single-vendor client/server network operating systems to independent, distinct, multi-vendor, client and server network operating systems. The functional characteristics of these distinct client and server network operating systems are described in detail later in this chapter. Figure 5-3 illustrates this architectural shift in network operating system development.

Client Network Operating Systems: The Universal Client   **Client network operating systems,** as illustrated in Figure 5-3, integrate traditional operating system functionality with highly configurable networking features to enable communication with a variety of network operating system servers. The client workstation's ability to interoperate transparently with a number of different network operating system servers without the need for additional products or configurations breaks the traditional hard linkage between client and server NOS. This ability is commonly referred to as **universal client** capability.

Server Network Operating Systems   Because the client and server platforms have been decoupled, **server network operating systems** can be selected based on their performance characteristics for a given function. For example, NetWare servers are often employed as file and print servers, whereas Windows NT, OS/2, or UNIX servers are more likely to be employed as applica-

Client/Server Network Operating System

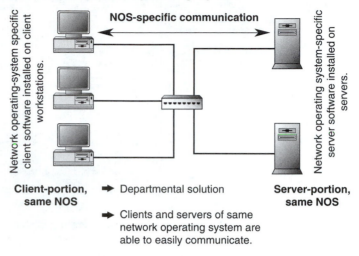

Client-portion, same NOS

➡ Departmental solution

➡ Clients and servers of same network operating system are able to easily communicate.

Server-portion, same NOS

Client Network Operating System
and
Server Network Operating System

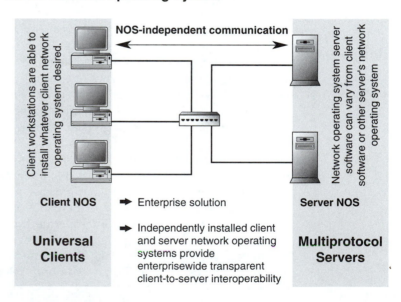

Client NOS

➡ Enterprise solution

➡ Independently installed client and server network operating systems provide enterprisewide transparent client-to-server interoperability

Universal Clients

Server NOS

Multiprotocol Servers

Figure 5-3 Client/Server NOS vs. Client *and* Server NOS

tion servers. Because the universal client has the ability to communicate with any server, and the server has the ability to communicate with any client, the choice of server network operating system can be based on optimizing functional performance rather than whether the system simply provides interoperability.

■ CLIENT NETWORK OPERATING SYSTEM FUNCTIONALITY

Having gained an understanding of the new architectural arrangement of network operating systems consisting of distinct, interoperable, multi-vendor, client and server network operating systems, the functional aspects of client network operating systems categories can be examined.

Client network operating systems such as Windows 9x, Windows NT Workstation, and the Macinstosh OS offer three major categories of functionality:

- Operating system capabilities

- Peer-to-peer networking capabilities

- Client software for communicating with various network operating systems

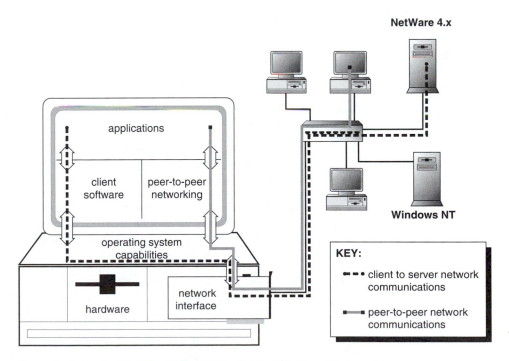

Figure 5-4   Logical Relationship of Client NOS Functional Categories

The logical relationship of these three distinct yet complementary categories of functionality is illustrated in Figure 5-4. This figure also points out potential areas for compatibility and protocol consideration where the various software and hardware layers interface.

The importance of each of these three functional categories to the overall network operating system is covered in the following sections together with key implementation differences between technologies. From such a review of network operating system functionality, the network analyst should be able to construct a logical network design listing the functionality required to meet the business objectives.

This logical network design is then used as an evaluation mechanism for selecting available technologies. Logical network design functionality can be compared to available technology's delivered functionality in a technology analysis grid such as Figure 5-15 (Server Network Operating System Technology Analysis Grid). As stated in previous chapters, the advantage to employing a technology analysis grid in such an endeavor is that it ensures that purchase decisions or recommendations are made based on facts rather than creative packaging or effective marketing.

Operating System Capabilities

Client operating systems concepts and capabilities are covered in the supplemental Chapter 2, located on the accompanying CD-ROM. The following operating systems characteristics are listed and briefly explained here from the perspective of each characteristic's importance to overall network operating system performance.

- 32-bit operating system—32-bit operating systems will allow more sophisticated and higher performance 32-bit applications to execute more quickly.

- Preemptive multitasking—Preemptive multitasking prevents misbehaving programs from monopolizing systems resources at the expense of the performance of other applications.

- Protected memory space—Protected memory space prevents application programs from accidentally writing into each other's or the operating system's memory space, thereby causing general protection faults and/or system crashes.

- Support for Symmetrical Multiprocessing—SMP support is especially important for server network operating systems due to the processing load imposed by multiple simultaneous requests for services from clients. Some high-powered client applications such as 3-D modeling or simulation software may warrant SMP support on client platforms as well.

- Multithreading—Multithreaded applications are able to achieve performance increases only if they are executed by an operating system that supports multithreaded applications, allowing more than one sub-process to execute simultaneously.

User Interface   Object Oriented User Interfaces present the user with a graphical desktop on which objects such as files, directories, folders, disk drives, programs, or devices can be arranged according to the user's whim. More important, as objects are moved around the desktop, they retain their characteristic properties. As a result, when a desktop object is clicked upon, only legitimate actions presented in context-sensitive menus appropriate for the object class are available.

Unlike object-oriented user interfaces, Windows-based user interfaces, although graphical, do not allow icons representing directories, files, disk drives, and such to be broken out of a particular Window and placed directly on the desktop.

Application Program Support   A very important aspect of any migration plan to a new client network operating system is the extent of support for **backward compatibility** in terms of application support, also known as **legacy application** support. It should be obvious that most companies cannot afford to replace or rewrite all of their application software in order to upgrade to a new client network operating system.

Although 32-bit client network operating systems are desirable and most current network-based applications are 32-bit, many custom software solutions are still 16-bit. In addition, many of these 16-bit application programs bypass supported API calls and commands in favor of directly addressing hardware devices. Initially done in the interest of increasing performance, these applications significantly limit multi-tasking and interoperability. Programs or subroutines that write directly to computer hardware are sometimes referred to as employing **real-mode device drivers.**

Many 32-bit network operating systems do not allow application programs to address or control hardware directly in the interest of security and protecting applications from using each other's assigned memory spaces and causing system crashes. Instead, these more secure 32-bit operating systems control access to hardware and certain system services via **virtual device drivers,** otherwise known as **VxDs.** Windows NT is perhaps the best example of a 32-bit network operating system that prevents direct hardware addressing. As a result, many 16-bit applications, particularly highly graphical computer games, will not execute over the Windows NT network operating system. On the other hand, Windows NT is extremely stable.

Another issue concerning the execution of 16-bit applications is whether or not those applications execute in a shared memory address space, sometimes referred to as a **16-bit sub-system.** If this is the case, then a single misbehaving 16-bit application can crash the 16-bit sub-system and all other executing 16-bit applications. Some 32-bit operating systems allow each 16-bit application to execute in its own protected memory execution area.

When it comes to 32-bit applications, client network operating systems may execute these applications in their own address space, otherwise known as **protected memory mode.** However, all of these protected mode 32-bit applications may execute over a single 32-bit sub-system in which case a single misbehaving 32-bit application can crash the entire 32-bit sub-system and all other associated 32-bit applications.

Whether or not an application is executable over a particular network operating system is dependent upon whether or not that application issues commands and requests for network-based services in a predetermined format defined by the network operating system's **application program interface (API).** Each network operating system has its own unique API or variation. For example, both Microsoft NT and Windows 9x support variations of the Win32 API.

Some client network operating systems, such as Windows NT, have the ability to support multiple APIs and multiple different operating system sub-systems, sometimes known as **virtual machines.** This feature allows applications written for a variety of operating systems such as OS/2, DOS, or POSIX to execute over a single client network operating system.

Figure 5-5 illustrates some of the concepts of Application Program Support by Client Network Operating Systems.

Plug-n-play Features   One of the largest problems with installing new devices into a computer was configuring the hardware's resource usage. **Plug-n-play (PnP),** included in varying degrees in most client network operating systems, is designed to free users from having to understand and worry about such things as IRQs (Interrupt Requests), DMA (Direct Memory Access) channels, memory addresses, COM ports, and editing CONFIG.SYS whenever they want to add a device to their computer.

Although the goal of automatic hardware configuration has not been fully realized, definite progress has been made. Ideally P-n-P functionality will:

- automatically detect the addition or removal of PnP devices

- set all of the previously mentioned settings so that they do not conflict with other devices

- automatically load necessary drivers to enable the particular device

PnP standards also include support for **dynamic reconfiguration** which enables

- PCMCIA cards being inserted into and removed from computers without a need to reboot

**Real Mode Drivers
versus API and VXD**

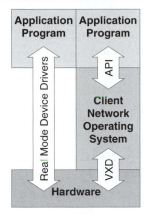

Shared 16-bit Subsystems versus Individual 16-bit Address Spaces

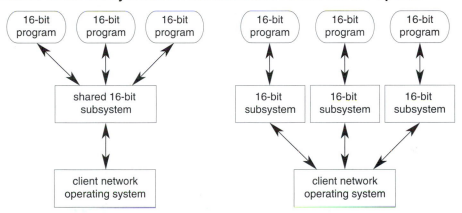

A single misbehaving program can crash the entire subsystem.

A single misbehaving program crashes only its own 16-bit subsystem.

Figure 5-5   Application Program Support by Client Network Operating Systems

- Hot docking (powered up) of laptop computers into docking bays or stations.

- Dynamic reconfiguration-aware applications software that could automatically respond to changes in system configuration

Compatibility issues are important to the achievement of full PnP functionality. To be specific, three distinct elements must all support PnP standards:

1. A **PnP BIOS** (Basic Input Output System) is required to interface directly to both PnP and non-PnP compliant hardware.

2. PnP capabilities must be supported by the client network operating system through interaction with the PnP BIOS. Windows 9x possesses the most PnP capability among currently available client network operating systems.

3. The devices installed must be PnP compliant. This basically means that the manufacturers of these devices must add some additional software and processing power so that these devices can converse transparently with the PnP operating system and BIOS. In some cases, PnP-compliant device drivers may also be required.

In order to cater to the vast majority of legacy (non-PnP compliant) devices, many PnP-compliant client network operating systems ease configuration hassles by using a variety of detection techniques. Non-PnP devices are detected by the client operating system through an assistant agent program, sometimes referred to as a hardware wizard, which walks the user through the configuration routine. Such programs are often capable of detecting and displaying IRQs and DMA addresses used by other devices, allowing users to accept supplied default answers in this semiautomatic configuration scenario.

Peer-to-Peer Networking Capabilities

Most current network client operating systems also include peer-to-peer networking capability. These features allow each client to interact at a basic level with other clients. By utilizing these features many small businesses can avoid the expense of implementing a large-scale server environment.

File and Printer Sharing   Perhaps the most basic peer-to-peer network function is file and printer sharing. In many cases, other resources such as CD-ROM drives and fax modems can also be shared. Network operating systems supporting peer-to-peer networking can vary widely in terms of file access security features. The level at which access can be controlled (disk, directory, or file level) is sometimes referred to as the **granularity** of the access control scheme. Access is controlled on a per user or per group basis. Sophistication of the printer management facility can also vary from one client network operating system to another.

As client network operating systems have grown in sophistication, file and printer sharing services are now available to client platforms other than those configured with identical client network operating systems. Figure 5-6 illustrates some of the cross-platform peer-to-peer file and printer sharing capabilities of Windows 9x.

WIndows '9x, WIndows NT/2000, and Windows for Workgroups Clients

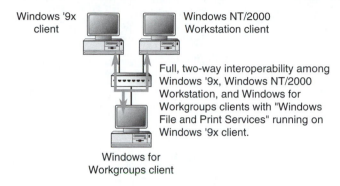

Windows '9x and NetWare Clients

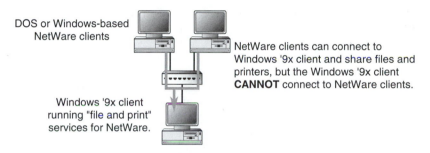

Figure 5-6   Cross-platform File and Printer Sharing

Practical Advice and Information

One important point to be made regarding cross-platform interoperability is that interoperability solutions cannot be assumed to be two-way or reversible. For example, as illustrated in Figure 5-6, although NetWare clients are able to connect to a Windows `95 client running File and Print Services for NetWare, the converse is not true. Windows 9x clients are not able to log into, or share the disks and files of NetWare clients.

Workgroup Applications   Ever striving to find new ways to differentiate themselves from the competition, client network operating systems are usually offered with bundled workgroup application software such as:

- Terminal emulation
- Calculator
- Clock
- Games

- Paintbrush

- Sound recorder

- Remote access software

- CD player

- Backup

- Chat

- Phone dialer

- Performance and network monitors

- Diagnostic software

- Screen savers

- Web browsers

- Fax access software

Managerial Perspective

The client network operating system that offers the greatest number of workgroup applications is not necessarily the best or most appropriate choice. Although free application software is nice, priority should be given to client network operating systems characteristics such as:

- Application program support and operating system characteristics

- Peer-to-peer networking capabilities

- Flexibility and ease of installation and use in acting as a client to a variety of different server network operating systems

Client network operating systems that are able to connect to many different server operating systems are sometimes referred to as a universal client. In support of multi-vendor, multi-platform, distributed information systems, this is probably the most important evaluation criterion when selecting a client network operating system.

Client Networking Capabilities

As illustrated architecturally in Figure 5-7, there are three distinct elements of client network functionality in addition to the previously mentioned required application support capabilities. In some cases, more than one alternative is offered for each of the following elements:

- Client software and network drivers that allow a particular client to communicate with a compatible server. These are MAC (Media Access Control) protocol specifications such as NDIS and ODI.

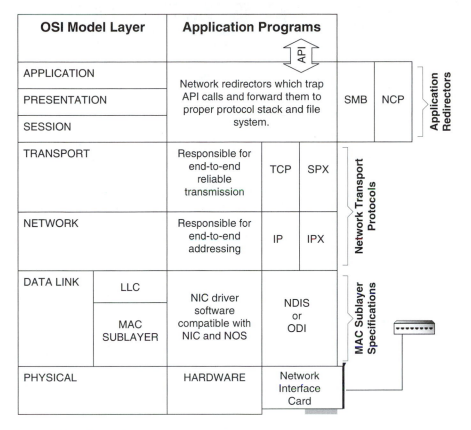

OSI Model Layer		Application Programs				
APPLICATION		Network redirectors which trap API calls and forward them to proper protocol stack and file system.			SMB	NCP
PRESENTATION						
SESSION						
TRANSPORT		Responsible for end-to-end reliable transmission	TCP	SPX		
NETWORK		Responsible for end-to-end addressing	IP	IPX		
DATA LINK	LLC	NIC driver software compatible with NIC and NOS	NDIS or ODI			
	MAC SUBLAYER					
PHYSICAL		HARDWARE	Network Interface Card			

Figure 5-7 Client Network Functionality

- Network transport protocols that package and transport messages between clients and servers. These protocols correspond to the network and transport layers of the OSI model.

- Network re-directors that trap API (application program interface) calls and process them appropriately. Redirectors are concerned with providing file system related services in support of application programs.

More than one alternative protocol may be provided in a given client network operating system for each of the three network protocol categories. Figure 5-8 displays the protocol stacks for the following four different client network operating systems:

- Windows for Workgroups

- Windows NT Workstation

- Windows 9x

Rather than organize protocols according to the OSI Network Reference Model, Figure 5-8 divides the protocols into layers according to networking functionality.

Connecting Clients to Multiple Servers   In most client network operating systems, the combination of these three elements of network functionality combine to allow client platforms to automatically find and connect to servers. For example, a properly configured Windows NT client will be able to automatically display network connections and connect to Windows NT and Net-Ware servers which are physically reachable and to which the client has been assigned access privileges. The client software does not have to be pre-configured with any information about these servers. The server discovery and access are handled transparently by the client network operating system.

In addition to network operating system client software for specific server network operating systems such as NetWare and Windows NT Server, special-

	Windows for Workgroups	Windows NT/2000 Workstation	Windows '9x
Application Support	WIN16 API 16-bit Windows applications supported	WIN32 API 32-bit and some 16-bit Windows applications supported	WIN32 API 32-bit and most 16-bit Windows applications supported
Application Redirectors and File Systems	SMB (Server Message Block Redirector (Microsoft)); FAT (File Allocation Table File System (DOS/Windows))	NCP (Netware Core Protocol Redirector (Novell)); SMB (Server Message Block Redirector (Microsoft)); FAT (File Allocation Table File System (DOS/Windows)); NTFS (NT File System)	NCP (Netware Core Protocol Redirector (Novell)); SMB (Server Message Block Redirector (Microsoft)); FAT (File Allocation Table File System (DOS/Windows))
Network Transport Protocols	IPX/SPX; NETBEUI (NetBIOS Extended User Interface (Microsoft)); TCP/IP	IPX/SPX; NETBEUI (NetBIOS Extended User Interface (Microsoft)); TCP/IP; Apple-Talk	IPX/SPX; NETBEUI (NetBIOS Extended User Interface (Microsoft)); TCP/IP
MAC Sublayer Specifications	NDIS (Network Data-Link Interface Specification (Microsoft/3Com)); ODI (Open Data-Link Interface (Novell))	NDIS (Network Data-Link Interface Specification (Microsoft/3Com))	NDIS (Network Data-Link Interface Specification (Microsoft/3Com)); ODI (Open Data-Link Interface (Novell))

Figure 5-8   Supported Protocol Stacks for Major Client Network Operating Systems

ized application-oriented client software is often also included in client network operating systems. Examples of such network applications include:

- Web browsers

- FTP (File transfer protocol) client software

- E-mail client software

- Scheduling systems client software

In the case of the e-mail and scheduling clients, compatible e-mail and scheduling application servers must be available to achieve maximum benefit. The client portion is merely the front-end to a back-end application engine executing in some other network-accessible location. Most e-mail clients do support the POP3 and SMTP protocols required to connect to Internet mail servers.

Remote Access   With the advent of telecommuting, access to network data from outside the network has become a key concern. Specialized client software written to allow remote access to data contained on network servers is included with or available for most client network operating systems. These remote access clients connect to remote access servers. Remote access servers can be implemented as either specialized software running on a network server operating system or as a specialized hardware solution. The remote access server is specifically designed to handle incoming remote access clients and usually contains specialized security features to ensure the integrity of network data. Common remote access servers that run on typical server platforms include:

- Windows NT Remote Access Server

- NetWare Connect and Border Manager

These servers can be installed either on a dedicated communications server, or as an additional service on existing application servers. Specialized hardware solutions are stand-alone devices also known as **dial-up servers** or **remote node servers.** Such a self-contained unit includes modems, communications software, and NOS-specific software combined into a turnkey system. Vendors of such hardware remote access solutions provide software that runs on the remote client required to access the network through the remote access server.

Some client network operating systems include not only remote access client software, but also remote access server software. With this capability, other remote access clients can dial-in to each other for file sharing, e-mail exchange, schedule synchronization, and such. Windows NT Workstation extends this scenario by offering limited local server capability, as well as remote access server capability. Figure 5-9 illustrates the relationship

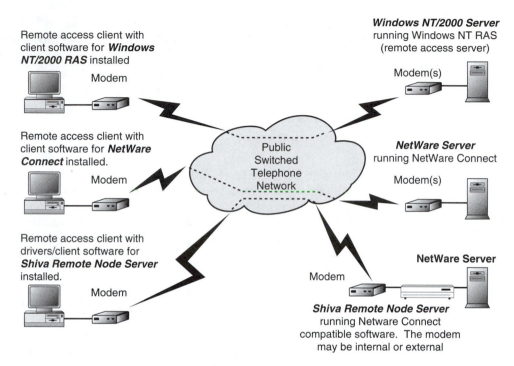

Figure 5-9   Remote Access Client Software

between remote access client and remote access server software as well as the architectural differences between applications server-based and remote-node server-based remote access.

Laptop Synchronization   Because mobile computing on notebook computers has grown exponentially, a need to synchronize versions of files on laptops and desktop workstations has quickly become apparent. Such **file synchronization software** was initially available as a stand-alone product or included as a feature on remote access or file transfer packages. Also known as **version control software** or **directory synchronization software,** this valuable software is now often included as a standard or optional feature in client network operating systems.

Laptops may be linked to their related desktop system in a number of different ways:

- The laptop and desktop computer systems may be locally linked directly via serial or parallel cables.

- The laptop and desktop computer systems may be remotely linked via modems and a dial-up line.

- The laptop and desktop computer system may be remotely linked via a local area network running a network operating system such as NetWare, Windows for Workgroups, or Windows NT.

Client network operating systems should support laptop synchronization in all of the aforementioned connectivity options, especially LAN-based alternatives. Laptop synchronization should happen automatically when the laptop computer is docked in its docking station. E-mail clients and scheduling system client software should automatically synchronize with the LAN-attached e-mail and scheduling application servers.

Some of the important functional characteristics or differences among laptop synchronization software are the following:

- Copy by date option, in which files and directories can be selectively synchronized by selected data range.

- Bi-directional option, in which file synchronization can occur from laptop to desktop, desktop to laptop, or both (bidirectional).

- Cloning option, which guarantees that the contents of a directory on one system exactly match the contents of the same directory on another system.

- Refresh option, copying only newer versions of files that are already located on both systems from one system to another.

- **Delta file synchronization,** perhaps the most significant file synchronization option in terms of its potential impact on reducing required bandwidth and file transfer time to accomplish the synchronization. Rather than sending entire files across the dial-up or LAN link, delta file synchronization transfers only the changes to those files.

Applied Problem Solving

Client Network Operating System Technology Analysis

Figure 5-10 is a technology analysis grid comparing key architectural and functional characteristics of the following client network operating systems:

- Windows for Workgroups

- Windows NT Workstation

- Windows 9x

This grid is included as an example of how technology analysis grids can be used to effectively map required networking functional requirements to available technology solutions in an objective manner. This technology

Client Network Operating System Category	Windows for Workgroups	Windows 9x	Windows NT Workstation
Hardware and Platform			
Required-Recommended Memory	4MB–8MB	16MB–32	32MB–64 MB
16 or 32 bit	16 bit	32 bit	32 bit
User Interface	Windows	Object-oriented desktop	Windows
Operating System Capabilities			
Preemptive Multitasking	no	yes	yes
Supports SMP	no	no	yes
Protected Memory Program Execution	no	yes	yes
Multithreading	no	yes	yes
Runs 32-bit Applications	no	yes	yes
Runs 16-bit Applications	yes	yes	Some. Won't support real-mode drivers
Peer-to-Peer Networking			
File and Printer Sharing	yes	yes	yes
Workgroup Applications	yes	yes	yes
Client Networking			
Network Clients	Windows NT, Microsoft Mail and Schedule	Windows NT, NetWare, Microsoft Exchange	NetWare, FTP, Internet
Network Transport Protocols	NetBEUI	NetBEUI, TCP/IP, IPX/SPX	NetBEUI, TCP/IP, IPX/SPX, Appletalk
Remote Access	yes	yes	yes
Laptop Synchronization	no	yes	no

Figure 5-10   Client Network Operating System Technology Analysis Grid

analysis grid is not meant to be absolutely authoritative or all-inclusive. Its primary purpose is to provide a concrete example of the type of analysis tool used in a professional, top-down, network analysis and design methodology. It is expected that network analysts will create new technology analysis grids for each networking analysis opportunity based on their own networking functional requirements and the latest technology specifications available from buyer's guides or product reviews.

The client network operating system technology analysis grid is divided into the following major sections:

- Hardware/Platform-Related Characteristics

- Operating System Capabilities

- Peer-to-Peer Networking Capabilities

- Client Networking Capabilities

▓ SERVER NETWORK OPERATING SYSTEM FUNCTIONALITY

Changing Role of the Server Network Operating System

Traditionally, file and printer sharing services were the primary required functionality of server-based network operating systems. However, as client/server information systems have boomed in popularity, **application services** have become one of the most important criteria in server network operating system selection. The distributed applications of the client/server model require distinct client and server portions applications to interact in order to perform the required task as efficiently as possible. It is the server network operating system that is responsible for not only executing the back-end portion of the application, but also supplying the messaging and communications services that enable interoperability between distributed clients and servers. Figure 5-11 illustrates the evolving role of the server network operating system from an architectural perspective.

The examination of server network operating system functionality in the remainder of the chapter will focus on those aspects of functionality that are most important to the support of distributed applications and their associated distributed clients and users.

In terms of currently available technology, NetWare and Microsoft Windows NT Server are the predominant server network operating systems. When comparing these two network operating systems, it is important to note the historical strong points of each. Novell NetWare has traditionally been stronger in file and print services than in the area of application services. Microsoft NT Server has traditionally been stronger in terms of application services than file and print services. With the release of the latest versions of each product, both are rapidly overcoming their weaknesses.

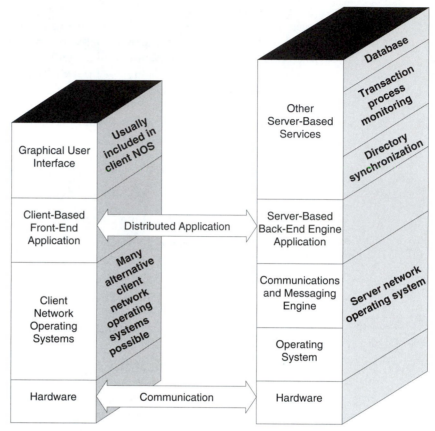

A server network operating system must be
capable of communicating transparently with
many different client network operating system
platforms.

Figure 5-11   Role of Server Network Operating Systems in Distributed Applications

Specific information on these two product lines will be covered in Chapters 6 and 7 respectively.

Various flavors of UNIX combined with TCP/IP as a network protocol and NFS as a file system have also been a popular choice of an applications server platform. However, this combination of operating system, network protocols, and file system is not as integrated or feature-rich as either NetWare or Windows NT Server and probably does not deserve the label of "next-generation" NOS. UNIX and NFS will be covered in detail in Chapter 8.

Directory Services

Network operating systems depend on some sort of naming service or directory in which to store information about users and system resources such as disks, servers, and printers. NetWare 3.x servers stored this type of information in a **bindery.** NetWare 4 and 5 employ a **global directory service** known as **NDS** or **NetWare Directory Services** while Windows NT uses a **domain directory service.**

Global Directory Services vs. Domain Directory Services   Global and domain directory services differ primarily in the organization of information concerning network users and resources. Global directory services organize all network user and resource data into a single hierarchical database, providing a single point of user and resource management. The hierarchical database is based upon a hierarchical tree structure. All servers that participate in the directory are part of the global hierarchy and can see all other parts of the network. In this sense, the hierarchical directory database is merely a reflection of the hierarchical network itself.

The global directory database is often **distributed;** different portions of the data are physically stored on multiple servers connected via the network. In addition, the global directory database is often **replicated** among multiple servers for redundancy and fault tolerance. In terms of a logical view of the network, global directory services provide a view of a single, enterprise network.

In contrast, domain directory services see the network as a series of linked subdivisions known as **domains.** Domain directory services associate network users and resources with a primary server known as a **PDC** or **Primary Domain Controller.** Each domain's directory must be individually established and maintained. Domains can be individually maintained and controlled in terms of how much of other domains can be seen.

Directory services can also vary in the types of information that are stored in the directory services database. In some cases, all users and network resources are considered **network objects** with information concerning them stored in a single database, arranged by object type. Object attributes can be modified and new network objects can be defined. In other cases, network users and network resources are kept in separate databases. Frequently, separate databases are maintained for network user account information and e-mail user account information.

![In Sharper Focus icon] **In Sharper Focus**

DIRECTORY SERVICES COMMUNICATION

In a global directory service implementation, a remote server performs a lookup in the NDS database to authenticate the user's right to the requested service. This NDS database lookup is repeated for every request for service from remote users. Recalling that the NDS database is distributed, the physical location of the server which contains the rights information of the requesting user may be located anywhere in the hierarchical distributed network.

In the case of a domain directory service such as Windows NT's, the remote or foreign server receives the user authentication from the user's primary domain controller (local server) in a process known as **Interdomain**

Trust. By having servers act on behalf of their local users when verifying authenticity with remote and foreign servers, every user ID does not have to be entered and maintained in every domain's directory service. In addition, once the interdomain trust has been established for a particular user, the remote domain server does not repeat the request for authentication.

The current trend is toward global directory services and away from domain directory services. Although each vendor's directory services solution is proprietary, all are loosely based on the OSI **X.500** directory service standard. A subset of the X.500 standard, known as the **Lightweight Directory Access Protocol or LDAP** and standardized by both OSI and the IETF, promises to provide a means of achieving some degree of interoperability between various vendors directory services offerings. LDAP runs over TCP/IP on ports 389 and 636. Any client that supports LDAP can access information in any LDAP compliant directory service. All major vendors have promised LDAP support in their various directory services offerings. The jury is still out as to whether LDAP will provide true integration between directories, but it appears to be a promising start.

Application Services

Recalling that the primary objective of the next-generation server NOS is to provide high-performance application services, the most important enabling NOS characteristic required to deliver that objective is the ability to support symmetrical multiprocessing. As numbers of users and sophistication of application programs continue to increase, the only real solution is for the application to be able to utilize more processing power simultaneously. Not all server network operating systems support symmetrical multiprocessing and those that do may vary in the maximum number of processors supported. Other server network operating system characteristics that are essential to optimization of application program performance are:

- Preemptive multitasking

- 32-bit execution

- Multithreaded application support

- Program execution in protected memory space

File Services   Application programs are stored in a particular file system format. In addition, when these application programs execute, they may request additional services from the resident file system via API calls. Server network operating systems vary in the types and number of supported file systems. Some network operating systems can have multiple partitions on a disk drive supporting multiple file systems. Figure 5-12 lists file systems supported by the various server network operating systems in the marketplace.

File System Name	Associated Network Operating System
FAT—File Allocation Table	Windows NT Server
NetWare File System	NetWare 3.x and 4.x
NetWare Storage System	NetWare 5.x
NFS	UNIX (native); most other NOS (optional)
NTFS—NT File System	Windows NT Server
Vines File System	Banyan Vines

Figure 5-12   File Systems and Associated Server Network Operating Systems

Other file services offered by some server network operating systems include file compression utilities and **data migration** utilities that manage the migration of data among different types of storage devices as part of a comprehensive hierarchical storage management (HSM) program.

Just as client network operating systems were either bundling or offering optional workgroup software as part of their package, server network operating systems are offering a variety bundled back-end engines as part of their offerings. For example, as an option or add-on to Windows NT Server, a bundled product known as Microsoft Back-Office offers the following suite of server applications:

- Exchange server

- System management server

- SQL server

- SNA gateway to IBM mainframe networks

Application Integration   Applications integration refers to the extent to which applications programs are able to integrate or take advantage of the capabilities of the operating system in order to optimize application program performance. Successful applications integration with operating system can yield both increased convenience and performance.

From a convenience standpoint:

- Does the application integrate with the operating system's security system allowing single UserIDs and user accounts, or must two separate security databases be maintained?

- Does the application integrate with the operating system's monitoring capabilities allowing it to be monitored from within the operating system?

- Can the application be configured and maintained from within the operating system's control panel or setup sub-system?

From a performance standpoint:

- Can the application take advantage of the multithreaded capabilities of the operating system?

- Can the application automatically detect the presence of multiple processors and respond accordingly?

- Can the application use the multitasking capabilities of the operating system, or does it supply its own multitasking environment?

- How easily, and to what extent, can adjustments be made to the operating system in order to optimize the performance of the application?

- Does the application run as a 32-bit or 16-bit application?

Managerial Perspective

New versions of server operating systems are released on an annual basis, if not more frequently. When in the market for a server operating system, it is important to take a fresh look at all currently available products. When making this analysis, consider current technology investment, business objectives, the applications that will be executed in the proposed server environment, as well as the stability and strategic product development direction of the operating system vendor. After completing this analysis, the best solution should be apparent.

Networking and Connectivity Services

Network Client Supported   In addition to the client network operating systems that were previously reviewed, server network operating systems may also have to communicate with client platforms with only the following operating systems installed:

- DOS

- Windows 9x

- Windows NT

- Macintosh

- UNIX

Because these operating systems possess no native networking functionality, the server network operating system must provide client software that supplies the necessary operating system-specific network communications capabilities. This software is loaded on the intended networking client, and the required network communication capabilities are merged with the native operating system.

Network Protocol Support The key question concerning network protocols and server network operating systems is not how many different network protocols are supported, but more important, how many network protocols can be supported simultaneously? As the trend toward heterogeneous multivendor enterprise networks continues, it is essential that server network operating systems possess the ability to support multiple network protocols simultaneously. This ability maximizes not only the different types of clients that can be supported, but also the number and type of other servers with which a given server can communicate. The ease with which multiple network protocols can be supported or whether multiple network protocols can be supported at all, can vary among different server network operating systems.

Related to the ability of a server network operating system to simultaneously support multiple protocols is the ability of a server network operating system to support multiple network interface cards. If a single NIC is the bottleneck to network communications, additional NICs can be added provided the NOS and computer bus supports them. As PCI buses and PCI-based NICs have increased in popularity, PCI cards containing up to four NICs have been produced. Unless the server network operating system has the ability to communicate with four NICs simultaneously, this four NIC PCI card would be of little use.

Multiprotocol Routing Underlying a server network operating system's ability to process multiple protocols simultaneously is the presence of **multiprotocol routing** software. This multiprotocol routing software may be either included, optional, or not available, depending on the server network operating system in question. Multiprotocol routing provides the functionality necessary to actually process and understand multiple network protocols as well as translate between them. Without multiprotocol routing software, clients speaking multiple different network protocols cannot be supported. Routing in general and multiprotocol routing in particular will be covered in great detail in Chapter 14, "Remote Access and Wireless Networking". Figure 5-13 illustrates the relationship between multiple network protocols, multiple network interface cards per server, and multiprotocol routing software.

Remote Access and Gateway Services Just as client network operating systems supplied the client portion of a remote access communication, server network operating systems can supply the server side of remote access communication. These remote access servers may be included with the server NOS or may be available for an additional fee. It is important that these remote access servers be tightly integrated into the server network operating system to ensure reliable performance, full functionality as offered to locally con-

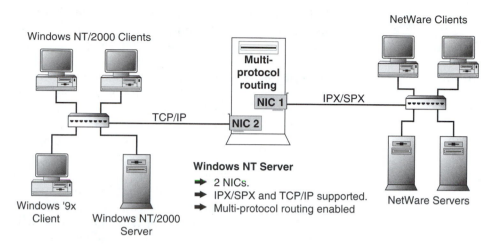

Figure 5-13 Multiple Network Protocols and Server Network Operating Systems

nected users, and tight security. Windows NT RAS (Remote Access Server) is integrated with Windows NT Server and NetWare Connect is the remote access server that integrates with NetWare.

In some cases, it may be necessary for either clients or servers to access IBM mainframe computers or AS/400s that are linked on IBM's proprietary network architecture known as **SNA (Systems Network Architecture).** In such cases, it makes more sense for the translation software necessary to access the SNA network to reside on a single server than on multiple clients. In this scenario, the server with the SNA translation software installed becomes a **gateway** to the SNA network. Windows NT's product for IBM mainframe access is called SNA Gateway, whereas NetWare's product is called NetWare for SAA (Systems Application Architecture).

Management and Administration Services

Installation, Configuration, and Administration Reviews of server network operating systems consistently list **autodetection and configuration** of installed controllers, interface cards, and peripherals as the most important installation-related feature. The ability of a server network operating system to automatically configure a controller, adapter, or peripheral is dependent on the network operating system possessing a compatible driver for that device. It should stand to reason that the greater the number of drivers supported by a given network operating system, the greater the probability that autoconfiguration will be successful.

Another hardware compatibility issue related to installation is which CPUs a given server network operating can operate. For example, although

NetWare can only operate on Intel chips, Windows NT Server can operate on Intel chips and DEC Alpha chips.

In order to appreciate the differences in ease of administration offered by server network operating systems, it is important consider multiserver enterprise network serving hundreds, if not thousands, of users. Simple items that are merely a nuisance on a smaller network can easily become major issues in such a large implementation. With this scenario in mind, some pertinent questions might be:

- How many steps are involved in creating a new user account?

- What is involved in giving a user access to remote servers?

- How easily can a user profile be copied and used as a template to automatically generate other user profiles? This feature is particularly important in academic settings where user profiles must be constantly generated in large numbers.

- What tools are available to assist in managing multiple servers simultaneously?

Server network operating systems can vary widely in the sophistication of the **performance monitoring** software included or available as an add-on. Ideally, the monitoring software should offer the ability to set thresholds for multiple system performance parameters. If these thresholds are exceeded, alerts or alarms should notify network management personnel of the problem, and offer advice as to possible diagnoses or solutions. Event logging and audit trails are often included as part of the performance monitoring package.

In multiple-server environments, it is particularly important that all servers can be monitored and managed from a single management console. Desktop and server management software offers capabilities beyond the monitoring software included in server network operating systems. For example, performance statistics are often gathered and stored in databases known as **MIB**s **(Management Information Base).** In addition, this performance management information can be communicated to Enterprise Management Systems such as HP OpenView, Computer Associates UniCenter, or Tivoli's Management Framework using SNMP **(Simple Network Management Protocol).** In addition to these enterprise network management platforms, both Microsoft and Novell offer tools designed to ease system administration across large network installations such as Microsoft System Management Server (SMS) and Novell ManageWise.

Integration and Migration   **Migration** features are aimed at easing the transition from one server NOS to another. Key among the migration concerns is the conversion of the directory services information. Utilities are available from third-party software vendors as well as from the NOS vendors themselves to help automate directory data conversion.

Integration refers to the transitionary period of time in the migration process when both network operating systems are running simultaneously and interacting to some degree. Integration utilities or strategies include:

- NetWare File and Print Services for NT, which allows a Windows NT server to appear to be a NetWare server by offering native file and print services to NetWare clients.

- NW-Link, which allows Windows NT Workstation clients and Windows `95 clients to communicate with NetWare 3.12 servers.

- File Access Protocols for NCP (NetWare Core Protocol) and SMB (Server Message Block) can be loaded simultaneously as redirectors allowing either NetWare or Windows compatible programs to be executed.

Monitoring As more mission-critical applications are deployed on LAN-attached servers, server operating systems must offer more sophisticated management tools in order to manage those applications effectively. Monitoring ability is essential in determining where potential performance bottlenecks might occur and to react accordingly. Among the server attributes that should be capable of being monitored and logged include:

- processor utilization

- network I/O

- disk I/O

- memory usage including L2 cache

- individual application performance and system impact

- process and thread performance

The monitor tool should be able to display data in a variety of ways:

- as a graph

- as a report

- as alarms or alerts if preset thresholds are crossed

A strong and flexible alert system is essential to keeping applications running and users happy. Some alert systems have the ability to dial particular pagers for particular alerts and can forward system status information to that pager as well.

A monitoring tool should support multiple open monitoring windows simultaneously so that multiple attributes or applications can be observed. The monitoring or management tool should be open and support industry standard management protocols and APIs so that application-specific management tools can be easily integrated into the overall operating system monitor.

Performance   In order to take advantage of the increased processing powers of multiple processors, server operating systems must be written to operate in a symmetrical multiprocessing (SMP) environment. Server operating systems can differ as to the maximum number of processors they can support. Figure 5-14 summarizes the number of processors supported by some currently available server operating systems.

UNIX-based server operating systems such as Solaris and others have been offering SMP capabilities for many more years than operating systems that have been developed in the Intel chip environment. As a result, UNIX-based server operating systems tend to be more stable with servers having more than 16 or 32 processors.

In order to allow greater freedom of choice in matching SMP server hardware with SMP server operating systems, a SMP specification for the hardware/software interface known as **Multiprocessing Specification 1.1 (MPS)** has been proposed by Intel and is widely supported by SMP hardware and software vendors. Clustering has become available for LAN-based servers as more powerful and performance-hungry applications are migrated from the mainframe environment to client/server architectures. By truly distributing applications, on a thread level, as well as associated data, over multiple CPUs physically located on multiple machines, clustering-capable operating systems can truly harness all of the available computing power in a client/server environment.

Practical Advice and Information

When it comes to optimizing performance in a symmetrical multiprocessing environment, the most important thing to remember is that the operating system and application program must support not only SMP but also multithreading in order ensure that the application program runs as efficiently as possible. Applications or operating systems that do not support multithreading may leave some CPUs idle, thereby negating the positive impact of SMP.

Server Operating System	Vendor	Number of Processors Supported
Windows NT Server	Microsoft	2 to 16
Solaris	Sun Microsystems	2 to 64
OpenServer MPX	SCO (Santa Cruz Operation)	2 to 30
NetWare 5.x	Novell	2 to 32

Figure 5-14   Number of Processors Supported by Server Operating Systems

Security

As local area network operating system based client/server systems have replaced traditional mainframe type applications, the need for effective security has increased. Overall security features fall into three broad categories:

- Authentication
- Authorization
- Encryption

Authentication   **Authentication** is concerned with determining which user is attempting to access the system. There are two key components to authentication: identification and proof of identification. In most network operating system environments, identification is provided by a UserID and proof of identification is provided by a password. Collectively, the UserID and password are known as a set of **Authentication Credentials.** In the login process, the server NOS checks the supplied authentication credentials against the directory service to determine if the credentials are valid. If so, the user is allowed to log into the system.

Most server network operating systems have the facility to support a guest user that is not authenticated. Although such a user usually is assigned minimal access rights to network resources, some situations, such as Internet publishing, require a nonauthenticated user be given access to files and resources on a network server. When browsing the web, users typically don't need to log onto each server they wish to access.

Authorization   **Authorization** is the process that controls access rights to network resources. **Access Control Lists** (ACLs) are the most commonly used authorization technique for local area network operating systems. In an ACL based authorization scheme, a list of users and groups is attached to each network resource along with their permitted access level. When a user attempts to access a network resource, the server checks the supplied authentication credentials against the access control list. If the credentials support the desired access level, the action is completed. If the credentials do not support the desired access level, the action is prohibited and an error is displayed to the user. A second authorization method is Kerberos, a multi-server authorization method that provides increased security for large client/server applications. Although traditionally used only in mainframe type applications, Kerberos is rapidly being integrated into PC local area network operating systems to increase the level of available security as more high end applications are ported to these platforms.

In addition to individual user accounts, it is also possible to create user groups accounts. A group account is a place holder that allows for a single change in user permissions or rights to affect multiple users at a time. By assigning all authorization rights to groups rather than users, it is possible to greatly reduce the amount of effort required to administrate a system while increasing consistency and alleviating potential security holes. When creating user accounts, considerable time can be saved if UserIDs can be created or modified using a template or group name instead of having to answer numerous questions for every individual UserID.

Encryption   **Encryption** is the process of "scrambling" data before they are sent across a network and "unscrambling" them at the destination. Encrypting data protects them from anyone who may make a copy of them along the way. There are multiple methods of data encryption in the marketplace. The two most common are DES and RSA public key encryption. DES is a single key system whereby a single key is used to encrypt and decrypt the message. In RSA public key encryption a combination of private and public keys is used to encrypt and decrypt the message, effectively eliminating potential problems with the transmission of a single key from the source to the destination.

Encryption is especially important when authentication credentials are entered. Encrypted passwords are unreadable while being transmitted between a client workstation and the authorizing server. There are two main methods used to encrypt authentication credentials: PAP and CHAP. The **Password Authentication Protocol (PAP)** provides for the transmission of encrypted passwords between network nodes. The **Challenge/Handshake Authentication Protocol (CHAP)** provides a more secure environment for the transmission of authentication credentials by encrypting the UserID as well as the password. Before PAP or CHAP can be implemented, both the client and server must be configured to support the protocol. Some clients cannot support one or the other, so a careful examination of the available options is required before implementing either solution.

In Sharper Focus

C LEVEL SECURITY

Security can be classified as to security level. Server operating systems often claim to implement **C2 level security.** C2 level security is actually part of a specification known as "Trusted Computer System Evaluation Criteria," which is specified in a Department of Defense document commonly known as *The Orange Book.* The book concentrates on seven levels of data confidentiality from D (low) to A1 (high).

In C level security users can control the access to their own files. C2 level security more specifically implies that although users can control access to their files, all file access can be monitored and recorded, or audited. Furthermore, these file-access audit records are reliable and verifiable and are therefore able to track and prove unauthorized file access. C2 level systems can also:

- identify and authenticate users

- have hidden passwords

- provide for resource isolation

- audit user activity

Systems claiming to be C2 *compliant* are judged so by the vendor, whereas systems claiming to be C2 *evaluated* or *certified* means that these systems (hardware and software) have undergone rigorous testing taking as long as two years.

The Orange Book only addresses security concerning file access and confidentiality of data. The security of networked systems is addressed in another Department of Defense document known as *The Red Book.* Encrypting passwords before transmitting them from client to server is a *Red Book* specification. Some server operating systems also claim "*Red Book* compliance".

Applied Problem Solving

SERVER NETWORK OPERATING SYSTEM TECHNOLOGY ANALYSIS

A network analyst's job is to always seek out the latest information that the industry has to offer before making recommendations for purchases which could have a significant bearing on both the company's prosperity as well as personal job security. The following Server Networking Operating System Technology Analysis Grid (Figure 5-15) is given as an example but is not meant to be either authoritative or all-inclusive. NetWare, Windows NT Server, and UNIX will be covered in greater detail in Chapters 6, 7, and 8, respectively. The technology analysis grid is divided into the following major categories:

- Hardware/Platform Characteristics

- Installation and Configuration

- Networking and Connectivity

- Management and Administration

Server Network Operating System Characteristic	Windows NT (2000) Server	NetWare	UNIX
Hardware/Platform			
Required Memory	32–64 MB	32–64 MB	64 MB +
CPUs	Intel, DEC/Compaq Alpha	Intel	Intel, Sparc, Power PC, DEC/Compaq Alpha, MIPS, etc.
Symmetrical Multiprocessing	yes	no	yes

(continued)

Preemptive Multitasking	yes	no	yes
Multithreading	yes	yes	yes
Protected Memory Application Execution	yes	yes, but not with NLMs	yes
Installation and Configuration			
Automatic Detection and Configuration of Adapters and Peripherals	yes	no	no
Requires a Separate Administrator Console	no	yes	yes
Networking and Connectivity			
Clients Supported	DOS, Windows, Windows for Workgroups, OS/2, Windows NT, Mac, UNIX	DOS, Windows, Windows for Workgroups, UNIX, OS/2, Windows NT, Mac	UNIX, DOS, Windows, Windows for Workgroups, OS/2, Windows NT, Mac
Network Protocols Supported	TCP/IP, IPX/SPX, NetBEUI, Appletalk, TCP/IP encapsulated NetBIOS	TCP/IP, IPX/SPX, Appletalk, TCP/IP encapsulated IPX, IPX encapsulated NetBIOS	TCP/IP, IPX/SPX
Routing Supported	TCP/IP, IPX/SPX	TCP/IP, IPX/SPX, Apple Talk	TCP/IP, IPX/SPX
Remote Access Services	Windows NT RAS	NetWare Connect	Optional
E-mail Gateways	Mail server optional	MHS included	Sendmail
Clients Able to Access Remote Resources	yes	yes	yes
Management and Administration			
Can Act as SNMP Agent for Enterprise Management System	yes	Optional	yes
Can Set Performance Thresholds and Alerts	yes	yes, with ManageWise (optional)	yes
Central Management of Multiple Servers	yes	yes	yes
Audit Trails and Event Logs	yes	yes	yes

Figure 5-15   Server Network Operating System Technology Analysis Grid

■ NETWORK OPERATING SYSTEM INTEROPERABILITY

Because of increased demands to be able to share information more quickly and easily within a company, as well as the increased number of corporate mergers and acquisitions, interoperability between different types of network operating systems has become an increasingly important functional characteristic.

Transparent interoperability between different network operating systems does not happen by magic. Compatibility on a variety of levels must be reconciled. A model should be devised that details how identified incompatibilities are to be dealt with. A separate model should be completed for each representative client and server system. Figure 5-16 illustrates representative models for NetWare, Windows NT (2000), and UNIX.

Once the layer 1 media (UTP, Fiber, Coax) and layer 2 network architecture (Ethernet, Token Ring, FDDI, Fast Ethernet) incompatibilities have been settled, the options for eliminating remaining incompatibilities are straightforward. Incompatibilities on layers 4 through 7 can be dealt with in any combination of the following ways:

- **Communication protocols:** In the case of NetWare/NT interoperability, IPX/SPX or TCP/IP can be supported by both network operating systems, dependent on NOS version numbers.

- **Server-side software or gateways:** Can NT or NetWare clients access each other's servers without adding special client software? Are server-based gateway products available that will give clients access to foreign servers?

Although not specifically noted on a particular layer of the OSI model, at least two other interoperability issues must be resolved before true transparent interoperability can be achieved:

	NetWare	**Windows NT (2000)**	**UNIX**
Directory Services	Bindery, NetWare Directory Services (NDS)	Domains, Active Directory	Stand-Alone, Network Information System (NIS)
File Systems	NWFS, NSS	FAT, NTFS	UNIX File System
Application Protocols	NCP	SMB	NFS
Network Protocols	IPX/SPX, TCP/IP	IPX/SPX, TCP/IP, NetBEUI, AppleTalk	TCP/IP

Figure 5-16   Sample Compatibility Model

- **File system interoperability** allows servers of different network operating systems and their respective clients to be able to share each other's files. Server-to-server interoperability is not automatically two-way. For example, one interoperability product may be required to allow server A to share server B's file system, while a different product may be required in order to allow server B to share server A's file system.

- **Directory system interoperability** allows two different network operating systems to share and synchronize their respective directory systems. As was the case with the file system interoperability, two separate products may be required to ensure two-way directory systems interoperability.

SUMMARY

Network operating systems have traditionally provided shared file and print services among networked clients. With the increase in client/server architectures and the associated increase in distributed applications, network operating systems are now also providing application services, directory services, and messaging and communications services in support of these distributed applications.

Network operating systems were once classified as either peer-to-peer or client/server. As network operating systems have evolved, this categorization no longer holds true. Network operating systems are now classified by their function: client network operating systems or server network operating systems.

Client network operating systems functionality can be categorized into operating systems capabilities, peer-to-peer networking capabilities, and client networking capabilities. Client networking capabilities are largely measured by the number of different server network operating systems with which the client can transparently interoperate. Remote access capability is also important.

Server network operating systems are now primarily concerned with high performance application services for back-end application programs. Enterprisewide directory services must also be provided. The two major approaches to enterprise directory services are global directory services and domain directory services.

In order to communicate with numerous client platforms, server network operating systems must support a variety of different network clients as well as a variety of different network transport protocols. Multiprotocol routing and remote access services are also essential to deliver transparent interoperability to the greatest number of client platforms. In the multiple server environments of the enterprise network, monitoring, management and administration tools play a critical role.

KEY TERMS

16-bit sub-system
ACL
Acess Control List
application program interface
application services
authentication
authentication credentials
authorization
autodetection and
    configuration
backward compatibility
bindery
C2 level security
CHAP
Challenge/Handshake
    Authentication Protocol
client network operating
    systems
client/server network
    operating
data display channel
data migration
DDC
delta file synchronization
dial-up server
directory services
directory synchronization
    software
domain directory services

domains
dynamic reconfiguration
encryption
file synchronization software
global directory services
granularity
integration
integration/migration services
Inter-domain Trust
IT
LDAP
legacy applications
Lightweight Directory Access
    Protocol
management information base
MIB
migration
multiprotocol routing
NDS
NetWare Directory Services
network objects
object-oriented user interfaces
PAP
Password Authentication
    Protocol
PDC
peer-to-peer network operating
    systems
performance monitoring

Plug-n-play
PnP
PnP BIOS
primary domain controller
protected memory mode
RAS
real-mode device drivers
remote node server
SCAM
SCSI configured automatically
server network operating
simple network management
    protocol
small business network
    operating systems
SNA
SNMP
Systems Network Architecture
universal client
version control software
virtual device drivers
virtual machines
VxDs
Windows NT Remote Access
    Server
X.500

REVIEW QUESTIONS

1. What effect has the adoption of client/server architectures and distributed applications had on network operating systems architectures?
2. Differentiate between peer-to-peer network operating systems and client/server network operating systems.
3. Differentiate between today's client network operating system and the client portion of traditional client/server network operating systems.
4. How does the combination of today's client and server network operating systems differ from a traditional client/server network operating system implementation?

5. What is a universal client?
6. Why is a universal client important to enterprise computing?
7. What new demands for services are being put on today's server network operating systems?
8. Describe the importance of the following service categories in more detail: directory services, applications services, integration/migration services.
9. Describe the major categories of functionality of client network operating systems.
10. What are the major differences between an object-oriented user interface and a graphical user interface?

11. Explain the difficulty in supporting legacy applications while offering protected memory mode execution.
12. What are real-mode device drivers and how do they differ from applications that interact with the operating system via APIs?
13. Why do many computer games use real-mode device drivers?
14. Why don't some client and server network operating support real-mode device drivers?
15. Describe how 16-bit or 32-bit applications running in their own protected memory space can still cause system crashes.
16. What is the objective of PnP standards?
17. Describe the components required to deliver a PnP solution, and the relationship of the described components.
18. Which client network operating system is most PNP compliant?
19. What is meant by the statement "Interoperability is not two-way"?
20. Describe the three elements of networking functionality belonging to client network operating systems, paying particular attention to the relationship between the elements.
21. Why is it important for a client network operating system to be able to support more than one network transport protocol?
22. Describe the importance of laptop synchronization as a client network operating system feature.
23. Describe the major differences between global directory services and domain directory services in terms of architecture and functionality.
24. What is accomplished by having directory services databases be both distributed and replicated? Differentiate between the two techniques.
25. What is interdomain trust?
26. How does interdomain trust save on network administration activity?
27. What is LDAP?
28. What is relationship between file systems, APIs, and application services?
29. What are the two basic parts of an authentication credential set?
30. What is the difference between authentication and authorization?
31. What is the purpose of an ACL?
32. Why might it be important for a network operating system to support more than one file system?
33. What is the role of NCP and SMB redirectors in offering application services?
34. What is the difference in terms of functionality and communication between a client running only an operating system such as Windows and a client running a network operating system such as Windows `95?
35. What is the role of multiprotocol routing in a server network operating system?
36. What is the role of gateway services such as SNA server?
37. What are some important functional characteristics of server network operating systems related to installation and configuration?
38. What are some important functional characteristics of server network operating systems related to integration and migration?
39. Name and describe the issues surrounding at least four areas of NOS functionality that must be addressed when designing interoperability solutions.

ACTIVITIES

1. Using back issues of a publication such as *PC Magazine*, prepare a presentation tracing the functionality of peer-to-peer LANs from 1994 to the present. Prepare a graph detailing price, number of supported users, and required memory over the research period.
2. Using back issues of a publication such as *PC Magazine*, prepare a presentation tracing the functionality of client/server LANs from 1994 to the present. Prepare a graph detailing price, number of supported users, and required memory over the research period.
3. Gather current market share statistics for the following market segments and prepare a presentation: peer-to-peer NOS, client NOS, server NOS.

4. Analyze the results of the previous activity. Which products are gaining market share and which are losing market share? Relate the market shifts to product functionality. Present your results in a top-down model format.

5. Prepare a presentation on the comparative functionality of Windows 9x vs. Windows NT Workstation. Compare marketing campaigns and current market share.

6. Review advertisements and catalogs for devices that support the PnP standard. Prepare a listing detailing which types of devices have the most PnP offerings. Which network operating system (if any) do devices claim to be compatible with?

7. Prepare a product review of dial-up or remote node servers, paying special attention to the source and compatibility of client software. Are most dial-up servers NOS specific? Why or why not?

8. Research and prepare a presentation on LDAP. What software categories supported LDAP specs originally? Currently? What key vendor groups or standards bodies (if any) support LDAP? What is your prediction as to the widespread adoption of LDAP?

9. Compare the performance monitoring capabilities of various server network operating systems. Which are best at monitoring a single server? Multiple servers? Which are best at setting thresholds and alerts? Which are best at linking to enterprise management systems such as HP Open View, CA Unicenter, or Tivoli NetView?

10. Compare the functionality of Microsoft Systems Management Server and Novell Manage Wise. Contrast these programs with enterprise management systems such as HP Open-View, CA Unicenter, and Tivoli SystemView in terms of functionality and price.

11. Investigate and compare the structures of NetWare 3.12 bindery and NetWare 5.x NDS database.

12. Prepare a product review of software tools designed to automate the migration from NetWare to Windows NT Server.

CASE STUDY

Campus Web Site Built in a Flash

Next time the University of Connecticut wins the NCAA title, you'll be able to buy victory T-shirts right off the Web.

Sports fans, college students and the curious can soon satisfy their cravings through ecampus.com, a Web site that will sell university apparel, textbooks and educational material from all over the country. Surprisingly, it has taken the start-up less than five months to assemble the infrastructure for what could become a multimillion-dollar site.

The ecampus.com idea came about when Wallace's Bookstores thought about going online, says Steve Stevens, president and CEO of ecampus.com and president of Wallace. A competitive analysis revealed that almost no one online was taking advantage of the $100 billion textbook market.

Stevens turned to Oracle's Advanced Technology Solutions, a consulting group primed to put businesses on the Web—fast. The Oracle group runs a large test lab in Herndon, Va. According to Brent Tuttle, director of operations at ecampus.com, the Oracle consultants put together a mixture of Oracle

Application Servers, Oracle database servers, Radware server load balancers and Cisco switches to form the back end of the ecampus.com site.

Because ecampus.com started with no network gear, it could afford to take all of Oracle's advice. That made putting up the Web site almost easy. "It enabled us to unpack the boxes, screw them into the racks and plug them in, and from a Friday to a Sunday we were up," Tuttle says. It wasn't a no-brainer—

Tuttle says no one's gotten much sleep in the past few months—but it meant everything worked out of the box.

Ecampus.com is running Fast Ethernet over Cisco 3000 series routers on the edge, Cisco 2000 switches inside, and Radware WSD Pro server loadbalancing devices in front of several flavors of Sun servers running Solaris 2,6 and 7. The company is also using Oracle 8.05 and Oracle Application Server 4.0.7.

The Radware WSD Pros are called server load bal-

ancers, but they're also being used for fault tolerance and scalability. While most networks using server load balancers deploy them in front of a server farm or hanging off a switch, ecampus.com is putting the WSD Pros between two internal Cisco switches.

All this doesn't come cheap. The company won't divulge the names of its investors, but it will spend $23 million in advertising this year alone.

Source: Robin Schreiber Hohman, "Campus Web Site Built in a Flash," *Network World,* vol. 16, no. 24 (June 14, 1999), p. 33 Copyright (June 14, 1999), Network World.

BUSINESS CASE STUDY QUESTIONS

Activities

1. Complete a top-down model for this case by gleaning facts from the case and placing them in the proper layer of the top-down model. After completing the top-down model, analyze and detail those instances where requirements were clearly passed down from upper layers to lower layers of the model and where solutions to those requirements were passed up from lower layers to upper layers of the model.
2. Detail any questions about the case that may occur to you for which answers are not clearly stated in the article.

Business

1. What products does Ecampus.com market?
2. How does Ecampus.com sell these products?

Application

1. What is the primary application used at Ecampus.com?
2. What application development environment was used to create the system?

Data

1. What types of data does the system manage?
2. What database engine is used by the system?

Network

1. Why was it possible for Ecampus.com to quickly get the network up and running?

Technology

1. What network technologies does Ecampus.com use?
2. How does Ecampus.com manage fault tolerance?

CHAPTER 6

NOVELL NETWARE

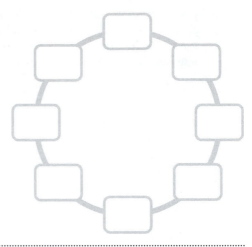

Concepts Reinforced

OSI Model

LAN Software

Network Architecture

Network Operating System
  Architectures

Client/Server Technology Model

Network Protocols and Standards

Network Operating System
  Functionality

Concepts Introduced

NetWare Loadable Modules

Bindery

NetWare Migration

Virtual Loadable Modules

NetWare Directory Services

Novell Distributed Print System

OBJECTIVES

After mastering the material in this chapter you should:

1. Understand the major architectural and functional similarities and differences between NetWare 3, NetWare 4, and NetWare 5

2. Understand the application layer protocols that support the NetWare network operating system

3. Understand the architecture and design of NetWare Directory Services

4. Understand the issues and options surrounding migration between NetWare versions

5. Understand remote access options associated with NetWare

6. Understand file system interoperability options between NetWare and other network operating systems

7. Understand directory service interoperability options between NetWare and other network operating systems

INTRODUCTION

Having gained an overall understanding of network operating systems architecture and functionality in Chapter 5, the intricacies of Novell's NetWare network operating system architecture and functionality are explored in this chapter.

Novell NetWare has been a key network operating system since its original release in 1983. Novell claimed its largest market share with NetWare 3 in the early 1990s. While new competitors have fragmented the network operating system market and eroded NetWare's market share, NetWare remains a major network operating system player.

There are three major release families of NetWare in the marketplace at this time: NetWare 3, NetWare 4, and NetWare 5. Each of these versions will be covered in detail throughout the course of this chapter. Special attention is paid to the communications protocols that perform the bulk of the work in any network operating system. Remote access and interoperability with other network operating systems such as Windows are explored from both architectural and functional perspectives as well. Finally, issues and options surrounding the migration between NetWare versions are detailed.

This chapter is intended to provide the reader with an in-depth knowledge of the underlying architecture and protocols associated with NetWare; it is not intended as a "how-to" guide for NetWare installation and configuration. To be more specific, listing the particular NetWare commands required to accomplish certain tasks is not the purpose of this chapter.

NETWARE 3

The importance of the NetWare 3 family cannot be overestimated. Released in the early 1990s, NetWare 3 was the most successful network operating system in history in terms of market share. Although newer versions of NetWare have added many features that improve scalability and Internet interconnectivity, many companies are still running the venerable NetWare 3.

Designed as a single server, stand-alone network operating system, NetWare 3 was a direct descendant of earlier NetWare releases. In terms of the modern network operating system, NetWare 3 provides a limited suite of services with a focus on file and print services. Due to its limited scalability and inability to perform well as an application server, most remaining NetWare 3 installations are in small office environments providing centralized file and print services to small workgroups.

Network Operating System Characteristic	NetWare 3
Hardware and Platform	
Supported Processors	Intel (386 or better)
Min Memory	8 MB
Min Disk	75 MB
Symmetrical Multi-Processing	Not natively supported
Operating System	
Program Structure	32 Bit
Memory Architecture	Flat (NLMs and Operating system reside in same ring)
Preemptive Multi-tasking	Yes
File System	NetWare File System *(File allocation table based)*
User Interface	Text
Network Drivers	ODI
Application Program Interface(s)	NetWare Loadable Modules (NLM) *pre-emptive multi-tasking not supported for NLM's*
CD-ROM Support	Version 3.12 or greater
Management and Administration	
Network Object Management System	Independent servers
Administrative Location	Performed from clients using utility applications residing on the server
Network Services	
Network Protocols Supported	IPX/SPX TCP/IP (not available for client/server communication)
Multiprotocol Routing	Yes
Native Services	File and print services
Common Third-party Services	Electronic mail, FTP, etc.
Clients Supported	DOS Windows 3.x Windows 9x Windows NT UNIX OS/2 Macintosh

Figure 6-1 NetWare 3 Technology Analysis Grid

Overall Architecture

NetWare 3 is a single-server, stand-alone network operating system designed for small to medium local area network systems. Figure 6-1 lists the key characteristics of the NetWare 3 platform.

Figure 6-2 illustrates the architecture of a typical NetWare 3 implementation.

Operating System Architecture and Characteristics

The NetWare server offers services such as file sharing and printer sharing to clients through the NetWare network operating system engine, or kernel.

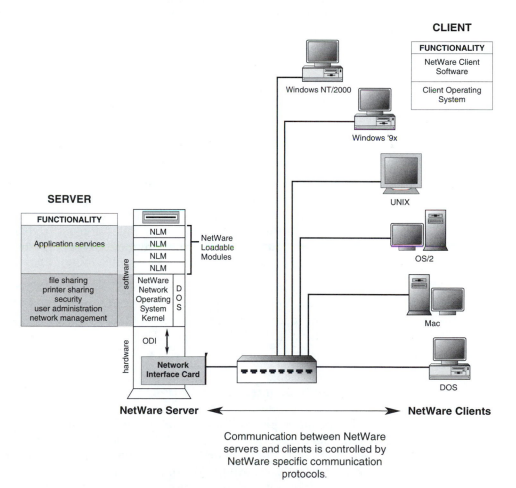

Figure 6-2   Generalized Overall NetWare Architecture

The NetWare kernel resides in a section of the server's disk drive known as the **NetWare partition.** This is the only portion of the disk the NetWare kernel is physically able to access. However, in order to initially install the Net-Ware server software, the native operating system of the server must be present in a bootable disk partition. When the server is powered on, the native operating system is booted and used to load the NetWare kernel into memory. After the NetWare kernel has initialized, the native operating system is ignored. The example in Figure 6-2 shows a **DOS partition,** but the native operating system could just as easily have been UNIX or Windows NT.

NLMs—NetWare Loadable Modules Additional functionality can be added to the basic NetWare kernel through the use of **NetWare Loadable Modules** or **NLMs** NLMs are programs written to interact with and add functionality to the NetWare kernel. Because the NLM application program interface (API) specification is available to third-party software developers, a wide variety of NetWare are available. These NLMs fall into three major categories:

- Operating system enhancements: The NetWare kernel itself needs additional operating system features such as virus protection, network interface card drivers and disk drivers in order to be fully operational and ready to interact with client workstations. This additional operating system functionality can be added in a platform-specific fashion thanks to the use of NLMs.

- Application programs: These programs, which actually execute on the NetWare server as opposed to being transferred to the client for execution, are written in the form of NLMs. As a result, they are loaded into memory only as called for and dynamically removed from memory following program execution, thus allowing that memory to be reused by other applications.

- Relational Database Management Systems: Perhaps considered a subcategory of application programs, an entire RDBMS engine can be loaded in the form of an NLM, thus allowing a NetWare server to act as a database server.

Management and Administration

The primary job of the server network operating system is to fulfill requests for services as received from NetWare clients. In order to fulfill such requests, the network operating system must have some method for keeping track of individual users, user groups, file and directory access rights, print queues and printers, and other available resources and services that may be requested by clients. In a NetWare 3 environment, this type of security and network resource information is stored in **bindery files.**

Bindery Services   All requests for services are first verified against the information in the bindery files for authorization. User logins and password verification are also handled by the bindery. In a multiple server environment, servers advertise available services via a specialized communication protocol known as the Service Advertising Protocol or SAP, which was described in detail in Chapter 4. Bindery services on a particular server are able to receive SAP broadcasts and update bindery files with the latest information regarding available services on other reachable servers.

NetWare's bindery service is organized around the relationship of three important concepts:

- **Objects** can be thought of as the system resources that are to be controlled or managed. User groups, users, printers, print servers, print queues, and disk volumes can all be considered objects by bindery services.

- **Properties** are associated with objects and those aspects of objects that can or must be controlled. Examples of properties include such things as login time restrictions, network address restrictions, e-mail address, print job configuration, file and directory access rights, or user group membership.

- **Values** are associated with properties and, in turn, with objects. For example, a value of Monday through Friday, 8:00 A.M. to 5:00 P.M. would be a value associated with the login time restriction property associated with a particular user or user group object.

The information related to these three important bindery services concepts is stored in three separate files linked by pointers on every NetWare server:

- NET$OBJ.SYS contains object information

- NET$PROP.SYS contains property information

- NET$VAL.SYS contains value information

The structure of the bindery is illustrated in Figure 6-3.

An important point to remember is that these bindery service files are associated with a single NetWare server. In multiple server environments, bindery files on each server must be established and maintained independently if users are to have access to multiple servers. This implies that when user information or other system resource information changes, these changes must be made to all associated servers in order to keep the bindery

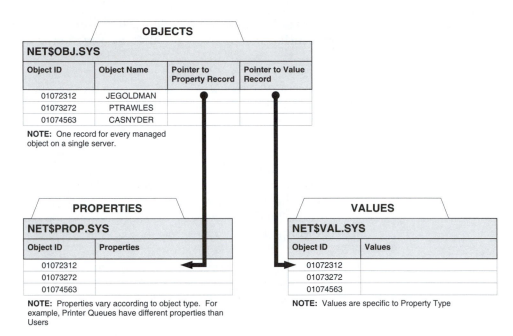

Figure 6-3   NetWare Bindery Services

services of the overall server environment synchronized. This manual synchronization across multiple servers can be a management nightmare as the number of servers continues to grow. This dilemma was addressed with the introduction of NetWare Directory Services in NetWare 4.

Communications Protocols

NetWare servers use the ODI (Open Datalink Interface), reviewed in Chapter 8, to allow network interface cards to support multiple transport protocols, such as IPX/SPX and TCP/IP simultaneously. In the case of Ethernet network interface cards, ODI also allows the NICs to support multiple Ethernet frame types such as Ethernet 802.3, Ethernet 802.2, Ethernet II, and Ethernet SNAP simultaneously.

NetWare clients communicate with NetWare servers via predetermined communication protocols that are supported or understood by both the NetWare clients and servers. The application layer protocol used by NetWare for client/server communication is known as the NetWare Core Protocols (NCP). Although a NetWare 3 server can be configured to communicate via TCP/IP to provide e-mail or FTP services, under NetWare 3 NCP is supported only by the IPX/SPX protocol suite for client/server communication.

NCP   NCP provide a standardized set of commands or messages that can be used to communicate requests and responses for services between clients and servers. When a NetWare client determines that a request from an application program should be directed over the network to the server, it encapsulates that message in an NCP packet which is, in turn, encapsulated within an IPX packet for delivery. NCP fulfills a similar role for NetWare networks as NetBIOS does for DOS-based LANs by extending the client workstation's operating system capabilities out onto the network. Figure 6-4 illustrates the packet layout and encapsulation of a NCP packet while Figure 6-5 provides descriptions and explanations of the fields within the NCP packet.

Network Services   NetWare 3 is primarily a file and print services platform. Although the NLM API allows additional applications to be added to the server, in NetWare 3 all NLMs run in the same memory space, allowing a single misbehaving NLM to crash the entire server. Because of this significant architectural limitation, NetWare 3 is rarely used as an application server.

▒ NETWARE 4

NetWare 3 was a highly successful network operating system but it had many limitations that restricted its usage. Lack of scalability, the independent nature of each server, poor memory protection, and protocol limitations effectively limited NetWare 3 to small workgroup-style applications. To overcome these limitations and create a large-scale enterprise NOS, Novell developed and released NetWare 4 in the mid-1990s.

There were two releases of NetWare 4: NetWare and **IntraNetWare.** The core of the two products is identical, the key difference being the bundling of NetWare/IP and a web server into IntraNetWare. From the perspective of this section NetWare 4 will refer to both plain NetWare and IntraNetWare. The features bundled into IntraNetWare will be noted.

Rather than examine NetWare 4 from the ground up, this section will focus on the significant upgrades and new features introduced in NetWare 4.

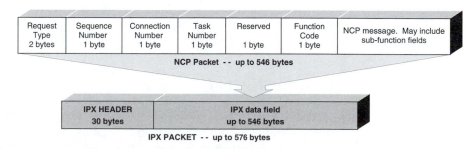

Figure 6-4   NCP Packet Layout and Encapsulation

NCP Packet Fields	Function/Importance
Request Type	This field indicates the general category of NCP communication contained within this packet as distinguished by different hexadecimal values. Among the possible types are:

Request Type	Hex Value	
Create a service connection	1111	Created at login time
Service request from workstation	2222	
Service response from server	3333	
Terminate a service connection	5555	Performed at logout time
Busy message	9999	

NCP Packet Fields	Function/Importance
Sequence Number	This field is incremented for each request sent from a particular workstation. The server uses this same number in its response so that the client knows which request is being responded to.
Connection Number	This is a number that is associated with the connection established when the user first logged into the server. It is used together with the sequence number and task number to uniquely identify requests and associated responses.
Task Number	This number identifies which particular program on a workstation issued the request for services.
Reserved	
Function Code	This field indicates which of the more than 100 standard NCP messages or commands is being executed or requested in this packet. Entries are indicated by hexadecimal numbers representing requested services. An extended listing of sub-functions will always insert 16hex in this field and then list the desired sub-function later in the NCP message packet. Some possible functions include:

Function	Hex Value
Get file size	40
Close a file	42
Delete a file	44
Rename a file	45
Open a file	4C
Create a file	4D
Get a directory entry	1F

NCP Packet Fields	Function/Importance
NCP Message	This field contains additional information transferred between clients and servers including possible sub-function hex codes.

Figure 6-5 NCP Field Descriptions and Explanations

Overall Architecture

NetWare 4 improves on NetWare 3 in many ways. Most notable are the introduction of NetWare Directory Services, a mechanism for multiple servers to share user data and improvements in memory structure and protocol support. Figure 5-6 lists the key characteristics of the NetWare 4 platform.

Network Operating System Characteristic	NetWare 4
Hardware and Platform	
Supported Processors	Intel (386 or better)
Min Memory	8 MB
Min Disk	75 MB
Symmetrical Multiprocessing	Yes (up to 4 processors with optional NetWare SMP product)
Operating System	
Program Structure	32 Bit
Memory Architecture	Ringed *Operating system and NLMs reside in separate rings*
Preemptive Multi-tasking	Yes
File System	NetWare File System (*File allocation table based*)
User Interface	Text
Network Drivers	ODI
Application Program Interface(s)	NetWare Loadable Modules (NLM) *Preemptive multi-tasking not supported for NLMs*
CD-ROM Support	Yes
Management and Administration	
Network Object Management System	Directory services
	Independent servers (*bindery emulation*)
Administrative Location	Performed from clients using utility applications residing on the server
Network Services	
Network Protocols Supported	IPX/SPX
	IPX/SPX Encapsulated in IP (*NetWare/IP*)
Multiprotocol Routing	Yes
Native Services	File and print services
	FTP, Web (IntraNetWare)
Common Third-party Services	Electronic mail, FTP, etc.
Clients Supported	DOS Windows 3.x Windows 9x Windows NT UNIX OS/2 Macintosh

Figure 6-6   NetWare 4 Technology Analysis Grid

Managerial Perspective

Whenever a new technology or an update of an existing technology is introduced, it is important to evaluate that technology from a somewhat skeptical, business-oriented perspective. When examining the new features of the new technology, a few key questions should be kept in mind:

1. What functional features are being newly delivered?

2. What are the benefits of these features?

3. Do these features offer potential cost savings?

4. Are there migration or installation issues involved to take advantage of these new features or are they implemented transparently to the user?

Operating System Architecture and Characteristics

Although file and print services have always been a traditional NetWare strength, improvements have been made in these areas in NetWare 4. Additional improvements have been made to NetWare 4 in order to compete more effectively with network operating systems such as Windows NT and UNIX in the applications services arena. In response to some well-publicized security holes in NetWare 3, security has also been beefed up in NetWare 4. Each of these feature upgrades is explained in more detail in the following sections.

Memory Architecture   Unit NetWare 4, the operating system or kernel portion of NetWare ran in the same general memory area or ring as the application programs loaded as NLMs (NetWare Loadable Modules). In this scenario, a misbehaving NLM could write into the operating systems memory space and crash the entire system. NetWare 4 introduces **ring memory protection** which seeks to isolate and protect the operating system from potentially dangerous NLMs. The area reserved for the operating system is known as **Ring 0,** otherwise known as **domain OS** (operating system). The area reserved for NLMs is known as **Ring 3** or **domain OSP** (operating system protected). NLMs executing in Ring 3 access operating systems services in Ring 0 by issuing structured **inter-ring gate calls,** thereby protecting the operating system from misbehaving NLMs overwriting its memory space.

RING MEMORY PROTECTION

Practical Advice and Information

Ring Memory Protection should not be confused with protected memory as implemented in Windows NT or UNIX. First, some NLMs must still run in Ring 0 and therefore still have the potential to crash the operating system. Second, if an NLM running in Ring 3 crashes, it has the potential to crash all other NLMs running in Ring 3. True protected memory means that each application runs in its own protected memory space rather than in a shared protected memory ring. Bottom line: although improved over NetWare 3, NetWare 4 is still not a good application server platform.

NETWARE 4 SMP

High-powered application servers require network operating systems that can support multiple CPUs, otherwise known as **symmetrical multiprocessing** or **SMP.** Since the original NetWare 4 did not have SMP capability, some way had to be found to support SMP while still ensuring backward compatibility with all existing NLMs. This was done by having **NetWare 4 SMP** load a second operating system kernel, known as the **SMP kernel,** which works cooperatively with the first or native operating system kernel. The native kernel works on processor one while the SMP kernel works on processors two through four. Because the SMP kernel has to be able to take full advantage of multiple processors, it also must support multithreading, although the native kernel does not.

The two kernels must cooperate when data must be shared between threads executing on the two kernels. If data needed by a thread executing in the SMP kernel belong to code executing in the native kernel, then that thread must be migrated from the SMP kernel to the native kernel in order to retrieve the required data. Once the required data have been retrieved, the thread is returned to the SMP kernel for further processing on CPUs two through four.

Disk Sub-System Upgrades   Several enhancements have been added to the NetWare 4 disk sub-system. **File compression** is incorporated into NetWare 4 and is controllable on a file-by-file basis. The file compression process is highly customizable with adjustable settings for how often compression takes place as well as minimum acceptable disk space gained by compression. Because the number of simultaneous file compressions as well as compression time of day can be controlled in order to minimize system impact, this entire file compression process is transparent to the user in terms of both file access time and CPU performance.

Disk Block Sub-Allocation is a process aimed at optimizing the use of disk space for file storage. Disks in a NetWare environment are divided into **disk allocation blocks** that range in size from 4 KB to 64 KB. In the past, when a file needed a portion of a disk allocation block in order to complete file storage, the remainder of the partially occupied disk allocation block could not be used by other files and was effectively wasted. By dividing all disk allocation blocks into 512 byte (.5 KB) **sub-allocation blocks,** multiple files are allowed to occupy single disk allocation blocks and disk storage efficiency is maximized. Figure 6-7 illustrates how disk block sub-allocation can minimize wasted disk space.

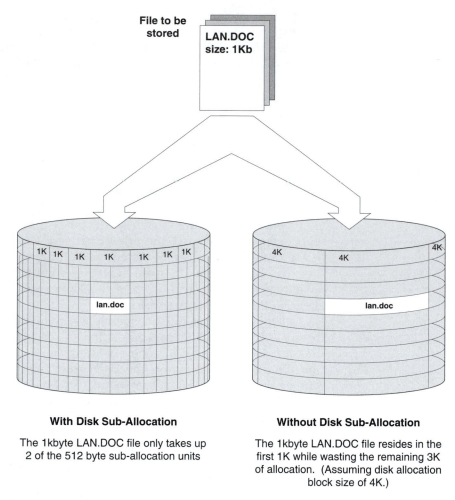

File to be stored

LAN.DOC size: 1Kb

With Disk Sub-Allocation

The 1kbyte LAN.DOC file only takes up 2 of the 512 byte sub-allocation units

Without Disk Sub-Allocation

The 1kbyte LAN.DOC file resides in the first 1K while wasting the remaining 3K of allocation. (Assuming disk allocation block size of 4K.)

Figure 6-7   Disk Sub-Allocation

Support of CD-ROMs has become increasingly transparent to the user in NetWare 4. CD-ROMs are mounted as just another disk volume and can be accessed by users like any other network-attached resource. NetWare 4 supports popular CD-ROM file systems such as ISO 9660, High Sierra (DOS), and HFS (Macintosh). Driver software included with NetWare 4 supports approximately 95% of all CD-ROM readers.

This transparent integration of CD-ROMs into the NetWare 4 file system has enabled the use of the **DynaText On-Line Help** system as the means of accessing all of the NetWare 4 manuals. In applications involving large sequential accesses such as reading manuals via CD-ROM, another NetWare 4 feature known as **read ahead cache buffering** improves performance by reading ahead in the sequentially accessed file and caching that information in anticipation of the next request for information from the user. In the case of the DynaText help system, the read ahead caching would buffer the next few pages of a document, thereby avoiding the delay of a physical disk seek in order to retrieve the next page that the user wishes to read. It is important to note that read ahead caching is likely to have a positive effect on performance on large sequential accesses only.

This same improved support of access to optical drives includes access to optical storage devices such as optical jukeboxes. As a result, **data migration** features have been added to NetWare 4, which allow files to be automatically migrated and archived in a structured fashion to the archival storage media of choice such as optical drives. Which files get migrated and when are totally controlled by parameters set by the system manager.

Fault Tolerance   Fault tolerance is another characteristic increasingly important to corporate application services. Although such fault tolerant features as disk duplexing and disk mirroring were reviewed in Chapter 5, **NetWare 4 SFT III** offers a unique fault tolerant feature known as **server duplexing.** In such a case, not only are the contents of the disks synchronized, but the contents of the servers' memory and CPUs are also synchronized. In case of failure of the primary server, the duplexed server takes over transparently.

The synchronization of the servers is accomplished through a dedicated link known as the **Mirrored Server Link** (MSL). The use of the dedicated MSL link and dedicated MSL adapters prevents the server duplexing from adversely affecting LAN traffic. The largest cost of such an arrangement is obviously the second identical duplexed server. However, the fact remains that this feature offers a level of fault tolerance not achieved by other network operating systems. Figure 6-8 illustrates server duplexing with NetWare 4 SFT III.

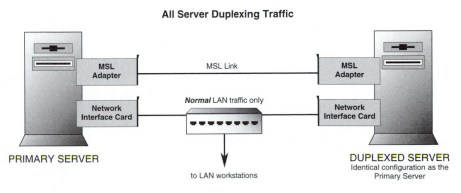

Figure 6-8   Server Duplexing with NetWare 4 SFT III

Security   Several important security enhancements have been added to NetWare 4. Due to a well-publicized security hole in NetWare 3 that allowed impostors to gain supervisory privileges, **authentication** is perhaps the most important of the security innovations. Using a combination of private encryption keys and passwords, the VLM requester security agent on the client workstation and NDS file server combine to ensure that users are properly authenticated before being logged in. Should even higher security be required, every packet transmitted from a particular client workstation can have a unique, encrypted digital signature attached to it which can only be authenticated by the server in a process known as **packet signing.** However, a performance price of 5 to 7% is paid for the increased security as valuable CPU cycles are spent encrypting and decrypting digital signatures.

While authentication and packet signing ensure that only valid users are accessing system resources, an extensive **auditing system** monitors and reports on what those valid users are doing. The auditor acts independently of the supervisor in an effort to ensure a proper system of checks and balances in which no single person could remain undetected while performing potentially harmful acts. The auditing system separately monitors activity on both the file system, as defined by volumes, and the NetWare Directory Services database as defined by container units. Figure 6-9 illustrates the organization and capabilities of the NetWare Auditing System.

Management and Administration

Like its predecessors, NetWare 4 is administered from client workstations via utilities shared from the network server. NetWare 4 simplifies the administration process compared to earlier versions of NetWare by combining the functionality of many different text-based utilities into a single graphical user interface utility known as nwadmin. Located in the SYS:PUBLIC directory on the NetWare server, **nwadmin** allows a system administrator to manage user accounts, groups, disk volumes, and printers from a single application. While the traditional text-based utilities such as syscon and printcon are retained from NetWare 3, management of NetWare Directory Services is greatly simplified through the use of nwadmin.

One of the primary problems with NetWare 3 was the inability of multiple servers to share user account data contained in the system bindery. With the release of NetWare 4, Novell improved upon the bindery model in two different ways: the introduction of NetWare Directory Services and bindery synchronization and emulation.

NetWare Directory Services   **NDS** or **NetWare Directory Services** was arguably the most significant feature introduced in NetWare 4. NDS is a single logical database containing information about all network-attached resources, which replaces the independently maintained, server-specific bindery files. The term *single logical database* is used because portions of the

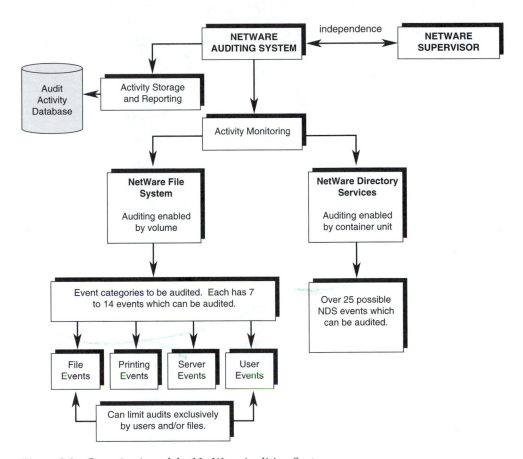

Figure 6-9   Organization of the NetWare Auditing System

NDS database may be physically distributed on different servers throughout the network. This section is meant to familiarize the user with the key features of NDS, and is not meant to serve as a tutorial on how to design an NDS database structure.

From a user perspective, the single database design allows a single user login for access to all authorized network attached resources rather than separate logins for each server. In other words, with NetWare 4, a user actually logs into the NDS database from any network attached server, whereas in previous versions of NetWare that same user logged in multiple times into particular servers. From a management perspective, NDS allows administrative tasks to be performed only once rather than numerous times on multiple servers as was required with bindery-based administration. Figure 6-10 summarizes some of the differences between the Bindery and NDS.

	Bindery	**NDS**
Logical Structure	Flat	Hierarchical
Users/Groups	Single server	Network-wide
Volumes	Single server	Global objects
Authentication Model (Login)	Password for each server with single password	System-wide login
Location	Single server	Distributed

Figure 6-10   Bindery vs. NDS

One thing that NDS and bindery services have in common is the organization of network resources according to objects, properties, and values. Examples of network resources include users or user groups:

- File servers
- Volumes on a File Server
- Printers
- Printer Queues
- Print Servers
- NetWare Servers
- Communication Servers
- Database Servers

Categories of information that can be used to describe or control objects are referred to as properties. For example, the following are some of the properties that can apply to user objects:

- Identification
- Environment
- Login Restrictions
- Login Time Restrictions
- Network Address Restrictions
- Mailbox
- Foreign E-Mail Address
- Intruder Lockout
- Group Memberships
- Rights to Files/Directories

- Postal Address
- Login Script
- Print Job Configuration
- and so on…

Entries for a specific object (user) for any of these properties are known as values.

NDS actually defines two types of objects. Network resources are considered **leaf objects,** whereas organizational units such as companies, divisions, and departments are referred to as **container objects.** Container objects can be cascaded and can contain leaf objects. Leaf objects cannot be cascaded.

Because NDS is a **global directory service,** organizing and managing all networked resources over an entire enterprise, a method had to be found to organize this myriad of network resources in some logical fashion. As a result, the NDS database is organized in a **hierarchical** fashion, which can be thought of as a tree. The hierarchical design of the NDS database can be roughly equivalent to the hierarchical and geographical organization of the corporation in question. The tree hierarchy starts at the top with the **root** object. There is only one root object in an entire global NDS database. Branches off of the root object are represented by container objects. Container objects were added to NDS in order to allow leaf objects to be logically organized into container objects such as buildings, campuses, departments, or divisions. Figure 6-11 represents a sample NDS database including root, container, and leaf objects.

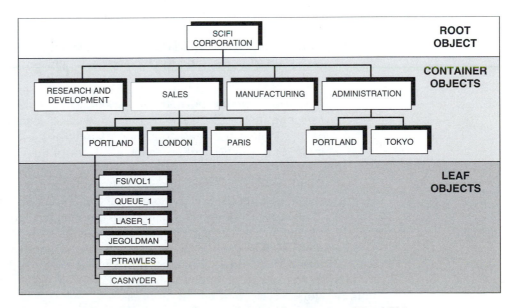

Figure 6-11   NDS Database Structure with Root, Container, and Leaf Objects

**Practical Advice
and Information**

NDS STRUCTURE DESIGN

An important thing to remember when developing the NDS structure is that the structure does not have to perfectly mirror the organizational structure of the corporation. Early adopters of NetWare 4 were overwhelmed trying to create massive NDS database structures designed to exactly match the proper placement of every employee in a corporate structure. The purpose of the NDS database structure is to logically organize network resources, including users, in a manner that will optimize both the ease of administration by the network manager and the ease of use by the network users. The NDS structure need not reflect reporting responsibilities or corporate hierarchy and need not be approved by the human resources department. The design of the NDS structure should be simply organized from the perspective of logically grouping network resources from a network management perspective.

Continuing with the metaphor of a tree to describe the overall hierarchical structure of the NDS database, utilities are provided within NetWare 4 to modify the structure as necessary. Entire branches of the tree, designated as **partitions,** and including all subordinate container objects and leaf objects, can be **pruned** (removed) from one point in the NDS structure and **grafted** to another branch. In fact two entire trees can be merged together into a single tree.

One of the key characteristics of the NDS database is its ability to have partitions be **replicated,** or physically stored on multiple file servers. Replication implies that these multiple copies of the same NDS partition are kept synchronized. There are two primary benefits of replicating NDS partitions:

- Fault tolerance is achieved due to the availability of a second copy of the NDS partition should the file server on which the primary copy of the partition is stored fail.

- In situations where portions of the enterprise network are linked over long distances by a wide area network, it would be advantageous to allow user authentication at login to be able to access a replica of the NDS partition on the local side of the WAN link.

One final benefit to NDS' one-stop shopping for network resource information is that application programs such as e-mail are able to access the NDS databases. Although this may seem obvious from a commonsense standpoint, the fact is that most e-mail programs have their own separate databases of UserIDs, passwords, and security restrictions that must be set for every user. These **integrated messaging services** offered by NDS allow network managers to maintain a single database of user information for both network services and e-mail services.

Bindery Synchronization and Emulation   Although NDS represents a giant step forward in functionality, it is often impractical to migrate all NetWare 3 servers simultaneously to NetWare 4. At the same time, it would be nice if the migration of a few servers to NetWare 4 would make the management of the multitude of remaining NetWare 3 servers more manageable. **Bindery synchronization** allows a single NetWare 4 server to be automatically and transparently synchronized with up to 12 NetWare 2 or NetWare 3 servers. By running NETSYNC NLMs on both the NetWare 4 and NetWare 3 servers, all administration of the NetWare 3 servers, or **NetSync Cluster,** is done through NDS on the NetWare 4 server with changes automatically replicated to the binderies on the NetWare 3 servers. The only caveat to this scenario is that when the NetSync Cluster is created, the binderies of the 3.12 servers must be searched for duplicate object names. Any duplicate names found must be eliminated, because the entire NetSync cluster is seen as a single bindery context container unit within NDS, and no duplicate object names can exist within the same container unit. Figure 6-12 illustrates bindery synchronization.

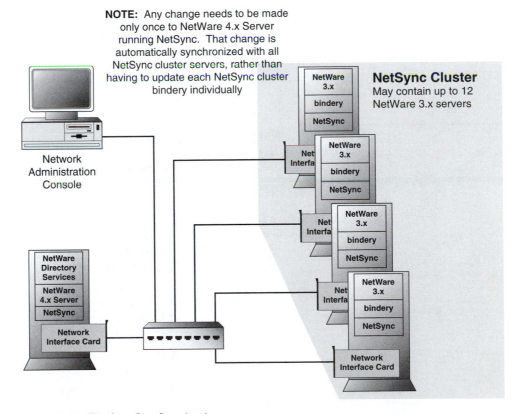

Figure 6-12   Bindery Synchronization

While bindery synchronization allows NetWare 4 servers to manage NetWare 3 servers, **bindery emulation** allows newly migrated NetWare 4 servers to enjoy most of the benefits of NetWare 4 without having to fully convert NetWare 3 bindery objects into a NetWare 4 NDS database. Bindery emulation allows the use of NetWare 2 or NetWare 3 software, NLMs, and clients while still offering many NetWare 4 benefits. NDS users are still able to access files and services managed by bindery emulation. In bindery emulation, NetWare 4 NetWare Directory Services emulates the flat, non-hierarchical structure of the bindery, thereby allowing transition time for the development of the hierarchical NDS database structure. Figure 6-13 summarizes the availability of NetWare 4 features under bindery emulation.

Communications Protocols

NetWare was originally designed when local area networks emphasized the term *local* in their architectures. Little consideration was given to the impact of NetWare communications protocols on the limited bandwidth, relatively expensive WAN (wide area network) links that connect multiple LANs. As a result, NetWare 4 introduced a number of new network communications protocols in an effort to make more efficient use of wide area network links.

Although NetWare 4 added new network protocols, the application layer protocol used continued to be NCP. As illustrated in the previous section on NetWare 3, NCP is the protocol used for communication between NetWare clients and servers. The file-and-print services and client redirec-

Effect of Bindery Emulation on Availability of NetWare 4 Features	**NetWare 4 Features**
Only available in NDS	• NetWare Directory Services • Enhanced Security
Available in Bindery Emulation but Enhanced by NDS	• Virtual Loadable Modules • Improved Print Services • Network Auditor
Available in Both Bindery Emulation and NDS	• Improved Memory Usage • Sub-allocation Block • File Compression • Data Migration • Better Administrative Tools • LIP • Packet Bursts • CD-ROM Support • DynaText On-Line Documentation

Figure 6-13   Bindery Emulation

tors use the NCP protocol to support seamless access to server-based resources.

Packet Bursts   Error detection and correction have always been important in data communications. Most error detection/correction schemes depend on the sending workstation waiting for an acknowledgment from the receiving station of the error-free receipt of a packet of data before being allowed to send the next packet of data. This is sometimes referred to as a stop-and-wait protocol.

In large file transfers or other high volume data broadcasts, a considerable amount of time is wasted waiting for acknowledgments, and a non-trivial amount of bandwidth is consumed by the multitudes of acknowledgments. In order to alleviate both of these situations, NetWare 4 introduced **packet bursts** otherwise known as **Burst Mode IPX.** This capability is built into the NetWare kernel and allows the NetWare 4 VLM requester on the clients and the NetWare 4 kernel on the servers to negotiate how many packets can be transmitted before an acknowledgment is required; 10 to 20 packets prior to acknowledgment is not uncommon. By allowing multiple packets to be transmitted before requiring acknowledgment, NetWare 4 is able to significantly reduce idle waiting time as well as remove significant numbers of acknowledgments from the data traffic stream, leading to overall greater transmission efficiency. Burst Mode IPX would have a positive impact on both local area as well as wide area traffic

LIP   LIP or **Large Internet Packets** applies only to NetWare 4 LANs that are linked to each other via a wide area network through routers. LIP, also known as **Large Packet IPX,** allows NetWare clients to negotiate with the routers as to the size of the IPX frame. From the NetWare client's perspective, the larger the IPX frame, the larger the IPX frame's data field, leading to a greater amount of data the client can cram into a single IPX frame. This philosophy will lead to greater efficiency provided the packet doesn't become too long, thereby introducing data errors that would necessitate retransmission of the large packet and negating the previous gains in efficiency. As discussed in Chapter 4, IPX frames are normally limited to 576 bytes.

One potential drawback of LIP is that it must be supported by all installed routers. Although Novell's software-only router known as **MPR, Multi-protocol Router,** supports LIP, there is no guarantee that large router vendors such as Cisco or Bay Networks will support such a network operating system specific protocol.

NLSP   The **NLSP** or **NetWare Link Services Protocol** was introduced in NetWare 4 in an effort to overcome the inefficiencies introduced by RIP. When dealing strictly with local area networks and their megabit-per-second bandwidths, protocols such as RIP and SAP that broadcast every 60 seconds are nothing more than a slight nuisance. However, when expensive, limited bandwidth WAN links are involved, chatty protocols such as RIP and SAP become intolerable. Refer to Chapter 4 for more detailed information on NLSP.

TCP/IP As discussed in Chapter 4, TCP/IP (Transmission Control Protocol/Internet Protocol) is the protocol of choice for internetworking a variety of LANs together over wide area network links. As interoperability with other network operating systems over inter-networks has become more important to NetWare customers, NetWare has been forced to support TCP/IP in conjunction with or as a replacement for its own communication protocols: IPX/SPX.

NetWare/IP (NWIP) provides a means of implementing NCP (NetWare Core Protocols) over TCP/IP. NetWare/IP can be implemented in a variety of different ways as illustrated in Figure 6-14. NetWare/IP clients can support IP, IPX, or both as their network communications protocols. Depending on the protocols supported by internetwork routers, NetWare/IP servers may support both IP and IPX or just IP.

NetWare/IP allows TCP/IP to be used as the network layer protocol for NetWare networks by encapsulating IPX into IP. Each IP network segment is assigned a logical IPX address, and the server creates an IPX packet then places it into an IP packet for delivery over the network. At the destination the IPX packet is removed from the IP shell and processed as a native IPX packet.

The encapsulation of IPX into IP creates a problem with disseminating server information. In a pure IPX environment servers use the broadcast SAP and RIP protocols (see Chapter 4) to share information about the other servers and networks. NetWare/IP makes use of **Domain SAP/RIP Servers (DSS Servers)** to provide this functionality. Essentially all information that would have been broadcast via SAP and RIP packets is sent to the DSS server. Servers periodically poll the DSS server to discover any pertinent changes. The DSS service is implemented as an NLM running on a NetWare 4 server. Whenever NetWare/IP is implemented, at least one DSS server must be present.

NetWare/IP allows the TCP/IP stack within itself to be swapped with other commercially available TCP/IP products at the users' discretion. Novell's LAN Workplace TCP/IP protocol stack is included with NetWare/IP, but Chameleon TCP/IP from NetManage, Inc. and Microsoft's Windows 9x TCP/IP protocol stacks also work with NetWare/IP.

Although the encapsulation of IPX into IP adds overhead to the communication process, Novell claims NetWare/IP only experiences an 8% performance decrease compared with NetWare 4 using native IPX.

Application Layer Services

Printer Services Upgrades The print server program known as PSERVER.NLM has been improved to support up to 255 printers in addition to executing up to three times faster than older versions of the same

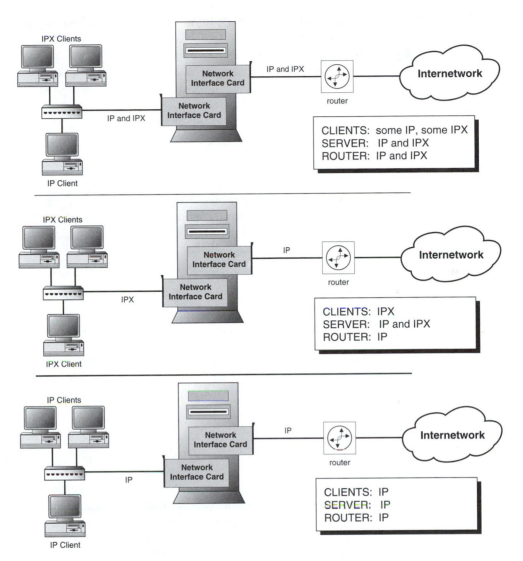

Figure 6-14   NetWare IP Implementation Options

program. Part of the reason for this improvement in performance is because the printer services information is stored in the NetWare Directory Services database rather than in bindery files. Print queues can also be more flexibly managed in NetWare 4. In past versions of NetWare, printer queues had to be stored as sub-directories on the SYS:SYSTEM volume with sufficient disk space allocated to handle the largest print job. In NetWare 4, the location of the print queue sub-directories is up to the network manager and can be changed as necessary should disk space issues warrant such a change.

Internet Services and IntraNetWare   In response to the bundled Internet services in the competing Windows NT Server platform, Novell released IntraNetWare. The IntraNetWare version of NetWare 4 combines NetWare 4, NetWare/IP, and FTP and web servers. These Internet services run as NLMs in the shared NLM memory ring. These services provide reasonable functionality, although the performance is limited and the lack of a protected memory space limits their robustness.

▨   NETWARE 5

Although NetWare 4 addressed many of the weaknesses of earlier versions of NetWare, several weaknesses remained. As the role of the server network operating system continued to evolve from simple file and print services to the more complete role of application server, the weaknesses of the memory architecture and multi-tasking abilities of NetWare 4 began take on increasing importance.

The introduction of NDS in NetWare 4 had made NetWare the best network operating system in terms of file and print sharing for large organizations, these weaknesses in NetWare's ability to function as an effective application server began to affect implementation decisions. Faced with declining market share to the rival Windows NT Server network operating system, Novell began the largest revision of NetWare in its history.

In mid-1998, NetWare 5 was released and was immediately heralded as a breakthrough for Novell. Improvements in memory structure, multi-tasking, protocol support, printing, and disk systems, along with an enhanced version of NDS, an improved graphical user interface, and improved installation and migration tool combined to make NetWare 5 a significant product in the network operating system marketplace. In fact, NetWare 5 can be thought of as taking NetWare and turning it into a world-class application server.

Faced with the realization that Internet enabling features were now standard network operating systems components, Novell abandoned the IntraNetWare product and rolled all of the optional IntraNetWare features directly into the base version of NetWare 5. Even though NetWare 5 has only been on the marketplace a short period of time as of the date of this writing, it appears to be the most significant release of the operating system in terms of market share since NetWare 3.

Rather than covering NetWare 5 from the ground up, this section will focus on the improvements in NetWare 5.

Overall Architecture

NetWare 5 improves on NetWare 4 in many significant ways. Most notable are the improvements in memory structure and multi-tasking that greatly improve NetWare's ability to serve as an application server. Figure 6-15 lists the key characteristics of the NetWare 5 platform.

Network Operating System Characteristic	NetWare 5
Hardware and Platform	
Supported Processors	Intel (Pentium or better)
Min Memory	64 MB
Min Disk	1 GB
Symmetrical Multi-processing	Yes (up to 32 Processors)
Operating System	
Program Structure	32 Bit
Memory Architecture	Ringed with protected memory spaces
Preemptive Multi-tasking	Yes
File System	NetWare Storage System *(Journaled File System)*
User Interface	Graphical *(Console One)* Text
Network Drivers	ODI
Application Program Interface(s)	NetWare Loadable Modules (NLM)
CD-ROM Support	Yes
Management and Administration	
Network Object Management System	Directory services
	Independent servers *(bindery emulation)*
Administrative Location	Performed from either the server or from clients using applications located on the server
Network Services	
Network Protocols Supported	IPX/SPX IPX/SPX Encapsulated in IP *(NetWare/IP)* TCP/IP
Multi-protocol Routing	Yes
Native Services	File and print services
	DNS, FTP, Web
Common Third-party Services	Electronic mail, etc.
Clients Supported	DOS Windows 3.x Windows 9x Windows NT UNIX OS/2 Macintosh

Figure 6-15 NetWare 5 Technology Analysis Grid

Operating System Architecture and Characteristics

The NetWare 5 operating system architecture is significantly improved over NetWare 4. Improvements in the kernel, memory architecture, and disk subsystem combine to create an operating system that is significantly more robust. Collectively these improvements make NetWare 5 much better suited to the role of application server than its predecessors.

Multi-processing Kernel The NetWare 5 kernel supports both uniprocessor and symmetrical multiprocessor systems, greatly increasing scalability. The kernel detects multiprocessor systems at boot time and loads SMP support automatically. The kernel supports up to 32 processors per server.

In addition to SMP support the NetWare 5 kernel adds support for **virtual memory.** Using virtual memory server code that is not currently running can be swapped out to disk to free memory for active processes. Previous versions of NetWare did not include this ability since they were designed and optimized to perform file and print services almost exclusively.

Memory Architecture NetWare 5 adds the ability to run NLMs in **protected address spaces** (sometimes referred to as virtual address space or virtual machines). When an NLM is run in such a protected address space, it is completely insulated from all other NLMs running on the server. If a single NLM crashes, it will not affect any other NLM.

When an NLM is loaded into a NetWare 5 protected memory space, both the module itself and any other required supporting modules (such as CLIB) are automatically loaded in the memory space. As modules are added to memory spaces the system automatically dedicates memory to the space as required up to the 512 MB maximum. NLMs loaded into protected memory spaces are under the control of the server's virtual memory system and can be swapped out to disk if the module is not currently in use. This allows rarely used services to remain available while minimizing the amount of required server memory.

Another key feature of maintaining highly available application services on the NetWare 5 platform is the ability of a memory space to automatically reset itself if an error occurs. If a module is loaded into a protected memory space with the RESTART option, the system will automatically close the address space, clean up the module(s) resources, restart the address space, and reload all modules in the space if a module abends (crashes).

Disk Sub-System NetWare 5 introduces the **NetWare Storage Services (NSS),** a journaled file system that increases disk reliability while reducing the time required to create and maintain disk volumes. NSS delivers the ability to create large volumes that span multiple physical disks while minimizing access time, repair time, and required memory. A comparison of the legacy NetWare File System and NSS is shown in Figure 6-16.

Item	Legacy NetWare File System	NetWare Storage System (NSS)
Volumes	64 mounted concurrently 1 terabyte (TB) maximum volume size	253 mounted concurrently 8 terabyte (TB) maximum volume size for 32-bit disk systems 8 exabyte (XB) maximum volume size for 64-bit systems
Maximum File Size	4 GB	8 TB
Maximum Number of Files	16 million	1 trillion
Maximum Open Files	100,000 per server	1,000,000 per server
Maximum Subdirectory Depth	100 levels	Limited only by client O/S
Character Set Support	ASCII double byte	UNICODE

Figure 6-16   NWFS vs. NSS

In addition to the dramatic increase in capacity achieved with NSS, the time required to create, mount, and repair volumes is dramatically decreased. While NetWare 5 includes many kernel and memory protection features that make it less likely to crash, server crashes are inevitable. Eventually a RAM segment will flip a bit, a critical kernel component will hiccup, or the power will go off. Under the legacy NWFS disk system such an unplanned system shutdown leaves the disk volumes in a dirty state that must be repaired before the server can be brought back on-line. For NetWare 3 and 4 systems this volume repair process can take hours and may require multiple iterations to completely repair all of the errors present in the volume. In comparison, an NSS volume can be completely repaired in seconds.

Other key features of NSS include reduced memory requirements for caching and international language support via UNICODE support.

NSS DISK DRIVERS

Practical Advice and Information

While NSS represents a revolutionary improvement over the older NWFS disk system, it is not without issues. NSS uses a new driver technology (.ham drivers) that is incompatible with NWFS (.dsk) drivers. While the selection of NSS drivers will undoubtedly increase over time, currently there are many disk adapters supported by NWFS that are not yet supported by NSS. Be sure to check the compatibility list before upgrading to NetWare 5 or purchasing new hardware.

Server Based Java Support   NetWare 5 includes server-based Java support. **Java,** Sun Microsystem's platform independent programming language, is used extensively in the new generation of NetWare utilities. In addition to this native use of Java, NetWare 5 contains support for serving third-party

Java applications to clients. A built-in Java engine on the server itself allows graphical administration tools to be written that can be run on the server or any client with a Java engine.

Novell has also added **Java Beans** that allow third-party developers to write Java applications that interact with NetWare directly. There are two Java Beans that ship with NetWare 5:

- NWDirectory—Allows a Java application to gain access to the NDS database

- NWSession—Allows a Java application to gain access about current sessions, such as login information and file services

Additional Java support includes Java Database Connectivity (JDBC) and the Novell Trader, a CORBA-based object broker. For more information on CORBA, see Chapter 9.

Security NetWare 5 includes many improvements to the NetWare security model. An enhanced authentication model combined with support for new encryption technologies combine to strengthen NetWare 5's ability to serve as an application server.

Secure Authentication Services (SAS) is a new authentication API. SAS currently supports the Secure Sockets Layer (SSL), the Internet standard for encrypted authentication. The modular design of SAS allows for new authentication standards (such as biometrics) to be added to NetWare as they are developed and standardized.

Public Key Infrastructure Services (PKIS) further NetWare's abilities as an e-commerce server and ensure secure transfer of user data. PKIS is a set of services that enable a NetWare system to use RSA public-key encryption and digital certificates to verify data sources and ensure secure transmission. The certificate authority features of PKIS allow a NetWare server to manage digital certificates and public keys, thus enabling certificate-based services such as SSL security for LDAP servers.

Management and Administration

While powerful, NetWare 4 was somewhat difficult to work with. Installation, configuration, and administration were problematic at best; this was especially true in terms of printing support. In addition to being difficult to work with, the NetWare licensing model was restrictive, forcing users to purchase large blocks of licenses.

Installation, Upgrade, and Server Based Administration NetWare 5 features new installation and upgrade utilities. Written in Java, these new utilities use a graphical user interface to create a common installation and configuration tool for all NetWare components and add-on products. Hardware autodetection is also greatly improved over NetWare 4, easing installation and configuration tasks.

One of the key issues with implementing a new version of any network operating system is the process of upgrading or migrating existing servers. All too often what appears to be a simple upgrade can degenerate into complete chaos as a technical snag develops. Novell has traditionally been very good at providing a robust upgrade path to newer versions of NetWare, and the upgrade path to NetWare 5 is no exception.

The **Novell Upgrade Wizard** is a graphical utility designed to aid in the migration of NetWare 3 and NetWare 4 servers to NetWare 5. It upgrades bindery and volume contents while maintaining user passwords, thus eliminating the need to reset each user's password as is common with other upgrade techniques. The printing sub-system is also upgraded automatically to NDPS (see the following section). The wizard performs a verification check before initiating the upgrade, thus identifying potential upgrade concerns before the upgrade is started.

A key administration upgrade in NetWare 5 is the release of **ConsoleOne.** Designed to replace nwadmin, ConsoleOne is a Java based graphical administration utility. Similar to nwadmin in look and feel, ConsoleOne can be run on the server or any Java enabled client. ConsoleOne is an intuitive, easy to use interface light years ahead of the text-based server utilities provided with earlier versions of NetWare.

NDS Enhancements   The NDS database is a hierarchical structure that is not easily searched. To find a particular object you have to navigate your way through the tree, opening containers and looking for the desired object. **NDS Catalog Services** provides a means of storing information from a distributed NDS database into a flat (ASCII) file that can be quickly searched.

Catalogs are defined in terms of what type of information they should contain. Once a catalog is defined, NDS Catalog Services dredges the distributed NDS database on a daily basis to update the catalog. Since the catalogs are stored in a flat file format, they are easy to search. Another key benefit to creating catalogs over searching the distributed NDS database is that a catalog can be stored on a local server. In the case of widely distributed NDS trees, this eliminates the need to go out over the WAN links to search for data in the tree.

There are two types of catalogs: master catalogs and slave catalogs. The master catalog is the main catalog that is built as a result of the dredging process. Slave catalogs are copies of the master catalog that are automatically copied when the master catalog is updated. In a distributed NDS tree, slave catalogs can be placed on remote servers, giving them local catalog access to the data contained in the NDS tree while eliminating the need to send data across the WAN.

NetWare 5 includes another new feature that can help reduce WAN traffic associated with NDS. Under normal circumstances changes in the NDS tree proliferate through the network as soon as they are posted to the local server. WAN Traffic Manager Services allow these NDS updates to be scheduled.

WAN Traffic Manager Services control traffic based on a WAN policy. Although WAN policies can be manually defined, NetWare 5 ships with several policies that can simply be activated. WAN policies can either be attached directly to a server or servers can be grouped into LAN areas with a WAN policy assigned to the area. In this manner all servers in the LAN area are automatically assigned the same WAN policy.

Using ConsoleOne, administration capabilities can be divided into various roles and spread among users. Similar to the manner in which users are granted access to various resources, administrators can be granted limited administrative rights. Compared to the traditional single level administrator account, this **role based administration** approach allows for tighter security since each administrator can be assigned only those rights that their position requires.

Another key improvement in NetWare 5's NDS implementation is support for **LDAP (Lightweight Directory Access Protocol)** version 3. An IETF and OSI standard, LDAP allows any compliant application to gain access to the data stored in the NDS database provided proper authentication credentials are presented. More detailed information on LDAP can be found in Chapter 5.

LDAP CLIENTS

In Sharper Focus

Both Netscape Communicator and Microsoft Internet Explorer contain address book utilities that are LDAP compliant. By opening the address book and pointing it at the IP address of a NetWare server running LDAP services, directory information can be accessed. Depending on need, the server can be configured either to allow anonymous access to the directory or to require an SSL connection to authenticate the user before allowing access.

Z.E.N. Works   Total Cost of Ownership (TCO) is a growing concern of network administrators. TCO is basically defined as the sum total of all costs associated with purchasing, installing, and maintaining a local area network system. Not surprisingly one of the major components of TCO is the cost associated with administering and maintaining network client workstations.

System administrators commonly have to visit each workstation on the network to perform updates whenever new software is deployed or whenever a workstation becomes "confused." Many of these visits to the workstations are the direct result of users altering critical configuration data, often by mistake. To reduce these costs Novell released **Z.E.N. Works** (Zero Effort Networking) concurrently with NetWare 5.

While Z.E.N. Works is technically an add-on to NetWare, the client that ships with NetWare 5 includes the Z.E.N. Works starter pack, a subset of the overall package that focuses on setting system policies to limit what administrative tasks a user can perform. By implementing this starter pack a system administrator can implement roaming (server based) profiles and system policies to prevent users from altering network settings, screen resolutions, or a multitude of other critical system configurations.

Policy files are created on the server that determine the features that are restricted from user intervention. Workstations are then assigned to policies through nwadmin or ConsoleOne. When the workstation connects to the server the updated policy is downloaded and the features are set. In this manner, limitations can be set on a per workstation or per user basis.

Software Licensing and Accounting   Another key component of Total Cost of Ownership is software costs. NetWare 5 adds a new licensing service known as **NetWare Licensing Service (NLS).** NLS is a distributed, enterprise network service that allows the use of licensed applications to be monitored and controlled. NLS contains a software metering tool that not only monitors and controls Novell products, but is also capable of limiting access to third-party software.

In addition to software metering, NetWare 5 includes an advanced accounting system that makes it possible to charge for usage of network services in terms of:

- Connection time

- Disk usage

- Disk access

- Applications run

Rates can be set to vary based on time of day or day of the week.

Communication Protocols

Changes to underlying communications protocols in NetWare 5 continue the trend established with NetWare 4: improved support for TCP/IP and improvements designed to reduce WAN traffic.

Pure IP   While NetWare/IP provided a mechanism to use IP as the network layer in NetWare networks, it required IPX to be encapsulated in IP. This encapsulation process increases latency and increases the amount of processor time required to encapsulate and de-encapsulate data on both the client and the server. This increased latency is especially critical on the server where a far greater number of connections must be concurrently maintained.

IP support in NetWare 5 has been enhanced to eliminate the need to encapsulate IPX in IP. Using the new **Pure IP** protocol support, the NCP application protocol can be placed directly into an IP packet. This approach avoids the issues associated with IPX encapsulation such as increased latency and the need to use DSS servers.

Most applications will work transparently over Pure IP. However, the potential exists that some applications may require IPX. The developers of these applications have written code that access IPX directly rather than following the recommended rules of protocol independence. If such an application attempts to make a call directly to IPX, the NetWare protocol stack will automatically revert to an IPX encapsulation compatibility mode for that particular application. In this manner all applications will continue to operate using the Pure IP stack.

To support the Pure IP protocol stack, changes were made to the NCP protocol to eliminate all IPX specific hooks. NDS was also modified to support DNS as a naming system. If IP is selected as a network protocol a DNS server must be running somewhere on the network. NetWare 5 includes a DNS server, although any DNS server is adequate, regardless of the operating system on which it is running. Additional information on DNS can be found in Chapter 4.

Despite the inherent advantages of Pure IP, it is unlikely that organizations are going to replace their entire IPX and NetWare/IP networks overnight. To allow Pure IP environments to work with these legacy protocol environments, NetWare 5 includes a Migration Agent. The **Migration Agent** can be thought of as a network protocol gateway running on a NetWare 5 server. On multi-homed servers the agent automatically converts between IPX, NetWare/IP, and Pure IP packets. The NCP packet is removed from the incoming packet and rewritten into a packet appropriate for the other side of the gateway. This process is illustrated in Figure 6-17. Packets from a work-

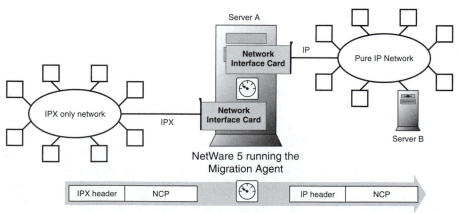

As the packet is sent from one network to the next, the NCP content is copied from the IPX packet to the IP packet by the Migration Agent; only the header is changed.

Figure 6-17   Migration Agent Functionality

station on the legacy IPX network destined for server B are automatically converted to Pure IP by server A and sent across the IP network to server B.

THE FEWER NETWORK PROTOCOLS THE BETTER

The advent of Pure IP is significant because it allows clients to use a single protocol for all network services. Use of a single protocol is preferred over using multiple protocols for the following reasons:

- Reduces latency associated with protocol selection

- Simplifies the process of binding services and protocols

- Eliminates potential protocol conflicts

- Reduces the amount of memory required by the network sub-system

Since TCP/IP is the protocol of the Internet, it makes sense to standardize on IP as the network protocol of choice for most local area networks.

Service Location Protocol   The development of Pure IP created a problem with servers sharing information: The SAP protocol is exclusive to the IPX protocol; it is not supported on IP networks. To resolve this problem the IP compatible **Service Location Protocol (SLP)** is used. An IETF standard, SLP registers service information in a database that is queried by clients looking for a specific service. Services register with SLP when they are initially started. The use of SLP greatly decreases network broadcast traffic compared with the SAP paradigm where every service announced itself every 60 seconds.

In addition to converting packets from IP to IPX, the Migration Agent also handles the conversion between SAP and SLP. SAP packets arriving from an IPX network are analyzed, and the service is registered in the SLP database. The agent queries the SLP database for services that are on a Pure IP segment and automatically sends a SAP packet on their behalf to the IPX network.

Application Layer Services

As previously mentioned changes to the NetWare 5 memory model and kernel have greatly enhanced NetWare's ability to serve as an application server. While IntraNetWare was a start toward a true Internet-enabled NOS, NetWare 5 expands this functionality by adding new web servers and integrating them with industry standard database services. Printing, long a NetWare strength, is also vastly improved in NetWare 5.

NetWare Distributed Print System   The **NetWare Distributed Print System (NDPS)** represents a revolutionary improvement in printing services over the traditional NetWare queue-based printing system. Developed jointly with Hewlett-Packard and Xerox, NDPS introduces several new features:

- Bidirectional communication with printers enables remote users to check the status of the printer. Items such as jams, paper outages, and toner shortages can now be queried in real time.

- Centralized print management through nwadmin rather than multiple utilities.

- Clients automatically download the correct printer device driver when initially attaching to the printer or whenever the driver is updated. This feature virtually eliminates incorrect driver problems, the source of many help desk inquiries.

- Increased support for network printers using the LPR protocol.

In addition to adding these new features, NDPS printing is significantly easier to set up and manage than the previous queue-based system.

The NDPS printer architecture consists of three parts: brokers, managers, and printer devices/gateways. The **NDPS Broker** is the key component of the NDPS architecture. The broker controls the following services that run on the NetWare file server:

- The **Service Registry Service (SRS)** stores information about public access printers available on the network. This information includes manufacturer, model, and printer type.

- The **Event Notification Service (ENS)** sends customizable messages to users about printer status and events. Examples of such printer events include out-of-paper errors, paper jams, and low toner alerts. ENS is capable of sending events via pop-up messages, e-mail, or simply logging the event to disk.

- The **Resource Management Service (RMS)** provides a centralized storage location for printer resources such as fonts, banner pages, client printer drivers, and printer definition files. By accessing these components clients are able to automatically install the required printer drivers for the printer.

NDPS Managers manage the communication between the broker and the printer. At least one manager must be present on the network to support printing. A single NDPS Manager can manage multiple printers, but only one manager can be installed per server.

NDPS Managers can only talk to NDPS aware devices. If a printer contains an NDPS aware network print server (such as an HP Jet Direct card), the manager can send data directly to the printer and report status information and printer events to the NDPS broker. For printers that are either not directly attached to the network or do not contain an NDPS aware print server an NDPS Gateway is required. The **NDPS Gateway** provides a means of translating information between the NDPS manager and the printer's native interface.

Three NDPS Gateways are provided with NDPS: the HP Gateway, the Xerox Gateway, and the Novell Gateway. The HP Gateway provides a means of communicating with older Jet Direct cards that do not natively support NDPS. These printers usually use the LPR protocol for network connections. Similarly, the Xerox Gateway provides a means of communicating with Xerox printers. The Novell Gateway is designed to manage the connection to printers that are either directly attached to a port on the server or on a network client workstation.

Printer Agents represent the printer on the network. Combining the role of print server, queue, and spooler, Print Managers interface the printer with the print manager. Each printer on the network must have a print manager. In the case of NDPS aware printers, the print manager is located in the printer itself. For printers that require a gateway the print manager resides on the server. Figure 6-18 shows the overall NDPS architecture with examples of each type of HDPS gateway.

Internet Servers   IntraNetWare represented a good starting point for an Internet aware NOS. However, the previously mentioned limitations of the NetWare 4 architecture limited the viability of NetWare in this role. With the release of NetWare 5, NetWare has become a capable Internet NOS. In recognition of the fact that Internet servers are now a standard part of any enterprise NOS, Novell dropped the IntraNetWare label. All versions of NetWare 5 now come standard with Internet servers.

Another key difference between the previous IntraNetWare release and NetWare 5 are the servers themselves. Where IntraNetWare used a proprietary web server developed by Novell, NetWare 5 uses a specialized version of Netscape's **FastTrack** web server developed by **Novonyx,** a joint venture between Novell and Netscape. By adopting an industry standard web server, Novell has further positioned NetWare as an Internet aware NOS.

NetWare 5 also contains a full function DNS server. Inclusion of these features combine to make NetWare a single solution for Internet connectivity.

■ NETWARE WAN/REMOTE ACCESS

As telecommuting and an increasingly mobile workforce have become more commonplace, network operating system architectures have had to adjust to these business-level requirements. Although LAN remote access solutions will be explored in depth in Chapter 14, NetWare's current approach to remote access is briefly discussed here. NetWare currently offers or supports two distinct product categories to cater to the WAN and remote access needs of NetWare clients.

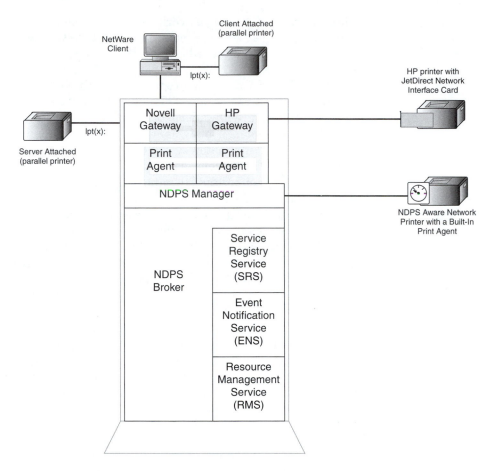

Figure 6-18   NDPS Architecture

- NetWare Internet Access Server/NetWare Connect
- Border Manager

NetWare Internet Access Server/NetWare Connect

Prior to version 5 of NetWare, remote access services were provided in the NetWare environment by implementing the **NetWare Connect** add-on product. NetWare 5 integrates this functionality in the renamed **NetWare Internet Access Server (NAIS),** a built-in option. Conceptually these products provide identical functionality although there are some slight installation and configuration differences. For the remainder of this section they can be thought of as identical.

NIAS is a software-only remote access server solution providing both dial-in and dial-out access capabilities for up to 128 simultaneous users. NIAS runs as an NLM on the server. Client software is available for DOS, Windows, and Macintosh client workstations. Remote access implies that a dialed-in client has the same functionality available to it as a locally attached client. NIAS allows the establishment and support of modem pools that preclude the need for every client workstation to have a directly attached modem and phone line. Following are some of the key operational features or advantages of NIAS:

- *Installation:* Autodetection of modems provides ease of installation. Ordinarily, linking modems and communications software can be a tedious chore while seeking the correct modem set-up string of Hayes AT commands unique to a particular modem.

- *Management:* Multiple servers can be managed from a single console. In addition, provided auditing software tracks system statistics such as users, port usage, line conditions, call duration, and modem speed. NIAS is integrated with NDS, thereby allowing network managers to control and assign both remote and local user access rights from a single location.

- *Security:* Since the passwords between the remote clients and local server must traverse public phone networks, the passwords are encrypted.

- *Supported Protocols:* In order to support the goal of remote access to grant remote clients the same functionality as local clients, specialized protocols are required that can encapsulate upper-layer protocols such as IPX/SPX and NCP and deliver them over the serial WAN links between remote clients and local servers. In other words, in a totally local setting, upper-layer protocols are encapsulated in data-link layer protocol frames such as Ethernet or Token Ring depending on the installed network interface card. In the case of WAN-attached remote access clients, that data-link layer protocol is either **PPP (Point-to-Point Protocol)** or **SLIP (Serial Line Internet Protocol),** both members of the TCP/IP family, more correctly referred to as the Internet Suite of Protocols. NIAS also supports Packet bursting, allowing more efficient use of potentially expensive WAN links while improving overall performance.

- *Usage Analysis:* Network managers can analyze usage trends to spot possible abuse or to prepare reports for cost analysis or charge back purposes.

- *Supported WAN Services:* In addition to normal phone service, otherwise known as POTS (Plain Old Telephone Service) or PSTN (Public Switched Telephone Network), NetWare Connect also supports

ISDN (Integrated Services Digital Network) which can deliver up to 144 Kbps of digital bandwidth over long distances.

Figure 6-19 illustrates a typical NIAS/NetWare Connect application.

BorderManager

BorderManager is NetWare's add-on solution for managing access to remote networks. BorderManager is designed to protect the private network from threats from external networks (such as the Internet) and to provide a means to manage how internal users access external networks. Available for both the NetWare 4 and NetWare 5 platforms, BorderManager functionality includes the following key features:

- *Packet Filtering:* Packets containing certain types of data can be prevented from leaving the internal network. This approach can be used to prevent data from being transferred out of the internal network.

- *Application Proxy Services:* Application protocols such as HTTP and FTP can be proxied to support secure connections between internal and external nodes. When using application proxy services, the internal and external node talk to BorderManager rather than each other. The application proxy service takes the application data from incoming packets on one side and forwards it to the other side.

- *Network Address Translation (NAT):* Using NAT a private network address range can be used on the internal network. Any requests to

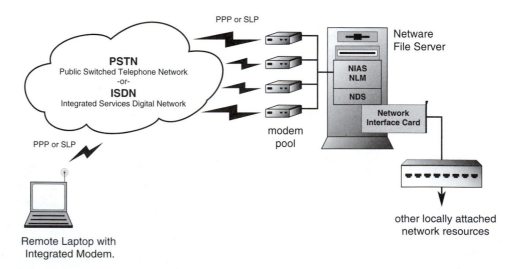

Figure 6-19   NIAS/NetWare Connect

the external network are processed to replace the original source address with the external interface of the BorderManager server. When the BorderManager server receives a response to the request, it readdresses and forwards the packet to the original requester.

- *IPX/IP Gateway:* For IPX only internal networks, BorderManager can translate requests to external networks running the IP protocol. This feature is especially useful for legacy NetWare networks that need access to the Internet.

- *Virtual Private Network (VPN):* Two private networks can be connected across a public, unsecured network (such as the Internet). VPN support requires either another BorderManager or some other VPN gateway be installed at the other VPN location(s).

- *Web Caching:* To maximize bandwidth efficiency to outside networks, web data requested by any client are cached on the BorderManager server. When another internal client requests the data, the cached data are presented instead of retrieving the data from the external network. Caching can be optimized for time to live and always allows a client to refresh data directly from the external source.

- *Web Content Filtering:* Web requests are analyzed against a list of allowed or disallowed sites. Only those requests that meet the criteria are filled. Content filtering can be used to eliminate access to questionable materials or to prevent access to high bandwidth resources such as Internet games.

- *Integrated NDS Management:* BorderManager integrates directly with the NDS security model. Access to external networks can be managed in the same policies using the same tools as internal security.

Figure 6-20 illustrates a typical BorderManager application architecture.

▣   NETWARE CLIENT SUPPORT

In the case of NetWare clients, the native operating system of the particular client workstation serves as the foundation for the operating system-specific version of the NetWare client software.

DOS/Windows 3.11

Unlike the DOS client software of previous NetWare versions known as the NETx shell, which acted as a replacement redirector, the current NetWare DOS client software is referred to as a **requester.** The change in name is relatively minor when compared with the architectural changes to the NetWare

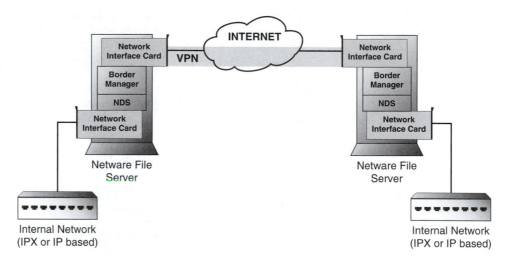

Figure 6-20   BorderManager Application

client software. Rather than remaining as a monolithic, stand-alone operating system, the requester has taken on a more flexible modular appearance. NetWare client functionality can be added or updated on an incremental basis thanks to the introduction of **Virtual Loadable Modules** or **VLM**s. Some VLMs depend on other VLMs and must be loaded in a particular order, whereas other VLMs are totally optional.

In fact, the **NetWare DOS Requester** actually works through DOS by having a VLM management program known as VLM.EXE interrupt DOS as appropriate and request services. The DOS requester uses DOS tables of network-attached resources rather than creating and maintaining its own as was the case with the NETx shell. DOS serves as the primary redirector passing only those requests for network attached resources on to the NetWare DOS Requester. The DOS requester also uses DOS' file handlers to open files on network attached volumes. In this manner, the NetWare DOS Requester combines with DOS to make a transparently interoperating client operating system. Numerous VLM modules are loaded separately onto the DOS client to offer such combined functionality as:

- IPX and NCP protocol stacks

- TCP/IP and NCP protocol stacks

- Security function calls

- NDS services

- Bindery based services

- NetWare Protocol Multiplexer for handling multiple protocol stacks

- File Management

- DOS Redirector

- Printer redirection to network print queues

- NETx Shell emulation

An upgrade to the NetWare DOS Requester known as the **Client32 Requester** is able to offer a wider variety of VLM-based services while using client memory resources more efficiently. DOS, Windows, and Windows 9x versions are based on a 32-bit architecture known as **NetWare I/O Subsystem** or **NIOS.** Figure 6-21 illustrates a conceptual view of the relationship between the NetWare DOS Requester and DOS.

Because Microsoft Windows for Workgroups 3.11 is an operating environment rather than a true operating system, adding NetWare support to Windows for Workgroups requires that the DOS NetWare client be installed. After the DOS client is configured, NetWare extensions to Windows networking are added to support access to NetWare servers via the DOS NetWare client.

Microsoft Windows 9.x and Windows NT Workstation

For Microsoft Windows NT and the Microsoft Windows 9x series of operating systems, there are two client choices available for connecting to NetWare 3 servers. Microsoft ships a NetWare client with Windows that integrates into the existing Windows network stack and Novell ships a separate NetWare client (Client 32). Although there are issues with the native Microsoft client when connecting to NetWare 4 and 5 servers that will be discussed later, it works well with NetWare 3.

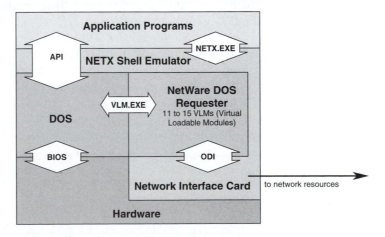

Figure 6-21 The NetWare DOS Requester

If the Novell client is installed, it replaces the native Windows NDIS network drivers with their ODI equivalents. ODI compliant network protocols also replace the native Windows protocols. A "shim" is placed between the ODI drivers and any remaining Microsoft network applications. The shim makes the ODI drivers appear to be NDIS drivers to the Microsoft network applications, allowing them to continue to function normally, although a slight performance penalty is incurred in the translation.

WHICH CLIENT SHOULD BE USED: MICROSOFT'S OR NOVELL'S?

Practical Advice and Information

The decision on which network client to use depends on two factors: workstation function and the predominant client on the workstation. If the workstation is going to be used to administer a NetWare 4 or 5.x server via the nwadmin utility, the Novell NetWare client must be installed.

If the station is not used to administer a NetWare 4 or 5.x server, the predominant network client should be considered. If the main source of network traffic on the station is NetWare, installing the NetWare client is the preferred solution. Conversely, if only occasional access to a NetWare server is required while the majority of network traffic is devoted to Windows networking or general Internet traffic, leaving the native Microsoft NetWare client in place is the preferred solution.

Apple Macintosh

Support for the Apple Macintosh platform varies by NetWare version. NetWare 4 includes Macintosh support and an NDS aware Macintosh client. NetWare 5 unbundles Macintosh support in favor of **NetWare for Macintosh,** an add-in product from Pro Soft Engineering that tightly integrates Macintoshes into the NetWare environment. Although similar in concept to the NetWare 4 Macintosh support, the remainder of this section focuses on the NetWare for Macintosh product.

NetWare for Macintosh is a client/server product containing both a series of NLMs that support Apple-specific networking technologies and a Macintosh NetWare client. Collectively, the client and server portions of NetWare for Macintosh allow for tight integration between the Macintosh and NetWare environments. Supported features include:

- Macintosh users can access files on NetWare servers

- Macintosh clients can send print jobs to NetWare printers

- Non-Macintosh clients can send print jobs to AppleTalk printers on AppleTalk networks

In addition to providing a means for Macintoshes to natively access NetWare servers, NetWare for Macintosh includes the ability for NetWare servers to speak the AppleTalk protocol and appear as a Macintosh server. For more information on AppleTalk, refer to Chapter 4.

MACINTOSH CLIENT INTEROPERABILITY

Practical Advice and Information

NetWare for Macintosh allows files to be shared between Macintosh and Windows computers. It does not provide the ability for Macintoshes to run Windows software or vice versa. Documents can only be shared if the Macintosh application software and Windows application software share a common file format. Fortunately common file formats are becoming more standard. Both Microsoft Office and WordPerfect Office share file formats between their Windows and Macintosh offerings.

■ NETWARE SERVER INTEROPERABILITY

Because of increased demands to be able to share information more quickly and easily within a company, as well as the increased number of corporate mergers and acquisitions, interoperability between different types of network operating systems has become an increasingly important functional characteristic. NetWare natively includes interoperability tools for Windows NT and UNIX.

NetWare/Windows Interoperability

Interoperability with Windows NT Server can be achieved either through the Microsoft **Gateway Services for NetWare,** an optional component of Windows NT Server or installing NDS for NT on all NT servers. Gateway services for NT allows an NT server to present NetWare resources as if they were NT resources and will be covered in Chapter 7.

NDS for NT integrates the Windows NT domain system directly into NDS. By extending the NDS schema to include NT domain information, NDS for NT allows for a single, unified directory. In this manner, NDS for NT is acting as a gateway between the two directory systems. By consolidating to a single administrative platform the cost of administering a heterogeneous NetWare/NT environment can be greatly reduced.

NDS for NT runs on NetWare 4.11 and above and integrates NetWare with NT Server version 3.51 and above. NDS for NT consists of two main components on the NT Server: the **NDS for NT Client** and SAMSRV.DLL. **SAMSRV.DLL** replaces the original NT SAMSRV library and automatically reroutes calls that would normally go to the NT user database to the NDS tree. The NDS for NT Client and SAMSRV.DLL must be installed on every domain controller in the NT network.

After NDS for NT is installed, all existing NT users can be automatically ported to the NDS tree via the **Domain Object Wizard.** The Domain Object

Wizard runs on the NT server one time after NDS for NT is installed. After this initial run, all NT user information is synchronized with the NDS tree. Running the Domain Object Wizard a second time will uninstall NDS for NT.

Managing the NT domain objects that have been ported to NDS is accomplished via the NetWare Administrator (nwadmin). NDS for NT installs extensions to nwadmin that provide this functionality. Additional extensions are added to nwadmin to allow it to create, edit, and delete Microsoft Exchange mailboxes. Using these extensions any changes made in nwadmin are automatically synchronized with the Exchange server. Figure 6-22 illustrates the NDS for NT architecture.

NetWare/UNIX Interoperability

UNIX typically uses the **NFS** or **Network File System** as its file sharing application layer protocol, while NetWare uses the NCP application layer protocols. To support true interoperability either NetWare needs to speak NFS or UNIX needs to speak NCP. The remainder of this section will focus on configuring NetWare to speak NFS. UNIX support of NCP will be covered in Chapter 8.

In order to offer interoperability between NFS and NetWare's native file system, Novell offers NetWare NFS Services. **NetWare NFS Services** allow UNIX systems to access NetWare file servers as if they were native NFS servers. NetWare NFS Services are actually a group of NLMs that run on a NetWare server. This software allows UNIX workstations to access NetWare

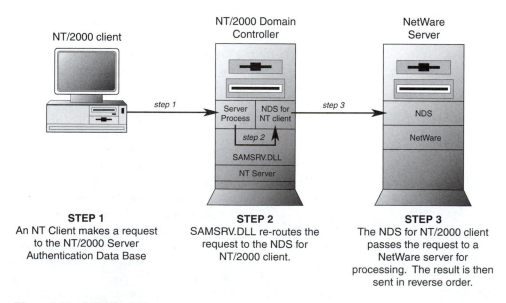

STEP 1
An NT Client makes a request to the NT/2000 Server Authentication Data Base

STEP 2
SAMSRV.DLL re-routes the request to the NDS for NT/2000 client.

STEP 3
The NDS for NT/2000 client passes the request to a NetWare server for processing. The result is then sent in reverse order.

Figure 6-22   NDS for NT

NetWare NFS Services

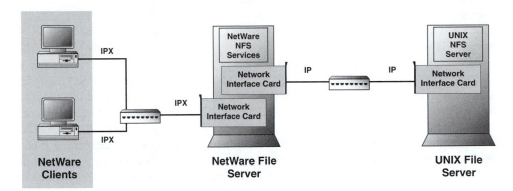

Figure 6-23   NetWare NFS Services

servers via TCP/IP without requiring any software changes to the UNIX clients. NetWare NFS Services is illustrated in Figure 6-23.

Similar to NDS for NT, **NDS for Solaris** allows servers running the Sun Microsystems Solaris UNIX style operating system to be tightly integrated into an NDS directory. By integrating with the Solaris NIS system, NDS for Solaris allows all Solaris accounts to be managed directly from nwadmin.

In addition to these point solutions designed to tightly integrate directory information from NT and Solaris, NetWare's LDAP support provides a common API for application programmers that wish to interact directly with the directory data while maintaining compatibility with other directory service offerings. Available as a standard feature in NetWare 5 or as an add-on in NetWare 4, the application flexibility that LDAP support offers cannot be overestimated.

SUMMARY

Novell NetWare has been a key network operating system since its original release in 1983. Novell claimed its largest market share with NetWare 3 in the early 1990s. While new competitors have fragmented the network operating system market and eroded NetWare's market share, NetWare remains a major network operating system player.

There are three major release families of NetWare in the marketplace at this time: NetWare 3, NetWare 4, and NetWare 5. NetWare 3 was originally designed as a single server Network Operating System (NOS). Using a file based structure called the bindery to house user data, each server operates in a stand-alone environment. There is no integration between two or more NetWare 3 servers.

NetWare 4 introduced NetWare Directory Services, a directory service based data structure for user data. The single control point characteristics of NDS are in sharp contrast to the bindery. By implementing NDS, NetWare 4 is infinitely more scalable that NetWare 3.

Additional improvements have been made in the NetWare kernel, file and print sharing, security, and network protocols. Support for TCP/IP was added in the form of IPX encapsulation in IP.

Despite the improvements made in NetWare 4, NetWare remained a poor application server based on the memory architecture. To address this weakness, Novell introduced NetWare 5.

NetWare 5 improves upon NetWare 4 in almost every NOS category. The most significant improvement is the memory architecture that has been modified to support protected memory spaces for applications running as NLMs. Under NetWare 5, these applications can be insulated from each other and from the operating system itself, resulting in NetWare

becoming a more viable application server platform.

Other key improvements in NetWare 5 include the introduction of NetWare Storage Services and Pure IP. NetWare Storage Services significantly increases the reliability of the NetWare disk storage model, whereas Pure IP greatly improves NetWare's ability to operate in an IP only network environment.

Interoperability with other network operating systems is becoming increasingly important since enterprise networks must deliver transparent interoperability to users regardless of installed network operating systems. Through the release of NFS for NetWare, NDS for NT and NDS for Solaris, NetWare 5 solves many interoperability issues.

KEY TERMS

Auditing system
Authentication
Bindery emulation
Bindery files
Bindery synchronization
BorderManager
Burst Mode IPX
Client32 Requester
ConsoleOne
Container objects
Data migration Netware 4
SFT III
Directory system
   interoperability
Disk allocation blocks
Disk Block Sub-Allocation
Domain Object Wizard
Domain OS
Domain SAP/RIP Server
DSS Server
DynaText On-Line Help
ENS
Event Notification Service
FastTrack
File system interoperability
Global directory service

Grafted
Hierarchical
Integrated messaging services
Inter-ring gate calls
IntraNetWare
Java
Java Beans
Large Internet Packets
Large Packet IPX
LDAP
Leaf objects
Lightweight Directory Access
   Protocol
LIP
Migration Agent
Mirrored Server Link
MPR
Multiprotocol Router
NDPS
NDPS Broker
NDPS Gateway
NDPS Managers
NDS
NDS Catalog Services
NDS for NT
NDS for NT Client

NDS for Solaris
NetSync Cluster
NetWare 4 SMP
NetWare Connect
NetWare Directory Services
NetWare Distributed Print
   System
NetWare DOS Requester
NetWare for Macintosh
NetWare I/O Subsystem
NetWare Internet Access Server
NetWare Licensing Service
NetWare Link Services
Protocol
NetWare Loadable Modules
NetWare NFS Services
NetWare partition
NetWare Storage Services
NetWare/IP
Network File System
NFS
NIAS
NIOS
NLMs
NLS
NLSP

Novell Upgrade Wizard
Novonyx
NSS
NWAdmin
NWIP
Objects
Packet bursts
Packet signing
Partitions
PKIS
Point-to-Point Protocol
PPP
Printer Agents
Properties
Protected address spaces
Pruned
Public Key Infrastructure
Services

Pure IP
Read ahead cache buffering
Replicated
Requester
Resource Management Service
Ring 0
Ring 3
Ring memory protection
RMS
Role based administration
Root
SAMSRV.DLL
SAS
Secure Authentication Services
Serial Line Internet Protocol
Server duplexing
Service Location Protocol
Service Registry Service

SLIP
SLP
SMP
SMP kernelFile compression
SRS
Sub-allocation blocks
Symmetrical multiprocessing
TCO
Total Cost of Ownership
Values
Virtual Loadable Modules
Virtual memory
VLM
WAN Traffic Manager Services
Z.E.N. Works
Zero Cost Networking

REVIEW QUESTIONS

1. What is the purpose of the separate NetWare and DOS partitions on a NetWare server?
2. What is the functional difference between NLMs and VLMs?
3. What is the relationship between objects, properties, and values in a bindery?
4. What is a bindery?
5. What is the function of NCP?
6. What are the major functional differences between NDS and bindery-based directory services?
7. What is a NetSynch Cluster?
8. What are the major architectural differences between NDS and bindery-based directory services?
9. What are the benefits of distribution of the NDS database?
10. What are the benefits of replication of the NDS database?
11. Describe the differences between bindery synchronization and bindery emulation.
12. Describe NetWare 4's attempts at memory protection for the operating system kernel.
13. What are the shortcomings of this memory protection scheme?
14. Describe the implementation of SMP in NetWare 4 SMP.
15. Evaluate the pros and cons of server duplexing.

16. What is the benefit of disk sub-allocation?
17. Differentiate between encryption, authentication, and packet signing.
18. What are the benefits of packet bursts?
19. What are the benefits of LIP?
20. How does NetWare 4 provide support for IP connected clients?
21. Describe NetWare 5's memory protection scheme. How does this approach affect NetWare's ability to act as an application server?
22. Explain NetWare 5's SMP capabilities.
23. What are the key differences and advantages of NSS compared to NWFS?
24. How do SAS and PKIS improve security in the NetWare environment?
25. What is ConsoleOne and why is it significant?
26. How does NetWare 5 improve NetWare's ability to operate efficiently over WAN connections?
27. What is the purpose of Z.E.N. Works?
28. How has support for IP been changed in NetWare 5 compared to NetWare 4?
29. How has printing support in NetWare 5 been improved?
30. Explain the parts of the NDPS system and how they integrate.
31. What functionality is delivered by NAIS/NetWare Connect?

32. What features are provided by BorderManager?
33. What features are added by the installation of NetWare for Macintosh?
34. Compare the options of UNIX/NetWare interoperability in terms of functionality, architecture, and installed software.
35. Compare the options of Windows NT/NetWare interoperability in terms of functionality, architecture, and installed software.
36. Explain why LDAP support is important to NetWare users.

ACTIVITIES

1. What are the hardware requirements for a NetWare 5 server?
2. How large must the NetWare and DOS partitions be on a NetWare 5 server?
3. Find examples of NLMs from sources other than Novell.
4. Draw an OSI diagram, properly placing all communications protocols associated with NetWare.
5. Find installations currently running NetWare 4 or 5 and interview networking personnel. Focus questioning on migration issues and perceived benefits. Include as much measurable, objective data in your report/presentation as possible.
6. Find and interview installations currently running NetWare 3. Focus questioning on migration planning, timetables, and perceived benefits. Why (or why not) is this installation migrating to NetWare 5?
7. Interview NetWare network managers that have fully implemented NDS. Focus questioning on the managers' perceptions of the benefits/shortcomings of NDS. Analyze your results.
8. Research the implementation of SMP in either Windows NT or UNIX. Compare and contrast this implementation with the SMP implementation in NetWare. Analyze your results.
9. Prepare a budget for server duplexing. How available are the Mirrored server link adapters? Are they actually special adapters? How much do they cost? What are the names of some vendors that sell them?
10. Prepare a payback period or breakeven analysis for investment in NetWare SFT including hardware and software. State assumptions as to MTBF (Mean Time Between Failures) and lost revenue per hour.
11. Research the cost of hot sites and compare that cost and functionality with the cost of the NetWare SFT implementation.
12. Interview a NetWare network manager to investigate the use of the auditing system. What features are being audited? What have the benefits been?
13. Find a NetWare installation supporting bindery synchronization and/or bindery emulation. Investigate the motivations for implementing this functionality as well as the perceived benefits.
14. Find an installation of NetWare/IP. Why was this product chosen? Report on the benefits, draw protocol stacks for both clients and servers, and draw a network architecture map highlighting the communication protocols.
15. Find an installation that has upgraded to NetWare 5. Interview the people who made the upgrade decision and determine the key reasons the upgrade was made. Prepare a report on your findings.
16. Find an installation of NAIS/NetWare Connect. Interview the people who use NetWare Connect remotely as well as the network manager. Report on functional benefits and drawbacks and draw a detailed network architecture highlighting communications protocols.
17. Find an installation of NDS for NT. Interview the administrators and prepare a report on the benefits to this organization from the installation of the product.
18. Research new or upcoming releases of NetWare. What new features are planned? What are the key benefits of these new features?

CASE STUDY

How Firm Stays Atop 25,000 Updates Per Second

If you think your network puts you in a tough spot, consider Len Monteleone's position. Externally, his network is about to serve up-to-date financial information over the World Wide Web. Internally, he has to deal with a network application called "the beast."

Monteleone is director of IT at Tullett & Tokyo Forex, an international securities trading company, which is upgrading its network to reach out to large customers over the Web. But because timing decides whether money is made or lost on a trade, the company's first priority is to make sure its own traders have real-time pricing data.

Securities prices are updated 25,000 times per second, and that's why the application that delivers the updates to the trading floor has earned the moniker of "the beast."

"Early on with the beast, we blew up every piece of equipment that we had," Monteleone says. Cisco routers and 3Com network interface cards were among the devices that couldn't keep up with the high volume.

Two years ago, Tullett & Tokyo installed Xylan switches to tame the beast. About a dozen Windows NT servers connect through four of Xylan's OmniSwitch LAN and ATM switches. The OmniSwitches in turn connect to Xylan PizzaSwitches at every trading desk via 155M bit/sec ATM. The Pizza-Switches provide 10M bit/sec and 100M bit/sec Ethernet connections to the desktops.

Monteleone says one of the biggest advantages of this approach is that there is no wiring closet on the trading floor. The company didn't have to buy a large box for the closet and doesn't have cables running out to every desktop. Instead, there are only 23 fiber-optic strands running to the PizzaSwitches at the trading desks. Short cables connect each PizzaSwitch to the 10 or 12 workstations at each desk.

The whole shebang cost about $250,000, whereas other vendors' solutions would have been two or three times that amount, Monteleone says. Much of the savings came from not having to recable the trading floor.

The switches have kept pace with the beast, delivering all updates to traders in real time. "You can't believe the amount of information you're looking at," Monteleone says.

A PEEK INSIDE

The new challenge is presenting market data to the outside world. Monteleone recently spent about $50,000 for six Foundry Networks Fast Ethernet switches, as part of the company's initiative to make select information available on the Web. This information includes end-of-day pricing and historical data related to different securities markets and foreign exchanges.

The Foundry switches provide redundant connections so if a switch fails, Web traffic will still be able to get through to the servers. There ought to be more than enough bandwidth to handle the load because the switches will have 100M bit/sec Ethernet links between them. The routers connecting the switches to the Internet will probably have a DS-3 (45M bit/sec) pipe, with a T-1 (1.5M bit/sec) backup, Monteleone says.

Tullett & Tokyo will continue to use Cisco routers to connect to the Internet because the Foundry gear doesn't have WAN connections.

Currently, the company is still trying to determine the right number of servers to hook up. It will probably choose to connect five to 10 of the "latest and greatest" Intel-based servers, Monteleone says. Foundry Server-Iron switches include a load-balancing function for distributing Web requests among the servers in a round-robin fashion.

CHEAPER TO BUY NEW

Tullett & Tokyo is now planning to install another Foundry switch to provide access from the Xylan network to the rest of the company. Currently a Cisco 7000 router fills that role.

But Monteleone found that upgrading the router to prepare it for the date change to 2000 was more expensive than buying a Foundry Big-Iron switch; updating software, memory and CPU would be factors. Plus, the router only supported 10M bit/sec Ethernet. Monteleone wants to migrate to faster speeds and is looking at Fast Ethernet and Gigabit Ethernet.

Faster speeds will be key as Tullett & Tokyo moves forward, with the Web and the beast at its heels.

"With trading information, delays are just not acceptable," Monteleone says.

Source: Jeff Caruso, "How Firm Stays Atop 25,000 Updates per Second," *Network World,* vol. 16, no. 6 (February 8, 1999), p. 17. Copyright (February 8, 1999), Network World.

BUSINESS CASE STUDY QUESTIONS

Activities

1. Complete a top-down model for this case by gleaning facts from the case and placing them in the proper layer of the top-down model. After completing the top-down model, analyze and detail those instances where requirements were clearly passed down from upper layers to lower layers of the model and where solutions to those requirements were passed up from lower layers to upper layers of the model.
2. Detail any questions about the case that may occur to you for which answers are not clearly stated in the article.

Business

1. What is the business need for 25,000 updates per second?
2. Why are network delays not acceptable in this environment?

Application

1. What is "the beast"?
2. What new application is Tullett & Tokyo Forex preparing to launch that will require additional bandwidth?

Data

1. What type of data does the system manage?

Network

1. What key features does the logical network design for "the breast" implement?
2. What server load balancing features are critical in the new application?

Technology

1. What network architecture(s) did Tullet & Tokyo Forex use in the initial system?
2. Why is there not a wiring closet on the trading floor?

CHAPTER 7

WINDOWS NT (2000)

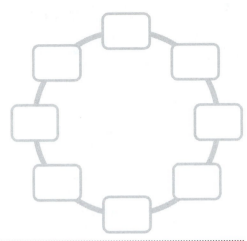

Concepts Reinforced

OSI Model	Client/Server Technology Model
LAN Software	Protocols and Standards
Network Architecture	Network Operating Systems
Network Operating Systems	Functionality
Architectures	

Concepts Introduced

Hardware Adaptation Layer	NT Communication Protocols
NT Architecture	NT Functionality
NT Servers	NT Clients
NT Interoperability	NetWare/NT Interoperability

OBJECTIVES

After mastering the material in this chapter you should:

1. Understand the major architectural and functional features of Windows NT

2. Understand the key differences between Windows NT 4.0 and Windows 2000 Professional

3. Understand the communication protocols underlying the Windows NT network operating system

4. Understand the options and limitations for interoperability between Windows NT and other platforms such as UNIX, NetWare, and Macintosh

5. Understand the remote access options associated with Windows NT

■ INTRODUCTION

Like NetWare, Windows NT is a fully integrated network operating system, incorporating both standard operating system and network operating system functionality into a single integrated product. Unlike NetWare, Windows NT was designed from the outset to be both portable and scalable. **Portability** is evidenced by Windows NT's unique ability to execute over multiple different CPUs such as Intel x86, and DEC Alpha. **Scalability** is provided through symmetrical multiprocessing support. Portability and scalability are only two of the important architectural characteristics exhibited by Windows NT that will be explored in this chapter. Windows NT distinguishes itself from NetWare by its ability to successfully support high-powered applications such as database engines, in addition to admirably performing print and file services.

The overall purpose of this chapter is to introduce the reader to the important architectural and functional characteristics of Windows NT. While direct comparisons between NetWare and Windows NT will be made throughout the chapter, the outline of the chapter is similar to that of the chapter on NetWare (Chapter 6) in order to ease comparison.

The current version of Windows NT is NT 4.0. Microsoft is readying Windows 2000 (a.k.a. Windows NT 5.0) for release sometime in early 2000. This chapter will focus on the basic characteristics of Windows NT as implemented in NT 4.0 and announced for Windows 2000.

Having carefully reviewed the chapter on NetWare and Windows NT as part of an overall top-down, business-oriented networking analysis, the reader should feel comfortable making recommendations as to whether either of these two powerful and popular network operating systems will meet their identified networking needs.

■ WINDOWS NT 4.0

Windows NT was developed by Microsoft as a "New Technology" (NT) platform to address the shortcomings of the Windows 3.x and LAN Manager product lines. The key new technologies introduced in Windows NT were preemptive multi-tasking and virtual machines. NT quickly gained acceptance in small to mid-size environments where its ease of use features outweighed its network object management architectural limitations.

The initial release of Windows NT was 3.1 (to correspond to Windows 3.1) rather than the traditional 1.0. After releasing versions 3.5 and 3.51, Microsoft released NT 4.0 in mid-1996. NT 4.0 combines the user interface initially released with Windows 95 with the stability of the Windows NT architecture.

Overall Architecture

Windows NT 4.0 is an integrated network operating system designed to support single server environments through enterprise-wide deployments. Windows NT 4.0 is available in three versions:

- Windows NT Workstation

- Windows NT Server

- Windows NT Server Enterprise Edition

Windows NT Workstation is architecturally identical to NT Server. The differences in the two platforms are available services and performance tuning. Since NT Workstation is designed to serve as a user workstation, some NT Server network services are not included. Examples of NT Server service that are not available in NT Workstation include Web, FTP, and DNS services. Similarly, in NT Workstation, processor priority is focused on foreground applications at the expense of background services.

Windows NT Workstation is just one of the possible client platforms that can interact with Windows NT Server. In addition, several computers running Windows NT Workstation can be linked to each other in a peer-to-peer network architecture. Windows NT Workstation computer supports only 10 incoming connections.

Windows NT Server Enterprise Edition expands NT Servers' scalability. SMP extensibility is increased to support up to 32 processors on systems on special hardware. Clustering and load balancing support allow multiple NT Servers to be tightly integrated. Using Windows NT Load Balancing Services (WLBS), up to 32 NT Servers can be clustered into a single network address, greatly increasing processing capacity. From the perspective of a network client this cluster of servers appears to be a single machine.

Windows NT Server Terminal Server edition includes special extensions that support ultra-thin clients. Ultra-thin clients, also known as network computers (NC), act as a graphical terminal to applications that are actually running on the server. Compared to traditional client/server applications a network computer solution required significantly more server resources because the server runs the applications for each client. A complete description of network computers is provided in Chapter 10. Figure 7-1 lists the key characteristics of the NT 4.0 platform.

Operating System Architecture and Characteristics

In addition to scalability and portability, stability is a very important functional characteristic of Windows NT. Compared to Windows 3.x and Windows 9x, Windows NT is relatively crash proof. This system stability can be largely attributed to rigid enforcement of structured access to hardware resources. Application programs and APIs are prohibited from interacting directly with hardware resources in Windows NT. Instead, applications and APIs must access hardware resources by requesting services through system services collectively referred to as the **NT Executive.**

As illustrated in Figure 7-2, communication between the various NT Executive sub-systems and the I/O manager is controlled by the **NT Kernel,**

Network Operating System Characteristic	Windows NT 4.0 Server	Windows NT 4.0 Server Enterprise Edition	Windows NT 4.0 Server Terminal Server Edition
Hardware and Platform			
Supported Processors	Intel x86 (386 or better) Digital Alpha PowerPC (While originally supported, support was dropped with Service Pack 3)	Intel x86 (386 or better) Digital Alpha PowerPC (While originally supported, support was dropped with Service Pack 3)	Intel x86 (386 or better) Digital Alpha PowerPC (While originally supported, support was dropped with Service Pack 3)
Required Memory	32 MB	64 MB	128 MB
Symmetrical Multi-Processing	4 processors	16 Processors (Up to 32 processors is possible with special hardware)	16 Processors (Up to 32 processors is possible with special hardware)
Operating System			
Program Structure	32 Bit	32 Bit	32 Bit
Memory Architecture	Virtual Machines	Virtual Machines	Virtual Machines
Preemptive Multi-tasking	Yes	Yes	Yes
Clustering	No	Yes	Yes
Load Balancing	No	Yes	Yes
File System	FAT NTFS	FAT NTFS	FAT NTFS
User Interface	GUI	GUI	GUI
Network Drivers	NDIS	NDIS	NDIS
Application Program Interface(s)	Win 32	Win 32	Win 32
CD-ROM Support	Yes	Yes	Yes
Management and Administration			
Network Object Management System	Domain Name Services	Domain Name Services	Domain Name Services
Administrative Location	Administration can be performed either from the server, from clients using utility applications, or via HTTP (WWW)	Administration can be performed either from the server, from clients using utility applications, or via HTTP (WWW)	Administration can be the performed either from server, from clients using utility applications, or via HTTP (WWW)
Network Services			
Thin Client (Network Computer) Support	No	No	Yes

(continued)

Network Protocols Supported	IPX/SPX NetBEUI TCP/IP Apple Talk (Macintosh support only) DLC (Printing only)	IPX/SPX NetBEUI TCP/IP AppleTalk (Macintosh support only) DLC (Printing only)	IPX/SPX NetBEUI TCP/IP Apple Talk (Macintosh support only) DLC (Printing only)
Multiprotocol Routing	Yes (Capabilities can be expanded via add-on product)	Yes (Capabilities can be expanded via add-on product)	Yes (Capabilities can be expanded via add-on product)
Native Services	File and print FTP Web	File and print FTP Web	File and print FTP Web
Common Third-party Services	Electronic mail Database Firewall etc.	Electronic mail Database Firewall etc.	Electronic mail Database Firewall etc.
Clients Supported	DOS Windows 3.x Windows 9x Windows NT UNIX OS/2 Macintosh	DOS Windows 3.x Windows 9x Windows NT UNIX OS/2 Macintosh	DOS Windows 3.x Windows 9x Windows NT UNIX OS/2 Macintosh

Figure 7-1   Windows NT 4.0 Server Technology Analysis Grid

sometimes referred to as the microkernel. Communication with hardware resources is allowed to occur by either of the following methods:

- Through the systems services layer, through the NT kernel, through the hardware abstraction layer, to the hardware resources

- Through the systems services layer, through the I/O manager and its sub-systems, through the hardware abstraction layer, to the hardware resources

This stable architecture with structured communication between sub-systems affords NT another architectural characteristic known as **modularity of design,** which allows entire sub-systems to be easily added or replaced. For example, replacement of the current Windows NT security sub-system with a Kerberos enabled authentication system would be a relatively straightforward modification.

Hardware Abstraction Layer   As illustrated in Figure 7-2, most of the hardware-specific portions of Windows NT are isolated in a sub-section known as the **hardware abstraction layer** or **HAL.** The hardware abstraction layer in Windows NT provides similar functions as the BIOS in DOS. The HAL can

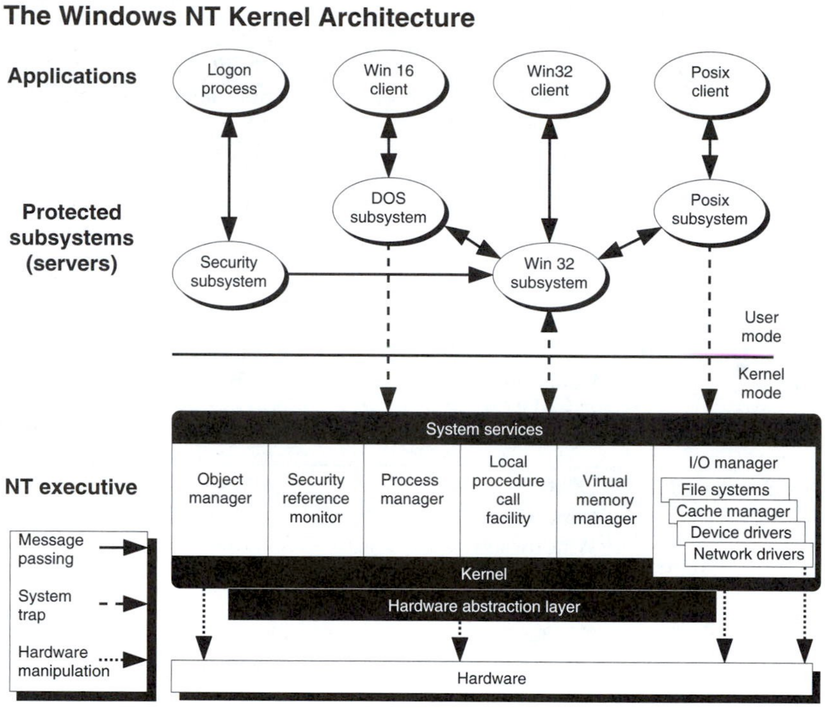

The Windows NT Kernel Architecture

Figure 7-2   Windows NT Architecture

be thought of as a hardware API. It takes standard calls from the kernel and converts them into specific instructions for the underlying hardware. From the perspective of the kernel, every HAL looks identical. To execute Windows NT on any given CPU chip, the following major steps are required:

- Develop a hardware-specific version of the hardware abstraction layer

- Supply a compatible Microsoft C compiler since Windows NT is written in C

- License the Windows NT source code from Microsoft

- Recompile the Windows NT source code on the C compiler that executes on this new CPU

Routines or system calls embedded within the HAL can be called from either the NT kernel or from device drivers included in the NT I/O manager.

NT Executive   The NT executive is comprised of the NT kernel plus a variety of sub-systems known collectively as system services. Among these system services are the following:

- I/O Manager

- Local Procedure Call Manager

- Object Manager

- Process Manager

- Virtual Memory Manager

- Security Reference Monitor

NT Kernel   The NT kernel runs over the hardware abstraction layer and controls the overall traffic flow of messages throughout the operating system. The NT kernel is more specifically concerned with handling interrupts and exceptions for communication between sub-systems and between hardware resources and the operating system. As part of the management of all inter–sub-system communication, the kernel is responsible for constantly checking the NT executive's security sub-system to ensure that requests for services have been properly authorized. More specifically, the NT kernel is responsible for:

- Thread scheduling in NT's multithreaded environment

- Multiple processor synchronization when NT runs on a SMP capable computer

- Interrupt and exception handling

- System crash recovery

- Security checking and enforcement

Interrupt handling occupies the majority of the NT kernel's time since an interrupt to the NT kernel is generated for every NT executive sub-system interaction. The NT kernel runs in **privileged mode** and is therefore never paged out of memory.

I/O Manager   The **I/O Manager** is in charge of managing all input and output for the Windows NT operating system. As illustrated in Figure 7-2, the I/O manager is particularly concerned with managing the communication between:

- Device drivers

- Network drivers

- Cache Manager

- File Systems Drivers

Device drivers, otherwise known as hardware device drivers, are specifically written to support a particular hardware device such as a printer, keyboard, or mouse. Windows NT provides a standardized environment within the I/O manager in which these device drivers can execute. Thanks to this standardized environment, device drivers will operate on any platform on which Windows NT is supported. Device drivers are written in C, like Windows NT, and can be easily swapped or added.

Network drivers will be discussed in more detail in the Communication Protocols section of this chapter. Many of the network drivers supported by Windows NT have been previously mentioned. For example:

- NetBIOS, Redirector, and the SMB server interface to applications and file systems.

- Communication protocols such as TCP/IP, NetBEUI, and IPX/SPX provide transport services.

- NDIS provides the ability for a network interface card to support multiple protocols as well as the ability for a network operating system to communicate with more than one NIC in a single computer.

The **cache manager** works closely with the file systems supported by NT to optimize file services offered to applications. By effectively managing cache memory, the cache manager can minimize the number of physical read/writes to disks, thereby optimizing the performance of application programs. Cache management becomes especially critical when NT is operating in an SMP environment due to the increased processing speed.

Windows NT supports multiple different file systems including FAT (DOS) and NTFS. In order for NT to communicate with these multiple different file systems, an intermediate layer of software interacts with both NT and the particular file system that is required. These specially written intermediate layers of software are known as **file system drivers.** When file systems services are required by applications, the file system is accessed by the I/O manager via the proper file system driver.

The modular design of the I/O manager allows these categories of drivers to be changed and allows simultaneous support of multiple file systems and drivers. Often, requests for I/O services come from application programs indirectly via the Win32 subsystem. The I/O manager oversees the interaction among the various categories of drivers to ensure that application programs are delivered requested services in a timely fashion. Communication among these various drivers is standardized by the I/O manager through the use of **I/O request packets.**

Local Procedure Call Facility Windows NT adheres to a client/server model internally. Application programs that request services of the NT operating system via sub-system services are considered clients, whereas the NT operating sub-systems that service those requests are considered servers. The internal communication within Windows NT between internal client requests and server responses is controlled by the **Local Procedure Call Facility,** a message-passing system. The exact nature of the message passing between application programs and NT system services will be explored further in the Application Services section of this chapter.

Object Manager   Objects in the context of Windows NT are anything that the NT operating system or any of its sub-systems can manipulate, access, or use in any way. Files, directories, and application program threads are all examples of objects. Object categories differ in the type of operations that can be performed on them and in the authorization level required to perform the given operation. The **object manager** is responsible for overall management of all NT objects including enforcement of naming conventions and authorization. In a very real sense, the object manager is responsible for object security.

Process Manager   A process can be thought of as the execution environment of an application program. The process includes the executable code of the application as well as the required memory space in which to execute the program. The **process manager** is ultimately responsible for the creation, maintenance, and termination of processes within Windows NT and communicates with the object manager and virtual memory manager in order to provide the required resources and protection for processes.

Virtual Memory Manager   To allow application programs to easily access large amounts of memory space beyond the limits of the physically installed memory, Windows NT uses portions of the disk drive as virtual memory. Every process is able to access up to 4 GB (gigabytes) of virtual memory provided adequate disk space is available. In a process known as **demand paging,** the **Virtual Memory Manager** transparently moves program code and data between assigned physical RAM and the disk-based paging file unbeknownst to the unsuspecting process. Much like the object manager and the process manager, the virtual memory manager also ensures that processes are protected from each other by preventing processes from writing into each other's memory space.

Security Reference Monitor   Yet another source of security for processes and the objects they manipulate is the **security reference monitor.** The security reference monitor is primarily concerned with performing authentication and authorization for processes that wish to access objects and users that wish to access the system via the logon process. The security reference monitor also generates audit reference messages to ensure proper records are kept that accurately record a wide variety of system activities.

Multiprocessing, Multitasking, Multithreading   Thanks to its limited functional focus on the management of overall traffic flow through the operating system, the NT kernel can be executed on any CPU in a SMP (Symmetrical Multi-Processing) computer. This arrangement allows any processor in an NT multiprocessor arrangement to offer full multithreaded operating system functionality. Windows NT 4.0 is able to run on as many as 16 processors simultaneously.

Windows NT is a preemptive multitasking operating system implying that applications are preempted or replaced with other application programs once their allotted amount of CPU cycles has been consumed. In this scenario, the Windows NT operating system never relinquishes full control of the CPU or memory resources to the application programs. Windows NT retains the ability to interrupt any application program.

Memory Architecture   Windows NT offers protected memory application execution via the use of Ring 0 and 3 assignments. Windows NT applications are normally executed in **user mode** (ring 3) where they are limited to their own protected memory area. This prevents applications from writing into each other's memory space and thereby causing general protection faults and system crashes. In order to access the I/O manager portion of the NT executive, applications must enter **kernel mode** (Ring 0). Architecturally, user mode and kernel mode processes and sub-systems are illustrated in Figure 7-2.

MULTITHREADED KERNELS AND SMP SCALABILITY

In Sharper Focus

SMP scalability refers to the percentage of increased performance achieved for each additional CPU. For example, 100% SMP scalability implies that adding a second CPU will double the original performance or computing power of a computer and that adding a third CPU will triple the original performance of a computer. In reality, due to the operating system overhead caused by having to coordinate the efforts of multiple CPUs, 100% scalability is impossible to achieve.

Not all network operating systems achieve the same level of SMP scalability. Network operating systems vary in their level of SMP scalability depending on whether or not the network operating system's kernel is multithreaded. Although OS/2 and Windows NT are both considered multithreaded operating systems capable of SMP, only Windows NT's kernel is multithreaded. In other words, although multiple threads can execute simultaneously across multiple CPUs in user mode in OS/2, when a thread requires I/O services and is required to enter kernel mode, only a single thread can be in kernel mode at any single point in time. In contrast, in Windows NT, multiple threads executing on multiple CPUs can be in kernel mode simultaneously. Figure 7-3 illustrates the effects of single-threaded and multithreaded kernels within multithreaded operating systems.

Single Threaded Kernel

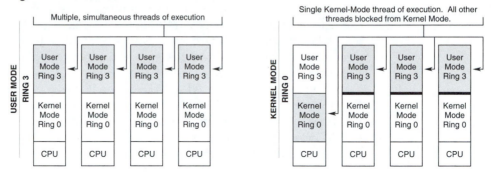

Multi-Threaded Kernel

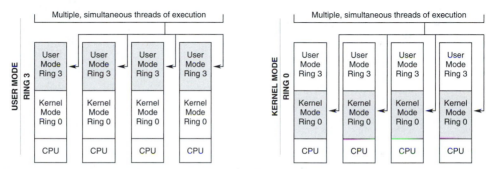

Figure 7-3   Single Threaded vs. Multithreaded Kernels

File Systems   As previously mentioned, NT supports the following file systems:

- **FAT** (File Allocation Table)—Compatible with DOS (only file system supported on diskettes)

- **NTFS** (NT File System)—Windows NT

- **CDFS** (CD File System)

Windows NT can also support simultaneous access to NetWare files stored on NetWare servers thanks to a layer of software that acts as a sort of redirector for file system requests known as the **Multiple Provider Router (MPR).** The MPR is an open interface that accepts requests to any supported file system from application programs adhering to the Win32 API. It is the MPR's responsibility to examine each request for file system services and route the request to the server housing the requested file system.

FAT   The FAT filesystem provides support for the legacy DOS file system. Using FAT, filenames are limited to eight characters plus a three-character extension, whereas filenames in Windows NT can be up to 256 characters in length. To resolve this difference in available length, a FAT-compatible eight-plus-three conventional name is automatically created for files with long filenames. For example, although this chapter was created as "Chapter 7.doc" on an NT computer with NTFS, when it is edited on a laptop running Windows 98 with FAT, the file is loaded as "Chapter~1.doc". Both FAT and NTFS partitions can be created on the same disk and files can be easily copied between the two file systems by NT. NT's FAT file system allows filenames of up to 256 characters on floppy diskettes.

NT FAT VERSUS FAT32

Practical Advice and Information

It is important to differentiate between the traditional 16 bit FAT file system as implemented in DOS, Windows NT, and the original release of Windows 95 and FAT32, the revised FAT filesystem introduced in Windows 95 OEM Service Release 2 (SR2 or Windows 95B) and Windows 98. Windows NT 4.0 can only access disk partitions formatted with FAT16. FAT32 partitions created with Windows 95 or 98 are not accessible by Windows NT 4.0.

■ NTFS

NTFS took the positive attributes of the FAT file system and added features required to support very large files and disk drives and features to increase security, reliability, and recoverability. Figure 7-4 summarizes the key features of NTFS.

NTFS FILE SYSTEM RECOVERABILITY

In Sharper Focus

NTFS treats its file system activity in a manner similar to distributed database transactions: If transactions are not successfully completed for any reason, a mechanism is in place to either re-post or roll-back those transactions to maintain database integrity.

The same scenario applies to NTFS. File system activity is looked upon as a series of transactions that is documented by the **log file service** of NTFS. In the unlikely event of a Windows NT system crash, two types of file system transactions would require scrutiny:

- Transactions that were being held in disk cache for lazy-write posting and were therefore not physically written to disk when the system crashed.

- Transactions that were is the midst of posting when the system crashed.

NTFS Feature	Explanation/Importance
Access Control	Access control permissions can be assigned to individual files as well as to directories.
Master File Table	• Contains records for each file and directory in NTFS. • Records concerning the organization of NTFS and the Master File Table (MFT) are redundant in case the primary record becomes corrupted. • Small files (less than 1500 bytes) are stored entirely within the MFT for faster access.
NTFS File Attributes	File attributes are contained with a file's MFT record. The list of file attributes can be customized for particular environments (Mac, UNIX) and can be added to in order to extend NTFS functionality.
Filenames	NTFS allows filenames up to 255 characters but also generates 8-plus-3 names for FAT/DOS compatibility.
POSIX Compliance	POSIX compliance allows UNIX applications to access files stored in NTFS on Windows NT. In order to do this, NTFS needs to support some unique POSIX file attributes such as: • case-sensitive filenames • hard-links that allow a given file to be accessed by more than one filename • additional time stamp attributes to show when a given file was last accessed or modified
Macintosh Support	Windows NT Services for Macintosh allows files to be accessed by both Macintosh users and Windows NT clients. To the Mac users, the NT server looks like an AppleShare server. NTFS supports unique Mac file attributes such as resource and data forks as well as the Finder utility. Macintosh access control permissions are also supported.
Hot Fixing	If NTFS finds a bad sector on a SCSI disk, it will automatically move the affected files and mark that segment as bad without the need for any user intervention.
File System Recovery	NTFS uses the cache manager to buffer disk writes in a process known as lazy-write, and also runs a transaction log on all disk writes to allow NTFS to recover quickly from system crashes.

Figure 7-4 NTFS Features

The log file service records two types of information: Re-do information allows transactions that were still sitting in disk cache to be re-posted. Periodically, NTFS checks the cache to note the status of transactions that had been physically written to disk. In the event of a system crash, these checkpoints make the recovery process more expedient. Undo information allows transaction entries that were in the midst of posting to be rolled-back or undone.

The NTFS file system is self-recovering. No file clean-up utility needs to be run by the users. Upon initialization, NTFS checks to see if it went down dirty. If the filesystem is determined to be dirty, it performs an analysis pass with the help of the log file service to determine where it left off when the system crashed. NTFS then re-posts filesystem transactions based on the log file service's re-do and checkpoint information and removes partial or corrupted transactions based on the log file service's undo information. This entire process of file system recovery takes only a matter of seconds. In contrast, a file recovery on a 1.2 GB NWFS partition under NetWare 4 takes approximately 35 minutes.

In Sharper Focus

MASTER FILE TABLE DESIGN ENSURES FAST ACCESS AND RELIABILITY

The design of the Master File Table attempts to accomplish two key, often contradictory, objectives:

- Fast performance and lookups, especially on small files and directories

- Reliable performance thanks to numerous redundant features

Interestingly, the **Master File Table** is able to accomplish both of these objectives quite well. First, the definition of the records within the MFT allows small files and directories to actually be included on the MFT record, thereby precluding the need for any further searches or disk accesses. For larger directory files, NTFS uses a hierarchical B-tree structure to ensure fast performance and directory lookups on larger directories as well.

Reliability is ensured through the relationship of the following redundant features as illustrated in Figure 7-5:

- Redundant MFT Master Records—MFT Mirror Record

- Redundant MFT Files and Data segments—MFT Mirror File

- Redundant boot sectors

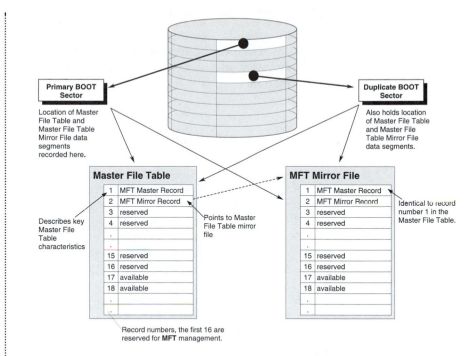

Figure 7-5   Built-in Reliability in the Master File Table Design

Fault Tolerance   Windows NT offers the following fault-tolerant features, most of which have been described in detail in previous chapters:

- Disk Mirroring, in which all data written to one disk are also written to a second redundant disk. In the event that the primary disk fails, the redundant disk takes over immediately.

- Disk Duplexing, which improves upon disk mirroring by ensuring that the two mirrored disks are also supported by separate disk controllers, thereby eliminating another potential point of failure.

- Disk Striping with Parity, otherwise known as RAID 5, allows data to be reconstructed from among the redundant array of disks in the event of a disk failure. Software-based RAID offers a less expensive alternative to hardware RAID sub-systems available from a variety of vendors.

- UPS support is especially important because of the function of the cache manager within Windows NT. In order to optimize system performance, physical writes to disk are not always performed immediately upon the execution of a "save" command. This information is often stored in cache memory until a convenient time to access the disk. If the system should shut down unexpectedly, all information stored in cache memory is lost. By having the ability to support uninterruptable power supplies, NT can execute an orderly system shutdown when necessary, thereby saving all cached information.

Management and Administration

Windows NT 4.0 uses a domain naming system approach to network object management. While this approach provides greater scalability than independent servers, it is not as scalable as a complete directory service solution.

Administration of NT systems is made easier by the graphical nature of the system. NT systems can be administered from the server itself, from clients on the network using optional tools, or via the web using the webadmin package in conjunction with the optional NT web server.

Domains and Workgroups   Unlike NetWare 4 and 5, Windows NT does not have a single, universal database in which all user and network resource information is stored and maintained. Instead, Windows NT networks are organized around the concept of **domains.** A domain is a collection of Windows NT servers that share a single security sub-system that controls access to all resources in the domain.

Information concerning the resources in a domain and the users allowed access to those resources is housed in a Windows NT server designated as the **primary domain controller.** All domains must have one, and only one, primary domain controller. Other NT servers in the domain can be designated as backup domain controllers for increased reliability, or they can simply be designated as resource servers to offer a variety of services to authorized users.

Windows NT computers, especially Windows NT Workstation clients, can alternatively belong to **workgroups,** rather than domains. The key difference between workgroups and domains is that in a workgroup, there is no domain controller, and therefore each workgroup computer must maintain its own security sub-system. In a workgroup, users log into a particular computer, whereas in domains, users log into the domain. This difference is not unlike the differences between the logging into particular servers in NetWare 3 and logging into the universal NDS database in NetWare 4 and above. Figure 7-6 illustrates some key features of domains and workgroups.

Trust Relationships   In order for users to access network resources located in remote domains without the need to duplicate the local user account and security information into the remote domain, a mechanism for domains to coordinate authentication must be established. The mechanism used to coordinate authentication between domains is known as a **trust relationship.** In a trust relationship (or **trust** for short), the trusting domain trusts the trusted

Domain

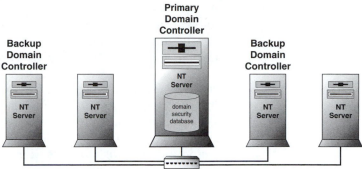

➡ All security and access control list information is maintained on the **Primary Domain Controller**. Copies are stored on **Backup Domain Controllers** for reliability.

➡ **Backup Domain Controllers** promoted in case of **Primary Domain Controller** failure.

➡ Any **Primary** or **Backup Domain Controller** can log you in.

Workgroup

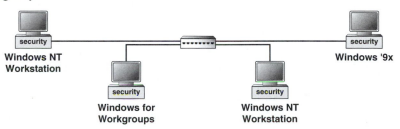

➡ Files and directories can be shared among the workgroup, but each workstation is responsible for maintaining their own user accounts and access control lists.

Figure 7-6 Domains and Workgroups

domain to properly authenticate its users. If a domain trusts another domain, it will allow users from the trusted domain to be included in access control lists for its resources.

Take the example of domain B trusting domain A. When a user from domain A wishes to access a resource in domain B, domain B will ask for the user's authentication credentials. The user will respond with their credentials for domain A. Domain B will then send this credential set to domain A and ask if they are correct. If they correct the resource server on domain B will grant the appropriate access level as determined by the access control list for the resource. This process is known as **passthrough authentication.**

Interdomain trust relationships are defined separately for each direction, meaning domain A granting trust to domain B and its users is a separate issue from domain B granting similar trust to domain A. Interdomain trust relationships are strictly point-to-point. In other words, just because domains A and B have a two-way trust relationship and domain B also has a two-way trust relationship with domain C, this does not mean that users on domain A have access to domain C.

Interdomain trust accounts that allow NT server domain controllers to perform passthrough authentication to other domains are, in fact, only one of three types of trust accounts supported by Windows NT. The other two are:

- **Workstation trust accounts** allow the workstation to connect to a domain by providing passthrough authentication for a Windows NT server in the domain. In essence, the workstation is able to authenticate itself, or remote users who have logged directly into the workstation and now wish to access domain-based resources.

- **Server trust accounts** allow NT servers to download copies of the master domain database from a domain controller. This trust relationship enables backup domain controllers.

Figure 7-7 illustrates a variety of trust relationships supported by Windows NT.

DOMAIN ARCHITECTURES

In Sharper
Focus

The number and structure of domains and interdomain trust relationships can vary significantly from one organization to another. Decisions as to the proper domain architecture for a given organization will hinge largely on the number and location of users, and the number and location of system administrators. Following are descriptions of five major models for possible domain architectures as well as some key positive and negative attributes of each:

- **Single Domain Architecture**—As the name implies, all users and network resources are organized into a single domain of up to 10,000 users. This is a flat architecture with no interdomain trust relationships involved. All security management is performed from a single location.

- **Multiple Non-Trusting Domains Architecture**—If multiple divisions or departments within a given organization do not need access to each other's data or network resources, then multiple independently managed domains can be established without defining any trust relationships between the domains.

- **Master Domain Architecture**—This is a hierarchical architecture in which a single master domain is established into which all users are defined. Multiple sub-domains all offer interdomain trust accounts to the single master domain, but the master domain does not allow trusted access from the sub-domains. The advantage of this architecture is that access to departmental data can be controlled by trust relationships, and all management is performed from a single cen-

Workstation Trust Accounts

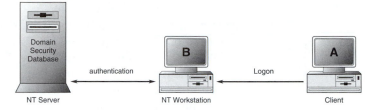

➡ NT Workstation *"A"* wishes to access Workstation *"B"*
➡ Workstation *"B"* passes login information to the domain controller for authentication."

Server Trust Accounts

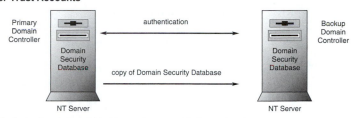

➡ The Backup Domain Controller is able to receive a copy of the Domain Security
   Database due to Server Trust Account.

Interdomain Trust Accounts

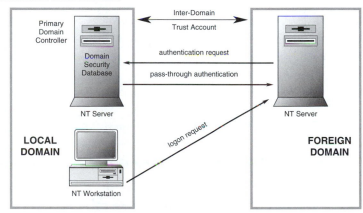

➡ Local workstation requests access to Foreign Domain Server.
➡ Foreign Server Requests authentication from Local Domain Controller
➡ Local Domain Controller performs pass-through authentication.

Figure 7-7   Trust Relationships in Windows NT

tralized location. Because all user information is managed by the single master domain, this architecture is limited to 10,000 total users.

• **Multiple Master Domains Architecture**—This two-tiered architecture supports multiple master domains, with up to 10,000 users each. All sub-domains offer interdomain trust accounts to all master domains. This architecture is appropriate for very large organizations and involves increased maintenance of the multiple master domains and the interdomain trust relationships.

- **Multiple Trust Architecture**—In this idealistic, flat architecture, all domains offer interdomain trust accounts to all other domains. The difficulty with this architecture is that all domains are independently administered and trust relationships must be established for every possible domain-domain combination. This architecture can grow quite large, since 10,000 users per domain are permitted. However, the totally decentralized management of the domains may not be appropriate for all organizations.

Figure 7-8 illustrates these various alternative domain architectures.

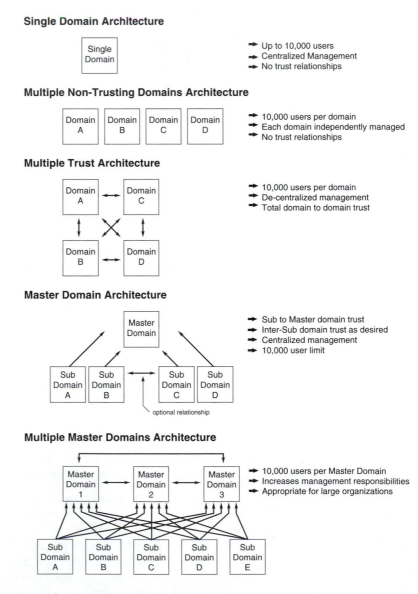

Figure 7-8   Alternative Domain Architectures

Security Security is an integral part of the Windows NT operating system. As a result, security in Windows NT offers not only user authentication and authorization services typically associated with network operating system security, but also an assurance that the programs and processes launched by those authorized users will only access system resources to which they have appropriate permissions. In Windows NT, no interprocess communication takes place without the knowledge and approval of the Windows NT security system.

The overall security system is organized around the concept of objects. In Windows NT, examples of objects are files, directories, print queues, and other networked resources. All objects are assigned permission levels that are associated with individual users or user groups through access control lists. Examples of permission levels are:

- read

- delete

- write

- change permission level

- execute

- take ownership

- no access

- print

By monitoring permission levels, the NT security system can monitor and control who accesses which objects as well as how those objects are accessed. In addition to monitoring and control, NT security can also audit and report on these same object accesses by users according to permission level. The components of the Windows NT security model are illustrated in Figure 7-9.

◼ COMPONENTS OF THE WINDOWS NT SECURITY MODEL

A logical start for introducing the interacting components of the Windows NT security model is the **logon process.** This is actually a client presentation layer function, identified as a separate component in order to allow login processes for a variety of different computer platforms to interact with the Windows NT security model in a standardized manner.

The platform-specific login process interacts with the **local security authority** that actually provides the user authentication services. Specifically, the local security authority generates a **security access token** for authorized users which contains **security IDs (SID)** for this user and all of the user groups to which this user belongs. This security access token accompanies every process or program launched by this user and is used as a means to

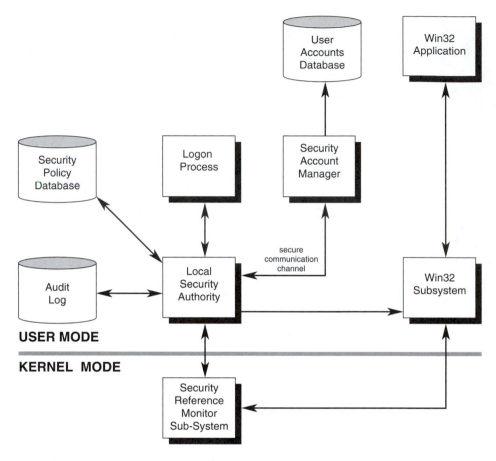

Figure 7-9 Windows NT Security Model

reference whether or not this user and their spawned processes have sufficient permissions to perform requested services or access requested resources. The local security authority also controls the security model's audit policy and generates audit messages that are stored in the audit log.

All of the user and user group ID and permission level information is stored in and maintained by the **security account manager** which interacts with the local security authority to verify user IDs and permission levels. The **user accounts database** is physically stored on the primary domain controller except in cases where an individual workstation may have a need to verify specific User IDs for remote access to that workstation. The links between components of the NT security model involved in the logon process are designed as secure communication channels in order to ensure that traffic which is supposedly received from a given workstation or computer is actually from that computer. This authentication is accomplished in Windows NT by a process similar to the Challenge Handshake Authentication

Protocol (CHAP), which is employed in NetWare 4.1 for a similar purpose. Passwords are encrypted before being transmitted during the logon process.

The only kernel mode portion of the NT security model is the **security reference monitor (SRM)** which serves as the security engine or back-end application for all of the previously mentioned security client applications. It is the security reference model that has the ultimate responsibility for ensuring that users have the proper authority to access requested network resources. The SRM is able to meet this responsibility by comparing the requested object's security description as documented in **access control lists (ACL)** with the requesting user's security information as documented on their security access token. Besides access validation the SRM is also responsible for audit checking and generating audit messages.

Communication Protocols

As illustrated in Figure 7-10, Windows NT offers not just a choice of multiple communication protocols, but the ability to run multiple communication protocols simultaneously. Windows NT supports the following communication protocols:

- TCP/IP
- NWLink (IPX/SPX)
- NetBEUI (NBF)

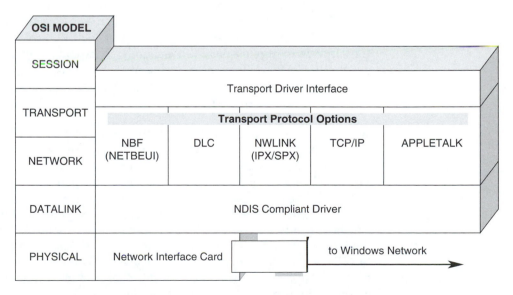

Figure 7-10   NT Communication Protocol Architecture

- DLC

- AppleTalk

Collectively this protocol selection not only provides connectivity between NT clients and servers, but also provides compatibility with other network operating systems.

This section focuses on the implementation of these protocols in the Windows NT environment. Refer to Chapter 4 for more detailed information on each of these protocols.

NWLink (IPX/SPX)   IPX/SPX is the traditional communication protocol stack for NetWare. IPX/SPX is supported in the Windows NT environment through a protocol stack known as **NWLink** that allows IPX/SPX to serve as the native communication protocol for all communication between NT clients and NT servers. As a result of having IPX/SPX serve as NT's native transport protocol, interoperability with NetWare clients and servers is easily enabled through NetWare interoperability products available from Microsoft such as:

- Gateway Service for NetWare

- File and Print Services for NetWare

Each of these NetWare interoperability products will be described in more detail in the Windows NT Interoperability section of this chapter.

NetBEUI (NBF)   **NetBEUI Frame (NBF)** is the Windows NT version of the NetBEUI protocol stack included for backward compatibility purposes with such NetBEUI-based network operating systems as Microsoft LAN Manager and OS/2 LAN Server. As the expansion of NetBEUI (NetBIOS Extended User Interface) implies, NetBEUI is merely an extended version of the original NetBIOS API. NBF can also be chosen as the native transport protocol for Windows NT, thereby supplying transport services for all communication between NT clients and NT servers.

AppleTalk   **AppleTalk** is included as a communication protocol in order to support NT's **Services for Macintosh (SFM).** These independently controlled services, which include File Server for Macintosh and Print Server for Macintosh, allow an NT server to act as an AppleShare server for Macintosh clients. Files can be easily retrieved and maintained from the NT server by the Mac clients. To the Mac clients, the connection is totally transparent. No additional software needs to be added to the Mac clients. At the same time, the files stored in the AppleShare section of the NT server are also accessible to NT clients with proper permission levels. Thus, Services for Macintosh plus the AppleTalk communication protocol provide a transparent interoperability environment for NT and Mac clients.

DLC   **DLC** or **Data Link Control** is a Windows NT communication protocol that has been traditionally reserved for communication with IBM mainframe computers. Recently, this same communication protocol has been used to communicate between Windows NT servers and printers that are attached directly to the network by network interface cards such as the Hewlett-Packard LaserJet 4Si equipped with a JetDirect card. In order to successfully complete such a communication, the mainframe or network-attached printer must also support the DLC protocol as well.

Figure 7-11 is a functional illustration of the use of the IPX/SPX, NBF, AppleTalk, and DLC communication protocols.

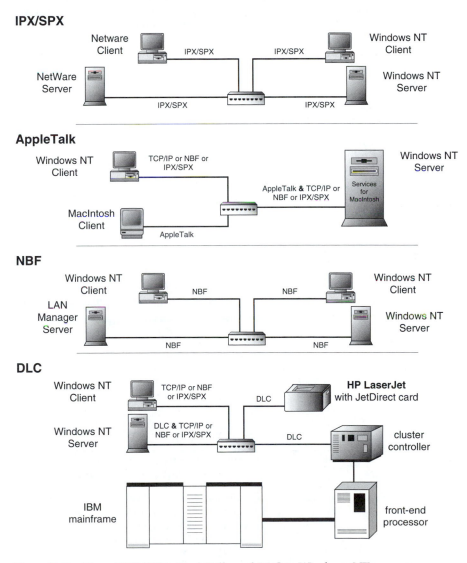

Figure 7-11   Use of IPX/SPX, AppleTalk, and DLC in Windows NT

TCP/IP and Related Protocols   Although the intricacies of TCP/IP and the related protocols of the Internet Suite were covered in Chapter 4, a brief description of supported protocols and services will be given here. In addition, significant issues related to Windows NT's implementation of TCP/IP-related protocols such as the **Dynamic Host Configuration Protocol (DHCP)** and the related **Windows Internet Naming Service (WINS)** will also be discussed. Figure 7-12 summarizes some of the TCP/IP protocols and services supported by Windows NT.

Protocol/Service Category	Details/Explanation
Communication Protocols	• TCP-Transmission Control Protocol: transport layer protocol that ensure reliability of IP transmission • IP – Internet Protocol: network layer communication protocol which provides end to end addressing and communication • UDP – User Datagram Protocol – Transport layer alternative protocol to TCP for transmission of short datagram messages that don't require reliability checking overhead of TCP
Special Delivery Protocols	• ARP – Address Resolution Protocol • ICMP – Internet Control Message Protocol
Remote Access Protocols	• PPP – Point-to-point protocol • SLIP – Serial Line Internet protocol • Both PPP and SLIP can be used for remote access of TCP/IP-based computers
APIs	• Windows Sockets 1.1 and 2.0
Utilities	• FTP – file transfer protocol • TFTP – trivial ftp – simpler version of FTP • Telnet – remote terminal login protocol • LPR – line printer protocol – used to print a file to a host print server • RCP – remote copy protocol • REXEC – Remote execution protocol allows commands to be executed on remote hosts • Note: some utilities may only be available from add-on product – Windows NT Resource Kit.
Diagnostics	• LPQ – used to obtain status of a print queue • PING – used to verify connections to a particular host • Tracert – used to trace the route of a packet from source to destination • Netstat – displays protocol statistics and network connections • Nbtstat – displays protocol statistics and network connections using NetBIOS over TCP/IP
Services	• WINS – Windows Internet Name Service • DHCP – Dynamic Host Configuration Protocol
Management Protocols	• SNMP – Simple Network Management Protocol. NT actually supplies an SNMP agent which is able to forward network statistics in SNMP format to enterprise network management systems such as HP Openview, Sun Sunnet Manager, and IBM Systemview.

Figure 7-12   TCP/IP Protocols and Services in Windows NT

Practical Advice and Information

TCP/IP can be used as the native communication protocol between all NT clients and servers. However, this is not the real advantage to using TCP/IP as a communication protocol. The real benefits to TCP/IP are apparent only when one looks outside the local NT clients and servers. TCP/IP is the communication protocol of the Internet, as well as most other public and private inter-networks. As a result, communication outside of the local NT network becomes much easier when TCP/IP is chosen as the communication protocol. In addition, TCP/IP has become the de facto common communication protocol across almost every computing platform imaginable. Although many computers use communication protocols other than TCP/IP, most computers are also able to speak to each other using TCP/IP.

DHCP AND WINS

TCP/IP, like any network operating system communication protocol, depends on an organized addressing scheme in order to know where to find intended recipients of interprocess communication. Traditionally, IP addresses were associated with the network interface cards within computers and were therefore more or less permanently associated with a physical machine. Two forces contributed primarily to the need for an alternative to the permanent, physically oriented IP addressing scheme:

- An overall lack of possible IP addresses due to the explosive growth of the Internet which depends on IP addressing. As a result, a solution was sought that could assign IP addresses dynamically as needed from a pool of available IP addresses, rather than having IP addresses permanently assigned to computers that were not being used.

- The explosive growth of remote and mobile computing. Some way had to be found to give remote and mobile users IP addresses as needed without having to permanently assign unique IP addresses to everyone's office computer as well as their laptop or notebook computer.

The solution was the Dynamic Host Control Protocol, or DHCP. DHCP allows NT servers using TCP/IP to dynamically assign TCP/IP addresses to NT workstations, Windows for Workgroups clients, Windows 9× clients, or DOS clients running the TCP/IP-32 protocol stack. The DHCP server is included as part of the TCP/IP protocol stack for NT server and references a DHCP database for lists of available IP addresses. IP addresses issued by DHCP are leased, rather than being permanently assigned, and the length of time that IP addresses can be kept by DHCP clients is known as the **lease duration.** Dial-in users are typically assigned an IP address only for the duration of their call. If necessary, specific IP addresses can be reserved for specific clients. DHCP must be enabled on Windows clients supporting the TCP/IP protocol stack in order to be able to request IP addresses from the DHCP server. For more information on BOOTP and DHCP, please refer to Chapter 4.

Because users and their workstations are easier to remember and access by name rather than address, NT keeps track of user names and associated IP addresses with a service known as WINS (Windows Internet Name Service). WINS is a Microsoft proprietary client/server name resolution system. Each client is configured with the address of at least one WINS server. At boot time the client registers its name and IP address with the WINS server. In this manner the WINS server builds a comprehensive database of names and IP addresses of the machines on the network regardless of the manner in which they received their IP address.

When a WINS enabled client wants to connect to another station, it sends a name query to the WINS server which responds with the current IP address of the destination computer. The client is then able to connect directly to the destination via IP.

The Internet uses a different naming service known as **DNS** or **Domain Name System.** While DNS normally only works with machines whose IP addresses never change (static addresses), use of the Microsoft DNS server for NT allows DNS to query the WINS database to present accurate DNS information on dynamically assigned hosts. As a result, users assigned DHCP addresses who are logged into the WINS database will still be accessible from the Internet via the DNS database. The DHCP server, WINS server, and DNS server can all be physically located on different server computers. Figure 7-13 illustrates the interaction of DHCP, WINS, and DNS clients and servers.

Network Services Windows NT network services provide the transport mechanism by which other services such as printing, security, file systems, and application support are delivered. These multipurpose network services are the result of a structured, modular architecture of interacting components as illustrated in Figure 7-14.

Following is a layer-by-layer description of the Windows NT Network Services Architecture:

- The network interface card at the base of the Windows NT Network Services Architecture provides the physical connectivity from every Windows NT client and server to the Windows NT network.

- The first layer of software in the architecture is the NDIS (Network Datalink Interface Specification) driver software that supports both multiple transport protocols per network interface card and multiple network interface cards per computer.

- Support for a variety of different transport protocols allows Windows NT to interoperate successfully with most popular client and server networking platforms. These protocols will be explained in more detail in the Communication Protocols section of this chapter.

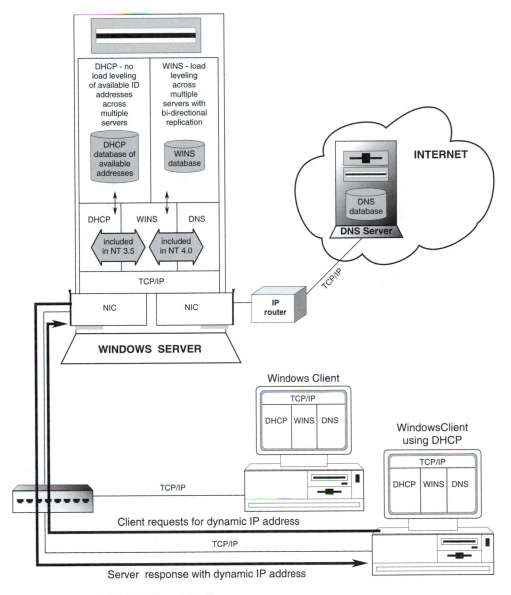

Figure 7-13   DHCP, WINS, and DNS

- The **transport driver interface (TDI)** is actually a protocol specification that provides a layer of transparency between session layer redirectors and transport layer protocols. It fulfills a role similar to the NDIS specification's role between the network and data-link layer protocols. This allows session layer redirector software to be written independently of the particular transport layer software with which the redirector software will need to communicate.

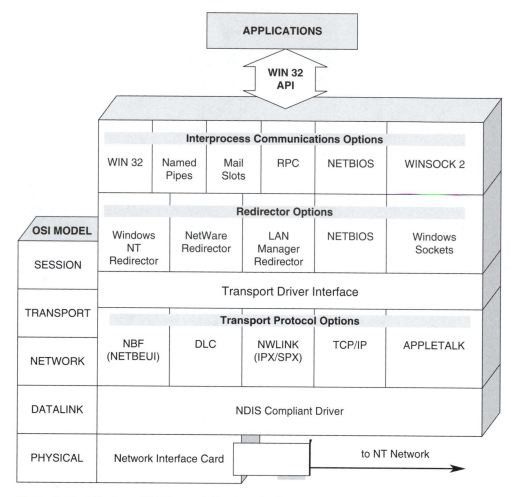

Figure 7-14 Windows NT Network Services Architecture

- Just as Windows NT is able to support multiple transport protocols simultaneously, it is also able to support a variety of redirectors simultaneously. It is the redirector's job to determine whether requests for files and services can be handled on the local computer or if they must be forwarded to a particular remote computer via the appropriate transport protocol. Redirectors in Windows NT are also able to request additional services from any of the systems services available in the NT executive. The various options for redirectors will be described further in the Applications Services section of this chapter.

- Finally, Windows NT applications must have some way to pass their requests for files and services to the redirector layer. The Win32 API, described in previous chapters, is the standard interface specification by which NT applications pass requests for services to the NT network operating system.

Application Services   Application services within Windows NT are primarily concerned with providing support for distributed or client/server applications. More specifically, Windows NT is responsible for providing communication services between the client and server portions of distributed applications. Communication between client and server portions of distributed applications fall into two major categories:

- **Synchronous I/O** or interprocess communication refers to the situation where a client application spawns a thread for information or processing and waits for the results of that thread before continuing with the execution of the client application. Synchronous I/O is sometimes also referred to as connection-oriented communication.

- **Asynchronous I/O** refers to the situation where a client application spawns a thread for information or processing and proceeds with the execution of the client application without waiting for the results of the spawned thread. Depending on how the client application is written, the server portion may notify the client application when the requested information has been delivered, or the client program may be required to check back for any newly delivered information on a regular basis. Asynchronous I/O is sometimes also referred to as connectionless communication.

As illustrated in earlier chapters on client/server software architectures, distributed applications interact with network operating systems via APIs or application program interfaces. In the case of Windows NT, this API is the Win32 API.

■ INTERPROCESS COMMUNICATION

The next requirement in establishing a distributed application between a client and server is to offer some type of mechanism for interprocess communication. Some way needs to be offered for the application to spawn threads and establish links from clients to servers in order to receive requested files and services. Windows NT offers at least six different options for interprocess communication establishment as illustrated in Figure 7-14.

The **Windows Sockets** interprocess communication mechanism, more commonly known as **WinSock,** is the most flexible of all of the interprocess mechanisms currently supported by Windows NT.

The term *sockets* in the name of this interprocess communication mechanism is a reflection of this protocol's derivation from Berkeley UNIX sockets.

Earlier versions of the WinSock protocol were able to allow programs written to support this protocol to operate transparently over a variety of different vendors' TCP/IP protocol stacks. **WinSock2** added to this functionality by allowing WinSock-compliant applications to operate transparently over IPX/SPX, AppleTalk, DECnet, and OSI transport protocols as well. The importance of this multiprotocol support from an application developer's standpoint is that only one version of an application needs to be developed and maintained rather than several network protocol specific versions.

A WinSock-compliant application uses the WinSock interprocess communication mechanism by loading the WinSock.DLL file. A DLL or **dynamic link library (DLL)** file is loaded into memory as needed at run time by Windows NT rather than having to be compiled into, and permanently added to the application programs themselves. As illustrated in Figure 7-15, the WinSock.DLL file includes two distinct interfaces:

- The WinSock API is used by applications developers for including appropriate commands within their WinSock compliant applications.

- The WinSock SPI (Service Provider Interface) translates the API calls to enable WinSock compliant applications to access multiple different network transport protocols through the transport driver interface.

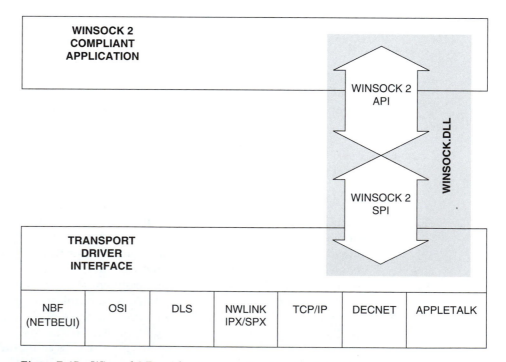

Figure 7-15 Winsock2 Provides Network Transport Independence

NetBIOS can also be used by application to establish client to server or interprocess communication. NetBIOS is an API that allows NetBIOS compliant applications to communicate with the NetBIOS redirector which, in turn, establishes communication via the NetBEUI Frame (NBF) transport protocol. The NetBIOS API is implemented by the NetBIOS DLL. NetBIOS establishes sessions between client and server computers which are then able to exchange messages that adhere to the SMB (Server Message Block) format.

Two other interprocess communication mechanisms included in Windows NT, primarily for backward compatibility with applications written for other network operating systems, are as follows:

- **Named Pipes** is included as an interprocess communication mechanism used by the OS/2 operating system.

- **Mailslot** is an interprocess communication mechanism used by the OS/2 LAN Manager network operating system.

The Open Software Foundation (OSF) has developed an entire architecture for the development of distributed applications known as the **Distributed Computing Environment (DCE).** DCE will be explored in detail in Chapter 9. The interprocess communication service defined within DCE is known as **RPC** or **Remote Procedure Call.** Windows NT, along with many other operating systems, supports RPC. Remote Procedure Calls is more like a "super" interprocess communication mechanism in that it has the ability to use other interprocess mechanisms such as named pipes, NetBIOS, or WinSock, should that be what a particular application requires. Client and server programs that wish to use the RPC service simply issue program calls for that service via specialized calls to the RPC mechanism known as **stubs.**

While the stub calls are compiled within the program, the interprocess communication is executed with the help of the RPC runtime module. All computing platforms that support the RPC interprocess communication mechanism must have a compatible RPC runtime module. In this way, the RPC runtime module becomes the common interprocess communication mechanism across all of the various computing platforms attempting to communicate with each other.

Application Layer Services

In addition to offering basic file and print services, Windows NT is well suited to use as an application server. Many different applications have been ported to the Windows NT platform, including multiprotocol routers; Internet services such as web servers, proxies, and firewalls; and database servers. It is in the installation of these applications that Windows NT truly distinguishes itself. This section will focus on the major services included in the Windows NT 4.0 distribution.

File and Print Services   File and print services represent an entry into the server NOS market. Windows NT provides basic file services to clients. Standard file service capabilities such as security and concurrent access are provided. File services are accessed by clients through redirectors using the SMB protocol as discussed in the preceding section.

Recalling that printer sharing is a key NOS application, it should come as no surprise that Windows NT does an especially good job of offering managed print services to client workstations. In keeping with the overall modular design of Windows NT, printer services are organized around the Windows NT printing model as illustrated in Figure 7-16.

The importance of the modular design of the Windows NT Printing Model should be clearly evident from Figure 7-6. At many layers of the model, a variety of options are available, depending on the particular environment of the user. For example, choices can be made for:

- print providers for interoperability with Macintosh, NetWare, or UNIX-based printers

- printing monitor programs compatible with a variety of management platforms

- a wide variety of types and brands of printers

If not for the modular design of the Windows NT Printing Model, monolithic printing spoolers would have to be developed for every possible unique combination of spooler, monitor, and printer—a mammoth undertaking. The basic building blocks of the Windows NT Printing model are:

- Clients are any application program able to produce a request for print services and pass that request to the spooler. The clients may be local or network attached.

- The router receives all requests for print services and determines whether this print request can be fulfilled locally or if it must be shipped out to another print provider more qualified to deal with this print request.

- Print providers, whether local or remote, examine the spooled print request and determine which print processor should be used to process the print job. In addition, the print provider also determines which print monitor is in charge of dealing with printer port output.

- Finally, the appropriate print monitor actually forwards the print job to the proper print device, whether local or network attached.

Internet Services   NT Server 4.0 comes bundled with **Internet Information Server (IIS),** a full-feature Internet server. IIS provides web, FTP, and Gopher server capabilities natively and is written in a modular format to

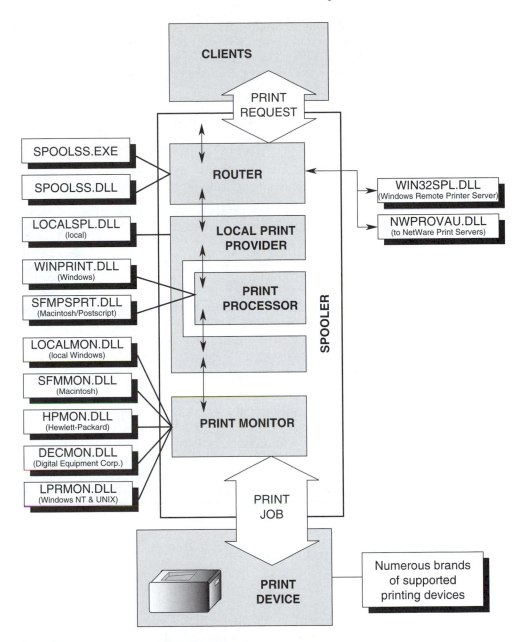

CLIENTS

PRINT
REQUEST

SPOOLSS.EXE

SPOOLSS.DLL

ROUTER

WIN32SPL.DLL
(Windows Remote Printer Server)

NWPROVAU.DLL
(to NetWare Print Servers)

LOCALSPL.DLL
(local)

LOCAL PRINT
PROVIDER

WINPRINT.DLL
(Windows)

SFMPSPRT.DLL
(Macintosh/Postscript)

PRINT
PROCESSOR

SPOOLER

LOCALMON.DLL
(local Windows)

SFMMON.DLL
(Macintosh)

HPMON.DLL
(Hewlett-Packard)

DECMON.DLL
(Digital Equipment Corp.)

LPRMON.DLL
(Windows NT & UNIX)

PRINT MONITOR

PRINT
JOB

PRINT
DEVICE

Numerous brands
of supported
printing devices

Figure 7-16   Windows NT Printing Model

allow other Internet services (such as a proxy server) to be added. Benefits of
IIS include its tight integration with the Windows NT security model. Access
to web pages can be set in the same manner as access to other files. Other key
IIS features include support for Active Server Pages (ASP), integrated Java
support, and a built-in message queue manager.

Database and BackOffice Services   To facilitate Windows NT Server's use as an application server, Microsoft has released the **BackOffice** family of products. BackOffice is a collection of server products that support the development of enterprise applications on the Windows NT platform. BackOffice services include:

- Exchange Server—e-mail services

- Proxy Server—an extensible firewall and web cache server

- Site Server—a web site environment for development and deployment of web applications via IIS

- Systems Management Server—a collection of centralized management tools for computer inventory, software distribution, and diagnostic services

- SNA Server—an integration platform for Microsoft networks and legacy SNA systems

- SQL Server—a relational database management system (RDBMS) for development of client/server applications

■ WINDOWS 2000 (NT 5.0)

The next generation of the Windows NT family is Windows 2000. Known in development as Windows NT 5.0, Windows 2000 expands upon many of the capabilities of Windows NT 4.0. Improvements in SMP capability, clustering, load balancing, and the replacement of the domain naming system with a true directory service allow Windows 2000 to scale to larger enterprises. This section will focus on the changes in Windows 2000 compared with Windows NT 4.0.

Overall Architecture

Windows 2000 will be available in four different versions: Professional, Server, Advanced Server, and Datacenter Server. Similar to Windows NT 4.0 Workstation, Windows 2000 Professional is designed to serve as a robust network client operating system. Windows 2000 Server is the introductory server platform. Delivering file, print, web and communication server functions, Windows 2000 Server is designed for small to medium-size enterprises.

Windows 2000 Advanced Server is designed to scale to larger enterprises. The replacement in the product line for Windows NT 4.0 Enterprise Edition, Windows 2000 Advanced Server adds clustering, load balancing, and doubles SMP support as compared to the Windows 2000 Server platform.

Windows 2000 Datacenter Server is designed for large enterprise deployments. With support for increased numbers of processors and memory along with clustering and load balancing, Windows 2000 Datacenter Server is optimized for large data warehouses, transaction processing, and scientific calculations. The key features of each server version of Windows 2000 are listed in Figure 7-17.

Network Operating System Characteristic	Windows 2000 Server	Windows 2000 Advanced Server	Windows 2000 Datacenter Server
Hardware/Platform			
Supported Processors	Intel x86 (386 or better) Digital Alpha	Intel x86 (386 or better) Digital Alpha	Intel x86 (386 or better) Digital Alpha
Min Memory	64 MB	128 MB	128 MB
Min Disk	1 GB	1 GB	1 GB
Symmetrical Multiprocessing	2 Processors	4 Processors	16 Processors
Operating System			
Program Structure	32 Bit	32 Bit	32 Bit
Memory Architecture	Virtual Machines	Virtual Machines	Virtual Machines
Preemptive Multi-tasking	Yes	Yes	Yes
Clustering	No	Yes	Yes
Load Balancing	No	Yes	Yes
File system	FAT FAT 32 NTFS	FAT FAT 32 NTFS	FAT FAT 32 NTFS
User Interface	GUI	GUI	GUI
Network Drivers	NDIS	NDIS	NDIS
Application Program Interface(s)	Win 32	Win 32	Win 32
CD-ROM Support	Yes	Yes	Yes

(continued)

Management and Administration

Network Object Management System	Domain Name Services Directory Services (Active Directory)	Domain Name Services Directory Services (Active Directory)	Domain Name Services Directory Services (Active Directory)
Administrative Location	Administration can be performed either from the server, from clients using utility applications, or via HTTP (WWW)	Administration can be performed either from the server, from clients using utility applications, or via HTTP (WWW)	Administration can be performed either from the server, from clients using utility applications, or via HTTP (WWW)

Network Services

Network Protocols Supported	IPX/SPX NetBEUI TCP/IP AppleTalk (Macintosh support only) DLC (Printing only)	IPX/SPX NetBEUI TCP/IP AppleTalk (Macintosh support only) DLC (Printing only)	IPX/SPX NetBEUI TCP/IP AppleTalk (Macintosh support only) DLC (Printing only)
Multiprotocol Routing	Yes (Capabilities can be expanded via add-on product)	Yes (Capabilities can be expanded via add-on product)	Yes (Capabilities can be expanded via add-on product)
Native Services	File and print FTP Web	File and print FTP Web	File and print FTP Web
Common Third-party Services	Electronic mail Database Firewall etc.	Electronic mail Database Firewall etc.	Electronic mail Database Firewall etc.
Clients Supported	DOS Windows 3.x Windows 9x Windows NT UNIX OS/2 Macintosh	DOS Windows 3.x Windows 9x Windows NT UNIX OS/2 Macintosh	DOS Windows 3.x Windows 9x Windows NT UNIX OS/2 Macintosh

Figure 7-17   Windows NT 2000 Server Technology Analysis Grid

Operating System Architecture and Characteristics

The operating system architecture improvements in Windows 2000 are designed to extend Windows NT 4.0's architectural stability and enhance scalability. While maintaining the virtual machine memory architecture used in Windows NT 4.0, Windows 2000 increases addressable memory. Windows 2000 provides support for up to 4 GB of physical RAM on Intel Pentium II Xeon processors and up to 32 GB of RAM on 64-bit processor systems such as the Digital/Compaq Alpha family and future Intel processors. By expanding the amount of physical memory supported, more data can be cached in memory, providing greatly increased data processing performance.

Multi-processing   One of the main differences between the various versions of Windows 2000 lies in SMP support. The base Windows 2000 Server product is limited to two-way (two-processor) SMP, whereas the mid-range Windows 2000 Advanced Server offers four-way SMP. For large enterprise applications, Windows 2000 Datacenter Server supports up to 16-way SMP. Regardless of the number of processors supported, Windows 2000 is tuned for better efficiency and provides enhanced support for newer hardware configurations.

In addition to SMP improvements, better processor utilization is made possible through support for the Intel I2O architecture. In an I2O-compliant system a separate processor, complete with its own memory, handles all I/O requests, allowing the main processor(s) to focus on application services. Input/Output performance is further enhanced through the use of "scatter/gather" I/O that increases access speed to data held in noncontiguous memory locations.

Clustering   While SMP and I2O support allow a single server to scale for critical enterprise level applications, large SMP servers present a single point of failure. If client/server computing is to succeed, servers must provide both high availability and be fail-safe. To provide such fail-safe high availability, two servers can be clustered. As illustrated in Figure 7-18, a server cluster consists of two servers that contain identical information. From the perspective of a network client, the cluster appears to be a single server.

When a client requests data from the cluster, the request is sent to the primary server for fulfillment. In the event that the primary server fails, the backup server will automatically pick up the active cluster connections. Ideally, this process happens so quickly that users don't realize that a failure occurred. Windows 2000 provides support for such fail-over clustering through the **Microsoft Clustering Services (MSCS).**

A second use for clusters is to increase scalability. If a single SMP server cannot provide adequate processing power for a large-enterprise application, multiple servers can be clustered together to collectively meet these processing requirements. As shown in Figure 7-19, when a client makes a request to the cluster, a cluster controller reroutes the request to one of the servers that makes up the cluster for execution. When a change is made on one server in the cluster, the change is automatically propagated through the cluster to ensure data integrity.

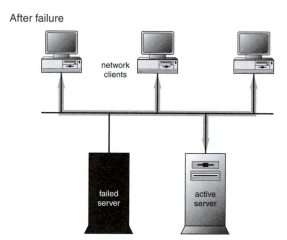

Figure 7-18   Fail Over Clustering

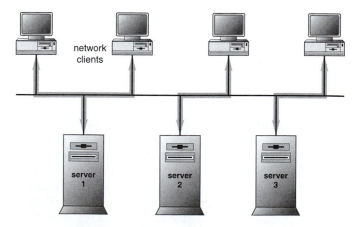

Figure 7-19   Scalability Clustering

Closely related to clustering is the concept of load balancing, which is the process of ensuring that the members of a cluster receive similar levels of use. Ideally the workload of the cluster should be balanced across the individual members of the cluster. In this environment the cluster's constituent servers not only provide increased scalability, but also provide fail-over support. Although MSCS does not currently support such clustering, Microsoft has stated intentions to include such capability in future releases of MSCS for the Windows 2000 Server family.

Storage Services   Windows 2000 presents multiple improvements in storage services. The NTFS file system has been enhanced in several ways:

- Dynamic Partition Allocation—Additional space can be allocated to an NTFS partition dynamically without the need to re-boot the system.

- Distributed Link Tracking—If the name or path to a link or shortcut is changed, the system can automatically search for the intended destination.

- Disk Quotas—Maximum disk usage and policies can be set on a per-user basis.

- Encryption—Data encryption can be set on a per-file or per-directory basis to secure sensitive data. The public key encryption system runs as an integrated service in a manner completely transparent to the user.

Windows 2000 introduces **Remote Storage Services (RSS),** a **Hierarchical Storage Management (HSM)** application. RSS provides an inexpensive method to increase storage capacity by constantly monitoring file usage and the level of free disk space on an NTFS partition. As shown in Figure 7-20, RSS automatically moves data that have not been accessed recently to remote media when the level of free space on a disk falls below a set level. By moving infrequently used data to slower, less expensive media such as optical disk or magnetic tape, RSS frees local disk space for newer, more commonly accessed files. The RSS service keeps a pointer on the local disk that points to the file on the remote media. When a user has to access the remote file, it is automatically copied back to local disk. From the perspective of the user, the entire process is seamless, although access to data that have been archived is slower due to the latency of the remote media.

The capabilities of RSS are expanded upon by the **Removable Storage Manager (RSM)** service. RSM provides a standard interface to multiple tape autoloaders and robotic tape and optical disk changers. Through the use of such hardware and the TSM service, the amount of data RSS can archive is increased beyond the capacity of a single tape or disk.

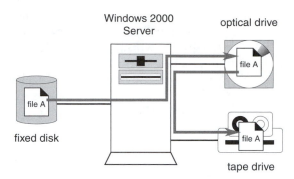

Figure 7-20   Remote Storage Services

The **Distributed File System (DFS)** is a network storage service that allows resources on multiple servers to be combined into a virtual directory tree. From the perspective of a network user, it appears that all of the resources are in a single directory. DFS simplifies the process of finding data on the network. Users are no longer required to remember server and share names; they need only remember the location of the data within the DFS directory.

Management and Administration

As mentioned in Chapter 6, Total Cost of Ownership (TCO) is one of the key concerns of network administrators. Windows 2000 provides several management and administrative features that allow it to reduce the cost of implementing and maintaining a Windows-based network system. Enhancements to the Windows NT Server 4.0 web-based administration capabilities, a new directory service, and new client and user synchronization tools combine to strengthen the management capabilities of Windows 2000.

Active Directory   The biggest change in Windows 2000 is undoubtedly the release of Microsoft's directory service. Dubbed the active directory, the change from the previous domain system to a directory service resolves many scalability issues that were prevalent in Windows NT 4.0. Similar in functionality to NDS in NetWare environments, the **Active Directory (AD)** is distributed database containing information about network resources.

Active Directory is designed to be a single solution for all of an organization's directory needs. As shown in Figure 7-21, the Active Directory not only provides authentication services for the network, but also integrates directly into e-mail and other services. This unified directory approach presents an administration point for the network, thus eliminating the overhead associated with maintaining duplicate directory structures.

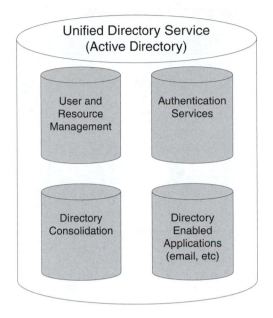

Figure 7-21   Active Directory—A Unified Directory Service

While the Active Directory is similar in functionality to NDS, it is quite different in structure. Where NDS is designed from a top-down perspective where a single tree is divided into multiple branches (organizational units), Active Directory works from a bottom-up perspective where multiple organizational units are combined into trees and trees are combined into forests.

As shown in Figure 7-22, the smallest physical section of the Active Directory is a **domain.** Similar to a Windows NT 4.0 domain, an Active Directory domain consists of a group of closely related network objects. To increase granularity, Active Directory domains can be broken into multiple sections, or organizational units (OU), each of which can be further broken down into additional OUs, creating a multilevel structure.

With the ability to contain up to 10 million objects, a single domain may provide enough capacity for many smaller, single location organizations. If an organization requires more than 10 million objects, or if the organization has multiple locations, multiple domains can be arranged into a **tree.** An Active Directory tree consists of multiple domains arranged in a hierarchical manner.

For very large enterprises, multiple trees can be combined into an Active Directory forest. A **forest** is a collection of trees. This bottom-up, build-it-as-you-go approach to directory structure allows an organization to start with a simple directory design and grow it as the company expands. As will be discussed in a subsequent section, it also is a great help in migrating from Windows NT Server 4.0 or NetWare to Windows 2000.

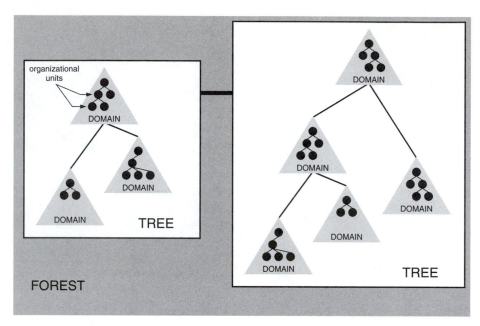

Figure 7-22   Active Directory Structure

Complete data about a domain are kept on each domain's controllers. Unlike Windows NT 4.0, which used primary and backup domain controllers, the Active Directory uses multiple domain controllers (DC) that act as peers. To ensure high availability, each DC can perform all domain controller duties. Domain changes automatically proliferate across domain controllers using multi-master replication.

In addition to a complete copy of all information pertaining to the domain, each domain controller contains meta-data (high-level data) about the other domains in the directory hierarchy. In this manner, client requests for data from other domains can be routed to the domain controller for the destination resource.

The Active Directory uses a DNS namespace. As illustrated in Figure 7-23, each Active Directory domain is analogous to a DNS domain (i.e., acme.com). Each server and workstation within an AD organization unit must be in the same DNS domain. A tree is similarly analogous to a DNS sub-domain (i.e., laf.acme.com and indy.acme.com). Forests can combine trees from different second-level DNS domains (i.e., acme.com and corp.com).

One of the main problems with the NT 4.0 Domain system was that administration was limited to the domain level. Active Directory has resolved this issue by allowing administrative control to be assigned on a per-OU basis to further the administrative granularity within a domain. To make security configuration easier to manager, permissions can be also be set to flow down AD trees and domains.

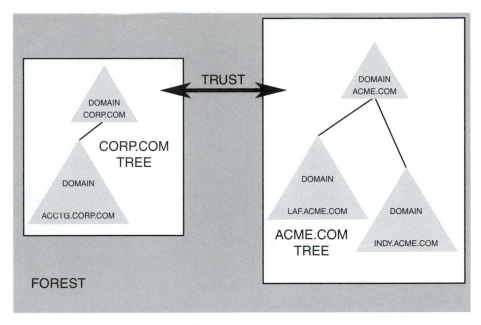

Figure 7-23   Active Directory to DNS Namespace Mapping

Although Active Directory is not an X.500 style directory, it does support the Lightweight Directory Access Protocol (LDAP). An IETF and OSI standard, LDAP allows any compliant application to gain access to the data stored in the NDS database provided proper authentication credentials are presented. More detailed information on LDAP can be found in Chapter 5.

In Sharper Focus

LDAP CLIENTS

Both Netscape Communicator and Microsoft Internet Explorer contain address book utilities that are LDAP compliant. By opening the address book and pointing it at the IP address of a NetWare server running LDAP services, directory information can be accessed. Depending on need the server can be configured either to allow anonymous access to the directory or to require an SSL connection to authenticate the user before allowing access.

Applied Problem Solving

MIGRATION TO ACTIVE DIRECTORY

The Active Directory solves many scalability and manageability problems associated with Windows NT 4.0. However, a clean migration path is required to convert the many NT 4.0 domain installations to Active Directory.

Windows 2000 takes a two-phase approach to migrating older Windows domain-based networks to Active Directory. The existing NT 4.0 Primary

Domain Controller is migrated to Windows 2000. Once the Primary Domain Controller migration is completed, all Backup Domain Controllers can be migrated. To maintain operation during the migration process, Windows 2000 server emulates an NT Server 4.0 domain controller. Once the domain is migrated, existing network clients will see the Windows 2000 Active Directory domain as a Windows NT 4.0 domain. Newer client network operating systems will include the ability to view the domain as an Active Directory domain and expand the client capabilities.

In addition to migrating from this older Microsoft directory solution, a means of migrating Novell solutions to Active Directory adds to the viability of Windows 2000 as a NetWare alternative for larger organizations. Windows 2000 also includes a NetWare migration utility that can migrate both bindery-based NetWare 3 and NDS-based NetWare 4 and 5 servers to Active Directory.

Client and User Tools   One of the key concerns for distributed computing users is providing a consistent desktop and network view for users regardless of which node they log into. This problem is exacerbated by the rapid adoption of notebook computers. These portable machines are consistently moved around the network and often are not even connected to the network. To provide as consistent an environment as possible, Windows 2000 introduces three new technologies: the application installation service, IntelliMirror, and client-side caching.

The **Application Installation Service** is designed to provide a consistent set of applications to be available to a user. Applications are assigned to users or groups of users. Whenever a user logs into a network station, the application installation service will ensure that the required applications are installed on the station. If not, the service will install the applications as part of the login sequence. In addition to providing a more consistent environment to users, the application installation service promises to greatly reduce time and expense associated with the distribution and maintenance of network applications.

To further enhance the capability of Windows to provide a consistent desktop and operating environment to mobile users, IntelliMirror services can be deployed. **IntelliMirror** can be thought of as a next-generation roaming profile that ensures a user's desktop, data, and applications are available wherever they log into the network. To ensure that a user's environment is always available, IntelliMirror caches user data on each workstation and automatically synchronizes updates to a central server.

Although these technologies can greatly increase the consistency of a user's operating environment, another issue with notebook computers is access to data when the notebook is not connected to the network. The Microsoft Briefcase service, introduced in Windows 95, provided a means of synchronizing manually selected files between a notebook and the network. Windows 2000 expands on the capability of Briefcase with the introduction of Client-side caching. **Client-side caching** transparently synchronizes data between the notebook and the network. Whenever the user logs into the network, the system will analyze the cached data and automatically synchronize with the network copy of the data, ensuring that an updated copy of the user's data is always available regardless of whether the user is connected to the network.

While these features address many of the administrative concerns of client systems, Microsoft provides the Systems Management Server product for larger systems that require tighter administrative control.

Security   In the Internet age, one of the most dynamic network operating system areas is security. NT Server 4.0 provides excellent security in stand-alone mode, but network security has been problematic with new vulnerabilities exposed and patched on a consistent basis. As mentioned in a previous section, NT 4.0 uses a modular security system. Windows 2000 utilizes this modular system to enhance network security by integrating standardized authentication and encryption technologies.

In addition to the standard Microsoft password authentication and access control list authorization system, Windows 2000 integrates support for **Kerberos** Version 5 directly into the operating system. A standardized authentication and authorization system, Kerberos support allows Windows 2000 to directly integrate with other client/server and mainframe-based security systems while enhancing the security model of a Windows only network. Please refer to Chapter 16 for additional information on Kerberos.

In addition to Kerberos support, the Windows 2000 authentication model provides a public key server and integrates smart card support directly into the security infrastructure. By providing a **public key certificate server,** Windows 2000 allows an organization to implement public key encryption technologies in their organization without the hassle and expense of relying on external commercial certificate servers. Smart card support integrates into the certificate services to allow the use of smart cards to enhance the standard software-only solutions for client authentication, logon, secure storage, and system administration.

In addition to these enhancements to the Windows security infrastructure, support for the NTFS file encryption and the IP Security Protocol (covered in other parts of this section) further enhances the security of Windows-based networks.

Communication Protocols

Although communication protocol support was one of the strengths of Windows NT 4.0, keeping up to date with evolving protocols is required to remain a viable network operating system choice. The continued expansion of the Internet into mainstream corporate computing has made TCP/IP the de facto network protocol. Windows 2000 enhances the NT TCP/IP implementation to add support for the IP Security protocol, network address translation, IP telephony, and dynamic DNS.

Support for the **IP Security Protocol (IPSec)** is added in Windows 2000. Designed to improve security over Internet connections, the IP Security Protocol is an IETF protocol for encrypting TCP/IP traffic. Windows 2000 integrates IPSec usage into the Windows security policies, making its usage completely transparent to the end user. By implementing IPSec, communication to trusted hosts on the Internet and on Virtual Private Network (VPN) links across the Internet can be protected.

Windows 2000 introduces the **Network Address Translator (NAT).** As mentioned in Chapter 4, the number of IPv4 addresses available is rapidly dwindling. As a means to increase security and eliminate the need to assign officially registered IP addresses to all internal clients, many organizations are assigning special IP address ranges that have been reserved as private addresses. These addresses will never be assigned to an actual Internet host. As shown in Figure 7-24, the NAT service is a special firewall/proxy server used to allow internal hosts with such private addresses to access external Internet hosts. Additional, detailed information on Network Address Translation can be found in Chapter 12.

While alternative services running on both NT and other operating systems also provide this functionality, the Windows 2000 NAT service has the advantage of seamlessly integrating with the Windows DHCP and DNS system. Internal hosts are automatically assigned appropriate configuration information to access the Internet through the firewall. Integration with the Windows security model also allows Internet access to be assigned as part of the overall Windows security policy, thus streamlining Internet security management.

Another major communication protocol improvement is the implementation of Dynamic DNS. **Dynamic DNS (DDNS)** is an IETF standardized extension to DNS that allows a client to register its IP address with the DNS server. When a client acquires an IP address in a dynamic means from either a LAN-based DHCP server or from a dial-in remote access server, the client registers the IP address and the computer's domain name with the DDNS server.

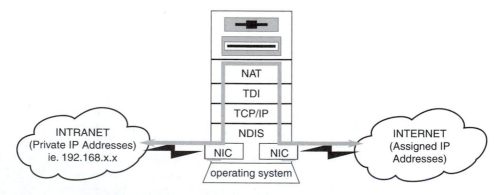

Figure 7-24   Network Address Translator

By adopting DDNS, the proprietary Windows Internet Naming System (WINS) is no longer required, allowing a single standards-based naming system for use not only by Windows networking and the Active Directory, but by all other TCP/IP-based application layer protocols.

Application Layer Services

The strength of NT has traditionally been its ability to act as an application server. Support for virtual machines and a strong service model have allowed NT to become a key application server for many organizations. The key application services included in Windows 2000 are file and print services, transaction and message queuing services, and Internet and streaming multimedia services.

While Windows 2000 introduces few changes to the Windows print system, a couple of items are noteworthy. The addition of the Active Directory makes it easier for users to locate printers by navigating AD trees. Out of the box driver support has been expanded to include more than 2,500 different printers. The Introduction of the Internet Printing Protocol enhances Windows 2000's ability to work with Internet technologies.

The **Internet Printing Protocol (IPP)** offers features that tightly integrate the Internet with the Windows 2000 printing model. Using IPP Windows 2000, users can print directly to a URL over the Internet, thus easing the process of locating and submitting jobs to the print system. IPP also includes the ability to publish printer status and job information in an HTML format, allowing any web browser to be used to manage the print system.

Windows 2000 includes integrated transaction services that provide client/server application developers a standardized means of ensuring that all transactions are successfully completed. Windows 2000 transaction services include the ability to process transactions across a wide range of data sources including SQL databases, CICS/VMS applications, or message queues. More information on these technologies can be found in Chapter 9.

Internet Information Server (IIS) has been enhanced with the release of Windows 2000. Support for new Internet technologies such as dynamic HTML (DHTML), XML, and DAV have been added to IIS. A new management console enables all Internet services to be integrated and managed not only at the server, but also via the web itself. The integrated streaming media services allow the delivery of high-quality audio, illustrated audio, and video to clients across the TCP/IP networks.

■ NT WAN/REMOTE ACCESS

As telecommuting and an increasingly mobile workforce have become more commonplace, network operating system architectures have had to adjust to these business-level requirements. Although LAN remote access solutions will be explored in depth in Chapter 14, Windows remote access is briefly discussed here.

Windows provides the **Remote Access Service (RAS)** that allows remote clients to connect to the network via a wide range of technologies including:

- Dial-up phone service, sometimes referred to as **POTS** (Plain Old Telephone Service)

- ISDN (Integrated Services Digital Network)

- X.25 packet switched network

The RAS server software is responsible for authentication of remote users and overseeing the communication sessions established with remote clients. In simple terms, it is the job of the RAS server to make sure that the remote client is provided all required services as if it were a local client. The actual servicing of the remote client's requests is performed by the NT network operating system. The RAS server is responsible for ensuring that the remote client's requests reach the NT server and that server responses reach the remote client. The RAS server is able to support up to 256 simultaneous connections and also supports data compression in order to optimize the throughput of information between the local server and the remote client. Figure 7-25 illustrates the interaction of the components of a RAS architecture. More details concerning the hardware, media, and network services required to enable remote access to LANs in general will be covered in Chapter 14.

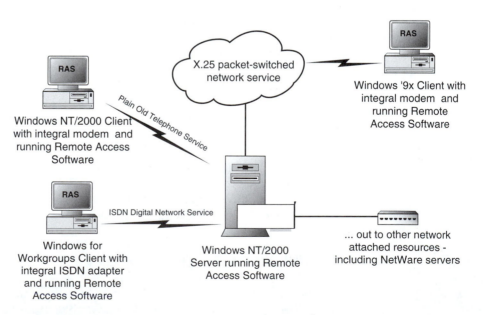

Figure 7-25   Windows NT Remote Access Service Architecture

In keeping with the overall objective of RAS to allow the remote client all of the functionality of local clients, RAS allows remote clients to run NBF, TCP/IP, or IPX/SPX communication protocols in any combination. As illustrated in Chapter 4, the only layer that must change for the trip across the WAN is the data-link layer. In this case, the wide area data-link layer protocols that encapsulate the upper layer protocols are **PPP (Point-to-Point Protocol)** and **SLIP (Serial Line Internet Protocol).**

Because RAS supports TCP/IP, NBF(NetBEUI), and IPX/SPX, NetWare applications, NT applications, and NetBIOS applications can all be accessed and executed by the remote client. NetWare servers available to local clients are equally available to remote clients. Any additional gateway services offered by the local NT server such as Internet gateways or SNA gateways to IBM mainframes are equally accessible by remote clients. Figure 7-26 illustrates the communication protocol architecture of RAS clients and servers.

■ WINDOWS SERVER INTEROPERABILITY

Because of increased demands to be able to share information more quickly and easily within a company, as well as the increased number of corporate mergers and acquisitions, interoperability between different types of network operating systems has become an increasingly important functional characteristic. Windows natively provides tools design to promote interoperability with NetWare and UNIX systems.

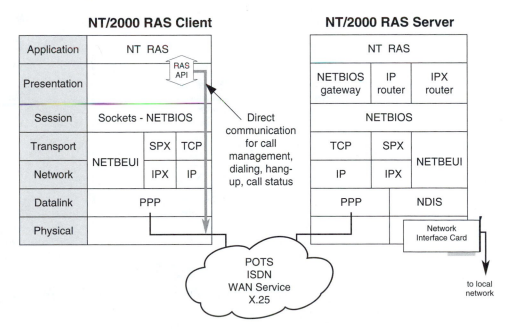

Figure 7-26   NT Client/Server Communication Protocols

Windows/NetWare Interoperability

Windows interoperability with NetWare is provided through Gateway Services for NetWare and File and Print Services for NetWare, optional components of Windows NT Server. Gateway Service for NetWare provides Windows clients access to NetWare resources, while File and Print Services for NetWare provides NetWare clients access to Windows resources.

As illustrated in Figure 7-27, **Gateway Services for NetWare** attaches to the NetWare server as a standard NetWare client. Once connected, the Windows server presents the NetWare resources as locally attached Windows resources. The clients request access to the resources via standard Windows shares using the SMB protocol. Upon receiving the request, Gateway services for NetWare restructures the request for transmission to the NetWare server using the NCP protocol. The response from the NetWare server is similarly translated from NCP to SMB for transmission to the Windows client. As can be seen, this process is very inefficient. If the Windows and NetWare servers are both on the same network segment, each request results in double the network traffic—once for the SMB request and once for the corre-

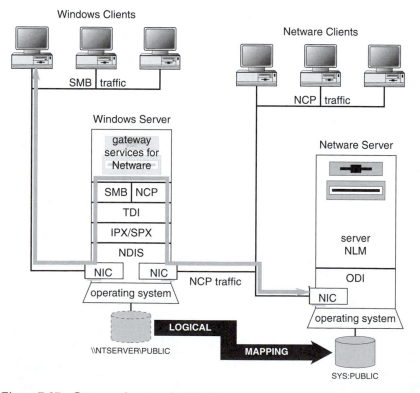

Figure 7-27 Gateway Services for NetWare

sponding NCP request. In addition to network traffic inefficiency, Gateway Services for NetWare also uses significant amounts of the Windows server's processor to translate information between SMB and NCP. Despite these issues, Gateway services for NetWare works well and provides a solution for the occasional traffic or an excellent migration path from NetWare to Windows.

Practical Advice and Information

SETTING GATEWAY SERVICES FOR NETWARE RIGHTS AND PERMISSIONS

The Gateway Services for NetWare service authenticates to the NetWare server using preset authentication credentials. Every request forwarded from the Windows server will appear to the NetWare server to be coming from this user. Therefore, the rights given to this account provide an upper limit to the rights Windows clients have to the NetWare resources. When the NetWare resources are re-shared by Gateway Services for NetWare, more restrictive permissions can be assigned to individual Windows users. The best solution is to give the Windows server all rights to the NetWare resource and set permissions for individual Windows users on the Gateway for NetWare server.

NetWare clients can gain access to Windows resources through File and Print Services for NetWare. **File and Print Services for NetWare** allow a Windows server to appear as a NetWare 3 server. NetWare clients authenticate and attach to the Windows server just as they would a NetWare server.

Managerial Perspective

By examining the array of products available from Microsoft, it should become clear that although interoperability with NetWare is certainly achievable, their primary purpose is to form a suite of products that make the transition from NetWare to NT as painless as possible.

Windows/UNIX Interoperability

With the emergence of Windows NT as an application server, interoperability with UNIX has become a key issue. There are two basic approaches to UNIX/NT interoperability: making NT speak UNIX upper-layer protocols (NFS) and making UNIX speak NT upper-layer protocols (SMB). The remainder of this section will focus on NFS implementations on NT. Technologies that allow UNIX to integrate into a native Windows environment will be covered in Chapter 8.

The **Network File System (NFS)** is UNIX's native network file system. Interoperability with UNIX is dependent on making Windows speak the NFS protocol. There are many different NT NFS solutions available. In addition to Microsoft's UNIX services for NT, many third-party software vendors have developed versions of the NFS file system that run on the Windows platform, thereby offering file system interoperability as well as client and server interoperability. These products should be reviewed carefully since they can differ in:

- Support for the Network Information System (NIS)

- Level of compatibility with standard NFS functionality

- Performance on reads, writes, copies, and deletes can vary significantly

- Number of simultaneous clients supported

- Support for multithreaded architecture

- Pricing policy

In addition to allowing Windows clients to connect to UNIX resources, another key Windows/UNIX interoperability issue is support for the UNIX X-Windows system. **X-Windows** is the system used by UNIX system to present a graphical user interface to UNIX applications. There are several products on the market that allow Windows clients to integrate into X-Windows. Detailed information on UNIX networking, NFS, and X-Windows is provided in Chapter 8.

SUMMARY

Windows NT is a powerful network operating system gaining significant market share thanks to its ability to serve as a powerful applications server as well as offering file and print services. The reliability, scalability, and portability that characterize Windows NT are directly attributable to its architecture, including a CPU-specific hardware abstraction layer and strict enforcement of program access to hardware resources through the NT kernel. One of NT's big advantages over market leader NetWare is its ability to support SMP with its multithreaded kernel.

Windows NT is designed for interoperability or extensibility on a number of levels. For example, NT support numerous file systems including FAT, NTFS, and AppleShare. In addition, it is also able to communicate

with native NetWare file systems as well. In terms of communications protocols, NT is able to support TCP/IP, IPX/SPX, or NBF (NetBEUI Frame) as its native communication protocol providing all transport services between NT clients and servers. In addition, NT also supports DLC and AppleTalk communications protocols for interoperability with IBM mainframes, networked printers, and Macintosh computers.

Unlike NetWare 4, which organizes an entire enterprise network's objects into a single NDS database, an NT enterprise network is divided into numerous independent domains. User accounts and access lists for each domain are administered by designated computers known as primary domain controllers. Users are able to access network attached resources on numerous domains thanks to specialized trust relationships established between domain controllers.

An upcoming release of Windows NT, now called Windows 2000, will expand on the shortcomings of Windows NT 4.0 by implementing a comprehensive directory services solution. Improvements in SMP capability, clustering, and load balancing are designed to allow Windows 2000 to scale to larger enterprises.

In recognition of the increased emphasis on remote and mobile computing, Windows NT includes remote access services that provide both outstanding security as well as sophisticated interoperability thanks to support of multiple communications protocols. In short, NT RAS offers full functionality to remote clients equivalent to that available to locally attached Windows clients.

Market surveys are consistently showing increased interest in Windows NT as an enterprise network operating system particularly well suited to high-end applications or database server roles.

KEY TERMS

access control lists
ACL
Active Directory
AD
AppleTalk
Application Installation
Backoffice
cache manager
CD File System
CDFS
Client-side caching
Data-Link Control
DCE
DDNS
demand paging
Device drivers
DFS
Distributed Computing
Distributed File System
DLC
DLL
DNS
Domain Name System
Domains
Dynamic DNS
Dynamic Host Configuration
Dynamic Link Library
Environment
FAT
File Allocation Table

File and Print Services for
    NetWare
file system drivers
forest
Gateway Services for NetWare
HAL
hardware abstraction layer
Hierarchical Storage
HSM
I/O Manager
I/O request packets
IIS
IntelliMirror
Interdomain trust accounts
Internet Information Server
Internet Printing Protocol
IPP
Kerberos
kernel mode
lease duration
Local Procedure Call Facility
local security authority
log file service
Logon process
Mailslot
Management
Master File Table
MFT
Microsoft Clustering Services
modularity of design

MPR
MSCS
Multiple Master Domains
    Architecture
Multiple Non-Trusting
    Domains Architecture
Multiple Provider Router
Multiple Trust Architecture
Named Pipes
NAT
NBF
NetBEUI Frame
Network Address Translator
Network drivers
Network File System
NFS
NT Executive
NT File System
NT Kernel
NTFS
NWLink
object manager
passthrough authentication
Point to-Point-Protocol
portability
POTS
PPP
primary domain controller
privileged mode
process manager

Protocol DHCP
public key certificate server
RAS
Remote Access Service
Remote Procedure Call
Remote Storage Services
Removable Storage Manager
RPC
RSM
RSS
scalability
security access token
security account manager
security ID

security reference monitor
Serial Link Internet Protocol
Server trust accounts
Service
Services for Macintosh
SFM
SID
Single Domain Architecture
SLIP
SMP scalability
SRM
Stubs
TDI
transport driver interface

tree
trust
trust relationship
user accounts database
user mode
Virtual Memory Manager
Windows Internet Naming
Windows Sockets
WINS
WinSock
WinSock2
workgroup
Workstation trust accounts
X-Windows

REVIEW QUESTIONS

1. What is meant by the NT characteristic of portability? Give examples.
2. What is meant by the NT characteristic of scalability? Give examples.
3. Differentiate between the various versions of NT 4.0.
4. Differentiate between the following: NT Executive, NT Kernel, and Hardware Abstraction Layer.
5. How does the NT kernel ensure system reliability?
6. How do the various sub-systems of the kernel interact and what controls this interaction?
7. Differentiate between user and kernel mode in NT.
8. Explain the implication of SMP scalability.
9. How is it possible for NT to support multiple file systems simultaneously?
10. Differentiate between FAT and NTFS.
11. Describe both the importance and functionality of NTFS file system recoverability.
12. Describe the function of each module or layer of the NT printing model.
13. Differentiate between domains and workgroups in NT 4.0.
14. Why are trust relationships important to NT 4.0 domain-based user accounts?
15. What is passthrough authentication?
16. Differentiate between the various NT 4.0 domain architectures in terms of domain

management, number of users supported, functionality offered, and target organization.
17. Describe each layer of the NT network services architecture. How does each layer contribute to NT's ability to support multiple transport protocols?
18. What is the role of interprocess communication in general and what advantage, if any, does WinSock 2 offer over alternative IPC protocols?
19. Explain the relationship between the various modules of the NT security model.
20. What functionality is offered by Services for Macintosh?
21. What architectural elements are required on NT in order to implement Services for Macintosh without requiring any hardware or software changes to the Mac clients?
22. What is Backoffice? What functionality is included in Backoffice?
23. Differentiate between the various editions of Windows 2000.
24. Explain the difference between fail-over clustering and scalability clustering. Which is native to Windows 2000?
25. What is the primary benefit of Windows 2000 clustering?
26. Explain how Remote Storage Services allows for better utilization of hard disk space.
27. What is the Active Directory?

28. Explain the difference between domains, trees, and forests in terms of the Active Directory.

29. How are the Active Directory and DNS related?

30. How would an NT 4.0 domain consisting of six NT Servers be migrated to Windows 2000 and the Active Directory?

31. What improvements in security were introduced in Windows 2000?

32. What is different about DDNS compared to normal DNS? Why is this difference significant?

33. Explain what NAT is and how it is most often used.

34. What are the key features of the Internet Printing Protocol?

35. What is NFS and what alternatives are available for support of NFS by NT?

36. What are the business layer issues behind the demand for tightly integrated remote access services?

37. Describe NT RAS in terms of supported communication protocols, WAN services, functionality, and architecture.

ACTIVITIES

1. Interview several organizations that have implemented NT. Determine the domain architecture employed in each case. Describe the organization structure and relate the organization size and structure to the chosen domain architecture. In your opinion, was the domain architecture implemented the best alternative? Why or why not?

2. Interview several organizations that have implemented NT. Document the chosen communications protocol in each case. Draw network diagrams indicating the communications protocols that must be supported at clients and servers. Determine why each communication protocol was chosen in each case. Were there alternatives that could have been implemented in any cases?

3. Interview several organizations that have implemented NT. Determine the functional use of NT. Is it being used as an application server? database server? file server? print server? more than one? What other network operating systems are being employed for which function?

4. Investigate DLC as implemented on network attached printers such as the HP 4Si. What functionality does DLC offer? What is required on both the printer and NT in order to implement it? Are alternatives to DLC available?

5. Interview several organizations that have implemented NT. Focus especially on those organizations that have implemented DHCP. What was their motivation? What has been their experience with DHCP to date? What unique requirements come into play when DHCP must be supported across networks using internetworking devices such as routers?

6. Interview several organizations that support both NT and NetWare LANs. Which interoperability products are employed and what functionality is delivered by each product? Is each product employed more for interoperability or transition? Be sure to note whether NetWare LANs are 3.x or 4.x.

7. Investigate several organizations that have implemented NT RAS. Draw detailed diagrams of their architecture including any additional hardware or software required. Be sure to also include business motivation and delivered functionality. Were alternatives to NT RAS considered?

8. Interview several organizations that are considering, or have recently upgraded to Windows 2000. What were the business reasons for the upgrade?

9. Interview several organizations that are considering or have recently upgraded to Windows 2000. What were the business reasons for the upgrade?

10. Interview several organizations that are considering or have recently upgraded to Windows 2000. What is/was their migration plan?

11. Interview several organizations that installed Windows 2000. How did they implement the Active Directory? How is their directory structure designed?

12. Interview several organizations that have upgraded to Windows 2000. Did they find any unexpected problems in the upgrade process?

13. Research products designed to integrate Windows and UNIX. Prepare a technology analysis grid describing the key features of these products.

14. Gather information concerning comparative market share of NetWare and NT from professional periodicals. Present your findings in graphical format. Explain your results. What trends are developing? Is NetWare or NT being adopted more in some market segments than in others? As a network manager, what would be your strategic plan for a network operating system given the results of your research?

CASE STUDY

Georgia Public Broadcasting Gets with the ATM Program

Georgia Public Broadcasting (GPB) believes the arrival of IP convergence is no longer a question, but rather, simply a matter of time.

This conclusion has driven the public radio and television station to build a high-speed ATM network designed to handle data, voice and video.

As a public broadcasting company, GPB isn't used to having a lot of money for its projects. But when the company moved into new facilities a couple of years ago, GPB gave its IT department $500,000 to build a corporate network that would last well into the next century.

The station began by wiring the building with multimode fiber-optic cable at a cost of $250,000. While the fiber network chewed up half the project budget, the organization figured fiber cable would provide a solid infrastructure for at least 15 years.

The fiber infrastructure is the foundation for the new ATM network that GPB started rolling out about a year ago. The organization previously ran an FDDI and Ethernet network.

The station chose ATM because it deemed the technology best suited to handling multiple protocols and highspeed multimedia applications. While GPB is in the midst of migrating to an all-IP network based on NetWare 5.0, the need for multiprotocol support is key because certain IPX and other applications are likely to be around for a while.

The network is anchored by 16 Madge Networks Collage 750 ATM switches, which support a batch of servers and 180 workstations. The ATM network lets GPB deliver 155M bit/sec to the desktop—plenty of bandwidth even for emerging multimedia applications, says Bill Burson, the organization's assistant director of IT.

GPB is awaiting tools from Madge that will let the company monitor the ATM network's performance via Hewlett Packard OpenView, says Burson, who is part of a three member team responsible for GPB's entire network.

GPB chose Madge because the vendor offered its products at one-third of the list price. Also, at the time of the transaction, Madge was the only major player supporting Novell's IPX protocol, Burson says. The one catch with the Madge deal was that GPB had to agree to be a showroom for the vendor.

"It hasn't been a problem at all," Burson says. "Madge representatives were in here half a dozen times when we first moved in, and that's about it."

While ATM to the desktop is rare, Burson's group decided ATM was the only technology that would let GPB send voice and video on the network over which all of its data is running. ATM has proven standards, such as Multi-Protocol over ATM, that let users support mixed protocol environments. While technologies such as Gigabit Ethernet are fast, they've yet to be tested like ATM, Burson says.

Today the network is supporting typical applications, such as Microsoft Office, and Oracle database applications used to store GPB member information.

But the station plans to begin running video over its network by year-end. GPB is considering hooking up a Real Networks RealVideo server to its ATM network. Video applications on tap include online video editing and the exchange of videos with other educational organizations.

"We should be streaming video internally instead of handling VHS tapes," Burson says. "But until recently, video servers were cost-prohibitive and the quality wasn't good enough."

Burson is awaiting available bit rate software from Madge that will let GPB guarantee bandwidth to desktop users, an important consideration for time-sensitive applications such as video.

Next year, GPB expects to add voice to its ATM network traffic mix. The organization plans to attach its Mitel SX2000 PBX, which comes equipped with an ATM interface, to the ATM net. The station figures it will connect its voice system to its membership database server, Burson says. This plan will enable callers to be identified by their phone numbers and will let GPB put members' latest information in the hands of call center agents more quickly.

It remains to be seen how ATM handles voice and video. But to date, ATM has proven to be more stable and far less complicated to deal with than people might think, Burson says.

Source: Denise Pappalardo, "Georgia Public Broadcasting Gets with the ATM Program," *Network World,* vol. 16, no. 14 (April 5, 1999), p. 14. Copyright (April 5, 1999), Network World.

BUSINESS CASE STUDY QUESTIONS ··

Activities

1. Complete a top-down model for this case by gleaning facts from the case and placing them in the proper layer of the top-down model. After completing the top-down model, analyze and detail those instances where requirements were clearly passed down from upper layers to lower layers of the model and where solutions to those requirements were passed up from lower layers to upper layers of the model.

2. Detail any questions about the case that may occur to you for which answers are not clearly stated in the article.

Business

1. What was the key business driver for Georgia Public Broadcasting?
2. What are Georgia Public Broadcasting's plans for telephony integration?

Application

1. What applications are currently running over the network?
2. What applications are expected to be running over the network when completed?

Data

1. What types of data are going to be supported over the network?

Network

1. Why did Georgia Public Broadcasting select ATM?

2. Georgia Public Broadcasting has an all ATM network. Is this typical?

Technology

1. What was the key reason for selecting Madge as a technology vendor?
2. What types of clients are used in the network?
3. What protocols are supported on the network?

CHAPTER 8

UNIX

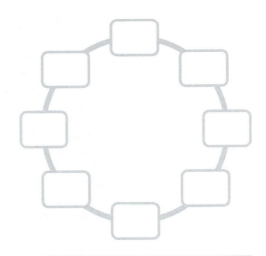

Concepts Reinforced

OSI Model
Internet Suite of Protocols Model
Network Operating Systems
   Functionality

Network Operating System
   Architecture
Protocols and Standards
Interoperability

Concepts Introduced

UNIX Architecture
UNIX Implementations
NFS Functionality

UNIX Functionality
X Windows
NFS Architecture

OBJECTIVES

After mastering the material in this chapter you should:

1. Understand the functionality, application, advantages and disadvantages of the currently available versions of UNIX

2. Understand how UNIX, TCP/IP, and NFS can combine to offer functionality equivalent to a fully-integrated network operating system

3. Understand the unique functional and architectural aspects of UNIX

■ INTRODUCTION

UNIX refers to a large family of related operating systems descended from work initially done by Ken Thompson and Dennis Ritchie at Bell Laboratories in the late 1960s and early 1970s. The name UNIX was derived as a play on words from another Bell Labs/M.I.T. project of the same era which produced a mainframe computer utility known as Multics.

Although the term UNIX itself is a trademark of The Open Group, a UNIX standards organization, it is commonly used in a general sense to refer to all UNIX-like operating systems regardless of vendor. These operating systems are also commonly referred to as the "ux"'s, since most of the product names end in ux or x: AIX, HPUX, Linux, and such.

Although not distributed as a ready-to-run network operating system solution, a network operating system can be built using UNIX as a foundation. Combined with NFS to provide a network aware file system, UNIX can offer the majority of the functionality of commercially available single-product network operating systems.

This chapter focuses on the architecture of UNIX style operating systems and their application as a network operating system. Each of the following key elements will be explored from both architectural and functional perspectives:

- UNIX operating systems

- NFS (Network File System)

Figure 8-1 conceptually illustrates how UNIX, TCP/IP, and NFS can be combined to offer full network operating system functionality to network-attached clients and servers.

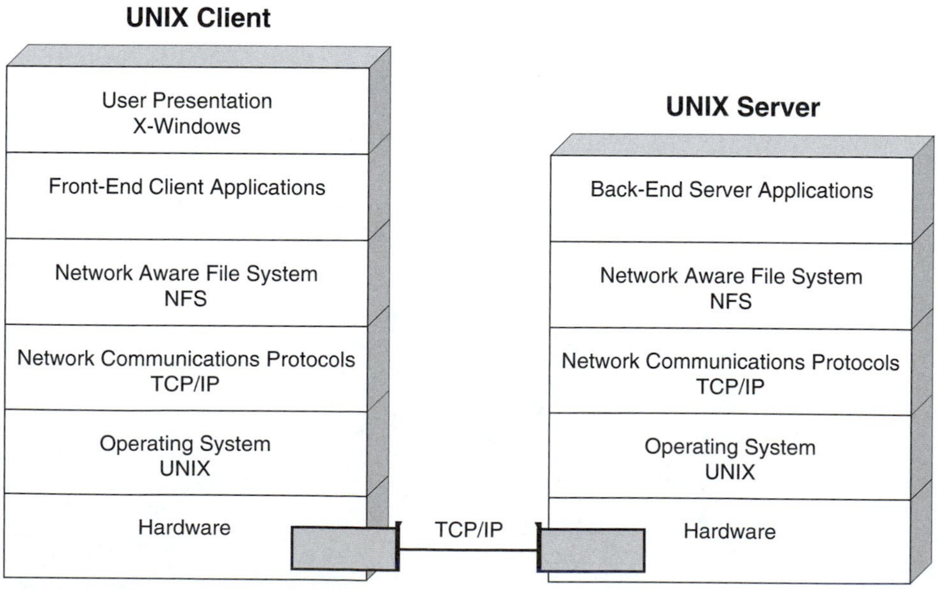

Figure 8-1   UNIX, TCP/IP, and NFS as a Network Operating System

■ OVERALL ARCHITECTURE

Unlike NetWare and Windows-based solutions, UNIX is not a product, but a family of similar operating systems. Conceptually the term UNIX can be thought of as product type (such as an automobile). Just as everyone understands what an automobile is and basically how to operate one, there are many subtle differences between vendors and models. The location of the gas and brake pedals is consistent across automobile implementations, but the locations of the headlight switch, windshield wipers, and other controls can vary greatly. Similarly, although the basic structure of all UNIX implementations is consistent, there are significant operational differences between vendors and implementations.

UNIX implementations can be broadly categorized into two major divisions or families: System V and Berkeley Standard Distribution (BSD). As shown in Figure 8-2, both System V and BSD share a common background in Bell Labs UNIX version 6, the first UNIX version widely available outside of Bell Labs. The split between the two occurred in 1977 when computer scientists at the University of California-Berkeley developed an alternative version of UNIX based on the version 6 source code, while Bell Labs continued to develop the original version of UNIX in version 7, System III, and System V.

UNIX Compatibility and Open Systems

As UNIX started to gain success in the commercial sector, the need to resolve the differences between UNIX implementations became paramount. University researchers were willing and able to rewrite software for different versions of UNIX, but commercial end users were not, so the task of maintaining software versions for each UNIX distribution rapidly became burdensome to UNIX application vendors.

In the late 1980s, two initiatives were developed to create a standard version of UNIX: UNIX International and The Open Software Foundation. **UNIX International** was created by AT&T, the owner of Bell Labs and UNIX System V, and Sun Microsystems, the leading proponent of BSD UNIX to integrate BDS functionality into System V. Other UNIX vendors viewed UNIX International as a threat and banded together under the guise of **The Open Software Foundation (OSF),** which was also working to merge BSD and System V into a single UNIX version known as OSF/1. As a result of the two competing groups and the participating UNIX system vendor's desire to make the resultant UNIX operating system as similar to their proprietary UNIX offering as possible, little progress was made in creating a single version of UNIX.

Other approaches to solving the UNIX distribution compatibility issue through standardization of interfaces proved more fruitful. **X/Open,** now merged with OSF as **The Open Group,** created the **single UNIX specification** that standardizes more than 1,000 UNIX APIs. Now in its second edition, the single UNIX specification allows software to be easily ported between compliant UNIX implementations. Before an operating system can be labeled and marketed as UNIX, it must conform to the single UNIX specification.

The Open Group is also responsible for the **Common Desktop Environment (CDE),** an effort by a consortium of UNIX vendors to establish standards for a unified graphical user interface, which allows those UNIX varieties that support the CDE to present an identical interface to users. Applications developers will be able to write applications to the CDE API

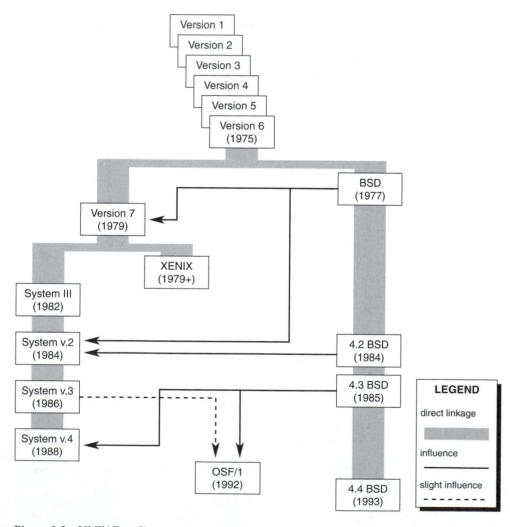

Figure 8-2   UNIX Families

rather than having to develop separate versions of their application for each UNIX variant.

A broader industry compatibility initiative is the POSIX standard. POSIX (Portable Operating System Interface) is an IEEE standard designed to facilitate application portability across operating systems by standardizing system calls and I/O. Although initially aimed at the splintered UNIX marketplace, non-UNIX operating systems such as Windows NT support POSIX. Collectively POSIX and the single UNIX specification have made porting applications across UNIX variations significantly easier.

■ COMMON UNIX IMPLEMENTATIONS

As illustrated in Figure 8-3, there are tens of UNIX implementations currently available in the marketplace. Each hardware vendor has its own version of UNIX optimized for their hardware. Although all UNIX implementations differ somewhat from each other, implementations from a given family are usually fairly close in file structure and command syntax. Although many of these UNIX implementations combine characteristics of both BSD and System V, most can still be categorized as one or the other. The heritage of some common UNIX implementations is summarized in Figure 8-4.

UNIX Implementation	Vendor	Hardware Platform	POSIX Compliant	Number of Bits
AIX	IBM	IBM RISC/6000 workstations and servers	Certified	32/64
Digital UNIX	Compaq	Compaq Alpha workstations & servers	Compatible	32/64
HP-UX	Hewlett-Packard Corporation	HP 9000 workstations and servers	Compatible	32/64
IRIX	Silicon Graphics	Silicon Graphics Indy workstations and servers	Compatible	32/64
Solaris	SunSoft	Sun Sparc stations and Intel ×86	Compatible	32/64
Linux	Multiple Open Source Vendors	Intel ×86 and various RISC platforms	Compatible	32/64 (32 on ×86)
UNIX Ware	SCO	Intel ×86 platforms	Compatible	32

Figure 8-3   UNIX Implementation Descriptions

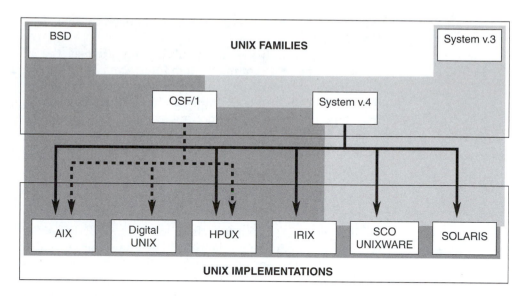

Figure 8-4   UNIX Implementation Heritage

AIX

AIX is IBM's POSIX certified 64-bit UNIX implementation. A stable, high-performance UNIX, AIX takes an innovative approach to easing the transition from 32-bit to 64-bit hardware through a clever design that allows a single executable to run on either 32- or 64-bit hardware. Traditional AIX strengths include system management and e-commerce enabling applications. Running on IBM's POWER and POWER/PC RISC platforms, AIX was the first UNIX release to support super scalar (more than one operation per clock cycle) processing. IBM has recently partnered with the Santa Cruz Operation (SCO), a longtime vendor of Intel x86 UNIX, to port AIX to Intel's upcoming IA-64 processor.

Digital UNIX

Digital UNIX (DUNIX) is a POSIX compatible 64-bit UNIX implementation originally developed by Digital Electronics Corporation (DEC) which was acquired by Compaq Corporation. Formerly known as Digital OSF/1, Digital UNIX is a direct result of the Open Software Foundation OSF/1 initiative. Digital UNIX runs on Compaq's Alpha.

Running on Compaq Alpha platforms, Digital UNIX has traditionally been a performance leader in the UNIX marketplace. Compaq has announced plans to port Digital UNIX to the upcoming Intel IA-64 platform as soon as it becomes available. Digital UNIX was the first 64-bit UNIX to ship and has continued to be a leader in the 64-bit UNIX field, with a strong combination of performance and overall operating system functionality.

HP-UX

HP-UX is Hewlett-Packard's POSIX compatible 64-bit UNIX implementation. Hewlett-Packard has historically marketed HP-UX as a business class operating system known for its quality and widely available consulting and support. Because of this business orientation, Hewlett-Packard is traditionally relatively slow to add new functionality to HP-UX, instead focusing on reliability and investment protection. HP-UX runs on Hewlett-Packard PA-RISC based systems. Hewlett-Packard has also announced plans to support the forthcoming Intel IA-64 architecture with a version of HP-UX.

IRIX

IRIX is Silicon Graphics' POSIX compatible 64-bit UNIX implementation. Designed to run on MIPS processor-based systems, Silicon Graphics and IRIX are known for excellent graphics performance and high performance. IRIX has traditionally boasted the highest UNIX scalability and performance with SMP systems that support up to 128 processors. Cellular IRIX, a new high-performance architecture that tightly integrates groups of SMP machines into a single logical system promises to further IRIX's reputation as a computing performance leader.

Linux

Linux is a POSIX compatible 32-bit UNIX implementation with SYSV and BSD extensions. Originally developed as a programming exercise by Linus Torvalds, Linux (Linus' UNIX) has grown into a high end UNIX implementation in a relatively short time.

Linux was originally developed for the Intel x86 platform. It is still primarily an x86 operating system, but the kernel has been ported to other processor architectures including Motorola 680x0, Sun SPARC, IBM PowerPC, and DEC Alpha. Other ports to ARM and MIPS processors are under development. With support for almost any computing platform, Linux represents a common API for the majority of today's computing hardware.

Strictly speaking the term Linux only refers to the Linux kernel. Multiple companies have written operating systems based on the Linux kernel. These Linux derivatives, or distributions, each have their own look and feel. Some have more in common with BSD, whereas others are more like System V UNIX implementations. A table of major Linux distributions is shown in Figure 8-5.

Distribution	Vendor	URL
RedHat Linux	Red Hat Systems	www.redhat.com
Open Linux	Caldera Systems	www.caldera.com
Debian Linux	Debian	www.debian.org
S.u.S.E. Linux	S.u.S.E.	www.suse.com
Slackware Linux	Slackware	www.slackware.com

Figure 8-5   Major Linux Distributions

One of the key differences between Linux and other UNIX implementations is the licensing model. Rather than being a product of a single company, Linux has been developed as **open source** software. The kernel is maintained by a loose knit team of system programmers collaborating via the Internet. The resulting code is then distributed under the GNU public license which ensures that the software must remain open source and freely available.

Because Linux is free and supports such a wide variety of hardware, a significant amount of development for UNIX is being done on Linux. Many new UNIX system programs are initially released for Linux followed later by ports to commercial UNIX implementations. At the same time most traditional UNIX applications such as SendMail and Bind have been ported to Linux.

The current market for Linux is for print services, software development workstations, and network infrastructure services. Linux, like all UNIX derivatives, is still too difficult to install and administer to replace Windows on the average user's desktop. However, the price is certainly right and a horde of emotional, highly motivated developers are currently working to overcome these issues and make Linux the operating system of choice for all users.

Managerial Perspective

OPEN SOURCE SOFTWARE

Great debate exists within the computing community about the viability of open source software in commercial computing environments. Open source software, such as Linux, is developed by a loosely connected group of programmers usually collaborating via the Internet.

One of the main problems with open source software is that there is no "company" standing behind the software. Open source software products come and go with amazing speed. A product that was virtually a standard last year may no longer be under development this year. In most cases, there is no centralized help desk that a user can call or support services that a company can contract with to ensure high availability. If a product dies, in many cases there is no way to get support since the developers have no obligation to support the product and it is no longer their main interest. Another issue hindering corporate adoption of open source software is liability. Because the developers have no financial stake in the product, many companies are concerned about quality and bug correction. If something goes terribly wrong, there is no one who can be held responsible for damages caused by software problems.

Although these are valid issues, in practice there are usually multiple means of finding support for open source software. Most products have newsgroups devoted to them that are monitored by the developers themselves. In several cases questions or problems pass directly from the user to the developer, far faster than would happen with traditional software. A problem posted to a news group might generate a patch to the product within days or even hours.

Another issue with open source software is version control. Open source software is constantly being updated and modified. The version downloaded from the Internet today very likely will be different than the version downloaded a week ago. With this high rate of change, compatibility issues and support for older software versions become very important for corporate users. While a single user might be able to constantly upgrade to have the latest features, a company with thousands of computers cannot afford to upgrade all of them even on a monthly basis.

The concept of open source software is still in its infancy. Any significantly different approach to software development takes time to mature and be sorted out by the marketplace. With companies working to provide support to corporate adopters (such as Red Hat and Caldera systems in the Linux marketplace), many of the issues hindering open source software's deployment in corporate environments may be overcome.

Solaris

Solaris is Sun Microsystems' POSIX compatible 64-bit UNIX implementation. Although Solaris is a System V implementation, it supports many BSD style features remaining from SunOS, its BSD-based predecessor. Sun is arguably the company that made UNIX a commercial success. Both NFS and NIS (discussed in detail later in this chapter) were originally developed by Sun before being adopted as multi-vendor standards.

Available in versions for Sun SPARC-based RISC workstations and Intel ×86 processor-based PCs and workstations, Solaris is a widely used general purpose UNIX platform. Almost all UNIX software can be purchased precompiled for Solaris, making it a safe choice for most UNIX applications.

■ OPERATING SYSTEM ARCHITECTURE AND CHARACTERISTICS

Originally developed as an operating system for engineering workstations, UNIX provides many high-end operating system characteristics. It natively supports multiprocessing, multi-tasking, and multithreading. In addition to these key NOS characteristics UNIX is also a multi-user operating system: more than one user can be concurrently executing applications on the same station as long as more than one user interface is attached to the computer. Collectively, these characteristics allow UNIX to serve as an excellent server platform for large applications.

From an operating system architecture perspective UNIX is a two-layered operating system consisting of a kernel and a series of System Programs. UNIX systems programs and utilities deliver requested functionality to users by issuing system calls to the kernel. UNIX system programs, utilities, and end-user applications are hardware-independent. They can run on any hardware that supports a compatible kernel. Figure 8-6 illustrates the basic components of the UNIX operating system architecture.

Multiprocessing Kernel

The UNIX kernel sits between the underlying hardware and the system programs. In addition to providing a common API to the system programs, the kernel performs lower-level operating system functions including memory management, process control, and I/O management. The majority of UNIX kernel functionality is concerned with managing files or devices of some type. In order to simplify and standardize system calls, the UNIX kernel

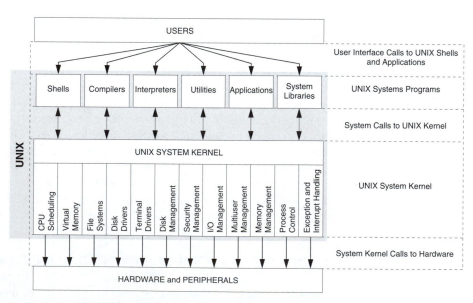

Figure 8-6   UNIX Operating System Architecture

treats devices as a special type of file. From the perspective of system or user programs, devices *are* files.

Memory Management   UNIX provides sophisticated memory management capabilities to manage multiple tasks for multiple users. The key memory management issue for any kernel is supporting virtual memory. The two primary methods employed for virtual memory management by UNIX systems are swapping and paging.

Swapping implies that entire processes are swapped between physical memory and a swap space partition on one or more disk drives. Swapping occurs when multiple processes are contending for the same limited amount of primary memory. The **scheduler process,** also known as the **swapper,** decides which processes should be removed from primary memory to the swap partition and which should be moved from the swap partition back into main memory.

One of the major problems with swapping is that adequate contiguous memory must be found in which to fit the swapped processes to optimize the speed and efficiency of the swapping process. The difficulty with this process is that as contiguous blocks of memory of varying sizes are continuously cut out of a finite amount of primary memory, the primary memory suffers from **fragmentation** where numerous, small leftover pieces of contiguous memory remain unused.

Paging seeks to eliminate, or at least minimize, memory fragmentation, by allowing processes to execute with only portions of a process, rather than the entire process, physically present in primary memory. Fixed-size portions of the process are loaded into primary memory as required. These application portions are known as **pages,** and the entire process is sometimes referred to as a **demand-paged virtual memory system.**

Process Control   Processes in UNIX are controlled by the **fork** system call. Fork calls are initiated through the shell interface, which allows **parent processes** to spawn multiple sub-processes (also known as **child processes**). In this manner new processes are launched from the basic shell interface. Access to system calls and applications are controlled according to UserID and groupID privileges. Described in more detail later in the chapter, these privilege levels are checked by the kernel prior to fulfilling requested system calls.

Exception and interrupt handling in UNIX is performed by the **signals** facility. In addition to handling exceptions, the signals facility is used for starting and stopping sub-processes and for allowing a shell to manage more than one process simultaneously. The shell sends signals to its child processes to manage the processes. Processes can be organized into **process groups** for the purpose of easily and effectively accomplishing a common goal. These process groups can then be managed as a single logical unit.

I/O System   The kernel is responsible for controlling all access to hardware. This means that whenever new hardware is added to the system, the kernel must be configured or altered to conform to the interface specification of the new hardware. The job of the I/O system is to minimize the amount of hardware specific interaction required of the UNIX kernel. As a result, most of the hardware specific device drivers are located in the I/O system.

Device drivers for specific block and character-oriented devices are stored outside of the kernel in arrays and are accessed with the assistance of pointers known as device numbers, which point to the correct array location, or entry point, of a particular device driver. Storing device drivers outside of the kernel helps contribute to the portability of the UNIX kernel.

The UNIX I/O system is comprised of three major types of I/O:

- The sockets interface used for interprocess communications.

- The block-device driver used for communications with block-oriented devices such as disk drives and tape drives. Block-oriented devices transfer data back and forth in fixed-length blocks, most commonly 512 or 1024 bytes.

- The character-device driver used for communications with character-oriented devices such as terminals, printers, or other devices that transfer data one byte at a time rather than in fixed-length blocks.

Figure 8-7 illustrates a representative UNIX I/O system.

Both block-oriented and character-oriented I/O have raw and cooked interfaces. Data that bypass all buffers and queues and interact directly with hardware devices go through the **raw interfaces.** In the case of character I/O, terminals and editing programs that interact on a keystroke-by-keystroke basis would use the raw TTY interface. The acronym **TTY** refers to terminals in general but actually stands for teletypewriter and is a holdover from the days before terminals had video monitors.

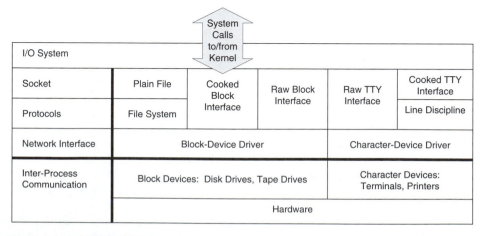

Figure 8-7   UNIX I/O System

Alternatively buffers and queues can be used to organize the transfer of data from the operating system to hardware devices. The interface to hardware that uses buffers and queues is known as a **cooked interface,** the term *cooked* being an analogy to food where cooked is the opposite of raw. The cooked interface provides auxiliary processing rather than merely providing access to the hardware as is the case with a raw interface.

System Programs

System programs include shells, compilers, interpreters, utilities, and system libraries. Residing just above the kernel, system programs interact directly with the kernel and therefore must adhere to an individual kernel's API set. Although the functionality of each system program is fairly standard, each UNIX implementation has its own set of specialized system programs written expressly for that version of the UNIX kernel.

System programs are the user's main interface to the system. From the shell used by the user to pass commands to the system through the utilities used to manage and run the system to the compilers used to create user applications, system programs represent the majority of the operating systems functionality.

In addition to providing services to users directly, system programs also provide APIs to user applications. As shown in Figure 8-8, system programs serve as a bridge between user application code and the kernel. As long as the user application makes standard API calls to a particular system pro-

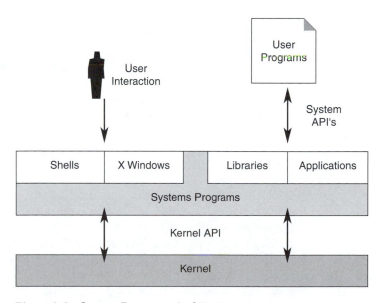

Figure 8-8   System Programs Architecture

gram, the application will work on any UNIX implementation that supports the system program.

Interprocess Communications

Interprocess communication in UNIX is accomplished via pipes and sockets. **Pipes** provide an interprocess communication mechanism to allow the output of one process to be used as the input for another process. Pipes are limited to communication between two processes executing on the same local computer and are initiated by a pipes system call. The two processes that communicate via the pipes interprocess communications mechanism must be related (parent-child) as enabled by the fork system call. The parent process must initiate the child process with a fork command to be able to pipe data into it.

A common example of a pipes system call is the redirection of the output of a command into the "more" system application to display the output in screens of information rather than sending the entire output to the screen at once, scrolling the data off the screen. This is accomplished using the pipe "|" symbol. The previous example is performed by issuing the "ls | more" command string.

Sockets is a more powerful and flexible interprocess communications mechanism than pipes. The key difference between pipes and sockets is that sockets are capable of providing interprocess communications across network interfaces between processes running on distributed computers. Sockets can also be used as a more generalized interprocess communications mechanism between processes running on a single computer.

Sockets is the IPC mechanism used to establish communications between a process on a server and multiple processes on multiple clients in a client/server architecture. The sockets IPC mechanism is implemented through a series of system calls that establish the network addresses of the processes that will communicate via sockets. Different types of sockets can be established for different types of interprocess communications. Some common socket types are described in Figure 8-9.

UNIX Filesystem

UNIX implements a hierarchical, multilevel tree file system with a common root directory. This hierarchical system is illustrated in Figure 8-10. The term **filesystem** has two meanings in UNIX: the overall filesystem and any subdirectory structure housed in a separate disk partition. UNIX is capable of supporting multiple file systems on a single disk. A disk is divided into multiple **slices** (or partitions) that can contain a file system, a swap area, or a raw data area. Each disk can have one and only one root file system, each file system

Socket Type	Explanation
Stream Sockets	Provides reliable, connection-oriented, two-way (full-duplex), sequenced packet interprocess communications through use of TCP (Transmission Control Protocol) as the transport layer protocol.
Datagram Sockets	Provides unreliable, connectionless, datagram interprocess communications through the use of UDP (User Datagram Protocol) as the transport layer protocol.
Raw Sockets	Provides direct interprocess communication from sockets to other layer protocols such as IP on the network layer or Ethernet on the data-link layer. Raw sockets is sometimes referred to as the **DIY (Do-it-Yourself)** interface since the functionality supplied by higher (transport) layer protocols such as TCP or UDP must be supplied by the programmer.

Figure 8-9   Socket Types

can have one and only one root directory, and each system can have only one root filesystem.

The basic job of the UNIX file system is to offer a consistent file services interface to user application programs without requiring them to worry about the particulars of the physical storage hardware used. The UNIX kernel treats files as a nonstructured sequence of bytes. In other words, although application programs may require files of a particular structure, the kernel merely stores files as a collection of sequenced bytes organized into directories. In the UNIX filesystem, directories are implemented as specially formatted files containing location information about the files in the directory.

Path names are used in UNIX to identify the specific path through the hierarchical file structure to a particular destination file. **Absolute path names** start at the root directory and provide a complete path to the destination directory while **relative path names** start at the current directory. When specifying relative paths, the "·"directory is the current directory and the "··" directory is the parent directory. The difference between absolute and relative path names is illustrated in Figure 8-10.

Links are another unique aspect of the UNIX file system that allow a given file to be known and accessed by more than one name. A link is actually an entry in a directory that points to another file. The target can be a file in the same directory, a file in another directory, or another whole directory. Two basic types of links are available in UNIX: hard links and symbolic links (also known as symlinks). A hard link means that anything done to the link (such as deleting it) will cause the same action to be performed on the link's target. Symbolic links are merely "pointers" to the target. Changes made to the symbolic link have no effect on the target. Links are illustrated in Figure 8-10.

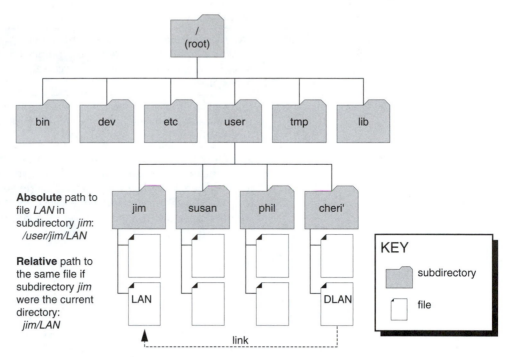

Figure 8-10   UNIX File System

Filesystem Layout   While the layout of the UNIX filesystem can vary significantly between UNIX implementations, most implementations adhere at
least in part to a common functional layout. This common layout enables a
system administrator to better understand and configure different UNIX
implementations. Figure 8-11 lists the common usage of each directory in the
UNIX filesystem.

User Interfaces

UNIX was originally developed as a command line operating system.
While extensions have been developed that add graphical operating system capabilities to UNIX, it retains a strong command line focus. In fact
there are many functions that are best performed or can only be performed
from the command line. The UNIX command line function is provided by
shell programs.

UNIX Shells   In UNIX, the command interpreter that provides the user's
interface to the system is a specialized user process known as a **shell.**
Because shells are applications, users are able to write their own shells or

Directory	Usage
/bin	UNIX system programs
/dev	Links to devices
/etc	Configuration information
/sbin	Configuration information
/lost+found	Lost files directory—When the UNIX filesystem locates a lost file it places it into this directory
/proc	Processes directory—Files represent active processes running on the system.
/usr	Locally generated programs—Usually where third-party applications are installed
/home	User home directories where user data are stored
/var	Temporary storage for spooling files and system queues

Figure 8-11   UNIX Filesystem Layout

modify existing shells to add particular functionality they might desire. Although such modification is possible, more users use a standard shell. Popular standard UNIX shells include:

- Bourne shell

- C shell—Uses shell scripting syntax similar to the C programming language

- Korn shell—Combines features of Bourne and C shells

- BASH—The Bourne Again Shell

Each of the aforementioned shells has its own scripting languages that can be used to automate operations or write simple system utilities. To create cross-shell, cross-platform scripts and programs either Perl or Rex can be used.

Developed to provide a powerful **Perl language** common scripting language that works on all shells on all UNIX implementations, the (Practical Extraction and Reporting Language) adds the following functionality to that offered by the Korn and Bourne shells:

- list processing

- associative arrays

- modern subroutines and functions

- more control statements

- better I/O

- full function library

Perl is distributed under the GNU software license and is free via download from the Internet. While Perl accomplished many of its aims, it is similar in syntax and commands to the more cryptic UNIX shells that it sought to improve upon.

The **Rexx** scripting language offers an easier to learn and use alternative to Perl that supports structured programming techniques such as modularity while still offering access to shell commands.

X Windows Although UNIX is historically a command line operating system, researchers at MIT developed the X Windows system to provide a graphical user interface (GUI) to UNIX. **X Windows** is a software solution that provides a standard graphical console for UNIX applications. Although X Windows provides all of the standard graphical user interface capabilities of other GUI interfaces, there is one significant difference: Unlike other GUI implementations, X Windows allows the output of an application to be displayed on any X compliant computer. The output of an application running on one computer can be displayed on another computer.

X Windows can be thought of as a client/server GUI solution. The output of an application running on one computer can be displayed on the graphical screen of another computer. However, the terminology used in X Windows is significantly different from a standard client/server application. In fact, the terminology is completely the reverse of a standard client/server environment.

As illustrated in Figure 8-12, the computer running the application is known as the **host** and the application program itself is known as the **client.** The output of the application is shown on a computer running special software known as the **display server** that interfaces to the computer's graphics system. The computer running the display server must have at least one **display** consisting of a keyboard, mouse, and graphical display. To simplify management of multiple graphical applications, multiple logical screens can be shown on one display. Similar to a desktop in a Windows environment, a **screen** represents a container for the output of multiple graphical applications. It is common for a single display to contain four logical screens.

Management of the X Windows display is performed by the **window manager.** Responsible for launching, moving, resizing, and iconifying application programs, the window manager controls the appearance and function of the display. Many different display managers are available including managers that emulate the Windows and Macintosh environments. Common display managers include the Motif Window Manager (mwm) and the Tab Window Manager (twm) among many others. Because the window manager is system software, users can tailor their window manager to their liking while maintaining interoperability. While the choice of window man-

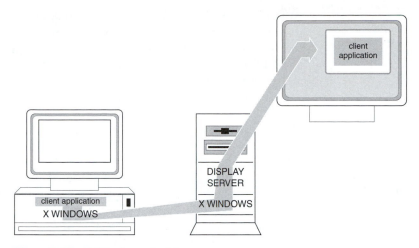

Figure 8-12   X Windows Architecture

ager is up to the user, only one window manager can be run on a display server at any given time.

When using X Windows, an additional parameter is required when launching an application: the user must specify on which display the application's output will appear. Although an application's output can be shown on the same computer running the application, the user must still specify the output location. This can be done manually when each application is launched, or automatically by setting an environment variable. It should be noted that while X Windows was originally developed for UNIX, display server software is available for many different applications including Microsoft Windows and Macintosh. These platforms cannot run UNIX software natively, but they can display the output of X-compliant UNIX applications as windows on their native GUI.

Modularity, Portability, and Scalability

The source code to the kernel and system programs is readily available, allowing individual programmers to enhance and modify UNIX. Most UNIX systems programs and kernels are written in C. This common development environment allows for easy portability of software to any available hardware platform as long as a C compiler is available for the new hardware. The ability to enhance and modify UNIX as desired or required is due to the layered, modular design as illustrated in Figure 8-6. New utilities or systems programs can be added as long as they issue standard system calls to the kernel. Even the kernel itself can be modified provided the modifications are compatible with the locally installed hardware and the local C compiler.

The use of C as a common development environment and the availability of the UNIX source code combine to make UNIX the ultimate open system. Other operating systems claim to be open systems based on the availability of published application programming interfaces (APIs). The ability of UNIX to allow modification of the operating system itself makes it the most flexible of all operating systems.

Practical Advice and Information

UNIX SOURCE CODE MODIFICATION AND FORWARD COMPATIBILITY

The ability to modify UNIX is a double-edged sword. While it makes it possible to tailor the operating system to meet an organization's *exact* needs, it can create significant version control and compatibility problems when upgrading to a new version of the operating system. A change (or patch in UNIX parlance) that works perfectly for the current version of UNIX may create problems when applied to the next version. A system administrator must carefully weigh the benefits of altering the operating system against the potential forward compatibility complications.

The modular nature of UNIX also allows increases its scalability. Scalability is further enhanced by the multiprocessing capabilities built into most UNIX kernels. UNIX can be quickly ported to newer and faster hardware as hardware technology matures, which is why most large database and application servers used in client/server environments are UNIX based.

It could be concluded from the previous discussion of the major architectural characteristics of UNIX that the operating system's chief positive attributes are:

Portability—Portability is a characteristic of UNIX on two distinct levels. First, UNIX itself is portable across numerous hardware platforms. Second, application programs written for UNIX are also inherently portable across all UNIX platforms.

Modularity—UNIX is a viable, dynamic, operating system to which functionality can be added in the form of new system utilities or system programs. Even modifications to the UNIX kernel itself are possible.

Scalability—UNIX can easily scale to larger and faster hardware to increase processing capabilities.

■ MANAGEMENT AND ADMINISTRATION

Management and administration of UNIX systems is significantly more complex than either NetWare or Windows systems. The command line nature of UNIX combined with the subtle differences between UNIX

Implementations make UNIX administration somewhat convoluted. Commands that work on one system may not work on another. To make matters worse, even when the commands are the same between implementations the command's parameters may be significantly different. Care must be taken to research each command to determine the exact parameters and syntax before issuing the command. Fortunately UNIX provides excellent on-line documentation through man pages. Typing man <command> will display a comprehensive list of the command's parameters and examples of its use.

One of the key shortcomings of using UNIX as a NOS is the limited resolution of administrative rights: to administer a UNIX server, you must become the superuser. The **superuser account** (or **root** account) is a special account that has ultimate rights over a UNIX system. Unlike other NOSes where administrative rights can be given to any users, in UNIX only the root account can administer the system. It is difficult to divide administrative rights among multiple users. If users have the root password, they are capable of fully administering the UNIX server.

Practical Advice and Information

ROOT PASSWORD MANAGEMENT

Anyone who knows the root password can completely manage a UNIX system including managing users, controlling processes, shutting the system down, and altering disk partitions. The root password should therefore be guarded diligently to ensure that it is not compromised to anyone who may intentionally or inadvertently harm the system through its use.

On the other hand, the root password is required to administer the system. Without the root password, it is impossible to even cleanly shut down the server. At least two people should always know the current root password to ensure the ability to administer the system in the event that the main administrator is unavailable due to vacation, sickness, or injury.

Server Grouping and User Authentication

UNIX is natively designed as a stand-alone operating system. Originally developed before the widespread availability of networks, UNIX systems were designed to support multiple users attached via serial terminals. Although network support has been tightly integrated into UNIX, each machine logically stands alone in terms of user authentication and authorization.

Each UNIX computer maintains a list of users in its/etc/passwd file. The contents of this file are used to authenticate users to the system. User authorization is performed through file ownership. A file has two owners: an individual owner and a group owner. Therefore granularity of access rights in a UNIX system is limited to three levels: individual, group, and public access. While it is possible to effectively manage resource authorization using these three levels, it represents additional complexity and more work than the multiple-user and group authorization schemes used in other network operating systems.

Because each system maintains its own user list, there is no native means to group UNIX systems. If users need to access resources on multiple systems, they must have an account on each system. While a semblance of seamlessness can be achieved by synchronizing the password on each system, this represents a significant limitation compared to the domain name and directory service schemes used in other network operating systems. Fortunately third-party add-ons have been developed to solve this scalability problem.

Sun Microsystems developed the **Network Information System (NIS)** to solve the integration issues between multiple UNIX servers running the Solaris UNIX implementation. Originally known as the yellow pages (yp), NIS provides a facility to synchronize the user authentication and authorization functions of UNIX systems. Even though the details of implementing NIS are beyond the scope of this book, by using NIS or the newer NIS+, a user can be defined to a system of UNIX computers in one location and have transparent access to all of the other computers in the system.

■ COMMUNICATION PROTOCOLS

Originally developed on UNIX, TCP/IP is natively supported by all UNIX implementations. In fact, UNIX is synonymous with TCP/IP. Many of the common TCP/IP-based utility applications now widely used on multiple operating systems were originally developed to solve connectivity issues on UNIX systems. Although support for IPX/SPX and AppleTalk have since been ported to UNIX, the vast majority of UNIX network traffic is IP based.

For UNIX to serve as a network operating system, both TCP/IP and a means of transparently offering file access to clients must be implemented. File transfer products such as FTP have been used to transfer files to and from UNIX hosts, but the native UNIX network file access solution is the Network File System or NFS.

NFS—Network File System

Originally developed by Sun Microsystems as part of their Open Network Computing (ONC) environment, **NFS** or **Network File System** allows multiple computing platforms to share files. To all of the heterogeneous computers that support NFS, a remote NFS file system appears as a transparent extension of their local operating system. By implementing a NFS, client remote disk drives appear as local. Print jobs can also be redirected from local workstations via NFS. Although originally developed for the UNIX operating system, NFS is now supported on a variety of platforms including PCs. This has allowed network operating systems such as NetWare and Windows NT to transparently support NFS as well, thereby offering transparent interoperability with UNIX workstations, minicomputers, and mainframes.

Although NFS is often considered functionally equivalent to the file systems of a fully integrated network operating system such as NetWare or Windows NT, NFS derives much of its functionality from the native operating system of the platform on which the NFS server is installed. While NFS is capable of supporting basic file sharing between different computing platforms, more advanced file sharing and management features such as user and group access rights, file and record locking, and file type conversion may not be universally supported. In other words, in some cases NFS is the lowest common denominator; only able to implement features common to all linked file systems and computing platforms as opposed to the most advanced file management functionality of any particular computing platform.

NFS Protocols   The term *NFS* is generally used to refer to a collection or suite consisting of three major protocols:

- **NFS**—Network File System

- **XDR**—eXternal Data Representation

- **RPC**—Remote Procedure Call

Strictly speaking, NFS is only the API portion of a collection of programs and utilities that offer the transparent file management interoperability associated with the NFS suite of protocols. Transparency is a key point since the client application requesting files does not know that the files are not located locally. The NFS client software automatically communicates with a remote NFS server to deliver the requested files to the application. Each NFS client protocol stack interacts with the native operating system of the computing platform on which it is installed, translating requests and responses for NFS services into standardized NFS protocols for communication with NFS servers. NFS is an OSI application layer protocol.

XDR (External Data Representation) is a presentation layer protocol responsible for converting the underlying data format to a standard NFS format. This is required to ensure that all NFS clients and servers can process the data, regardless of the computing platform or operating system on which the NFS client or server may be executing.

RPC (Remote Procedure Call) is a session layer protocol responsible for establishing, maintaining, and terminating communication sessions between distributed applications in a NFS environment. NFS protocols may use either UDP or TCP for transport layer services. The architectural relationship between the NFS suite of protocols and the TCP/IP suite of protocols is illustrated in Figure 8-13.

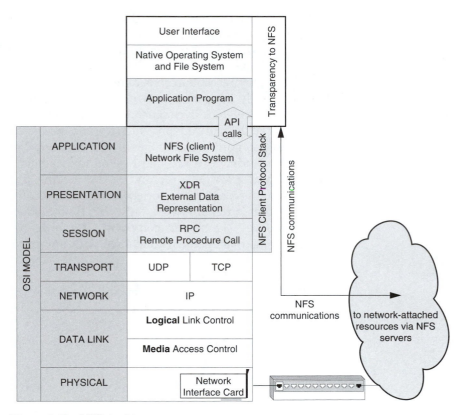

Figure 8-13   NFS Architecture

UNIX AND NFS AS A NOS ALTERNATIVE

Practical Advice and Information

Traditionally the main reason that UNIX/NFS was used as a NOS was to support the TCP/IP protocol or to solve scalability issues with PC-based file/print servers. As comprehensive network operating systems such as NetWare and Windows have continued to evolve, the need for using UNIX and NFS as a NOS has diminished. With current versions of both NetWare and Windows natively supporting the IP protocol and multiprocessing, the need for using UNIX/NFS as a NOS has decreased. While NFS remains a valid alternative for organizations predominately UNIX based, most organizations that are primarily PC based will find either NetWare or Windows nominally represent a better alternative.

UNIX/PC Integration Beyond NFS

While it is possible to create a NOS look-alike by installing NFS client software on PC client computers to allow them to connect to standard UNIX NFS services, recent developments in UNIX network services represent an alternative method of using UNIX as a scalable network server for PC clients. Developed as part of the Linux initiative, UNIX services have been developed that emulate PC Network Operating Systems. From the perspective of the client stations, UNIX hosts running these services appear to be PC NOS servers. Although these packages were originally developed for Linux, they can be ported and compiled on most UNIX implementations. One of the key benefits of these services is that PC clients can connect to the server using the existing network client software.

For predominantly NetWare environments the **Mars_nwe** package emulates a bindery-based NetWare server (i.e., NetWare 3). NetWare clients will view the UNIX server as a NetWare server. Mars_nwe implements the NCP application layer protocol on IPX/SPX only—neither NWIP nor Real/IP is supported (for detailed information on NetWare communication protocols please refer to Chapter 6). While this solution simplifies client configuration for organizations that are NetWare based, the limitation of the bindery significantly reduces scalability. New NetWare emulation packages promise to add NDS compliance to UNIX.

For predominantly Windows NT/2000 server environments, the **Samba** package emulates a Windows NT 4.0 server. Implementing the SMB protocol on both TCP/IP and IPX/SPX, Samba is a sophisticated NT server emulation capable of serving as a primary domain controller and participating in trust relationships. Development of Samba is ongoing and there is significant reason to believe that it will be able to participate actively in Active Directory trees and forests when the final APIs are implemented.

Another solution that adds support for NT Network services on UNIX is AT&T **Advanced Server for UNIX.** Designed as a commercial solution supported by the major commercial UNIX implementations, Advanced Server for UNIX considerably eases Windows NT/UNIX integration. Additional information on Windows networking protocols and structures is given in Chapter 7.

In addition to the obvious benefits of easy integration into existing Windows server environments, Samba or Advanced Server for UNIX is also an excellent solution for connecting a workgroup of Windows-based clients to a single UNIX host. Because each Windows client comes natively with an SMB-based network client that will work with Samba, it can be much easier and more economical to install an SMB server on a UNIX host rather than purchasing and installing NFS client software on each Windows workstation.

■ APPLICATION LAYER SERVICES

Figure 8-14 illustrates the placement of many of the TCP/IP family of protocols into their respective layers of the TCP/IP model. Each application layer protocol has a corresponding application service or utility that implements the protocol. This section focuses on these application layer protocols and services.

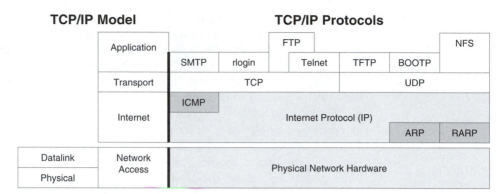

Figure 8-14   TCP/IP Family of Protocols

TCP/IP utilities, otherwise known as Application Layer Services, adhere to a distributed processing or client/server model in that it takes two distinct pieces of software, a client piece and a server piece, running on two different computers, in order to deliver a given application layer service. The server piece is usually referred to as a **daemon,** and is named with a "d" suffix. For example, the client piece of the FTP utility is known as FTP, whereas the server piece is known as ftpd. The following paragraphs offer brief descriptions of several popular application layer services.

User Interaction

Because UNIX is a multi-user operating system, a means of allowing multiple users to access a UNIX host concurrently is required. Serial terminals were originally used for this purpose, but the advent of low-cost LAN technologies has resulted in LAN-attached computers replacing serial terminals for most applications. In addition to the graphical X Windows solution discussed previously, there are two network enabled command line applications are used for user interaction: Telnet and the R commands.

Telnet   Strictly speaking, **Telnet** is terminal access API that allows remote terminals to connect to hosts running Telnetd (the Telnet server program). If the remote terminal accessing the Telnet server is not truly a "dumb" terminal, then terminal emulation software must be executed in order to make it appear to be just a "dumb" terminal to the Telnet server host. The real purpose of Telnet is to make this remote terminal, which may be something other than a typical terminal, appear to be a normal terminal to the login host.

Because Telnet must be able to operate with a variety of terminal types, it contains an adaptive negotiation mechanism known as **Telnet negotiation.** Telnet negotiation allows Telnet to establish sessions assuming very basic functionality known as the **Network Virtual Terminal,** and progressively negotiate more advanced terminal features supported for the particular terminal and application in question. This process ensures that a session is established and that the highest level of functionality is used for each session.

R Commands   The term **R commands** describes a group of application layer service commands that can be executed remotely. For example, rlogin allows a user to remotely login to another computer and rexec allows the same user to execute a program on that remote computer. The major problem with the R commands is their lack of sophisticated authentication and security features. As a result R commands are often disabled, especially on PC-based TCP/IP clients to prevent a breech of system security.

File Transfer Services

One of the first network applications developed was software to allow files to be transferred from one host to another. UNIX implements two approaches to file transfer: FTP and TFTP.

FTP—File Transfer Protocol   FTP or the **File Transfer Protocol** provides a mechanism for transferring files between a variety of different types of networked computers. Strictly speaking, FTP does not provide a user interface but rather an API for FTP services. An application program must be written that invokes the FTP commands and executes the FTP services. In order to accomplish this, both FTP client and FTP server software (ftpd) must be available on any given networked computer.

FTP provides a platform nonspecific means of transferring files between computers. Although the computers may differ in a variety of ways, such as underlying operating system commands, FTP becomes the language that all the computers have in common. For example a user may type "dir" on a DOS-based terminal, which translates locally and travels across the network as an FTP "list" command, where it is translated by FTP into an "ls" command for the remote UNIX operating system. The only commands actually defined by the FTP protocol are those exchanged between the FTP client and FTP server. FTP user commands vary according to the vendor of the FTP software but generally conform to the commands of the operating system on which the FTP user software is installed. To ensure that files are transferred error-free, FTP uses TCP for its transport services. Figure 8-15 differentiates between FTP client software, FTP server software, and FTP user software.

TFTP—Trivial File Transfer Protocol   TFTP or **Trivial File Transfer Protocol** is another file transfer utility. TFTP was designed to be a simpler and less memory intensive alternative to FTP. It does not offer nearly the sophistication or functionality of FTP and is used primarily for computer-to-computer

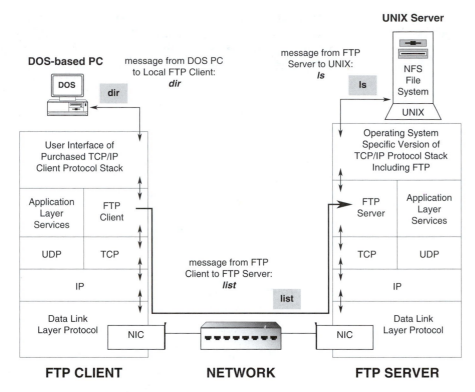

Figure 8-15   FTP Software and Communication

communication of small messages. TFTP uses UDP rather than TCP and, as a result, must provide its own error correction mechanism.

Management

As the complexity and importance of networked computer systems continue to increase, a means of effectively managing the network infrastructure, clients, and servers has become paramount. With networks spanning the globe, it has become almost impossible to manage them by observation. To support network-based management, the SNMP protocol was created.

SNMP—Simple Network Management Protocol   Client/server architectures have been implemented using a variety of different server platforms and internetworking devices from a multitude of vendors. Although enterprise network management systems are discussed in more detail in Chapter 15, the role of the TCP/IP family's **Simple Network Management Protocol (SNMP)** in the successful implementation of enterprise network management systems is introduced here.

A multi-vendor enterprise network management system requires the interaction of a number of different components as illustrated in Figure 8-16. SNMP offers a standardized protocol for the transport of management information such as device status, device activity, and alarm conditions. The decision as to which information should be requested, transported, and stored for a variety of different devices is defined by a standard closely related to SNMP known as the **MIB (Management Information Base).**

The MIB is a database of information about a network device. The fields and values of the MIB are known as MIB objects. While the basic values for the MIB are defined via IETF standards, individual vendors have added their own fields or MIB extensions to the standardized MIB definitions. Although these extensions offer product differentiation and increased functionality, they can also make SNMP interoperability difficult.

SNMP is a client/server style protocol; however, there are far more servers than clients. Each device that is to be managed via SNMP must be equipped with an SNMP server capable of reporting required performance statistics in standardized SNMP format. This embedded SNMP server is known as a software **agent,** SNMP agent, or management agent. Any device that contains an agent is said to be SNMP compliant. **SNMP managers** collect and parse data from the various agents. Managers are specialized software applications that run as applications on computer platforms.

SNMP managers poll the agents for information and present network configuration and operational status in a meaningful manner. In some cases, enterprise network management systems can be programmed to react to certain SNMP reported conditions by dialing pager or cellular phone numbers of network managers.

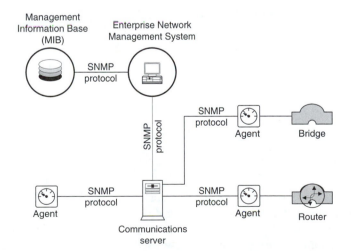

Figure 8-16   SNMP, MIB, Agents, and Enterprise Network Management System

Other Common Services

In addition to the aforementioned services, UNIX and TCP/IP also include support for many other application services. Many network applications that are currently widely implemented utilize services and protocols developed in the UNIX/TCP/IP environment.

SMTP—Simple Mail Transfer Protocol   The **Simple Main Transfer Protocol (SMTP)** provides a means of transferring electronic mail between computers. Just as the FTP client required a separately written application program to provide an interface between users and the FTP client, the SMTP client requires a separately written user front-end. SMTP allows different computers that support the TCP/IP protocol stack to exchange e-mail messages. It is important to understand that SMTP is only able to establish connections, provide reliable transport of e-mail messages via TCP, notify users of newly received e-mail, and terminate connections—SMTP is not used to read e-mail. SMTP establishes reliable point-to-point connections between SMTP clients and their destination SMTP servers

If sophisticated e-mail translation is required, this functionality must be provided by the end-user's e-mail application. Strictly speaking, SMTP only defines communication between the SMTP client service (requests) and the SMTP server service (responses). Extensions to SMTP such as **Multipurpose Internet Mail Extension (MIME)** allow binary files to be attached to SMTP delivered e-mail messages.

Line Printer Services   **LPS** or **Line Printer Services** are also available in client (requests) and server (responses) versions. The client portion runs on the client PC requesting services and the server portion runs on the print server. Basically LPS supplies the printer services typically supplied by network operating systems such as NetWare, Windows for Workgroups, or Windows NT. LPS utilities allow users to send or remove a print job to/from a print queue attached to another computer, or to display the status of the print jobs in a print queue, among other typical print queue management commands.

SUMMARY

Although not truly fully-integrated network operating systems, Unix plus TCP/IP and NFS offer equivalent functionality to many fully integrated network operating systems. The standardized, open systems orientation of Unix, TCP/IP, and NFS has made this combination of technology a popular choice for high-performance network-based computing. Unix offers a preemptive multitasking operating system, TCP/IP offers the network communications and management functionality, whereas NFS offers the ability for a variety of network attached computers to share disk drives and file systems.

Rather than a single product, UNIX refers to a family of similar operating systems or implementations. There are two major families of UNIX implementations: BSD and System V. Software can be ported between implementations by recompiling the source code to work with the target system's kernel.

The architecture of the Unix operating system is hierarchical in nature, consisting of the Unix systems programs and the Unix kernel. User interfaces are known as Unix shells. The two key functional characteristics enabled by this architecture are portability and modularity. Unix has a native file system of its own.

X Windows provides a client/server graphical interface to UNIX systems. Applications running on one system can be displayed on another system via X Windows.

File-sharing services are added to UNIX via NFS. NFS is a networked file system that can be shared by a variety of distributed computing platforms. Any computing platform that supports a NFS client can access files from an UNIX NFS server.

In addition to NFS, UNIX provides many other network application layer services, including Telnet for network terminal emulation, FTP for file transfer, SNMP for network system management SMTP for e-mail messaging, and LPS for printer sharing services.

KEY TERMS

Absolute path names
Advanced Server for UNIX
Agent
CDE
child processes
client
Common Desktop Environment
cooked interface
Daemon
demand-paged virtual memory
    system
display
display server
External Data Representation
File Transfer Protocol
filesystem
fork
fragmentation
FTP
host
Line Printer Services
Links

LPS
Management Information Base
Mars_nwe
MIB
MIME
Multipurpose Internet Mail
    Extension
Network File System
Network Information System
Network Virtual Terminal
NFS
NIS
open source
OSF
pages
Paging
parent processes
Path names
Perl language
Pipes
process groups
R commands

raw interfaces
relative path names
Remote Procedure Call
Rexx
root
RPC
Samba
scheduler process
screen
Shell
signals
Simple Network Management
    Protocol
single UNIX specification
slices
SNMP
SNMP managers
Sockets
superuser account
swapper
Swapping
Telnet

Telnet negotiation   Trivial File Transfer Protocol   window manager
TFTP   TTY   X Windows
The Open Group   UNIX   X/Open
The Open Software Foundation   UNIX International   XDR

REVIEW QUESTIONS

1. How is the combination of Unix, TCP/IP, and NFS functionally equivalent to a fully integrated network operating system such as Windows NT?
2. What are the two main families of UNIX implementations?
3. List six UNIX implementations and their respective strengths.
4. What standards are used to increase portability of UNIX applications between UNIX implementations?
5. What reasons are commonly given as reasons not to include open source software in mission critical applications?
6. What is the relationship between the Unix systems programs, Unix system kernel, Unix shells, and Unix applications programs?
7. Describe which architectural features of Unix contribute to its portability.
8. Describe which architectural features of Unix contribute to its modularity.
9. Describe some of the unique features of the Unix file system.
10. Differentiate between swapping and paging. Which do you feel is more efficient? Justify your answer.
11. What is the relationship between the fork system call and the multithreading capabilities of Unix?
12. What is the purpose of X Windows? What are the main parts of an X Windows system?
13. List two non–shell-specific scripting languages and their respective strengths.
14. Explain the statement "UNIX is limited in terms of permission granularity."
15. What is NIS?
16. What is the difference between pipes and sockets?
17. What is the relationship between the Unix file system and NFS?
18. Differentiate between the various types of sockets in terms of functionality and proper application.
19. Why are TCP/IP application layer services considered to be running in a client/server architecture?
20. What is a daemon?
21. Describe the relationship between an FTP client, an FTP server, and the operating systems of the computing platforms on which each is installed.
22. Differentiate between FTP and TFTP.
23. Why is SMTP not considered to be a fully functional e-mail system?
24. Describe the relationship between SNMP, MIB, agents, and enterprise network management systems.
25. Explain the relationship between the various layers of the NFS architecture.

ACTIVITIES

1. Research UNIX implementations and prepare a chart showing the currently available implementations, supported hardware, vendor, and specific strengths and weaknesses.
2. Interview the IT manager at your company or school to learn his or her attitudes and plans for the inclusion of Open Source Software into the corporate network.

3. Draw a diagram comparing the functionality of a fully integrated network operating system such as Windows NT and the combination of Unix, TCP/IP, and NFS. Use the OSI model as a frame of reference.
4. Draw a diagram illustrating the relationship between Unix systems programs, Unix system kernel, Unix shells, and Unix applications programs.
5. Investigate and report on the differences between the various Unix shells as well as lan-guages such as Perl and Rexx. What is the relationship between Unix and languages such as C, C++, and Visual C++?
6. Prepare a chart or time line showing the major events in the history of Unix. Pay particular attention to standardization efforts or other efforts to make Unix more commercially acceptable.
7. Research and report on any current efforts to offer increased standardization to the Unix environment.

CASE STUDY

Software Helps Resort Manage Growth

Sunterra Resorts may have great places to go for holidays, but running the company's network and systems hasn't been much of a vacation.

Buying up resorts all over the world, the $450 million company has grown by leaps and bounds—from nine resorts two years ago to 87 today.

The buying spree resulted in a decentralized IT system that had no good way of keeping companywide information in one place.

It also became difficult to track what was going on at the growing number of servers, and that was causing problems, says Mike Wester-field, senior network analyst at the Orlando company. "The servers couldn't stay up for more than a day or two at a time," he says.

BRINGING IT TOGETHER

Last year Sunterra started to bring all of its reservation, accounting and contract information into its corporate headquarters, making admin-istration easier and improv-ing access for centralized reservations and collections departments.

The plan is to create a cen-tralized Oracle database run-ning on an HP 9000 server, accessed by Citrix WinFrame servers based on Windows NT. The task became more difficult when the corporate site went from six of these application servers last year to 13 today.

The job will get harder still when the corporate site expands to as many as 50 servers in coming months.

To pull off the centraliza-tion, Sunterra's IT staff needed answers to some basic ques-tions, such as: Do the servers have enough disk space or memory? and, How well are applications performing?

To provide some answers, Westerfield last year installed Heroix's RoboMon software, which resides on servers and alerts systems managers to potential problems.

The software uses a set of rules to determine if there is a problem. Then RoboMon can fix the problem or notify a systems manager via e-mail or a page. It also sends events back to a central monitor.

PROACTIVE PUSH

Westerfield says RoboMon is helping Sunterra move from fixing problems reactively to proactively stopping problems before they occur. As a result, servers are much more stable.

RoboMon has already discovered a couple of problems. One server "came dangerously close to running out of disk space," Westerfield says. Before RoboMon raised a red flag, "nobody had any idea that was happening."

The warning gave the systems managers an opportunity to make space on the drive.

RoboMon also helped show how Microsoft Exchange was using too much memory, Westerfield says.

Sunterra also uses the software to detect if a user has been idle for a long time. RoboMon can then automatically log off that user.

To maintain network performance, Westerfield made the company's Cisco routers give a higher priority to Win-Frame packets, which use Citrix's Independent Computing Architecture protocol.

LOOKING AHEAD

As Sunterra continues to bring its data into a central location, there will be less traffic on the links from headquarters to each of the resorts.

This fact means many of these links can be cut back from full 1.5M bit/sec T-1s to

512K bit/sec frame relay lines, Westerfield says.

Over the long term, Sunterra is using RoboMon to generate reports about usage on the servers, so the company will know when it needs more server capacity. However, the reports may not be enough.

Westerfield says he'd like to see RoboMon generate graphs in the future to make it easier for nontechnical people to see trends.

"That way, we can have some backing when we go to management and say, 'We need more servers,'" he says.

At the rate the company is growing, chances are Sunterra will probably need many more.

Source: Jeff Caruso, "Software Helps Resort Manage Growth," *Network World,* vol. 16, no.13 (March 29, 1999), p. 27. Copyright (March 29, 1999), Network World.

BUSINESS CASE STUDY QUESTIONS

Activities

1. Complete a top-down model for this case by gleaning facts from the case and placing them in the proper layer of the top-down model. After completing the top-down model, analyze and detail those instances where requirements were clearly passed down from upper layers to lower layers of the model and where solutions to those requirements were passed up from lower layers to upper layers of the model.
2. Detail any questions about the case that may occur to you for which answers are not clearly stated in the article.

Business

1. What was the business reason for centralizing Sunterra's systems?

Application

1. What does the RoboMon software do?
2. What database system is used at Sunterra?

Data

1. What types of data are carried over the network?

Network

1. What are the advantages to centralizing the systems?
2. What thin client technologies are used in the system?

Technology

1. How has RoboMon helped Sunterra implement and manage their system?

CHAPTER 9

MIDDLEWARE

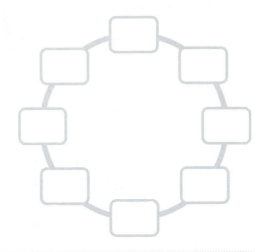

Concepts Reinforced

Middleware
Asynchronous Communication
N-Tier Client/Server Architecture

Synchronous Communication
Two-Tier Client/Server Architecture
Application Programming Interfaces

Concepts Introduced

Structured Query Language
Universal Data Access
Transaction Processing
Message Queuing
CORBA

ODBC
Remote Procedure Calls
Message Passing
DCOM

OBJECTIVES

After mastering the material in this chapter you should:

1. Understand the role of middleware in a client/server system

2. Understand middleware categorization techniques

3. Understand middleware selection techniques

4. Be able to make a middleware selection based on business requirements

■ INTRODUCTION

Middleware can be considered the "/" in client/server computing: the glue that binds the clients and the servers together into a cohesive system. Middleware is an enabling software layer that provides a transparent means of accessing information between clients and servers. Residing between the business application and the network transport layer on both client and server systems, middleware insulates the business application from the intricacies of the various operating environments on which the application is running.

In this chapter various categories of middleware will be introduced. Although a fairly detailed technical description of each is presented, the main factor in a middleware decision must be based on the business implications of each potential solution. Regardless of the perceived technical superiority of a solution, if it does not allow the installed clients and servers to communicate, it is of no value.

■ THE NEED FOR MIDDLEWARE

To gain a better understanding of the need for middleware, consider the major differentiating factor between client/server applications and traditional applications: In a client/server system, processing takes place on two or more computers connected by some form of communication link rather than on a single computer as in a traditional application. Therefore both the client and server portions of the distributed application must be able to "talk" to one another over the communication link between them.

Without middleware, both client and server applications would have to be programmed to access the platform-specific communication protocol stack directly. Although it is certainly possible to develop client/server systems in this manner, it adds considerable complexity for the application programmer who probably does not have significant communication programming experience. This approach requires every client and server application to contain routines to facilitate communication, directly tying the application to the lower-level communication protocols. If a lower-level protocol is changed, the application must be rewritten.

This approach also directly ties a client application to a specific server application. Each client application is written to access a specific server application. If a change is made on either end, a corresponding change may be required at the other end. This direct tie eliminates one of the key advantages of client/server systems: the ability to develop modular systems.

What is needed is a new layer of software that interfaces with the lower-layer communication protocol stack, formats data for transmission between the client and server applications, and provides a standard interface for the application programmer to access. Software that provides these services is known as **middleware.**

■ MIDDLEWARE ARCHITECTURE

The combined functionality of client and server middleware is to provide a transparent means for the client application to access the services of the server application. In this case, middleware can be thought of as a translator between the language of the client application and that of the server application.

Logical Architecture

Regardless of application or type, all middleware implementations share a common architecture. Aptly named, middleware resides on both clients and servers in the middle of the application stack: between the network operating system and the business application. As shown in Figure 9-1, middleware has a direct interface to the *underlying* network operating system and the user application and a logical interface to other middleware via the network operating system's communication sub-system.

The interfaces to the network operating system and the application program represent **vertical integration.** Vertical integration refers to integration of components within a single computer. The interface to the network operating system, labeled *Interface 1* in the diagram, is the simplest interface in the middleware architecture. From the perspective of the middleware consumer, *Interface 1* is a binary selection: a middleware solution will either run on a particular network operating system or it will not. All subsequent discussion will assume middleware to NOS compatibility.

The other vertical integration interface, labeled *Interface 2* in Figure 9-1, represents integration with the business application. For servers, this interface provides a means for the middleware to communicate with the applications that maintain and serve resources to the clients. For clients, this interface represents the interface used by client applications to access resources on the remote servers.

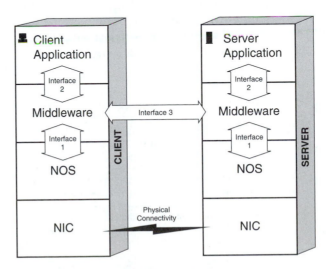

Figure 9-1   Logical Middleware Architecture

The interface between middleware and the application is an **Application Programming Interface (API).** An API is a published specification that details the interface to a software component. Through use of the API, an application programmer can write software compatible with the software component in question. The API used between two software components is determined by whichever component is completed first. In the case of client/server computing, server software is usually written before client software. Therefore the server-side middleware usually is written to conform the API presented by the existing server application. Client-side middleware is then written to provide an API to the client application developer that provides access to the functionality of the server via the server middleware.

The final interface in a middleware solution, labeled *Interface 3* in Figure 9-1, is a logical interface between the client and server middleware. This is labeled a logical interface because the two software components do not directly communicate with one another. All communication physically takes place on the network interface within their respective network operating systems as accessed by the middleware through *Interface 1.*

Interface 3 provides **horizontal integration** between the middleware components. The capabilities of the completed client/server solution will depend heavily upon the functionality of this interface. Particularly important is the relationship between the API the middleware solution presents to the application developer *(Interface 2)* and the logical communication interface *(Interface 3.)* The functionality represented in *Interface 2* is limited to the capabilities of *Interface 3.*

Managerial Perspective

INTERFACES AS MIDDLEWARE SELECTION CRITERIA

Selection of a middleware solution will depend largely on the standards to which the three interfaces adhere. A middleware solution must be compatible with the target environment for all three interfaces. The best middleware in existence is worthless if it will not run on the desired platform or does not support the desired development environment. A compatibility checklist is shown in Figure 9-2.

Interface	Usage	Example
1 – Network Operating System	Client Network operating system Server NOS	Windows NT Workstation Windows NT Server
2 – Business Application	Development Environment (API)	Visual BASIC, C/C++, etc.
3 – Communication	Middleware Communication Technique	ODBC, RPC, CORBA, etc.

Figure 9-2 Middleware Interface Compatibility List

To better understand the flow of data through the middleware architecture, consider a data request from a client application to a database located on a remote server. The client application makes a request via the middleware API to retrieve the desired data. The middleware takes the request and formats it into a message that can be understood by the server application and passes it to the network operating system's communication subsystem for delivery. Upon arriving at the server, the message is passed up to the middleware by the server network operating system's communication subsystem. The server middleware then takes the request and reformats it for submission to the server application for processing through the server's application API. The response will return through the same path in reverse order.

Physical Architecture

Client/server applications can be built using either a two-tier or *n*-tier physical architecture. The choice of physical architecture directly affects the mid-

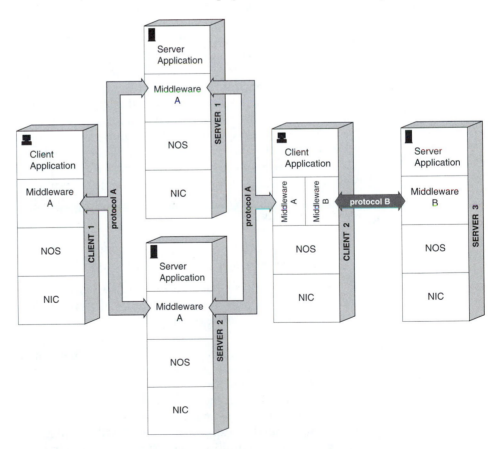

Figure 9-3   Two-Tier Middleware Architecture

dleware solution. As defined in the middleware logical architecture, each computer in a client/server environment contains middleware. As shown in Figure 9-3, in a two-tier client/server scenario each client communicates directly to each server.

Although there are potential issues regarding the number of open connections that are beyond the scope of this chapter, this solution works well as long as each server uses the same middleware solution. As shown in Figure 9-3, clients one and two can directly communicate with servers one and two via the same middleware stack (Middleware A).

However, client two must also communicate with server three, which is running a different middleware solution (Middleware B.) Therefore client three must run two different middleware solutions concurrently—one for communication with servers one and two and another for communication with server three. This solution adds significant complexity to both the installation and maintenance of the client middleware. This is further complicated by the potential assortment of client network operating systems. If an organization needs to support the client application on UNIX, Windows, and the Macintosh platform, two middleware stacks must be installed, tested, and debugged on three different platforms. In some cases, it may not even be possible to run the two middleware solutions concurrently due to base-level incompatibilities between the solutions.

N-tier client/server architectures provide a middleware advantage by providing a means to eliminate the need to run multiple middleware solutions on the same client. Figure 9-4 illustrates the clients and servers from the two-tier architecture of Figure 9-3 reorganized into a three-tier solution. In this configuration, each client communicates with an application server that formats the requests for further processing by the resource server. Each application server supports at least two middleware stacks: one for communication to the clients and one for communication to resource servers. This approach provides two major advantages from the middleware perspective:

- The resource server only has to communicate with a few application servers rather than potentially thousands of clients.

- The client only has to communicate with an application server via a single middleware interface rather than multiple resource servers via multiple middleware interfaces.

In this scenario, client two only has to have a single middleware stack loaded to communicate with servers one and three even though they are running different middleware solutions. The translation between middleware formats occurs at the application server, greatly simplifying client configuration and maintenance. Another benefit is that there is only one platform required to support multiple middleware formats (the application server) rather than multiple platforms as required in a two-tier architecture.

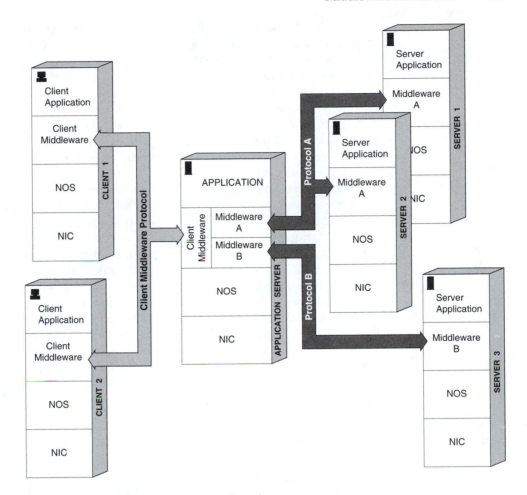

Figure 9-4   *n*-Tier Middleware Physical Architecture

Synchronous vs. Asynchronous Middleware Communication

When a client makes a request to a server, two things can happen: the client can halt all processing while waiting for a reply or it can continue to perform other processes. If the client application waits for a reply before continuing processing, the middleware communication is said to be synchronous. If other processing can continue while waiting for the reply, the middleware communication is classified asynchronous.

Synchronous communication is the most common approach taken in middleware solutions. In this scenario, the client application issues a request to the server application. While waiting for a reply to the request, the client is prevented from performing other application tasks. This process is known as **blocking.** A client waiting for a response from a server is referred to as being blocked. While the client application waits for the reply, it will appear to be stalled. In Windows-based applications an hourglass mouse pointer will commonly appear to indicate that the client is waiting.

In an **asynchronous communication** model, the client application can continue to process other requests while waiting for a reply. In this manner a client application can continue to respond to user input providing the next request does not depend on information for which the client is waiting. Asynchronous communication can represent a significant improvement in responsiveness to the user providing the development environment can take advantage of this capability.

Synchronous communication is most commonly used with structured, procedural programming languages such as COBOL, Pascal, and C. In these single-threaded environments, application processing passes linearly through various routines. When a routine makes a call to middleware to process an information request, the application waits until a response is received. Most synchronous communication middleware solutions generate a time-out error if a response from the server is not received within a certain period. Although synchronous communication is easier to program and ensures requests are processed, application responsiveness is dependent on the speed of the communication link and the server.

Asynchronous communication is most commonly used with event-driven application development environments such as Visual BASIC, Delphi, and Visual C. In these multithreaded environments, each event procedure is free to initiate a communication link to the server.

■ MIDDLEWARE CATEGORIZATION

By its very nature middleware categorization is complicated. There are as many different middleware implementations as there are server platforms and development platforms multiplied together. In order to make some sense out of this muddle of middleware, a means of categorizing middleware must be developed.

Middleware categorization is a two-part process based on the applications integrated and the communication methodology used to achieve integration. Categorizing middleware by application type focuses on discriminating between the different types of client and server applications the middleware supports. This categorization strategy focuses on the vertical integration within each host, specifically on the type of business application used with the middleware. Some common application categories of middleware are listed in Figure 9-5.

Middleware is also categorized by the communication techniques used to integrate the clients and servers. This categorization technique is independent of the applications supported by the middleware. As of this writing there are four major communication-based categories of middleware, although the middleware market is relatively young and consolidation of

Category	Application Type	Technology
Database Middleware	Integrates database clients to relational database servers	SQL ODBC
Legacy/Application Middleware	Integrates any type of client to existing applications	TP MONITOR
Web Middleware	Integrates WWW clients to any type of resource server	CGI Active X Java

Figure 9-5   Application-Based Middleware Categories

techniques is likely to reduce the number of commonly used approaches in the future. The four major middleware communication categories are listed in Figure 9-6. Every middleware solution falls into an application-based category and a communication-based category.

APPLICATION-BASED MIDDLEWARE CATEGORIES

Database Middleware

The earliest application of client/server systems was the deployment of distributed database applications. The clients in these systems represent front-end applications accessing data located on remote database servers. These database servers, commonly referred to as database engines, provide a central data repository and ensure that data entered into the system are consistent with the data model as defined in the database schema.

Category	Application/Development Environment	Example/Standard
Remote Procedure Calls	Procedural Development Languages (COBOL, C, etc.)	DCE
Message-Oriented Middleware	Event Driven Development Environments (Visual BASIC, etc.)	Message Queuing Message Passing
Transaction Process Monitors	Mainframe Integration High Reliability Applications	CICS, IMS, ACMSxp
Object-Oriented Middleware	Object-Oriented Development Environments (Smalltalk, etc.)	CORBA DCOM

Figure 9-6   Communication-Based Middleware Categories

These systems originally were designed and implemented as two-tier architectures with each client conversing directly with any servers containing required data. In such systems, the client processes data entered directly into the system and formats the data for display. The servers represent a repository containing all data required to support client functionality. Middleware for such database systems is limited to providing a means for the application programmer to access and manipulate data located on the remote database servers.

In a database middleware solution, the majority of the business logic (such as data analysis and report generation) takes place at the client. Some business logic can take place on the server through stored procedures, an approach especially useful for queries of large data tables. Rather than transmitting the entire contents of the table across the network for processing by the client, the server can select the subset of data required and transmit only that data. No business logic is performed in the middleware portion of the system.

Structured Query Language   **Structured Query Language (SQL)** is a standard language developed to facilitate querying relational database servers. SQL is a comprehensive relational database language providing a means of performing common database operations such as record additions, updates, and database design modifications in addition to query capabilities. The SQL standard includes methodologies for embedding SQL calls into other programming languages and systems to create client/server applications. The American National Standards Institute (ANSI) has standardized the SQL language. Through the use of ANSI standard SQL syntax, transparent data access between different vendors' database servers can be achieved.

Practical Advice and Information

SQL STANDARDIZATION

Don't be misled by features lists that state an SQL implementation is ANSI compliant, yet list features that are not in the ANSI standard. While SQL is an ANSI standard, each database vendor has added its own proprietary extensions to the language in an effort to add functionality and create a competitive advantage. This additional functionality only works when using products from that specific vendor. The advanced features are not supported when connecting to third-party applications. If true inter-vendor connectivity is required, base ANSI SQL syntax is usually required.

As shown in Figure 9-7, the application programmer writes an SQL compliant query and presents it to the client middleware. The client middleware passes the query across the network to the server middleware. The server middleware then executes the query against the database server, which replies with a data set. The data set is then sent back across the network to the client middleware and presented to the client application. From the client application's perspective, the data are located locally.

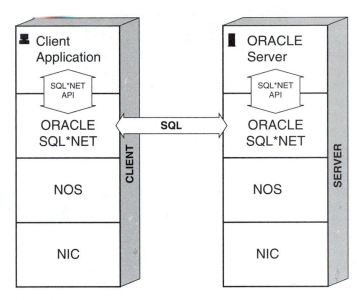

Figure 9-7   SQL Middleware Architecture

Most database server vendors provide personal computer network operating system-based client middleware compatible with their database server systems such as SQL*Net from Oracle. This client middleware provides a proprietary API for use by application programmers in the development of client applications. Because of the proprietary nature of the API, the resulting application is in effect linked exclusively to that particular database server. If a decision is made to replace the database server software, the client application may have to be rewritten to support the new database server. A list of proprietary SQL database middleware is listed in Figure 9-8.

Open Database Connectivity   In order to eliminate this direct tie between the client application and the database server, Microsoft developed **Open Database Connectivity (ODBC).** Designed around the relational database/SQL model, ODBC provides a standard means of accessing data residing on a relational database server. As shown in Figure 9-9, ODBC is a dual interface

Database Vendor	Database Server	Middleware
Oracle	Oracle	SQL*Net
CA-Ingres	Ingres	Open Ingres
Informix	Dynamic Server	Informix Connect
Sybase	Adaptive Server	Open Client

Figure 9-8   Proprietary SQL Middleware

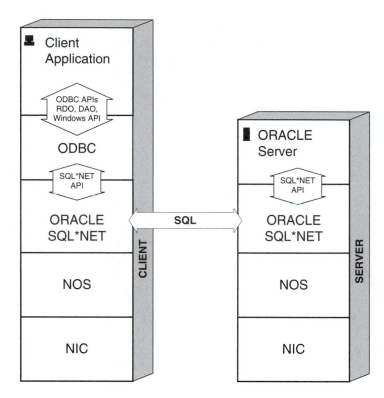

Figure 9-9 ODBC Logical Architecture

API residing between the user application and the proprietary database middleware on the client workstation. ODBC provides a set of non-vendor specific APIs that the application programmer can use to create open applications. When a client application needs to access data it makes an ODBC-compliant request to the ODBC layer. The ODBC layer translates the request to a format compatible with the underlying proprietary client database middleware. ODBC has achieved such market acceptance that most database vendors have suspended further development on their proprietary middleware solutions.

The ODBC architecture consists of two parts: the ODBC driver manager and the actual ODBC driver for the underlying database connectivity layer. The driver manager keeps track of which drivers are connected to which underlying database connectivity software. The ODBC driver makes the actual translation between the standard ODBC APIs and the vendor-specific SQL implementation. ODBC allows each client to access multiple data sources by binding multiple ODBC drivers to the driver manager to create separate ODBC stacks for each data source. However, each client must be individually configured for each data source, creating significant administrative overhead. Combined with increased latency through the various

ODBC stacks, this administrative overhead is one of the main problems with ODBC.

Open database connectivity presents three separate APIs to the application programmer. The initial ODBC release was designed as a Windows API, making it accessible only via the Microsoft Jet database engine or to system level programmers. To provide greater access to the benefits derived from ODBC, the second release added two high-level programming APIs: **Data Access Objects (DAO)** and **Remote Data Objects (RDO).** Data access objects are most commonly used in the Microsoft Access personal computer database platform. Remote data objects are readily accessible via windows programming languages such as Visual BASIC and Delphi. As long as the application programmer maintains strict adherence to the ODBC API standards, the database server and associated database connectivity software can be changed independently of the application.

Once a Microsoft proprietary protocol, ODBC has now been ratified as an official standard by the **SQL Access Group (SAG).** There are more than 700 ODBC drivers available for most relational database servers either from the database vendor, Microsoft, or third-party ODBC driver suppliers. There are also ODBC drivers on the market that include the capability to provide a relational database interface to nonrelational database servers. Drivers are available for flat files and most mainframe data definition languages record and block based access methods such as **VSAM** and **ISAM**. Although these drivers require significant configuration, by using them an application programmer can access data from a nonrelational data store through ODBC in the exact same manner as from a relational database. An applications programmer with ODBC experience can readily create an application that accesses data on database platforms with which the programmer has no practical experience.

Although ODBC greatly increases the portability of client applications, it does not solve all issues related to transparent data access. As shown in Figure 9-10, if a client application needs to access data from two different database engines, two ODBC drivers and transport stacks must be maintained on the client. Maintaining multiple ODBC stacks on each client represents a considerable managerial headache for the systems administrator. In order to eliminate this need, third-party vendors such as Intersolv have developed three-tier ODBC systems that allow for even greater database transparency than the original ODBC specification.

These new proprietary ODBC solutions move the translation to vendor-specific syntax from the client to an application server. As shown in Figure 9-11, this solution removes the need for any client to run multiple ODBC stacks, greatly simplifying client configuration. The client application requests data from the ODBC-compliant middleware interface, which sends the data to the application server as an ODBC request. The ODBC-compliant middleware on the application server then translates the request to vendor-specific syntax, issues the request to the database server, formats the response, and replies to the originating client.

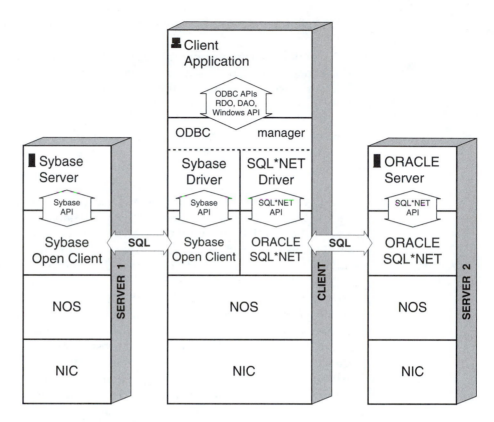

Figure 9-10 Accessing Multiple ODBC Sources

Practical Advice and Information

ODBC PORTABILITY

Third-party vendors are also porting ODBC from the Windows environment to other operating environments such as Mainframes, UNIX, and the Macintosh. Although ODBC is not yet present on all platforms, it is positioned to become the predominant database translation tool across all major platforms, replacing such platform-specific solutions as Apple's DAL on the Macintosh solution.

Universal Data Access While ODBC has greatly improved the flexibility and portability of relational database client applications and has some capabilities to access data from nonrelational data sources through specialized ODBC drivers, it is not a complete data access solution. As the importance of accessing data across the enterprise continues to grow, the relational limits of ODBC become evident. Microsoft is in the process of growing ODBC into a more feature-rich environment known as **Universal Data Access (UDA).** Universal Data Access is designed to provide a comprehensive means to access data from both relational and nonrelational data stores.

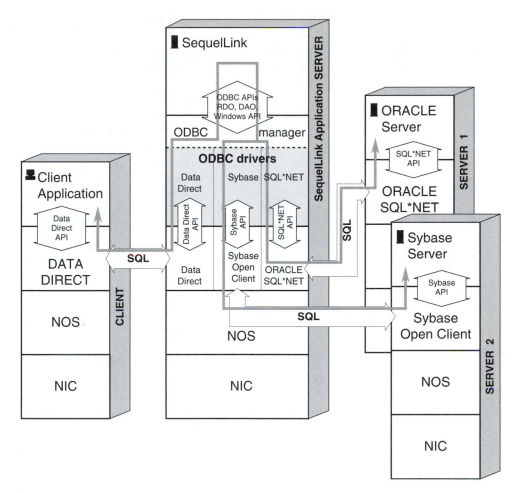

Figure 9-11   Distributed ODBC Architecture

Universal Data Access is an umbrella term covering **Object Layering and Embedding Database** services **(OLE DB)** and **Active Data Objects (ADO).** OLE DB defines a collection of interfaces that encapsulates various database management system services. These interfaces enable the creation of software components that enable these services. OLE DB components are categorized as data providers, data consumers, and service components. Figure 9-12 shows a distributed system built using Universal Data Access components.

Data providers are components that store and serve data. Data providers can range from traditional flat files to relational database servers to object-oriented databases. **Data consumers** are components that use the data stored on the data providers. A typical data consumer is a distributed database client application. Service components are those components that

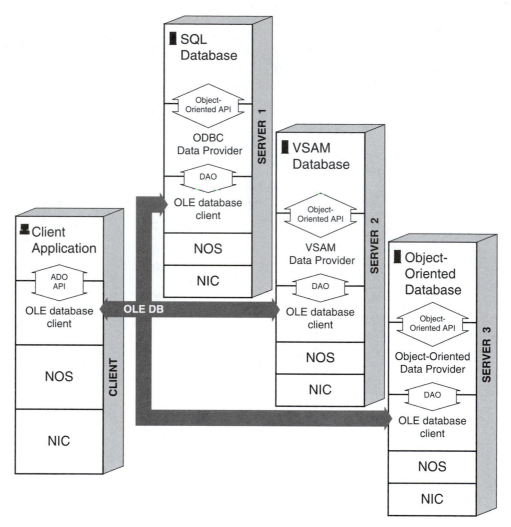

Figure 9-12   Universal Data Access Architecture

process and transport data between data providers and data consumers. To ensure compatibility with existing ODBC technology, the first data provider released was an ODBC provider. Through this provider OLE DB can utilize any data source supported by ODBC.

In order to provide access to nonrelational data, OLE DB replaces the ODBC APIs with a new application layer API known as Active Data Objects (ADO). As illustrated in Figure 9-12, Active Data Objects replace the DAO and RDO APIs used in ODBC. Active Data Objects combine the functionality of DAO and RDO along with new functionality to access nonrelational data. The ADO interface also includes functionality designed to ease integration with web browsers. Collectively, the latest versions of ODBC, OLE DB, and

ADO are packaged together in a suite called **Microsoft Data Access Components (MDAC).**

Legacy Application Middleware

In addition to new systems built on the client/server model, there is a desire to modify existing large-scale monolithic systems to operate in a client/server paradigm. Middleware that helps facilitate this integration is collectively known as legacy application middleware. This modification is accomplished by replacing traditional terminal input screens with client applications. Client applications vary from simply replacing the text-based terminal interface with a similar client-based interface to providing front-end processing of data. In either case, the client application usually sends data to the host application in traditional "screens" of information.

Web Middleware

With the explosion of the Internet, many companies are interested in creating a web browser-compatible interface to their existing business systems. Middleware that helps facilitate this integration is collectively known as web middleware. Web middleware varies in scope from simple graphical web clients to applications distributed in real time over the network. Common development environments include **Common Gateway Interface (CGI),** Microsoft **ActiveX,** and **Java.**

■ COMMUNICATION-BASED MIDDLEWARE CATEGORIES

Remote Procedure Calls

The first communication-based middleware category is **Remote Procedure Calls (RPC).** Remote procedure calls evolved from UNIX and are a widely accepted technology for building client/server applications. RPC-based middleware products have been standardized as one of the distributed services of the **Distributed Computing Environment (DCE),** an open standard middleware architecture. DCE is represented by a single source code currently owned and maintained by The Open Group (formerly the Open Software Foundation).

**In Sharper
Focus**

THE DISTRIBUTED COMPUTING ENVIRONMENT (DCE)

The Distributed Computing Environment architecture is illustrated in Figure 9-13.

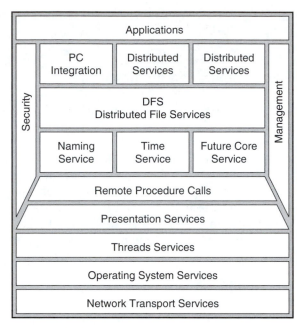

Figure 9-13   Distributed Computing Environment Architecture

DCE is actually a collection of services that are operating-system and network operating system-independent and that allow distributed applications to be developed, deployed, and managed in a secure environment. Among the key components of the DCE architecture are the following:

Distributed File Services—The purpose of DFS is to offer a consistent interface and consistent services for allowing users to access files from any node on the DCE-based enterprise network. DFS acts as a sort of translator between the native file system of the DCE host node and the DCE requesting client by using other DCE services such as the DCE Naming service which guarantees a consistent naming convention for all DFS accessible files. Similarly, DFS depends on the DCE security services to provide authorization and authentication controls over file access by any DCE client. The RPC messaging sub-system is used to set up point-to-point connections between client and server in order to optimize file transfer efficiency. In order to further improve file transfer efficiency, a DFS cache manager resides on the client workstation to minimize the amount of client to server communication. Since the file system is distributed and the possibility exists for more than one client to request access to the same file simultaneously, a token manager is used to ensure that file updates are synchronized to prevent unintentional file corruption.

Naming Service or Directory Service—Just as DCE was responsible for presenting a consistent interface for file access regardless of the native file system of the DCE node, consistent directory services are also required in order for all DCE-compliant clients to quickly and easily access required services. DCE's directory service is not unlike Novell's NDS. Any service or device that can be accessed is referred to as an object, is described by a series of attributes, and is listed as an entry in a directory. Directories themselves are considered objects and can therefore be listed as entries in other directories, thereby supporting a hierarchical directory structure. Through a gateway service known as the Global Directory Agent, local or cell directory services are linked to global directory services such as the X.500 international directory service.

Remote Procedure Calls Service is the interprocess communications mechanism supplied with DCE. In order to ensure consistency and interoperability, the RPC services in DCE are not alterable by users or licensees of DCE. As a result, some proprietary RPC services may offer more sophisticated interprocess communications services. RPC provides the basic transport or messaging mechanism for all DCE services as well as for DCE-compliant client applications. RPC provides consistent support for communications via distributed enterprise network connections regardless of the platform or protocol of either the source or destination node. This transparency means that programmers do not have to worry about platform specific network communications while developing distributed applications for the DCE environment. RPC works with the DCE security services to provide for secure client/server communications across the enterprise network.

Threads Services are provided to offer multithreaded capabilities to those DCE nodes whose native operating systems are not multithreaded. Threads services are stored as functions that can be called from within a threads library. Although not as efficient as a native multithreaded capability contained within an operating system kernel, the threads service does provide a homogeneous multithreaded environment supported by all DCE nodes. Like most multithreaded environments, DCE threads allow multiple sub-processes of a single application to execute simultaneously. This is particularly useful when RPCs have created a link to a distant server, thereby allowing the local application to continue processing in the interim. Other DCE services such as RPC, security, time and directory services use the threads service.

Distributed Time Service—DCE services such as DFS and security services depend on time and date stamps as part of their functionality. It is important given the distributed, multinode nature of a DCE implementation, that there is a source for an "official" time by which all connected systems can be synchronized. DCE provides three types of time servers in order to coordinate system time across a DCE environment. Local time servers coordinate with other local servers on the same LAN, while global time servers offer similar services across WAN or inter-LAN links. A courier time server is responsible for coordinating with global time servers at regular intervals.

Security Services for DCE are divided into two general categories. Authorization grants users access to objects based on the contents of ACLs (Access Control Lists) while authentication guarantees the identity or authenticity of a user or object. Authentication in DCE is based on **Kerberos** authentication system, which provides multi-level authentication and encryption services dependent on the level of security required. Authentication can be established only at connection time, or can be enforced for each and every network message that traverses that connection.

RPC Architecture RPCs were designed to work with procedural programming languages such as COBOL or C. From the client perspective, RPCs can be thought of as remote subroutines. The application programmer calls a link to a subroutine or procedure located on a remote server. The local link to the remote procedure is known as a **stub function.** The stub function transfers the calling parameters to the RPC-based middleware on the server and waits until the server responds. Therefore, RPCs are synchronous and blocking by nature. A client application or thread must wait for the server to reply before continuing program execution.

A similar operation takes place on the server. The incoming data request from the client stub goes to a matching server stub. The server stub then calls the actual procedure and waits for the server to complete the task. From the server application's perspective the request appears as if it were called by a local procedure. The server runs the procedure and replies to the server stub which sends the result across the network to the client stub. The client stub then sends the reply to the actual calling routine. This process is illustrated in Figure 9-14.

The distributed nature of the RPCs is transparent to the client application. The client application calls the remote procedure in exactly the same manner it would call a local procedure. The application programmer does not need to worry about data synchronization, since the client application is blocked until the server application returns a result to the RPC. This makes RPCs a very straightforward approach to use with procedural languages like COBOL and C.

Although the server application sees the incoming RPC as if it were being called locally from the server host, the server must perform some housekeeping logic before it can complete the incoming procedure. The

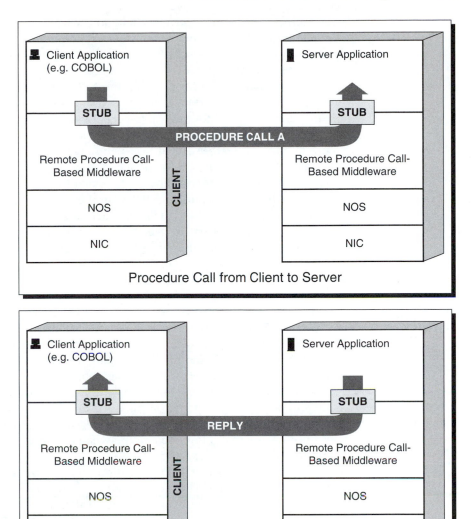

Figure 9-14   Remote Procedure Call Architecture

server application must register the availability of the service with the directory and authenticate all incoming connections to verify that the requesting user and application have authorization to access the desired server resources.

The middleware functionality of RPCs takes place in the stub routines. Located on both the server and the client, stub routines represent a one-to-one direct relationship between client and server. In order for RPCs to be language independent a common means of defining the interface between the stubs and a detailed description of all data that need to be passed between the stubs must be defined.

The responsibility for defining the RPC interface belongs to the server programmer. The interface is comprised of definitions for the function name and parameters for the data passed between the stubs including variable name, type, format, and length. This description of the RPC interface is provided via the **Interface Definition Language (IDL).** IDL is a high-level universal notation language that operates independently of the client and server application programming languages. Once the IDL parameters have been defined, they are input into an IDL compiler for the desired application programming language that creates the actual stub routines. The application programmer merely has to call the RPC and pass parameters via the standard constructs for the chosen application programming language.

Managerial Perspective

RPC ANALYSIS

Although straightforward to program, RPC-based middleware provides extremely limited flexibility. Because the client and server stubs have to match one-for-one, an RPC-based client application is bound to a specific server application. To modify this binding the applications must be modified and recompiled. This problem is exacerbated when a single RPC is potentially called by multiple client applications. Each client application would have to be rewritten and recompiled for the change to take effect. This is a significant drawback to RPC-based middleware compared with other types of middleware that allow linkages between clients and servers to be created and torn down on a dynamic basis.

Another drawback to RPC-based middleware solutions is their synchronous blocking nature. The blocking behavior of RPCs eliminates many data consistency problems, but it adds significant latency to the client application. Rather than continuing to work, the user must wait until each RPC call is completed before moving on. This added latency has a tendency to make RPC-based solutions seem sluggish as compared with other middleware communication methodologies.

Message-Oriented Middleware

Message-Oriented Middleware (MOM), or simply **messaging middleware,** refers to middleware solutions that transport information through the network as independent messages. Unfortunately, unlike other middleware categories that are standards based, there are no definitive standards that define message formats. As of this writing there are more than a dozen different messaging middleware products in the marketplace. Each set of server and client applications is free to develop its own specific messaging language.

This makes messaging middleware one of the more confusing middleware areas and one of the most difficult to integrate across platforms. Messaging middleware is broken into three basic categories:

- Message Passing
- Message Queuing
- Publish and Subscribe

Messaging Middleware Architecture   Each category of messaging middleware shares a common architecture. Each message consists of a string of bytes that have some meaning to the applications that exchange them. Messages can consist of either data or control parameters designed to store, route, deliver, retrieve, and track the data payload. Messaging is one of the most flexible middleware communication models with the ability to support both synchronous and asynchronous communication. The ability to support asynchronous communication makes messaging middleware a good fit for event-driven programming environments.

Message Passing **Message passing** uses a direct program-to-program communication model. Message passing is connection oriented. The client and server applications must maintain a logical connection at all times. Care must be taken to ensure both applications are running before communication is attempted since a message-passing client immediately initiates a connection to the server on application launch. If the server is not available, the connection will time out and the application will fail. For this reason, message passing works best with tightly coupled, time-dependent applications.

Message-passing middleware architectures support both synchronous (blocking) operation and asynchronous operation. In synchronous mode a message-passing client application will wait for a response from the server before continuing. In asynchronous mode, the client application will send a message to the server then go about other business while periodically polling the server to see if the request has been completed. When a reply message becomes available it will be pulled from the server to the client. These processes are illustrated in Figure 9-15.

Message-passing middleware architectures typically support concurrent connections to multiple servers. However, each client and server must support the overhead of maintaining the connection. Message-passing MOM architectures rely on connection-oriented transport protocols such as TCP and SPX. An example of message-passing middleware is PIPES from Peer-Logic.

Message Queuing **Message Queuing** replaces the direct connection between applications with a message queue. Each application attaches to a message queue that holds all incoming and outgoing messages until they can be processed. Because the message queue exists independently of the

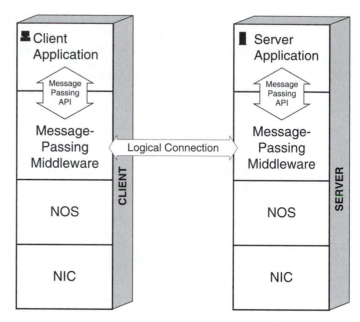

Figure 9-15 Message-Passing Middleware Architecture

application, this removes the message-passing requirement that both applications be running before communication is attempted.

As shown in Figure 9-16, each application attaches to a message queue on the local host. Each host in turn runs a special process known as a **Queue Manager** that manages the message queues and handles delivery of messages. In a message-queuing middleware implementation, all interprocess communication takes place via the message queues. For messages between processes on a single host, the queue manager processes delivery internally. For messages bound for processes on remote hosts, the queue manager manages the communication to a remote message queue attached to the remote process.

The queue manager is the heart of a message-queuing middleware system. In addition to simply processing inbound and outbound messages from the network, they actively control the message delivery process. Queue managers work together to determine the best route through a network and to find backup routes in the event of a partial network failure. Other network services provided by the queue manager include:

- Reliable message delivery—ensures no messages are lost in transit

- Guaranteed message delivery—ensures messages will get to the destination either immediately if the network is available, or eventually if the network is not currently available

- Assured non-duplicate message delivery—ensures messages are delivered only once

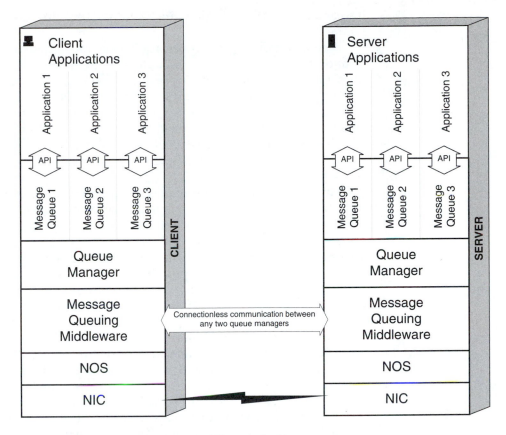

Figure 9-16 Message-Queuing Middleware Architecture

Queue managers also add support for different **Quality of Service** levels. Quality of service refers to the acceptable level of network latency for a particular message. Quality of service can be thought of as a message prioritization scheme whereby time critical messages are processed prior to non–time-critical messages. Queue managers prioritize messages by quality of service level in both outgoing and incoming message queues.

Queue managers can either be nonpersistent or persistent in nature. **Nonpersistent message queues** are memory based and are lost in the event of queue manager failure or whenever the host is shut down. **Persistent message queues** are disk based and remain intact when the queue manager is not running. As soon as the queue manager is restarted, it will begin to process the messages remaining in the queue. In general, nonpersistent queues impart better performance than persistent queues, while persistent queues are more reliable. The decision as to which queue type to use depends on the application requirements. A banking application is an example of an application that requires a persistent queue—you wouldn't want the bank to forget that you deposited your paycheck due to a queue manager failure.

Because message queuing relies on queues rather than on direct communication between clients, it is connectionless in nature. The remote process does not even have to be running in order to send it a message. The message will arrive at the remote host and be put into the process's incoming message queue for processing. Some message-queuing implementations support **triggers** that will "awaken" a process that is not running and alert it that a message has arrived for processing. In this manner, unused processes can be unloaded from memory to conserve system resources yet still remain available when needed.

Most message-queuing products support **network message concentration.** By using this technique a single connection is established between queue managers regardless of the number of message queues each supports. As illustrated in Figure 9-17, network message concentration allows a queue manager to concentrate the communication requirements from multiple applications. This approach greatly reduces communication overhead, resulting in lowered network bandwidth requirements and communication costs compared with the direct connection requirements of message passing.

Message-queuing middleware presents a highly flexible, relatively simple API to the client application developer. Because of its connectionless nature, message-queuing middleware is an ideal solution for event-driven applications. An event in one application can cause a message to be sent to a second application, leading to a specific result in the second application.

Message-queuing middleware is rapidly outdistancing message-passing middleware in most applications. The advantages of a looser coupling between applications and the reliability advantages of persistent queues combine to make message-queuing middleware more flexible for most applications. Example message-queuing middleware solutions include BEA Systems DECmessageQ, IBM's MQSeries, and Microsoft Message Queue (previously known as Falcon).

Publish and Subscribe   **Publish and subscribe** middleware relies on a distribution model similar to that of a newspaper. In a publish and subscribe messaging system there are no servers or clients in the traditional sense. Each host on the network is a potential source and consumer of messages. As shown in Figure 9-18, each host connects to a **logical message bus.** When a host has a piece of information potentially of interest to other hosts, it broadcasts (publishes) it to the message bus. Any host that subscribes (listens) to the message bus receives the message and passes it to an application for further analysis and subsequent action.

Publish and subscribe systems have the ability to rapidly propagate a message through a system with minimal messaging overhead. Publishers and subscribers need not even know of each others' existence, making it possible to dynamically reconfigure the network. Although publish and sub-

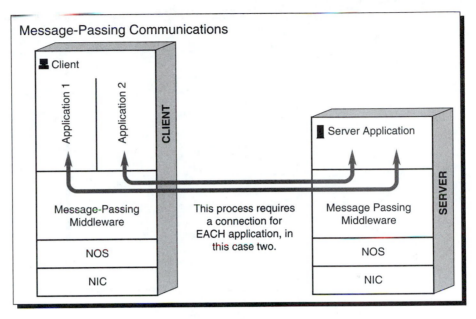

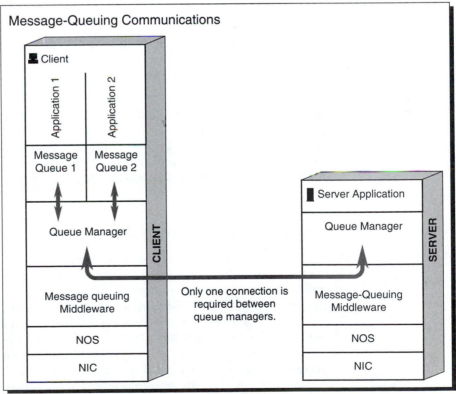

Figure 9-17 Network Message Concentration

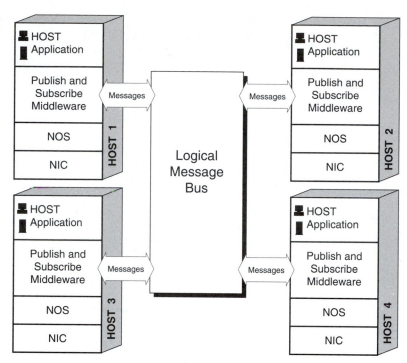

Figure 9-18 Publish and Subscribe Messaging Middleware Architecture

scribe is a relatively new category of messaging middleware, it has great potential as a technique to integrate a new generation of loosely coupled, flexible business systems such as distributing pricing information to automated stock trading systems. An example publish and subscribe middleware solution is Tibco's Software Rendezvous (formerly Teknekron Information Bus).

MESSAGE-ORIENTED MIDDLEWARE ANALYSIS

Managerial Perspective

The message orientation of message-oriented middleware makes it especially flexible. Messages can be defined on a per-application basis, enabling messaging to solve many complex middleware problems. However, this flexibility makes message-oriented middleware difficult to integrate varying applications since there are no definitive messaging standards. Message-oriented middleware supports both synchronous and asynchronous communication modes. This makes it an especially good solution for event-driven application development environments such as Visual BASIC. As shown in Figure 9-19, each of the three basic types of messaging middleware has specific strengths and weaknesses.

	Synchronous Communication	Asynchronous Communication	Procedural Languages	Event-Driven Languages	Message Concentration	Security	Fast Broadcasts
Message Passing	●		●	●		●	
Message Queuing		●		●	●	●	
Publish and Subscribe		●		●	●		●

Figure 9-19   Message-Oriented Middleware Technology Analysis Grid

Message passing is the most basic messaging middleware type and provides basic middleware functionality. The requirement that all applications which need to share data via message passing be available at all times makes message passing less flexible and more system resource intensive than other messaging middleware solutions. Message-passing solutions also tend to be more bandwidth intensive than the other choices.

Message queuing provides the most flexibility and reliability of the messaging middleware categories. The ability to utilize persistent queues allows the application of message-queuing systems to applications requiring high reliability such as financial applications. Under most circumstances, message-queuing middleware provides the best mix of flexibility and functionality.

Although publish and subscribe represents a niche in the overall middleware marketplace, it provides a unique solution to applications where data security is not as important as quick, efficient distribution of information. Final messaging middleware selection criteria will depend on achieving the balance of flexibility, reliability, and efficiency required by the distributed application.

Transaction Processing Monitors

Transaction Process Monitors (TP monitor) are a mature technology with roots in mainframe-based monolithic applications and UNIX database applications. Transaction process monitors are used with database systems to oversee (monitor) the database transactions between clients and servers.

One of the key features of transaction process monitors is their ability to ensure secure database transactions across heterogeneous database servers. In order to provide this integration capability all current transaction process monitors conform to the X/Open standard for **Distributed Transaction Processing (DTP).**

In Sharper Focus

TRANSACTION PROCESSING

Transaction processing refers to series of operations that take place in response to a business transaction. For example, let's consider the case of a customer entering a furniture store and purchasing a couch on the store's in-house credit plan. This single business transaction will result in postings to several information systems. The inventory control system must be updated to reflect the sale of the item. A pick slip must be sent to the warehouse to indicate the couch is to be brought to the dock for pick-up. The accounts receivable system must be updated to reflect the credit purchase. Collectively these operations make up a single transaction.

As their name would suggest, TP monitors monitor the processing of database transactions. The main purpose of transaction processes is to ensure that the transaction is processed completely. If any aspect of the transaction cannot be completed, the entire transaction process must be reversed or "rolled back." In this manner the TP monitor ensures data integrity throughout the system.

Transaction roll-back is made possible through a two-phase commit process. In a two-phase commit the transaction is sent to the affected database servers. The transaction process monitor then issues a "pre-commit" command to each server. Upon receipt of the "pre-commit" command, the database servers test to see if the commit can be completed and report the result to the TP monitor. If every database server can complete the commit, the TP monitor then issues a "commit" command and the database servers permanently make the changes. If any server responds negatively to the "pre-commit" command, the entire transaction is rolled back from all of the servers.

Database Requests versus Transaction Management   Every database transaction must conform to a set of rules or traits to ensure the transaction is completed successfully. These rules ensure that data integrity is maintained when a transaction updates multiple databases. Commonly referred to as the **ACID test,** these rules collectively constitute transaction management:

- **Atomicity**—A database transaction is considered to be single unit of work that must be wholly completed. If any portion of the transaction fails, the entire system must be **rolled back** (restored) to its state before the transaction attempt began.

- **Consistency**—At the end of a transaction, all resources that participated in the processing of the transaction should be left in a consistent state.

- **Isolation**—Each transaction should be isolated from all other transactions. Concurrent access to shared resources should be coordinated to ensure independence.

- **Durability**—All updates to resources that have been performed within the scope of a transaction will be persistent or durable.

In all other middleware categories transaction process management is performed by the database engines themselves. The function of the middleware is limited to providing a means of transporting the request to the database engine for transaction processing. Transaction process monitors perform transaction process management as a function of middleware. In addition to reducing the processing requirements of the database server, transaction process monitors provide a means to manage transactions across heterogeneous database servers. Transaction process monitors can also ensure transaction processing rules are met for record-oriented files and queues as well as relational databases.

Transaction Process Monitor Architecture   The DTP standard defines a standard transaction process monitor architecture. As shown in Figure 9-20, transaction process monitors are usually implemented as a three-tier middleware solution. The client application accesses TP monitor middleware through the **Standard Transaction Definition Language (STDL).** STDL provides a vendor-independent transaction definition language. STDL is analogous to SQL in a relational database environment.

The TP monitor middleware processes the STDL request and makes a request to the transaction process monitor through the TX protocol. The transaction process monitor takes the incoming TX requests from each client and groups them into logical units of work to be performed by server applications or by the database servers themselves. The TP monitor then forwards the requests to the database server(s). The TP monitor can connect to database servers directly via the XA protocol or to a server application via the TX protocol. Each of these scenarios is illustrated in Figure 9-20, with the Oracle connection being direct and the VSAM data connection going through a back-end server application.

The ability of a TP monitor to consolidate database requests is one of the key features of the technology. The TP monitor maintains connections to each client and concentrates the requests for each database server into a single database server connection, freeing the database server from the overhead of maintaining the connections itself. This three-tier architecture also allows the TP monitor to manage transactions across heterogeneous data-

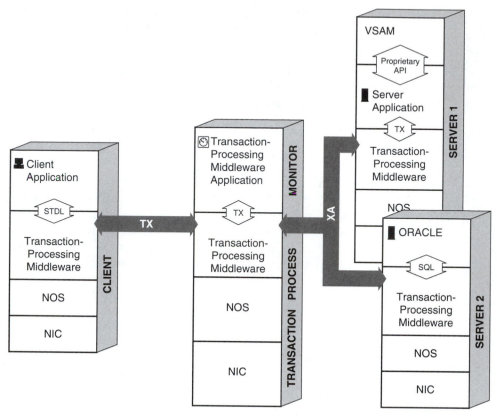

Figure 9-20 Distributed Transaction Process Monitor Architecture

base servers and technologies. Figure 9-21 shows the functional characteristics of transaction process monitor systems.

Applied Problem Solving

CHARACTERISTICS OF TRANSACTION PROCESS MONITOR SYSTEMS

Transaction Process Monitor Functional Characteristic	Importance/Implication
Communications Models	• The transaction monitor must communicate with all servers in the system • What protocols and models does the TP monitor support?
Resource Managers	• The TP monitor must support the application interfaces of the resource servers.

(continued)

	• Most transaction process monitors will support the XA standard, but what about record-oriented file systems, journal-based files, and RDBMS systems?
Client Platforms	• The TP monitor must include client support for all clients that need to post transactions. • Most will currently support Windows NT and Windows 95, but what about DOS, Macintosh, UNIX, web clients?
Network and Systems Management	• Distributed transaction process monitor systems can be complex to manage and administrate. • Does the TP monitor support Simple Network Management Protocol (SNMP)? • Is there a means to automatically update all clients with newer versions of the client software?
Security	• Does the TP monitor support encryption?
Server Development Characteristics	• What server side development environments does the TP monitor support (C/C++, COBOL, Java)?

Figure 9-21   Transaction Process Monitor Functional Characters

Managerial Perspective

TRANSACTION PROCESS MONITOR ANALYSIS

Transaction process monitors off-load transaction processing from the database server to a separate task. This allows for transactions to occur between heterogeneous database server environments ranging from list-based files to relational databases. This capability is especially important when a client application needs to access and update data controlled by monolithic mainframe-based applications.

Implementation of transaction process monitor-based middleware has several additional benefits. Transaction process monitors serve as a network connection concentrator to reduce the number of incoming connections to a server application, resulting in increased server capacity and responsiveness. The ability to dynamically start additional transaction process management processes allows a system to automatically scale to meet demand. As is the case with other middleware categories, the key compatibility issue is that the transaction process monitor be compatible with the platform operating environment.

One of the first TP Monitors widely deployed was IBM's Customer Information Control System (CICS). Originally developed to monitor transactions for mainframe applications, CICS has been ported to the AS/400, OS/2, and UNIX platforms. In addition to its role as a TP Monitor, CICS also provides mainframe programmers with a method to develop screen displays without detailed knowledge of the terminals being used.

In addition to CICS, many other TP Monitors are available in the marketplace. Current generation products are designed to be implemented as a middle tier in *n*-tier client/server systems. These products include Tuxedo from BEA Systems, IBM Transaction Server, and NCR Top End.

Object-Oriented Middleware

While remote procedure calls, messaging middleware, and transaction processing monitors provide excellent middleware functionality, they are all designed to work with procedural or event-driven programming environments. Many software developers are in the process of transitioning to object-oriented (OO) programming environments. These OO programming environments represent a significantly different development environment. Object-oriented programming environments require a middleware solution that provides a high level of abstraction. Such middleware is referred to as **Object-Oriented Middleware.**

Object-Oriented Middleware Architecture   There are two major Object-Oriented Middleware solutions currently available in the marketplace: CORBA and DCOM.

CORBA   The **Common Object Request Broker Architecture (CORBA)** is a set of object-oriented middleware specifications published by the Object Management Group (OMG.) The CORBA specifications define the way objects are defined, created, dispatched, and invoked, as well as how they communicate with one another.

There are four main service components in a CORBA system: object services, common facilities, domain interfaces, and application interfaces. The key difference between these services is the level at which they are available. Services can exist within an application, within a domain of related applications such as manufacturing or telecommunications, or at the global inter-domain level.

Object services are domain-independent interfaces used by distributed object programs to locate available objects and services. Example object services include the naming service that allows clients to find objects based on names and the trading service that allows clients to find objects based on their properties.

Common facilities are also domain-independent interfaces. However, common facilities provide interfaces directed toward end-user applications rather than the underlying objects. An example common facility is the Distributed Document Component Facility (DDCF). DDCF provides a method of linking multiple objects together into a single compound object. For example, a spreadsheet may be linked into a word processing document.

Domain interfaces fill roles similar to object services and common facilities at the domain level. These services are tailored for specific industries. One of the first domain interfaces standardized by the OMG was the Product Data Management enabler for the manufacturing domain. Any object that conforms to the manufacturing domain standards can access data through this service.

Application interfaces are interfaces developed specifically for a given application. Because they are application specific, they are not standardized by the OMG. However, if certain broadly useful services emerge within an application domain, they may be integrated into the domain standard and become domain interfaces.

The key communications component in the CORBA architecture is the **Object Request Broker** or **ORB.** An ORB is a distributed software component that provides an interface through which objects make requests and receive responses. An ORB is installed on each host to provide services to the OO-based applications running on that host. Depending on the solution, ORBs are either included in the network operating system or supplied by third-party vendors.

As shown in Figure 9-22, the distributed ORB middleware represents a logical ORB bus connecting all objects in the system. All communication

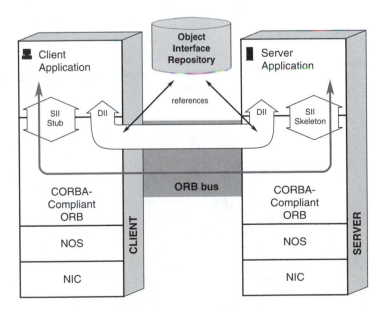

Figure 9-22   ORB Architecture

between objects is accomplished via the ORBs, allowing the location of the destination object to be masked from the programmer. From the perspective of the source object, both local and remote objects are accessed in the same manner.

Objects can be accessed via static interfaces or dynamic interfaces. Static interfacing implies that the object's interfaces do not change over time. This is the most commonly implemented CORBA interface technique and takes place via the **Static Invocation Interface (SII).** The static invocation interface works very much like remote procedure calls in a procedural programming environment. The interface characteristics for an object are defined using the **Object Management Group Interface Description Language (OMG IDL).** OMG IDL is a derivative of the IDL language used in DCE standard RPCs. As in an RPC implementation, the IDL code describes the interfaces of the object.

The IDL code is input into an IDL compiler, which creates a stub object that is implemented on the client and a skeleton object that is implemented on the server. The IDL code is also stored in an object interface repository. Just as in RPC-based middleware, the application development environments supported are determined by the IDL compiler. Currently, CORBA-compliant IDL compilers exist for C, C++, Smalltalk, and JAVA. Mappings for COBOL and ADA 95 are under development.

As illustrated in Figure 9-22, a client using the SII accesses a remote object via the stub object. The information sent to the stub is sent to the actual remote object by the ORB through the server skeleton object. As with RPCs, SII only supports synchronous communication. The client application is blocked until the server application responds to a request.

CORBA also supports dynamic interfacing of objects via the **Dynamic Invocation Interface (DIL).** DII-based applications support both synchronous and asynchronous communication. Using the DII a client looks up the IDL code for the destination object in the object interface repository to determine the destination object's interface capabilities. In this manner a client application can be built with a generic interface that automatically adapts to changes in the server application. Although DII has tremendous potential for the development of intelligent, self-configuring information systems, the high complexity of building the multitude of CORBA calls required to traverse the object interface repository practically limit the feasibility of this approach.

As object-oriented applications continue to expand, developing a means of communicating between ORBs from different vendors increases in importance. The second version of the CORBA standard focuses on such ORB interoperability. As shown in Figure 9-23, an SII invocation from a client of ORB 1 passes through its IDL stub into the ORB. The ORB examines the object reference and looks up the location of the destination object in the object implementation repository. If the implementation is local to ORB 1, it passes the invocation through the appropriate skeleton for processing by the destination object. If the implementation is remote, ORB 1 passes the invoca-

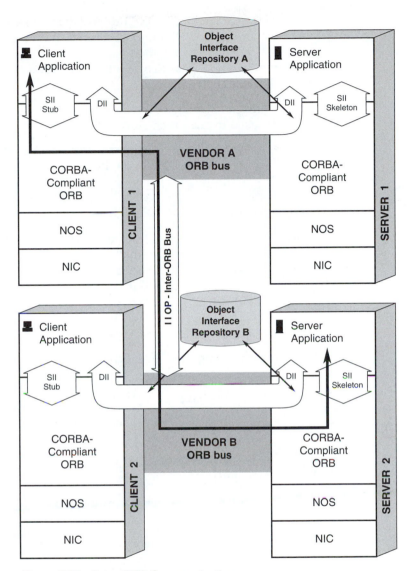

Figure 9-23   Inter-ORB Communication

tion across the communication pathway to ORB 2, which routes it to the appropriate skeleton for processing.

Passing of the invocation implies that there is a mechanism through which the two ORBs communicate. There are two such mechanisms that enable inter-ORB communication: ensuring each ORB supports the same protocol or installing bridges to translate between protocols. CORBA 2.0 addresses both of these issues. All CORBA 2.0-compliant ORB implementations must support the **Internet Inter-ORB Protocol (IIOP),** an implementation of the General Inter-ORB Protocol that runs on TCP/IP-based networks. The General Inter-ORB Protocol consists of three specifications:

- Common Data Representation (CDR)—defines representation of all OMG IDL data types

- GIOP Message Formats—defines seven specific message formats used to carry the invocation

- GIOP Message Transport Requirements—requires a connection-oriented transport protocol that supports reliable communication

In Sharper Focus

CORBA SERVICES

In addition to the core CORBA specification, the OMG has specified additional middleware services that can be implemented. These services, collectively known as CORBA Services, provide additional functionality to ease the development of distributed object-oriented applications. CORBA Services include:

- Naming—binds names to objects

- Events—provides event channels for asynchronous communication

- Transactions—provides transactional capabilities for communication between objects

- Concurrency control—enables multiple clients to coordinate their shared object access

- Relationships—provides the capability to represent entities and relationships

- Externalization—defines protocols for externalizing and internalizing objects

- Life cycle—defines conventions for creating, deleting, copying, and moving objects

- Persistence—provides a means of storing the state of objects

- Object trader—supports routing of client requests to servers based on rules

- Security—defines the security interfaces required for distributed client/server applications

DCOM The **Distributed Common Object Model (DCOM)** is a Microsoft proprietary solution for building distributed object-oriented applications. Providing similar functionality to CORBA-based solutions, DCOM allows objects to be defined, created, dispatched, invoked, and communicate with one another. However, rather than being a set of specifications like CORBA, DCOM is a software product. Because DCOM is a product rather than a set of specifications, it provides binary compatibility between objects that have been built using varying programming environments, allowing a software developer to purchase software objects from multiple vendors and integrate them into a custom application with certainty that they will interoperate successfully.

At the center of the DCOM architecture is the **Component Object Model** or **COM.** As illustrated in Figure 9-24, the component object model consists of a library of objects, a service control manager, a proxy manager, and a stub manager. Similar to an ORB in CORBA-based solutions, the Service Control Manager (SCM) manages all communication between objects.

Like CORBA, object invocations can either be static or dynamic. In the case of a static invocation, the client issues a request for an object. The SCM on the client determines if a server containing the desired object is currently running. If not, it will search the registry for the location of a server containing the object. Once the destination server location is identified, the client SCM establishes an RPC connection with the server SCM. The SCM on the client and server then load specific proxy stubs into the client and server processes via the proxy and stub managers on each node. Just as in CORBA SII, static invocations in DCOM rely on a version of IDL to define an object's interfaces. Microsoft's IDL implementation supports the COM notation that an interface is defined as a family of logically related operations or methods.

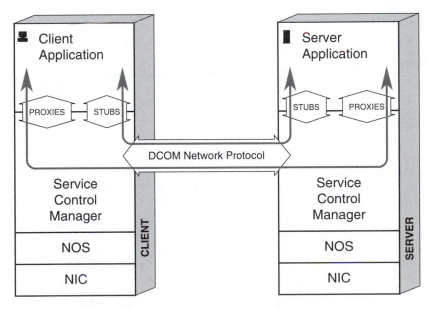

Figure 9-24 DCOM Architecture

Dynamic object invocations occur through Object Layering and Embedding Automation (OLE Automation). OLE Automation allows a client to dynamically build a request and issue it against a remote object. As with CORBA, the client can retrieve all of the required interface information from a repository. However, OLE Automation also provides a means to interrogate an object at runtime about the interfaces it supports. In this manner, client applications can discover new server objects and ask them about their interfaces dynamically without updating the client's object information store.

Managerial Perspective

OBJECT ORIENTED MIDDLEWARE ANALYSIS

Object-oriented middleware solutions provide a means of integrating middleware functionality into object-oriented development environments. If an object-oriented development environment such as C++ or Smalltalk is used, the middleware solution of choice is either CORBA or DCOM. These two middleware solutions share many features, but there are several significant differences.

Applied Problem Solving

CORBA VERSUS DCOM TECHNICAL ANALYSIS

Although they provide similar functionality, CORBA is a standard set of specifications, whereas DCOM is a proprietary product. DCOM supports binary compatibility between all objects, enabling complete program language independence. A C++ client can use an object written in Smalltalk transparently. CORBA's binary compatibility is on a product-by-product basis: objects written in the same language are binary compatible providing the development environment supports binary compatibility. Otherwise, platform independence is achieved through communication between ORBs using the IIOP protocol.

DCOM does not support multiple implementation inheritance; only interface definitions can be inherited. However, DCOM supports multiple interface definitions per object. This can be of significant use for upward compatibility. When a revised server object is implemented, it will continue to support its old set of interfaces in addition to any new interfaces changed or added in the upgrade. Existing client applications can continue to use the old interfaces until they are upgraded. This greatly simplifies version control in a distributed application environment.

DCOM is currently limited to the Microsoft Windows NT network operating system. However, third parties are currently porting DCOM to non-Windows platforms. CORBA solutions are available for all major operating environments. DCOM is bundled in the NT network operating system at no additional cost, whereas CORBA-based solutions must be purchased separately. It remains to be seen see what the pricing strategy will be for non-Windows implementations of DCOM. However, Microsoft has indicated that it will work with the third-party developers to keep costs low in order ensure the technology becomes pervasive. Most CORBA products charge a fee per development module and in most cases require a run-time license for all hosts using the product.

DCOM supports late binding through OLE automation that eliminates the need to write IDL code and bind stubs into applications. While similar capabilities exist in CORBA via DII, it is substantially more complex to develop DII compliant applications. Therefore, most CORBA implementations rely on SII static binding through stubs written in IDL.

Managerial Perspective

MIDDLEWARE SELECTION

Middleware is a relatively immature software category. Competing standards and varying technologies combine to make middleware selection a complicated decision. In order to clear up the technology muddle, the relationship between the middleware and applications must be examined.

The first question that must be addressed is the types of applications the middleware solution must support. Are you working on a distributed relational database project or does the middleware need to provide access to data on non-relational servers such as VSAM and ISAM data?

The second question to address is the application development environment. Is the client going to be written in a traditional procedural language such as COBOL, an event-driven language like Visual BASIC, or an object-oriented environment such as C++? Figure 9-25 illustrates the relationship between application types, application development environments, and middleware communication categories.

	Remote Procedure Calls	Messaging Middleware	Transaction Process Monitors	Object-Oriented Middleware
Application Type				
• **Database**	X	X	X	X
• **Web**	X	X	X	X
• **Legacy Application**	X	X	X	
Development Environments				
• **Procedural (COBOL, C, Pascal)**	X	X	X	
• **Event-Driven (Visual BASIC, Delphi)**	X	X	X	
• **Object-Oriented (C++, Smalltalk)**				X
Middleware Services				
• **Multiple**	X	X		

(continued)

Communications Protocols

• **Consistent Cross-Platform API**	X	X	X	X
• **Security Service**	X		X	
• **Synchronous Communications**	X	X	X	X
• **Asynchronous Communications**		X	X	
• **Publish and Subscribe**		X		
• **Network Session Concentration**		X		X
• **Dynamic Binding**		X	X	X
• **Load Balancing**			X	
• **Broadcasting/Multicasting**		X		
• **Naming Services**	X		X	
• **Quality of Service**		X		
• **Triggering**		X		X
• **Fault Tolerance**			X	
• **Message Prioritization**		X	X	

Figure 9-25   Application Development Environment to Middleware Mapping

SUMMARY

Middleware can be thought of as the "/" in client/server computing—the glue that holds the clients and servers together. Middleware is classified in two different ways: by application type and by communications methodology.

There are three basic middleware application types: database, web, and legacy application middleware. Database middleware is the predominant application in most systems, with web middleware rapidly gaining in importance.

Database middleware relies heavily on SQL to provide a means of communication between clients and servers. In order to iso-late the client application from specific database server implementations, ODBC was developed. ODBC is a vendor-independent programming interface accessible from most application programming environments. Recently ODBC has been superseded by Universal Data Access, a superset of ODBC that includes methodologies to access nonrelational data.

There are four basic middleware communications types: remote procedure calls, messaging middleware, transaction process monitors, and object-oriented middleware. Each middleware technology implementation can be categorized as being from one application category and from one communications category. For example, a middleware solution can be referred to as database–transaction process monitor middleware.

Remote procedure calls are a blocking, synchronous communications method best suited for procedural programming environments such as COBOL and C. Messaging middleware relies on communicating computers to exchange data via a series of messages. Messaging middleware is further divided into three subcategories: message passing, message queuing, and publish and subscribe.

Transaction process monitors are a specialized middleware solution designed to ensure that database transactions are posted across distributed database servers in a reliable manner. Object-oriented middleware is used with object-oriented programming environments such as C++ and Smalltalk. There are two categories of object-oriented middleware: CORBA-compliant solutions and Microsoft DCOM.

CORBA-compliant object-oriented middleware solutions are based on a standard

from the object management group. Compliance to the CORBA standard allows middleware solutions from different vendors to interoperate. CORBA compliant middleware can use many different communications protocols, but each solution must comply with the IIOP protocol that runs over TCP/IP.

DCOM is a series of products released by Microsoft for the Windows environment. DCOM utilized the common object model to provide binary compatibility between objects and object programming environments. In this manner, a programmer can purchase objects and know they will work with whatever programming language they wish to use. DCOM is currently only supported on the Windows platform, although third-party vendors are in the process of porting it to other operating environments such as UNIX.

Regardless of the specific middleware technology used, the key concept in middleware is to select a solution that allows the required applications to communicate in a manner consistent to the overall needs of the system.

KEY TERMS

ACID Test
ActiveX
ADO
Application programming
   interface
Asynchronous communications
Blocking
CGI
COM
CORBA
DAO
Data consumers

Data providers
DCE
DCOM
DII
Distributed transaction
   processing
Horizontal integration
IDL
IIOP
ISAM
Java
Kerberos

MDAC
Message queuing
Messaging middleware
Middleware
Network message
   concentration
Nonpersistent queues
ODBC
OLE
OLEDB
ORB
Persistent queues

Quality of service
Queue manager
RDO
Roll-back
RPC
SAG

SCM
SII
SQL
STDL
Stub function
Synchronous communications

Transaction process monitor
Triggers
Universal data access
Vertical integration
VSAM

REVIEW QUESTIONS

1. Compare and contrast vertical and horizontal middleware integration.
2. Differentiate between synchronous and asynchronous communications.
3. What programming environments are best suited for synchronous communications?
4. What programming environments are best suited for asynchronous communications?
5. What are the three basic middleware application categories?
6. What are the four basic middleware communications categories?
7. What language is most commonly used to query relational database systems?
8. Are all SQL implementations compatible? Why or why not?
9. What is the primary benefit to ODBC?
10. What are the two APIs associated with ODBC?
11. Can ODBC be implemented as a three-tier solution? How?
12. What are the components of universal data access?
13. What APIs are associated with universal data access?
14. What development environments are associated with web middleware?
15. What is the relationship between DCE and RPCs?
16. In terms of RPCs, what is a stub?
17. What is the purpose of IDL?
18. Are RPCs synchronous or asynchronous?
19. Explain the concept of blocking.
20. What are the three categories of message-passing middleware?
21. Which category of message-passing middleware supports QOS?
22. Compare and contrast message passing with message queuing.
23. Differentiate persistent and nonpersistent message queues. For what types of applications are each best suited?
24. Explain network message concentration.
25. In terms of middleware, what is a trigger?
26. What types of applications are best suited for publish and subscribe middleware solutions?
27. What does transaction processing mean?
28. Explain the ACID test of database transaction management.
29. What is STDL?
30. What are the X/Open standard interfaces for portable transaction monitors?
31. What programming environments are best suited for object-oriented middleware?
32. What is an ORB?
33. In terms of CORBA-compliant middleware, differentiate between SII and DII.
34. What is IIOP used for?
35. What functionality does CORBA services provide?
36. Does DCOM support dynamic binding of objects? If so, how?
37. What is IDL used for in DCOM?
38. Is DCOM a standard?
39. Differentiate between DCOM and CORBA.
40. Explain the middleware selection process.

ACTIVITIES

1. Investigate VSAM and ISAM data files and report on their usage.
2. Research the ANSI SQL standard. Prepare a report on how closely individual SQL implementations follow the standard.
3. Prepare a report on SQL functional areas and the basic statements used in each area.
4. Prepare a chart outlining the middleware interface model. As new middleware solutions are encountered, map them to the model.
5. Research ODBC implementation. What platforms currently support ODBC?
6. After completing the previous activity, research universal data access implementation. Have universal data access implementations significantly eroded the ODBC market share?
7. Prepare a report on DCE. Is DCE gaining or losing market share?
8. Research RPC-based communications. Which middleware solutions rely on RPC communications techniques?
9. Research message-oriented middleware solutions. Create a chart of the available solutions and categorize each solution as message passing, message queuing, or publish and subscribe.
10. Prepare a report on the X/Open transaction processing standard.
11. Research transaction process monitors. Create a chart describing the available solutions and the data types they support.
12. Create a chart of the CORBA model. Research CORBA-compliant middleware solutions and map them onto the chart.
13. Prepare a report on the DCOM architecture. What are the underlying technologies used?
14. Report on the current state of CORBA and DCOM implementations. Has either solution increased their market share in the past 12 months?
15. Create a series of questions that can be used as a middleware selection tool. Contact a representative of your company or school and work through the selection process with him or her to select the best middleware solution currently available.

CASE STUDY

Mariamba Solves Home Depot Data Dilemma

Next time you saunter into Home Depot looking for a can of paint in Gustavian blue gray, think about this: the IT department in the retailer's Atlanta headquarters has to send updated databases to 754 stores—every night.

And not just for paint. IT also has to send the databases for design systems for kitchen cabinets, decks and mill work (windows and doors).

"We were killing our WAN sending out these data sets," says Curtis Chambers, manager of distributed architecture at Home Depot. The company uses STA, a File Transfer Protocol-type system that doesn't allow incremental downloads.

The company faced a dilemma: either figure out a way to speed up the nightly updates or upgrade the network.

That kind of upgrade wouldn't be just wood shavings for a company like Home

Depot. It had sales of nearly $8 billion in the third quarter of 1998 alone and is adding a new retail store nearly every two days.

The IT department has four IBM mainframes linked together, and the headquarters' databases reside on Hewlett-Packard servers. Each store has its own HP D270 Unix server, and often no IT employee.

Mike Anderson, Home Depot's vice president of technology, tries to schedule updates when the stores are closed. This is still a chore because the databases can hold 60M to 80M bytes. So Anderson took a look at Marimba's Castanet Infrastructure Suite and did the math.

The Castanet Transmitter sits on a server and automatically sends applications and data over an intranet, extranet or the Internet. The most important feature for Home Depot is the ability to send differentials—just the changes to a database or a file.

With four databases per store, Anderson is sending around 320M bytes of information to each store, every night. If a connection fails, the system has to resend the entire update; there's no way to resume the download. But with Castanet, he can send just the differential data. So instead of sending 80M bytes, he can transmit a total of about 1.2M bytes, about the amount of data that fits on single floppy disk. Instead of taking hours to update one database, Anderson says he'll be able to do it in 30 seconds.

At each store, Castanet's Tuner will automatically receive the updates and merge them with the store's databases. The Tuner also has built-in protection so it doesn't overlay an active file. Instead, it downloads the file, and the Tuner keeps trying to update it until it succeeds. The Tuner can also install and launch applications. Home Depot may eventually use this feature to update code.

Currently, Home Depot runs an AT&T frame relay network with T-1s to every store, sending data and voice traffic on different channels. Anderson is looking to switch to ATM so he can multiplex data and voice.

Chambers has been lab-testing Castanet for several months and says he's had no problems running it over IBM AIX, Sun Solaris, HP Unix and Windows NT because the code is written in Java. The rollout is scheduled for later this month.

Chambers says payoffs will not just be speedier downloads: "It's letting us use our existing network technology for a little while longer."

Source: Robin Schrier Hohman, "Marimba Solves Home Depot Data Dilemma," *Network World,* vol. 16, no. 5 (February 1, 1999), p. 29. Copyright (February 1, 1999), Network World.

BUSINESS CASE STUDY QUESTIONS

Activities

1. Complete a top-down model for this case by gleaning facts from the case and placing them in the proper layer of the top-down model. After completing the top-down model, analyze and detail those instances where requirements were clearly passed down from upper layers to lower layers of the model and where solutions to those requirements were passed up from lower layers to upper layers of the model.

2. Detail any questions about the case that may occur to you for which answers are not clearly stated in the article.

Business

1. What were the key business reasons for changing the system to use Marimba?

Application

1. What does Marimba Castanet do?

Data

1. What data are updated nightly?
2. What percentage of the data typically is updated each night?

Network

1. What is the logical network design for Home Depot?

Technology

1. What were the main reasons for selecting Marimba?
2. What new Marimba features are potentially going to be utilized by Home Depot in the future?

CHAPTER 10

CLIENT/SERVER APPLICATION DEVELOPMENT AND INTEGRATION

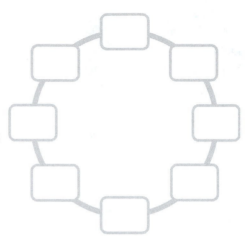

Concepts Reinforced

Middleware	ODBC
HTML	Web Development

Concepts Introduced

Procedural Programming	Event-Driven Programming
Object-Oriented Programming	Application Distribution
JAVA	Active X
Network Computing	Legacy Application Integration
SNA/LAN Integration	

OBJECTIVES

After mastering the material in this chapter you should:

1. Understand structured programming

2. Understand event-driven programming

3. Understand object-oriented programming

4. Be able to explain application deployment techniques

5. Understand network computing techniques

6. Evaluate legacy application integration techniques

7. Understand SNA/LAN integration

■ INTRODUCTION

By definition, client/server systems consist of two applications joined together by middleware. In this chapter various categories of application development environments and methods of deploying the resulting applications throughout the network will be introduced. Although many of the discussed development environments can be used to develop stand-alone applications, emphasis will be placed on the features required to develop and deploy client/server applications. Methods of integrating client/server applications with existing applications will also be covered.

■ APPLICATION DEVELOPMENT ENVIRONMENTS

Client/server applications (or programs) consist of a specialized list of instructions. Applications can be thought of as recipes for business functions. When the application is executed, these instructions cause the computer to complete a predetermined task. Through the use of statements and variables, the application performs a business task. Regardless of the sophistication of the computer system, it is only as useful as the application it's executing. Business applications are developed using computer languages. There are two types of computer languages: low level and high level.

Low-Level Languages

Low-level languages are languages close to the actual code the computer executes. **Machine language** is the most basic language, and the only language a computer can natively understand. Machine language code consists of binary instructions for the computer's central processing unit (CPU). Each CPU has a different machine language. Although easily understood by the CPU, machine language is almost impossible for human programmers to develop because it consists entirely of binary numbers. In order to ease the development of business applications, a means of abstracting machine language type CPU instructions into something more meaningful to humans is required.

The next level of language abstraction is assembly language. **Assembly language** is similar to machine language since it uses the same basic instructions as machine language. However, assembly language uses names for instructions rather than numbers, making assembly language much easier for human programmers to understand. Before it can be executed, assembly language code must be converted to machine language code by a specialized program called an assembler.

Assembly language is significantly easier for programmers to use than machine language, but it is still very abstract. Using assembler, the programmer must manually manipulate the CPU's data stack. It can take multiple lines of assembly language code to perform even the simplest of operations such as adding two numbers together. Assembly language is difficult to write, but it has the advantage of creating very small, efficient code. Assembly language is also very powerful, because it allows the programmer to manipulate the CPU at the most basic levels. There are some tasks that can only be performed in assembly language.

Assembly language is basically an alphanumeric abstraction of a particular CPU's machine language. As shown in Figure 10-1, each machine language instruction is represented by a short pneumonic code, thus making assembly language easier for humans to understand. However, there is a one-to-one mapping between assembly language codes and machine language instructions, so assembly language is also CPU dependent. Because they are difficult to program and are CPU dependent, low-level languages are typically only used to write operating systems and specialized programs that convert higher-level languages into machine language.

High-Level Languages

The complexity and CPU-dependent nature of low-level languages make them a poor choice for writing business applications. What is needed are languages that provide a higher level of abstraction from the CPU. Such **high-level languages** are significantly closer to human language, making them

```
            mov sign,0                  ;initialize sign
            mov di,buf;                 set first character of buffer to dummy
            mov byte ptr [di],'*'       ; value to guarantee first character not null
            mov bx,control              ;get address of control string
            inc bx                      ;skip over initial %
            cmp byte ptr [bx],'c'       ;is it a character?
            je character                ;if so, output character
            cmp byte ptr [bx],'h'       ;is it a short int?
            je short_int                ;if so, output short int
            cmp byte ptr [bx],'d'       ;is it an int?
            je norm_int                 ;if so, output integer
            cmp byte ptr [bx],'l'       ;is it a long int?
            jne next
            jmp long_int                ;if so, output long int
    next:   cmp byte ptr [bx],'s'       ;is it a string?
            je string                   ;if so, output string
```

Figure 10-1   Sample Assembly Language Program

much easier for programmers to use. High-level languages have a larger and more powerful set of commands than low-level languages, easing the programmer's job. When converted to machine language, each high-level language command requires multiple lines of machine code to implement.

High-level languages are also CPU independent, allowing a programmer to write programs that can run on multiple types of computers. The high-level language written by the programmer is called source code. Because a computer cannot natively understand high-level language, the source code must be converted into machine language before it can be executed. Two tools can make this conversion: interpreters and compilers.

An **interpreter** is a special program that runs whenever the high-level language program is executed. As its name implies, an interpreter converts the high-level language commands into machine language commands in real time. However, just as there is a delay when a human language interpreter is used to allow two people who speak different languages to communicate, there is an inherent latency associated with high-level language interpreters. The interpreter must convert each high-level command into machine language every time it is run. For code segments that are run repeatedly, this conversion must occur during each iteration.

A **compiler** is a specialized program that converts the entire high-level language program into a machine language "executable." Given high-level language source code, the compiler creates a machine language executable. Because a compiler must convert the whole program into machine language before program execution can begin, it takes longer for program execution to begin than in an interpreted environment. Because the whole program is already converted into machine language, however, the resulting executable normally runs much faster than the same code would run using an interpreter.

Practical Advice and Information

INTERPRETERS VERSUS COMPILERS

All things being otherwise equal, a compiled application will always deliver better performance than an interpreted environment. Some development environments allow for the use of an interpreter for application development and debugging, then provide a compiler for the creation of the application executable.

Managerial Perspective

COMPILER SELECTION

Because compilers translate high-level languages into a CPU-dependent machine language, a separate compiler is required for each high-level language/CPU combination. For example, there is a C compiler for Intel-based personal computers, another for Apple Macintosh computers, and still another for UNIX computers. To make compiler selection more interesting, the compiler industry is quite competitive. There are actually many compilers for each language on each type of computer. For instance, more than a dozen companies develop and sell C compilers for the Intel x86 platform.

Many different high-level programming languages and environments are available for use in building client/server applications. A recently published list included more than 120 different high-level programming languages from Ada to ZPL. Each of these languages has specific strengths and weaknesses, making them better for some types of development than others. To better understand the differences between programming languages, they can be broken into three major categories: procedural languages, event-driven environments, and object-oriented environments.

Procedural Languages   Procedural languages (also known as imperative languages) were the first application development environments to be developed. Originally developed for single-tasking, single-threaded operating environments, these languages allow the programmer to maintain total control over the execution of the code. As the name would imply, procedural languages follow a specific set of instructions exactly in order.

In a **procedural language** the programmer determines the sequence of instructions (the procedure) a program will execute at design time. The user can affect operation of the program only when the program requests input. This complete control over the program's execution is the key differentiating factor between procedural languages and other application development environments.

If software developed in a procedural language contains more than one feature, a methodology for users to select the feature they wish to utilize must be included in the program. The most common method used to allow such selections is a menu. However, even when a menu is used, the programmer is still in control of the process. The programmer determines when the user can select a choice from the menu, and what code will run when any given menu item is selected.

Structured Programming   When developing applications using procedural languages, structured programming techniques are used. **Structured programming** is a method of organizing a computer program as a series of hierarchical modules, each having a single entry and exit point. Processing within a module takes place in a step-by-step manner without unconditional branches (such as GOTO statements) to higher levels within the module.

Program flow within a module is based on three basic structures: sequence, iteration, and test. If a line of code requires no decision, program execution continues with the next line of code in the sequence. If a line of code is to execute multiple times, a structure such as For-Next is used to control iteration. Without the ability to test conditions and take action based on the outcome of such a test, computers would be worthless. If a code structure involves a test, it must contain instructions for the computer to take for all possible outcomes of the test. The *if* command is used to trigger test structures in most high-level computer languages.

Within a structured program, a main routine is automatically entered when the program is executed. From within this main routine, control is passed to the various modules of the program. Modules within a structured program interact with other modules by the passing of **parameters.** When a module calls another module, it passes control and parameters containing any information the called module needs to execute. There are two basic types of structure program modules: functions and subroutines.

Functions are modules that return a single result based on the parameters passed to them. An example of a function would be a module that determines a monthly car payment. When the function is called, the calling module passes the following parameters: cost of the vehicle, the amount of any down payment, the length of the term, and the annual interest rate. Based on these parameters, the function determines the monthly payment.

The second type of structured program module is subroutines. **Subroutines** are code modules that perform general processing. Unlike functions, subroutines can return any number of items to the calling module, including none. Subroutines can be nested so that one subroutine calls another subroutine. By dividing frequently used code segments into subroutines, a programmer can greatly reduce code repetition within a structured program. An example of a subroutine would be a module that creates a message box to display information and ask for input from the user. The information displayed by the message box can be passed to the subroutine, and the resulting user input can be passed back to the calling routine. In this manner, this one subroutine can process all requests for information from the user, regardless of topic.

The use of structured programming techniques allows a programmer to develop an application that includes minimal code repetition. Such code can be interpreted or compiled into efficient machine language code. Structured programming also makes it easier for programmers to understand each other's work. This is especially important if more than one programmer is working on a single application development project. Although structured programming techniques originated with procedural languages, the basic concepts are used in all programming environments.

Common Procedural Languages There are many procedural languages currently used to develop client/server applications. The following is a brief list of the more common languages and the type of applications for which they are most often used.

COBOL **COBOL** (COmmon Business Oriented Language) is the second oldest high-level programming language in use today (FORTRAN is the oldest). Developed in the late 1950s, COBOL has traditionally been the language of choice for business-oriented mainframe applications. In fact, COBOL is inextricably linked to text-based mainframe applications. Compared with other high-level languages, COBOL is a verbose language. This wordiness makes COBOL code easier to understand, but it reduces the efficiency of programs written in the language. Due to the size and limited efficiency of COBOL, it has typically not been used on the personal computer platform. In terms of client/server computing, COBOL is most commonly used as a development environment for mainframe-based server applications.

Managerial Perspective

COBOL AND THE YEAR 2000

Although COBOL is rarely used to develop new applications today, the vast majority of existing business applications are written in COBOL. As long as these systems remain in production, there will be a demand for COBOL programmers to update and maintain these systems. In fact, in the late 1990s the demand for COBOL programmers increased significantly as business tried to solve the "year 2000" glitch.

In the 1960s and 1970s, many business applications written in COBOL were designed to represent dates as two-digit numbers in order to save disk space, which was costly at the time. However, the approach of the year 2000 represented a significant problem for applications written in such a manner. Many applications perform operations such as subtracting a person's two-digit birth year from a two-digit representation of the current year. When the two-digit representation of the current year is 00, such calculations return negative numbers—creating a host of other problems. While the so-called year 2000 problem is not the direct result of the use of COBOL, most of the affected business systems were written in COBOL.

Pascal   Named after Blaise Pascal, a seventeenth-century French mathematician who constructed one of the first mechanical adding machines, the Pascal programming language was created in the late 1960s. Because **Pascal** requires programmers to design programs that conform to the concepts of structured programming, it is a very popular teaching language. Although Pascal itself has had limited use in the development of business applications, many popular business programming languages (such as C) have their roots in Pascal. Recently, Pascal has reemerged as a business programming language as the structured language used in Borland's Delphi event-driven programming environment.

C   **C** was developed at Bell labs in the 1970s during the development of the UNIX operating system. C was originally designed as a systems programming language used to write operating systems and systems programs. Although it is a high-level language, C is much closer to assembly language than most other high-level languages. This allows C to create very compact, efficient code that requires fewer system resources than most other high-level languages. Because of this efficiency, C has gained considerable usage as a business application language on the personal computer and UNIX platforms.

BASIC **BASIC** (Beginners All-purpose Symbolic Instruction Code) was developed at Dartmouth College in the 1960s. One of the first high-level languages, BASIC is also one of the easiest languages for a beginner to understand and is therefore often used as an introductory teaching language. BASIC was extensively used during the 1970s and early 1980s as a programming language for business applications, but was largely supplanted in the market by C until the release of Microsoft Visual BASIC, an event-driven programming environment.

Event-Driven Languages Procedural languages work well with text based operating environments, but they are limited in their ability to work with graphical user interface (GUI) environments. Graphical user interface environments are typically object-based applications consisting of multiple objects, such as text boxes and buttons. The user manipulates these objects in no specific order. The programmer is no longer in control of program execution.

Unlike procedural languages, an event-driven application does not ask for input from the user. The user provides input to the application then initiates an **event** that triggers an event handler (or procedure) within the application to process the input. Each **event handler** is effectively a separate program that should follow structured programming rules. The **window manager,** part of the GUI operating system, monitors the application for events. When an event occurs, the event manager starts a process to complete the code associated with the event handler for the triggered event. In effect the user controls execution of the program.

Just about anything the user does triggers an event. Such user events include clicking the mouse, pressing a key, moving the scroll bar, moving the mouse pointer, and changing windows. In addition to user events, there are also many system events triggered automatically by the window manager when certain system functions occur. System events include clock ticks and system shutdown. By using the system shutdown event an application can be programmed to automatically ask users if they wish to save their changes when the shutdown command is issued.

Event-driven programming languages are mainly used for the development of client applications for GUI-based operating systems such as the Apple Macintosh, X-Windows, and Microsoft Windows. An example event handler and the screen from which it is called are shown in Figure 10-2.

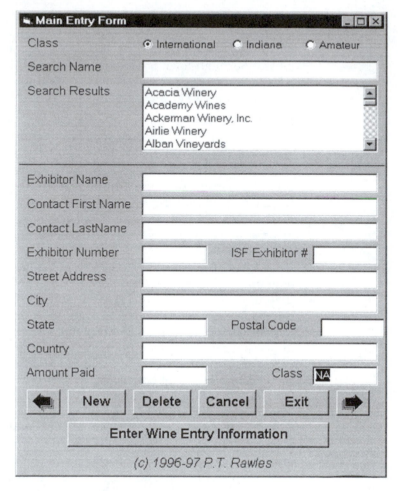

The following code is the event handler for a change in the **Exhibitor Name** control:

```
Private Sub txtExhibitorName_Change()
'declare variables
Dim I As Integer
I = 0
'clear lstnamelookup list box
1stNameLookup.Clear
'check for' in box – trap if there
If Right$(txtExhibitorName, 1)= "'" Then
    txtExhibitorName = Left$(txtExhibitorName, (Len(txtexhibitornmame) – 1))
End If
'find the first match in the rsExhibitorName recordset
rsName.FindFirst SearchFieldName & "like'" & txtExhibitorName & "*'"
If Not rsName.NoMatch Then
    'there was at least one match
    While Not rsName.NoMatch And I <21
```

```
'put next match into array
If Class <> "AW" Then
    MatchName(1, I) = rsName.Fields(SearchFieldName)
Else
    MatchName(1, I) = rsName.Fields("ContactLast") & "," &
rsName.Fields("ContactFirst")
End If
MatchName(2, I) = rsName.Fields("Number")
'put matched field into listbox
lstNameLookup.AddItem MatchName(1, I)
'find next match
rsName.FindNext SearchFieldName & "like'" & txtExhibitorName & "*'"
'index I
I = I + 1
Wend
Else
    1stNameLookup.AddItem "New Record"
End If
End Sub
```

Figure 10-2   Example Event Handler Code

Common Event-Driven Languages   There are many event-driven languages currently in use for the development of client/server applications. The following are some of the more common languages and the applications for which they are typically used.

Visual BASIC   **Visual BASIC** is one of the most popular event-driven languages for the development of business applications. Designed for the Microsoft Windows family of operating environments, Visual BASIC provides a powerful development platform, yet it is easy to program. As the name would suggest, Visual BASIC utilizes the BASIC language for the development of event handlers.

Visual BASIC is not a true object-oriented programming language, but it is an object-based programming environment. By using objects, Visual BASIC can be extended to provide additional capabilities. In addition to the base objects that ship with Visual BASIC such as text boxes, buttons, lists, and labels, Visual BASIC has the ability to use third-party objects. These third-party objects are packaged as **OCX**es (Object layering and embedding custom controls or simply custom controls). Custom controls provide a means of modularizing code within Visual BASIC. As shown in Figure 10-3, multiple applications can include a custom control and make use of its functionality.

Developers can create custom controls that provide specific services and package them separately from an application. Many different software developers are currently developing custom controls that range from user interface extensions to special input/output objects that manage connections to remote devices. The ability to use this large selection of third-party software objects is one of the attractions of Visual BASIC.

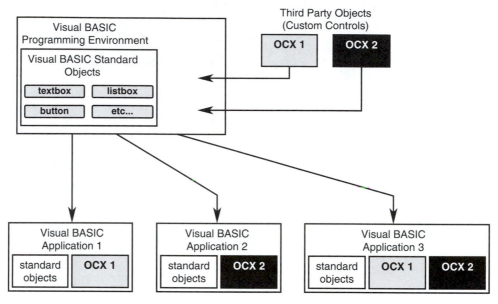

Figure 10-3 OCX Packaging

Visual BASIC integrates with database server applications through the use of Open Database Connectivity (ODBC). As described in Chapter 9, ODBC is a database independent API that allows a client application programmer to develop database applications that will work with any database engine that implements the relational database design. Combined with ease of development, adherence to the ODBC standard is one of the main reasons Visual BASIC has enjoyed significant market success. The sample event-driven code shown in Figure 10-2 was developed in Visual BASIC.

VISUAL BASIC EXECUTION

Practical Advice and Information

Visual BASIC currently operates in an interpreted manner. Therefore, Visual BASIC is better suited for the development of business applications than for the development of general purpose Windows programs such as word processors and spreadsheets. Although newer versions of Visual BASIC have significantly increased execution speed by converting the BASIC code to native code, a quasi-compiled mid-tier language, Visual BASIC application execution speed remains slower than compiled environments.

Delphi **Delphi** is an event-driven language from Borland designed for the Windows family of operating systems. Delphi event handlers are written in a derivative of the Pascal language. Delphi event handlers are compiled directly into machine language for faster execution.

Delphi also supports OCXes as a means of including third-party objects into the operating system. Delphi is also well equipped for use as a database client. In addition to ODBC, a series of native SQL database drivers for most major relational database management systems are presented to the programmer. Although use of the native database drivers limits flexibility to easily move to nonsupported database servers, they can result in significant performance gains compared with using ODBC.

Object-Oriented Languages   One of main problems facing the developers of business applications is decreasing the duration of application development while increasing the ability of the resulting code to be easily maintained. As mentioned in the preceding section, one method of accomplishing these goals is to package code into reusable objects that can then be used in multiple applications. Although object-based event-driven languages provide significantly more modularity and potential for code reuse than procedural languages, code reuse is still somewhat limited.

One of the chief limitations with event-driven languages is that there is no way to dynamically create objects at run time, forcing the programmer to create all objects at design time. **Object-oriented** programming environments address this shortcoming by including a mechanism to dynamically create objects at run time. For instance, an object called *car* that provides a framework for information about a car can be used to create new cars. By entering values for the information defined in the car object, a user can create a new object called Mustang that describes a specific type of car.

Properly implemented, object-oriented programming environments can provide faster development, increased quality, easier maintenance and understandability, and enhanced modifiability compared to procedural languages or event-driven languages. However, object-oriented programming environments are still a developing technology. As such, the features and mechanisms supported by object-oriented programming environments are still being developed. New techniques, concepts, and executions will continue to be developed as the paradigm continues to evolve.

Object-oriented programming is dependent on the concept of abstract entities called software objects. Software objects, just objects for short, range from items on a screen such as text boxes and buttons to more advanced items such as stacks and queues. Objects typically have **state,** or parameters that describe the current condition of the object (such as whether it is selected). While an external force to change state must act for most objects to change their state, some objects are capable of changing state independently of any such external manipulation. Such objects are referred to as **active objects** or actors. An example of an active object is a timer. When the duration of the timer has expired, the state of the timer will automatically change.

There are two major categories of objects: classes and instances. A **class** is an object that contains information on the structure and capabilities of another object along with a mechanism for creating objects based on these instructions. Classes create objects based on these rules. The objects created by a class are **instances** of the class. The process of creating an instance is sometimes referred to as **instantiation.** For example, consider an application that controls a CD jukebox. An object-oriented programmer could create a class called CD that describes the required information for a CD button. The CD button for each CD installed in the jukebox based on the CD class would be considered an instance of CD.

Through the use of classes, an object-oriented programmer can allow the application to create new objects during program execution. In this manner, the application can automatically adapt to any changing requirements placed upon it. In the preceding example, when a new CD is inserted into the system, the application can automatically create a new instance of CD and add the button to the screen for selection by the user.

All objects have a well-defined set of commands. These commands are referred to as the **methods** of the object. An object's methods determine what the object is capable of doing and how it will behave within a system of objects. Objects interact with one another by passing messages to each other to invoke methods much in the same manner subroutines pass parameters between one another in a structured programming environment. Objects can pass messages within a program on a single computer or between distributed applications across a network. For instance, when a CD button from the previous example is pressed, it can send a message to load the CD to the object that controls the CD changer. After the changer has placed the appropriate CD in the player, it can send a message to the CD player to begin playing the disc.

One of the key concepts in maintaining software modularity is **encapsulation,** which is the process of packaging an object so that only the details that affect the object's use are accessible. An object should be a self-contained entity with only state and methods available. The underlying implementation details should not be accessible to the object programmer. Objects can be thought of as the proverbial black box—an item that performs a task through some unknown process. A programmer using the object to perform a task cannot alter the object. In this manner object independence and reusability can be maintained.

Objects interact with one another through **interfaces.** Every object has a public interface that is accessible by all other objects. By accessing an object's public interface, the state of the object can be altered or the methods of the object can be invoked. A second interface exists on classes for use exclusively by instances of the class to gain access to information about the class. This interface is known as the **inheritance interface.** As its name would suggest, the inheritance interface provides a means to automatically gain information from their parent class. Through inheritance a change in a class can quickly proliferate through all its child instances. The interaction between objects through their interfaces is illustrated in Figure 10-4.

Object-oriented applications are built by assembling a group of objects into a system. Such an object system allows each object to interact with the other objects within the system to modify state and invoke methods.

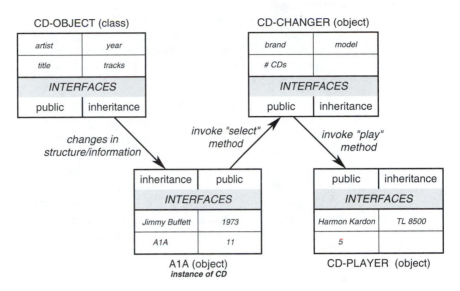

Figure 10-4   Object Interfaces

Common Object-Oriented Languages   Object-oriented programming techniques are less mature than either procedural languages or event-driven languages. Therefore, there are fewer object-oriented languages available. The two object-oriented languages most commonly used to develop client/server applications are Smalltalk and C++.

Smalltalk   **Smalltalk** was developed in the late 1960s at the Xerox Palo Alto Research Center (PARC), the same facility that has developed many other important information technologies such as Ethernet. As the first object-oriented programming language, many people still believe Smalltalk to be the only true object-oriented development language. Because Smalltalk was written from the ground up as an object-oriented programming language rather than having object extensions added after the fact, it provides the most complete object implementation of any object-oriented programming language.

After getting little use for the greater part of 30 years, Smalltalk has emerged as the most commonly used object-oriented programming environment for business applications. With interest in object technologies at an all-time high, many MIS shops are converting from COBOL to Smalltalk as their predominant application development environment. Based both on technical merit and its ability to handle large projects, Smalltalk is an excellent fit for business application development.

There are many different versions of Smalltalk commercially available. As of late 1999, VisualWorks from ParcPlace was the most commonly used version for business application development. Built on top of VisualWorks is Distributed Smalltalk, a version that adds CORBA (see Chapter 9) compliant object distribution. For applications intended for the Microsoft Windows environment, IBM's VisualAge provides a good balance of functionality, speed, and Windows integration. Another Smalltalk implementation optimized for speed on Microsoft Windows platforms is VisualSmalltalk, also from ParcPlace.

C++   Originally developed in the mid-1980s, C++ adds object orientation to the C procedural programming language. Because of this relationship, C++ programs were originally "precompiled" into standard C source code, then compiled using any C compiler. Modern compilers have eliminated this precompilation by integrating it into the C compiler itself.

As this relationship would indicate, C++ is a superset of C. This allows a C programmer to begin using C++ by simply including C++ statements in their code. C++ has a weaker object model than Smalltalk and is more difficult to program. Although some business application development is occurring in C++, it is most commonly used for applications that have traditionally been developed in C such as operating systems and system applications.

Many different versions of C++ are currently available in the marketplace. Most versions of UNIX include C++ capability in their C compilers. Borland and Microsoft both market C++ compilers for personal computer environments. Microsoft Visual C++ combines many advantages of event-driven languages with true object orientation.

Applied Problem Solving

DEVELOPMENT ENVIRONMENT SELECTION

Rarely are application development environment questions a black-and-white issue. Many factors, including personal bias, combine to make development environment selection more of an art than a science.

The process of selecting an application development environment can be eased by asking a few key questions:

1. Upon what platform will the final program execute?

2. What are the characteristics of the application?

3. Are programmers available with knowledge of the environment?

The first question is inherently obvious: the development environment selected must be capable of producing machine language code for the platform upon which the application will execute. If the target platform is a mainframe, Visual BASIC can automatically be removed from consideration since it doesn't run in a mainframe environment.

The second question takes the characteristics of the application into account. As discussed in the preceding section, different languages have different strengths and weaknesses. Neither Visual BASIC, Delphi, nor COBOL would be good choices to write a system-level application or operating system. Conversely, C++ is more difficult to develop a simple database application with than any of the preceding choices. Another key issue to address is the maintainability of the final application. It is certainly possible to write a business application in Assembler, but it would be exceptionally difficult and expensive to maintain.

The final question focuses on human resource issues. If no one is available to write the application in a particular language, it might make sense to select an alternate language for which developers are available. However, if the reasons to use a particular language are compelling, it might make sense to either train an existing developer on the new system or to hire a new developer who already has the required skills.

CASE Tools   Each of the programming environments discussed so far requires a human programmer to develop the business application. Originally **CASE** (Computer-Aided Software Engineering) tools were specialized computer applications designed to assist the application programmer in the development of business applications. These earlier CASE tools focused on the development of mainframe applications, most commonly using the COBOL procedural programming language.

Newer CASE implementations have become more specialized and support specific parts of the overall software development process. The various levels of CASE are illustrated in Figure 10-5. While a few CASE tools continue to automate the entire systems development process, the trend is for specialized tools that focus on specific sections. Such systems are commonly referred to as upper CASE, middle CASE, or lower CASE tools. This new approach has resulted in a change in the meaning of the CASE acronym to computer-aided systems engineering. Although the focus and acronym may have changed, the goal of CASE tools remains to help increase the productivity of application developers.

Computer-Aided Systems Engineering

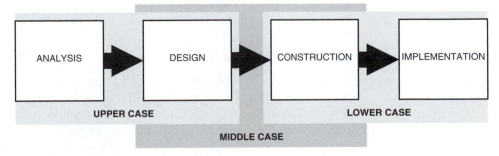

Figure 10-5   CASE Classification

Managerial Perspective

THE NEED FOR CASE

The development of business applications is an arduous, time-intensive task. Programmers must determine the requirements of the application, create a logical application design that fulfills these requirements, and then create the code to implement the finished solution. This process has changed little throughout the duration of the modern computer era.

As organizations become more dependent on their information technology systems, the need for reliable business applications that can be easily maintained and upgraded has increased dramatically. According to a report by the National Research Council, computer software is now in excess of a $1-trillion-a-year business with an annual growth rate in excess of 8%. This tremendous growth has led to a shortage of qualified computer programmers. In order to meet the needs of this rapidly expanding market, a means of increasing the accuracy and productivity of software developers must be developed. CASE tools are a means of helping achieve this quality and productivity increase.

Before determining exactly what a CASE tool is, it is imperative to understand what a CASE tool is not. CASE is not a means of eliminating or replacing application programmers with computer programs that write other computer programs. CASE is a means of providing an advanced tool kit to assist an application developer throughout the application development life cycle—from analysis through code development. CASE tools provide many different capabilities to the application developer. Common CASE functionality includes:

- Summarizing initial requirements
- Developing flow diagrams
- Scheduling development tasks
- Preparing documentation
- Controlling software versions
- Developing program code

Managerial Perspective

KEEPING CASE IN PERSPECTIVE

Although many CASE tools are marketed as a panacea for the software industry with promises to increase productivity while increasing quality, in reality they are just another tool in the application developer's arsenal. Recent research has found that the highest levels of quality and efficiency are reached by using a combination of CASE and manual development. It has also been determined that CASE techniques work best on large projects. Projects with fewer than four developers rarely, if ever, see a benefit from the use of CASE technologies. Contrary to the implications of some trade publications, CASE tools do not represent a silver bullet to solve the labor shortage currently faced by the software industry. Instead, CASE tools should be thought of as specialized project management platforms for software development.

There are literally hundreds of different CASE tools in the marketplace, making the selection of a tool a difficult task. It is impossible to determine a single best CASE tool, since different applications types and development environments lend themselves to different requirements and hence different tools. When a development project is determined to be a candidate for CASE, a careful selection process should be used to determine the tool best suited for the application type, development language, development environment, and personnel involved.

■ APPLICATION DEPLOYMENT

Regardless of the development environment used, both client and server applications must be deployed throughout the network. Server applications are typically easier to deploy since they are relatively few in number and are often centralized in location. Client applications, in contrast, can be very difficult to deploy as they are spread throughout the network. The deployment of client applications is further complicated by the fact that there can be many different client applications, running on many different platforms, connected to the same server application.

Server Application Deployment

Server applications usually support multiple instances of a client application. It is not uncommon for a single server application to process data for thousands of clients. In order to meet the demands for such large numbers of clients, server applications are implemented on large hardware platforms ranging in scale from uni-processor PC-based servers that sit under a desk to mainframes that can take up hundreds of square feet of space.

Because of the size and operational requirements of server applications and their hardware, they are commonly deployed in a few centralized locations. By consolidating server applications, the overhead required to maintain these large systems can be spread across multiple applications. This is particularly important because each location not only needs to have physical space and adequate power to install the server, but must also provide operations staff to maintain the hardware and software.

Server applications can run on many different operating system platforms, ranging from Windows NT to UNIX to full-scale mainframe operating systems such as IBM's MVS. Many commercially available server

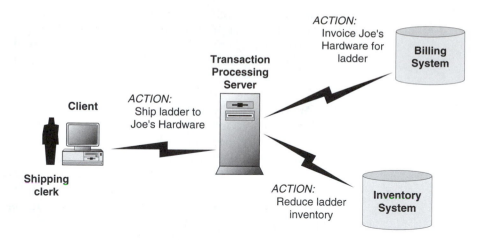

Figure 10-6 Transaction Processing Nature of Server Applications

applications, such as relational database management systems, are supported on multiple hardware platforms depending on the number of clients that need to attach. In this manner a server application can be scaled up to meet the needs of the users as demand increases.

The main purpose of a server application is to store and process data while exchanging it with multiple client applications. Server applications are optimized to interact with client applications rather than humans. Therefore, the chief development parameter for most server applications is processing speed with user interface a secondary consideration. The application programmer focuses his or her attention on the client interface (through middleware) and the physical interface with the server hardware. Because of this focus, most server applications are written in efficient languages such as C or C++.

The server application must maintain the system's data integrity and perform transaction processing for items that cross the boundaries between user applications. As illustrated in Figure 10-6, a user in the shipping department might enter that a particular item was shipped. At that time, the server application would perform many postings, such as removing the item from inventory, adding the value of the sale to accounts receivable, and generating an invoice for the customer. All of this processing takes place at the server without the knowledge of the shipping clerk, who has started us to prepare the next item for shipping.

TRANSACTION PROCESSING

In Sharper Focus

Transaction processing refers to a series of operations that take place in response to a business transaction. For example, let's consider the case of a customer entering a furniture store and purchasing a couch on the store's in-house credit plan. This single business transaction will result in postings to several information systems. The inventory control system must be updated to reflect the sale of the item. A pick slip must be sent to the warehouse to indicate the couch is to be brought to the dock for pickup. The accounts receivable system must be updated to reflect the credit purchase. Collectively these operations make up a single transaction. Please refer to Chapter 9 for further discussion on transaction processing.

Client Application Deployment

Many different client applications often access a common server application. In our shipping example from Figure 10-6, the shipping clerk is working on an application specifically designed to assist in shipping product. It may include the ability to print shipping labels and automatically notify the transportation company that there is a package ready to ship. At the same time, someone in the accounting department is using a different client application tied to the same server application to determine who is currently behind in paying for goods shipped. If an invoice exceeds a certain age, the accounting user can deny credit to the customer, effectively changing the behavior of the shipping clerk's client system.

Not only can multiple client applications access a single server application, but each client application can be written in a different language and run on a different hardware platform. In the previous example, the shipping clerk could be using an application written in C on a UNIX terminal, while the accountant is using a Windows NT application written in Smalltalk on an Intel-based personal computer. Collectively, this ability to mix and match software components is what gives client/server systems their flexibility. It also makes distribution and maintenance of client/server systems difficult.

In sharp contrast to server applications that are optimized for processing, client applications are primarily concerned with providing user access to the underlying data. As such, the user interface for such systems is critical to the usability and the final success or failure of the system. Users of client applications want simple systems that are easy to operate and provide a means of entering data into the server applications. Although speed is certainly a factor in client application design, it is secondary in importance to user interface issues. If a user cannot understand how to use a client application effectively, it is irrelevant if the application can perform a transaction in less than a tenth of a second.

Client application programmers typically utilize development environments that take advantage of the graphical user interfaces common to most modern client operating systems. Visual BASIC, Visual C++, and Smalltalk are all commonly used to develop client applications for windowed application environments. Procedural languages are rarely used for the development of client applications at this time.

In addition to custom developed applications, standard productivity software can be programmed to serve as a rudimentary client. For instance, the Microsoft Office productivity suite for Windows and Macintosh clients provides an advanced macro development environment. A subset of Visual BASIC called VBA (Visual BASIC Application edition) can be programmed to access data from many server applications. For relational database servers supported by ODBC (see Chapter 9 for more detail), a tool called Microsoft Query can be used to retrieve and update data records for processing within spreadsheets and word processing documents. In many cases, it is possible to rapidly create applications in this manner to either solve a pressing need or prototype a more robust, full-featured solution based on a more traditional development environment.

Client Software Distribution   No matter what application development environment is used, the resulting application must be distributed to all of the client systems that will execute it. Managing the distribution of such client-based applications throughout a large network is a daunting task. Traditionally, an administrator would have to physically visit every client to install and test each application, representing considerable cost and expense. The cost of maintaining client/server systems has been estimated as being up to three times the cost of purchasing the enabling hardware and software. In fact, the cost of maintaining client/server systems in this manner can easily surpass the cost of maintaining mainframe-based systems.

In order to reduce this cost, many organizations have opted to run applications from file server systems rather than installing them directly on each client. In a file server-based system the actual client application code is kept on a file server and each client accesses it through the network. This approach also allows for increased application security. If a user does not have adequate authorization the file server will not allow them to execute the client application.

In Sharper Focus

CLIENT-BASED APPLICATIONS VERSUS SERVER-BASED APPLICATIONS

In a client-based application environment, the executable application is stored on the client's local hard drive. When the application is executed, it is loaded directly from the hard drive. Only data are sent across the network. Client-based solutions minimize network usage requirements, but require each client to be individually maintained.

In a server-based application environment, the executable application is stored on a file server. When the application is executed, it is pulled from the file server to the client. Both the application and data are sent across the network. Server-based applications reduce the cost and time required to maintain the clients, but require additional network resources to transport the application to the clients.

The architectural differences between client-based applications and server-based applications are illustrated in Figure 10-7.

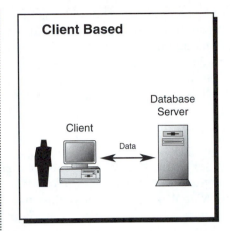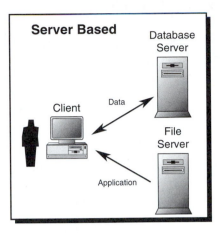

Figure 10-7   Client-Based Applications vs. Server Based Applications

File server systems do not completely eliminate client configuration issues, however. What is needed is a means of automatically distributing software to client workstations. Several products now in the marketplace perform automatic software distribution. These products, such as Microsoft System Management Server, have the ability to "push" software from a distribution server to the client. Use of these products effectively eliminates the requirement that an administrator physically visit each client.

Although automatic software distribution reduces the labor cost of maintaining client-based software, it utilizes significant network capacity. For this reason, most automatic software distribution tools allow client updates to be scheduled at times when the network is not heavily loaded. Updates can be scheduled to take place after-hours or on weekends to minimize the network impact on business applications.

REQUIREMENTS FOR AUTOMATIC SOFTWARE DISTRIBUTION

Practical Advice and Information

Automatic software distribution represents a tremendous time savings if properly implemented, but several factors must be considered for it to reach its potential.

- A relatively large number of stations must exist. It takes considerable time to develop an error-resistant software distribution package. For networks of fewer than 100 clients, automatic software distribution rarely delivers a reduction in either time or effort unless the clients are widely distributed. If physically going to each of five clients would require five flights to five different cities, it might make sense to use an automatic distribution system despite the low number of clients.

- The distribution environment should be as homogeneous as possible. Each different configuration must be fully tested prior to distribution. If a large population of clients is comprised of several groups of different system types, the time spent developing distribution packages for each system type could once again surpass the time it would take to distribute the software manually. For some environments, it might make sense to use automatic software distribution for some client types and manually distribute software for others.

Web Applications Another method to solve the software distribution problem is to use Internet technologies to provide client services. In addition to web surfing, World Wide Web browsers have the capability to serve as client application environments. However, the web paradigm convolutes the separation between clients and servers somewhat, since the web itself is a client/server system.

Web-based solutions are categorized based on the location of the web in the business system client/server architecture. If the business application client resides at the WWW server, the implementation is considered a server-side solution. Conversely, in client-side solutions, the business application client is distributed directly to the end user's computer through the web.

Server-side solutions are similar in concept to traditional terminal-based mainframe applications. The business client resides on the web server and connects to the business server in the same manner as any other client. The difference is that interaction with the user requires the business client to send and receive data through the web server to the user's web browser. The server-side web application architecture is illustrated in Figure 10-8.

The most common method of implementing server-side solutions is through the **Common Gateway Interface (CGI)** specification. The CGI specification allows a web page designer to create a web page that represents the client application's data. The business client running on the web server,

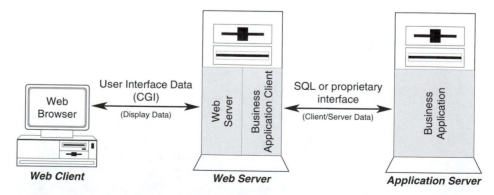

Figure 10-8 Server-Side Web Application Architecture

referred to as a CGI application, dynamically interfaces with the fields on the end user's web browser at run time. In addition to connecting to the business server, CGI applications must run on the web server platform and conform to the CGI specification. CGI applications can be written in any high-level programming language.

In contrast to server-side solutions, client-side solutions do not introduce the web paradigm into the overall client/server architecture. In this model, the web server acts as a distribution server to distribute a copy of the business client to the user's computer through the web. The client application then runs locally on the web client just as in a traditional client/server environment. The server-side web application architecture is illustrated in Figure 10-9.

There are currently two main technologies used to develop web-distributed applications: JAVA and ActiveX.

Java Originally developed as a programming language for hand-held devices, Java was developed by Sun Microsystems in the mid-1990s. **Java** is a general purpose, object-oriented, high-level programming language. Roughly based on C++ in terms of syntax and command structure, Java has a simplified command structure designed to ease application development and reduce many common programming errors.

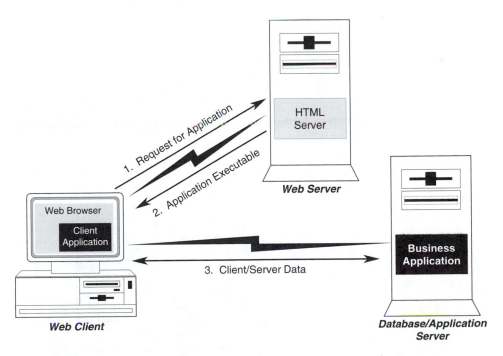

Figure 10-9 Server-Side Web Application Architecture

The major difference between Java and other high-level programming languages is the manner in which the completed application is executed on the client. Java is an interpreted language. Rather than being directly compiled into an executable, Java applications are compiled into **bytecode,** an intermediate format capable of running on any platform that supports a Java interpreter, or **virtual machine.** Figure 10-10 illustrates the JAVA run-time environment.

By using Java, a programmer can write a single client application that can be run on any client regardless of hardware or software platform providing the client supports a Java virtual machine. As virtual machines are included in the latest versions of all major web browsers, a user merely has to click on an item on a web page and the application is automatically downloaded to the computer and executed. By using Java, almost all client distribution issues can be eliminated. The downloaded Java executable is often referred to as a Java applet. An **applet** is a small application that runs inside of another application. In this case, the Java applet is running on the virtual machine inside of the web browser.

While the ability to configure a client to automatically download a portable application and execute it directly on the client greatly simplifies software distribution, it creates the potential for serious security problems. Because the applet is running directly on the client computer, the potential exists for it to damage or steal data from the client's storage system. Such applets are referred to as malicious or hostile applets and will be discussed in more detail in Chapter 16, "Local Area Network Security." Java addresses these issues by limiting the client system resources a Java applet can address. In a Java virtual machine, a limited environment called the **sandbox** is created for the exclusive use of the applet. The applet cannot access any system resources beyond the domain of the sandbox.

Although Java represents an architecturally efficient method of creating web-enabled client applications, it is currently somewhat of a limited programming environment. Because of its hardware independence and the limitations of the sandbox, mechanisms to write to local disk or access a local printer are highly limited. In order to accomplish these functions, the Java

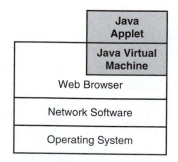

Figure 10-10   JAVA Run-Time Environment

programmer must often make calls directly to the underlying system. However, such action leads to the application being tied directly to a specific hardware/software platform, effectively removing one of the chief advantages of Java. If these issues can be resolved, the write-once-run-anywhere nature of Java, combined with the ease of web-based software distribution, could combine to make Java a serious contender for business client application development.

JAVASCRIPT

Practical Advice and Information

JavaScript is the name of a scripting language, originally named LiveScript, developed by Netscape Communications. After Java gained popularity, Sun and Netscape renamed LiveScript to JavaScript to capitalize on the market appeal of the Java name. In fact, Java and JavaScript have little in common other than the name *Java* and their ability to run on multiple operating systems.

JavaScript is an interpreted scripting language. The main function of JavaScript is to allow multiple parts of a web page to work together to form a cohesive whole. Using JavaScript, parameters can be sent to a Java application based on the result of other web page activity.

ActiveX   An alternative web application development environment is **ActiveX** from Microsoft. While the term *ActiveX* actually refers to a wide variety of distributed software technologies including the Component Object Model (COM) and the Distributed Component Object Model (DCOM), the key ActiveX technologies for building web-based applications are ActiveX Controls.

An extension of Object Layering and Embedding (OLE) custom controls, ActiveX controls are precompiled software objects that can be embedded into other applications. ActiveX controls can be written in a variety of programming languages including C, C++, Visual BASIC, and Java. They can be embedded into any application that supports DCOM, including web browsers, productivity applications, and high-level programming environments such as Visual BASIC or Smalltalk. By using ActiveX controls a web designer can add local functionality to a web page, making it look and feel more like an application running on the user's local computer.

Distribution of ActiveX controls depends on the application within which they are embedded. For high-level programming environments such as Visual BASIC, the control is distributed with the executable. For web-based applications, the web page designer references the control from within the web page. Upon loading the web page, the web browser will check if the control is present on the client. If so, it is executed. If not, the browser downloads a copy of the control to the client, then executes the control.

In sharp contrast to Java applets that play in a specific sandbox, ActiveX controls are designed to interface directly with the operating system. They are therefore operating system dependent rather than being platform independent. Although this ability allows ActiveX Controls to perform tasks that require direct system interaction such as printing and disk access, it constitutes a potential security exposure. A hostile ActiveX control could be written that erases all of the data from the client's disk drive. This exposure is relatively low for high-level programming environments, because all of the required ActiveX controls are distributed with the application. However, the risk is substantially higher for web pages that download controls through the network.

To minimize the risk of downloading a hostile control, ActiveX uses a security model known as **trust.** Before a web browser downloads an ActiveX control it displays a digitally signed certificate that acts as an authentication tool by stating who developed the control and its function. The user then has the option of downloading and installing the application or deciding not to execute the object. From a practical perspective, a user can trust that ActiveX controls coming from a known server are safe. Java applets are also beginning to make use of trust security as the need to access system resources increases.

To build web-based applications using ActiveX controls, a web page designer creates a basic web page layout and adds references to the required ActiveX controls using HTML. The various controls and other elements of the page are then tied together into a cohesive application through the use of VBScript, a scripting language based on Visual BASIC. Web-based applications built using these technologies offer exceptional integration between components, but they will only run on Microsoft Windows operating systems.

XML Regardless of whether CGI, Java, or ActiveX is used to develop a web-based application, some type of markup language must be used to define the basic structure of the page. The HyperText Markup Language **(HTML)** is currently the standard markup language for the web.

HTML was originally designed to provide a means of structuring document content and controlling document presentation. Implemented as a compromise between these two functions, HTML currently has limited capabilities in both areas. In response to the shortcomings of HTML in the presentation area, browser vendors expanded HTML to include presentation management functionality. Elements that control the font type of the text and various layout elements were added to the language. Despite these changes, HTML remains a very limited language in terms of controlling document presentation.

In response to these shortcomings, browser vendors have adopted a new mechanism to separate content structure and document presentation. To separate presentation and content, document presentation is controlled by cascading style sheets while document structure is defined by HTML. By separating presentation and content, it becomes significantly easier to update either aspect of a web page. The roles of content generation can be divided among several people with assurances that the resulting web pages will have a consistent look and feel.

The use of style sheets can greatly improve HTML's presentation management ability, but HTML also has shortcomings in the area of document structuring. One of the issues is that HTML is not extensible: there is no means of creating user-defined elements, thus limiting a web page designer's ability to cleanly structure data. If a web page designer is developing content about cars, they must manually manage and format all of the information about each aspect of every car.

If a means of creating user-defined elements is provided, the web page designer could define data **tags** for body styles, engines, transmissions, and other aspects of a car. The information within the web page could then be structured (and ultimately formatted) based on these tags. Upon opening the web page, the browser would download the tag description, enabling it to properly process the page content.

The **eXtensible Markup Language (XML)** solves these issues by adding extensibility to web page design. Rooted in the Standard Generalized Markup Language (SGML), the same language that originally spawned HTML, XML has the potential of easing the creation and structuring of data on the web while maintaining the same basic feel as HTML. XML also eases the task of building web-based applications that share data between multiple applications. As long as the applications agree on a common set of user-defined tags, the structured XML data can be used as an intermediate file format to transfer complex data structures between applications across the web. However, XML is not a direct replacement for HTML. In most applications XML would contain the document content, while HTML would retain control over document presentation.

Despite the technical advantages associated with XML, it remains to be seen if the language will ever gain widespread adoption. The sheer volume of existing HTML code and the number of designers who are familiar with HTML development ensure HTML's short-term market dominance. With new features consistently being added to HTML, it is possible that HTML may evolve into an extensible markup language in its own right. If that is the case, however, the odds are high that it would share much with XML.

Network Computers   One of the key issues associated with the application, administration, and maintenance of client/server computing technologies has been cost. Client/server computing technologies have certainly allowed systems to be created that have had a significant positive impact on business operations, but operating cost has almost universally exceeded estimates.

There are three major expense categories associated with the deployment of distributed client applications platforms: initial implementation costs, user training costs, and administration and maintenance costs. Collectively these costs are referred to as **total cost of ownership.** In order to make the client/server computing model more affordable, each aspect of total cost of ownership must be addressed.

Traditionally, initial implementation costs were considered the largest expense associated with the deployment of distributed systems. This category includes the cost of computer hardware, operating systems, application software, and required network infrastructure. Easy to quantify and cost justify, initial implementation costs are commonly used as the economic model upon which client/server decisions are made.

Unfortunately, initial implementation costs are just the tip of the iceberg in terms of total cost of ownership. Over the life of the client, system administration and maintenance costs have been proven to reach up to four times the initial implementation cost. The high cost of administration and maintenance is the result of the high labor quotient of these tasks. At a time when the demand for people with such training is outpacing supply, the overall cost of administration and maintenance is consistently trending upward.

Many factors combine to make client system administration and maintenance such a labor-intensive, significant expense. The personal computer technology typically used for network clients is inherently difficult to configure and troubleshoot. The operating system must be installed locally and the network interfaces must be properly configured before the client can participate on the network. To make matters worse, configuration files are typically stored locally on the machine where any user can alter them either intentionally or by attempting to install additional software.

After the client system is initially configured, application software must be installed before it can be deployed into the field. Although there are now methods to automate this process (as mentioned in a previous section), a systems administrator must test and debug each installation procedure prior to releasing it to the network. Then whenever a change is made to any deployed application, each client system must be upgraded, often all at one time to ensure data integrity.

Another issue with traditional client/server computing is that clients require a personal computer. For users who only need to run a few basic programs, the power of a complete personal computer platform, with the configuration and administrative costs associated with it, is often overkill. Rather than deploying a personal computer for such applications, a specialized computer designed to run a few applications over the network would suffice. This new paradigm is known as **network computing.**

There are many different opinions as to what constitutes network computing. At the low end are computer platforms that have minimal memory, no disk storage, and an operating system specifically designed to run software downloaded at application run time. Such systems, known as **NCs**, or Network Computers, include a Java-based OS designed to run Java applications. As illustrated in Figure 10-11, in NC environments, all configuration information and applications are kept in a centralized location and sent across the network as required, eliminating almost all client configuration and software distribution issues. A consortium of companies including Sun Microsystems, Oracle, Apple, IBM, Netscape, and Acorn are currently supporting the development of NCs built around the Java model.

Although Java applications fit the NC model well, they are unable to run existing Windows applications. Users who have an investment in existing

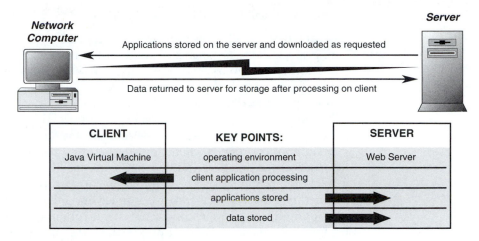

Figure 10-11   Network Computer Architecture

Windows applications could alternatively investigate **Windows terminals.** Windows terminals are similar to Java-based NCs, since they also contain a minimal amount of hardware and software. However, instead of running the application locally, Windows terminals act as a graphical terminal for Windows applications running on a remote host. As shown in Figure 10-12, this approach is conceptually similar to mainframe style processing. Terminals display the output of client applications running on a remote host and serve as input devices to the remote client application.

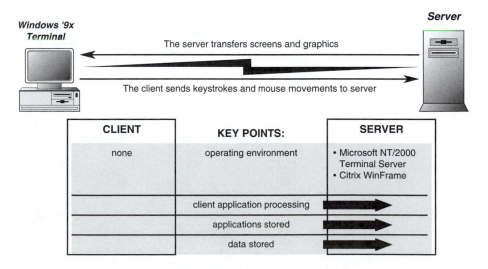

Figure 10-12   Windows Terminal Architecture

Practical Advice and Information

WINDOWS TERMINAL SERVER CONFIGURATION

Windows terminal servers or hosts are typically Windows NT servers running special software such as Citrix Win-Frame or Microsoft Terminal Server, previously known as Hydra. Because the server must execute the applications for all of the attached Windows terminals, a Windows terminal server can support far fewer clients than a typical Windows file server. Although the exact number of clients a server can support will depend on the nature of the applications executed, most Windows terminal manufacturers recommend no more than 50 clients be attached to a single server, with 15 clients per server the practical limit for most early installations.

When configuring servers for use in supporting Windows terminals, it is imperative that adequate processor speed and memory be provided. A server configured to support 50 concurrent clients running Office 97 would require a multiprocessor server with approximately one gigabyte of memory.

At the opposite end of the network computing spectrum are **Net PCs.** Net PCs are low-end personal computers optimized to run applications from a network file server. Similar in concept to diskless workstations, these platforms are designed to run existing Windows applications directly on the distributed platform. The main difference between Net PC clients and full-featured PC clients is that Net PCs are designed from the ground up to be centrally administered. Like NCs and Windows terminals, they boot across the network and rely on the server to maintain their configuration information. The Net PC architecture is illustrated in Figure 10-13.

NCs, Windows Terminals, and Net PCs are all designed for deployment in areas where a few basic applications are required. General applications

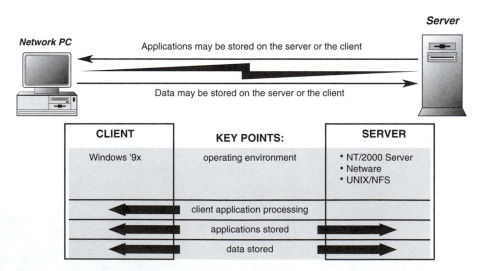

Figure 10-13   Net PC Architecture

such as word processing and web browsing, along with specific applications such as a bank teller application or customer service application, are excellent candidates for these technologies. For larger applications such as computer-aided design or environments that require a large number of supported applications, traditional PC clients will continue to the platform of choice.

Managerial Perspective

DOES NETWORK COMPUTING REPRESENT THE END OF THE PC?

Although none of these network computing technologies are going to make personal computers obsolete anytime in the near future, they have resulted in the development of many new technologies designed to make distributed personal computer systems easier to administer and maintain. Microsoft has announced the Zero Administration Windows effort and Novell has responded with Zero Effort Networking. Each of these initiatives includes multiple utilities designed to reduce the effort and cost associated with supporting distributed PC systems. These initiatives to reduce the total cost of ownership of client/server systems will be the legacy of network computing systems regardless of the final level of network computing technology adoption.

Practical Advice and Information

NETWORK IMPACT OF NETWORK COMPUTING

Network computing techniques can greatly reduce administration and maintenance expenses for small homogeneous environments, but they do so at the cost of increased network traffic. At a bare minimum these devices boot and transfer configuration information and applications across the network. In the case of Windows terminals, whenever the user enters data or the screen is updated, data are sent between the terminal and the host. Special care must be exercised in the design and implementation of data networks that will support these technologies.

■ INTEGRATION WITH EXISTING APPLICATIONS

Third-Party Software

Rather than developing extensive client/server based business applications in-house, many companies are purchasing complete systems from external vendors. Although these systems represent a significant investment, they are typically less expensive than hiring a team of programmers to design, develop, test, and debug a custom application suite. Another major reason for purchasing business systems is implementation time. A third-party application can be selected and installed in less time than most development efforts can define system objectives and modules.

There are many different third-party business application suites available in the marketplace, but three applications represent the majority of the packaged business software market: BAAN, Peoplesoft, and SAP R/3. A brief description of each of these products is shown in Figure 10-14.

Although third-party software has the potential to significantly reduce development and implementation expenses, there are potential drawbacks that must be considered before making a purchase decision. One of the key issues with purchased software is configuration and extensibility. Most third-party application suites support modularized modification through the use of scripting languages. In this manner, modifications can be made within the structure of the application without modifying the application's source code. Such modifications can typically be carried forward into new versions of the software without causing compatibility issues.

If customers need to add functionality that exceeds the capability of the configuration and scripting capabilities of the application, they may need to write a separate application. Such a custom application would access the underlying data structures of the purchased application. The purchased application is left unmodified, allowing an easy upgrade path, while the customer is able to add the required functionality into the system. With this approach it is typically better to write the custom application to access data through a vendor-defined API. All major application suite vendors support such an API through which a customer can access data from custom applica-

Vendor	Major Product	Application Areas
BAAN	BAAN	• Manufacturing • Finance • Project • Distribution/Transportation • Service
Peoplesoft	Peoplesoft	• Human Resource • Financials • Distribution • Materials Management • Manufacturing • Supply Chain Management • Student Administration
SAP	R/3	• Accounting and Controlling • Production and Materials Management • Quality Management and Plant Maintenance • Sales and Distribution • Human Resources Management • Project Management

Figure 10-14 Major Third Party Applications

tions. By using the customer API, the custom application developer is assured that data integrity will remain intact.

If the needs of the custom application exceed the ability of the API to deliver data or if the customer wishes to create an application that will run independently of the purchased application, the custom application can be written to directly access and potentially modify the purchased application's database. This approach requires extensive knowledge of the data structures and operation of the purchased application. The application programmer must be careful to properly lock any data resources opened for write access and minimize the duration that any such resources are locked, since the main application is expecting to control access to the data store.

Writing custom applications to interface with purchased applications either through the application's API or directly through the application's data store requires significant knowledge of the purchased application. Since such in-depth knowledge is usually beyond a new customer, consulting firms that specialize in the development of such custom solutions have entered the marketplace. In fact, many companies that implement purchased solutions contract the implementation and operation of the systems to such consulting firms, thus eliminating the need to train operations personnel to maintain the application.

Although purchased solutions are gaining in popularity, most organizations continue to maintain their own proprietary business solutions. This is particularly evident in niche industries where the marketplace is too small for the major application developers to realize an adequate return on their investment.

Legacy Applications

Before the advent of client/server computing, most business applications ran on **mainframe** systems. Unlike client/server systems that distribute processing among multiple computers, mainframe systems centralize all processing on a large central computer. This computer is responsible for maintaining the data and running applications to access and modify the data for each user. Users connect to the mainframe from terminals through specialized communications networks designed and optimized for terminal traffic. Mainframe applications are commonly referred to as **legacy applications** because they predate client/server development efforts.

Legacy applications represent the majority of the business systems at most companies. Typically written in COBOL, many of these applications are decades old and have been extensively modified through the years. While they are sometimes patched together, these systems are typically very effective at performing the business functions of the company. Rather than replacing these venerable workhorses, companies are looking for ways to develop client applications that access the data processing capabilities and existing data stores of their mainframes.

Managerial Perspective

MAINFRAMES AREN'T DEAD YET

It has been estimated that as of December 1997, more than 80% of corporate data remain on mainframes. While client/server computing continues to gain popularity, mainframe applications will remain significant for the foreseeable future.

The process of taking a legacy application and making its functionality and data accessible in a client/server environment is known as **wrapping** the application. A new software envelope that hides the actual implementation details from the end user is developed to surround the legacy application. Wrapping can be considered the process of developing new user interfaces for existing legacy applications. There are many applications for wrapping.

- Making legacy applications available in client/server environments
- Enabling client applications to access existing mainframe data
- Creating a single application from a group of related legacy applications
- Eliminating access to parts of a host application
- Making legacy systems amenable to new productivity tool technologies such as business process reengineering and workflow management

There are four main methods of wrapping legacy systems into client/server environments:

- Database wrapping
- API wrapping
- Scripting
- Screen scrapers

Database wrapping is the process of developing a new client application that integrates with the legacy system directly through the legacy application's data store. When accessing a mainframe data store, care has to be taken to ensure data integrity, because most legacy systems do not use relational database technologies. Data are kept in indexed files, and resource locking and data integrity are the responsibility of the legacy application itself, which is why database wrapping typically only allows read only access to the legacy data. Database wrapping is illustrated in Figure 10-15.

However, the ability to read legacy data can be extremely useful. Applications can be built that periodically pull data from the legacy application into relational database structures that can be queried by multiple client

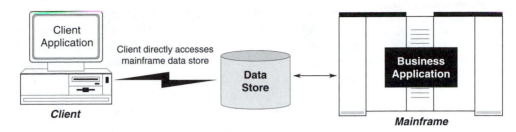

Figure 10-15   Database Wrapping

applications. Customer service applications can be written that allow a customer service representative to easily see all pertinent data about a customer's account on a single screen, regardless of the legacy systems that maintain each data point. This process can be extended to allow a customer to connect via a Touch-Tone phone or via the web to access account data.

Many legacy applications have their own APIs designed to allow other legacy applications to exchange information. For these applications, an **API wrapper** can be built to convert between client application calls and legacy application functions. From the perspective of the legacy application, the wrapper is viewed as another mainframe application, whereas the wrapper application is viewed as an application server from the perspective of the distributed client. As shown in Figure 10-16, the application acts as a gateway, converting between requests from the client and API calls for the legacy application.

API wrapping allows significant flexibility in the creation of client/server systems, but there are several issues. As each invocation of a legacy application typically served one user, supporting multiple client applications through an API wrapper can create data consistency problems. When an error occurs in the legacy application, it must be properly handled to preserve data integrity and inform the final client application of the severity and result of the error condition.

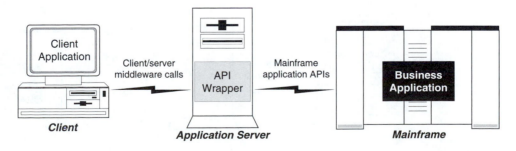

Figure 10-16   API Wrapping

Some legacy applications do not have an API. Such applications, typically smaller in scope, have multiple command line options that can be specified when the application is executed. Depending on the option given, the application performs different tasks. As illustrated in Figure 10-17, **script wrapper** can be used to interface to these types of legacy applications. Similar to an API wrapper, a script wrapper executes the legacy application for each potential command line flag. This can lead to difficulties with the handling of varying complex I/O and potential performance problems on both the application server and the legacy system.

For legacy applications that cannot be accessed in any other way, a screen driven interface can be developed to execute the legacy application and exchange data fields between the terminal screen and the client application. A **screen scraper** is a piece of software used to provide interaction between a legacy application and a client through the terminal screen interface originally designed for human use of the legacy system. As shown in Figure 10-18, the screen scraper presents an API to the application programmer and emulates a user terminal session to the business application. From the perspective of the mainframe application, the screen scraper appears as a human operator.

The screen scraper converts between API calls for the client application and data screens for the mainframe application. Depending on the characteristics of the mainframe application(s) being accessed, the screen scraper may have maintain multiple virtual terminal sessions with the mainframe(s). Due to the significant overhead associated with screen scraping, it should be used only as a last resort when no other methods of wrapping a legacy application are available.

SNA/LAN Integration   Before any of the listed legacy application techniques can be implemented, a means of communicating with the mainframe must be implemented. Originally designed as multi-user platforms, mainframes were designed to interact with users via stand-alone terminals rather than via a peer-to-peer network. Strictly speaking, micro-mainframe connectivity and internetworking are two different concepts. In **micro-mainframe con-**

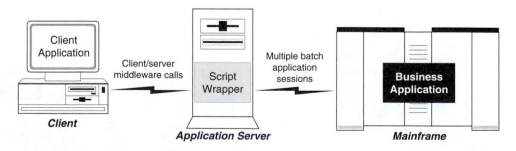

Figure 10-17   Script Wrapping

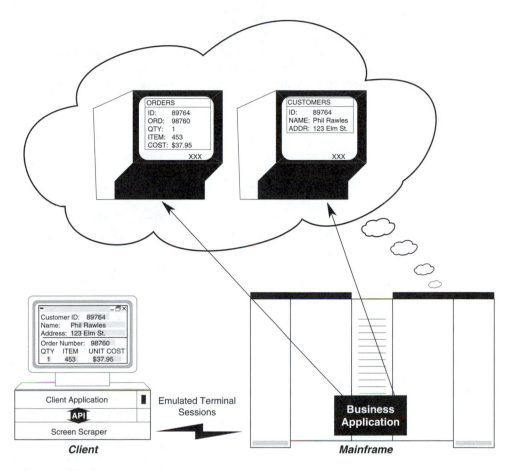

Figure 10-18   Screen Scraping

nectivity, the micro (Standalone or LAN-attached PC) pretends to be or "emulates" a mainframe terminal such as an **IBM 3270** attached and logged into the mainframe. Although file transfer utilities may allow more capability than mere remote login, this is not the peer-to-peer networking implied by the term *internetworking*.

With full **peer-to-peer internetworking,** the PC can exchange data with any mainframe or any other PC on a host-to-host level rather than acting like a "dumb" terminal as in the case of micro-mainframe connectivity. Although these two mainframe connectivity alternatives have their differences, they still have much in common. The truth is that most "IBM Shops" have a mixture of 3270 terminal connections, mainframes, and LANs that must communicate with each other on a number of different levels.

IBM, the largest vendor of mainframe systems, uses a hierarchical network called SNA (Systems Network Architecture) to connect terminals and other devices to the mainframe. SNA is centered around the mainframe. If two devices other than the mainframe on an SNA network wanted to communicate, they would have to establish, maintain, and terminate that communication through the mainframe. This model is in direct contrast to the peer-to-peer network communications structure used in most LANs.

SUMMARY

There are many different ways to write and deploy client/server applications. Traditional client and server applications can be developed using procedural languages, event-driven languages, or object-oriented languages. Regardless of the development method used, client applications must be distributed throughout the network in some manner. Although some techniques are available to reduce the labor-intensive nature of delivering and maintaining distributed applications, it still represents a considerable portion of the total cost of ownership of client/server systems.

In an effort to ease software distribution and reduce the cost of maintenance, some companies have turned to web technologies. The web can be used as either a "terminal" to a client application running on the web server or as a means of distributing the client application through the network. These technologies have been further extended to create a new class of network computing devices that function only as network-based clients. Although these devices can function well for specific applications, they are not going to replace personal computers in the near term, if ever.

Mainframes still maintain the majority of corporate data. There are several methods of creating client applications that access this data, ranging from directly attaching to the mainframe's data store to creating applications that work with a terminal emulator to interact with existing mainframe applications. Before a client can interact with a mainframe, a means of physically communicating with the mainframe must be in place. Because most mainframe systems in the marketplace run IBM's SNA network, this means a technique to convert between SNA and LAN protocols must be installed.

With all of these choices for developing and deploying client/server applications, it might appear difficult to make a development decision. However, the best development method is usually easily distinguishable as long as the developer remembers that the method chosen should be based upon the requirements of the application in question.

KEY TERMS

Activex	BASIC	C++
API wrapper	Broadcast filtering	CASE
Applet	Bytecode	Central Directory Server
APPN	C	CGI

Channel-Attached Gateways
COBOL
Compiler
Data-Link Switching
Database wrapping
Delphi
DLUR/S
Encapsulation
End nodes
Event
Event handler
Functions
Gateway
High-level languages
HTML
IBM 3270
Inheritance interface
Instances
Instantiation
Interfaces
Interpreter

Java
Legacy applications
Low-level languages
Machine Language Assembly
Language
Mainframe
Methods
Micro-mainframe
Connectivity
NC
Net PC
Network computing
Network nodes
Object oriented
OCX
Parameters
Pascal
Peer-to-peer internetworking
Poll spoofing
Procedural language
Protocol conversion

Proxy polling
Sandbox
Screen scraper
Script wrapper
SDLC conversion
Smalltalk
State
Structured programming
Subroutines
Tags
TCP/IP encapsulation
Total Cost of Ownership
Trust
Virtual machine
Visual BASIC
Window manager
Windows terminal
Wrapping
XML

REVIEW QUESTIONS

1. What is a low-level language?
2. List two types of low-level languages.
3. What is a compiler?
4. What is an interpreter?
5. Which provides faster application execution, an interpreter or a compiler?
6. What are the characteristics of a procedural language?
7. What is structured programming?
8. Compare and contrast a function and a subroutine.
9. List procedural languages and the applications for which they are best suited.
10. Who controls program execution in an event-driven application environment?
11. What is an event handler?
12. What is the function of the window manager?
13. List two event-driven languages.
14. What is the difference between an object-based programming language and an object-oriented programming language?
15. What is the difference between classes and instances?
16. What is inheritance?
17. Which object-oriented programming language has the best object model?
18. Which object-oriented programming language used to require a pre-compiler?
19. What is a CASE tool?
20. Will CASE tools replace programmers?
21. What development languages are most commonly used to develop server applications?
22. How are server applications most commonly distributed?
23. What development languages are most commonly used to develop client applications?
24. List two problems associated with the distribution of client applications.
25. For automatic distribution of client applications to be cost-effective, what conditions must be met?
26. How is CGI implemented in a client/server environment?
27. Compare and contrast server-side and client-side web-based solutions.
28. What is a Java virtual machine?
29. What is the main appeal of Java?
30. How closely are Java and JavaScript related?

31. What is the security model used with ActiveX?
32. Compare and contrast Java and ActiveX.
33. In terms of markup languages, what does the term *extensibility* mean?
34. Will XML replace HTML? Why or why not?
35. Explain total cost of ownership.
36. What are the three main categories of network computing?
37. Under what circumstances do network computers make sense?
38. Where does a client application run in a Windows terminal environment?
39. Compare and contrast NCs and NetPCs.
40. What is the impact on the network of network computing technologies?

41. List two methods of integrating with third-party applications.
42. What is a legacy application?
43. Explain database wrapping.
44. Explain API wrapping.
45. Explain script wrapping.
46. What is a screen scraper? How are they used?
47. What is SNA?
48. What does the term *3270 emulation* mean?
49. Which is less expensive: front-end processors or channel-attached gateways?
50. List four solutions to integrate SNA and local area networks.

ACTIVITIES

1. Research and report on assembly language.
2. Research structured programming techniques and prepare a guide to structured programming.
3. Investigate COBOL usage. Is COBOL truly going away?
4. Contact business application developers at your company or school and research the application development languages they're currently using.
5. Prepare a paper on object-oriented programming technologies.
6. Research CASE tools. Prepare a chart listing the major tools and their key features.
7. Visit the machine room at your company or school. Draw a map of the various servers and their purposes.
8. Research client software distribution strategies. What products currently on the market help automate this process?
9. Research total cost of ownership for distributed systems. Draw a pie chart that breaks total cost of ownership into categories.

10. Connect to a web site that uses CGI. Download the source HTML code and identify the embedded CGI commands.
11. Research Java. Prepare a report on the state of Java related to business application development.
12. Research ActiveX. What operating system environments currently support ActiveX?
13. Research SGML, the parent of both HTML and XML. Why is SGML not used for web page design?
14. Research third-party business software. Create a chart that describes the major third-party business software vendors and their products.
15. Research legacy application wrappers. What techniques are currently in use? Which products have the largest market share?
16. Contact the data center at your company or school. What techniques are they using to connect their LANs to their mainframes?

CASE STUDY

Thin Clients Transform National Semiconductor

National Semiconductor has been so impressed with the thin-client technology it has deployed over the past 18 months that the company this week is hosting a CIO get-together at its headquarters to show off its new computing environment.

The chip maker expects to save millions of dollars per year by converting end users' desktop systems from full-blown PCs to Windows-based terminals that rely on server-based applications. So far, the company has converted about 800 of its roughly 8,000 desktop systems to thin clients in one form or another.

But desktop savings aren't the only thing National plans to brag about to the Silicon Valley executives invited to view the company's data center and see how thin clients perform. The company says its thin-client environment enables the easy exchange of documents and attachments around the world because all users now have the same server-based version of applications such as Microsoft Word.

The thin-client scheme also supports the fast deployment of new and improved applications. That's because the IS group can now load software on a few servers instead of thousands of PCs.

Until recently, most of National's desktop machines were Windows PCs running Microsoft applications and some home-grown programs. About 18 months ago, incoming CIO Ulrich Seif and other top National executives decided that the company's computing environment needed to be more efficient and that costs had to be more controlled. That meant the emergence of a new corporatewide IS focus on centralizing operations and creating enforceable standards for all levels of computing, Seif says.

To meet these needs, managers decided on server standards, such as four-CPU Compaq (and now Dell) servers running Citrix Systems' WinFrame multiuser version of Windows NT and, in the future, Microsoft NT Server, Terminal Server Edition. The desktop standards include existing PCs running a client program that lets them access WinFrame servers or new Wyse Technologies Windows-based terminals powered by Cyrix MediaGX processors. The desktops can access a standard applications suite, including Microsoft Office.

National's internal studies concluded that each Windows PC cost the company between $7,500 and $8,000 each year over the course of the PC's life. That figure, which accounts for everything from software upgrades to support costs, stunned executives.

"It was very hard to glue credibility to that number," says Kay Marsh, National's manager of desktop integration.

Based on the company's experience to date, the thin-client model cuts about $2,000 from the average desktop cost.

This is not to say that the thin-client deployment has been simple. To forestall a rebellion among the company's PC users, National allowed end users to move to terminals on a voluntary basis and simply added a small client program to existing PCs. The program let PC users access WinFrame servers and see firsthand how much faster the same software ran on the powerful servers.

Another challenge has been to pump up network bandwidth to support increased traffic between clients and servers. National has deployed 10/100Base-T technology, including switches, to keep traffic flowing.

Source: John Cox, "Thin Clients Transform National Semiconductor," *Network World*, vol. 15, no. 48 (November 30, 1998), p. 19. Copyright (November 30, 1998), Network World.

BUSINESS CASE STUDY QUESTIONS

Activities

1. Complete a top-down model for this case by gleaning facts from the case and placing them in the proper layer of the top-down model. After completing the top-down model, analyze and detail those instances where requirements were clearly passed down from upper layers to lower layers of the model and where solutions to those requirements were passed up from lower layers to upper layers of the model.
2. Detail any questions about the case that may occur to you for which answers are not clearly stated in the article.

Business

1. What was the business reason for implementing the thin client system?
2. How much money does National Semiconductor feel they save on each client per year?

Application

1. What applications are supported on the network?
2. On which operating systems do the applications run?

Data

1. What type of data is carried on the network?
2. Is the amount of data carried increased or decreased as a result of the new system?

Network

1. How many locations does National Semiconductor have using the new system?
2. What is the scope of the network?

Technology

1. What thin client technology is currently being used?
2. What thin client technology is planned for future use?

CHAPTER 11

LOCAL AREA NETWORK APPLICATIONS SOFTWARE

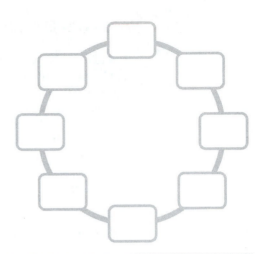

Concepts Reinforced

OSI Model
Protocols and Standards
Client/Server Technology Model

Top-Down Model
Hardware/Software Compatibility
Network Architectures

Concepts Introduced

LAN Software Architecture
LAN Productivity Software
GroupWare
Network Backup
Electronic Software Distribution
E-Mail

LAN Resource Management
 Software
Multi-Protocol Network Printing
Network Faxing
License and Inventory
 Management

OBJECTIVES

After mastering the material in this chapter you should:

1. Understand the categorization of GroupWare and LAN resource management software

2. Understand the analysis involved in properly applying GroupWare and LAN resource management software

3. Understand the compatibility issues involved with implementing LAN software

4. Understand the functionality and potential business impact of GroupWare and LAN Resource Management Software

◼ INTRODUCTION

Local Area Network application software is software that operates only in a LAN environment. LAN software is distinguished from other application software by its ability to communicate across the LAN between clients and servers, between two or more servers, and/or to enterprise management workstations. In other words, software that can be run on a stand-alone machine is by definition not LAN software. Although most software is now "LAN aware," with optional features that run only in a LAN environment, the software discussed in this chapter can only be run on LAN attached computers.

◼ LAN SOFTWARE ARCHITECTURE

In order to organize and illustrate the interrelationships among the various categories of LAN software, a **LAN Application Software Architecture** as illustrated in Figure 11-1 can be constructed. **Application software** on a LAN is divided into client front-ends and server back-ends or engines and is concerned with accomplishment of a specific type of task or transaction. LAN applications software can be divided into two major subcategories: GroupWare and LAN resource management software.

GroupWare is the name of a category of software that seeks to take advantage of the fact that workers are networked together electronically in order to increase communication and maximize worker productivity. In other words, this is the software that people use to not only get their work done, but more important, to get their work done more quickly, effectively, accurately, or at a lower cost than if they did not have the benefit of this software.

In contrast to the user focus of GroupWare, **LAN resource management software** provides access and management to shared network resources and services. Examples of such shared network-attached resources include printers, fax machines, CD-ROMs, modems, and a variety of other devices and services.

Two overlying elements required in any LAN software configuration are security and management. **Security** is especially important in networked, LAN software environments, as logged-in users can be physically dispersed over large areas. Increased deployment of remote workers has led to increased need for remote access to corporate information resources. As important corporate data are transferred over network links, precautions must be taken to prevent unauthorized access to transmitted data, as well as to corporate networks and computer systems.

Finally, **management software** is incorporated into the network to provide a single, consolidated view of all networked resources, both hardware and software. From a single location, all of the distributed elements that comprise today's client/server information systems must be able to be effectively monitored and managed. This single enterprise management platform

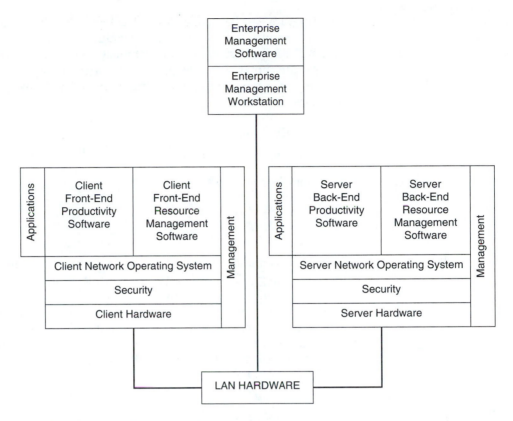

Figure 11-1   LAN Software Architecture

must be able to integrate management information from not just networking components, but also application programs, database management systems, and client and server hardware.

■ GROUPWARE

Because it is impossible to give an exhaustive review of each of the major categories of GroupWare within the space constraints of a reasonably sized text, a practical approach from the perspective of a network analyst will be offered while focusing primarily on the following key areas:

- Key current issues and trends in each GroupWare category that are important to the network analyst

- Examples of how each category of GroupWare actually increases worker productivity

- Key criteria for GroupWare product decisions and recommendations

GroupWare can be defined as technologies that allow people to work together electronically to become more productive and increase communication regardless of physical location or time. GroupWare products are collaborative products that allow people to work together and share information in a variety of ways. There are four fundamental technologies that Group-Ware builds on:

- Electronic mail

- Calendaring and scheduling

- Workflow

- Conferencing

- Electronic meeting support

Each of these technologies will be covered in detail throughout this section. Although no single GroupWare product incorporates all of the preceding technologies, products are becoming more advanced and are incorporating new technologies while improving upon the technologies already included.

There are several benefits to implementing GroupWare technologies. The benefits outlined in Figure 11-2 can be achieved if the top-down model has been followed to first identify the business objectives and what is to be accomplished with the new technology.

Benefit	Example/Explanation
Increase Information Access	• Employees can obtain timely information and increase their communication and collaboration efforts with others.
Eliminate Redundant Information	• By using GroupWare technology a company can have one "container" of information.
Improve Business Processes	• Companies can improve their business processes and in doing so can enhance their customer service, improve communication, and reduce costs.
Automate Routine Processes	• This can increase productivity by allowing employees to work on other duties instead of doing routine processes over and over.
Improve Decision Making	• By having one "container" of information people know where to get the information they need in order to make decisions. This can increase customer service and make a company more flexible and make it easier for them to respond to changes and opportunities.
Increase Organizational Learning	• By allowing employees to have access to the latest company information along with historical data on the company, increased learning and cross-training will develop.

Figure 11-2   Benefits Associated with GroupWare

Potential Problem	Example/Explanation
Not Enough Properly Trained People	• Since GroupWare is a relatively new technology, the number of properly trained people in the business community is limited.
Lack of Upper Management Support	• Get support from top-level managers before implementing the GroupWare technology so that employees can see that management is not only behind the idea but also using the technology themselves.
No Clear Business Objective	• Many companies fall into the trap of buying new technology but having no predetermined business need for it. Make sure to use the top-down model to ensure that the implemented technology meets the defined business objectives.
Confusion As to What GroupWare Really Is and What It Really Does	• This goes back to the problem of having very few educated businesspeople who really understand how GroupWare technology works.
Lack of Standards	• This can make a company have to rely on one given vendor, which doesn't sit well with many companies.
Lack of Affordability	• GroupWare is a client/server technology and with any new client/server technology there are training and support costs involved, so many small and mid-size companies can't afford GroupWare.
Less Human Interaction	• GroupWare technologies can lead to reduced human interaction and reduced socialization, which is an important aspect of business. Also, it is much easier to misinterpret electronic communication than it is to misinterpret face-to-face communication.
Resistance to Change	• People get used to doing their job one way and don't like it when new technology is introduced that will change the way they work. Plan for people to resist the new technology by having training sessions and discussion forums on how the new technology will be beneficial.

Figure 11-3   Negatives Associated with GroupWare

Along with the benefits of any new technology there are some problems that can arise. Some of the potential problems are outlined in Figure 11-3. These should be remembered when selecting or implementing GroupWare technology.

E-Mail

E-mail is the most commonly implemented GroupWare technology. In fact, most surveys show e-mail as the second most popular use of local area networks after printer and file services. Although many new users are frightened of e-mail technology initially, they quickly become convinced of the positive attributes of LAN-based e-mail:

- Correspondence can be accomplished on an ad hoc basis rather than having to coordinate face-to-face meetings, or catch persons at their desks for a phone call. The old game of telephone tag is effectively eliminated.

- E-mail enables more concise correspondence. People tend to get directly to the point in e-mail messages rather than engaging in idle conversation. These concise questions can be quickly answered.

- Overall productivity is increased as specific issues are handled via e-mail rather than an endless series of meetings, appointments, and lengthy conversations.

Managerial Perspective

E-MAIL IS A DOUBLE-EDGED SWORD IN TERMS OF PRODUCTIVITY

Although e-mail can greatly increase productivity by enabling the quick and easy exchange of information, it also enables the quick and easy forwarding of non-business material. One of the tangential effects of widespread e-mail deployment on the Internet is that the time it takes for a joke to cross the country has been reduced from months to a few days. Left unchecked, these nonproductive uses of e-mail quickly eliminate any productivity gains while increasing Internet bandwidth requirements.

A personal e-mail policy is helping to resolve this issue. It is difficult at best to completely eliminate all personal e-mail, but having a stated policy forces employees to consider their e-mail usage. Sometimes the perceived threat of monitoring is enough to entice employees to self moderate their e-mail usage.

E-mail is a **store-and-forward messaging technology.** Messages are sent, received, replied to, and delivered in discrete steps performed in a disjointed fashion over a period of time. This series of events is sometimes described as an asynchronous messaging system. In contrast, a phone conversation would be considered a synchronous messaging system since calling parties are speaking to each other in a "live" fashion: both parties must be available concurrently for the communication to take place.

E-mail systems can be categorized in a number of ways. One particularly effective technique is to divide e-mail functionality based on the user of function. In this manner e-mail functionality can be divided into two major subcategories: end-user features and administration features.

End-User Features   In order to understand which features are important to an e-mail system, one needs only to examine the types of things one ordinarily does when creating, mailing, receiving, sorting, storing, and retrieving paper-based correspondence. Effective e-mail systems should deliver the same functionality plus increased productivity enabled by the speed and electronic, computer-based nature of an e-mail system. End-user features of e-mail can be logically divided into four general categories:

- Features related to the ease with which e-mail can be created, addressed, and edited.

- Features related to how flexibly a variety of different types of files and documents can be attached to e-mail messages.

- Features related to how easily received e-mail can be organized for retrieval at a later time.

- Integration with supplementary or advanced systems such as scheduling systems or workflow automation systems.

Figure 11-4 summarizes some important end-user e-mail features according to the previous categorization.

Remote End-User Features   With the increased emphasis on mobile computing and virtual offices, the needs and constraints of remote or mobile e-mail users are becoming increasingly important. Chief among the constraints faced by remote e-mail users is the comparatively limited bandwidth offered by dial-up telecommunications services compared to local area network bandwidth. As a result, some e-mail systems offer specialized **remote e-mail client software** offering specialized features such as:

- Built-in phone number storage and communications software

- Support for large numbers of modem and wide area network services

- The ability to download only the headers of received e-mail which indicate the source, data, time, and subject of e-mail. Based on such header information the user can decide which messages to invest the time of downloading the message body. This feature conserves both bandwidth and time.

- The remote end-user client software can be automatically updated and synchronized with corporate-based e-mail that might be installed in a docking station or workstation at corporate headquarters.

Administration Features   Administration features can be logically divided into three subcategories:

- Installation features are concerned with such issues as how many platforms the e-mail system can operate and how easily the e-mail system can be implemented.

End-User Features Category	Features/Importance
E-Mail Creation, Editing, and Addressing	• Group addressing capabilities to easily send the same e-mail to a number of individuals • E-mail routing capabilities to control the order in which users receive, revise, and pass-along e-mail • E-mail flags and options: Urgent, Return receipt requested, Message delivery confirmation vs. message open and read confirmation • Private electronic Rolodex organization • Automatic e-mail replies "I won't be able to check e-mail for two weeks" • E-mail easily forwarded and/or replied to • Separate login, authentication and security system for e-mail system • Is the e-mail desktop environment customizable? Can custom toolbars be created for individual users which include icons for features most often used by a particular user? • Can rules be established that automatically handle incoming or outgoing messages? • Can e-mail be screened by administrative assistants or by the e-mail system? • Carbon copy, blind copy, priority setting • Can individual messages be encrypted or password protected?
E-Mail Attachments	• Types of files that can be attached for both sent and received mail • Multiple files can be attached to single e-mail message • Attachments can be saved and edited • Attachments can be encrypted
E-Mail Organization and Retrieval	• Multiple hierarchical folders for organization of e-mail by topic or project • Received e-mail can be sorted or selected by date, sender, topic, keywords, or message content
Integration with Supplementary Systems	• Integrated with scheduling system so that meeting requests are sent via e-mail system • Integrated with workflow automation software for automatic routing of attached documents • Integrated with FAX server sub-system so that messages and documents may be either faxed or e-mailed from a single screen • Integrated with voice-mail system so that voice messages can be digitized, stored on disk, listed along with e-mail in a single received messages in-box, and replayed • Integrated with forms design software so that customized forms can be created and routed via the e-mail system

Figure 11-4   E-Mail User Features

- Operation features are concerned with how easily can the system be maintained on an ongoing basis including ease of user administration, troubleshooting, security management, and message delivery management.

- Interoperability features are concerned with how easily the e-mail system can exchange e-mail and attachments with a variety of other e-mail systems. This is especially important with the increase in Internet e-mail.

E-Mail System Interoperability   E-mail is a client/server solution. The client portion of any e-mail system software runs on a particular type of client workstation to send and receive e-mail messages. **Multi-platform e-mail client software,** the first stage of interoperability for e-mail systems, can be objectively evaluated by the number of different computing platforms for which client e-mail software is available. In a similar fashion, the server portions of most e-mail systems can use the file management systems of numerous different network operating systems.

When an e-mail message created on one e-mail system needs to be sent to a destination workstation running a different e-mail system, some translation between the two systems is obviously necessary. This system-to-system translation is accomplished through specially written software known as **e-mail gateways.** E-mail systems vary in the number of e-mail gateways supported and whether or not the gateway software must be run on a dedicated server. Figure 11-5 summarizes key e-mail administration features.

E-Mail Systems Architectures   The end-user and administration features listed in the previous sections are the most overt evidence of e-mail system functionality. However, the underlying messaging architecture of the e-mail system can determine both how efficiently the e-mail system operates as the number of users increases and how easily the system can be managed. There are two primary messaging architectures for LAN-based e-mail products: Shared File E-Mail Systems and Client/Server E-Mail Systems.

In a **shared file e-mail system** architecture, the e-mail software uses the native file system included with the network operating system over which the e-mail software executes. This approach easily allows a single e-mail package to run over different network operating systems. Often, a single file server can be used for e-mail system operation for a given network, thereby affording relative ease of installation and operation. In this approach e-mail messages are simply files transferred to the proper destination post office, or file server, by **message transfer agent** software. To ensure rapid response, MTA software is usually run on a dedicated computer. The file server (post office) is frequently used only as a storage device in this type of e-mail system architecture and does not execute back-end e-mail engine software. As a result, it is the client-based e-mail software that must poll the post office (file server) periodically to see if any new mail (files) has arrived.

Administration Features Category	Features/Importance
Installation	• E-mail system can read network operating system UserID directories such as the NetWare bindery in order to ease establishment of e-mail UserIDs • Are User directories integrated so that only a single user account needs to be maintained? • Can a single e-mail user profile be copied to create multiple new e-mail UserIDs? • How easy is the e-mail server installation? • Is there a maximum number of mailboxes per post office?
Operation	• Is a separate login required to access the e-mail system? • Must separate e-mail system user accounts be maintained? • Are users automatically notified of newly received mail? • Can the administrator manage the e-mail system remotely? • Can the administrator manage multiple e-mail systems from single management console? • Can the administrator read all user e-mail? • Can the administrator limit connect times to/from remote post offices? • Can the administrator monitor statistics on links to remote post offices or clients? • Can the administrator track system usage by individuals or groups? • Can the administrator delete old messages? • Is a remote client module available to allow access via modem • Does the remote client module interface match the local client interface? • Does the remote client module cost additional money? • Can the mail system files be backed up while users are logged in? • Can the post office disks be compressed while the system is up?
Interoperability	• Availability of client software for: Macintosh, OS/2, UNIX, and VAX workstations? • Which network operating systems can the post office run over? Options: NetWare, Windows NT/2000, various flavors of UNIX • Availability of gateways to: NetWare E-Mail (MHS), AT&T Mail, CompuServe, IBM DISOSS, IBM PROFS, MCI Mail, Wang MailWay.X.400 • Options supported for inter-post office links: LAN-to-LAN, leased lines, dial-up lines, X.25, ISDN

Figure 11-5   E-Mail Administration Features

In **client/server e-mail systems,** the server plays a more active role in the operation and management of the e-mail system. Rather than just serving as a passive file-server used only for message storage, the server in a client/server e-mail messaging architecture executes specialized back-end e-mail engine software supporting real-time communication links to e-mail clients and other e-mail servers. Client/server e-mail systems interact with a network operating system's communication protocols rather than merely with its file management system. Allowing real-time communication between e-mail clients and servers on an as-needed basis eliminates the need for polling and its associated bandwidth usage. Due to the processing power provided by a server-based e-mail engine, client/server e-mail messaging architectures are more efficient in terms of installation, operation, and interoperability for larger numbers of users. Figure 11-6 illustrates some of the key architectural differences between shared-file and client/server e-mail messaging architectures.

Electronic Mail Standards   Before selecting e-mail software for a company to run on their clients and servers, it is important to spend some time researching and understanding the different standards, protocols, and APIs involved. Standards cover a broad area and can be defined in different ways. The most important standards related to messaging are explored in more depth below:

X.400—This standard was defined by the Consultative Committee for International Telephony & Telegraphy (CCITT). This standard was used mainly by large companies that have geographic locations around the globe. The X.400 standard covers the exchange of electronic messages between computer systems. It includes information on all of the three main areas handled by the messaging server. The X.400 standard is losing ground to the increasingly popular SMTP/MIME standard. This standard is described below.

X.500—This is also a CCITT standard. The X.500 standard is designed to provide directory information in a global setting. Many people feel the X.500 standard is too complex to use. Another standard regarding directory information is the Lightweight Directory Access Protocol (LDAP). LDAP is currently the favored protocol in directory access protocols.

LDAP—Lightweight Directory Access Protocol. This protocol is currently the favorite of directory access protocols. It can be used to consolidate personnel information profiles, application and device, and security management. It provides for a single point of administration across multiple directory systems.

SMTP—Simple Mail Transport Protocol. This messaging protocol is used in TCP/IP networks to exchange e-mail messages. In conjunction with TCP/IP, it is able to establish connections, provide reliable transport of messages, and terminate connections. SMTP is the e-mail language of the Internet and will continue to gain support as the Internet and intranets continue to grow.

Shared File EMAIL System

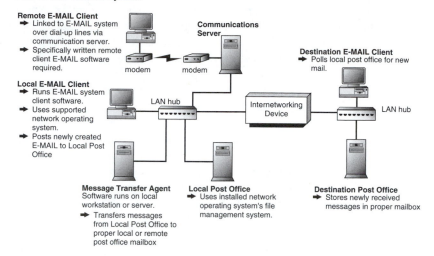

Remote E-MAIL Client
➡ Linked to E-MAIL system over dial-up lines via communication server.
➡ Specifically written remote client E-MAIL software required.

modem   modem

Communications Server

Destination E-MAIL Client
➡ Polls local post office for new mail.

Local E-MAIL Client
➡ Runs E-MAIL system client software.
➡ Uses supported network operating system.
➡ Posts newly created E-MAIL to Local Post Office

LAN hub

Internetworking Device

LAN hub

Message Transfer Agent
Software runs on local workstation or server.
➡ Transfers messages from Local Post Office to proper local or remote post office mailbox

Local Post Office
➡ Uses installed network operating system's file management system.

Destination Post Office
➡ Stores newly received messages in proper mailbox

Client/Server E-MAIL System

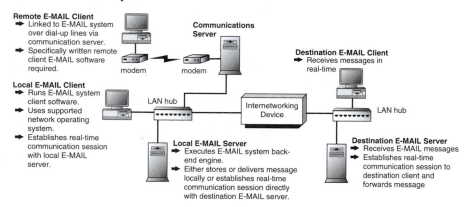

Remote E-MAIL Client
➡ Linked to E-MAIL system over dial-up lines via communication server.
➡ Specifically written remote client E-MAIL software required.

modem   modem

Communications Server

Destination E-MAIL Client
➡ Receives messages in real-time

Local E-MAIL Client
➡ Runs E-MAIL system client software.
➡ Uses supported network operating system.
➡ Establishes real-time communication session with local E-MAIL server.

LAN hub

Internetworking Device

LAN hub

Local E-MAIL Server
➡ Executes E-MAIL system back-end engine.
➡ Either stores or delivers message locally or establishes real-time communication session directly with destination E-MAIL server.

Destination E-MAIL Server
➡ Receives E-MAIL messages
➡ Establishes real-time communication session to destination client and forwards message

Figure 11-6   Shared File versus Client/Server E-Mail Systems

MIME—Multipurpose Internet Mail Extensions. This standard is an extension of SMTP. MIME provides each attachment of an e-mail message with its own header. The information included in the header is used to describe the type of information contained in the message and how the message was encoded. MIME is used for standardizing the exchange of files such as word processing documents or graphics via Internet mail. MIME has helped lead to the increased use of SMTP.

POP3—Post Office Protocol. POP3 is a client side e-mail protocol that facilitates offline operations. Messages are downloaded and manipulated on the client.

IMAP—Internet Mail Access Protocol. IMAP's features include selective downloading, server-side folder hierarchies, shared mail, and mailbox synchronization. IMAP does demand more from the server end than POP but if the server has the capacity, IMAP can save a lot of work for the users and increase the speed of e-mail communications.

Messaging APIs—There are numerous mail client and server packages to choose from today. How can all of the various clients and servers communicate? The answer is through the use of application programming interfaces (APIs). Using APIs makes it easier to mix and match multivendor mail clients and servers. In the messaging area there are three main APIs to choose from as outlined below.

Common Mail Calls (CMC)—CMC is a cross-platform messaging API. This API was released by the X.400 API association (XAPIA). This API provides a basic set of services, such as send, receive, and address lookups, through the 12 API calls it supports. This API was established as a result of the war between Microsoft and other vendors regarding messaging APIs. CMC provides a basic set of services, such as sending, receiving, and address lookup. CMC left out advanced functions to promote wide acceptance from vendors. An example of an advanced messaging function not supported by CMC is the ability to attach documents to e-mail messages.

Messaging Application Programming Interface (MAPI)—This is the most popular of the messaging APIs. It was developed by Microsoft and is supported by almost every vendor. MAPI provides a way for applications to access different types of messaging systems. There are two versions of MAPI: simple and extended. Simple MAPI calls provide a way to access various e-mail functions and provides for simple mail, address book, and message store services. Extended MAPI provides many more calls and provides interfaces to many mail systems and their address books, message transport, and message store areas.

Vendor Independent Messaging (VIM)—VIM is an API that is supported by Lotus, Borland, IBM, Apple, Oracle, MCI, Novell, and many other messaging vendors. VIM is a cross-platform interface that allows developers to create mail-enabled applications that work on various platforms. VIM supports address book services as well as message store and includes services for creating, reading, and sending messages. VIM can link with other messaging APIs including MAPI. Figure 11-7 illustrates the relationship between numerous e-mail messaging protocols and standards.

Calendaring and Scheduling

Calendaring or Group Scheduling software can be a very efficient way to schedule electronic or face-to-face meetings or conferences. By simply listing with whom one wishes to meet, a meeting could be scheduled without mak-

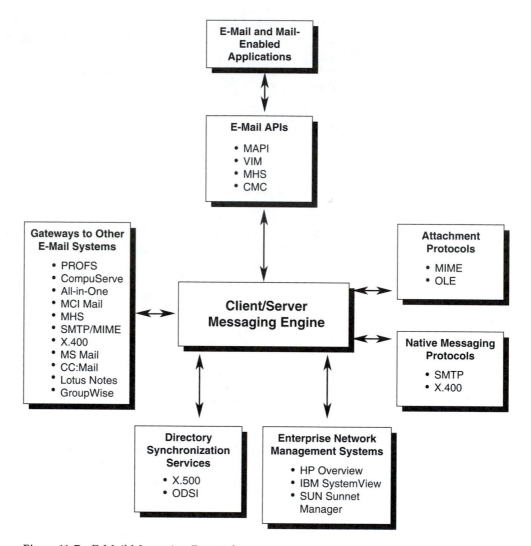

Figure 11-7   E-Mail Messaging Protocols

ing a single phone call. Some scheduling software even has the ability to work over inter-networks or wide area networks, allowing meetings to be scheduled with people across the country or around the world. Group scheduling software is often integrated with e-mail systems so requests for meetings can be automatically sent and replied to via e-mail. Most of the differences between group scheduling packages can be divided into the following categories:

- Platforms Supported/Installation
- Personal Schedule Management

- Group Calendar Management

- Meeting Scheduling

Figure 11-8 summarizes some of the key features included in calendaring software according to the aforementioned categories.

Practical Advice and Information

Although this electronic calendaring process may sound simple, be forewarned! Implementation of group scheduling software can fail miserably due to people factors. If everyone in a given organization does not make a firm commitment to keep their electronic schedule and calendar accurate and up-to-date, then the product simply cannot work. Controls must be put into place as to who has the authority to add commitments to someone else's schedule, to avoid constant meetings. The politics of calendaring can turn out to be much more complicated than the software.

Calendaring and Scheduling Standards   The Calendaring and Scheduling (calsch) working group of the Internet Engineering Task Force (IETF) is working on developing standards for calendaring and scheduling. The IETF calsch working group is working on three efforts: Calendar Exchange Format, Calendar Interoperability Protocols, and Calendar Access Protocol.

Calendar Exchange Format—The objective of this standard is to define a standard representation for calendaring and scheduling information. This format will allow different calendaring applications to communicate and interchange basic meeting and to do information. Some work has already been done in this area with vCard, vCalendar, and iCalendar. vCard and vCalendar were put together by the Internet Mail Consortium and their partners. The vCard is an industry format for describing and displaying information typically found on a business card. The vCalendar is an industry standard format for describing and displaying information about a calendar or schedule. Lotus and Microsoft are codeveloping the iCalendar document and it is currently in draft format in the IETF calsch working group.

Calendar Interoperability Protocols—These protocols are required so different calendaring and scheduling products can communicate with each other. The interoperability protocols will allow communication over Internet e-mail and other transports such as hypertext transport protocol (HTTP). Once the protocols are defined by the IETF calsch working group they will allow users using different calendaring products to send and reply to group meeting requests, search for free times on others' calendars, send and reply to do requests, schedule recurring meetings, and schedule meetings in different time zones.

Calendar Access Protocol—The objective of this protocol is to allow users to mix and match different calendaring and scheduling clients and servers. An example would be a cc:Mail client accessing a calendar on a Microsoft

Calendaring Feature Category	Feature/Implication
Platforms Supported/Installation	• Which network operating systems can this group scheduling software run over? Options: NetWare, Vines, LANManager, Windows NT, AppleShare, LANtastic, and other DOS-based LANs • Does the scheduling package support out-bound and in-bound wide area network links? Is this feature included or optional? • What options can be performed remotely? Edit or view schedule including appointments? • If a schedule is kept on a remote workstation, can the scheduling package automatically synchronize the remote schedule with new meetings, and appointments from the server? • Is the group scheduling system designed to integrate tightly with a particular e-mail or GroupWare package? Options: Lotus Notes, GroupWise, cc:Mail, Microsoft Mail • Are e-mail gateways available to send meeting and appointment messages across a variety of different e-mail platforms? • Can the scheduling package communicate directly with **PDA (Personal Digital Assistants)?** • Can the scheduling system output be incorporated into other documents such as word processing or spreadsheets?
Personal Schedule Management	• Can recurring appointments be easily and flexibly defined? • Are reminder alarms available and programmable? • Can tasks or projects be scheduled as well as meetings? • Can prospects or contacts be managed within the scheduling system? • Is an address book module integrated? • Can appointments be easily changed or rescheduled? • Are reports available in a variety of formats such as daily planner pages or to-do lists? • Are a variety of access levels available to control who can request meetings of whom? • Can administrative assistants be given control of one's schedule? • Can notes be attached to appointments?
Group Calendar Management	• Are reports available that show group activities and meetings scheduled for a given date range? • Can tasks and activities as well as meetings be assigned to groups? • Can other group members' calendars be viewed? • How are holidays and length of business day defined and displayed?
Meeting Scheduling	• Can rooms and resources be reserved/assigned as meetings are scheduled? • How powerful are the querying tools to find available meeting times for multiple attendees? • Does the program allow users to set up automated rules for response to meeting requests? • How are conflicts or double-bookings handled? • Can confirmed replies be requested? • How are nonresponses to meeting requests handled?

Figure 11-8   Key Features of Calendaring Software

Exchange Server. This protocol would allow companies to have true interoperability. Figure 11-9 illustrates the relationship between these various calendaring and scheduling standards efforts.

Workflow

Workflow (also known as **workflow automation) software** automatically routes information through the organization according to preprogrammed rules or workflow directives. As project assignments change, there is no need to move offices or workstations. The work from the new project simply flows to the current worker location thanks to workflow automation. Another aspect of workflow automation tracks time spent on given projects by individuals in order to simplify client chargeback and billing for professional or consulting organizations. Workflow automation software encourages business processes to first be reevaluated and/or reengineered before being programmed into the workflow automation software.

Workflow software can vary widely in both cost and capabilities and can be categorized in a number of ways. One criterion on which workflow automation software can be categorized is the type of business process that the workflow software is attempting to automate. Using this criterion, three major categories emerge:

- **Production Workflow**—This category of workflow software automates complicated business processes that are performed on a regu-

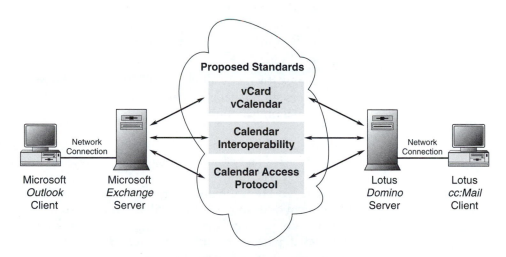

To ensure interoperability between different calendaring and scheduling products, some or all of these proposed standards need to be mutually supported.

Figure 11-9   Calendaring and Scheduling Standards

lar basis, perhaps daily. These processes are at the heart of a business' production capability. Examples might include building an automobile or building custom-made vinyl replacement windows.

- **Ad Hoc Workflow**—This category of workflow software automates more open-ended, creative, or flexible business processes that are done occasionally or in an unscheduled manner. Product design, marketing plan design, application software design, network design, or other brainstorming-based activities are examples of such processes.

- **Administrative Workflow**—This category of workflow software automates routine business processes that are common in most businesses. Examples include purchase order requisition and approval, accounts payable approval, review of job applicants' files, or expense report approval.

Related to the business process categorization of workflow automation software is categorization according to extent of routing supported by a given workflow product.

- **Sequential routing** is the simplest of the routing schemes in which business processes follow predictable paths with individual steps following each other in a linear fashion.

- **Conditional branch routing** introduces multiple possible routes to a process dependent on results or outcomes at a particular step in the process. Exception handling and sophisticated rules-based or expert systems can all be supported or integrated into conditional branch routing workflow automation software.

- **Parallel routing** adds a layer of sophistication to workflow automation software by allowing subprocesses to be completed by multiple users simultaneously. Parallel routing may be combined with conditional branch routing.

Figure 11-10 summarizes a few additional functional issues that should be considered when contemplating the purchase of workflow automation software.

When workflow involves a great deal of handling, storage, indexing, and retrieval of documents, an ancillary **document management and imaging** software package may be required. These software packages, also known as **departmental image management** software, seek to bring new levels of electronic efficiency to the classic manual filing cabinet by storing key information about stored documents which can then be queried, searched, and reported on by a multitude of differentiating indexing criteria. In some cases, the document management and imaging software includes workflow automation capabilities as well. Productivity gains from this soft-

Workflow Automation Software Feature Category	Feature/Importance
Platform/Scalability	• How many simultaneous users will the workflow automation software support?
	• Which LAN network operating systems will the software execute over?
	• Will the software perform over a variety of WAN links?
	• How many different computer platforms will the system run over?
	• Is this a stand-alone product or an add-on for Lotus Notes?
	• Does this software include a programming language?
	• Does this software integrate or include document management and imaging capabilities?
	• Does this software integrate or include faxing and scanning management capabilities?
	• What is the impact on network bandwidth as users are added and processes become more complicated?
Workflow Development	• How intuitive or easy to use are the workflow design tools?
	• How easily and flexibly can tasks or processes be assigned to individuals or groups of individuals?
	• How complicated can links and rules between dependent subprocesses be?
	• Can workflow rules be stored in a Notes database?
	• Does the software support a variety of security settings that can be varied for each different step in the overall workflow process?
	• Can batch moves and updates be processed between databases either as work is completed or at timed intervals?
	• Does the system integrate with existing e-mail system for delivery of forms and work in process? If so, which e-mail systems?
	• Can complicated conditional branching algorithms written in other languages such as Visual Basic be integrated with this product?

Figure 11-10   Workflow Automation Software

ware are achieved by the elimination of long searches through desks and filing cabinets for a given document.

Interoperability standards among document management packages are contained in a specification known as **DMA,** or **Document Management Alliance.** The DMA interoperability standard actually defines a series of common APIs and middleware that enable interoperable document management and services such as:

- **Query services** that will support access to documents stored in any DMA-compliant document management system

- **Library services** that will include interoperable version control and access control

- **Multilevel security services** that provide a variety of security levels for individual documents regardless of which DMA-compliant document management system they are stored in

Figure 11-11 summarizes some of the key features of document management and imaging software.

Managerial Perspective

WORKFLOW ONLY AUTOMATES EXISTING SYSTEMS

In truth, workflow automation software only mirrors the business processes designed by humans. It will not improve a poorly designed or inefficient work process. Poorly implemented workflow automation software can actually have the opposite of intended impacts by increasing headcount and decreasing worker productivity. Workflow automation software should be looked upon more as a toolbox for developing automated processes than a type of off-the-shelf, ready-to-go application software. Most workflow automation software requires setup and programming by properly trained individuals knowledgeable not only in the syntax of the particular workflow automation software package, but also knowledgeable in business process engineering in general. There are currently no interoperability standards between different workflow automation packages, and not all workflow automation software runs on all available computer platforms. A good method for evaluating the applicability of workflow software is to first map out a business process in need of automation then make direct inquiries of software vendors as to whether or not their workflow automation software will be able to successfully automate the business process in question. If the answer is in the affirmative, get it in writing.

Workflow Standards and Technology   The **Workflow Management Coalition (WfMC),** established in August 1993, is a body of software vendors, consultants, and user organizations responsible for the development and promotion of workflow standards. Its membership is open to all parties interested or involved in the creation, analysis, or deployment of Workflow Management Systems. The Coalition has proposed a framework for the establishment of workflow standards. This framework includes five categories of interoperability and communication standards that will allow multiple workflow products to coexist and interoperate within a user's environment.

Document Management and Imaging Feature Category	Feature/Importance
Platform/Scalability	• Does the document management package include or is it integrated with workflow automation software? • How many users can simultaneously be supported by the software? • Would this software be considered a workgroup or enterprise solution? both? • What is the network impact at various levels of numbers of users and documents? • How easy is the software to install and manage? • Is the document management software DMA compatible?
Document Management	• Is the document management software integrated with e-mail systems for delivery of documents? If so, which ones? • What is the nature or sophistication of the search engine or database used to categorize and search for documents? • Can searches be performed for keywords embedded within stored documents? • Is there a limit to the number of documents that the system can efficiently handle? • Is the query tool for finding documents intuitive and easy to use with a natural interactive language interface, or does it require entering search strings according to a particular syntax? • How flexible is the security system? Can different security levels be assigned to individual documents? • Are documents arranged logically in electronic files or folders? • Is the database in which document indexing information is stored open or proprietary? • Is the database accessible by other query, report generation, and application tools? • What is the nature and sophistication of the version control features?
Document Input/Output	• Does the software include **OCR (Optical Character Recognition)** software to turn faxed images into editable documents? • Can audio and video objects also be stored, indexed, and retrieved? • How well integrated is the system with fax machines, fax servers, and scanners? • Are optical storage devices supported?

Figure 11-11 Document Management and Imaging

The Coalition is currently working on four main objectives. The objectives are to:

- Develop standard terminology to describe workflow systems and their environment

- Enable interoperability between different workflow systems

- Help users understand workflow through the standard Reference Model

- Work with other related industry groups to set standards and communicate its work

The Workflow Management Coalition (WfMC) has unveiled its first standard client application programming interface (API). The workflow API provides a means of communication between workflow client applications and workflow engines to give users increased flexibility in implementing standards-based workflow systems. The Coalition has established various working groups to meet the objectives listed above, and each working group has a specific area of interest. The various working groups and their responsibilities are outlined in Figure 11-12.

Working Group	Responsibilities
Reference Model	• Specify a framework for workflow systems, identifying their characteristics, functions, and interfaces.
Glossary	• Development of standard terminology for workflow.
Process Definition Tools Interface (1)	• Define a standard interface between the process definition tool and the workflow engine(s).
Workflow Client Application Interface (2)	• Define standards for the workflow engine to maintain work items that the workflow client presents to the user.
Invoked Application Interface (3)	• A standard interface to allow the workflow engine to invoke a variety of applications.
Workflow Interoperability Interface (4)	• Definition of a variety of interoperability models and the standards applicable to each.
Administration and Monitoring Tools Interface (5)	• Definition of monitoring and control functions.

Figure 11-12 Working Groups Established by the Workflow Management Coalition

Conferencing

Conferencing technologies allow multiple people to work together across a network. By using conferencing technologies, people can closely collaborate across great distances. Client/server conferencing can be divided into two main areas: real-time conferencing and non–real-time conferencing.

Real-Time Conferencing   **Real-time conferencing** can be defined as people working together collaboratively using various technologies in real time. Real-time conferencing is also called **synchronous conferencing.** There are three main categories of real-time conferencing:

- Group document editing
- Data conferencing using whiteboards and shared screens
- Audio and video conferencing

These areas are explored in more depth below. With all of the different options available for conferencing which one or ones should one select? The answer is it depends. Following the top-down model should make selecting which technology to use very easy.

Group document editing can be very useful for teams that are collaboratively developing documents. It can also be very useful for teams that are geographically dispersed by allowing them to develop, edit, and revise documents remotely. Group document editing can take place within a word processing package. For example, in Microsoft Word users can make comments and add revisions as they review a document electronically. If multiple people are making comments and revisions to a document, each person's comments show up in a different color in order to make it easy to see who made what revision. When the document owner opens the reviewed document, he or she can easily see the comments made by various people, and the owner has the option of accepting or rejecting changes. This can save a huge amount of time and effort, since it is no longer necessary to route a hard copy of the document from person to person.

Data conferencing can be very beneficial to companies by allowing people to share data in real time and combine various collaborative technologies, such as electronic whiteboards and chatting, into one comprehensive product. It can provide an inexpensive way for employees to communicate and collaborate in real time. The main advantages in using data conferencing are that it is inexpensive, easy to install and maintain, and most of the time it is the appropriate choice for conferencing. Another advantage is that it allows groups the ability to collaborate about documents, make changes, and have discussions all in real time. Many meetings are conducted where it is not necessary to hear or see everyone involved in the meeting. Most data conferencing software includes a whiteboard and some chat capabilities. Some data conferencing software products also include true application sharing. A whiteboard can be used to discuss a diagram or document, and all the participants can write on the whiteboard and provide their input. (Electronic whiteboards are discussed below in more depth.) The chat rooms can be used to discuss what is on the whiteboard or can be used for separate discussions that do not concern everyone at the meeting. Some available data conferencing software also includes support for audio conferencing. When evaluating different data conferencing software, make sure what business situations the software will be used for and select the software that meets those needs.

Electronic whiteboard software is a hybrid category of GroupWare software combining elements of electronic meeting support, document conferencing, and videoconferencing. As a result, many electronic whiteboard software packages are incorporated into a variety of different types of software packages. In focusing strictly on the electronic whiteboard software aspects of these alternatives, functionality differs primarily in the level of collaboration required among session participants.

- **Collaborative or interactive work sessions** allow users connected via networks to participate in joint work sessions as if they were all in the same room working at the same whiteboard or conference table. These sessions may involve intensive document creation and modification work or may be more discussion oriented, in which case documents may need to be displayed only for all participants. The whiteboard aspects of the session allow participants to use the equivalent of whiteboard markers to annotate and draw on the networked whiteboard that appears on all participants' workstations. When electronic whiteboard software sessions involve collaborative development or review of documents by multiple users linked via LAN or WAN links, the software category is occasionally referred to as **document conferencing software.**

- **Networked group presentations** allow one individual to present a graphically oriented presentation to multiple network-attached group members as if all seminar participants were seated in a single room. Collaborative interaction is minimal in comparison to collaborative work sessions described previously.

Because of the bandwidth demands involved with electronic whiteboard software, one of the key technical differences among products is whether multi-point conferences are supported as opposed to being limited to two-user point-to-point links. As a result, the number of supported work session participants can vary widely from 2 to more than 50. Figure 11-13 summarizes the key features of electronic whiteboard software.

A nice benefit to using an electronic whiteboard during a meeting is that it can have multiple windows open and can contain information from a variety of sources. Electronic whiteboards can be set up as either point-to-point communication or multi-point communication. The advantage to using a

Electronic Whiteboard Software Feature Category	Feature/Importance
Network Communications	• What types of network connections are supported for work sessions? Options: dial-up modems, ISDN, LAN-to-LAN connections • For dial-up communications, are address books and auto-dialers included? • For LAN communications, what types of network operating systems are supported? Options: NetWare (IPX), Windows for Workgroups (NetBEUI), DOS-based LANs (NetBIOS), UNIX (TCP/IP) • Given the amount of network communications, what types of video compression are supported? Options: JPEG, MPEG, proprietary
Work Sessions	• How many work session participants are possible? Options: From 2 to 50+ • Does the work session software support facilitator functionality? • Can session participants join and leave once the session has started? • What is the nature of the security that controls access to sessions? • Can application programs be shared or controlled remotely as part of the work session?
Whiteboard and Tools	• Are slide sorters and slide-show software available for networked group presentations? • How many participants can be writing on the electronic whiteboard simultaneously? • How many markers or different types of annotation tools (erasers, etc.) are available? • How many different marker colors are available? • Can typed text be edited with annotation tools? • Can whiteboard contents be easily saved and printed? • Can certain regions of whiteboard be highlighted, saved, and printed? • How many different types of file formats can be imported into the whiteboard? Options: ASCII, .BMP, .DIB, .GIF, .PCX, TIFF, JPEG

Figure 11-13   Electronic Whiteboard Software

multi-point system is that it allows various groups to gain control of the whiteboard. Electronic whiteboards can be an excellent addition to other collaborative technologies to enhance the overall communication and collaboration efforts.

Audio and video conferencing software adds live audio and video images between communicating parties to the collaborative computing functionality offered by electronic whiteboard software. The level to which users can collaboratively share applications or documents varies among desktop videoconferencing systems. While some videoconferencing systems support full application sharing so that users can simultaneously edit a single document with full application functionality, others only support file transfer between parties or highlighting a non-editable document on an electronic whiteboard with electronic marking pens.

One of the key problems with LAN-based videoconferencing is the basic incompatibility between the video traffic and the LAN access methodologies and bandwidth. Video and its associated voice transmission are time-sensitive, streaming types of traffic that depend on guaranteed bandwidth and delivery times for smooth transmission. Neither 10 Mbps Ethernet nor Token Ring network architectures possess either the access methodology or sufficient bandwidth to ensure such guaranteed delivery times. If audio and video are deployed on a network, newer, faster network architectures such as Fast Ethernet are required. However, even on these more advanced network architectures, more than a few simultaneous videoconferences will saturate the network and render it unusable for data-only users.

Furthermore, if the videoconference is to extend beyond the LAN, then sophisticated wide area network services such as ISDN or Switched 56K must be available at all end points of the conference. The availability of such data services at all corporate locations is by no means a forgone conclusion. Quality of the transmitted video signal is another consideration and is usually measured in frames per second (fps). As a reference, standard broadcast television in the United States displays 30 fps. In comparison, most LAN-based videoconferencing systems achieve only half that number, with some displaying less than one frame per second.

At the heart of the videoconferencing system is the video **CODEC (COder-DECoder),** which digitizes not only analog video signals but also analog voice signals. **Video Digitization** is a process by which a sample of a video signal is digitized into an 8-bit binary code. In order to maximize the amount of video and audio information transmitted over limited bandwidth, the CODEC probably also performs compression and decompression of digitized video and audio. Additional required equipment beyond the "normal" workstation includes the following:

- A communications adapter card to merge the digitized video and voice signal with the digital data stream from the workstation and communicate this integrated stream of digital traffic over a specialized WAN link such as an ISDN or Switched 56K line.

- A microphone for audio input and speakers for audio output.

- A camera for video input.

Figure 11-14 illustrates a typical network architecture setup for an audio/video conference.

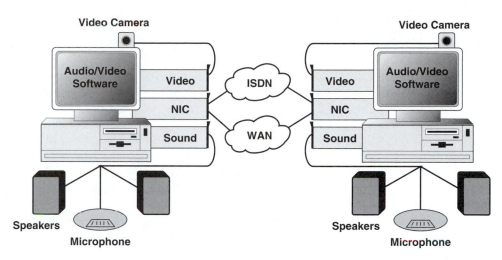

Figure 11-14   Typical Audio/Video Conference Configuration

LAN-based desktop videoconferencing systems differ primarily in the LAN network architectures over which they will operate, the number of simultaneous users supported, and the extent to which application sharing and collaborative computing is supported. Figure 11-15 summarizes the major feature categories of LAN-based desktop videoconferencing systems.

Videoconferencing Feature Category	Feature/Importance
Hardware	• What hardware is included with the videoconferencing workstation? Required: microphone, camera • Is the CODEC included? • What computer bus types is the CODEC compatible with? Options: ISA, EISA, PCI • Is the CODEC H.320 compliant?
Network	• What wide area network services are supported? Options: ISDN, Switched 56K, T-1, fractional T-1, analog dial-up • Is an ISDN adapter included? • Which LAN architectures can the videoconference be transmitted over? Options: Ethernet, Token Ring, FDDI, Iso-Ethernet, 100BaseT, 100VG-AnyLAN • Is a separate phone circuit required for audio transmission?
Application	• What is the maximum resolution of the video frames? • What is the maximum number of frames/second possible? • Can incoming and outgoing video be displayed simultaneously? • What is the maximum number of users per videoconference? • Is real-time application and collaborative computing supported? • Is electronic whiteboard highlighting supported? • Is file transfer supported? • Can linked application objects be embedded within other applications?

Figure 11-15   LAN-Based Desktop Videoconferencing Systems

Managerial Perspective

ISSUES IN REAL-TIME CONFERENCING

Several people and technology issues need to be addressed when a company is considering using some type of real-time conferencing. One major issue is the need to get input from various departments on what type of electronic collaboration is needed and potentially beneficial. Once the technology is selected and implemented, it is extremely important to train people on how to properly use the technology in order to ensure that they will use it and see the benefit. As discussed earlier in the chapter, GroupWare changes the way people work, so it is important to educate them on how the GroupWare technology can benefit them and make their jobs easier. Some other issues that should be considered when evaluating real-time conferencing tools are:

- How does the technology selected allow users to control the whiteboard and chat rooms?

- How many people or groups can the technology support at one time?

- How many people can be involved in the conference for it to be effective?

- Will the selected technology fit into the overall information technology architecture?

- Does the selected technology allow for action items, goals, and meeting outcomes to be stored, communicated, and integrated with other software applications such as project management software?

Non–Real-Time Conferencing   **Non–real-time conferencing** can be defined as people working together collaboratively using various technologies in non-real time. Non–real-time conferencing is also called **asynchronous conferencing.** A benefit to using this type of software is the increase in a company's ability to share information. This is a benefit only if the information that is collected is valuable to others. Non–real-time conferencing can be broken into two categories: electronic mail and bulletin board systems (BBS). Electronic mail was described in detail earlier in the chapter.

A **Bulletin Board System (BBS)** is a computer system that serves as an information center and message-passing center for users who have a connection to the system. The BBS can be accessed through a network connection or a through a dial-up connection. Once users are connected to the system they can read and post messages or they can upload or download files. A BBS provides an easy way for users who have common interests or work on the same projects to share information electronically. Users read and post information to the BBS when they have time. A BBS can be very beneficial to companies with many employees who are remotely located, since it allows them to exchange files and messages. When evaluating BBS software it is important to know who is going to use it and what they are going to use it for. Some features to look for when considering different BBS software packages are:

- How many users can be supported at one time?

- Can users have "real-time" conversations?

- Can the BBS share information with other BBSs?

- What type of security does the product offer?

- How does it prevent unauthorized users from gaining access?

- How does it prevent unauthorized access to messages and files?

- What are the system administration requirements?

Conferencing Standards and Technology The two main conferencing standards are T.120 and H.323. The T.120 standard contains a series of communication and application protocols and services that provide support for real-time communications. It was developed by the International Telecommunications Union (ITU) and is a family of open standards. Many key international vendors have committed to implementing T.120-based products and services. The T.120 standard is comprised of many components, including T.121–T.127. There are many benefits to using the T.120 standard including multi-point data delivery, network and platform independence, network transparency, interoperability, reliable data delivery, multicast enabled delivery, scalability, coexistence with other standards, and support for various topologies.

The H.323 standard provides a foundation for data, audio, and video communications across Internet Protocol (IP) networks. H.323 was recommended by the ITU and is very broad in scope. The standard addresses call control, multimedia management, and bandwidth management for point-to-point or multi-point conferences. The H.323 standard is part of a larger series of communications standards that address videoconferencing. The key benefits of H.323 are interoperability; application, platform, and network independence; multi-point support; bandwidth management, compression and depression of video and audio data; and inter-network conferencing. Figure 11-16 summarizes a variety of conferencing standards.

Electronic Meeting Support

Electronic meeting support software offers opportunities for workers to interact electronically. Brainstorming or idea generation sessions are conducted via the network and managed by the **workgroup conferencing software** package. Ideas can be generated on "private" screens and then shared

Videoconferencing Standard	Purpose/Explanation
H.221	• Framing and synchronization specification, which standardizes the CODEC's handshaking and interface to WAN services such as ISDN used for videoconference transmission.
H.230	• Multiplexing specification, which describes how audio and video information should be transmitted over the same digital WAN link.
H.231	• Multi-point control unit (MCU) specification, which defines standards for a device to bridge three or more H.320-compliant CODECs together on a single multi-point videoconference.
H.233	• Specification for encryption of video and audio information transmitted through H.320-compliant CODECs, also known as H.KEY.
H.242	• Specification for call setup and tear-down for videoconference calls.
H.261	• Also known as Px64, describes compression and depression algorithms used for videoconferencing. Also defines two screen formats: CIF (common intermediate format), 288 lines × 352 pixels/line, and QCIF (quarter common intermediate format), 144 lines × 176 pixels/line.

Figure 11-16   Conferencing Standards

with the group. Meetings can be held electronically, and thereby anonymously allow more honest interaction not subject to the political pressures of many face-to-face meetings. Ideas can be prioritized, consensus can be reached, action items can be established, and meeting minutes can be electronically recorded, edited, and approved.

Workgroup conferencing software may be a stand-alone application or may be integrated with other GroupWare modules such as document management or workflow automation. In addition to the obvious technical issue of which computing platforms are supported, there are three major functional categories for electronic meeting support software corresponding to the natural flow of meeting events:

- **Meeting Creation**—Meetings must first be created or established.

- **Idea Generation**—The major purpose of an electronically supported meeting is to generate ideas in a nonthreatening, politically neutral environment.

- **Meeting Results Reporting**—In order to benefit fully from the ideas generated at the meeting, results must be easily, accurately, and flexibly reported.

Electronic meeting support software has a unique vocabulary, and many software packages function in an overall similar manner. Discussion groups are called **forums.** Each forum would probably contain multiple topics for discussion known alternatively as **discussion categories** or **sections.** Specific discussion topics on which participants are welcome to comment are generally referred to as **threads.** User comments on topics are made up of a series of messages that may contain supporting material or documents known as **enclosures.** Meetings may be held in specially equipped **decision support rooms** in which all forum participants gather in what is known as a **same-place, same-time meeting** or may convene via a local or wide area network according to participants' availability in what is known as a **different-place, different-time meeting.** Figure 11-17 summarizes some of the key features to look for when purchasing electronic meeting support software.

Managerial Perspective

Electronic meeting support software is no substitute for effective leadership and excellent communications skills. This software must be looked upon as an enabling technology which, when properly implemented by trained individuals, can encourage open, unbiased discussion and idea generation leading to better overall collaboration and consensus building. When properly planned and implemented, electronic meetings tend to stay more focused on agenda items, generate more alternative ideas, reach consensus more quickly, and provide immediate electronic documentation of the entire meeting's proceedings. Electronic meeting support software can make good group leaders even better but will do little to improve ineffective leadership skills.

LAN RESOURCE MANAGEMENT SOFTWARE

LAN Resource Management Software provides the functionality required to administer and manage distributed network systems. While the area of LAN resource management software is constantly changing, the following functional areas are representative of the field: multiprotocol network printing, printer management, network backup, network faxing, electronic software distribution, license metering, and asset management.

Multiprotocol Network Printing

One of the first motivations for installing a local area network has historically been the need to share networked printers. As a result, the software

Electronic Meeting Support Feature Category	Feature/Importance
Platforms Supported	• What network operating system does the information sharing take place over? NetWare, Windows for Workgroups, Windows NT? • What clients are supported for meeting participation? Macintosh, Windows, DOS?
Meeting Creation	• Facilitators should be able to be designated in advance and should be allowed to structure the meeting's agenda and topics for discussion ahead of time. • Can threads be easily moved from one forum to another? • What are the security procedures for entry into a forum? • Can forums be built across multiple servers? • Can existing forums be merged or segmented? • Can users participate in forums via dial-up access? • Are tools available for agenda creation? • Can different-place, different-time meetings be supported as well as same-place, same-time meetings?
Idea Generation	• What types of functionality are supported during the meeting? Options: workflow automation, document management, interactive workgroup discussions, idea generation via collaboration and feedback. • Support for integrating documents with document tracking and version control may be very important since group discussion often centers around historical or proposed documentation • Are "viewers" for different types of documents included or must every forum participant have every document software package installed on his or her workstation? • Are tools available for alternative consolidation, evaluation, and voting? • Can ad hoc surveys of participants be quickly created, executed, and results evaluated?
Meeting Results Reporting	• Reports must be easily generated and interpreted for both meeting agendas as well as meeting results and follow-up.

Figure 11-17   Electronic Meeting Support Software

required to offer LAN-based shared printing services is usually included in network operating systems software.

When shared printing services are required across different network operating systems, specialized **multiprotocol network printing** hardware and software is required. Multiprotocol network printing software is not usually included with most network operating systems. As illustrated in Figure 11-18, multiprotocol printer servers need to be able to support:

- multiple network operating systems protocols

- multiple network architectures

- multiple vendors' printers

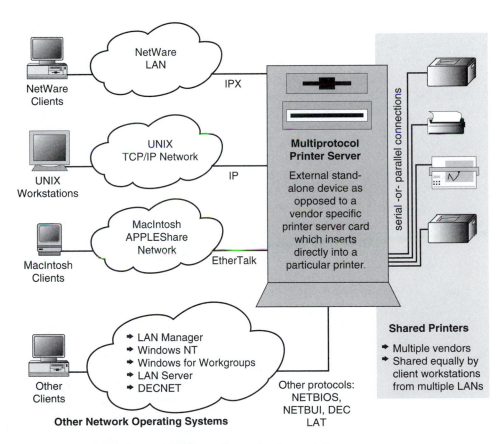

Figure 11-18   Multiprotocol Printer Server Implementation

Figure 11-19 summarizes some of the functional differences between multi-protocol printer servers of which network analysts should be aware.

Printer Management

Printer management in a multiprotocol, multi-vendor environment is in a state of evolution. Several of the larger printer vendors such as HP and Lex-Mark have their own printer management software packages. However, they offer extremely limited interoperability with printers from other

Multiprotocol Printer Server Feature	Feature/Implication
NetWare Support	• NetWare supports two different printing methods: PSERVER and RPRINTER. PSERVER spools print jobs to the NetWare file server, whereas RPRINTER transmits print jobs directly to the print server. • Multiprotocol print servers should support both PSERVER and RPRINTER
UNIX Support	• UNIX print services are performed via LPD or Line Printer Daemon. • Multiprotocol print servers should support LPD.
Macintosh Support	• Apple's print services protocol is known as PAP or Printer Access Protocol • Apple also expects bidirectional communication with printers • Multiprotocol printer servers should support both PAP and bidirectional communication
Network Architectures	• Which network architectures are supported? Options: Ethernet (10Base2, 10BaseT), Token Ring (4 Mbps, 16 Mbps) • Is more than one network architecture supported in a single multiprotocol print server?
Management	• Is the management console PC-based or UNIX workstation based? • Does the management protocol support SNMP and MIBs? • Is the MIB and management system proprietary? • Evaluate management systems based on ease of configuration, installation, and monitoring • Do the management systems support existing or emerging standards?
Price Range	• Prices can vary between $500 and $1000

Figure 11-19 Multiprotocol Printer Server Functionality

vendors. As printers have become another distributed resource to be managed in a multiprotocol network environment, the need for printer management standards has become evident.

Standardized printer management protocols would allow users with proper authorization to change paper trays or printer setup from their network-attached desktop computer. Users would see a replica of the printer control panel on their computer monitor. Multiprotocol printer management systems would also be able to monitor printer usage by user in order to spot abuse or for charge-back purposes.

Network Backup

With the shift to network operating system-based servers housing all user data, a means of effectively backing up multiple servers must be developed. Rather than install a separate backup solution in each server, it can be advantageous to install a network-based solution capable of backing up multiple servers. In order to evaluate network-based backup solutions, it is important to first establish objectives or expected outcomes of such a system. Among the possibilities are the following:

- Network backup systems should be designed so as to minimize the amount of required operational support.

- Network backup systems should be expandable or scalable so that additional clients and servers can easily be added to the backup plan.

- Since the entire purpose of backup systems is to be able to restore critical files in the event of a problem, file restoral must be efficient and effective.

- Network backup systems should be interoperable so that all backup can be managed from a single location regardless of the operating systems or network operating systems of backed-up devices.

Network Backup Architectures   There are two primary network backup architecture alternatives for multiple server environments:

- **Locally attached multiple tape drives** are attached directly to each server. The multiple tape drives provide both faster backup performance and fault tolerance. Depending on the capabilities of the backup software, multiple backup devices may be operational simultaneously. Locally attached tape devices perform at bus speeds rather than network backbone speeds.

- **Dedicated backup server** architectures allow multiple servers to be backed up across the network backbone onto a dedicated backup server linked to multiple backup devices. Dedicated backup servers provide the added benefit of being able to not only restore files but to also act as a contingency server for executing restored files in the event of primary server failures. Such an architecture is appropriate if multiple gigabytes of data must be backed up across multiple servers. Dedicated backup servers require multiple, high-speed, network connections to the network backbone. **Tape changers or tape autoloaders** are also required in order to swap tapes into/out of backup devices for multi-Gigabyte backup sessions.

Figure 11-20 illustrates these alternative network backup architectures.

Locally Attached Multiple Tape Drives

Dedicated Backup Server

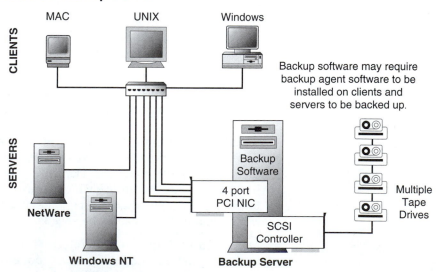

Figure 11-20 Network Backup Architectures

NETWORK BACKUP ANALYSIS

Figure 11-21 summarizes some of the key issues involved in analyzing and designing an effective network backup solution in addition to the primary issue of network backup architecture previously described.

Network Backup Analysis Issue	Importance/Implication
Potential Bottlenecks	• Network backup analysis must be performed with an eye for end-to-end system performance. Among the potential bottlenecks in a network backup solution are: tape drive/media capacity, tape drive speed, hard disk I/O speed, network bandwidth
Tape Drives to Server Ratio	• It is possible, depending on backup software capability, to have multiple tape drives attached to a single server simultaneously performing backup duties. The number of backup devices is limited by the number of SCSI controllers per server that a particular backup software package will support. Each SCSI controller will support 6 tape drives.
Servers to Tape Drive Ratio	• It is possible, depending on backup software capability, to have multiple servers (or clients) being backed up by a single tape device through a process known alternatively as **interlacing, interleaving,** or **tape streaming**.
Scheduling Backup Sessions	• Backups may be performed either during or after business hours. This decision can have a serious impact on available network bandwidth for dedicated backup server architectures. During business hours, 20%–30% of network capacity may be consumed by backup jobs, whereas up to 50% of network bandwidth may be available after business hours. • If backups are performed during business hours, is the backup software capable of retrying to backup open files?

(continued)

Computing Required Backup Time and Capacity	• In order to determine amount of backup capacity required to complete network-based system backups in an acceptable amount of time, multiply the available network bandwidth in bits per second by 60 seconds per minute and divide by 8 bits per byte. Results is expressed in terms of megabytes per minute. Most of today's servers contain storage capacities of gigabytes (1000 megabytes), leading to the need for substantial backup capabilities.
System Restoral	• How easy and fast is the system, or selected files to restore? • Can the restoral process be easily tested and benchmarked? • Can users restore their own files?
Fault Tolerance	• If a tape drive fails, can the backup software automatically shift the backup responsibilities of the failed drive to another functional drive?
Tape Library Management	• Can the backup software keep database or list of all files contained on all backup volumes? • Can the backup software keep multiple versions of the same files organized and display multiple versions for possible restoral?
Multi-Platform Support	• Which client operating systems are compatible with server-based backup software? Options: Windows, Windows NT, DOS, UNIX, OS/2, Macintosh, NetWare 3.12 or 4.1 • Does the backup software support interoperability standards such as NetWare's SMS and SIDF? (See Chapter 5.) • Can multiple locally attached tape drives, attached to multiple servers, be centrally administered from one single location?
Tape-to-Tape Backups	• Can the software automatically perform tape-to-tape backups between tape drives for redundant storage?

Figure 11-21   Network Backup Analysis

Network Faxing

Network Faxing Objectives   In order to choose a particular network faxing architecture or analyze network faxing requirements, it is necessary to first identify the objectives, or desired outcomes, of the implemented network faxing solution. Among the possible objectives are the following:

- Allow users to share FAX modems and phone lines in order to maximize worker productivity while simultaneously minimizing investment in modems and phone lines

- Allow users to FAX directly from PCs and workstations

- Allow users to receive faxes directly at PCs and workstations

Network Faxing Architectures   Providing FAX services to network-attached workstations requires a combination of network-aware FAX software in combination with FAX boards or FAX modems. PCs equipped with fax boards or fax modems and specially written faxing software that are dedicated to network Faxing are known as **FAX servers.**

Network faxing architectures can be divided into three basic alternatives:

- Software-only solutions in which the user supplies both the PC to execute the FAX software and compatible FAX boards or modems. The FAX software purchased for such an architecture must be network-aware or LAN-enabled. Such is not always the case, since most FAX software originated as single-server versions.

- Hardware/Software solutions in which the user supplies the PC to which vendor-supplied FAX boards and bundled software are loaded.

- Turnkey solutions that are specially made LAN-attached devices that are pre-configured with both software and all necessary FAX hardware.

Which of these three architectures is correct for any given situation will vary according to the budget and performance needs as determined by the network faxing needs analysis. In general, turnkey solutions are easier to configure, install, and operate, but are also more expensive than either of the other two options. Figure 11-22 illustrates these alternative network faxing architectures.

Network Faxing Standards   Network faxing software must adhere to two different sets of standards:

- Standards for FAX software APIs that define interfaces between FAX software and hardware components

- FAX transmission international standards known commonly as FAX Group I through Group IV as defined by the CCITT.

There are two **FAX APIs:**

Software Only Solution

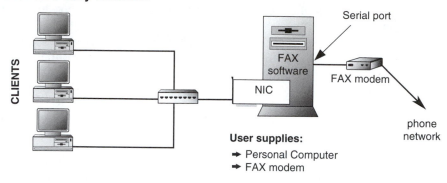

Hardware/Software Solution

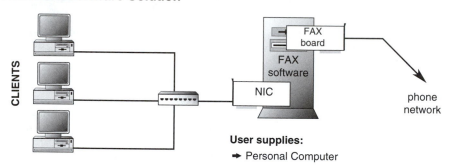

Turnkey FAX Server

Figure 11-22 Network Faxing Architectures

- **CAS—Communications Applications Specification** was developed by Intel and DCA. This API allows software vendors to integrate FAX capabilities into their application software by allowing the software to include standardized, embedded commands that are understood by FAX boards and FAX modems.

CCITT FAX Standard	Description/Features
Group 1	• Transmits an 8.5 × 11 inch page in 6 minutes • Outdated
Group 2	• Transmits an 8.5 × 11 inch page in 3 minutes • Outdated
Group 3	• Most common FAX standard • Transmits an 8.5 × 11 inch page in 20 seconds • Resolutions: 203 × 98 dots per inch (dpi) and 203 × 196 dpi • 9600 bps transmission rate
Group 3 bis	• Resolution: 406 × 196 dpi • 14.4 Kbps transmission rate
Group 4	• Transmission rate: 64 Kbps • Requires ISDN switched digital service • Transmits an 8.5 × 11 inch page in 6 seconds

Figure 11-23   FAX Transmission Standards

- **FaxBIOS** is an alternative FAX API developed and supported by the FaxBIOS Association, which is comprised of FAX circuit board vendors.

Figure 11-23 summarizes FAX transmission standards.

Applied Problem Solving

NETWORK FAXING ANALYSIS

Figure 11-24 summarizes some of the key analysis issues that must be examined prior to making recommendations as to Network faxing architectures.

Networking Faxing Analysis Issue	Importance/Implication
Incoming vs. Outgoing Faxes	• Allowing multiple users to access shared fax modems for outgoing faxes is far less complicated than automatically routing faxes to users' network-attached workstations. • Not all FAX software packages or FAX servers can provide both outgoing and incoming FAX capability

(continued)

Application Integration	• How easily/transparently does the FAX software integrate with application software such as word processing, spreadsheet, presentation graphics, and e-mail?
	• Can FAX capabilities be transparently accessed from within Windows applications?
	• Does the FAX software execute in the background allowing the user to continue working?
	• Is a FAX viewer included?
	• Is OCR (Optical Character Recognition) software included to convert FAX images to editable documents?
	• Does the FAX client run as a TSR (Terminate and Stay Resident) program, thereby always taking up memory?
Hardware Interface	• Are users able to choose modems and phone lines manually or are outgoing lines automatically selected by the software?
	• Can a fax be sent to multiple destinations simultaneously by using multiple modems simultaneously?
	• Does the FAX software require a dedicated FAX server?
	• How many different types of fax modems and fax boards are supported?
	• How many modem setup strings are included?
	• Can the modems be shared for data transmission as well as FAX transmission?
Capacity/Expandability	• What is the maximum number of fax modems per server, workgroup, and LAN?
	• How easily can additional modems and phone lines be added?
Licensing	• What is the licensing policy? Server-based or client-based?
	• Are client licenses only available in fixed increments such as 10, 25, 50?
	• Are unlimited client licenses available?
NOS Compatibility	• How many network operating systems are supported? NetWare, Windows for Workgroups, LANtastic
	• Is a 32-bit version available for Windows NT networks?
	• Does the NT version support multitasking? symmetrical multiprocessing?

(continued)

E-Mail Compatibility	• Which e-mail systems and associated e-mail protocols does the FAX software support? Microsoft Mail (MAPI), Lotus cc:Mail (VIM), NetWare (MHS)
Management Capabilities	• What is the extent of administrative features? Call logging, summary reports, departmental chargeback reports
Scheduling	• Can faxes be scheduled for transmission at later dates and times to accommodate reduced phone rates and changing time zones?
Internet Capabilities	• Does the FAX software include Telnet, FTP, and TCP/IP support for transparent interfacing to the Internet?
Security	• Can faxes be secured by password protection?

Figure 11-24   Network Faxing Analysis

Electronic Software Distribution

As the Client/Server architecture has taken hold as the dominant information systems paradigm, the increased processing power possessed by client workstations had been matched by increasing the sophistication of the client software. The distribution of client software to multiple locally and remotely attached client workstations could be a very personnel-intensive, and expensive, task were it not for a new category of LAN-enabled software known as **ESD** or **Electronic Software Distribution.** ESD software can vary widely in the types of services and features offered as well as the costs for the convenience offered. For example, in addition to simply delivering software to LAN-attached clients, ESD software may also:

- Update configuration files

- Edit other files

- Capture commands entered during a manual software installation and convert the captured text into an automated script to control subsequent electronic software distribution

Figure 11-25 summarizes some of the key functional characteristics of ESD software.

License Metering Software

Although **license metering software** was originally intended to monitor the number of executing copies of a particular software package versus the

ESD Software Functional Category	Description/Implication
NOS Support	• Since ESD software distributes software via the LAN, it is important to know which network operating systems are supported.
Update Control	• Can updates be scheduled? • Can updates be selectively done based on hardware configuration? • Can updates be done only on selected machines? • Can only certain files be searched for and replaced? • Can files be edited or updated? Examples: CONFIG.SYS, AUTOEXEC.BAT, WIN.INI, SYSTEM.INI • Can files in use be replaced? • Can files be moved and renamed? • Can the update be done in the background on client workstations? • How secure is the update control? • Can updates be scripted? • Can update keystrokes be captured and converted to an automated update control file? • Can users perform their own selected updates from a distribution server? • Are unattended updates possible? • Are in-progress status screens available? • Can outside distribution lists be imported? • Can remote workstations be shut down and rebooted? • How extensive are the update reporting and logging capabilities?
Interoperability	• Is the ESD software integrated with License Metering or LAN Hardware/Software Inventory software? • Are other software packages required in order to execute the ESD software?
Licensing	• Are licensing fees based on numbers of clients or numbers of distribution servers?

Figure 11-25   Electronic Software Distribution Functionality

number of licenses purchased for that package, an interesting and beneficial side effect of license metering software has occurred. In recognition of this beneficial side effect, this category of software is now sometimes referred to as **license management software.** The previously mentioned beneficial side effect stems from the realization that at any one point in time, fewer than 100% of the workstations possessing legitimate licenses for a given software product are actually executing that software product.

As a result, with the aid of license management software, fewer licenses can service an equal or greater number of users, thereby reducing the numbers of software licenses purchased and the associated cost of software ownership. License management software is able to dynamically allocate licenses to those users wishing to execute a particular software package in a process known as **license optimization.** Three of the most popular license optimization techniques are as follows:

- **Dynamic allocation** gives out either single-user or suite licenses based on the number of suite applications used. As an example, if a user starts a word processing package within an application suite, the user would be issued a single user license for the word processing package. However, if a user were to subsequently also execute a spreadsheet package within the same suite, he or she would be issued a suite license rather than a second single user license.

- **Load balancing** shifts licenses between servers to meet demands for licenses put on those servers by locally attached users. Licenses are loaned between servers on an as-needed basis. In this way, every server need not have a full complement of licenses to meet all anticipated user demands. This technique is also known as **license pooling.**

- **Global license sharing** recognizes the opportunity for license sharing presented by the widely distributed nature of today's global enterprise networks. While users on one side of the globe are sleeping, users on the other side of the globe are sharing the same pool of licenses.

License metering and management software have traditionally been supplied as add-on products written by third-party software developers. This trend may change abruptly, however. Novell and Microsoft have cooperated (an unusual circumstance in itself) on a **licensing server API (LSAPI).** This API would build license-metering capability into Microsoft and Novell's network operating systems and thereby eliminate the need for third-party license metering software.

LSAPI-compliant applications would communicate with a specialized **license server** which would issue **access tokens,** more formally known as **digital license certificates,** based on the license information stored in the license server database. Applications wishing to take advantage of the NOS-based license metering service would only need to include the proper commands as specified in the LSAPI.

Asset Management Software

Asset Management Software is often included or integrated with Electronic Software Distribution or License Metering software. However, it has a unique and important mission of its own in a widely distributed client/server architecture where hardware and software assets are located throughout an enterprise network. A quality asset management system is especially important in the planning efforts for network hardware and software upgrades. An enormous amount of human energy, and associated expense, can be wasted going from workstation to workstation determining the hardware and software characteristics of each workstation. An effective asset management system can do the job automatically and report gathered data in useful and flexible formats. Figure 11-26 lists several functions of asset management software.

Asset Management Functional Category	Description/Functionality
Platforms	• Client platforms supported: DOS, Macintosh, Windows, OS/2 • Server platforms supported: NetWare, Windows NT/2000, UNIX
Data Collection	• Scheduling: How flexibly can inventory scans be scheduled? • Can inventory scans of client workstations be completed incrementally during successive logins? • Does the inventory software flag unknown software that it finds on client workstations? • How large a catalog of known software titles does the inventory software have? 6,000 titles is among the best. • Can software titles be added to the known software list? • Are fields for data collection user-definable? • Can the inventory management software audit servers as well as client workstations? • Is hardware and software inventory information stored in the same database? • What is the database format? • Can the inventory management software differentiate between and track the assets of multiple laptop computers that share a single docking bay?
Reporting	• How many predefined reports are available? • Are customized reports available? • How easy is it to produce a customized report? • Can reports be exported in numerous formats such as popular word processing, spreadsheet, and presentation graphics formats?
Query	• How user-friendly and powerful are the query tools? • Can queries be generated on unique hardware and software combinations? • Can inventory information be gathered and displayed on demand?

Figure 11-26 Asset Management Software Functionality

SUMMARY

Local area network software categories include network operating systems and LAN-enabled application software. LAN-enabled application software written specifically to take advantage of networked nature of clients and servers can be further subdivided into GroupWare and LAN resource management software categories.

GroupWare is a category of LAN productivity software that offers a collection of integrated software packages to enable geographically dispersed coworkers to be at least as productive as if they all worked at a single location. GroupWare is an emerging category of software that may contain any or all of the following software modules: electronic mail, calendaring and scheduling, workflow, conferencing, and electronic meeting support. From a network analyst's standpoint, sufficient bandwidth is a key concern for supporting the many bandwidth-intensive GroupWare applications.

LAN-based e-mail systems are currently in an architectural transition from simple shared-file architectures to more complex client/server messaging-based e-mail systems. Interoperability features that allow any e-mail system to interoperate with any other e-mail system and that allow multiple diverse documents to be attached to e-mail messages are among the key functional e-mail developments.

LAN resource management software seeks to optimize the use of network-attached hardware resources such as printers, fax modems, and backup devices. The LAN resource management software written for this optimization must be compatible with the installed network operating systems and their associated communications protocols, as well as with the network-attached hardware the software seeks to manage.

LAN-based software resources represent a significant capital investment and can potentially benefit from the use of LAN resource management software as well. Electronic software distribution seeks to reduce the time required to distribute software across widely dispersed client workstations on an enterprise network by using the network itself as a distribution mechanism.

License management software uses a variety of license optimization techniques to allow users to execute desired applications while minimizing the number of purchased software licenses. The final LAN resource management category, LAN inventory management software, automatically scans network-attached workstations and inventories the hardware and software assets contained therein. By knowing exactly what hardware and software is currently installed, users can make more cost-effective planning and purchasing decisions.

KEY TERMS

Access tokens
Ad-hoc workflow
Administrative workflow
Application software
Asset Management Software
Asynchronous conferencing

Audio and video conferencing
BBS
Bulletin Board System
Calendar Access Protocol
Calendar Exchange Format
Calendar Interoperability

Protocols
Calendaring
CAS
Client/server e-mail systems
CMC
CODEC

COder-DECoder
Collaborative work sessions
Common Mail Calls
Communications Applications
  Specification
Conditional branch routing
Data conferencing
Decision support rooms
Dedicated backup server
Departmental image
  management
Different-place, different-time
  meeting
Digital license certificates
Discussion categories
DMA
Document conferencing
  software
Document management and
  imaging
Document Management
  Alliance
Dynamic allocation
Electronic meeting support
Electronic Software Distribution
Electronic whiteboard software
E-mail
E-mail gateways
Enclosures
ESD
FAX APIs
FaxBIOS
Forums
Global license sharing
Group Document Editing
Group Scheduling software

GroupWare
Idea Generation
IMAP
Interactive work sessions
Internet Mail Access Protocol
LAN application software
  architecture
LAN resource management
  software
LDAP
Library services
License management software
License metering software
License optimization
License pooling
License server
Licensing server API
Lightweight Directory
Access Protocol
Load balancing
Locally attached multiple tape
  drives
LSAPI
Management software
MAPI
Meeting Creation
Meeting Results Reporting
Message transfer agent
Messaging APIs
Messaging Application
  Programming Interface
MIME
MTA
Multilevel security services
Multi-platform e-mail client
  software

Multiprotocol network printing
Multipurpose Internet Mail
  Extensions
Networked group presentations
Non–real-time conferencing
Parallel routing
POP3
Post Office Protocol
Production Workflow
Query services
Real-time conferencing
Remote e-mail client software
Same-place, same-time meeting
Security
Sequential routing
Shared file e-mail system
Simple Mail Transport Protocol
SMTP
Store-and-forward messaging
  technology
Synchronous conferencing
Tape autoloaders
Tape changers
Threads
Vendor Independent Messaging
Video Digitization
VIM
WfMC
Workflow
Workflow Automation
Workflow Management
  Coalition
Workgroup conferencing
  software
X.400
X.500

REVIEW QUESTIONS

1. How can LAN-enabled application software be developed to interoperate with a variety of different network operating systems?

2. What type of services does network applications software request from network operating systems?

3. Differentiate between GroupWare and LAN resource management software in terms of intended benefits.

4. What are the basic categories of GroupWare?

5. What are the areas of compatibility with which remote e-mail client software must be concerned?

6. What is the importance of attachment capabilities to overall e-mail system usefulness?

7. What are some of the e-mail features or functions important to remote e-mail client software?

8. Why are e-mail interoperability features important?

9. In which types of corporate environments would e-mail interoperability features be most important?

10. Differentiate between the two major e-mail system messaging architectures in terms of complexity, interoperability with a variety of network operating systems, and scalability.

11. Distinguish between SMTP, POP, and IMAP.

12. What is calendaring?

13. What are the three product classification areas regarding calendaring and scheduling?

14. What is workflow?

15. Distinguish between ad hoc and process workflow.

16. What are the four main elements contained in a workflow application?

17. What are the four main objectives of the workflow management coalition?

18. What are the key functional areas of workflow products?

19. What is real-time conferencing?

20. What are some examples of real-time conferencing?

21. What is non–real-time conferencing?

22. What is data conferencing?

23. What is an electronic whiteboard?

24. What is group document editing?

25. What are the benefits to using audio and video conferencing?

26. What is a bulletin board system?

27. What are the key functional areas of conferencing?

28. List the issues surrounding videoconferencing that should be of concern to a network analyst.

29. Why are ISDN and Switched 56K popular WAN services for videoconferencing?

30. What is the business justification for purchasing workflow automation software?

31. Differentiate between the various types of workflow automation software in terms of the type of workflow to be automated. Is one type of workflow more likely to benefit from automation than another?

32. What is the relationship between business process reengineering and workflow automation software?

33. Why is interoperability important to document management systems from a business perspective?

34. What is the intended business impact of computer telephony integration software?

35. Differentiate between advisory agents and assistant agents.

36. What are the various levels of compatibility that multiprotocol printer servers must address?

37. Differentiate between alternative network backup architectures in terms of advantages, disadvantages, and delivered functionality.

38. What are some of the key network backup issues with which network analysts should be concerned?

39. Differentiate between the alternative network faxing implementation solutions in terms of ease of installation and expense.

40. Why would shared network access for incoming faxes be more difficult to automate than shared network access for outgoing faxes?

41. What is the purpose of a Fax API?

42. What is the business justification for the purchase and implementation of electronic software distribution software?

43. What types of issues should a network analyst be concerned with regarding the implementation of electronic software distribution?

44. Why has license metering software now taken on more of a license management or license optimization role?

45. What are the business benefits that can be gained through implementing LAN inventory management software?

1. Research the topic of e-mail etiquette and report on your findings or prepare a brochure for distribution of e-mail etiquette tips.
2. Consult buyers' guides or product directories regarding e-mail systems. Differentiate among available products in terms of architecture. Focus on messaging protocols and services used in each system and relate your findings to the level of interoperability offered by each e-mail system.
3. Investigate and report on installed e-mail systems at a school or business. Pay particular attention to interoperability with other e-mail systems. How is mail prepared for transmission over the Internet? Are e-mail gateways employed?
4. Research unsolicited e-mail or SPAM. What are the major issues associated with SPAM?
5. Investigate the electronic whiteboard software category of GroupWare. Pay particular attention to functionality delivered and bandwidth requirements. Report on the relationship between bandwidth requirements, network architectures and WAN service supported, and number of simultaneous users supported.
6. Prepare a survey of schools or companies that employ videoconferencing. Report on video-conference network infrastructure, videoconference usage or applications, and payback or cost/benefit analysis. Is the video traffic sharing network bandwidth with data transmission?
7. Find a school or business that has implemented workflow software. Analyze the implementation in terms of type of workflow, type of routing, implementation history, and perceived benefits.
8. Investigate the Computer telephony integration category of software in terms of current market size, estimated market growth, key vendors, standards efforts, intended business impact, and report on your results.
9. Investigate and report on the current status of printer management standard development efforts.
10. Investigate network faxing software, paying special attention to comparative abilities to support automatic routing of incoming faxes. Contrast the various approaches found for auto-routing of incoming faxes.
11. Investigate and report on installed software license management systems at a school or business.
12. Investigate and report on the current status of efforts to develop a standardized license server embedded within popular network operating systems.

CASE STUDY

State University Webifies Its Widespread Networks

The University of California is serving its far-flung networks new courses of intranets, workflow systems and high-speed ATM LANs.

For example, the MIS team at the university system's Office of the President built a Web-based "benefits rep calculation tool." Through a browser, administrators can remotely access the university's IBM RS/6000 financial application to calculate benefits for 200,000 employees.

A new interactive voice response (IVR) system is easing the process of applying for loans. The state school system has a $22 billion retirement fund that employees can borrow against. Instead of heading down to an office, employees can simply dial an 800 number. "We took the whole process and put it up on IVR," says Bruce James, IS maintenance manager in the Office of the President.

With the dial-a-loan process, the caller can begin to apply by punching the keypad for the amount he wants. The IVR loan application, designed by university staff using Edify Corp. workflow tools, sends each loan request to the school's Sybase database, which kick-starts a "work object" on the loan administrator's LAN. Prompted by an item in his work queue, the administrator mails off loan documents to the applicant. The forms are scanned into the university's FileNet imaging system once they are signed and returned by the applicant.

The imaged documents are added to the loan workflow process, which has cut the approval process to days instead of weeks, James says.

Throughout the state, the University of California campuses are working on network modernization projects.

Gary Forman, director of administrative IS at UC San Francisco, says his campus last year installed the PeopleSoft 7.0 financial reporting application on a Sun server to replace the mainframe ledger system. Now MIS staff is adding the NetDynamics 4.0 application server as the front end so administrators on and off the campus can get PeopleSoft financial data in Web format (see graphic).

At the larger campuses of UC Davis and UC San Diego, MIS staff has installed multi-megabit ATM-based campus backbones. The high-speed backbones handle the ever-growing traffic from students and faculty.

For the Davis campus, American Management Systems custom-designed a set of Web-based financial applications running on Hewlett-Packard Unix servers for use by about 20,000 people, according to Tony Flores, associate vice chancellor there.

But UC San Diego chose to build its own set of intranet applications, dubbing them the Link family of Web applications, according to Elazar Harel, UC San Diego's assistant vice chancellor for computing and telecommunications.

These applications include Student-Link, which lets more than 18,000 students enroll for classes or change addresses; FinancialLink, which lets administrators review ledgers and budget statements; and TravelLink, for submitting expenses for reimbursement.

Next up? Tightening security. "All of the Link family is based on passwords, but we want to migrate over to digital certificates," Harel explains. Certificates offer better security than passwords, and the entire university system would like to share a common public-key infrastructure (PKI) for issuing and revoking certificates to students and employees.

A TOUGH TEST

The Office of the President has launched a pilot PKI project, based on Netscape certificate-management and Lightweight Directory Access Protocol servers, to certificate-enable a handful of Web applications. Jim Dolgones, assistant vice president of IS in the Office of the President, says getting applications to use certificates is not the toughest task. The hardest issue is administrative: properly checking out the would-be user's identity and distributing the certificate to him.

In addition to its Netscape pilot, the university is looking into whether Veri-Sign could supply and manage certificate distribution for the entire university system.

Source: Ellen Messmer, "State University Webifies Its Widespread Networks," *Network World,* vol. 16, no. 10 (March 8, 1999), p. 31. Copyright Network World.

BUSINESS CASE STUDY QUESTIONS

Activities

1. Complete a top-down model for this case by gleaning facts from the case and placing them in the proper layer of the top-down model. After completing the top-down model, analyze and detail those instances where requirements were clearly passed down from upper layers to lower layers of the model and where solutions to those requirements were passed up from lower layers to upper layers of the model.
2. Detail any questions about the case that may occur to you for which answers are not clearly stated in the article.

Business

1. What business features have been addressed in the work described in the case study?
2. What is the key business feature of the dial-a-loan system?
3. What is the key business driver for the People-Soft system?

Application

1. What are the components of the Link system?
2. What new features does the state university system plan to bring on-line in the near future?

Data

1. What types of data are accessible through the Link system?
2. What types of data are managed in the dial-a-loan system?

Network

1. What is the logical network design at UC Davis and US San Diego?

Technology

1. What network technologies have been adopted at the various campuses?
2. What security technologies is the state university system considering for future implementation?

LOCAL AREA NETWORK CONNECTIVITY

INTRODUCTION

Part 3 of the text builds on the knowledge of LAN infrastructure and software gained in Parts I and 2 by exploring the issues, challenges, and solutions involved with getting LANs, remote clients, and other types of computing systems to communicate with each other. These issues are thoroughly explored from logical design through physical implementation.

Chapter 12, Network Design Using TCP/IP, seeks to inform the reader on how network design is actually performed in a TCP/IP based network. The importance of how to use IP addressing to properly define subnet masks and how the logical distribution of IP addresses must correlate to the physical topology of the network are key issues stressed in this chapter. Issues that are critical to network design in the real world such as the shrinking pool of IP addresses and the need to minimize the size of routing tables are analyzed and potential solutions are provided. By the completion of this chapter, the reader should be comfortable designing IP based networks in both a classful and classless addressing environment.

Chapter 13, Local Area Network Internetworking, introduces the reader to the complexities and basic principles of internetwork design such as bridging, routing, and switching. Internetwork design and technology issues are explored for both LAN-to-LAN internetworking as well as LAN-to-mainframe internetworking.

Chapter 14, Local Area Networking Remote Access and Wireless Networking, outlines a methodology for the proper design of remote access solutions based on a thorough understanding of user needs, network architecture alternatives, available remote access technology, and available WAN services.

CHAPTER 12

NETWORK DESIGN USING TCP/IP

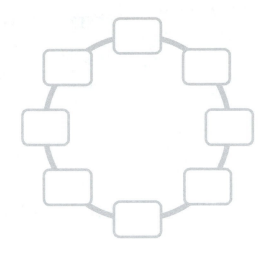

Concepts Reinforced

Classfull Addressing	Subnet Masks

Concepts Introduced

Classless Addressing	Variable Length Subnet Masks
Reserved Subnets	Classless InterDomain Routing
Extended Network Prefixes	Route Summarization
Longest Match Lookups	Static Routing
Dynamic Routing	

OBJECTIVES

After completing this chapter, the reader should be able to:

1. Define proper classfull subnet masks for a given IP address that will meet network design requirements

2. Understand the advantages and proper use of variable length subnet masking

3. Define proper variable length subnet masks for a given IP address that will meet network design requirements

4. Understand the advantages and proper use of classless interdomain routing addresses

■ INTRODUCTION

Having thoroughly introduced TCP/IP from a conceptual standpoint in Chapter 4, this chapter seeks to inform the reader on how network design is actually performed in a TCP/IP-based network. The importance of how to use IP addressing to properly define subnet masks and how the logical distribution of IP addresses must correlate to the physical topology of the network are key issues stressed in this chapter. Issues that are critical to network design in the real world such as the shrinking pool of IP addresses and the need to minimize the size of routing tables are analyzed and potential solutions are provided. By the completion of this chapter, the reader should be comfortable designing IP-based networks in both a classfull and classless addressing environment.

■ CLASSFULL ADDRESSING—A BRIEF REVIEW

Address Classes

Classfull addresses are broken apart on octet boundaries. Therefore, there are three basic classes of addresses. As illustrated in Figure 12-1, these classes are known as class A, B, or C networks. To distinguish among classes, the first few

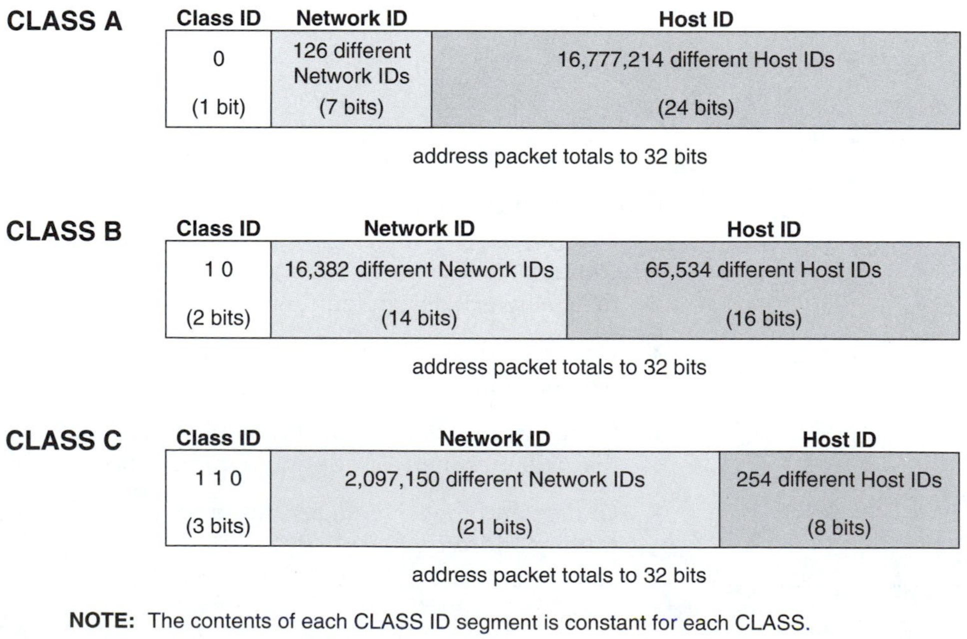

CLASS A

Class ID	Network ID	Host ID
0	126 different Network IDs	16,777,214 different Host IDs
(1 bit)	(7 bits)	(24 bits)

address packet totals to 32 bits

CLASS B

Class ID	Network ID	Host ID
1 0	16,382 different Network IDs	65,534 different Host IDs
(2 bits)	(14 bits)	(16 bits)

address packet totals to 32 bits

CLASS C

Class ID	Network ID	Host ID
1 1 0	2,097,150 different Network IDs	254 different Host IDs
(3 bits)	(21 bits)	(8 bits)

address packet totals to 32 bits

NOTE: The contents of each CLASS ID segment is constant for each CLASS.

Figure 12-1   IPv4 Address Classes

bits of each segment address are used to denote the address class of the segment. The class ID plus network ID portions of the IP address are also known as the network prefix, the network number, or the major network. As illustrated in Figure 12-1, Class A addresses have an 8-bit network prefix, sometimes referred to as "/8" (slash eight); Class B addresses have a 16-bit network prefix and are sometimes referred to as /16 addresses, and Class C addresses have a 24-bit network prefix and are sometimes referred to as /24s.

As illustrated in Figure 12-1, Class A addresses can be identified if the first bit is a 0 in binary notation or has a decimal value between 1 and 126. Class B addresses can be identified if the first two bits are 10 or if the first decimal octet is between 128 and 191. The first octet address of 127 is reserved for loopback tests on network interface cards and routers. Class C addresses can be identified if the first three bits in binary notation are 110 or if the first octet's decimal value is between 192 and 223, inclusive.

In addition to these basic address classes, there are two additional classes, class D and class E, that can be used for IPv4 addressing. Class D addresses are reserved for multicast systems such as routers, whereas Class E addresses are reserved for future use.

The assignment of address classes and network ID ranges to a particular organization wishing to connect to the Internet is the responsibility of the Internet Activities Board (IAB). The IAB ensures that all organizations using the Internet for network communications have unique IP addresses for all of their workstations. If an organization has no intention of ever accessing the Internet, there may be no need to register with the IAB for an IP address class and range of valid network IDs. Even in this case, however, all workstations on all communicating networks must have IP addresses unique within the internal corporate network.

Subnetting—Why Subnet?   When the IP address classes were established in the early 1980s, before the widespread use of personal computers, computer networks were comprised of a relatively small number of relatively expensive computers. However, as time went on and the personal computer exploded into local area networks, the strict boundaries of the classfull addressing address classes became restrictive and forced an inefficient allocation of addresses. More specifically, a Class C address with its limit of 254 hosts (computers) per network is too small for most organizations, whereas Class B address with its limit of 65,534 hosts per subnet is too large. Unfortunately, Class B addresses were given out to organizations that would never need the 65,534 addresses.

A second issue arose as organizations' networks grew and needed to be divided or segmented in order to improve traffic flow. Two separate networks are joined by routers. Networks that are separated by routers must have different network IDs so that the router can distinguish between them. This would require all organizations that needed to install a router-based internetwork to go back to the IAB for more addresses, thereby accelerating the depletion of IP addresses.

In order to address both of these concerns, RFC 950 was defined in 1985. It provided a way to **subnet** or provide a third layer of organization or hierarchy between the existing network ID and the existing host ID. Since the network IDs were assigned by IAB and could not be altered, the only choice was to "borrow" some of the host ID bits that were under the control of the organization to which the address had been assigned. These "borrowed" bits are what constitutes the subnet portion of the address. The particular bits that are used for the subnet ID are identified through the use of a subnet mask.

Subnetting allowed organizations to use the one network ID assigned by the IAB and create multiple subnets within their private network. Although their internal routers had to remain aware of all of the internal subnets in order to properly deliver data, the Internet routing tables were not affected because all of these subnets existed behind the original network ID assigned by the IAB. As a result, organizations could build router-based internetworks without asking for additional network IDs and the Internet routing tables did not have to be overloaded with all the information about routes to all of the internal subnets.

■   NETWORK DESIGN WITH CLASSFULL IP ADDRESSING

Subnet Masks

By applying a 32-bit subnet mask to a Class B IP address, a portion of the bits that comprise the host ID can be reserved for denoting sub-networks, with the remaining bits being reserved for host IDs per sub-network. If the first 8 bits of the host ID were reserved for sub-network addresses and the final 8 bits of the host ID were reserved for hosts per subnetwork, this would allow the same Class B address to yield 254 subnetworks with 254 hosts each as opposed to one network with 65,534 hosts. Figure 12-2 provides examples of subnet masks. The overall effect of subnetworking is to create multiple network segments within the address space given by the IAB.

	Binary Subnet Mask	Decimal Subnet Mask	Number of Sub-Networks	Number of Hosts per Sub-Network
Default Class B Subnet Mask	11111111 11111111 00000000 00000000	255.255.0.0	1	65,534
Alternative Subnet Mask Used to Subnet Class B Network	11111111 11111111 11111111 00000000	255.255.255.0	254	254

Figure 12-2   IPv4 Subnetworking

As illustrated in Figure 12-2, to create a subnet mask, each bit position is reserved for either a network ID or a host ID. By default, in the case of a Class B address, the first 16 bits are reserved for network ID and the second 16 bits are reserved for host ID. Of the 16 bits originally reserved for host ID, those bits that we wish to use for a subnet ID are reserved by placing a 1 in that bit position. If we wish to retain the use of a bit position for host ID, then we reserve that bit position with a 0. In the example illustrated in Figure 12-2, we borrowed 8 of the 16 bits set aside for host ID and reassigned their function as subnet ID by reserving those 8 bit positions with a 1 in the subnet mask. Converting the binary place holder values to decimal yielded the decimal subnet mask 255.255.255.0.

This subnet mask yields 8 bit positions for subnet IDs and 8 bit positions for host IDs. Two to the eighth power is 256. However, as will be explained further, the all zeros and all ones subnet and host Ids are reserved thereby leaving 254 available subnets and 254 available host IDs as listed in Figure 12-2.

Extended Network Prefix   The classfull network prefix (/16 in the case of a Class B address) plus the number of bits borrowed from the host ID is called the **extended network prefix.** In the case of the example illustrated in Figure 12-2, the extended network prefix would be /24 (/16 network prefix + /8 subnet mask). As an example, if we were given the Class B address of 128.210.49.213/24 what would we know? Figure 12-3 illustrates the network prefix, extended network prefix, subnet mask in binary and decimal, network ID, subnet ID, and host ID.

The TCP/IP Subnet Definition Chart   Once the theory behind how subnet masks are defined is understood, it would be nice to be able to define appropriate subnet masks without having to perform binary arithmetic. Figure 12-4 provides a convenient chart that can be used to define the proper subnet mask dependent on the class of the original network ID, the number of required subnets, and the number of required hosts per subnet.

Working with Subnet Masks—Subnet Design   In order to illustrate the use of the TCP/IP Subnet Definition Chart, let's take a practical example:

The university where you work has six administrative offices, each on its own subnet and each requiring between 15 and 25 hosts. For your Class C

	Decimal	Network Prefix	Subnet ID	Host ID
IP Address	128.210.49.213	10000000.11010010	00110001	11010101
Subnet Mask	255.255.255.0	11111111.11111111	11111111	00000000
		← Extended Network	Prefix → =/24	

Figure 12-3   Extended Network Prefix

Number of Ones in Last Octet of Subnet mask	Subnet Mask Octet	Address Block Size	Number of Subnets	Number of Class C Hosts	Number of Class B Hosts	Number of Class A Hosts
2	192	64	2	62	16382	4,194,302
3	224	32	6	30	8190	2,097,150
4	240	16	14	14	4094	1,048,574
5	248	8	30	6	2046	524,286
6	252	4	62	2	1022	262,142
7	254	2	126	N/A	510	131,070
8	255	1	254	N/A	254	65,534

Figure 12-4   Classful IP Subnet Definition Chart

address, you create the subnet mask 255.255.255.240. How well does this solution address the problem? Explain.

Referring to the TCP/IP Subnet Definition Chart, we can see that if 6 subnets are required, then the last octet in the subnet mask should be 224, not 240, which would yield 30 hosts per subnet. In the example, the defined subnet of 240 would yield 14 subnets but only 14 host per subnet, which would not meet the requirement.

The correct answer, 224, has 3 ones in the subnet mask borrowed from the host ID. A Class C address is a /24 subnet mask by default. Adding the 3 ones yields a correct subnet mask of 255.255.255.224 or a correct extended network prefix of /27 (24+3).

In order to properly define a subnet mask for a given classfull address, one must know the following information:

1. What is the address class of the assigned network ID? This is important to know because the address class tells you how many bits are available for "borrowing" from the host ID for the subnet ID. Class A: 24 bits, Class B: 16 bits, Class C: 8 bits. Obviously, you can't borrow all of the available bits for the subnet ID because there won't be anything left for the host ID.

2. How many subnets are required both now and in the future? Future considerations are important. Although more flexible subnet definition alternatives will be examined later in the chapter, classfull subnet definition needs to be done exactly the same across all subnets in a given network ID.

3. How many host IDs per subnet are required now and in the future? Again, you must define your subnet mask based on the worst anticipated scenario. That is to say, what is the largest number of hosts that you anticipate having to support on your largest subnet? Remember, you can't just choose an arbitrarily large number of host Ids because every bit that gets reserved for host Ids means one less bit available for subnet IDs.

Let's try another example:

A retail chain of 80 stores expects to expand by 20 stores per year for the next eight years. Only one computer connected to a router at each site (total of two host IDs) will be needed to upload the daily sales figures to corporate headquarters. The IP address is 165.32.0.0 What should the subnet mask be? Explain.

Solution: The given IP address is 165.32.0.0. This is a Class B or /16 address, which means we have 16 bits available with which to define the subnet mask. In order to determine the number of required subnets, we take the 80 current stores and add 160 more (20 per year × 8 years) for a total anticipated number of stores or subnets of 240. We only need two host IDs per subnet. Using the TCP/IP Subnet Definition Chart, we see that in order to have 240 subnets, we will need 8 bits in the subnet mask. Adding the subnet mask to the default for a Class B address yields 255.255.255.0 or an extended network prefix of /24 (/16+8).

Defining Subnet Numbers   Once the subnet mask for a given major network or network prefix has been defined, the next job is to define the individual subnet numbers that are associated with the assigned major network number. From the previous example, the assigned major network was 165.32.0.0. We know we are going to use the next 8 bits, or the entire third octet, for the subnet ID. The subnet mask of 255.255.255.0 tells us this is so. Notice how the third octet, which is normally reserved for host ID is a Class B address, is all ones (255) in the subnet mask indicating that it will be used for defining the subnet ID. Since 2 raised to the eighth power is 256, we should be able to define 256 different subnet IDs. In fact, we can. As we'll soon see, however, two of those subnet addresses are reserved, yielding 254 available subnet IDs as stated on the TCP/IP Subnet Definition Chart. Figure 12-5 shows how individual subnet IDs are defined.

Reserved Subnet Numbers   Two subnet numbers, the all zeros subnet and the all-ones subnet are typically reserved, especially in routers that support classfull routing protocols. The all zeros subnet is labeled as Subnet 0 and the all ones subnet is labeled as Subnet 255 in Figure 12-5. As can be seen in Figure 12-5, the full address of subnet 0 (165.32.0.0) is identical to the Assigned network ID of 165.32.0.0. In order to differentiate between the two, one

	Network Prefix	Subnet Number	Reserved for Host ID	Decimal with Extended Network Prefix
Assigned Network ID	10100101.00100000	00000000	00000000	165.32.0.0/16
Subnet 0	10100101.00100000	00000000	00000000	165.32.0.0/24
Subnet 1	10100101.00100000	00000001	00000000	165.32.1.0/24
Subnet 2	10100101.00100000	00000010	00000000	165.32.2.0/24
Subnet 3	10100101.00100000	00000011	00000000	165.32.3.0/24
|				
|				
Subnet 254	10100101.00100000	11111110	00000000	165.32.254.0/24
Subnet 255	10100101.00100000	11111111	00000000	165.32.255.0/24

Figure 12-5 Defining Subnet Numbers

would have to know the extended network prefix in each case. Since routers supporting classfull routing protocols don't exchange extended network prefixes, there is no way for them to differentiate between the assigned major network ID (sometimes referred to as the default route) and Subnet 0 of the major network, leading the Subnet 0 address to be declared reserved. The all ones subnet ID is reserved because it has a special meaning to classfull routing protocol routers, namely, broadcast to all subnets. Later in the chapter we will discuss other types of routing protocols that are able to share extended network prefixes, thereby allowing routers to distinguish between the pairs discussed above and listed in Figure 12-6.

Defining Host Addresses for a Given Subnet Because the network ID with extended network prefix is 165.32.0.0/24 in the current example, that tells us that the last octet, or last 8 bits, has been reserved to define host IDs. Host IDs are defined within a given subnet. In Figure 12-7, we have chosen to

	Decimal with Extended Network Prefix
Assigned Network ID	165.32.0.0/16
All Zeros Subnet	165.32.0.0/24
Broadcast	165.32.255.0/16
All Ones Subnet	165.32.255.0/24

Figure 12-6 Reserved Subnet Numbers

	Extended Network Prefix	Host ID	Decimal
Host 1	10100101.00100000.00000001	00000001	165.32.1.1/24
Host 2	10100101.00100000.00000001	00000010	165.32.1.2/24
Host 3	10100101.00100000.00000001	00000011	165.32.1.3/24
Host 4	10100101.00100000.00000001	00000100	165.32.1.4/24
Host 5	10100101.00100000.00000001	00000101	165.32.1.5/24
Host 253	10100101.00100000.00000001	11111101	165.32.1.253/24
Host 254	10100101.00100000.00000001	11111110	165.32.1.254/24

Figure 12-7   Defining Host Ids for a Given Subnet

define host IDs for subnet #1. As a result we know that all host IDs will have the same first three octets in dotted decimal format, namely, 165.32.1. The only part that will vary will be the fourth octet which will contain unique host IDs. Since there are 8 bits in the fourth octet, we should be able to define 2 to the eighth power, or 256 different host IDs per subnet. However, as was the case with subnet IDs, we have two reserved host IDs as well leaving us with 254 usable host IDs.

Reserved Host Addresses   Just as when defining subnet numbers, there are also reserved host IDs, regardless of the length (number of bits) of the host ID, the all ones host ID is reserved as the broadcast address for a given subnet and the all zeros host ID is reserved as identifying the subnet number itself. As a result, the broadcast address for the number one subnet used in Figure 12-7 would be 165.32.1.255.

How Routers Use Classfull IP Address Information

Now that we understand subnetting from a conceptual perspective, let's see how it works in reality. As previously mentioned, network processing devices known as routers are employed to act as intelligent forwarding devices between subnets and networks. Figure 12-8 illustrates two subnets of the 165.32.0.0 network separated by a router. The router acts as a gateway to each subnet. The router actually has a network interface card that participates in each subnet. The IP address of the router's NIC in subnet 1 is 165.32.1.1, and the IP address of the NIC acting as a gateway to subnet 2 is 165.32.2.1. Associated with the IP address assigned to each NIC on the router is a subnet mask. As we will see shortly, the subnet mask is used by the

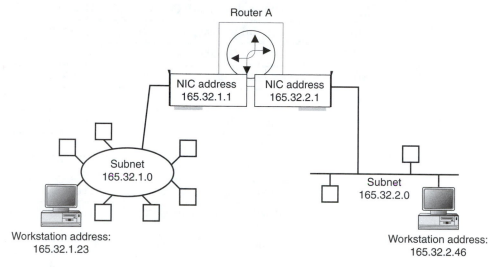

Figure 12-8   Single Router Scenario

routers to determine the subnet IDs of all traffic that it is asked to process. Note how the third octet distinguishes between subnets. Also notice the differences in workstation addresses on the respective subnets.

Determining if IP Addresses Are Part of the Same Subnet   In the example we have been using, the entire third octet was used for the subnet ID, so the subnet number is immediately evident just by reading the dotted decimal address. For example the subnet ID in the address 165.32.2.46/24 is 2 and the subnet ID in the address 165.32.1.23/24 is 1. What would happen if this were not the case? What if the entire third octet were not reserved for the subnet ID? How would we, or the routers for that matter, be able to determine what the real subnet address was when all we are given is the dotted decimal format?

Given the network ID 192.210.165.0 from the IAB, we need to define a subnet ID that will yield 30 subnets with up to six hosts per subnet. Noting that we are dealing with a Class C address and referring back to the Subnet Definition Chart (Figure 12-4), we should see that we need the last octet to be 248. Since this is a Class C or/24 address and we are reserving 5 of the remaining 8 bits for subnet ID, it should be evident that the extended network prefix will be /29 or the subnet mask in dotted decimal format would be equivalently expressed as 255.255.255.248. Figure 12-9 shows how the subnets would be defined.

Note that in Figure 12-9 there are only 5 bits available for subnet IDs and 3 bits reserved for host IDs for each subnet. As we will see, since an entire octet has not been reserved for the subnet ID, it will not be as immediately evident as in previous examples. Also notice in Figure 12-9 that with only 5

	Network Prefix	Subnet Number	Reserved for Host ID	Decimal with Extended Network Prefix
Assigned Network ID	11000000.11010010.10100101	00000	000	192.210.165.0/24
Subnet 0—Reserved	11000000.11010010.10100101	00000	000	192.210.165.0/29
Subnet 1	11000000.11010010.10100101	00001	000	192.210.165.8/29
Subnet 2	11000000.11010010.10100101	00010	000	192.210.165.16/29
Subnet 3	11000000.11010010.10100101	00011	000	192.210.165.24/29
Subnet 30	11000000.11010010.10100101	11110	000	192.210.165.240/29
Subnet 31—Reserved	11000000.11010010.10100101	11111	000	192.210.165.248/29

Figure 12-9   Subnet Definition with Less than an Octet

bits to work with, we are only able to define 32 total subnets, two of which are reserved.

Figure 12-10 defines host IDs for Subnet 1 from Figure 12-9. Since there are only 3 bits reserved for host ID, we can only define 8 different host IDs, 2 of which are reserved. Notice how the extended network prefix does not increase when we define host IDs for a given subnet the way it did when we defined additional subnet levels to existing subnets.

In the case of subnet 1 (subnet address 8), if we were to choose one of the full host IDs as defined Figure 12-10, we don't immediately see the subnet address of 8 in the full dotted decimal address of the host IDs. Where is the

	Extended Network Prefix	Host ID	Decimal
Host 1 - Reserved	11000000.11010010.10100101.00001	000	192.210.165.8/29
Host 2	11000000.11010010.10100101.00001	001	192.210.165.9/29
Host 3	11000000.11010010.10100101.00001	010	192.210.165.10/29
Host 4	11000000.11010010.10100101.00001	011	192.210.165.11/29
Host 5	11000000.11010010.10100101.00001	100	192.210.165.12/29
Host 6	11000000.11010010.10100101.00001	101	192.210.165.13/29
Host 7	11000000.11010010.10100101.00001	110	192.210.165.14/29
Host 8 - Reserved	11000000.11010010.10100101.00001	111	192.210.165.15/29

Figure 12-10   Defining Host IDs

Decimal Value	128	64	32	16	8	4	2	1
Power of 2	7	6	5	4	3	2	1	0
Subnet 1 Binary	0	0	0	0	1	Reserved	For	Host ID
Subnet 1 Decimal					8	Reserved	For	Host ID
Subnet 30 Binary	1	1	1	1	0	Reserved	For	Host ID
Subnet 30 Decimal	128+	64+	32+	16+	0 = 240	Reserved	For	Host ID

Figure 12-11   Hidden Subnet Ids

subnet address of 8 hiding? Why is the subnet address of subnet 1 defined as 8? As illustrated in Figure 12-11, it is due to the decimal place values of the binary digits used to define the subnet number.

Routers need to know the real subnet address of every piece of packetized data that they encounter in order to properly forward that data toward its ultimate destination. To do this, routers must know the subnet mask or extended network prefix of the address in question and then use a type of binary arithmetic known as a logical AND. If a 1 is present in a given place in both the IP address and the subnet mask, then a 1 is placed in the result; otherwise a 0 is placed in the result. This operation is illustrated in Figure 12-12. In this case, we will use the host ID defined in Figure 12-10 for host ID 6 on Subnet 1, with the full dotted decimal address of 192.210.165.13/29.

As illustrated in Figure 12-12, although the last octet of the full address had a value of 13, by using binary arithmetic, the router is able to determine the actual subnet ID of the address provided it also knows the subnet mask or extended network prefix.

If the subnet ID of the destination address on the data packet is the same as the subnet of the router interface, the router will do nothing. Because it is a local delivery, the router need not get involved. If after determining the

IP Address	192.210.165.13/29
Subnet Mask	255.255.255.248

	First Octet	Second Octet	Third Octet	Subnet Portion of Fourth Octet	Host ID Portion of Fourth Octet
192.210.165.13	11000000	11010010	10100101	00001	101
255.255.255.248	11111111	11111111	11111111	11111	000
Result Binary from Logical AND	11000000	11010010	10100101	00001	
Result Decimal	192	210	165	8	5

Figure 12-12   Determining if IP Addresses Are Part of the Same Subnet

real subnet ID of the destination address it turns out that the destination subnet is not the same as the local router interface's subnet, then the router needs to go to work consulting its routing tables and determining the address of the next hop router that will help this data packet on its way to its ultimate destination.

Static Routing versus Dynamic Routing   Routes to specific networks that are stored in a routing table can be entered into that routing table in two different ways. **Static routes** can be manually entered by a network administrator into a router's routing table. By definition, static routes do not change as network conditions change and are therefore unable to adapt to network failures. As networks grow, configuring and maintaining static routes on multiple routers can become a real challenge.

Dynamic routing is achieved when routers are allowed to build their own routing tables based on route advertisements received from other routers. This may be simpler to configure but risks having one misbehaving router create a potentially cascading negative impact on other routers. This is a greater concern when those other routers are controlled by other unknown organizations, as explained further in the section entitled "Hierarchical Networking and Autonomous Systems."

Longest Match Algorithm and Routing Table Organization   Routing protocols and routing table organization were first introduced in Chapter 4. To briefly review, Figure 12-13 differentiates between the two major categories of routing protocols: distance vector and link state.

At least some routers are capable of executing multiple routing protocols. This is often necessary, since various networks that had been designed and administered independently must subsequently find a way to interoperate transparently. Routers running more than one routing protocol simultaneously and sharing or translating routing information between those routing protocols are able to do so through a process known as **redistribution.**

Regardless of routing protocol, whenever a router consults its routing table in order to find the proper route on which to forward a given packet, it chooses that route via a method known as the **longest match algorithm.** Simply stated, this means that the more specific the direction, the better. For example, suppose a routing table contained the following two entries as illustrated in Figure 12-14.

Now suppose the router received a packet destined for a workstation with the address 192.210.165.32. The router would work its way down the routing table looking for the longest match. Addresses are sorted from most specific (longest) to least specific, so as soon as the router encountered the 192.210.0.0 entry it would have known that it had just passed the most specific or longest match entry. In this manner, the router does not have to read the entire routing table every time for every packet. It only reads until one entry past the longest match and back up one to its most specific entry.

	Distance Vector	Link State
Examples	RIPv1, RIPv2, IGRP	OSPF, NLSP, ISIS
Updates	Entire routing table exchanged with neighbor every 30–90 seconds, depending on protocol	Only updates to routing table are sent out only as needed
Processing	After receiving neighboring router's routing table, each router recomputes all routing table entries based on its distance from the sending router.	Link State Packets are processed immediately. Information contained therein is added to update the overall view of the network.
Extent of View	Only can see its neighboring routers which it depends on for broader view of network	Each router has a view of the entire network, since all link state packets are received and incorporated by all routers
Bandwidth Usage	More	Less
Processor and Memory Usage	Less	More
Metric	RIP: Hop Count IGRP: bandwidth, delay, load, reliability, max. transmission unit	Cost, shortest path algorithm
Advantages	• Low processing and memory usage • Simpler to implement	• No routing table exchange • No hop count limit • Link bandwidth and delay are considered in routing decisions • Fast convergence • Support for VLSM and CIDR • Hierarchical view of network scales better for large internetwork
Disadvantages	• Doesn't consider bandwidth of links when making routing decisions • Slow convergence • Hop count limit of 15, 16 = unreachable • Exchanging entire routing tables is inefficient • Don't support Variable Length Subnet Masks and Classless Inter Domain Routing (RIPv1) • No hierarchy to network view, can't scale to large internetworks	• More processor and memory intensive • More complicated to implement

Figure 12-13   Distance Vector versus Link-State Protocols

Network ID	Path
192.210.165.0/24	Path 1
192.210.0.0/16	Path 2

Figure 12-14   Routing Table for Longest Match Algorithm

Gateways of Last Resort   What if a router gets to the bottom of a routing table and still hasn't found a match? Certain routing protocols, such as IGRP, support a feature known as gateway of last resort. If a router cannot find a match in a routing table for a destination packet, it will forward that packet to the address of the gateway of last resort under the assumption that the gateway of last resort may know of additional networks that were unknown to the original router.

The danger in using a gateway of last resort is that the router may be forwarding traffic to destinations that are truly unreachable. Over time, this lost traffic could consume significant amounts of bandwidth. In order to avoid this, routers can be configured with a **null interface,** sometimes referred to as a bit bucket, so that undesirable traffic can be discarded rather than endlessly forwarded.

SPLIT HORIZON, POISON REVERSE, AND TRIGGERED UPDATES

RIP broadcasts its routing tables to all directly connected routers every 30 seconds. Those directly connected routers then propagate the new routing table information to the routers directly connected to them. This pattern continues, and after a matter of about 7 minutes (30 sec. intervals × 15 hop max.), all routing tables have been updated and, for the moment, are synchronized. However, the delay that occurs while all of the routers are propagating their routing tables, known as **slow convergence,** could allow certain routers to think that failed links to certain networks are still viable. In order to reduce the convergence time, the following optional approaches have been added to RIP:

- **Split horizon** prevents routers from wasting time broadcasting routing table changes back to the routers that just supplied them with the same changes in the first place. This can help prevent **routing loops** in which two routers continue to trade routing table updates for a route that is in fact no longer reachable. However, each router thinks the other router can still reach the unreachable network and continues to add an additional hop to its own routing table to that network and rebroadcast this erroneous information to the other router caught in this routing loop. When traffic destined for this unreachable network is received by either of these routers, they continually forward the traffic back and forth, each thinking the other router knows how to reach the unreachable network. Eventually, one of the routers will reach a hop count of 16 to the unreachable network. In distance vector protocols, a hop count of 16 means the network is unreachable. This is an important limitation to the physical design limitations of networks using distance vector protocols. The slow process of routers caught in a routing loop eventually figuring out that a network is unreachable is sometimes referred to as "counting to infinity." As previously mentioned, enabling split horizon on a router interface will prevent routing loops.

- Instead of just waiting for the counting to infinity process to eventually identify and shut down routing loops, **reverse poison** allows a router to immediately set a hop count on a given route to 16 (unreachable) as soon as it senses that it and a neighboring router are incrementing hop counts by 1 to a given network on successive routing table exchanges.

- **Triggered updates** allow routers to immediately broadcast routing table updates regarding failed links rather than having to wait for the next 30 second periodic update.

However, it should be pointed out that despite these improvements, RIP is still not as efficient or as scalable as link state routing protocols.

Private Addressing and Network Address Translation   As mentioned earlier in the chapter, IP address depletion has resulted from the explosion of the Internet as well as the inefficient use of existing IP addresses forced by Classfull addressing. One way to cope with the rapid depletion of IP addresses is through the use of **private addressing.**

When organizations connect to the Internet, the IP addresses they send out over the Internet must be globally unique. In most cases, these globally unique addresses are specified by an organization's Internet service provider.

However, traffic that remains only on an organization's private network does not need to be globally unique; it only needs to be unique across that organization's private network. In support of this the Internet Assigned Numbers Authority (IANA) has set aside the following three ranges of private IP addresses:

- 10.0.0.0 through 10.255.255.255   (equal to a single Class A Network ID)

- 172.16.0.0 through 172.31.255.255   (equal to 16 contiguous Class B Network IDs)

- 192.168.0.0 through 192.168.255.255   (equal to 256 contiguous Class C Network IDs)

Traffic using any of the preceding address ranges must remain on the organization's private network. Because anyone is welcome to use these address ranges, they are not globally unique and therefore cannot be used on the Internet.

Computers on a network using the Private IP address space can still send and receive traffic to/from the Internet by using **network address translation (NAT).** Network address translation can be provided by a router or by a stand-alone network translation software package running on a multi-homed server. A multi-homed server is the term used to describe a server that would have one network interface card that was a member of the internal private IP address space network and one network interface card that was assigned a globally unique IP address. A version of such a program that is included as a networking feature of Linux is known as IP Masquerade, while a version that runs on Windows NT is known as WinRoute (www.winroute.com). A Linux IP Masquerade resource page can be found at http://ipmasq.cjb.net/. An added benefit of NAT is that the organization's private network is not visible from the Internet. Figure 12-15 illustrates how network translation allows an organization to use private addressing yet still benefit from global Internet connectivity.

As can be seen in Figure 12-15, all of the workstations on the private network can share a single IP address (195.75.16.65) to the global Internet because the NAT software maintains a table of connections and maps each private workstation to a unique TCP port number. In the case of WinRoute, these port numbers are in the range of 61000 to 61600 so as not to be confused with more commonly used port numbers.

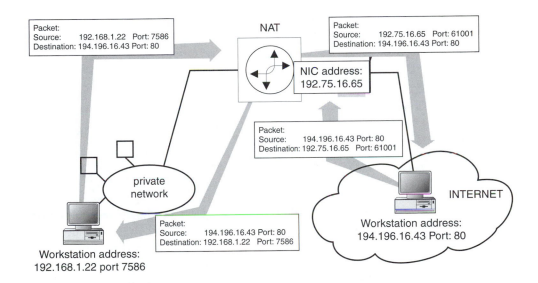

NAT Source/Destination Table

Private Source IP Address	Private Source Assigned Port ID
192.168.1.22	61001
192.168.1.23	61002
192.168.1.24	61003
192.168.1.25	61004
..and so on..	..and so on..

Figure 12-15   Network Address Translation

Hierarchical Networking and Autonomous Systems   Thus far, only two layers of network hierarchy have been discussed: the network ID and the subnet ID. These two layers are sufficient for many private organizations. However, global private internetworks or public networks such as the Internet need additional layers of hierarchy in order to organize such massive networks and to keep routing tables of a reasonable size.

The concept of **autonomous systems** was introduced to allow a more structured view of the Internet and to control the growth of Internet routing tables. An autonomous system is rather arbitrarily defined as a network under the authority of a single entity whose interior routing policies or **interior gateway protocols (IGP)** are independent of those of any other autonomous system. Autonomous systems talk to each other via mutually agreed-upon **exterior gateway protocols (EGP).**

The most common exterior gateway protocol currently is **BGP4 (Border Gateway Protocol Version 4).** BGP (Border Gateway Protocol) is an exterior gateway protocol that performs routing between multiple autonomous systems or domains and exchanges routing and reachability information with other BGP systems. To the outside world, the AS is seen as a single entity. Each AS runs its own IGP (interior gateway protocol) independent of any other AS. Simply stated, any network can talk to any other network via the Internet because, regardless of what routing protocols those networks may speak internally, they all speak the same language (BGP) externally. Strictly speaking, BGP is a **path vector protocol.** This means that BGP routers exchange path information, which is a series of AS numbers, to indicate paths between autonomous systems. Routing policy in BGP can be very finely defined by manipulating BGP attributes and by setting route filtering. Figure 12-16 is a simple diagram illustrating these concepts.

BGP depends on TCP for path vector information delivery, and is therefore considered a reliable protocol. BGP works on the concept of neighboring autonomous systems. Once a neighbor to a given autonomous system is discovered, keep-alive messages are continuously exchanged between neighboring autonomous systems to ensure the viability of advertised paths. In this manner, BGP routers know when neighboring routers fail and when path information becomes invalid. Each BGP router on an autonomous system is configured to advertise the summarized networks within that autonomous system and to define with which routers on neighboring autonomous systems it will exchange path vector information. Administrative weights can be assigned to different paths to make one path more attractive than another.

In the case of autonomous systems, static routing may be preferable over dynamic routing. Because routing information is not shared over the link connecting the various autonomous systems, the danger of having a misbehaving router from another autonomous system negatively affect the routers within a given autonomous system is minimized.

OSPF Areas   If the interior gateway protocol in a given network is OSPF, an additional layer of network hierarchy known as the **OSPF area** is intro-

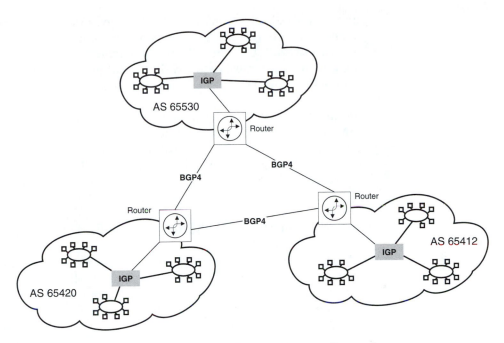

Figure 12-16   Autonomous Systems and Exterior Gateway Protocols

duced. All OSPF networks have at least one configured area, known as Area 0 or the backbone area. Depending on the size of the network, in order to keep the topological databases of manageable size, and to reduce the amount of OSPF information that needs to be transmitted between routers, additional areas can be defined. All areas would communicate with each other through Area 0, the backbone area. In terms of network hierarchy, an OSPF system would have four tiers: autonomous system, OSPF area, network ID, subnet ID.

Limitations of Classfull Addressing and Fixed Length Subnet Masks

Before moving on to classless addressing and variable length subnet masks, it is important to understand the problems that these techniques are attempting to fix.

Only One Subnet Mask per Network Prefix: Wasted Addresses   Routing protocols such as RIP that are unable to transmit subnet masks or extended network prefix information along with network IDs and IP addresses force all routers, servers, and workstations within a given network to all have the same subnet mask. Recalling that a subnet mask is the logical portion that relates to a physical network topology, it should be evident that a fixed subnet mask implies a fixed subnet size for all subnets of a given network ID. Naturally, subnets must be sized to accommodate the largest required subnet within a given network ID. As a result, all subnets, regardless of their requirements, are sized to this largest required size, resulting in wasted host addresses that cannot be recovered or used by other subnets.

Shrinking Pool of Available IP Addresses   Internet traffic is doubling every three to six months. Class A addresses are exhausted. Class B addresses are either exhausted or nearly so. All that remains is Class C addresses. However, as was seen in the IP Subnet Definition Chart, Class C addresses, with only an 8-bit host ID, don't leave much room for subnet definition.

■ CLASSLESS ADDRESSING AND VARIABLE LENGTH SUBNET MASKS

Clearly, something needed to be done to combat the potentially fatal situation caused by the combination of the shrinking pool of IP addressing and fixed length subnet masks. Two different techniques, described below, seek to mitigate the previously mentioned shortcomings of Classfull IP addressing.

Variable Length Subnet Masks

Variable Length Subnet Masks (VLSM), defined in 1987 as RFP1009, specified how a single network ID could have different subnet masks among its subnets. Used correctly, VLSM could minimize the wasted IP addresses forced by a single subnet mask per network ID as defined by the original RFC 950 Subnetting technique.

Benefits   The major benefit of VLSM is that subnets can be defined to different sizes as needed under a single Network ID, thereby minimizing, if not eliminating, wasted addresses. As a result, an organization assigned IP address space is more efficiently used. Second, when correctly defined to match the physical topology of the network, variable length subnet masks can be used to permit route aggregation which minimizes the number of distinct routes that need to be advertised and processed by network backbone or Internet routers. Route aggregation will be explained shortly.

Implementation Requirements   In order for VLSM to be successfully implemented there are three requirements. First, the routers on the network where VLSM is implemented must be able to share subnet masks and/or extended network prefixes along with each route advertisement. Routing protocols such as OSPF and IS-IS are able to do this, whereas RIP and IGRP are not. Without the subnet mask or extended network prefix for each route being shared, the receiving router would have to assume that the received route was using the same subnet mask as the receiving router itself. There was an improvement to the original RIP (RIPv1), known as RIPv2 (RFC 1388), which added support for VLSM.

Second, all routers supporting VLSM must support a longest match routing algorithm. This is particularly important in VLSM networks, since subnets can be embedded within subnets. As will be seen in the following sections, the deeper a particular subnet is embedded within the network topology, the greater its extended network prefix, and the more specific its route advertisement.

Finally, the implemented network topology must match the distribution of addresses and definition of subnets, meaning the network designers must decide in advance how many levels of subnets are required, and how many hosts per subnet must be supported at each level. As will be seen in the following sections on network design with variable length subnet masks, at each level of subnetting, all addresses can be summarized or aggregated into a single address block. This reduces the amount of routing information that needs to be shared among the routers on a given network.

Classless Interdomain Routing

As previously mentioned, the near exhaustion of Class B addresses and rapid depletion of the limited capacity Class C addresses, combined with the explosive growth of the Internet and an associated explosive growth in demand for Internet IP addresses, forced the IETF (Internet Engineering Task Force) to take decisive action. **Classless Interdomain Routing** was announced in September 1993 and is documented in RFCs 1517,1518,1519, and 1520. **CIDR** is also sometimes referred to as **supernetting.**

Benefits   CIDR (often pronounced "cider") eliminates the traditional concept of Class A, B, and C addresses. The first three bits of the IP address, which have traditionally been used to determine address class, are meaningless. Similarly, first octet address ranges no longer indicate a particular address class. In so doing, CIDR allows a more efficient allocation of the remaining Internet IP addresses. CIDR also supports route aggregation, which allows routing information for multiple network addresses to be represented by a single routing table entry. This can significantly reduce the number of routes that must be processed by Internet routers, thereby making the Internet perform more efficiently.

Implementation Requirements   CIDR addresses are issued in blocks known as CIDR blocks. Recall that the first octet is meaningless in determining how many subnets or host IDs can be defined for a given CIDR block. The only factor that determines the capacity of a CIDR block is the network prefix assigned by the Internet authorities when the CIDR block is issued. Just as with classfull addressing, the network prefix issued by the Internet authorities indicates the number of bits used for the major network ID. These bits are reserved and cannot be used by the end users for subnet IDs or host IDs. Think of the network prefix number as the "hands-off" area. For example, if a CIDR block were issued with a network prefix of /18, that would imply that the first 18 bits from left to right were reserved for the network ID. This would leave 14 bits (32–18) for subnet IDs and host IDs. Because 2 raised to the fourteenth power is 16384, that is how many host IDs or individual addresses can be defined for a CIDR block with a network prefix of /18.

An important point to remember is that it doesn't matter what the assigned major network ID is; all /18 CIDR blocks are equal in terms of capacity, regardless of network ID. This is where it becomes important to forget the traditional view of classfull addressing. As an example, the following three CIDR addresses are equivalent, even though they would not be from a classfull addressing standpoint:

- 10.46.64.0/18

- 128.210.0.0/18

- 204.17.192.0/18

Figure 12-17 summarizes the key information about the capacity of CIDR blocks with various prefix lengths. Remember that the assigned prefix indicates the number of left-most reserved bits. Much like subnetting, all bits reserved by the Internet authorities for the network ID prior to assignment to end users are designated with a 1 in the reserved bit positions. These reserved ones can then be converted to dotted-decimal format. Unlike subnetting where end users assign reserved bits to create a subnet mask, because these ones are assigned to reserved bits in a mask before assignment to end users, this could be called a supernet mask.

Another important implementation issue with CIDR is that the TCP/IP configuration programs on all servers and workstations must be CIDR compliant. In other words, they must be able to accept classless subnet masks, or masks that would be illegal from a classfull addressing standpoint. Many of the TCP/IP configuration programs associated with network operating systems have error-checking routines that assume that only classfull addressing is supported and will not allow subnet masks that appear to violate classfull addressing rules but are perfectly correct for CIDR.

Address Allocation Using CIDR

The impact of address allocation using CIDR is most obvious when Internet Service Providers must provide a block of addresses to an organization that wishes to connect to the Internet through their ISP. For example, let's start by assuming that an ISP has been issued the CIDR block of 207.32.128.0/17 by the Internet authorities. Referring to the CIDR Block Capacity Chart (Figure 12-17), it should be evident that this block equates 32,768 IP addresses or the

CIDR Prefix Length	Supernet Mask	Number of Host Addresses	Number of Bits Available for Subnetting	Equivalent Number of Classfull Networks
/13	255.248.0.0	524288	19	8 Bs or 2048 Cs
/14	255.252.0.0	262144	18	4 Bs or 1024 Cs
/15	255.254.0.0	131072	17	2 Bs or 512 Cs
/16	255.255.0.0	65536	16	1 B or 256 Cs
/17	255.255.128.0	32768	15	128 Cs
/18	255.255.192.0	16384	14	64 Cs
/19	255.255.224.0	8192	13	32 Cs
/20	255.255.240.0	4096	12	16 Cs
/21	255.255.248.0	2048	11	8 Cs
/22	255.255.252.0	1024	10	4 Cs
/23	255.255.254.0	512	9	2 Cs
/24	255.255.255.0	256	8	1 C
/25	255.255.255.128	128	7	1/2 C
/26	255.255.255.192	64	6	1/4 C
/27	255.255.255.224	32	5	1/8 C

Figure 12-17   CIDR Block Capacity Chart

equivalent of 128 separate C addresses. Remember that this is classless addressing and the value in the first octet of the CIDR block address has no significance. Obviously, the ISP wants to allocate these addresses in the most efficient manner possible.

Suppose an organization needed 1000 IP addresses from the ISP for Internet connection. If this were strictly a classfull environment, the ISP would have two choices:

- Give up a Class B address. This would effectively waste 64,534 addresses because a Class B address offers 65,534 and the organization only wanted 1000.

- Assign four separate Class C addresses that support up to 254 addresses each. The disadvantage of this approach is that it will take four additional advertised routes on all Internet routers to reach this organization. Although four additional routes may not sound like much, if multiple C class addresses were the only way to meet any organization's Internet connectivity needs, the impact on Internet routing tables would be very significant.

Thanks to CIDR, however, the ISP has the flexibility to more closely match the exact needs of the organization in terms of the number of required IP addresses while adding only a single entry to the Internet routing tables. Referring back to the CIDR Block Capacity Chart, it should be evident that a /22 CIDR block with 1024 IP addresses would fit the needs of the organization in question quite well. Figure 12-18 illustrates the relationship between the ISP's CIDR block, the client organization's CIDR block, and the equivalent Class C Addresses.

Reducing Route Advertisements with CIDR

Just as CIDR allowed addresses to be more effectively allotted to meet a given organization's needs, CIDR also allows route aggregation to effectively reduce the number of route advertisements from a given network. Using the example illustrated in Figure 12-18, the client organization could summarize all of the subnet information from its four assigned networks into a single route advertisement: 207.32.168.0/22. Similarly, the ISP in the example could summarize all of its routes for all of its client organizations into a single route advertisement: 207.32.128.0/17.

CIDR versus VLSM: Similarities and Differences

CIDR and VLSM are actually quite similar in that they both allow a given high-level network ID to be divided and subsequently subdivided repeatedly into smaller and smaller pieces. This division into subnets, sub-subnets, sub-sub-subnets, and so on, is done in such a way that the addresses that are contained within any lower-level subnet can be rolled up, or aggre-

	Binary	Available for Subnets and Hosts	Dotted Decimal with Extended Network Prefix
ISP CIDR Block	11001111.00100000.1	0000000.00000000	207.32.128.0/17
Client Organization's CIDR Block	11001111.00100000.101010	00.00000000	207.32.168.0/22
Class C Address 1	11001111.00100000.10101000	.00000000	207.32.168.0/24
Class C Address 2	11001111.00100000.10101001	.00000000	207.32.169.0/24
Class C Address 3	11001111.00100000.10101010	.00000000	207.32.170.0/24
Class C Address 4	11001111.00100000.10101011	.00000000	207.32.171.0/24

Figure 12-18 Address Allocation with CIDR

gated into a single address at the next higher level of addressing. This type of address segmentation is sometimes referred to as recursive division or **recursion.**

In terms of implementation, both VLSM and CIDR require that the extended network prefix information be transmitted with every route advertisement. All routers supporting VLSM or CIDR must use a longest match algorithm for determining which route should be chosen from among possible routes in a routing table. In order for route aggregation to effectively limit the number of route advertisements, addresses must be assigned in a manner that mirrors the physical topology of the network.

The key difference between CIDR and VLSM is when the recursion is performed. In the case of VLSM, the division of the addresses and definition of multiple levels of subnets of various sizes is done *after* the addresses were assigned to the end user. All of the addresses of the nested subnets are aggregated and the Internet has no knowledge of internal network structure of the VLSM environment. In the case of CIDR, the recursion is known as supernetting, and is performed by Internet authorities and higher-level ISPs and is done *before* the end user receives assigned addresses.

■ NETWORK DESIGN WITH VARIABLE LENGTH SUBNET MASKS

Recursive Division of a Network Prefix with VLSM

As previously described, VLSM allows an organization's assigned address space to be recursively divided into as many levels and sizes of subnets as required. In order to better understand this process, we will first show how the address space is divided and then show how the routes from that recursively divided address space can be aggregated to effectively reduce the amount of transmitted routing information. In addition to reducing the amount of transmitted and stored routing information, an added benefit is that the associated network topology and structure of one subnet is unknown to other subnets. Figure 12-19 illustrates how a single network prefix can be recursively divided thanks to VLSM.

Notice in Figure 12-19 how subnet sizes can be flexibly defined even on a given subnet level. On the sub-subnet level in Figure 12-19, the 121.1.0.0 subnet is divided into 254 sub-subnets, whereas the 121.253.0.0 subnet is divided into only 6 sub-subnets. Also, notice that subnet IDs can become "hidden" when subnet addresses do not fall evenly on octet boundaries.

Route Aggregation with VLSM

The benefits of flexible subnet size definition are illustrated in Figure 12-19, and the route aggregation benefits of VLSM are illustrated in Figure 12-20.

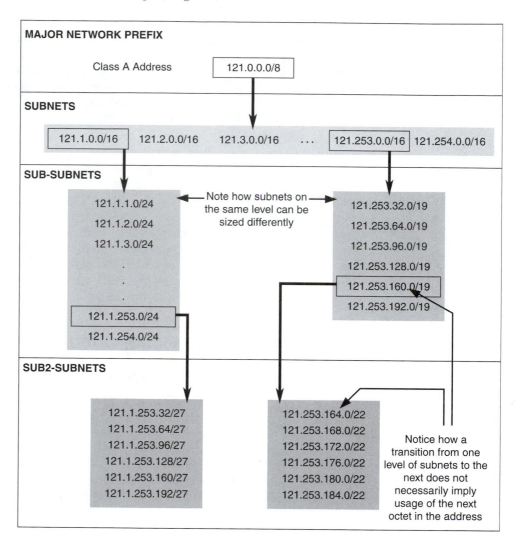

Figure 12-19   Recursive Division of a Network Prefix with VLSM

Often, the terms **summarization** and **aggregation** are used interchangeably to describe the process of reducing the number of routing advertisements between subnets by only advertising the common portion of subnet IDs. In other words, summarization and aggregation mean that subnet information is not shared between two networks when those networks are connected by a router.

In some cases, however, a distinction is made between the two terms. In such cases, the term *summarization* is reserved to describe those circumstances in which subnet addresses have been rolled up all the way to the major network prefix as assigned by the Internet authorities. In Figure 12-20,

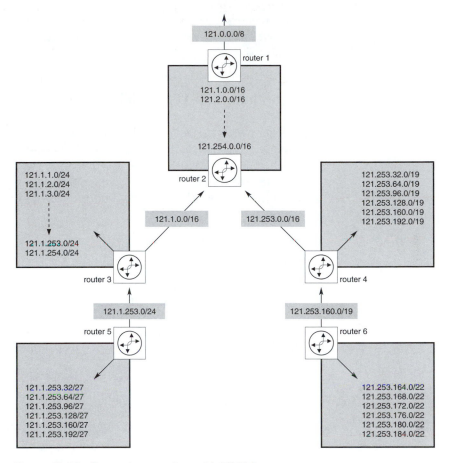

Figure 12-20   Route Aggregation with VLSM

this would be the 121.0.0.0/8 major network prefix. On the other hand, the term *aggregation* is used to describe any circumstance when a subnet's entire address space can be represented by only the common portion of those addresses in a routing advertisement. In Figure 12-20, Router 6's advertisement to Router 4 of the 121.253.160.0/19 route to represent six separate networks is an example of aggregation since 121.253.160.0/19 is not the major network prefix.

Notice in Figure 12-20 how each physical network that houses multiple subnet IDs can have its routing information summarized to a single route advertisement to the next higher layer of subnet. Finally, the entire internetwork can be advertised to the Internet routing tables by the single assigned network ID: 121.0.0.0. Such route aggregation and the efficiencies gained therein are possible only if subnet masks are assigned in a planned manner so that subnet address assignment mirrors the actual topology of the network as illustrated in Figure 12-20. If assigned addresses are not organized to mirror the physical topology of the network, address aggregation is not possible and the benefit of reduction of routing table size will not be realized.

Working with Variable Length Subnet Masks—Subnet Design

Subnet design with variable length subnet masks is similar to subnet design with fixed length subnet masks except that decisions made regarding subnets for the entire network in the fixed length subnet mask scenario are made independently at each level in the variable length subnet mask scenario. To elaborate, at each level (subnets, sub-subnets, sub2-subnets, etc.) two questions must be answered:

1. How many subnets are required at this level both now and in the future?

2. What is the largest number of hosts required per subnet on this level both now and in the future?

The answers to these questions will determine how many subnets with how much host ID capacity needs to be defined at each level.

Defining Sub-Subnet Numbers with VLSM   Figure 12-21 provides an example of how subnet numbers are defined in VLSM. In this example, it was determined that six sub-subnets were needed beneath the 121.253.0.0/16 subnet. Because two subnets are reserved, we need to be able to define eight sub-subnets. Two

	Network Prefix	Sub-Subnet Number	Reserved for Host ID	Decimal with Extended Network Prefix
Assigned Network ID	01111001.11111101			121.253.0.0/16
Sub-Subnet 0-reserved	01111001.11111101	000	00000.00000000	121.253.0.0/19
Sub-Subnet 1	01111001.11111101	001	00000.00000000	121.253.32.0/19
Sub-Subnet 2	01111001.11111101	010	00000.00000000	121.253.64.0/19
Sub-Subnet 3	01111001.11111101	011	00000.00000000	121.253.96.0/19
Sub-Subnet 4	01111001.11111101	100	00000.00000000	121.253.128.0/19
Sub-Subnet 5	01111001.11111101	101	00000.00000000	121.253.160.0/19
Sub-Subnet 6	01111001.11111101	110	00000.00000000	121.253.192.0/19
Sub-Subnet 7-reserved	01111001.11111101	111	00000.00000000	121.253.224.0/19

Figure 12-21   Defining Sub-Subnet Numbers with VLSM

to the third power is 8, so it will take 3 additional bits or /19 (/16+3 = /19) extended network prefix to provide the required six sub-subnets.

Defining Sub2-Subnet Numbers with VLSM   If it was then decided that the 121.253.160.0/19 sub-subnet needed to be recursively divided into 6 sub2-subnets, 3 additional bits of variable length subnet mask would be required. This is illustrated in Figure 12-22.

Defining Host Addresses for a Given Subnet   With VLSM, defining host addresses involves the same process for subnet, sub-subnets, or sub2-subnets. Figure 12-23 illustrates the host definition process for sub2-subnet 121.253.184.0/22 defined in Figure 12-22. The extended network prefix of /22 tells us that 1022 host IDs can be defined on this sub2-subnet (32 bit address – 22 reserved bits = 10 bits available for host ID; 2 to the tenth power = 1024– 2 reserved host IDs = 1022 available host IDs). If 1022 host IDs is much more than we could ever reasonably use, we would probably want to consider defining another subnet level so as not to strand or waste precious IP addresses.

Notice that the extended network prefix does not increase when we define host IDs for a given subnet the way it did when we defined additional subnet levels to existing subnets.

Notice how the third octet has changed from 184 to 187 on the last few host IDs. Does this mean that the subnet ID changed somehow? The answer is no. If you look in the extended network prefix column, you will see that the subnet ID has not changed. The third octet has changed because the extended network prefix was 22, leaving 2 bits of the third octet left over for

	Network Prefix	Sub-Subnet Number	Reserved for Host ID	Decimal with Extended Network Prefix
Assigned Network ID	01111001.11111101.101			121.253.160.0/19
Sub-Subnet 0-Reserved	01111001.11111101.101	000	00.00000000	121.253.160.0/22
Sub-Subnet 1	01111001.11111101.101	001	00.00000000	121.253.164.0/22
Sub-Subnet 2	01111001.11111101.101	010	00.00000000	121.253.168.0/22
Sub-Subnet 3	01111001.11111101.101	011	00.00000000	121.253.172.0/22
Sub-Subnet 4	01111001.11111101.101	100	00.00000000	121.253.176.0/22
Sub-Subnet 5	01111001.11111101.101	101	00.00000000	121.253.180.0/22
Sub-Subnet 6	01111001.11111101.101	110	00.00000000	121.253.184.0/22
Sub-Subnet 7-Reserved	01111001.11111101.101	111	00.00000000	121.253.188.0/22

Figure 12-22   Defining Sub2-Subnet Numbers with VLSM

	Extended Network Prefix	Host ID	Decimal
Host 0-Reserved	01111001.11111101.101110	00.00000000	121.253.184.0/22
Host 1	01111001.11111101.101110	00.00000001	121.253.184.1/22
Host 2	01111001.11111101.101110	00.00000010	121.253.184.2/22
Host 3	01111001.11111101.101110	00.00000011	121.253.184.3/22
|	|	|	|
|	|	|	|
Host 1022	01111001.11111101.101110	11.11111110	121.253.187.254/22
Host 1023 Reserved	01111001.11111101.101110	11.11111111	121.253.187.255/22

Figure 12-23 Defining Host IDs

use by the host ID. Because the host IDs start using the rightmost bits first, it was only when we got to the last few host IDs that we were forced to use the left-most bits, which happened to belong in the third octet. As a result, the third octet may have become 187, but the sub2-subnet ID is still 184.

Determining if IP Addresses Are Part of the Same Subnet Routers use the same algorithm to determine if IP addresses are part of the same subnet whether or not VLSM is used. A router must somehow know the extended network prefix or subnet mask as well as the IP address. In the case of fixed length subnet masks, the router could use its own interface's subnet mask since all subnet masks on a given network had to be the same, or it could assume the default subnet mask based on classfull address class. In the case of variable length subnet masks, no such assumptions can be made. Extended network prefixes must accompany every advertised route that is shared between routers. Only certain router-to-router protocols are able to support VLSM's requirement for sharing extended network prefixes. OSPF and IS-IS are link-state protocols that are able to support VLSM. RIPv2 is a distance vector protocol that is able to support VLSM. Neither RIPv1 nor IGRP is able to support VLSM.

Figure 12-12 illustrates how routers use the extended network prefix or subnet mask to determine if IP addresses are part of the same subnet.

SUMMARY

This chapter was intended to provide readers with an understanding of the correct way to use IP addressing when designing networks. Two key characteristics in which different IP network design techniques differ are the efficiency with which addresses can be allocated to minimize wasted IP addresses and the level to which route advertisements can be aggregated to minimize both router-to-router traffic and the size of routing tables. Classfull addressing is a simple technique for both people and routers to understand, but has the negative effect of not allowing subnets. Classfull or fixed length subnet masking allows the creation of subnets but has the undesirable characteristic of wasting precious IP addresses. Variable length subnet masking allows more efficient allocation of IP addresses by allowing subnets of appropriate sizes to be defined through an internetwork. The rapid depletion of classfull IP addresses is another issue of major concern. Classless Interdomain Routing allows blocks of addresses to be assigned in a flexible manner that supports both efficient allocation of addresses as well as reduction of route advertisements. Both variable length subnet masking and classless interdomain routing are dependent on the ability of routers to support these protocols, most specifically through the ability to forward extended network prefixes with all route advertisements.

KEY TERMS

Aggregation
Area 0
Autonomous systems
BGP4
Border gateway protocol
    version 4
CIDR
CIDR block
Classfull IP addressing
Classless Interdomain Routing
Dynamic routing
EGP
Extended network prefix
Exterior gateway protocols

Gateway of last resort
IGP
IGRP
Interior gateway protocols
Longest match algorithm
Major network ID
Network address translation
Null interface
OSPF area
OSPF
Path vector protocol
Private addressing
Recursion
Redistribution

Reverse poison
RIP
Routing loop
Slow convergence
Split horizon
Static routes
Subnet
Subnet mask
Summarization
Supernetting
Triggered updates
Variable length subnet masking
VLSM

REVIEW QUESTIONS

1. What are some of the situations that led to the need for subnetting?
2. What is the difference between a major network ID, a network prefix, and an extended network prefix?
3. How does subnetting work?

4. What is the purpose of a subnet mask?
5. What is the purpose of reserved subnet numbers and reserved host addresses?
6. How do routers use classfull IP address information?

7. How do routers determine if IP addresses are part of the same subnet?
8. What is the difference between static routing and dynamic routing?
9. What is the longest match algorithm and how is it implemented in routers?
10. What are the major differences between distance vector and link state protocols?
11. Give examples of distance vector and link state protocols.
12. What is redistribution?
13. What is a gateway of last resort?
14. What is a null interface?
15. What is the cause of slow convergence?
16. How does split horizon seek to reduce convergence time?
17. What are routing loops and how are they prevented?
18. How does reverse poison deal with routing loops?
19. How do triggered updates seek to nullify slow convergence?
20. What is the purpose of private addressing?
21. How does network address translation work?
22. What is an autonomous system?
23. What is the difference between interior gateway protocols and exterior gateway protocols? Give an example of each.

24. What are the key functional characteristics of BGP4?
25. What is meant by a path vector protocol?
26. How does a path vector protocol differ from a distance vector protocol?
27. What are OSPF areas?
28. What special role is reserved for OSPF area 0?
29. What are some of the limitations of classfull addressing?
30. What are some of the limitations of fixed length subnet masks?
31. How does VLSM overcome the limitations of fixed length subnet masks?
32. How does CIDR overcome the limitations of classfull addressing?
33. What are some of the implementation requirements of VLSM?
34. What are some of the implementation requirements of CIDR?
35. How is address allocation done with CIDR?
36. How can route advertisements be reduced with CIDR?
37. What are the similarities and differences between CIDR and VLSM?
38. What is recursive division of a network prefix?
39. How are routes aggregated with VLSM?
40. What is the difference between route aggregation and route summarization?

ACTIVITIES

1. Convert the following from binary to decimal values: 00110011, 01010101, 00011100, 01001100, 11001010.
2. Convert the following from decimal to binary values: 49, 220, 115, 134, 61.
3. Convert the following address to binary and identify the address class and network prefix: 128.210.42.20.
4. Convert the following address to binary and identify the address class and network prefix: 202.30.61.26.
5. Convert the following address to binary and identify the address class and network prefix: 10.44.126.124.
6. Your organization has been assigned the 165.32.0.0/16 network ID. You need to establish a total of 8 subnets from this network ID.

How many bits will need to be reserved in order to define 8 subnets?
7. What will be the extended network prefix once the required 8 subnets have been defined?
8. Create a table that defines the 8 subnets in both binary and dotted decimal format.
9. Pick a subnet from Question 8 and list the range of host addresses that can be assigned to that subnet in both binary and decimal. Identify the broadcast address for this subnet.
10. Your organization has been given the 165.32.0.0/16 network ID. Your largest subnet requires 64 hosts per subnet. What should the extended network prefix be that will meet this requirement?
11. How many subnets can be defined in Question 10?

12. Create a table that lists the first 8 subnets in both binary and decimal format for Question 10.
13. Your company has been assigned the network number 128.212.0.0/16. Your network supports VLSM. Specify the 8 subnets of 128.212.0.0/16.
14. List the host addresses that can be assigned to Subnet 3 (128.212.96.0).
15. Identify the broadcast address for Subnet 3.
16. Specify the 16 subnets of Subnet 6 (128.212.192.0/19).
17. List the host addresses that can be assigned to Subnet 6-3.
18. Specify the 8 subnets of Subnet 6-14.
19. List the host addresses that can be assigned to Subnet 6-14-2.
20. List the individual equivalent Class C addresses defined by the CIDR block 207.42.172.0/21.
21. Aggregate the following set of /24 addresses to the highest degree possible: 207.42.196.0/24, 207.42.197.0/24, 207.42.198.0/24, 207.42.199.0/24.

CASE STUDY

Massachusetts College Takes a Class in VPNS

Fitchburg State College is betting that its new virtual private network (VPN) will be able to handle an expected flood of remote users as the school opens its network resources to satellite campuses, telecommuters and local public schools.

Potentially, thousands of remote users will have to be authenticated and granted restricted rights to the campus network, says Joe Turner, associate director of MIS. And the Massachusetts college really isn't sure what network resources will be most in demand, he says.

"Do we have a driving application right now? No. How will we actually use the VPN? I don't know," says Turner, who designed the VPN with extreme flexibility in mind.

The VPN has been set up because:
- The college is negotiating with the City of Fitchburg to set up homeworkzone.com, a place where middle school kids can post academic questions to professors.
- The faculty is clamoring to work more at home. "They say, `We need to do more than just pick up our e-mail,'" Turner says.
- Fitchburg State is offering courses and degrees to students in Bermuda, which has no four-year college.

Currently, the VPN is being used only by a dozen staff members, while other remote users go through an existing firewall.

The VPN users call their ISPs locally and use the Internet to hit an Altiga Networks C10 VPN concentrator that sits at the Internet threshold to the college network.

The concentrator challenges users for name and password, authenticates them and then grants access. Remote users have VPN rights restricted according to which ATM virtual LAN they've been assigned.

The VLANs are managed by two 3Com Cellplex 7000 ATM switches that anchor the campus backbone.

As more users from outside the college community seek access, they may be segregated by new VLANs, Turner says. He will also go to a separate Remote Authentication Dial-In User Service server to handle authentication.

For example, a server to handle homeworkzone.com traffic might be assigned a VLAN of its own. User rights could also be set by class. So blocks of IP addresses could be assigned to each class, and IP filters could be configured to keep users out of LAN segments to which they are not authorized access.

Distributing VPN client software to remote users shouldn't be a problem, Turner says. Users whose machines are outfitted with Windows 95 or NT with Dialup Networking 1.3 will be able to establish an encrypted session over the Internet to the Altiga box via the Point-to-Point Tunneling Protocol.

For more sensitive traffic that needs stronger encryption, users will be able to download an Altiga client that supports the IP Security protocol with Data Encryption Standard (DES) and DES3 encryption.

Turner says the Altiga box handles up to 5,000 simultaneous sessions, and Altiga boxes can be stacked if traffic grows beyond that limit.

Turner says it took about an hour to install the Altiga box. "It's similar to configuring a PC on a local network," he says. List price for the concentrator is $10,000.

Until the VPN was set up late last year, the school's remote access system consisted of 32 modems used mainly for accessing e-mail and supporting terminal emulation.

Turner says the VPN is already being eyed to support a wider variety of applications, including filing electronic admissions applications, remote registration for classes and printing unofficial transcripts.

With enhanced security such as smart cards, Turner envisions the outside firm handling the school's payroll to access the administration database.

And Turner says he is already thinking about getting a second T-1 access link to the Internet from a different service provider. That would not only improve response times during peak loading, but it also would offer a diversely routed fallback if one of the links goes down.

Source: Jeff Caruso, "Managing the Tightest Ship in the Shipping Biz," *Network World,* vol. 16, no. 19 (May 10, 1999), p. 51. Copyright Network World. Reprinted with permission.

BUSINESS CASE STUDY QUESTIONS

Activities

1. Complete a top-down model for this case by gleaning facts from the case and placing them in the proper layer of the top-down model. After completing the top-down model, analyze and detail those instances where requirements were clearly passed down from upper layers to lower layers of the model and where solutions to those requirements were passed up from lower layers to upper layers of the model.
2. Detail any questions about the case that may occur to you for which answers are not clearly stated in the article.

Business

1. What was the change in the college's mode of doing business that prompted the change in its network?
2. What are some of the costs involved with this implementation?
3. How could benefits be measured?

Application

1. How many more users could potentially need to be authenticated and given access to the college's network?

2. What is the driving application that will be used by most remote users?
3. Who are some of the different user groups expected to use the VPN and how do their needs/demands differ?
4. What type of software must be installed on the VPN clients? Will this be a problem?
5. What are some future possible applications and what security technology might these apps require?

Data

1. What are the different types of data that will need to be carried over the VPN?
2. How many users can be served simultaneously by the VPN?
3. How scalable is this VPN solution?

Network

1. How do users get to the VPN from wherever they may be located?
2. How are IP addressing and IP filters potentially used to meet user and network needs?
3. What are some of the ways in which security issues will be addressed?
4. How much bandwidth to the Internet is required?
5. What would another T-1 to the Internet provide besides more bandwidth?

Technology

1. What types of technology are used to establish and manage the VPN?
2. What type of remote access capability did the VPN replace?

CHAPTER 13

LOCAL AREA NETWORK INTERNETWORKING

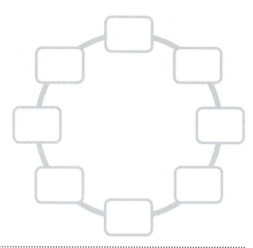

Concepts Reinforced

OSI Model	Internet Suite of Protocols Model
Protocols and Standards	Interoperability
Network Operating Systems Architecture	Network Operating Systems Functionality
Network Addressing	TCP/IP Protocols

Concepts Introduced

Internetwork Design	Internetworking Technology
Bridging	Routing
Switching versus Routing	Routing Protocols
Bridges	Routers
Repeaters	Bridging Protocols
SNA/SDLC	SNA/LAN Integration
Layer 2, 3, 4 Switches	ATM LAN Emulation
Virtual LANs	

OBJECTIVES

After mastering the material in this chapter you should:

1. Understand why an organization would want to implement LAN-to-LAN internetworking

2. Understand the basics of internetwork design including decisions as to bridging, routing, or switching

3. Understand the importance of protocols to successful internetworking design and implementation

4. Understand the functionality and proper application of the following types of internetworking technology: repeaters, bridges, branch office routers, edge routers, boundary routers, route servers, distributed routers, dial-up routers, ISDN bridges and routers, wireless bridges, source routing bridges, layer 2, 3, and 4 switches, and software-only routers

5. Understand the options available for integrating LAN traffic with SNA/SDLC mainframe traffic

▨ INTRODUCTION

Having gained an understanding of the majority of the protocol-related issues involved with internetworking in Chapter 12, this chapter will:

- Introduce the reader to the complexities and basic principles of internetwork design such as bridging, routing, and switching.

- Introduce the reader to the available technology with which to implement designed internetworking solutions.

These internetwork design and technology issues will be explored for both LAN-to-LAN internetworking as well as LAN-to-mainframe internetworking. In order to understand the importance of internetworking in general, it is first necessary to understand the business motivation for seeking internetworking solutions in the first place.

▨ INTERNETWORKING DESIGN

**Managerial
Perspective**

BUSINESS MOTIVATION AND INTERNETWORKING CHALLENGES

Local area networks tend to grow by a natural process until the shared media network architecture (Ethernet, Token Ring, FDDI, etc.) becomes too congested and network performance begins to suffer. This scenario is one of the two primary reasons for investigating **internetworking** solutions. The other situation that often leads to internetworking design is when independently established and operated LANs wish to begin to share information. Each of these scenarios boils down to business issues. The poor performance of the overloaded shared media LAN leads to a decrease in worker productivity with potential ripple effects to decreases in customer satisfaction, sales, market share, and so on.

The ability to provide decision makers with instantaneous access to the right information at the right place and time, regardless of the location of that information, is the key motivation for internetworking. The key challenge or stumbling block to achieving transparent information access is the numerous incompatibilities caused by the multiple vendor hardware and software technologies that comprise the individual LANs to be linked. The operational characteristics of LANs are defined by protocols, which when organized into a layered model such as the OSI model, are referred to as a protocol stack. A LAN's protocol stack is actually a definition of that LAN's personality. In other words, if transparent LAN-to-LAN interoperability is to be achieved, each protocol in a given LAN's protocol stack must be either matched or converted in order to transparently interoperate with the corresponding protocol in the neighboring LAN to which the given LAN is to be linked. Overall LAN-to-LAN transparent interoperability is realized only when corresponding protocols are able to achieve transparent interoperability.

Overall Internetworking Design Strategies

In order to improve performance on overburdened shared media LANs, several proven design strategies can be followed:

- **Segmentation** is usually the first approach to reducing shared media congestion. By having fewer workstations per segment, there is less contention for the shared bandwidth. Segmentation improves performance for both CSMA/CD (Ethernet) and token passing (Token Ring) access methodologies. Some type of internetworking device, such as a bridge or router, will be required to link the LAN segments.

- When segmentation is taken to the extreme of limiting each LAN segment to only a single workstation, the design strategy is known as **micro-segmentation.** A micro-segmented internetwork requires a LAN switch that is compatible with the NICs installed in the attached workstations. Both Ethernet and Token Ring switches are readily available.

- Instead of assigning all workstations to their own LAN segment as in micro-segmentation, only selected high-performance devices such as servers can be assigned to their own segment in a design strategy known as **server isolation.** By isolating servers on their own segments, guaranteed access to network bandwidth is assured.

- **Hierarchical networking** isolates local LAN traffic on a local network architecture such as Ethernet or Token Ring while transmitting internetwork traffic over a higher speed network architecture such as FDDI, Fast Ethernet, or ATM. Servers are often directly connected to the **backbone network,** while individual workstations access the backbone network only as needed through routers.

Figure 13-1 illustrates these overall internetworking design strategies.

Bridging, routing, and switching are the three primary internetworking processes that offer LAN segmentation and isolation of network resources. All three internetworking processes are basically address

Segmentation

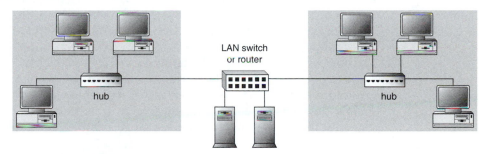

Micro-Segmentation

Server Isolation

Hierarchical Networking

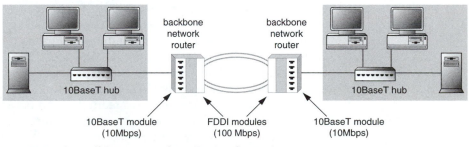

Figure 13-1   Overall Internetworking Design Strategies

processors, making decisions as to how to forward internetwork traffic based on data-link layer and network layer addresses. The three processes differ in their use of network addresses, in their overall sophistication, and in their advantages and limitations. The bridging, routing, and switching internetworking processes are reviewed here; differences between their associated internetworking technologies are reviewed later in the chapter.

Bridging

Bridging is often the first internetworking or LAN segmentation strategy employed because of its ease of installation and effective results. Dividing a single overburdened LAN into two LAN segments linked by a bridge must be done with some forethought in order to minimize the amount of internetwork traffic and thereby avoid having the bridge become an inter-network bottleneck. The 80/20 rule is often used in deciding which work-stations and servers should be assigned to each side of the bridge. The goal should be to have 80% of all LAN traffic stay on the local LAN with no more than 20% of overall traffic requiring processing and forwarding by the bridge.

Addressing   Bridging is a data-link layer process, making forwarding deci-sions based on the contents of the MAC layer or data-link layer addresses. Bridges are passive or transparent devices, receiving every frame broadcast on a given LAN. Bridges are known as **transparent** due to their ability to process only data-link layer addresses while transparently forwarding any variety of upper-layer protocols safely embedded within the data field of the data-link layer frame. Rather than merely transferring all data between LANs or LAN segments, a bridge reads the **destination address** (MAC layer address of destination NIC) of each data frame on a LAN, decides whether the destination is local or remote (on the other side of the bridge), and allows only those data frames with non-local destination addresses to cross the bridge to the remote LAN.

Data-link protocols such as Ethernet contain **source addresses** as well as the destination addresses within the predefined Ethernet Frame layout. A bridge checks the source address of each frame it receives and adds that source address to a table of **known local nodes.** In doing so, the bridge is learning, without having to be manually reconfigured, about new worksta-tions that might have been added to the local LAN. Some bridges broadcast requests to all locally attached workstations, thereby forcing responses that can then be stored in the known local nodes table.

After each destination address is read, it is compared with the contents of the "Known Local Nodes" table in order to determine whether the frame should be allowed to cross the bridge (whether the destination is local). Because only frames with destination addresses not found in the known

Data Link Layer Frame

Data Link Header		Data Link Data Field	Data Link Trailer
Source Address	**Destination Address**	**Upper layer protocols including network layer address information**	
Contains MAC address of original source workstation	Contains MAC address of ultimate destination workstation		
These addresses are used by bridges to determine whether or not packets should be forwarded across the bridge.			
Data Link layer addresses are *NOT* changed by bridges.			

Figure 13-2   Use of Data-Link Addressing by Bridges

local nodes table are forwarded across the bridge, bridges are sometimes known as **Forward-if-not-local** devices. Figure 13-2 illustrates the use of data-link layer frame addresses by bridges.

Advantages   Because of their ability to learn, bridges are relatively easy to install and configure, providing quick, cost-effective relief for overburdened network segments. In addition to providing logical segmentation of LAN traffic, bridges are able to extend network segment length by repeating, retiming, and regenerating received signals before forwarding them across the bridge. Bridges are also able to translate between different network architectures (Token Ring to Ethernet) and between different media types (UTP to fiber).

Bridges are most often used either to segment traffic between LANs or to segment traffic between a LAN and a higher-speed backbone network.

Limitations   The primary limitation of bridges is also one of their strengths. Because bridges learn and do not require ongoing configuration, they only know to forward all packets that are addressed to non-local nodes. In the case of a destination node, which is many LANs and connecting bridges away from its source workstation, all workstations on all LANs between the source and destination workstation will be broadcast with the frame bound for the distant destination. Forwarding messages to all workstations on all intermittent LANs is known as **propagation.** In the case of improperly addressed frames or frames destined for nonexistent addresses, frames can be infinitely perpetuated or flooded onto all bridged LANs in a condition known as a **broadcast storm.** Bridges are generally unable to support networks containing redundant paths since the multiple active loops between LANs can lead to the propagation of broadcast storms.

Routing

Although both processes examine and forward data packets discriminately, routing and bridging differ significantly in several key functional areas:

- Although a bridge reads the destination address of every data packet on the LAN to which it is attached, a router examines only those data packets that are specifically addressed to it.

- Rather than just merely allowing the data packet access to the inter-network in a manner similar to a bridge, a router is more cautious and more helpful as well.

Before indiscriminately forwarding a data packet, a router first confirms the existence of the destination address as well as the latest information on available network "paths" to reach that destination. Next, based on the latest network traffic conditions, the router chooses the best path for the data packet to reach its destination and sends the data packet on its way.

Addressing   Although bridges make their forwarding decisions based on the contents of the MAC layer addresses contained in the header of the data-link layer frame, routers make their forwarding decisions based on the contents of the network layer addresses embedded within the data field of the data-link layer frame.

The router itself is a data-link layer destination address, available to receive, examine, and forward data packets from anywhere on any network to which it is either directly or indirectly internetworked.

How do data packets arrive at a router? The destination address on an Ethernet or Token Ring packet must be the MAC address of the router that will handle further internetwork forwarding. Thus, a router is addressed in the data-link layer destination address field. The router then discards this MAC sub-layer "envelope" which contained its address, and proceeds to read the contents of the data field of the Ethernet or Token Ring frame. Data-link layer addressing is functionally referred to as point-to-point addressing.

Just as in the case of the data-link layer protocols, network layer protocols dictate a bit-by-bit data frame structure that the router understands. What looked like just "data" and was ignored by the data-link layer internetworking device, the bridge, is "unwrapped" by the router and thoroughly examined in order to determine further processing.

After reading the network layer destination address, which is actually the network address of the ultimate destination workstation, the router consults its **routing tables** in order to determine the best path on which to forward this data packet. Routing tables contain at least some of the following fields upon which to base their "best path" decisions:

- Network number of the destination network. This field serves as the key field or lookup field used to find the proper record with further information concerning the best path to this network.

- MAC address of the next router along the path to this target network

- Port on this router out of which the readdressed data-link layer frame should be sent

- Number of hops, or intermediate routers, to the destination network

- The age of this entry in order to avoid making routing decisions based on outdated information

Having found the best path, the router has the ability to repackage the data packet as required for the delivery route (best path) that it has chosen. Although the network layer addresses remain unchanged, a fresh data-link layer frame is created. The destination address on the new data-link layer frame is filled in with the MAC address of the next router along the best path to the ultimate destination and the source address on the new data-link layer frame is filled in with the MAC address of the router which has just completed examination of the network layer addresses. Network layer addressing is functionally referred to as end-to-end addressing.

Unlike the bridge that merely allows access to the internetwork (forward-if-not-local logic), the router specifically addresses the data packet to a distant router. However, before a router actually releases a data packet onto the internetwork it confirms the existence of the destination address to which this data packet is bound. Only when the router is satisfied with both the viability of the destination address as well as with the quality of the intended path, will it release the carefully packaged data packet. This meticulous processing activity on the part of the router is known as **forward-if-proven-remote** logic. Figure 13-3 illustrates routers' uses of data-link and network layer addresses.

Advantages   In comparison with bridging, routing is able to make more efficient use of bandwidth on large networks containing redundant paths. The effective use of a network's redundant paths allows routers to perform **load balancing** of total network traffic across two or more links between two given locations. Choice of "best path" by routers can be determined by a variety of factors, including number of hops, transmission cost, and current line congestion. Routers are able to dynamically maintain routing tables, thereby adjusting performance to changing network conditions. Thanks to the "forward-if-proven-remote" logic, routers are better able to keep misbehaving or misaddressed traffic off the network through filtering of network layer addresses. In this role, routers can be considered as firewalls between connected networks. Router-based networks are much more scalable than bridge-based networks. Routers are able to forward more sophisticated and informative management information to enterprise network management systems via SNMP.

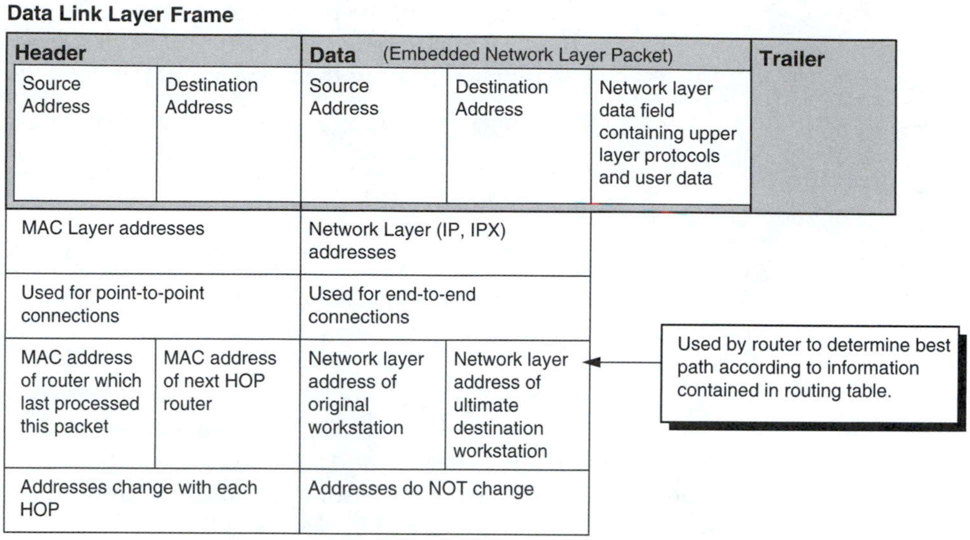

Data Link Layer Frame

Header		Data (Embedded Network Layer Packet)			Trailer
Source Address	Destination Address	Source Address	Destination Address	Network layer data field containing upper layer protocols and user data	
MAC Layer addresses		Network Layer (IP, IPX) addresses			
Used for point-to-point connections		Used for end-to-end connections			
MAC address of router which last processed this packet	MAC address of next HOP router	Network layer address of original workstation	Network layer address of ultimate destination workstation		
Addresses change with each HOP		Addresses do NOT change			

Used by router to determine best path according to information contained in routing table.

Figure 13-3   Router's Use of Data-Link and Network Layer Addresses

When LANs are connected over a long distance via WAN links, routers are more likely than bridges to be employed to interface to the WAN link. Thanks to the router's ability to more accurately identify upper-layer protocols, unnecessary or unwanted traffic can be kept off the relatively low-speed, high-cost WAN links.

Perhaps the most significant advantage of routers is their ability to process multiple network layer protocols simultaneously. A properly configured router could process IP, IPX, and Appletalk packets simultaneously while forwarding each protocol type to the proper destination network. In addition, some routers are also able to handle non-routable protocols such as NetBIOS, LAT, or SNA/SDLC which possess no network layer addressing scheme. In these cases, the data-link layer frames are either bridged or upper-layer protocols are encapsulated in a network layer envelope such as IP.

To summarize, routers provide the following services to the internetwork:

- Create firewalls to protect connected LANs

- Filter unwanted broadcast packets from the internetwork

- Discriminate and prioritize processing of packets according to network layer protocol

- Provide security by filtering packets by either data-link or network layer addresses

- Provide transparent interconnection between LANs

Limitations   Due to the sophisticated processing offered, routers are considerably more complicated to configure and manage than bridges. As the number of routers increases in a router-based network, the complexity level of network management increases proportionately. If routers are expected to be able to process multiple network layer protocols, they must have all supported protocol stacks installed and properly configured.

The router's sophisticated processing also has an impact in terms of the sophistication and cost of the router technology in comparison to bridging technology.

Switching

Switching, otherwise known as LAN switching, is similar in function to bridging. The key difference between switching and bridging is that switching is done in hardware, or ASIC (Application Specific Integrated Circuit) chips and is extremely fast in comparison to bridging. The primary purpose for employing a switch is to increase available bandwidth within a shared media LAN by implementing micro-segmentation on the local LAN. Because the switch creates point-to-point connections for each packet received, shared media LANs that employ switches become switched media LANs.

Addressing

Switching uses addresses in a manner similar to bridging. LAN switches read the destination MAC addresses on incoming data-link layer frames and quickly build a switched connection to the switched LAN segment that contains the destination workstation. The switch ports for LAN segments containing multiple workstations are able to discriminate between traffic between locally attached workstations and traffic that must be switched to another LAN switch port.

Switches work best when traffic does not have to leave the LAN segments linked to a particular LAN switch. In other words, in order to minimize the use of expensive WAN links or filter the traffic allowed onto high-speed backbone networks, layer 3 protocols will need to be examined by a router. In some cases, this routing functionality is being incorporated into the LAN switch. Basic LAN switches are layer 2 devices that must be complemented by either external layer 3 routers or by internal layer 3 routing functionality.

Much like a bridge would handle "non-local" traffic, when a LAN switch receives a data-link frame bound for a destination off the local network, it merely builds a switched connection to the switch port to which a router is connected, or to a virtual router within the switch where the switch's routing functionality can be accessed.

**Practical Advice
and Information**

In discriminating between the proper roles of switching and routing, the best advice may be: Switch for bandwidth; route for filtering and internetwork segmentation.

Advantages   LAN switches are able to produce dramatic increases in bandwidth in comparison to shared media LANs if sufficient thought has gone into organizing workstations and servers on LAN switch segments in a logical manner.

Virtual LANs, which will be thoroughly explored later in the chapter, are enabled by the LAN switch's ability to quickly make any two workstations or servers appear to be physically attached to the same LAN segment. Virtual LANs take advantage of this switching capability by logically defining those workstations and computers that belong to the same virtual LAN regardless of the physical location of those workstations and servers. A given workstation or server can belong to more than one virtual LAN.

Limitations   A LAN switch's limitations are largely a result of its bridging heritage. Switching cannot perform sophisticated filtering or security based on network layer protocols because LAN switches are unable to read network layer protocols. Switches are unable to discriminate between multiple paths and make best path decisions. Management information offered to enterprise network management systems by LAN switches is minimal in comparison with that available from routers.

Perhaps more important, because switched LAN connections may exist only for a matter of microseconds, monitoring and management of traffic within the LAN switch are considerably more challenging than performing similar tasks on routers. Traditional LAN analyzers constructed for use on shared media LANs are of no use on switched media LANs. Potential solutions to this and other switching limitations, such as buffering between high- and low-speed network architectures within a single switch, are covered in the LAN switch technology analysis section of Chapter 3.

▨ INTERNETWORKING TECHNOLOGY

Internetworking Technology and the OSI Model

Internetworking technology can be categorized according to the OSI model layer corresponding to the protocols that a given internetworking device is able to process. In this way, the following internetworking devices can be categorized with the following OSI layers:

- Repeaters— OSI Layer 1   Physical Layer
- Bridges—OSI Layer 2   Data-Link Layer
- Routers—OSI Layer 3   Network Layer

Each of these categories of internetworking devices will be explored in more detail in the following sections. Switching was discussed in this chapter as an internetworking design issue based on future directions such as virtual LANs and integrated routing, but LAN switch technology was previously explored in Chapter 3 on LAN Hardware because of its current deployment largely in local area networks, rather than in internetworks.

A few characteristics are true of all internetworking devices in relation to the protocols of the OSI layer with which they are associated.

- Any given network device can translate or convert protocols associated with OSI layers lower than or equal to the OSI layer of the internetworking device.

- Any given network device is unable to process protocols associated with OSI layers higher than the OSI layer of the internetworking device.

The relationship between the OSI model and internetworking devices is illustrated in Figure 13-4.

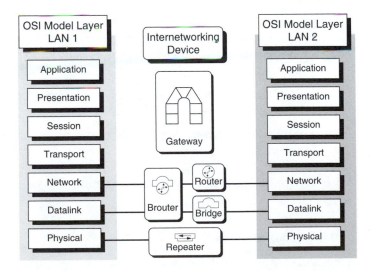

Figure 13-4   Relationship Between the OSI Model and Internetworking Devices

Repeaters

Functionality   All data traffic on a LAN is in a digital format of discrete voltages of discrete duration traveling over one type of physical media or another. The only exception to this statement would be in the case of wireless-based LANs where the transmission would be through the air in an analog format. Given this, a **repeater's** job is fairly simple to understand:

- Repeat the digital signal by regenerating and retiming the incoming signal.

- Pass all signals between all attached segments.

- Do not read destination addresses of data packets.

- Allow for the connection of and translation between different types of media.

- Effectively extend overall LAN distance by repeating signals between LAN segments.

A repeater is a non-discriminatory internetworking device. It does not discriminate between data packets. Every signal that comes into one side of a repeater gets regenerated and sent out the other side of the repeater. Repeaters are available for both Ethernet and Token Ring network architectures for a wide variety of media types. A repeater is a physical layer device concerned with physical layer signaling protocols relating to signal voltage levels and timing. The primary reasons for employing a repeater are:

- Increase the overall length of the network media by repeating signals across multiple LAN segments. In a Token Ring LAN, several MAUs can be linked together by repeaters in order to increase the size of the LAN.

- Isolate key network resources onto different LAN segments in order to ensure greater survivability.

- Translate between different media types supported for a given network architecture.

Figure 13-5 illustrates typical installations of repeaters.

Applied Problem Solving

TECHNOLOGY ANALYSIS

Figure 13-6 outlines some of the technology analysis issues that should be considered before purchasing Ethernet or Token Ring repeaters.

Installation - Ethernet Fiber-Optic Multiport Repeater

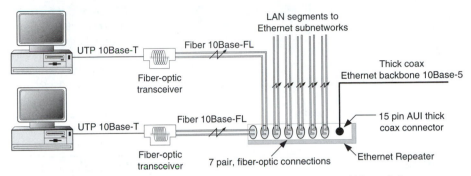

Installation - Token Ring Repeaters

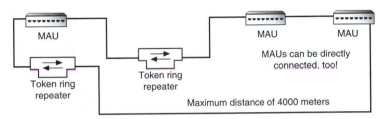

Figure 13-5   Repeater Installations

Network Architecture	Technology Analysis Issue	Importance/Implications
Ethernet	Media Type/Interface Support	• 10BaseT: UTP, RJ-45 • 10Base2: Thin coax, BNC • 10Base5: Thick Coax, AUI • 10BaseFL: Fiber-Optic Cable, ST or SMA connectors
	Long/Extended Distance Repeaters	• Work over single pair telephone wire • Extend Ethernet LANs up to 1250 feet • Must be used in pairs • Fiber-optic links yield distances of up to 1.2 miles
	Local Repeaters	• Used to extend and segment local LANs
	Modular Repeaters	• Hot-swappable modules allow flexible use for a variety of different media types and interfaces
	Workgroup Repeaters	• Used for media conversion

(continued)

	Auto-partitioning	• All possible media combinations are available
		• An important feature that prevents failure of one connected segment from affecting other segments
		• Auto-restoral upon segment reestablishment is often also included
	Number of Segments per Repeater	• Repeaters vary in segment capacity
		• Typical segment capacities range from 2 to 8
	Cascadability	• Some repeaters can be daisy-chained or cascaded to increase overall LAN length.
	Price Range	• $250–$2500
Token Ring	Transmission speed	• Token Ring is available in 4 Mbps and 16 Mbps
		• Some repeaters are able to convert between speeds
		• Repeaters must support proper speed
	MAU Ring Length vs. Lobe Length	• Token Ring repeaters can extend either the overall ring length as measured by the distance between MAUs, or the Lobe length that is the distance from the workstation to the MAU
		• Some Token Ring repeaters can be used to extend either ring length or lobe length
	Fiber-Optic Repeaters	• Token Ring fiber-optic repeaters can extend Ring length to 8200 feet
	Media Type/Interface Support	• Type 1 Cabling: STP, Type 1 connectors
		• Type 3 cabling: UTP, RJ-45 connectors
	Price Range	• $815–$2300

Figure 13-6 Repeater Technology Analysis

Bridges

Functionality When users on one LAN need occasional access to data or resources from another LAN, an internetworking device that is more sophisticated and discriminating than a repeater is required. From a comparative outlook on the functionality of **bridges** versus repeaters, one could say that bridges are more discriminating.

This reading, processing, and discriminating indicate a higher level of sophistication of the bridge, afforded by installed software, and also implies a higher price tag than repeaters. (Repeaters: $250–$2500; Bridges: $2,000–$6,000). Bridges come in many varieties as determined by the characteristics of the two LANs joined by a particular bridge. Physically, bridges may be network interface cards that can be plugged into an expansion slot of a PC along with additional bridging software, or they may be stand-alone devices.

Bridge performance is generally measured by two criteria:

- **Filtering Rate:** Measured in packets/sec or frames/sec. When a bridge reads the destination address on an Ethernet frame or Token Ring packet and decides whether or not that packet should be allowed access to the internetwork through the bridge, that process is known as **filtering.** Filtering rates for bridges range from 7,000 to 60,000 frames per second.

- **Forwarding Rate:** Also measured in packets/sec or frames/sec. Having decided whether to grant a packet access to the internetwork in the filtering process, the bridge now must perform a separate operation of **forwarding** the packet onto the internetwork media whether local or remote. Forwarding rates range from as little as 700 packets per second for some remote bridges to as much as 30,000 packets per second for RISC-based high-speed local bridges.

Although bridging functionality has already been reviewed in the section on Internetwork Design, two issues specific to bridging deserve further explanation:

- Dealing with redundant paths and broadcast storms
- Source Route Bridging

Spanning Tree Algorithm   The **Spanning Tree Algorithm (STA)** has been standardized as **IEEE 802.1** for the purposes of controlling redundant paths in bridged networks, thereby reducing the possibility of broadcast storms. When installing multiple bridges in a complex internetworking arrangement, a looping topology containing multiple active loops could be accidentally introduced into the internetwork architecture. The Spanning Tree Algorithm (IEEE 802.1), which is implemented as software installed on STA-complaint bridges, can sense multiple paths and can disable all but one. In addition, should the primary path between two LANs become disabled, the Spanning Tree Algorithm can re-enable the previously disabled redundant link, thereby preserving the inter-LAN link. STA bridges accomplish this path management by communicating with each other via **configuration bridge protocol data units** (Configuration BPDU). The overall effect of STA-compliant bridges is that they enable the positive aspects of redundant paths in bridged networks while eliminating the negative aspects.

Source Route Bridging   **Source Routing bridges** are not to be confused with routers since the capture of the routing information that delineates the chosen path to the destination address is done by the source device, usually a LAN-attached PC, and not by the bridge. The PC sends out a special **explorer packet** which determines the best path to the intended destination of its data message. The explorer packets are continually propagated through all source routing bridges until the destination workstation is finally reached by the explorer packet. Along the journey to the destination work-station, each source routing bridge enters its address in the Routing Information Field of the explorer packet. The destination workstation sends the completed RIF back directly to the source workstation. All subsequent data messages include the suggested path to the destination embedded within the header of the Token Ring frame. Having determined the best path to the intended destination, the source PC sends the data message along with the path instructions to the local bridge, which forwards the data message according to the received path instructions.

Data messages arrive at a source routing bridge with a detailed map of how they plan to reach their destination. One very important limitation of source routing bridges as applied to large internetworks is known as the **7 Hop Limit.** Because of the limited space in the **RIF (Router Information Field)** of the explorer packet, only seven hop locations can be included in the path to any remote destination. As a result, routers with larger routing table capacity are often employed for larger internetworks.

In order to avoid constantly flooding the network with explorer packets seeking destinations, source routing bridges may employ some type of **address caching** or RIF caching, so that previously determined routes to known destinations are saved and re-used.

Applied Problem Solving

TECHNOLOGY ANALYSIS

Bridges can be categorized in a number of different ways. Perhaps the major criteria for categorizing bridges is the network architecture of the LANs to be joined by the bridge.

First and foremost, are the two LANs that are to be bridged Ethernet or Token Ring? Bridges that connect LANs of similar data-link format are known as **transparent bridges.** Transparent bridges exhibit the following characteristics:

- **Promiscuous listen,** meaning that transparent bridges receive all data packets transmitted on the LANs to which they are connected.

- Store-and-forward bridging between LANs means that messages that are not destined for local workstations are forwarded through the bridge as soon as the target LAN is available

- Learning is achieved by examining all MAC source addresses on data-link frames received in order to understand which workstations are locally attached to which LANs through which ports on the bridge.

- The IEEE 802.1 spanning tree algorithm is implemented in order to manage path connectivity between LANs.

A special type of bridge that includes a **format converter** can bridge between Ethernet and Token Ring. These special bridges may also be called **multiprotocol bridges** or **translating bridges.**

A third type of bridge, somewhat like a translating bridge, is used to bridge between Ethernet and FDDI networks. Unlike the translating bridge, which must actually manipulate and rewrite the data-link layer frame, the **encapsulating bridge** merely takes the entire Ethernet data-link layer frame and stuffs it in an "envelope" (data frame) which conforms to the FDDI data-link layer protocol.

Source routing bridges are specifically designed for connecting Token Ring LANs that have source routing enabled. Not all Token Ring LANs are source routing LANs but only Token Ring LANs can be source routing LANs. Bridges that can support links between source routing Token Ring LANs or transparent LANs are known as **Source Routing Transparent (SRT) bridges.** These bridges are able to identify whether frames are to be bridged transparently or source routed by reading the flags setting in the data-link frame header.

Figure 13-7 illustrates typical bridge installations, whereas Figure 13-8 identifies some of the technology analysis issues that should be considered prior to purchasing bridge technology.

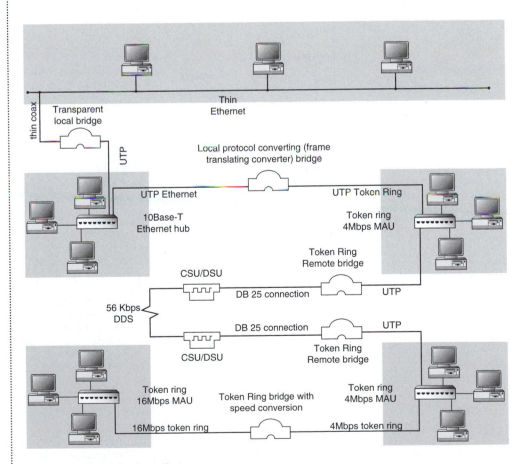

Figure 13-7   Bridge Installations

Bridge Technology Analysis Issue	Importance/Implication
Network Architectures to Be Connected	• Bridges for Ethernet and Token Ring are common. • Bridges for FDDI, 100BaseT, and 100VGAnyLAN are less common. • Network architecture determines LAN speed. • Network architecture determines supported network media.
Transparent Bridges	• Used for connecting Ethernet to Ethernet or non-source routing Token Ring to non-source routing Token Ring. • Must be able to support promiscuous listen, store-and forward bridging, learning, and spanning tree algorithm.
Translating Bridges	• Ethernet/Token Ring is the most common translating bridge. • Can become a serious network bottleneck owing to incompatibilities between Ethernet and Token Ring frame layouts, transmission speeds, and frame lengths.
Source Routing Bridges	• Used to connect two or more source routing enabled Token Ring LANs. • Source routes are determined by explorer packets broadcasts. • Explorer packet broadcasts can negatively affect network performance. • Routes are limited to 7 hops (intermediate bridges).
Source Routing Transparent Bridges	• An intelligent bridge which is able to distinguish between transparent bridge traffic and source routing bridge traffic and is able to bridge each appropriately.

Bridge Performance Testing	• Bridge performance can be measured in any of the following ways:
	  • Throughput: Maximum sustained transmission rate with zero errors or lost packets.
	  • Packet Loss Rate: % of packets lost at maximum theoretical transmission speed of the bridge.
	  • Latency: The time it takes for a bridge to process a single packet. In other words, the delay per packet introduced by the bridge.

Local Bridges	• Local bridges connect two or more LANs directly via network media. • Local bridges contain two or more network interface cards. • Local bridges are used to translate between media types.

Multiport Bridges	• Multiport bridges contain more than two network interface cards. • If the bridge has learned which ports a destination workstation is attached to (by building known local nodes table for each port), it will forward the data-link layer frame to that port. • If the bridge does not know which port a destination workstation is attached to, it will broadcast the data-link layer frame to all ports except the one from which it came.
Remote Bridges	• Remote bridges contain network interface cards as well as serial ports for connection to WAN links via modems or CSU/DSUs. • Most remote bridges contain one network interface card, specific to a particular network architecture, and one serial interface (RS-232 or V.35). • A compatible remote bridge must be used on the far end of the WAN link to complete the LAN-to-LAN connection. • Data compression is particularly important to remote bridges since the WAN links possess significantly less bandwidth than the LANs. Although compression rates depend on the file being compressed, 3:1 compression ratios are possible. • SNMP management information from remote bridges is important to allow these bridges to be monitored and managed by an SNMP-compliant enterprise network management system • In order to be able to configure remote bridges from a centralized support location, the remote bridges must support Telnet login.
WAN Services for Remote Bridges	• Among the WAN services available for remote bridges are 56K DDS, ISDN, T-1 (1.544 Mbps).
Hot Swappable Modules	• Some bridges may support hot-swappable modules, allowing users to flexibly configure the network interfaces in a bridge without disabling the network.
RISC Processors	• Bridge performance is directly related to the speed of the processor within the bridge. • RISC processors produce superior performance results.
Price Range	• $2000 to $6000

Figure 13-8   Bridge Technology Analysis

Wireless Bridges   When corporate LAN locations are located up to 3 miles apart, remote bridges linked by WAN services such as 56 Kbps or faster lines are a common internetworking solution. This design implies monthly recurring expenses of approximately $500 for the WAN services in addition to fixed costs for the acquisition of the remote bridges and associated transmission equipment. An increasingly popular alternative for bridging remote LANs up to 50 miles apart are **wireless bridges.** Wireless bridges use spread spectrum radio transmission between LAN sites and are primarily limited to Ethernet networks at this time. Although transmission ranges were generally limited to three miles in the past, new wireless bridges using the 2.4 1 GHz or 5.8 1GHzfrequency ranges can transmit at T-1 speed (1.544 Mbps) for up to 50 miles.

Like most Ethernet bridges, most wireless bridges support the spanning tree algorithm, filtering by MAC addresses, protection against broadcast storms, SNMP management, encryption, and a variety of different Ethernet network media. Like other remote bridges, wireless bridges must be used in pairs. List prices can range from $2700 to $13500 with the majority of wireless bridges in the $4000 to $5000 range. These prices make wireless bridges comparable to remote WAN bridges in initial cost, but have the added advantage of not requiring ongoing monthly expense for WAN services.

Routers

Functionality   Among the advanced functionality offered by routers, perhaps the most important is their ability to discriminate between multiple network layer protocols. For instance, remembering that multiple protocols can be "sealed" within Ethernet data-link layer "envelopes," a router may be programmed to open the Ethernet envelopes and forward all NetWare (IPX) traffic to one network and all TCP/IP (IP) or Appletalk (AFP) to another. In some cases, a certain protocol may require "priority" handling due to session time-out restrictions or the time sensitivity of the embedded data.

Routers are made to read specific network layer protocols in order to maximize filtering and forwarding rates. If a router has to route only one type of network protocol, then it knows exactly where to look for destination addresses every time and can process packets much faster. However, realizing that different network layer protocols will have different packet structures with the destination addresses of various lengths and positions, some more sophisticated routers known as **multiprotocol routers** have the capability to interpret, process, and forward data packets of multiple protocols.

In the case of an Ethernet data-link frame, the multiprotocol router knows which network layer protocol is embedded within the data-link frame's information field by the contents of the TYPE field in the Ethernet frame.

Some common network layer protocols and their associated network operating systems or upper-layer protocols are listed below:

- IPX   NetWare
- IP   TCP/IP
- VIP   Vines
- AFP   Appletalk
- XNS   3Com
- OSI   Open Systems

Other protocols processed by some routers are actually data-link layer protocols without network layer addressing schemes. These protocols are considered **non-routable.** Non-routable protocols can be processed by routers by either having the routers act as bridges or by encapsulating the non-routable data-link layer frame's upper-layer protocols in a routable network layer protocol such as IP. At one time, specialized devices that could either bridge or route were referred to as **brouters.** Today, however, most advanced routers include bridging functionality. Some of the more common non-routable protocols and their associated networking environments are listed below:

- LAT   Digital DecNet
- SNA/SDLC   IBM SNA
- NetBIOS   DOS-Based LANs
- NetBEUI

In Sharper Focus

ROUTING PROTOCOLS

Routers manufactured by different vendors need a way to talk to each other in order to exchange routing table information concerning current network conditions. Every network operating system contains an associated routing protocol as part of its protocol stack. Figure 13-9 lists common routing proto-

Routing Protocol		Network Environment
RIP	Routing Information Protocol	XNS, NetWare, TCP/IP
OSPF	Open Shortest Path First	TCP/IP
NLSP	NetWare Link State Protocol	NetWare 4.1
IS-IS	Intermediate System to Intermediate System	DECnet, OSI
RTMP	Routing Table Maintenance Protocol	Appletalk
RTP	Router Table Protocol	Vines

Figure 13-9 Router-to-Router Protocols

cols and their associated protocol suites or network environments. Routing protocols were explored in detail in Chapters 4 and 12.

RIP, Routing Information Protocol, at one time the most popular router protocol standard, is largely being replaced by **OSPF, Open Shortest Path First**. OSPF offers several advantages over RIP, including its ability to handle larger internetworks as well as a smaller impact on network traffic for routing table updates.

A major distinction between routing protocols involves the method or algorithm by which up-to-date routing information is gathered by the router. For instance, RIP uses a **distance vector** algorithm which only measures the number of hops to a distant router, to a maximum of 16, while the OSPF protocol uses a more comprehensive **link state** algorithm that can decide between multiple paths to a given router based on variables other than number of hops such as delay, and capacity, throughput, and reliability of the circuits connecting the routers. Perhaps more important, OSPF uses much less bandwidth in its efforts to keep routing tables up-to-date.

Distance vector routing requires each router to maintain a table listing the distance in hops, sometimes referred to as link cost, between itself and every other reachable network. These distances are computed by using the contents of neighboring routers' routing tables and adding the distance between itself and the neighboring router that supplied the routing table information. Routing tables must be kept up-to-date to reflect any changes in the network. The key problem with distance vector routing protocols is that changes in the network are not always known by all routers immediately because of delays in having routers recalculate their own routing tables prior to retransmitting updated information to neighboring routers. This phenomenon is referred to as **slow convergence.**

Link state protocols such as OSPF (TCP/IP) and NLSP (NetWare) are able to overcome slow convergence and offer a number of other performance enhancements as well. One important distinction between distance vector and link state routing protocols is that distance vector routing protocols only use information supplied by directly attached neighboring routers, whereas link state routing protocols employ network information received from all routers on a given internetwork.

Link state routing protocols are able to maintain a complete and more current view of the total internetwork than distance vector routing protocols by adhering to the following basic processes:

- Link state routers use specialized datagrams known as **link state packets (LSP)** to determine the names of and the cost or distance to any neighboring routers and associated networks.

- All information learned about the network is sent to all known routers, not just neighboring routers, using LSPs.

- All routers have all other routers' full knowledge of the entire internetwork via the receipt of LSPs. The collection of LSPs is stored in an

LSP database. This full internetwork view is in contrast to only a view of one's immediate neighbors using a distance vector protocol.

- Each router is responsible for compiling the information contained in all of the most recently received LSPs in order to form an up-to-the-minute view of the entire internetwork. From this full view of the internetwork, the link state routing protocol is able to calculate the best path to each destination network as well as a variety of alternate paths with varying costs.

- Newly received LSPs can be forwarded immediately, whereas distance vector routing protocols must recalculate their own routing tables before forwarding updated information to neighboring routers. The immediate forwarding of LSPs allows faster convergence in the case of lost links or newly added nodes.

Applied Problem Solving

TECHNOLOGY ANALYSIS

The most significant distinguishing factor among routers is directly related to the location and associated routing requirements into which the router is to be deployed. As a result, **central site routers,** otherwise known as **enterprise** or **backbone routers** are employed at large corporate sites, whereas **boundary** or **branch office routers,** are employed at remote corporate locations with fever routing requirements and fewer technical support personnel. For branch offices whose amount of internetwork traffic does not warrant the constant bandwidth and higher cost of leased lines, **dial-up routers,** often using ISDN, are employed. Figure 13-10 illustrates the installation of various types of routers.

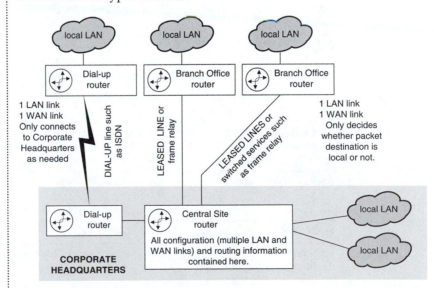

Figure 13-10   Router Installations

Boundary Routers and Branch Office Routers

In the case of boundary or branch office routers, all routing information is kept at the central site router. This allows the boundary router to require less technical configuration and to be available at a lower cost than central site routers. Boundary routers generally have just two interfaces—one WAN link and one LAN link. A boundary router's logic is fairly simple. All locally generated packets are either destined for the local LAN, in which case they are ignored, or they are non-local, in which case they are forwarded over the single WAN link to the central site router for further processing.

The obvious limitation of such a topology is that there is no direct communication between boundary routers, and that the central routers must include redundancy because all internetwork communication depends on them. Also, a particular vendor's boundary routers must be matched with that vendor's central office routers since there are no interoperability standards for this configuration. Figure 13-11 outlines some of the technical analysis issues to be considered with boundary routers.

Technical Analysis Issue	Importance/Implication
Ability to Deal with Non-Routable Traffic	• Must be able to deal with non-routable protocols such as SNA/SDLC and NetBIOS • Must be able to deal with timing requirements such as SDLC's session time-out limitation
Remote Configuration Support	• Must be able to be configured remotely • Software upgrades must be able to be performed remotely from central site • What happens if the transmission line or power fails during a remote update?
SNMP Compatibility	• Must be able to output SNMP compatible management information for interaction with enterprise network management systems
WAN Services Supported	• May be any of the following: 56K DDS, T-1, Frame Relay
Frame Relay Support	• If Frame Relay is to be used as the WAN service, can the device interact properly with Frame Relay's congestion control mechanism to avoid packet loss?
Backup WAN Services	• Are switched WAN services available for backup if the leased line fails? • Examples: ISDN, Dial-up Async, Switched 56K
WAN Protocols Supported	• Examples: HDLC, X.25, Frame Relay, PPP
LAN Network Architectures Supported	• Examples: Ethernet, Token Ring. Others?

(continued)

LAN Protocols Routed	• Examples: IP, IPX, DECnet, Appletalk, Vines, XNS, OSI
LAN Protocols Filtered	• Some LAN protocols are very chatty and can waste precious WAN bandwidth • Boundary routers should be able to filter these protocols to keep them off the WAN link: SAP, RIP, NetBIOS broadcasts, Source Routing explorer packets

Figure 13-11   Boundary Routers Technology Analysis

Dial-Up Routers   In cases where the amount of inter-LAN traffic from a remote site does not justify the cost of a leased line, dial-up routers may be the appropriate choice of internetworking equipment. This is especially true if the dial-up digital WAN service known as ISDN (Integrated Services Digital Network) is available at the two ends of the LANs to be linked. ISDN BRI (Basic Rate Interface) provides up to 128 (2 × 64) bps of bandwidth on demand, and ISDN PRI (Primary Rate Interface) provides up to 1.536 Mbps of usable digital bandwidth on demand. There are currently no interoperability standards for dial-up routers. As a result, dial-up routers should always be bought in pairs from the same manufacturer.

In addition to all of the technical features important to boundary routers, perhaps the most important feature of dial-up routers is **spoofing.** Spoofing is a method of filtering chatty or unwanted protocols from the WAN link while ensuring that remote programs which require ongoing communication from these filtered protocols are still reassured via emulation of these protocols by the local dial-up router. Among the chatty protocols most in need of filtering are:

- RIP (Routing Information Protocol): NetWare and TCP/IP

- SAP (Service Advertising Protocol): NetWare

- Watchdog, otherwise known as keep-alive messages: NetWare

- Serialization, looking for duplicate license numbers: NetWare

Filtering is very important to dial-up routers because these unwanted protocols can easily establish or keep a dial-up line open, thereby causing excessive line charges. Spoofing as a combination of filtering and emulation is illustrated in Figure 13-12.

Occasionally, updated information such as session status or services availability must be exchanged between dial-up routers so that packets are not routed in error and sessions are not terminated incorrectly. The manner in which these required updates of overhead information are performed can make a significant difference in the efficiency of the dial-up routers and the size of the associated charge for the use of dial-up bandwidth. It is important to remember that these routers communicate only via dial-up connections

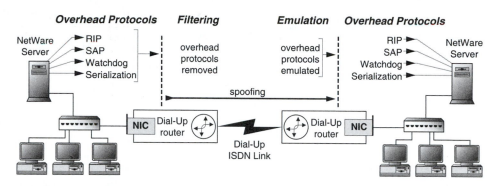

Figure 13-12   Dial-Up Router Spoofing

and that it would be economically unwise to create or maintain immediate dial-up connections for every update of overhead information. Different dial-up routers use different update mechanisms. Three primary methods for efficient updating are as follows:

- **Timed Updates** are performed at regular predetermined intervals

- **Triggered Updates** are performed whenever a certain programmable event, such as a change in available services, occurs.

- **Piggyback Updates** are performed only when the dial-up link has already been established for the purposes of exchanging user data.

Routing Evolution   Although no one knows for sure what the future of internetworking design and technology holds, most people seem to agree that some combination of switching and routing will be the likely scenario in the foreseeable future. Although switching is excellent at providing large amounts of switched LAN bandwidth, it is a layer 2 technology and is unable to offer advanced filtering, security, and internetwork segmentation associated with layer 3 routing technology.

Three different possible internetwork design evolutionary scenarios are as follows:

- **Distinct Layer 2 Switching and Layer 3 Routing** in which separate layer 2 switches and layer 3 routers cooperatively contribute what each does best in order to deliver internetwork traffic as efficiently as possible.

- **Distributed Routing** in which layer 2 switching and layer 3 routing functionality are combined into a single device sometimes referred to as a **multi-layer or Layer 3 switch.**

- **Route Servers** will provide a centralized repository of routing information, whereas **edge switches** deployed within the LANs will be programmed with minimal routing information. Edge switches will consult distributed route servers for "directory assistance" when they encounter routing situations they are not equipped to handle. In this scenario, routing information and processing overhead is kept to a minimum at the switches that are primarily responsible for providing local bandwidth.

In differing manners, each of these scenarios implements the future of internetwork design as described by the currently popular phrase, "Switch when you can, route when you must." These three internetworking design scenarios combining switching and routing are illustrated in Figure 13-13.

IP Switching and Quality of Service   Another possible evolutionary scenario combining switching and routing is known as **IP switching.** By implementing IP routing software directly on ATM switching hardware, IP switching combines switching and routing capabilities into a single device and discriminates between which traffic should be switched and which should be routed. For streaming data such as file transfers or multimedia sessions, ATM switched virtual circuits are established and the traffic is allowed to flow through the virtual circuit without the typical packet-by-packet processing associated with routers. For connectionless datagrams and shorter transmissions, IP routing software is implemented. Protocols to distinguish which traffic should be switched and which should be routed have been proposed by at least three different companies and will eventually be considered by the IETF. The early entries for IP switching management protocols are Flow Management Protocol from IPsilon Networks, Tag Distribution Protocol from Cisco, and Aggregate Route-Based IP Switching from IBM. IPsilon was an early promoter of IP switching that was later acquired by Nokia. Cisco's Tag Switching protocol became known as **MPLS (Multiprotocol label switching)** when it began deliberation by the IETF.

Although MPLS was originally intended for use within a switched internetwork environment, the scope of its application has broadened to include the Internet. MPLS provides the following functionality:

- Uses labels to provide shortcuts to specific circuits for fast routing of IP packets without the typical packet-by-packet routing table lookups.

- Labels can also be used to represent **QoS (Quality of Service)** requirements or a Virtual Private Network through the Internet.

- Defined for use over frame relay, ATM, and PPP (point-to-point protocol) WAN connections and IEEE 802.3 LANs

Distinct Layer 2 Switching and Layer 3 Routing

ENTERPRISE NETWORK   ROUTING   SWITCHING
                       LAYER   LAYER

Distributed Routing

ENTERPRISE NETWORK   ROUTING AND
                               SWITCHING LAYER

Route Servers

ENTERPRISE NETWORK   ROUTING   ROUTING AND
                       INFORMATION   SWITCHING LAYER

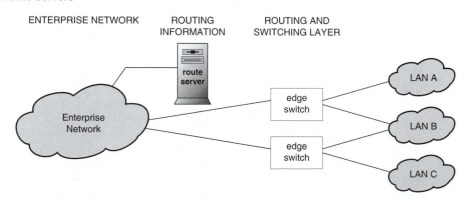

Figure 13-13   Routing Evolution Scenarios

- Supports explicit routing that allows certain types of traffic (e.g., video) to be explicitly assigned to specific circuits.

However, it is this last functionality, explicit routing, that may delay the adoption of MPLS. Cisco and Juniper Networks are in favor of using **RSVP (Resource Reservation Protocol)** to implement explicit routing, whereas other vendors such as Nortel and Ericsson are in favor of using **LDP (Label Distribution Protocol).**

As a total alternative to MPLS, **Diff-Serv (Differentiated Services)** is being prepared by another IETF working group. Diff-Serv provides the following functionality:

- Uses the type of service (ToS) bits already in the IP header to differentiate between different levels of service required by different applications.

- Allows service level agreements between users and service providers to be supported.

Using the OSI model to differentiate between MPLS and Diff-Serv, it should be noted that MPLS is a layer 2 solution, whereas Diff-Serv is a layer 3 solution. For this reason, the two standards are not really competing although many people perceive otherwise. MPLS, being a layer 2 service, will work with or without Diff-Serv on layer 3. In fact, the best solution may be for the two protocols to work together with MPLS-enabling switching labels for circuit assignment after reading the ToS bits in the layer 3 IP header.

Virtual LANs

Basic Functionality   The logical network design known as a virtual LAN is dependent on a physical device, the LAN switch, for its functionality. While the original LAN switches delivered abundant bandwidth to locally attached workstations and segments, they lacked the ability to partition the switch into multiple segregated broadcast zones and to segment users into corresponding separate workgroups.

Virtual LANs are software definable through configuration software contained within the LAN switch. The use of virtual LANs allows workgroup members to be assigned to more than one workgroup quickly and easily, if necessary. Subsequently, each virtual workgroup is assigned some portion of the LAN switch's backplane capacity. LAN switches that support virtual LANs use OSI layer 2 bridging functionality to logically segment the traffic within the switch into distinct virtual LANs.

Any message received by a LAN switch destined for a single workstation is delivered to that destination workstation via an individual switched network connection. The key difference between a LAN switch that does not support virtual LANs and one that does is the treatment of broadcast and multicast messages. In a virtual LAN, broadcasts and multicasts are limited to the members of that virtual LAN only, rather than to all connected devices. This prevents propagation of data across the entire network and reduces network traffic. To simplify, virtual LANs are nothing more than logically defined broadcast/multicast groups within layer 2 LAN switches, because point-to-point traffic is handled by switched dedicated connections.

Limitations A key limitation of virtual LANs is that when members of the same virtual LAN are physically connected to separate LAN switches, the virtual LAN configuration information must be shared between multiple LAN switches. Currently, no interoperability standards exist for transmitting or sharing virtual LAN information between layer 2 LAN switches. As a result, only proprietary switch-to-switch protocols between a single vendor's equipment are possible for multi-switch virtual LANs, although IEEE 802.10 (see below) may be an open standard for inter-switch communication.

Management and monitoring of virtual LANs are more difficult than traditional LANs due to the virtual LAN's dependence on LAN switches for physical connectivity. Because the switched LAN connections are established, used, and terminated in a matter of microseconds for most transmissions, it is almost impossible to monitor these transmissions in real time by traditional means. One solution to this dilemma is known as **traffic duplication** or port mirroring in which traffic between two switch ports is duplicated onto a third port to which traditional LAN analyzers can be attached.

Figure 13-14 illustrates the differences between a LAN switch, a virtual LAN, and a multi-switch virtual LAN.

In Sharper Focus

TRANSMISSION BETWEEN LAYER 2 LAN SWITCHES

Among the alternative methods used by switch vendors to share virtual LAN information across layer 2 LAN switches are the following:

- Signaling Message—Switches inform each other whenever new workstations come on line as to the MAC address and virtual LAN number of that workstation. In order to keep all switches' information synchronized, each switch's virtual LAN tables are broadcast periodically to all other switches. In larger switched networks, this virtual LAN table transfer can introduce significant amounts of broadcast traffic.

- Frame Tagging—A tag indicating the virtual LAN number of the source workstation is appended to every data-link layer frame that must travel between LAN switches. In this way, the recipient switch knows immediately to which virtual LAN workstations the received frame must be forwarded. One difficulty with frame tagging is that the added bits may exceed the maximum frame length of the data-link layer protocol, thereby requiring additional proprietary methods to cope with this limitation.

- Time Division Multiplexing—Each virtual LAN is assigned a specific portion of the bandwidth available on the LAN switches' backplanes. Only the assigned virtual LAN is allowed to use designated

LAN Switch

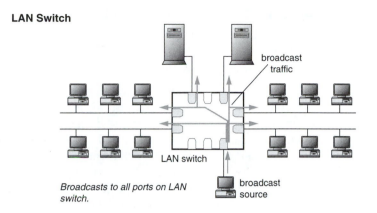

broadcast traffic

LAN switch

Broadcasts to all ports on LAN switch.

broadcast source

Single Switch Virtual LANs

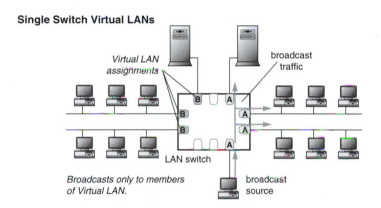

Virtual LAN assignments

broadcast traffic

LAN switch

Broadcasts only to members of Virtual LAN.

broadcast source

Multi-Switch Virtual LANs

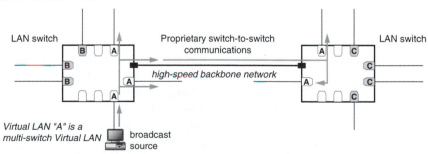

LAN switch

Proprietary switch-to-switch communications

LAN switch

high-speed backbone network

Virtual LAN "A" is a multi-switch Virtual LAN

broadcast source

Figure 13-14   LAN Switches and Virtual LANs

bandwidth. In this way, each virtual LAN has a virtual private back-plane and traffic from various virtual LANs does not interfere with each other. However, assigned but unused bandwidth cannot be shared among other virtual LANs.

One possibility for standardization of switch-to-switch communication in support of virtual LANs that span multiple switches is **IEEE 802.10.** Originally conceived as a standard for secure data exchange on LANs that would allow workstations to set encryption and authentication settings, this standard is of interest to virtual LAN switch vendors because of the addition of a 32-bit header to existing MAC sub-layer frames. Instead of holding just security information, this additional 32-bit header could hold virtual LAN identifiers. In order to overcome the limitation on maximum data-link layer frame length, IEEE 802.10 also includes specifications for segmentation and reassembly of any frames that should exceed maximum length due to the addition of the 32-bit header.

Transmission Between Virtual LANs   Virtual LANs are built using LAN switches that are OSI layer 2 devices only able to distinguish between MAC layer addresses. As a result, LAN switches are only able to offer the "forward-if-not-local" internetworking logic of bridges. In order to selectively transmit traffic between virtual LANs, routing functionality is required. This routing functionality may be supplied by an external router or by specialized router software included in the LAN switch. LAN switches with built-in routing capabilities are sometimes referred to as layer 3 switches. Because traffic cannot move between virtual LANs without the benefit of routing, the virtual LAN logical design has been credited with offering firewall functionality due to the filtering capabilities of intermediary routers.

Classification of Virtual LANs   Virtual LANs are often classified in terms of the OSI layer that represents their highest level of functionality:

Layer 2 Virtual LANs are built using LAN switches that act as microsegmenting bridges. In fact, some say that a layer 2 switch is nothing more than a multiport bridge. A LAN switch that supports a layer 2 virtual LAN distinguishes only between the MAC addresses of connected workstations. No differentiation is possible based on layer 3, network layer, protocols. One or more workstations can be connected to each switch port.

Layer 3 Virtual LANs are built using LAN switches that are able to process layer 3 network addresses. Such devices may be called **routing switches** or **layer 3 switches.** Because these devices are able to perform filtering based on network layer protocols and addresses, they are able to support multiple virtual LANs using different network layer protocols.

In other words, one virtual LAN might support only TCP/IP, whereas another might only support IPX/SPX. Since layer 3 switches understand layer 3 addressing schemes, they are able to use the subnetwork numbers embedded within layer 3 addresses to organize virtual LANs. These subnetwork numbers are previously assigned to workstations, so some layer 3 switches are able to query all connected workstations and auto-configure or automatically assign workstations to virtual LANs based on these subnetwork numbers. Workstations using nonroutable protocols such as LAT, NetBEUI, or NetBIOS are similarly segregated into their own virtual LANs.

Figure 13-15 illustrates the architectural differences between layer 2 and layer 3 virtual LANs, whereas Figure 13-16 details the functional differences between the two virtual LAN designs.

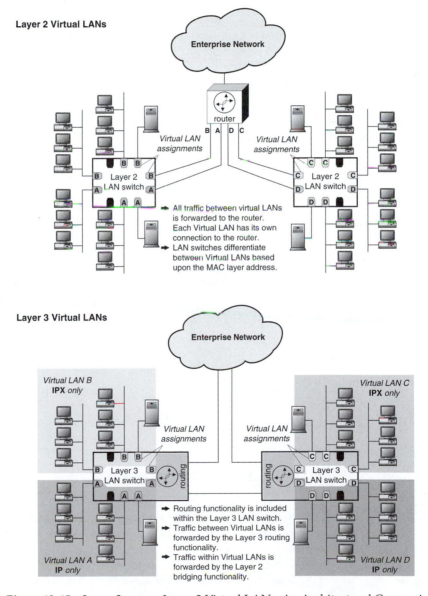

Figure 13-15   Layer 2 versus Layer 3 Virtual LANs: An Architectural Comparison

Virtual LAN Characteristic	Layer 2 Virtual LAN Functionality	Layer 3 Virtual LAN Functionality
Configuration	Simpler	More difficult
Expense	Less expensive, but may require external routers	More expensive, but include internal routing capability
Performance	Faster since they only process layer 2 addresses	Up to 30% slower since they must process layer 3 protocols
Non-routable Protocols	No problem since this is a layer 2 only device	May be able to segregate into a separate VLAN or may not be able to handle
Routable Protocols	No ability to differentiate between layer 3 protocols	Can differentiate between layer 3 protocols and can build separate virtual LANs based on the layer 3 protocol. Layer 3 switches vary in the number of routable protocols supported.
Multi-switch Virtual LANs	Must use proprietary switch-to-switch communication, which adds to networktraffic congestion in most cases	Able to use subnetwork numbers in network layer addresses to keep track of virtual LANs that span multiple switches without the need for proprietary switch-to-switch protocols
Broadcasts	Broadcasts to all segments that belong to a particular virtual LAN	Can broadcast to only appropriate subnetwork within a virtual LAN
Filtering	No filtering on network layer addresses or protocols possible	Filtering on network layer addresses and protocols for security and virtual LAN segmentation by protocol
Routing Capabilities	Must be supplied by external router	Included with built-in routing software that provides traffic management and protocol isolation. Some layer 3 switches are able to communicate with routers via RIP or OSPF while others are not able to.

Figure 13-16   Layer 2 versus Layer 3 Virtual LANs: A Functional Comparison

Managerial Perspective

VIRTUAL LAN REALITIES—THE BOTTOM LINE

Virtual LANs were initially touted as the ultimate solution for increasing LAN manageability and broadcast control. By implementing the "route once, switch many" concept, VLAN technologies promised to increase LAN performance while reducing management effort.

Based on OSI Network Reference Model layer 2 switching technologies, VLANs initially required a separate layer 3 routing device to allow traffic to flow between VLANs. To resolve this dependency on routing technologies, routing capabilities were added to layer 2 switches.

LAN switches that include routing capabilities, known as layer 3 switches or routing switches, perform the traditional routing process for the first packet in a series, add the layer 2 addresses (MAC addresses) to an address table, and switch the remaining packets in the data flow at layer 2. In addition to allowing a series of switches to handle all traffic within and between VLANs, layer 3 switching can provide routing between LAN segments at a speed much faster than traditional routers.

As layer 3 switching technologies matured, the ability to analyze traffic flows based on the type of flow (as defined by the port number) was added. The resulting layer 4 switches provide a means to prioritize traffic flows based on traffic type, increase security by filtering, and collect application level traffic statistics on a per port basis.

The promise of VLANs to provide broadcast control has been fully realized, but increasing manageability has been less successful. When a packet needs to be delivered to a VLAN node on a different physical switch, a means of identifying the VLAN to which the packet is to be delivered must be implemented.

One of the biggest issues with VLAN implementation has been the fact that standards for managing such multi-switch VLAN packet identification were late in arriving. In the absence of clear standards, VLAN technology manufacturers implemented various proprietary solutions. With these technologies currently in place, manufacturers are reluctant to replace their proprietary solutions with newer standard solutions such as IEEE 802.10 packet tagging. As a result, VLAN solutions are limited mostly to single vendor solutions. Manageability varies widely among vendors, making it impossible to draw a definitive conclusion about overall VLAN manageability.

In addition to the growing pains experienced by VLANs, several significant technological changes have been introduced since the advent of VLAN technologies that are of interest. Changes to both the normal broadcast environment and routing technologies have affected the viability of VLANs.

One of the primary reasons for implementing VLANs has traditionally been to control LAN broadcast traffic. Broadcast traffic has traditionally represented a high level of traffic overhead from ARP, RIP, and SAP broadcasts. Occasionally network nodes would error and propagate these broadcast packets repeatedly, wasting significant bandwidth. The control of broadcast activity was important because network bandwidth was limited. In addition to the network capacity issue, each broadcast packet sent causes the network stack of each node on the network segment to analyze the packet, generating interrupts and using CPU cycles.

Research indicates that broadcast control is no longer the important issue it once was. Newer network software has optimized ARP functionality, RIP is rapidly being replaced in favor of more efficient routing protocols, and IPX with its associated SAP broadcasts is rapidly being replaced in favor of IP. In conjunction with this reduction in broadcast frequency, bandwidth on

LAN segments has been increased to the point that the percentage of broadcast activity is now relatively inconsequential for most LANs. The need for broadcast management has been further reduced because the increased processing power and standardization of bus mastering NIC cards have reduced the amount of node processor power wasted to processing broadcast packets to irrelevant levels for most LANs.

Based on these data, a case can be made that a network based entirely on layer 2 switching technologies is a viable option. No longer constrained by broadcast traffic concerns, such a network is significantly easier to troubleshoot and manage than a series of VLANs. As long as the backbone capacity of the layer 2 switches used is adequate to meet the overall traffic needs, this type of solution would allow a node to simply be attached to any available switched port.

Routing technologies have also significantly changed. Newer routers that implement the routing function in hardware based application specific integrated circuits (ASICS) have greatly reduced the latency traditionally associated with routers. These new "wire speed" routers offer IP routing performance similar to layer 3 switches while maintaining the familiar, easy to troubleshoot and manage routing paradigm. These new products also include many layer 4 switching features for packet prioritization, security, and application level packet flow data collection purposes.

Although wire speed routing technologies are new to the marketplace, companies such as Rapid-City Communications, Foundry Networks, and Cisco Systems (with technology acquired from Granite Systems) have developed or are developing products using this approach. These products offer Gigabit speed LAN routing at costs relatively similar to layer 3 enabled VLAN switches. The use of such "wire speed" routers offers new life to the traditional routed network paradigm.

While VLANs continue to offer excellent broadcast control and reasonable (though not standard) manageability, changes in other LAN technologies have significantly clouded the VLAN issue. It is no longer necessary to implement a VLAN solution to obtain many of the results associated with VLAN technologies.

Traditional switched networks can now offer similar performance to VLANs with significantly less management overhead and no standards issues. One potential concern with such large switched network designs is network address allocation. For IPX-based networks this is not of concern since the node section of the network layer address is not fixed. For IP-based networks considerable network address redesign may be necessary to implement such a solution.

The advent of "wire speed" LAN routers also infringes on the market segment initially held by VLAN solutions. For an organization currently built on traditional shared media or switched LANs interconnected by routers, this solution has the added advantage of retaining the existing network design and time-tested analysis and troubleshooting techniques while increasing network performance. These solutions are new to the marketplace, however, and have little to no real-world record upon which to make definitive performance conclusions.

The final decision as to the best technologies to use to gain manageability and broadcast control is ultimately dependent upon the existing network design and exact features required. For IPX-based networks VLANs or large switched solutions are the only viable choices, since the market for wire speed IPX routers will probably never be strong enough to merit their development. For those solutions that require the collection of detailed information on data flows, layer 3/4-enabled VLAN solutions have the most mature data collection capabilities of the technologies reviewed.

Layer 3 and Layer 4 Switches   Although layer 3 switches process network layer (layer 3) IP addresses and quickly build point-to-point connections based on routing table information, layer 4 switches process TCP port numbers and can distribute multiple requests for a given service to multiple different physical servers, thus providing load balancing.

A layer 3 switch is nothing more than routing functionality delivered on ASIC (application specific integrated circuits) chips. By forcing the routing functionality onto silicon, significant price/performance gains can be realized when migrating from traditional software-based routers to layer 3 switches. Layer 3 switches also simplify moves, adds, and changes for network administrators through their support of layer 3 virtual LANs that don't require the network administrators to know to which physical ports the users are attached.

A layer 4 switch uses a virtual IP address to balance traffic across multiple servers based on session information and status. This process is sometimes referred to as service-based load balancing. Layer 4 switches are best used when multiple servers are offering the same applications and require load balancing across those multiple servers. The layer 4 switch is capable of determining which session is being requested and submitting that request to the most available server by substituting the IP address of the virtual server with the IP address of the actual server to which the request is being forwarded. However, because of the virtual IP address running NAT (network address translation), the multiple load-balanced servers in the background are transparent to users and their applications. Layer 4 switching is sometimes referred to as application redirection. In some cases, switches can examine content above layer 4 and make switching decisions accordingly. For example, HTTP (web traffic) could be identified on layer 4 (Port 80). However, layer 4 switches can also load balance or redirect based on actual session content, thereby allowing different types of web content to be stored on different physical servers even though they are all accessed via a single server address.

Layer 4 switches can also be used to provide filtering of unwanted layer 4 protocols such as IPX SAP (Service Advertising Protocol) or can also be used to provide prioritization. Depending on whether the packet is destined for a LAN or WAN, the layer 4 switch will assign prioritization with an

802.1p priority tag (layer 2) or set the priority in the IP ToS (Type of Service) field in the IP header (layer 3).

Still other layer 4 switches that use TCP and UDP port numbers to make decisions are more concerned with bandwidth management and traffic shaping. The PacketShaper from Packeteer classifies data traffic according to port number and then assigns guaranteed and excess bandwidth amounts along with a prioritization number to each of these traffic classes. The objective of such devices is a smooth and controlled traffic flow.

ATM Switching on the LAN

Although different vendors of enterprise networking equipment may be promoting their own view of the enterprise network of the future, one view shared by all of these vendors is that ATM will serve as the high-speed switched backbone network service used to connect geographically dispersed corporate networks. As was previously discussed in the section on virtual LANs, layer 2 switching, no matter how fast, is not by itself a sufficient enterprise network platform. As a result, routing capabilities must be added to the underlying switching capabilities offered by ATM. The basic differences between alternative enterprise network physical topologies are in the way routing capabilities are added to the ATM switching fabric and the subsequent enterprise network performance characteristics exhibited as a result of those routing capabilities.

ATM LAN Emulation   Because ATM acts as a layer 2 switching service, and because layer 2 LAN switches support virtual LANs, it would stand to reason that ATM switches ought to be able to support virtual LANs as well. In fact, through a process known as **ATM LAN Emulation,** virtual LANs are able to be constructed over an ATM switched network regardless of the geographic scope of that network. ATM LAN emulation is considered a bridging solution, like LAN switch-based virtual LANs, because traffic is switched based on MAC layer addresses. Unlike LAN switch-based virtual LANs, however, MAC layer addresses must be translated, or resolved, into ATM addresses in a process known as **ATM address resolution.** In ATM LAN emulation, the ATM switching fabric adds an entire layer of its own addressing schemes that it uses to forward virtual LAN traffic to its proper destination.

In Sharper Focus

ATM LAN EMULATION ARCHITECTURE

The way in which MAC layer addresses are resolved into ATM addresses is defined by an ATM Forum specification known as LAN emulation or more formally as L-UNI (LAN emulation User to Network Interface) or LANE (LAN Emulation). The ATM LAN Emulation Specification actually defines an entire architecture of interacting software components in order to accomplish the ATM to MAC layer address resolution. Among the interacting components that cooperate to accomplish ATM LAN emulation as illustrated in Figure 13-17 are the following:

- **LAN Emulation Client (LEC)** software may physically reside within ATM-to-LAN conversion devices or may be included within a router that supports ATM interfaces. The job of the LEC is to appear to be an ATM end-station on behalf of the LAN clients it represents. As a result, the LEC is sometimes referred to as a proxy ATM end-station. The LEC is also responsible for converting the LAN's data-link layer protocols (Ethernet, Token Ring, FDDI) into fixed length ATM cells. Once the local LEC knows the ATM address of the remote LEC that is acting as an ATM proxy for the remote LAN destination, it sets up a switched virtual circuit, or switched network connection, to the remote LEC that subsequently delivers the information payload to the remote LAN workstation in a **unicast** (point-to-point) transmission.

- **LAN Emulation Server (LES)** software resides on a server or workstation that is directly attached to the ATM network and has a unique ATM address. The LES software performs three major tasks or services that can actually be accomplished by separate software programs executed on separate servers:
  - LES **Configuration Services** are responsible for keeping track of the types of virtual LANs that are being supported over the ATM switching fabric and which LECs belong to which type of LAN. MAC addresses and corresponding ATM addresses of attached workstations are stored by the configuration server. LAN type (Ethernet, Token Ring, FDDI) is important to keep track of owing to the variability of the maximum frame length accepted by workstations attached to each type of LAN.
  - LES **Broadcast and Unknown Services (BUS)** are responsible for handling requests for broadcasts and multicasts within the virtual LANs that exist across the ATM switching fabric. In addition, should a LEC not know the destination ATM address of a destination LAN workstation, it will forward that frame to the Broadcast and Unknown Server, which will broadcast that frame throughout the virtual LAN on behalf of the LEC.
  - LES **LAN Emulation Services** receive address resolution protocol (ARP) requests from LECs seeking the ATM addresses of destination LAN workstations for which the MAC address is known. Once the LES responds to the LEC with the requested ATM address, the LEC is able to set up the point-to-point connection to the destination LEC. If the LES does not respond immediately, the LEC continues to use the BUS to broadcast the destination frame throughout the virtual LAN.

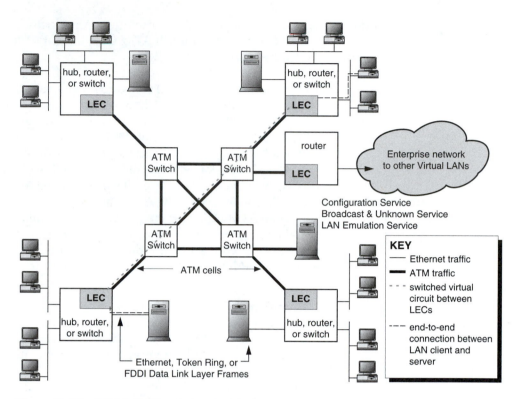

Figure 13-17 ATM LAN Emulation Architecture

Managerial Perspective

It is important to understand that ATM LAN emulation, like other virtual LAN architectures built on layer 2 switching, is basically a bridged topology that suffers from the same limitations as other layer 2 switched networks:

- Flat network topology

- Broadcast storms (although limited to a particular virtual LAN)

- No layer 3 filtering for security or segmentation

- No ability to differentiate between quality of service (QoS) requirements

On the other hand, because it does not discriminate between network layer (layer 3) protocols, ATM LAN emulation is able to support, or transport, multiple network layer protocols between virtual LANs.

Perhaps more important, however, ATM LAN emulation offers no routing capability. As a result, each virtual LAN that is emulated using ATM emulation must still have a dedicated connection to a router which is able to process layer 3 addresses and make appropriate route determination and forwarding decisions between virtual LANs.

Layer 3 Protocols Over ATM Networks   A variety of initiatives are underway by both the IETF (Internet Engineering Task Force) and the ATM Forum to somehow integrate layer 3 functionality with ATM networks. IETF RFC (Request for Comment) 1577 is known as **Classical IP over ATM.** The goal of Classical IP over ATM is to allow IP networks, as well as all upper-layer TCP/IP protocols, utilities, and APIs encapsulated by IP, to be delivered over an ATM network without requiring modification to the TCP/IP protocols. Using Classical IP over ATM, the ATM network is treated by IP like just another subnet or data-link protocol such as Ethernet or Token Ring. IP Routers see the entire ATM network as only a single hop, regardless of the actual size of the ATM network. IP subnets established over ATM networks using this protocol are known as **Logical IP Subnets** or **LIS.**

A significant limitation of Classical IP over ATM is that it only works within a given subnet. As a result, to use IP addresses to properly route data between Classical IP subnets, an IP router must still be employed. Just as with ATM LAN emulation, Classical IP over ATM also requires address resolution. In this case a new protocol known as **ATMARP (ATM Address Resolution Protocol)** runs on a server in the logical IP subnet and provides address resolution between IP addresses and ATM addresses. ATM addresses may actually be the virtual circuit ID numbers of the virtual circuits or connections that are established between two ATM end-points on the ATM network.

Understandably, Classical IP over ATM only supports IP as a network layer protocol over ATM networks. Other initiatives are underway to support multiple network layer protocols over ATM. The ATM Forum is currently working on **MPOA (Multi Protocols Over ATM),** which will not only support IP, IPX, Appletalk, and other network protocols over ATM, but will also be able to route data directly between virtual LANs, thereby precluding the need for additional external routers. Routing implemented on switches using protocols such as MPOA is sometimes referred to as **cut-through routing** and uses ATM LAN Emulation as its layer 2 switching specification. Like ATM LAN Emulation, MPOA operates transparently to end-devices and requires no hardware or software changes to those end-devices or their applications. Multiprotocol over ATM is actually an entire architecture, as illustrated in Figure 13-18, comprised of the following key components:

- **Edge Devices,** which might be a kind of hybrid hub, switch, and router, would act as interfaces or gateways between LANs and the ATM network. Once the ATM address is known, edge devices would be capable of establishing new virtual circuits over the ATM network.

- A **Route Server** would supply edge devices with their routing information including ATM addresses and virtual circuit IDs. The route server may actually be located within one of the ATM switches in the ATM backbone. Routing tables within the route server are organized

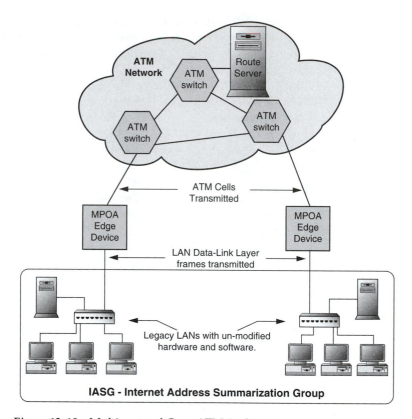

Figure 13-18   Multiprotocol Over ATM Architecture

according to layer 3 protocol specific subnets, which are referred to as **Internet Address Summarization Groups (IASG).**

While MPOA defines multiprotocol communications between ATM end-stations and a given route server, another ATM forum specification known as **Integrated Private Network-to-Network Interface (IPNNI)** defines how route servers are able to communicate path and address information to each other and to/from ATM switches over an ATM network. If multiple route servers are required on a given enterprise network, then a protocol such as IPNNI must be implemented to share the layer 3 information between ATM switches and route servers in order to allow the best path through the network to be selected dynamically.

The IETF is currently working on RFC 1483, **Multiprotocol Encapsulation over ATM Adaptation Layer 5.** One of the significant contributions of this proposal is that it defines two different ways in which multiple network layer protocols can be transmitted simultaneously over an ATM network. The first method, LLC/SNAP Encapsulation, places indicators in the ATM data-link layer frame to identify which network layer protocols are embedded within that data-link layer frame. The second method, Virtual Channel-based Multiplexing, establishes a separate virtual circuit, or connection, through the ATM network, for each network layer protocol transported from one workstation to another.

Another alternative to add routing capabilities to ATM switching fabrics is known as **IP switching.** IP switching technology distinguishes between the length of data streams and switches or routes accordingly on a case-by-case basis. In the case of long data streams associated with file transfers or voice or video transmissions, the IP switch sets up a virtual circuit through the ATM switching fabric and then forwards packets immediately via layer 2 switching to that virtual circuit. In the case of datagram-oriented, short messages, each message is forwarded through the layer 3 routing software located in the IP switch. Protocols to distinguish between the types of transmissions and to decide whether to switch or route were covered in the "IP Switching and Quality of Service" section of this chapter.

▨ LAN-TO-MAINFRAME INTERNETWORKING

Micro-Mainframe Connectivity versus Peer-to-Peer Internetworking

Strictly speaking, micro-mainframe connectivity and internetworking are two different concepts. In **micro-mainframe connectivity,** the micro (Standalone or LAN-attached PC) pretends to be or "emulates" a mainframe terminal such as an **IBM 3270** attached and logged into the mainframe. Although file transfer utilities may allow more capability than mere remote login, this is not the peer-to-peer networking implied by the term *internetworking*

With full **peer-to-peer internetworking,** the PC can exchange data with any mainframe or any other PC on a host-to-host level rather than acting like a "dumb" terminal as in the case of micro-mainframe connectivity. Although these two mainframe connectivity alternatives have their differences, they still have much in common. The truth is that most "IBM Shops" have a mixture of 3270 terminal connections, mainframes, and LANs that must communicate with each other on a number of different levels.

Hierarchical Networks and Peer-to-Peer Communications Networks

A hierarchical network structure such as the "classic" SNA (Systems Network Architecture) centers around the mainframe. If two devices other than the mainframe on an SNA network wanted to communicate, they would have to establish, maintain, and terminate that communication through the mainframe. This model is in direct contrast to a peer-to-peer network communications structure, typical of most LANs, in which any device may communicate directly with any other LAN attached device.

Classic SNA Architecture

Figure 13-19 illustrates a simple SNA architecture and introduces some key SNA network elements.

Two devices in a classic SNA environment as illustrated in Figure 13-19 are:

- **Front End Processor**—(IBM 3745, 3746) A front end processor is a computer that offloads the communications processing from the mainframe, allowing the mainframe to be dedicated to processing activities. A high-speed data channel connects the FEP to the main-frame locally, although FEPs can be deployed remotely as well. The FEP, also known as a communications controller, can have devices such as terminals or printers connected directly to it, or these end-user devices may be concentrated by another device known as a cluster controller. There are two options for high-speed data chan-nels between FEPs and IBM mainframes:
  - **Bus and Tag** has a transmission rate of 4.5 Mbps and has been available since 1967.
  - **ESCON II (Enterprise System CONnection)** has a maximum transmission rate of 70 Mbps, has been available since 1990, and is able to transmit up to 30 miles over fiber-optic cable.

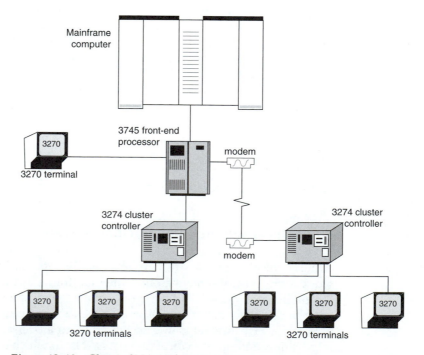

Figure 13-19   Classic SNA Architecture

- **Cluster controller**—(IBM 3174, 3274) A cluster controller is a device that allows connection of both 3270 terminals as well as LANs with possible wide area links to packet switched networks (X.25) or high-speed leased lines. A cluster controller concentrates the transmissions of its numerous input devices and directs this concentrated data stream to the FEP either locally or remotely.

The hierarchical nature can be seen in Figure 13-19 as data received from the lowly terminals are concentrated by multiple cluster controllers for a front end processor that further manages the data for the almighty mainframe. As additional processors and minicomputers such as an IBM AS/400 are added, the hierarchical nature of classic SNA can be seen even more clearly.

The network illustrated in Figure 13-19 will be modified one step at a time until the goal of an architecture that seamlessly transports SNA as well as LAN traffic is reached.

Micro-Mainframe Connectivity

PCs as 3270 Terminals   The first step of PC or LAN integration with classic SNA is allowing a stand-alone PC to emulate a 3270 terminal and conduct a communication session with the mainframe. In order to accomplish this, **protocol conversion** must take place to allow the PC to appear to be a 3270 terminal in the eyes of the mainframe.

A **3270 Protocol Conversion card** is inserted into an open expansion slot of a PC. Additional protocol conversion software, which may or may not be included with the protocol conversion card, must be loaded onto the PC in order to make the PC keyboard behave like a 3270 terminal keyboard (keyboard remapping). The media interface on the card is usually RG-62 Thin Coax for local connection to cluster controllers. Synchronous modems could also be employed for remote connection. Figure 13-20 illustrates possible configurations for stand-alone PC- 3270 terminal emulation.

LAN-Based SNA Gateways   The next scenario to be dealt with is how to deliver mainframe connectivity to LAN-attached PCs. One way would be to mimic the method for attaching stand-alone PCs. That is, for every LAN-attached PC, buy and install the 3270 protocol conversion hardware and software and provide a dedicated link to a cluster controller. Whereas most of these LAN-attached PCs need mainframe connectivity only on an occasional basis, this would not be a very cost-effective solution. Not only would it be wasteful in terms of the number of PC boards purchased, but also in the number of cluster controller ports monopolized but underutilized.

Instead, it would be wiser to take advantage of the shared resource capabilities of the LAN to share a protocol conversion attachment to the main-

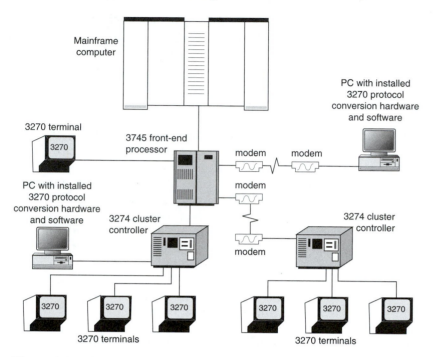

Figure 13-20   Standalone PC 3270 Terminal Emulation

frame. Such a LAN server-based, shared protocol converted access to a mainframe is known as a **gateway.** Two popular SNA gateway software packages associated with LAN network operating are as follows:

- Microsoft SNA Server for linking to Windows NT LANs
- NetWare for SAA for linking to NetWare LANs

Figure 13-21 illustrates both a LAN-based local gateway as well as a remote gateway.

As can be seen in Figure 13-21, a gateway configuration can allow multiple simultaneous 3270 mainframe sessions to be accomplished via a single gateway PC and a single port on the cluster controller. A remote PC-based LAN gateway needs additional hardware and software in order to emulate not only the 3270 terminal but also the 3274 cluster controller. Such remote 3274 Cluster Controller boards and software are as readily available as 3270 Terminal emulation hardware and software. As a slight variant on the PC-based emulation hardware and software previously mentioned, stand-alone protocol conversion devices for both 3270 terminal as well as 3274 cluster controller emulation are available as illustrated in Figure 13-21.

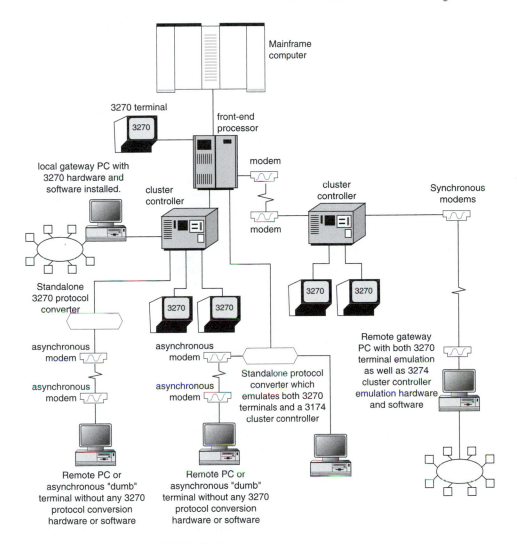

Figure 13-21   LAN-Based SNA Gateways

Mainframe Channel-Attached Gateways   As an alternative to LAN-based gateways, **channel-attached gateways** are able to interface directly to the mainframe's high-speed data channel, thereby bypassing the FEP entirely. Physically, the channel attached gateways are often modules that are added to enterprise routers. Depending on the amount of actual 3270 terminal traffic required in a given network, the use of channel-attached gateways may either preclude the need for additional FEP purchases or may allow FEPs to be replaced altogether.

The price difference between channel-attached gateways and FEPs is significant. An ESCON-attached IBM 3745 FEP costs approximately

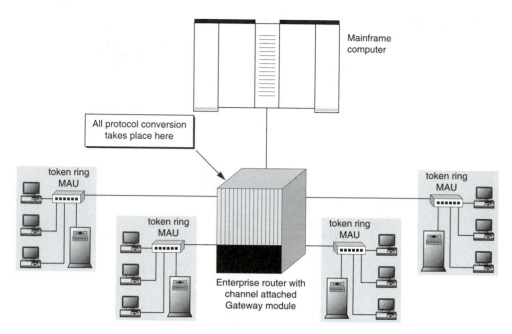

Figure 13-22 Channel-Attached LAN/SNA Gateways

$225,000, whereas an equivalent router-based Cisco Channel Interface Processor costs approximately $69,000. Figure 13-22 illustrates the installation of channel-attached gateways for linking LAN-based PCs as 3270 terminals to mainframes.

IBM's Answer to Channel-Attached Gateways In response to the challenge presented by channel-attached, router-based gateways, IBM has introduced a series of stand-alone devices that are able to interface SNA mainframes to IP networks. Enterprise router-based channel-attached gateways from companies such as Cisco are priced at $69,000, and the Network Utility devices from IBM, which cost $29,500, are capable of handling 16,000 SNA sessions simultaneously. These devices have the ability to interface to a variety of LAN architectures including Token Ring, Ethernet, FDDI, and ATM as well as interfacing to either ESCON or bus and tag channel interfaces.

The SNA Architecture

Figure 13-23 illustrates a seven-layer model of the SNA hierarchy. Like the OSI model, the SNA model starts with media issues in layer 1—the Physical Control Layer—and ends up at layer 7—the Transaction Services Layer, which interfaces to the end user. The layers in between, however, do not

Layer number	Sublayer number	Layer/Sublayer Name	Function
7		Transaction Services	Provide network management services. Control document exchange and distributed database access.
6		Presentation Services	Formats data, data compression, and data transformation.
5		Data Flow Control	Synchronous exchange of data supports communications session for end-user applications, assures reliability of session.
4		Transmission Control	Matches the data exchange rate, establishes, maintains, and terminates sessions. Guarantees reliable delivery of data between end points. Error control, flow control.
3		Path Control	Overall layer: Creates the link between two end-points for the transmission control protocols to manage. Divided into 3 sublayers.
	3	Virtual Route Control	Create virtual route (virtual circuit), manage end-to-end flow control.
	2	Explicit Route Control	Determines actual end-to-end route for link between end nodes via intermediate nodes.
	1	Transmission Group Control	If multiple possible physical paths exist between the end-points, this protocol manages to use these multiple lines to assure reliability and load balancing.
2		Data Link Control	Establishes, maintains, and terminates data transmission between two adjacent nodes. Protocol is SDLC.
1		Physical Control	Provides physical connections specifications from nodes to shared media.

Figure 13-23   The SNA Architecture Model

match up perfectly with the corresponding numbered layer in the OSI model, although general functionality at each layer is similar. "Similar general functionality" will not suffice when it comes to internetworking. As a result, options will be seen for merging SNA (SDLC) and OSI (LAN-based) data transmissions on a single internetwork involving various methods to overcome the discrepancies between the two architectures.

The SDLC Protocol   Figure 13-24 illustrates the structure of the **SDLC (Synchronous Data Link Control)** protocol. Although the protocol structure itself does not look all that unusual, the information block of the SLDC

Flag 1 byte	Address 1 byte	Control 1 byte	Information	Frame Check Sequence 2 bytes	Flag 1 byte

Figure 13-24   SDLC Data-Link Control Frame Layout

frame contains nothing equivalent to the OSI network layer addressing information for use by routers, which makes SDLC a **non-routable proto-col.** SDLC is non-routable because there is simply no network layer address information available for the routers to process. This shortcoming can be overcome in a number of different ways. However, it is important to understand that this non-routability is one of the key challenges facing SNA-LAN integration.

Since SDLC cannot be routed, network managers had no choice but to implement multiple networks among corporate enterprises. One network would carry SDLC traffic between remote cluster controllers and FEPs to local cluster controllers, FEPs and mainframe; while a second network would support remote bridged/routed LANs linking with local LANs between the same corporate locations. Such an implementation is sometimes referred to as a **parallel networks model.** Obviously, it would be advantageous from both business and network management perspectives to somehow combine the two traffic streams into a single network. Figure 13-25 illustrates this multiple network scenario.

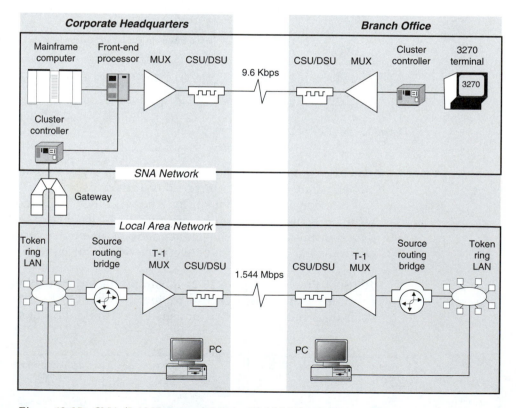

Figure 13-25   SNA/LAN Incompatibilities Yield Multiple Networks

Challenges to SNA/LAN Integration

In order to understand how SNA and LAN traffic can be integrated, the incompatibilities between SNA networks and local area networks must first be delineated.

- The first characteristic of SNA that can cause trouble on a LAN is the great amount of **acknowledgment and polling traffic** between SNA processors and SNA end-user devices. This constant chatter could quickly monopolize the better part of the LAN bandwidth.

- The second SNA characteristic that can cause problems when run over a shared LAN backbone is that SNA has **timing limitations** for transmission duration between SNA hosts and end-user devices. Thus on wide area, internetworked LANs over shared network media, SNA sessions can "time-out," effectively terminating the session.

- Another traffic contributor that can easily monopolize internetwork bandwidth comes from the LAN side of the house. As described earlier in this chapter, Token Ring LANs use an internetworking device known as a source routing bridge. In order to define their source routed internetworking paths, source PCs send out numerous explorer packets as a means of gaining a sense of the best route from source to destination. All of these discovery packets mean only one thing—significantly more network traffic.

- As previously stated, SDLC is non-routable protocol. In order to maximize the efficiency of the integrated SNA/LAN network, some way must be found to route SDLC or otherwise transparently incorporate it with LAN traffic.

Given the aforementioned incompatibilities, it would seem clear that there are three major challenges to allowing SNA and LAN traffic to share an internetwork backbone:

- Reduce unnecessary traffic (source routing explorer packets and SDLC polling messages)

- Find some way to prioritize SNA traffic in order to avoid time-outs

- Find a way to allow internetwork protocols to transport or route SDLC frames

SNA/LAN Integration Solutions

Several major categories of SNA/LAN Integration Solutions are currently possible. Each varies in both approach and extent to which SNA/LAN incompatibilities are overcome:

• Add a Token Ring adapter to a compatible cluster controller

• TCP/IP Encapsulation

• SDLC Conversion

• APPN—Advanced Peer-to-Peer Networking

Token Ring Adapter into Cluster Controller The first method, as illustrated in Figure 13-26, is the least expensive and, predictably, also the least effective in terms of meeting the SNA/LAN Integration Challenges. A Token Ring network adapter is attached to an available Cluster Controller port, and attached to a Token Ring network. The SNA traffic is transported using the standard source route bridging (SRB) to its destination.

However, that is only one of the three challenges to be met. The failure to deal with unnecessary traffic and prioritization of SNA traffic make this a less than ideal solution. This is a bridged approach, dealing only with OSI layer 2 protocols. Notice, however, the significant potential reduction to hardware and networking costs by this simple approach.

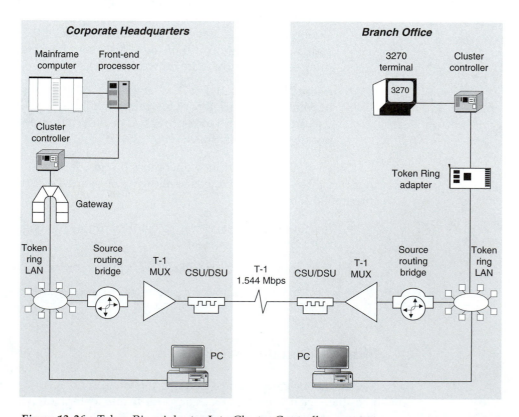

Figure 13-26 Token Ring Adapter Into Cluster Controller

TCP/IP Encapsulation   The second method is known alternatively as **TCP/IP encapsulation,** passthrough, or tunneling. Simply stated, each upper-layer SNA packet is "stuffed" into an IP "envelope" for transport across the network and processing by routers supporting TCP/IP internetworking protocol. This IP passthrough methodology for SDLC transport is a common feature or option on internetworking routers. In this methodology IP is supplying the network layer addressing that was lacking from the native SDLC protocol, thereby enabling routing. Figure 13-27 illustrates a Passthrough architecture. Upon close examination of Figure 13-27, it may become obvious that, in fact, there is no SNA/LAN integration. What the SNA and LAN traffic share is the T-1 wide area network between routers. The SNA traffic never travels over shared LAN media. Cost savings as compared with the parallel networks model (Figure 13-25) includes eliminating one wide area link and associated internetworking hardware. The actual TCP/IP encapsulation may take place in either a gateway or a router.

IBM's version of TCP/IP encapsulation is known as **Data-Link Switching** or **DLSw** and has been approved as a standard by the IETF (Internet Engineering Task Force) as RFC (Request for Comment) 934. DLSw does not

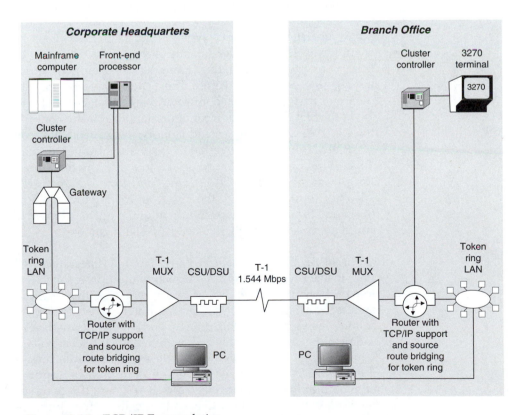

Figure 13-27   TCP/IP Encapsulation

propose anything radically new but incorporates many vendor-specific TCP/IP encapsulation features into a single standard which, it is hoped, will be widely supported. DLSw is implemented as a software feature on supported routers.

In addition to encapsulating SNA packets in IP addressed envelopes, DLSw also deals with the polling traffic and session time-out issues of SDLC traffic. **Poll spoofing** is the ability of an internetworking device, such as an SDLC converter or router, to respond directly to, or acknowledge, the FEP's constant polling messages to the remote cluster controller. By answering these status check messages locally, the inquiry and its answer never enter the wide area link portion of the internetwork. **Proxy polling,** on the other hand, emulates the FEP's polling messages on the remote side of the network, thereby assuring the remote cluster controller that it is still in touch with an FEP.

Broadcast filtering addresses a bad habit of the LAN side of SNA/LAN integration. In Token Ring source route bridging, individual PCs send out multiple broadcast packets or explorer packets, causing potential congestion on the internetwork links. Instead of allowing these packets onto the internetwork, routers can filter these broadcast packets out of the traffic, read the destination address to which the PC is seeking a route, and supply the PC directly with that information after consulting its own routing tables.

SDLC Conversion   The third possible solution to SNA/LAN traffic integration is known as **SDLC Conversion** and is characterized by SDLC frames actually being converted to Token Ring frames by a specialized internetworking device known as a **SDLC Converter.** The SDLC converter may be a stand-alone device or may be integrated into a bridge/router. As can be seen in Figure 13-28, in the SDLC Conversion configuration, the cluster controller is attached to the Token Ring LAN via a stand-alone or integrated SDLC converter.

SDLC frames are converted to Token Ring frames, transported across the Token Ring internetwork, and routed to a gateway that transforms the Token Ring frames back into SDLC frames and forwards them to the mainframe. Also notice the absence of the FEP from the illustration, a potential savings of several thousand dollars. Eliminating the FEP assumes that all 3270 traffic could be routed through attached LANs and gateways.

APPN: IBM's Alternative to LAN-Based SNA/LAN Integration   APPN-Advanced **Peer-to-Peer Network** is IBM's answer to multiprotocol networking on a peer-to-peer basis using the SNA architecture, rather than a LAN-based network architecture. Simply put, attached computers, whether PCs, AS/400s or mainframes, are welcome to talk directly with each other without having the communications session established, maintained, and terminated by the almighty mainframe as was required in the classic SNA architecture. Recent enhancements to APPN known as **HPR (High Performance Routing)/AnyNET** now allow multiple transport protocols such as IP and IPX to travel over the APPN network simultaneously with SNA traffic. In such an implementation, APPN rather than TCP/IP serves as the single backbone protocol able to transport

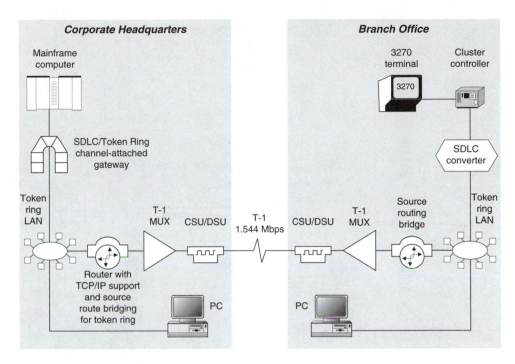

Figure 13-28   SDLC Conversion

multiple LAN protocols as well as SNA traffic simultaneously. The specific APPN protocol that deals with SNA/LAN integration is known as **DLUR/S (Dependent Logical Unit Requester/Server).**

APPN is a software-based solution consisting of only three basic components:

- **End Nodes** are end-user processing nodes, either clients or servers without any information on the overall network, available internetwork links, or routing tables.

- **Network Nodes** are processing nodes with routing capabilities. They have the ability to locate network resources, maintain tables of information regarding internetwork links, and establish a session between the requesting end node and the internetwork service requested.

- The **Central Directory Server** can save time as well as network traffic for the Network Nodes. Instead of each Network Node on an internetwork doing its own information gathering and internetwork exploration and inquiry, it can simply consult the Central Directory Server.

A simple example of an APPN network with HPR/AnyNET is illustrated in Figure 13-29.

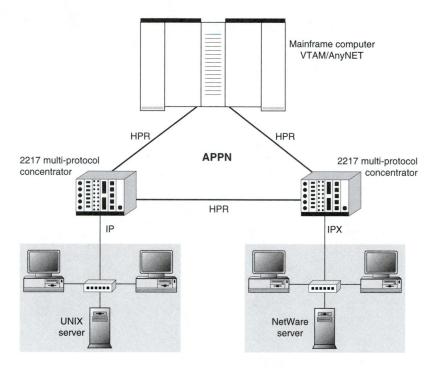

Figure 13-29   APPN with HPR/AnyNET for SNA/LAN Integration

If the functionality of APPN sounds a lot like what was just reviewed in the other SNA/LAN integration solutions, that should come as no surprise. IBM is not proposing any radical new methodologies. Rather, they are offering an IBM-backed migration from the hierarchical SNA network to a more effective peer-to-peer environment. In other words, rather than running SNA over a TCP/IP-based LAN internetwork, APPN runs TCP/IP, and other protocols, over an SNA mainframe-based internetwork.

Managerial Perspective

Although it now supports multiple protocols, APPN should not be misconstrued as an open architecture. APPN is a single vendor solution with only limited support from third-party internetworking hardware vendors.

SNA/LAN Integration and Frame Relay   Although all of the SNA/LAN integration solutions illustrated thus far have used a leased T-1 (1.544 Mbps) as their WAN service, this is by no means the only option. A WAN packet-switched network service known as **Frame Relay** has become a popular alternative SNA/LAN integration WAN service. The key positive attribute of Frame Relay is that charges are based on actual amounts of traffic transmitted rather than fixed monthly rates. The key negative aspect of using frame relay as a WAN service for SNA/LAN integration is that the frame relay network is being shared with numerous other subscribers and is subject to congestion. At such times, the access device to the frame relay network, known as a **frame relay access device** or **FRAD,** must be able to respond to requests from the frame relay network to "throttle back" or slow down the input to the network or risk losing transmitted packets due to network overload.

Specifications for the transmission of integrated SNA/LAN traffic over frame relay networks, including proper reaction to congestion notification is contained in the IETF RFC 990. Rather than converting SNA to IP and then using a FRAD before transmitting data over a frame relay network, RFC 1490 allows SNA traffic to be natively encapsulated from an IBM device directly onto a frame relay network. This method allows for less overhead than using DLSw as previously discussed. SNA/SDLC's need for prioritization in order to avoid session time-outs must still be addressed within the frame relay network. This is most often accomplished by circuit or bandwidth assignment capabilities offered by frame relay service vendors.

SUMMARY

Internetworking represents an evolutionary stage of LAN development brought on by either poor network performance or a need to share information between two different LANs. Internetworking design includes techniques such as segmentation and hierarchical networking as well as processing methodologies such as bridging, routing, and switching.

Bridging is an OSI layer 2 process that makes forwarding decisions based on the contents of data-link layer addresses. Routing is an OSI layer 3 process that makes forwarding decisions based on the contents of network layer addresses. Switching is actually an implementation of micro-segmented bridging designed to supply ample bandwidth to a local area network.

Switching and routing functionality must be combined in order to deliver optimal performance on the internetwork. Switching is used for supplying bandwidth, whereas routing is used for security, filtering by network layer protocols, and internetwork segmentation.

Repeaters are a physical layer internetworking device used to extend LAN segment length and to convert between media types. Bridges are a data-link layer internetworking device used to logically segment LANs, thereby supporting fewer workstations and more bandwidth on each LAN. Division of workstations onto bridged LANs should be done with some forethought in order to avoid having the bridge become an internetwork bottleneck.

Routers are network layer devices that are able to deal with larger internetworks than bridges and are able to determine best paths to destination workstations. Routers must keep routing tables up to date with the latest internetwork status through the use of routing protocols. Routing protocols can add significantly to bandwidth usage.

LAN-mainframe connectivity can be as simple as 3270 terminal emulation or as sophisticated as SNA/LAN integration via a single backbone protocol. In either case, alternatives are available which vary in their ability to meet the challenges of SNA/LAN integration as well as in their cost and complexity.

KEY TERMS

3270 protocol conversion card
7 Hop limit
acknowledgment and polling
    traffic
address caching
Advanced Peer-to-Peer
    Networking
APPN
backbone network
BGP
boundary router
bridge
broadcast filtering
broadcast storm
brouters
bus and tag
Central Directory Server
central site router
channel-attached gateways
cluster controller
configuration bridge protocol
    data unit
Data-Link Switching
destination address
dial-up router
distance vector
distinct layer 2 switching and
    layer 3 routing
Diff-Serv
distributed routing
DLSw
edge switches
EGP
encapsulating bridges
end nodes
ESCON
explorer packet
FEP

filtering
filtering rate
format converter
forward if not local
forward if proven remote
forwarding
forwarding rate
FRAD
Frame Relay
frame relay access device
front end processor
gateway
hierarchical networking
HPR/AnyNET
IBM3270
IEEE 802.1
IGRP
internetworking
IP Switching
known local nodes
layer 2 switch
layer 3 switch
layer 4 switch
link state
link state packets
load balancing
LSP
micro-mainframe
connectivity
micro-segmentation
MPLS
multi-layer switch
multiprotocol bridges
multiprotocol routers
network nodes
non-routable
non-routable protocol
open shortest path first

OSPF
parallel networks model
peer-to-peer internetworking
piggyback updates
poll spoofing
promiscuous listen
propagation
protocol conversion
proxy polling
QoS
repeater
RIF
RIP
router servers
Routing Information Field
routing information protocol
routing tables
SDLC
SDLC conversion
SDLC converter
segmentation
server isolation
slow convergence
source address
source routing bridge
source routing transparent
    bridge
Spanning Tree Algorithm
spoofing
Synchronous Data-Link Control
TCP/IP encapsulation
timed updates
timing limitation
translating bridges
transparent
transparent bridge
triggered updates
wireless bridge

REVIEW QUESTIONS

1. What is internetworking?
2. What are some of the factors that can lead an organization to seek internetworking solutions?
3. Differentiate between the four basic internetwork design strategies in terms of proper application.
4. Describe the use of data-link layer addresses by bridges.
5. What is meant by the phrase "forward-if-not-local"?
6. What are some of the key limitations of bridges?
7. How do routers overcome some of the key limitations of bridges?
8. Describe the use of data-link layer addresses by routers.
9. Describe the use of network layer addresses by routers.
10. What is meant by the phrase "forward-if-proven-remote"?
11. What are some of the key services that routers are able to provide to the internetwork?
12. Is switching more like bridging or routing? Explain.
13. What types of functionality are switches not able to deliver?
14. What can be said of all internetworking devices in relation to the OSI model layers and protocols?
15. What types of functionality is a repeater able to deliver?
16. What is auto-partitioning and why is it important to repeaters?
17. What is the difference between ring length and lobe length in Token Ring networks?
18. What is the difference between filtering and forwarding in bridge functionality?
19. What is the importance of the spanning tree algorithm?
20. What are the advantages and disadvantages of source route bridging?
21. Name and describe the functional characteristics of transparent bridges.
22. Differentiate between translating bridges and encapsulating bridges.
23. Differentiate between source routing bridges and source routing transparent bridges.
24. What implementation scenario is particularly well suited for wireless bridges?
25. What makes a protocol non-routable?
26. What is slow convergence and why is it a problem?
27. Differentiate between distance vector and link state routing protocols in terms of delivered functionality.
28. From a business standpoint, when should boundary routers and dial-up routers be employed?
29. What functionality is of particular importance to boundary or branch office routers? Why?
30. What functionality is of particular importance to dial-up routers? Why?
31. What is spoofing and why is it important?
32. Differentiate between the three major methods for updating spoofed protocols on dial-up routers.
33. Differentiate between the three major alternatives for combining routing and switching functionality.
34. Differentiate between micro-mainframe connectivity and peer-to-peer internetworking in terms of where presentation, data management, and application processing take place in each alternative.
35. Why is a classic SNA architecture considered hierarchical?
36. What is the difference in terms of functionality between a front end processor and a cluster controller?
37. Differentiate between LAN-based SNA gateways and Channel-attached SNA gateways in terms of cost and functionality.
38. What is SDLC?
39. Why is SDLC considered non-routable?
40. What is the parallel networks model and what is its cause?
41. Describe each of the challenges to SNA/LAN integration introduced by either SDLC or LAN protocols.
42. Differentiate between the four major SNA/LAN integration solutions in terms of their ability to meet the previously identified SNA/LAN integration challenges.
43. What is DLSw? Describe its functionality.

44. What is the importance of poll spoofing and proxy polling to DLSw?
45. Differentiate between TCP/IP encapsulation and SDLC conversion in terms of functionality, advantages, and disadvantages.
46. What are some of the major differences between APPN and TCP/IP encapsulation?
47. What is IP switching and how does it differ from conventional switching and routing?

ACTIVITIES

1. Find an organization that has implemented internetworking solutions. Interview the individuals who initiated the internetwork design. What were the motivating factors? Were they primarily business-oriented or technology-oriented?
2. Survey a number of organizations with internetworks to determine how many use primarily bridges vs. routers. Explain your results.
3. Research the expected market forecast for bridges, routers, and other internetwork technology. Many professional periodicals publish such surveys in January. Report on the results of your study.
4. Research broadcast storms and the Spanning Tree Algorithm. Draw diagrams depicting how broadcast storms are created, and how the Spanning Tree Algorithm controls multiple active loops.
5. Print out the contents of a routing table from two different routers on the same internetwork. Trace the logical path that a packet would take from a local workstation on a LAN connected to either router.
6. Conduct a survey among organizations with internetworks. Research how many organizations are currently employing or plan to implement LAN switches. What do all of the situations have in common? How do they differ?
7. Research the topic of source route bridging. What percentage of Token Ring LANs employ source route bridging? Is this percentage increasing or decreasing? How is source route bridging being dealt with in multiprotocol internetworks by either bridges or routers?
8. Conduct a survey of organizations with router-based internetworks as to the router-to-router protocol currently employed and planned within the next year. What percentage use RIP versus OSPF? What percentage are planning a change? Analyze and present your results.
9. Review trade magazines, professional periodicals, and product literature to determine the alternative methods for combining switching and routing technology. Is one method dominant? Report on and explain your results.
10. Conduct a survey of organizations with both SNA/SDLC traffic and LAN internetwork traffic. What percentage run parallel networks? What percentage have achieved SNA/LAN integration? How was SNA/LAN integration achieved? What are the plans for the one-year horizon? Report on and explain your results.
11. Research IP switching technology and protocol development efforts. Have protocols been standardized? Who are the technology market leaders? How widespread is the deployment of IP switching technology? What are the projected growth rates for the IP switching market? Report on and explain your results.

CASE STUDY

Bethlehem Steel Shows Its Network Mettle

Whatever your image is of a modern steel manufacturing plant, it's probably wrong.

"You would walk through one of our mills today, and you would not see a lot of people out there in harm's way," says Tom Conarty, director of IT at Bethlehem Steel, the second-largest integrated steel manufacturer in the U.S.

Plant workers still control the manufacturing process, but now they do so by monitoring the flow of data via PCs more than by directly overseeing the flow of steel itself. It is Conarty's job to ensure the data moves quickly and is accessible.

Four years ago, his department started moving the company away from a bridge-based network of 10M bit/sec Ethernet LANs to a zippy switched network anchored by 100M bit/sec FDDI backbone switches and Fast Ethernet links.

One of Conarty's first moves was to replace copper wiring with single- and multimode fiber from AT&T throughout four Bethlehem Steel plants and the company's headquarters.

Conarty looked at network gear from the usual suspects, including 3Com, Bay, Cabletron and Cisco, but ultimately chose ODS Networks as its supplier. ODS really caught Conarty's attention by offering to build a replica of Bethlehem Steel's network, complete with equipment from Cisco, Hewlett-Packard and other Bethlehem suppliers, at ODS in Richardson, Texas.

ODS also beat its competitors on price, though Conarty declined to get into specifics. However, he did say Bethlehem has bought close to $15 million worth of ODS gear to overhaul the net.

Bethlehem Steel now has installed dozens of ODS MicroInfinity Hubs and InfiniteSwitch 6000 switches throughout its plants. The chassis-based switches connect to each other via FDDI and link to the hubs, PCs, servers and process control computers via dedicated 10M bit/sec and 100M bit/sec Ethernet links, as well as some token-ring and ATM connections.

The process control computers, machines the size of small refrigerators made by

General Electric and Digital, sit on the manufacturing floor and act like supersensors, constantly monitoring the physical conditions in the plant. The machines measure molten temperature, gauge the width of a slab and adjust each step in the process to make up for imperfections and variations in the previous process. Some processes are monitored 30 to 50 times per second.

The machines are controlled by thousands of employees sitting at PCs. The employees type in instructions that tell the process control computers what they need to do to fulfill customer orders for everything from car doors to cans for food.

Conarty says the trend is definitely moving toward more reliance on robotics for handling physical labor, meaning the network will need to be more reliable than ever going forward. Fortunately for the steel company, there is still plenty of unlit fiber that can be turned on as more bandwidth is needed and high-speed LAN technologies such as Gigabit Ethernet become more proven, he says.

Source: Robin Scherer Hohman, "Bethlehem Steel Shows Its Network Mettle," *Network World*, vol. 15, no. 40 (October 5, 1998), p. 19. Copyright Network World. Reprinted with permission.

BUSINESS CASE STUDY QUESTIONS ···

Activities

1. Complete a top-down model for this case by gleaning facts from the case and placing them in the proper layer of the top-down model. After having completed the top-down model, analyze and detail those instances where requirements were clearly passed down from upper layers to lower layers of the model and where solutions to those requirements were passed up from lower layers to upper layers of the model.
2. Detail any questions about the case that may occur to you for which answers are not clearly stated in the article.

Business

1. How have computers and networks changed the way in which this organization conducts its core business?
2. What was the key criteria for ultimately choosing the vendor of network equipment?
3. Do you agree with this criteria? Why or why not?
4. Approximately how much has been spent on the network upgrade?
5. How could such an expenditure be cost-justified?

Application

1. What application is actually running over this network?

2. What type of devices are feeding data onto the network?
3. What kinds of data do these machines feed onto the network and how often?
4. How do users interact with these machines?
5. What are some possible future uses of the network?
6. What impact would these future applications have in terms of availability and reliability requirements?

Data

1. What are the data availability requirements in this business application?
2. Would you consider the data being transported over this network to be mission critical? Defend your answer.

Network

1. What was the previous network architecture in terms of bandwidth and technology?
2. What is the current network architecture in terms of bandwidth and technology?
3. What are the different bandwidths available for different types of links?

Technology

1. What changes in cabling had to be made?
2. What types of technology have actually been installed?

CHAPTER 14

REMOTE ACCESS AND WIRELESS NETWORKING

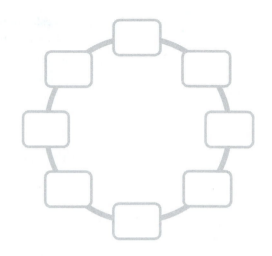

Concepts Reinforced

OSI Model	Internet Suite of Protocols Model
Top-Down Model	Protocols and Compatibility
Internetwork Design	Internetworking Technology
Network Operating Systems	

Concepts Introduced

Remote Access	Remote Control
Remote Node	Mobile Computing
Remote Access Security	Wireless LANs
Wireless WAN Services	Remote Access Technology
Remote Access Network Design	IEEE 802.11

OBJECTIVES

After mastering the material in this chapter you should:

1. Understand the difference between and proper application of remote node versus remote control computing

2. Understand the business motivation behind the need for remote access network design

3. Understand the importance of and networking implication of mobile computing

4. Understand how to successfully design logical and physical topologies for remote access networks, including wireless LAN and WAN services

5. Understand how to evaluate remote access technology including hardware, software, and WAN services

6. Understand the unique security issues introduced by remote access and mobile computing

■ INTRODUCTION

In order to understand the importance of remote access and wireless technology, it is first important to appreciate the business forces that have created the increased demand for such technology.

One of the most important things to understand about LAN remote access is the relatively limited bandwidth of the wide area network links that individuals will use to connect to corporate information resources. Although the goal of LAN remote access may be to offer transparent remote LAN connectivity, decreases in bandwidth by a factor of 100 on WAN links as compared with LAN links cannot be ignored.

The overall goal of this chapter is to outline a methodology for the proper design of remote access solutions based on a thorough understanding of user needs, network architecture alternatives, available technology, and available WAN services.

Managerial Perspective

BUSINESS ISSUES OF REMOTE ACCESS

As information has come to be seen as a corporate asset to be leveraged to competitive advantage, the delivery of that information to users working at remote locations has become a key internetworking challenge. Corporate downsizing has not only increased remaining employees' responsibilities, but pushed those responsibilities ever closer to the corporation's customers. As a result, the voice mail message, "I'll be virtual all day today," is becoming more and more common. The business-oriented motivations for remote access to local LAN resources fall into about three general categories:

The first category of remote LAN access is often referred to as **telecommuting,** or more simply, working from home with all the information resources of the office LAN at one's fingertips. This category of connectivity and computing is often referred to as **SOHO** or **Small Office Home Office.**

Studies have indicated that some of the ways in which telecommuting can increase overall worker productivity are the following:

• Better, faster, more effective customer service

• Increased on-time project completion and quicker product development

- Increased job satisfaction among highly mobile employees, which can lead to both greater productivity and employee retention

- Decreased worker turnover leads to decreased training and recruiting budgets

- Increased sales

A variation of telecommuting, **mobile computing,** addresses the need for field representatives to be able to access corporate information resources in order to offer superior customer service while working on the road. These field reps may or may not have a corporate office PC into which to dial.

Although some of the positive results of enabling remote access to corporate data for mobile workers are similar to those of telecommuters, the increased customer focus of the mobile worker is evident in the following benefits:

- Faster responses to customer inquiries

- Improved communications with coworkers and support staff at corporate offices

- Better, more effective customer support

- Increased personal productivity by the mobile workers such as being able to complete more sales calls

- Increased ability to be "on the road" in front of customers

- Allowed service personnel to operate more efficiently

The third major usage of remote computing is for **technical support** organizations that must be able to dial-in to client systems with the ability to appear as a local workstation, or take control of those workstations, in order to diagnose and correct problems remotely. Being able to diagnose and solve problems remotely can have significant impacts:

- Quicker response to customer problems

- Increased ability to avoid having to send service personnel for on-site visits

- More efficient use of subject matter experts and service personnel

- Increased ability to avoid revisits to customer sites owing to a lack of proper parts

- Greater customer satisfaction

Managerial Perspective

THE HIDDEN COSTS OF TELECOMMUTING

To fully understand the total costs involved in supporting telecommuters, it is first essential to understand which employees are doing the telecommuting. Telecommuting employees generally fall into either one of the following categories:

- Full-time, day shift, at-home workers
- After-hours workers who have a corporate office but choose to extend the workday by working remotely from home during evenings and weekends

Most studies indicate that more than 75% of telecommuters are of the occasional, after-hours variety. However, corporate costs to set up and support these occasional users are almost equal to the costs for setting up and supporting full-time at-home users—more than $4,000 per year. Among the hidden costs to be considered when evaluating the cost/benefit of telecommuting are the following:

- Workers may not be within local calling area of corporate resources, thereby incurring long distance charges.
- May need to add wiring from street to home or within home to support additional phone lines.
- If existing phone lines are used, personnel time is used to sort personal calls from business calls.
- In order to provide sufficient bandwidth, more expensive ISDN or ADSL lines are often installed, if available.
- Some applications, especially those not optimized for remote access, run very slowly over dial-up lines, leading to decreased productivity.

■ ARCHITECTURAL ISSUES OF REMOTE ACCESS

There are basically only four steps to designing a dial-in/dial-out capability for a local LAN:

- Needs analysis
- Logical topology choice
- Physical topology choice
- Current technology review and implementation

Logical Design Issues

Needs Analysis   As dictated by the top-down model, before designing network topologies and choosing technology, it is essential to first determine what is to be accomplished in terms of LAN-based applications and use of other LAN-attached resources. Among the most likely possibilities for the information sharing needs of remote users are the following:

- Exchange e-mail
- Upload and download files
- Run interactive application programs remotely
- Utilize LAN-attached resources

The purpose in examining information sharing needs in this manner is to validate the need for the remote PC user to establish a connection to the local LAN, which offers all the capabilities of locally attached PCs.

In other words, if the ability to upload and download files is the extent of the remote PC user's information sharing needs, then file transfer software, often included in asynchronous communications software packages, would suffice at a very reasonable cost. A network-based bulletin-board service (BBS) package is another way in which information can be shared by remote users easily. Similarly, if e-mail exchange is the total information sharing requirement, then e-mail gateway software loaded on the LAN would meet that requirement.

In order to run LAN-based interactive application programs or utilize LAN-attached resources such as high-speed printers, CD-ROMs, mainframe connections, or FAX servers, however, a full-powered remote connection to the local LAN must be established. From the remote user's standpoint, this connection must offer transparency. In other words, the remote PC should behave as if it were connected locally to the LAN. From the LAN's perspective, the remote user's PC should virtually behave as if it were locally attached.

Logical Topology Choice: Remote Node versus Remote Control   In terms of logical topology choices, two different logical methods for connection of remote PCs to LANs are possible. Each method has advantages, disadvantages, and proper usage situations. The two major remote PC operation mode possibilities are:

- Remote node
- Remote control

The term **remote access** is most often used to describe the process of linking remote PCs to local LANs without implying the particular functionality of that link (remote node versus remote control). Unfortunately, the term *remote access* is also sometimes more specifically used as a synonym for remote node.

Figure 14-1 outlines some of the details, features, and requirements of these two remote PC modes of operation, whereas Figure 14-2 highlights the differences between remote node and remote control installations.

Remote node or remote client computing implies that, in theory, the remote client PC should be able to operate as if it were locally attached to network resources. In other words, the geographic separation between the remote client and the local LAN resources should be transparent. That's a good theory, but in practice, the comparative bandwidth of a typical dial-up link (theoretically 56 Kbps for a V.90 modem, more likely 34–42 Kbps average) as compared with the Mbps bandwidth of the LAN, is anything but transparent. Whereas a NIC would normally plug directly into an expansion slot in a computer, a remote node connection merely extends that link via a relatively low-speed dial-up link. Client applications run on the remote client rather than a local LAN-attached client.

Client/server applications that require large transfers of data between client and server will not run well in remote node mode. Most successful remote node applications are rewritten to minimize large data transfers. For example, modified remote node e-mail client software allows just the headers of received messages, which include sender, subject, and date/time to be transferred from the local e-mail server to the remote client. The remote client selects which e-mail messages should have the actual e-mail message body and attachments transferred. Local e-mail client software, which assumes plenty of LAN bandwidth, does not bother with such bandwidth

Functional Characteristic	Remote Node	Remote Control
Also Called	Remote Client	Modem Remote Control
	Remote LAN Node	
Redirector hardware/s oftware required?	Yes	No
Traffic Characteristics	All client/server traffic	Keystrokes and screen images
Application Processing	On the remote PC	On the LAN-attached local PC
Relative Speed	Slower	Faster
Logical Role of WAN Link	Extends connection to NIC	Extends keyboard and monitor cables
Best Use	With specially written remote client applications that have been optimized for execution over limited bandwidth WAN links	DOS applications; graphics on Windows applications can make response time unacceptable

Figure 14-1 Remote Node versus Remote Control Functional Characteristics

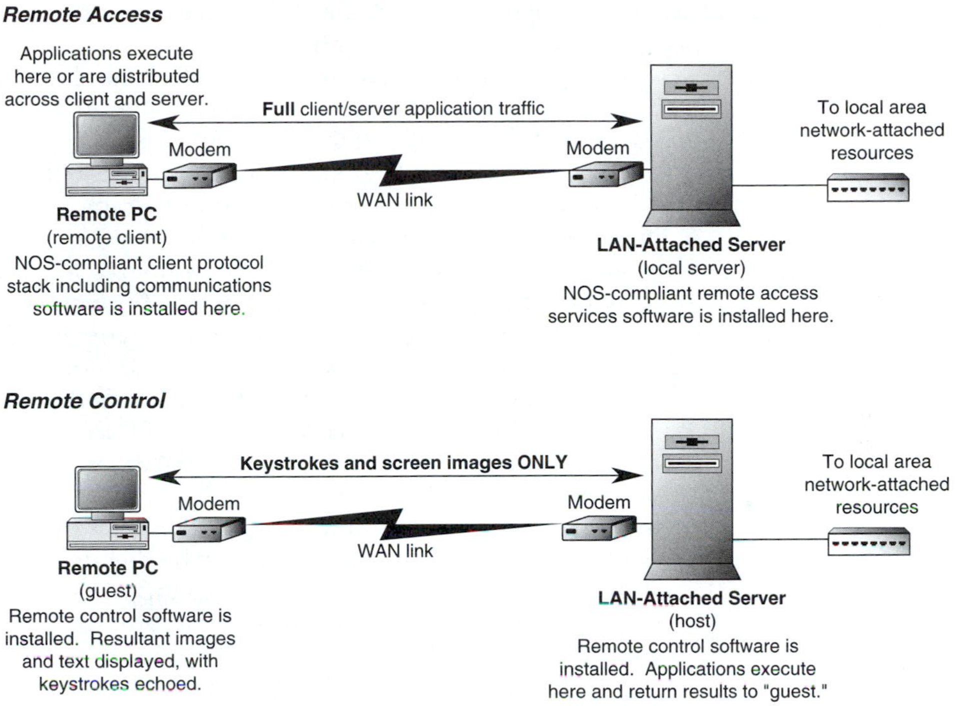

Remote Access

Applications execute
here or are distributed
across client and server.

Full client/server application traffic

To local area
network-attached
resources

Modem

Modem

Remote PC
(remote client)
NOS-compliant client protocol
stack including communications
software is installed here.

WAN link

LAN-Attached Server
(local server)
NOS-compliant remote access
services software is installed here.

Remote Control

Keystrokes and screen images ONLY

To local area
network-attached
resources

Modem

Modem

Remote PC
(guest)
Remote control software is
installed. Resultant images
and text displayed, with
keystrokes echoed.

WAN link

LAN-Attached Server
(host)
Remote control software is
installed. Applications execute
here and return results to "guest."

Figure 14-2   Remote Node versus Remote Control Installations

conserving modifications. Other client/server applications must be similarly modified if they are to execute acceptably in remote node mode.

Although transparent interoperability was discussed as one of the goals of remote access, that does not necessarily mean that a worker's mobile computer programs must be identical to those running on one's desktop at the price of terrible performance. One of the most commonly overlooked aspects in deploying remote access solutions is the need, and associated cost, to customize applications for optimal performance in a remote access environment.

Remote node mode requires a full client network operating system protocol stack to be installed on the remote client. In addition, wide area network communication software must be incorporated with the remote client NOS protocol stack. Remote node software often also includes optional support of remote control functionality.

Remote control differs from remote node mode both in the technology involved and the degree to which existing LAN applications must be modified. In remote control mode, the remote PC is merely supplying input and output devices for the local client, which interacts as normal with the local server and other locally attached LAN resources. Client applications still run on the local client, which is able to communicate with the local server at native LAN speeds, thereby precluding the need to rewrite client applications for remote client optimization.

Remote control mode requires only remote control software to be installed at the remote PC rather than a full NOS client protocol stack, which is compatible with the NOS installed at the local LAN. The purpose of the remote control software is only to extend the input/output capabilities of the local client out to the keyboard and monitor attached to the remote PC. The host version of the same remote control package must be installed at the host or local PC. There are no interoperability standards for remote control software.

One of the most significant difficulties with remote control software is end-users' confusion regarding logical disk assignments. Recalling that the remote PC supplies only the keyboard and monitor functionality, remote users fail to realize that a C: prompt refers to the C: drive on the local LAN-attached PC and not the C: drive of the remote PC they are using. This can be particularly confusing with file transfer applications.

Protocols and Compatibility   At least some of the shortcomings of both remote node and remote control modes are caused by the underlying transport protocols responsible for delivering data across the WAN link.

In the case of remote control, the fact that proprietary protocols are used between the guest and host remote control software is why remote control software from various vendors is not interoperable.

In the case of remote node, redirector software in the protocol stack must take LAN-based messages from the NDIS or ODI protocols and convert them into proper format for transmission over asynchronous serial WAN links.

Some remote node software uses TCP/IP as its protocol stack, and PPP as its data-link layer WAN protocol. In this manner, remote node sessions can be easily established via TCP/IP, even using the Internet as the connecting WAN service should that connection satisfy the security needs of the company in question. Once the TCP/IP link is established, the remote control mode of this software can be executed over TCP/IP as well, overcoming the proprietary protocols typically associated with remote control programs. In addition, due to PPP's ability to transport upper-layer protocols other than TCP/IP, these remote node clients can support communications with a variety of different servers.

Figure 14-3 illustrates the protocol-related issued of typical remote control and remote node links as well as TCP/IP-based links.

Security   Although security from an enterprise-wide perspective will be dealt with in Chapter 16, "Local Area Network Security", security issues specifically related to remote access of corporate information resources are introduced here. Security-related procedures can be logically grouped into the following categories:

- Password assignment and management—Change passwords frequently, even considering single-use passwords. Passwords should

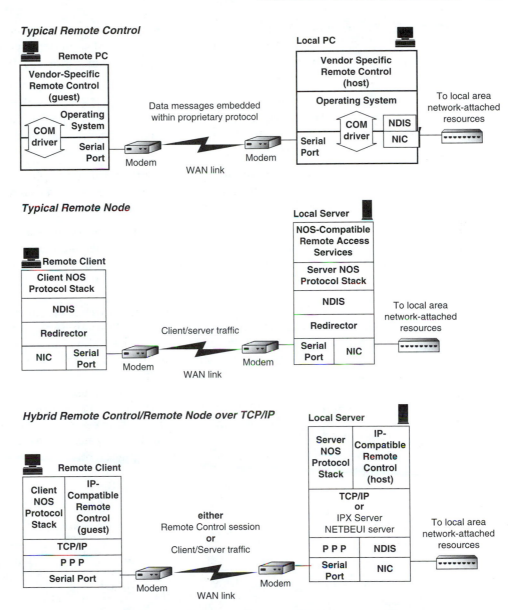

Figure 14-3   Protocol Issues of Remote Control and Remote Node Links

not be actual words found in a dictionary, but should ideally be a random or meaningless combination of letters and numbers. Consider two factor authentication such as Secure ID.

- Intrusion responses—User accounts should be locked after a preset number of unsuccessful logins. These accounts should only be able to be unlocked by a system administrator.

- Logical/physical partitioning of data—Separate public, private, and confidential data onto separate physical servers to avoid users with minimum security clearances gaining unauthorized access to sensitive or confidential data.

- Encryption—Although it is important for any sensitive or proprietary corporate data to be encrypted, it is especially important that passwords be encrypted to avoid interception and unauthorized reuse.

- Dial-back systems—After remote users enter proper UserID and passwords, these systems terminate the call and dial the authorized user back at preprogrammed phone numbers.

- Remote client software authentication protocols—Remote client protocol stacks often include software-based authentication protocols such as PAP (password authentication protocol) or CHAP (challenge handshake authentication protocol).

One remote access security category that deserves further explanation is hardware-based **token authentication.** Although exact implementation details may vary from one vendor to the next, all token authentication systems include server components linked to the communications server, and client components that are used with the remote access clients. Physically, the token authentication device employed at the remote client location may be a hand-held device resembling a calculator, a floppy disk, or it may be an in-line device linked to either the remote client's serial or parallel port. Figure 14-4 illustrates the physical topology of a typical hardware-based token authentication remote access security arrangement.

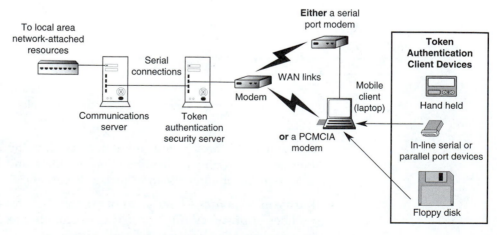

Figure 14-4 Token Authentication Physical Topology

In Sharper Focus

TOKEN AUTHENTICATION

Logically, token authentication schemes work in either of two different ways:

Token response authentication schemes work as follows:

1. Remote user dials in and enters private identification number (PIN).
2. Authentication server responds with a challenge number.
3. Remote user enters that number into hand-held client authentication unit or it is received automatically by in-line client authentication unit.
4. Client authentication unit generates challenge response number, which is either automatically transmitted back to the authentication server or is entered manually by the remote user.
5. Transmitted challenge response is received by the authentication server and compared with the expected challenge response number generated at the server. If they match, the user is authenticated and allowed access to network-attached resources.

Time-synchronous authentication schemes work as follows:

1. Random authentication numbers are generated in time-synchronous fashion at both the authentication server and client.
2. Remote user enters PIN number and the current random authentication number displayed on the client authentication unit.
3. Due to time synchronization, the server authentication unit should have the same current random authentication number, which is compared with the one transmitted from the remote client.
4. If the two authentication numbers match, the authentication server authenticates the user and allows access to the network attached resources.

A few other important operational issues concerning token-authentication security systems for remote access are as follows:

- Most authentication servers have a management console that provides supervisory access to the authentication security system. Transmission between the management console and the authentication server should be encrypted.

- Valid passwords and UserIDs may be stored on either the management console or on the authentication server. In either case, security-related data such as userIDs and passwords should be stored in encrypted form.

- The authentication server's response to failed attempts at remote login should include both account disabling and the ability to generate an alarm, preferably both audible and as a data message to the management console. Ideally, the authentication server should pass alarms seamlessly to enterprise management systems via SNMP to avoid having separate management consoles for every management function.

- Although this functionality is also supplied by such remote access server products as Windows NT RAS, the authentication server should also be able to limit access from remote users to certain times of day or days of the week.

- As can be seen in Figure 14-4, the authentication server must be able to transparently interoperate with the communications or remote access server. This fact should not be assumed, but demonstrated or guaranteed by the authentication server vendor.

Physical Design Issues

Physical Topology: Alternative Access Points   As Figure 14-5 illustrates, there are three basic ways in which a remote PC user can gain access to the local LAN resources.

- Serial port of a LAN-attached PC—Perhaps the simplest physical topology or remote access arrangement is to establish a communications link to a user PC located in the corporate office. However, many field representative or mobile computing users no longer have permanent offices and workstations at a corporate building and must depend on remote access to shared computing resources

- Communications server—As an alternative to having a dedicated PC at the corporate office for each remote user to dial into, remote users could attach to a dedicated multiuser server, known as a **remote access server** or **communications server** through one or more modems. Depending on the software loaded on the communications server, it may deliver remote node functionality, remote control functionality, or both. As telecommuting and demand for Internet access have increased, remote access servers have become the dominant means for accessing networks remotely. The 1999 revenue for remote access servers in the United States was $2.1 billion, growing at a 21% growth rate.

- LAN modem—Another alternative is to install a specialized device known as a **LAN modem,** also known as a **dial-in server,** to offer shared remote access to LAN resources. LAN modems come with all necessary software preinstalled and therefore do not require additional remote control or remote node software. LAN modems are often limited to a single network architecture such as Ethernet or Token Ring, and/or to a single network operating system protocol such as IP, IPX (NetWare), NetBIOS, NetBEUI, or Appletalk.

The physical topology using the communications server (Figure 14-5, illustration 2) actually depicts two different possible remote LAN connections. Most communications servers answer the modem, validate the UserID and password, and log the remote user onto the network. Some communications servers go beyond this to allow a remote user to access and/or remotely control a particular networked workstation. This scenario offers the same access capabilities as if the networked workstation had its own modem and software,

Access Point 1: Serial Port of LAN-Attached PC

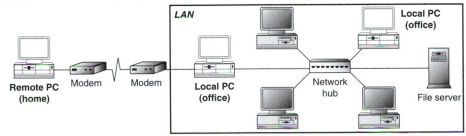

Access Point 2: Communications Server

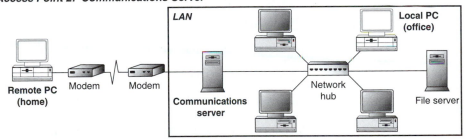

Access Point 3: LAN Modems

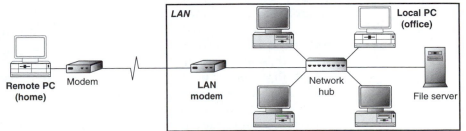

Figure 14-5   Physical Topology: Alternative Access Points

but also offers the centralized management, security, and possible financial advantage of a network attached communications server.

The three access arrangements illustrated are examples of possible physical topologies and do not imply a given logical topology such as remote node, remote control, or both. It is important to understand that the actual implementation of each of these LAN access arrangements may require additional hardware and/or software. They may also be limited in their ability to utilize all LAN-attached resources, or to dial out of the LAN through the same access point.

■ REMOTE ACCESS TECHNOLOGY

Hardware: Communications Servers and Remote Access Servers

As is often the case in the wonderful but confusing world of data communications, communications servers are also known by many other names. In some cases these names may imply, but don't guarantee, variations in configuration, operation, or application. Among these varied labels for the communications server are:

- Access servers

- Remote access servers

- Remote node servers

- Telecommuting servers

- Network resource servers

- Modem servers (usually reserved for dial-out only)

- Asynchronous communications servers

A communications server offers both management advantages as well as financial payback when large numbers of users wish to gain remote access to/from a LAN. Besides the cost savings of a reduced number of modems, phone lines, and software licenses, perhaps more important are the gains in control over the remote access to the LAN and its attached resources. By monitoring the use of the phone lines connected to the communications server, it is easier to determine exactly how many phone lines are required to service those users requiring remote LAN access.

Multiple remote users can dial into a communications server simultaneously. Exactly how many users can gain simultaneous access will vary with the sophistication and cost of the communications server and the installed software. Most communications servers service at least four simultaneous users and possibly more than 1,000.

Figure 14-6 provides an I-P-O (Input-Processing-Output) diagram illustrating options for the key functional components of a communications server.

As can be seen from Figure 14-6, the key hardware components of the communications server are:

- Serial Ports

- CPU(s)

- Network Interface Card(s)

Modems are sometimes included in the remote access server, usually in the form of multiport modem cards. The relative number of each of these three components included in a particular communications server is a key differentiating factor in communications server architectures or configurations. Although not guaranteed, the differentiation between communications servers and remote node servers is generally considered the following:

- Communications servers include several CPU boards inside a single enclosure. These servers combine both applications server functionality and remote node server functionality. Applications are physically loaded and executed on the communications server. Communications servers are often used for remote control functionality as an alternative to having several separate desktop PCs available for remote control. Consolidating the CPUs into a single

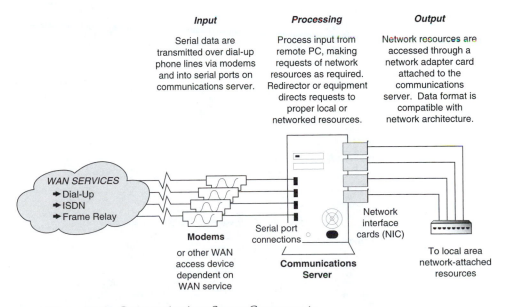

Figure 14-6 Communications Server Components

enclosure provides additional fault tolerance and management capabilities over the separate PCs model.

*   **Remote node servers** are strictly concerned with controlling remote access to LAN-attached resources and acting as a gateway to those resources. Applications services are supplied by the same LAN-attached applications servers that are accessed by locally attached clients.

The functional differences between communications servers and remote node servers are illustrated in Figure 14-7.

Currently, remote node server solutions fall into four major categories:

*   Software-only solutions in which the user supplies a sufficiently powerful server and adds a remote node server software package such as Windows NT RAS or NetWare Connect or other third party remote node software package. In some cases, a multiport serial board may be included with the software to add sufficient serial ports to the user's server. More information about software-only solutions is offered in the section on remote node software.

*   Turnkey or hardware/software solutions in which fully configured remote node servers are compatible with existing network architec-

Communications Server

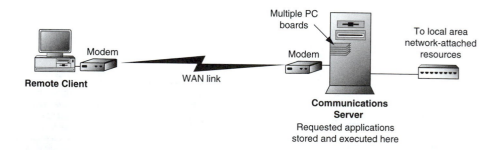

Remote Node Server

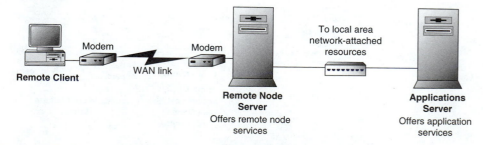

Figure 14-7   Communications Servers versus Remote Node Servers

tures and operating systems. Integrated modems may or may not be included. The remote node server software included on these turnkey systems must be compatible with the installed network operating system.

- LAN modems, also occasionally known as dial-up servers, could be thought of as a remote node server with one or more integrated modems. Included security and management software are also installed on the LAN modem. Given the rapid increase in modem transmission speeds owing to evolving modem transmission standards, integrating a modem that cannot be upgraded within a remote node server may be less beneficial than using external modems which can be more easily upgraded. Perhaps in a response to this need for convenient modem upgrades, some remote node servers now come with four or eight PC Card (PCMCIA) slots into which the latest modem technology can be easily inserted. LAN modems are generally included in reviews of remote node servers rather than being looked upon as a distinct product category.

- **Large Scale Remote Access Servers (RAS)** also known as **Monster RAS** are differentiated from previously mentioned RAS hardware by their scalability (number of modem ports), manageability, and security. These are enterprise class machines boasting modem port counts up to 1,344 per chassis, Fast Ethernet LAN interfaces, and ATM DS3 (45 Mbps) or OC3 (155 Mbps) WAN connections. This functionality doesn't come cheap, since fully configured prices range from $114,000 to $255,000. Among Monster RASs are: AS5800 from Cisco, MAX TNT from Ascend, Portmaster 4 from Lucent, CVX 1800 from Nortel, and Total Control Mutiservice Access Platform from 3Com.

When employing a self-contained remote node server including both hardware and software, compatibility with existing network resources on a number of different levels must be considered. These compatibility issues as well as key functional issues of remote node servers are outlined in Figure 14-8.

In Sharper Focus

DIALING-OUT FROM THE LAN

Normally, when a modem is connected directly to a PC, the communications software expects to direct information to the local serial port to which the modem is attached. In the case of a pool of modems attached to a remote node server, however, the communications software on the local clients must redirect all information for modems through the locally attached network interface card, across the local LAN, to the remote node server, and ultimately to an attached modem. This ability to re-direct information for **dial-out** modem applications from LAN-attached PCs is a cooperative task accomplished by the software of the remote node server and its corresponding

Remote Node Server Compatibility/Functional Issue	Importance/Implication
Network Architecture Compatibility	• Since the remote node server includes network interface cards, these must be compatible with the network architecture (Ethernet, Fast Ethernet, Token Ring) of the network in which it is to be installed. • Most remote node servers have Ethernet models, whereas fewer offer Token Ring models • Media compatibility must also be assured. For example, Ethernet may use AUI, BNC, or RJ-45 interfaces.
Network Operating System Compatibility	• The remote node server software installed in the server must be compatible with the network operating system installed in the network-attached applications servers. • Since these are third-party hardware/software turnkey systems, the remote node server software is not the same as the native software-only solutions such as Windows NT RAS or NetWare Connect, which imply guaranteed compatibility with their respective network operating systems. • The remote node server must also be compatible with the underlying transport protocols used by the installed network operating system. • Can the remote node server access the network operating system's user authorization files to avoid having to build and maintain a second repository of userIDs and passwords? • In the case of NetWare LANs, integration with NetWare Bindery (3.12) or NDS (4.1) should be provided.
Remote Client Software Compatibility	• The remote node server software must be compatible with the remote node software executed on the remote clients. • This remote client software must be compatible with the native operating system on the remote client. • If compatible remote client software is not supplied with the remote node server, is compatibility with third-party PPP client or remote client software guaranteed? • Cost of remote client software may be included in remote node server purchase cost or may be an additional $50/client.
Physical Configuration	• Number of serial ports: Most models start at 8, some are expandable to over 1,000 multiport modem ports • Serial port speed: Most support serial port speeds of 110.2 Kbps, while some support speeds of 230.4 Kbps.

Transmission Optimization	• Use of the limited bandwidth WAN link can be optimized in a variety of ways:
	  • Compression—Are both headers and data compressed?
	  • Spoofing—Are chatty protocols restricted from the WAN link?
	  • Are users warned before launching remote applications that may bog down the WAN link and offer poor performance?

(continued)

Routing Functionality	• Routing functionality would allow LAN-to-LAN or remote server-to-local-server connectivity rather than from a single remote client to the local server. • Routing functionality allows the remote node server to also act as a dial-up router. Dial-up routers must be used in pairs.
WAN Services Supported	• Is connectivity to ISDN, X.25, Frame Relay, ATM, SONET as well as dial-up lines supported? • Some remote node servers have high-speed serial ports for connection to higher-speed WAN services such as T-1 (1.544 Mbps) and T-3 (45 Mbps).
Call Management	• Are dropped calls automatically redialed? • Can connect-time limits be enforced? • Can status of all remote access calls be viewed and controlled from a single location? • Are event logs and reports generated? • Are status and alarm messages output via SNMP agents? • Is fixed and variable callback supported? • Is encryption supported?

Figure 14-8   Compatibility and Functional Issues of Remote Node Servers

remote client software. Not all remote node servers support dial-out functionality.

The required redirection is accomplished through the use of industry standard software re-direction interrupts. The interrupts supported or enabled on particular remote node servers can vary.

- **Int14,** or Interrupt 14, is one of the supported dial-out software redirectors and is most often employed by Microsoft network operating systems. Int14 is actually an IBM BIOS serial port interrupt used for the purpose of redirecting output from the local serial port. A TSR (terminate-and-stay-resident) program running on the client intercepts all of the calls and information passed to Int14 and redirects that information across the network to the modem pool.

- **NASI,** or NetWare Asynchronous Services Interface, is a software interrupt that links to the NetWare shell on NetWare clients. As with the Int14 implementation, a TSR intercepts all of the information passed to the NASI interrupt and forwards it across the network to the dial-out modem pool.

Figure 14-9 illustrates some of the issues involved in dialing out from the LAN.

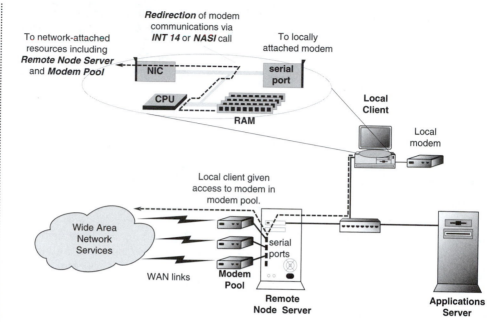

Figure 14-9   Dialing Out from the LAN

Wireless LANs   Although not limited to use strictly in a remote access setting, wireless LANs do play a role in the overall objective of untethering workers so as to increase productivity and customer satisfaction. Although wireless LANs may have been initially marketed as a means of replacing wire-bound LANs, that marketing strategy has not been reflected in their applied uses to date.

Mobile computing can be performed within the confines of a corporate or campus environment and over longer distances with the assistance of wireless bridges or WAN services. Portable or notebook PCs equipped with their own wireless LAN adapters can create an instant LAN connection merely by getting within range of a server-based wireless LAN adapter or wireless hub. In this way, a student or employee can sit down anywhere and log into a LAN as long as he/she is within range of the wireless hub and has the proper wireless adapter installed in their portable PC. These implementations are especially helpful in large warehouse or inventory settings.

Meeting rooms could be equipped with wireless hubs to allow spontaneous workgroups to log into network resources without running cables all over the meeting room. Similarly, by quickly installing wireless hubs and portable PCs with wireless adapters, temporary expansion needs or emergency/disaster recovery situations can be handled quickly and with relative ease—no rerunning of wires or finding the proper cross-connects in the wiring closet.

Finally, wireless LAN technology allows entire LANs to be preconfigured at a central site and shipped "ready to run" to remote sites. The nontechnical users at the remote site literally just have to plug the power cords into the electrical outlets and they have an instant LAN. For companies with a great number of remote sites and limited technical staff, such a technology is ideal. No pre-installation site visits are necessary. Also avoided are costs and supervision of building wiring jobs and troubleshooting building wiring problems during and after installation.

Although they have been called a technology looking for a market or, perhaps more aptly, a solution looking for a problem, they do offer significant flexibility and spontaneity not possible with traditional wire-bound LANs. It is important to note that, in general, wireless LANs cannot match the speed of their wired equivalent network architectures. For example, most Ethernet wireless LANs are limited to about 2 Mbps in comparison to Ethernet's 10 Mbps wire-based capacity.

Currently there are two popular wireless transmission technologies in the local area network technology area. They are:

- **Spread Spectrum Transmission**

- **Infrared Transmission**

In Sharper Focus

FREQUENCY HOPPING VERSUS DIRECT SEQUENCE SPREAD SPECTRUM

Spread spectrum transmission, as its name implies, spreads a data message across a wide range or spectrum of frequencies. This technique was originally employed as a security measure, since a receiver would need to know exactly how the message was spread across the frequency spectrum in order to intercept the message in meaningful form. Spread spectrum transmission for wireless LANs is most often limited to three frequency ranges:

- 902–928 MHz

- 2.4–2.4835 GHz

- 5.725–5.825 GHz

In addition, only two spread spectrum techniques are allowed by the FCC for wireless LANs:

- **Frequency hopping spread spectrum**

- **Direct sequence spread spectrum**

As can be seen in Figure 14-10, direct sequence spread spectrum is more commonly employed in wireless LAN technology, and in general, is capable of delivering higher data throughput rates than frequency hopping spread spectrum. Direct sequence spread spectrum (DSSS) transmits at a particular frequency within the allowable range. To distinguish between transmissions from multiple wireless workstations, DSSS adds at least 10 bits to the data message to uniquely identify a particular transmission. DSSS receivers must be able to differentiate between these bits, known as chips, in order to properly distinguish transmissions. The addition, removal, and interpretation of chips in DSS adds complexity, cost, and processing overhead. Nonetheless, DSSS generally delivers superior throughput to FHSS.

Frequency-hopping Spread Spectrum (FHSS) hops from one frequency to another throughout the allowable frequency range. The pattern of frequency hopping must be known by the wireless receiver so that the message can be reconstructed correctly. A given wireless transceiver's signal is on a given frequency for less than 1 second. Another desirable effect of all of the hopping from one frequency to another is that the transmission tends to be less affected by interference, an especially desirable characteristic for mobile computing applications.

Practical Advice and Information

Interference with wireless LANs using the 2.4–2.4835 GHz frequency range can be generated by microwave ovens. Other electronic devices such as cordless phones and wireless scanners are also licensed to use the 902–928 MHz frequency range.

Some of the technical and functional differences between these wireless LAN technologies are summarized in Figure 14-10. Internetworking devices that are able to link wireless LANs with wire-based LANs are known as wireless bridges or wireless access points and were reviewed in Chapter 13.

Some functional issues of wireless LANs not addressed in Figure 14-10 are as follows:

- Network Interface Cards—Because wireless LAN technology seems to be shifting toward an emphasis on mobile computing via laptops and portables, it should come as no surprise that most wireless LAN network interface cards are available as PC cards (PCMCIA). In such a case, card and socket services compatibility should be verified. Parallel port adapters that can also be attached to portable computers are also available on some wireless LANs, as are ISA adapters.

- Encryption—Because data are being sent through the air, it is especially important to consider security with wireless LANs. Some wireless LANs support DES (data encryption standard) encryption directly on the network interface card, usually through the installation of an optional encryption chip.

Wireless LAN	Manufacturer	Network Architecture	Wireless Transmission Technology	Data Throughput	Maximum Distance
AirLAN	Solectek Corp.	Ethernet	Direct-sequence spread spectrum 902–928 MHz	2 Mbps	800 ft.
ArLAN	Aironet Wireless Communications Inc.	Ethernet or Token Ring	Direct-sequence spread spectrum 902–928 MHz	860 Kbps	1000 ft.
			Direct-sequence spread spectrum 2.4–2.4835 GHz	2 Mbps	500 ft.
Collaborative	Photonics Corp.	Ethernet	Diffuse infrared	1 Mbps	30 ft. radius
FreePort	Windata	Ethernet	Direct-sequence spread spectrum 902–928 MHz	5.7 Mbps	260 ft.
Infranet	JVC	Ethernet	360-degree infrared	10 Mbps	16.5 ft radius
InfraLAN	InfraLAN Wireless	Ethernet	Line-of-sight Infrared	10 Mbps	90 ft.
NetWave	Xircom Inc.	Ethernet	Frequency hopping spread-spectrum 2.4–2.4835 GHz	1.6 Mbps	750 ft.
RangeLAN2	Proxim Inc.	Ethernet	Frequency hopping	1.6 Mbps	1000 ft.
Roamabout	Digital Equipment Corp.	Ethernet	Direct-sequence spread spectrum 2.4–2.4835 GHz	2 Mbps	800 ft.
WaveLAN	AT&T G.I.S.	Ethernet	Direct-sequence spread spectrum 902–928 MHz	2 Mbps	800 ft.

Figure 14-10   Wireless LAN Functional and Technical Analysis

In Sharper Focus

WIRELESS LAN STANDARDS: IEEE 802.11 AND MOBILE IP

One of the key shortcomings to date of wireless LANs has been a lack of interoperability among the wireless LAN offerings of different vendors. In an effort to address this shortcoming, a proposal for a new wireless LAN standard known as **IEEE 802.11** was approved in 1997 after seven years of debate. Key points included in the standard are as follows:

- Physical Layer: The standard defined physical layer protocols for each of the following transmission methods:
  - Frequency-hopping spread spectrum
  - Direct-sequence spread spectrum
  - Pulse position modulation infrared (diffuse infrared rather than line of sight)

- Media Access Control Layer: The standard defined **CSMA/CA (Carrier Sense Multiple Access with Collision Avoidance)** as the MAC layer protocol. The standard is similar to CSMA/CD except that collisions cannot be detected in wireless environments as they can in wire-based environments. CSMA/CA avoids collisions by listening to the network prior to transmission and not transmitting if other workstations on the same network are transmitting. Before transmitting, workstations wait a predetermined amount of time in order to avoid collisions, and set up a point-to-point wireless circuit to the destination workstation. Data-link layer header and information fields such as Ethernet or Token Ring are sent to the destination workstation. It is the responsibility of the wireless LAN access device to convert IEEE 802.3 or 802.5 frames into IEEE 802.11 frames. The wireless point-to-point circuit remains in place until the sending workstation receives an acknowledgment that the message was received error-free.

- Data Rate: 1 or 2 Mbps selectable either by the user or by the system, depending on transmissions conditions.

One important issue not included in the IEEE 802.11 standard is **roaming** capability, which allows a user to transparently move between the transmission ranges of wireless LANs without interruption. Proprietary roaming capabilities are currently offered by many wireless LAN vendors. **Mobile IP,** under consideration by the IETF, may be the roaming standard that wireless LANs require. Mobile IP, limited to TCP/IP networks, employs two pieces of software in order to support roaming:

- A mobile IP client is installed on the roaming wireless client workstation.

- A mobile IP home agent is installed on a server or router on the roaming user's home network.

The mobile IP client keeps the mobile IP home agent informed of its changing location as it travels from network to network. The mobile IP home agent forwards any transmissions it receives for the roaming client to its last reported location.

Practical Advice and Information

In January 1997, the Federal Communications Commission set aside an additional 300 MHz of bandwidth for a new class of wireless LANs and other wireless devices. The frequencies, from 5150 to 5350 MHz and from 5725 to 5825 MHz, commonly referred to as 5.8 GHz frequency range, are collectively known as the Unlicensed National Information Infrastructure (U-NII). Compliant devices could include PCs and laptops with built-in or external radio receivers.

Software

Remote Control Software   **Remote control software,** especially designed to allow remote PCs to "take-over" control of local PCs, should not be confused with the asynchronous communications software used for dial-up connections to asynchronous hosts via modems. Modem operation, file transfer, scripting languages and terminal emulation are the primary features of asynchronous communications software.

Taking over remote control of the local PC is generally only available via remote control software. Remote control software allows the keyboard of the remote PC to control the actions of the local PC with screen output being reflected on the remote PC's screen. The terms *remote* and *local* are often replaced by **guest** (remote) and **host** (local), when referring to remote control software.

Operating remote control software requires installation of software programs on both the guest and host PCs. Various remote control software packages do not interoperate. The same brand of remote control software must be installed on both guest and host PCs. Both the guest and host pieces of the remote control software may or may not be included in the software package price. Remote control software must have modem operation, file transfer, scripting language, and terminal emulation capabilities similar to those of asynchronous communications software. In addition, however, remote control software should possess features to address the following situations unique to its role:

- Avoid lockups of host PCs

- Allow the guest PC to disable the keyboard and monitor of the host PC

- Additional security precautions to prevent unauthorized access

- Virus detection software

Additionally, Windows-based applications pose a substantial challenge for remote control software. The busy screens of this graphical user interface can bog down even with V.34 or V.90 modems. Some remote control software vendors have implemented proprietary Windows screen transfer utilities which allow Windows-based applications to run on the guest PC as if they were sitting in front of the host PC, whereas others do not support Windows applications remotely at all.

Figure 14-11 summarizes the important features of remote control software as well as their potential implications. Among the more popular remote control software enterprise or LAN-enabled packages are:

Software	*Vendor*
COSessions Remote 32	Artisoft
ReachOut Enterprise	Stac
PCAnywhere32 8.0	Symantec
Timbuktu Pro	Netopia
Carbon Copy 5.0	Compaq
Proxy 3.0	Funk Software
LapLink 7.5	Traveling Software

Prices range from $119 to $199, with most in the $149 range.

Feature Category	Feature	Importance/Implication
Protocol Compatibility	Windows support	• How are Windows applications supported? Are full bit-mapped screens transmitted or only the changes? • Proprietary coded transmission of Windows screens?
	Windows '95 support	• Are Windows '95 applications supported?
	Network operating system protocols	• Which network operating system protocols are supported? (IP, IPX, NetBIOS)
LAN Compatibility	LAN versions	• Are specific multi-user LAN server versions available or required?
	Host/guest	• Are both host and guest (local and remote) versions included?
	Operating system	• Some remote control packages require the same operating system at host and guest PCs, whereas others do not.
Operational Capabilities	Printing	• Can remote PC print on local or network attached printers?
	File transfer	• Which file transfer protocols are supported? (Kermit, XModem, YModem, ZModem, Proprietary) • **Delta file transfer** allows only changes to files to be transferred.

(continued)

		•	Automated file and directory synchronization is important to mobile workers who also have desktop computers at home or at the office.
	Drive mapping	•	Can guest (remote PC) drives be mapped for host access?
		•	Can local (host PC) drives be mapped for guest access?
	Scripting language	•	Allows repetitive call set-ups and connections to be automated
	On-line help system	•	Context sensitive that gives help based on where the user is in the program is preferable.
	Color/resolution limitations	•	Different packages vary from 16 to 16 million colors and 800×600 to 2048×1280 pixels resolution.
	Terminal emulation	•	How many different terminals are emulated? Most common are VT100, VT102, VT320, TTY.
	Simultaneous connections	•	Some packages allow more than one connection or more than one session per connection, for example, simultaneous file transfer and remote control.
Security	Password access	•	This should be the minimum required security for remote login.
	Password encryption	•	Since passwords must be transmitted over WAN links it would be more secure if they were encrypted.
	Keyboard disabling	•	Since the local PC is active but controlled remotely, it is important that the local keyboard be disabled to prevent unauthorized access.
	Monitor blanking	•	Similar to rationale for keyboard disabling, since output is being transmitted to the remote PC, it is important to blank the local monitor so that processing cannot be viewed without authorization.
	Call-back system	•	Added security, although not hacker-proof, hangs up on dial in, and calls back at preprogrammed or entered phone number.
	Access restriction	•	Are remote users able to be restricted to certain servers, directories, files, or drives? Can the same user be given different restrictions when logging in locally or remotely?
	Remote access notification	•	Can system managers or enterprise network management systems be notified when remote access or password failures have occurred?
	Call logging	•	Can information about all calls be logged, sorted, and reported?
	Remote host reboot	•	Can the remote PC (guest) reboot the local host if it becomes locked up?

(continued)

Limited logon attempts	•	Are users locked out after a given number of failed login attempts?
Virus protection	•	This feature is especially important given file transfer capabilities from remote users.
	•	Can remote users be restricted to read-only access?
Logoff after inactivity time-out	•	In order to save on long distance charges, can users be logged off (and calls dropped) after a set length of time?

Figure 14-11   Remote Control Software Technology Analysis

The remote control software loaded onto a communications server for use by multiple simultaneous users is not the same as the remote control software loaded onto single remote (guest) and local (host) PCs. Communications servers' remote control software has the ability to handle multiple users, and in some cases, multiple protocols.

Remote Node Software   Traditionally remote node client and server software were supplied by the vendor of the network operating system on the server to be remotely accessed. **Windows NT RAS** (remote access service) and **Net-Ware Connect** are two examples of such NOS-specific **remote node server** software. It is important to note that these are software-only solutions, installed on industry standard, Intel application servers as opposed to the proprietary hardware of specialized remote access or communications servers. A representative list of remote node server software, required operating system or network operating system, and vendors are listed Figure 14-12.

Some of the important functional characteristics of remote node server software other than operating system/network operating system compatibility are listed in Figure 14-13.

Most of the remote node server software packages also include compatible **remote node client** software. A problem arises, however, when a single remote node client needs to login to a variety of different servers

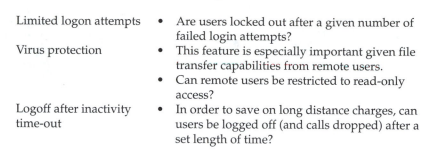

Remote Node Server Software	Required Operating System or Network Operating System	Vendor
Windows NT RAS	Windows NT 4.0	Microsoft
NetWare Connect	NetWare 4.1	Novell

Figure 14-12   Remote Node Server Software Operating System Compatibility

Remote Node Server Software Functional Characteristic	Importance/Implication
NOS Protocols Supported	• Although most remote node server software supports IP and IPX, support of NetBIOS, NetBEUI, Appletalk, Vines, LANtastic, and SNA was more limited. • If IP is supported, is the full IP protocol stack including applications and utilities supplied?
WAN Data-Link Layer Protocol	• Most remote node server software now supports PPP, while others support proprietary protocols. Proprietary protocols are fine in single-vendor environments.
Modem Support	• How many serial ports can be supported simultaneously? Numbers vary from 32 to more than 1,000. • How many modem setup strings are included? If the setup string for a particular type of modem is not included, configuration could be considerably more difficult. Numbers vary from 75 to more than 400. • Does the remote node server software support modem pools or must a modem be dedicated to every user? • Does the remote node server software support dial-out functionality over the attached modems?
Management	• How is the remote node server managed? via a specialized console or any attached workstation with proper software? • Does the remote node server software output management information in SNMP format? • Can remote users be limited as to connect time or by inactivity time-out?
Security	• Is forced password renewal (password aging) supported? • Are passwords encrypted? • Is the remote node server software compatible with third-party security servers such as token authentication servers? • Does the remote node server support callback (dial-back) capabilities?
Client Support	• Which types of client platforms are supported? (DOS, Mac, Windows, Windows for Workgroups, Windows95, WindowsNT, OS/2) • Are both NDIS and ODI driver specifications supported?

Figure 14-13   Remote Node Server Software Functional Characteristics

running a variety of different network operating systems or remote node server packages. What is required is some sort of universal remote access client. Such remote node clients are, in fact, available. These standardized remote clients with the ability to link to servers running a variety of different network operating systems are sometimes referred to as **PPP clients.** In general, they can link to network operating systems that support IP, IPX, NetBEUI, or XNS as transport protocols. Those that support IPX are generally installable as either NetWare VLMs (virtual loadable modules) or NLMs (NetWare loadable modules). In addition, these PPP client packages include sophisticated authentication procedures to ensure secure communications, compression to ensure optimal use of the WAN link, as well as most of the important features of remote control software. PPP client software is usually included with remote control software. The inclusion of remote control software allows users to choose between remote node and remote control for optimal performance.

Among the specialized compression and authentication algorithms included with a majority of these PPP clients are:

- **CIPX**—for compression of IPX headers

- **VJ**—for compression of IP headers

- **CHAP MD5**—for PPP encrypted authentication

- **CHAP MD80**—authentication for Windows NT RAS

- **SPAP**—Shiva's proprietary authentication protocol, which includes password encryption and callback capability

Mobile-Aware Operating Systems The mobile computer user requires flexible computing functionality to easily support at least three possible distinct computing scenarios:

- Stand-alone computing on the laptop or notebook computer

- Remote node or remote control computing to corporate headquarters

- Synchronization of files and directories with desktop workstations at home or in the corporate office

Operating systems that are able to easily adapt to these different computing modes with a variety of included supporting accessory programs and utilities are sometimes referred to as **mobile-aware operating systems.** Windows 95/98 is perhaps the best current example of such an operating system. Among the key functions offered by such mobile-aware operating systems are the following:

- Auto-detection of multiple configurations—If external monitors or full-size keyboards are used when at home or in the corporate office, the operating system should automatically detect these and load the proper device drivers.

- Built-in multiprotocol remote node client—Remote node software should be included that can automatically and transparently dial into a variety of different network operating system servers including, Windows NT RAS or NetWare Connect. The remote node client should support a variety of network protocols including IP, IPX, and NetBEUI as well as open data-link WAN protocols such as SLIP and PPP.

- Direct Cable Connection—When returning from the road, portables should be able to be easily linked to desktop workstations via direct connection through existing serial or parallel ports or perhaps an Infrared port adhering to the IrDA spec. The software utilities to initiate and manage such connections should be included.

- File transfer and file/directory synchronizations—Once physical connections are in place, software utilities should be able to synchronize files and directories between either the laptop and the desktop or the laptop and the corporate LAN server.

- Deferred printing—This feature allows printed files to be spooled to the laptop disk drive and saved until the mobile user is next connected to corporate printing resources. At that point, instead of having to remember all of the individual files requiring printing, the deferred printing utility is able to automatically print all of the spooled files.

- Power management—Since most mobile computing users depend on battery-powered computers, anything that the operating system can do to extend battery life would be beneficial. The demand for higher resolution screens has meant increased power consumption in many cases. Power management features offered by operating systems have been standardized as the **advanced power management (APM)** specification.

- Infrared connection—To avoid the potential hassle of physical cable connections, mobile aware operating systems are including support for infrared wireless connections between laptops and desktops. In order to ensure multi-vendor interoperability the infrared transmission should conform to the **IrDA (Infrared Data Association)** standards. The IrDA standard defines line-of-sight infrared transmission parameters rather than diffuse infrared transmission as defined by IEEE 802.11 IR. IrDA is currently limited to point-to-point distances of only 3 feet.

Mobile-Aware Applications   Beyond the shortcomings of remote node applications already delineated, mobile applications that depend on inherently unreliable wireless transmission services must be uniquely developed or modified in order to optimize performance under these circumstances.

Oracle Mobile Agents, formerly known as Oracle-in-Motion is perhaps the best example of the overall architecture and components required to produce **mobile-aware applications.** As illustrated in Figure 14-14, the Oracle Mobile Agents architecture adheres to an overall **client-agent-server** architecture, as opposed to the more common LAN-based client/server architecture. The overall objective of such an architecture is to reduce the amount of client-to-server network traffic by building as much intelligence as possible into the server-based agent so that it can act on behalf of the client application. Oracle's testing of applications developed and deployed in this wireless architecture has produced performance improvements of up to 50:1.

The agent portion of the client/agent/server architecture consists of three cooperating components:

- The **message manager** executes on the mobile client and acts as an interface between client applications requesting services and the wireless link over which the requests must be forwarded. It keeps track of requests pending on various servers that are being handled by intelligent agents. Oracle Mobile Agents also operates over LAN links or PPP-based dial-up links.

- The **message gateway** can execute on the local server or on a dedicated Unix or Windows workstation, and acts as an interface between the client's message manager and the intelligent agent on the local server. The gateway also acts as a holding station for messages to and from temporarily unreachable mobile clients. The client-based message manager and the message gateway communicate with each other via a communications protocol developed by Oracle, which provides reliable message delivery over wireless transmission services while minimizing acknowledgment overhead.

- The **agent event manager** is combined with a customer-written transaction handler to form an entity known as the **intelligent agent,** which resides on the local server. Once the agent event manager receives a request from a mobile client, it acts on behalf of that client in all communications with the local server until the original client request is totally fulfilled. During this processing time in which the intelligent agent is representing the mobile client, the wireless connection can be dropped. Once the original client request has been fulfilled, the entire response is sent from the intelligent agent to the client-based message manager in a single packet, thereby conserving bandwidth and transmission time. Having received the response to a pending request, the client-based message manager deletes the original request from its pending request queue.

Mobile Middleware An emerging category of software that seeks to offer maximum flexibility to mobile computing users while optimizing perfor-

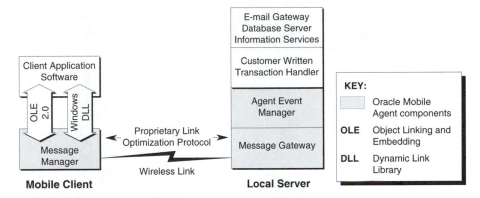

Figure 14-14   Client/Agent/Server Architecture Support Mobile-Aware Applications

mance is known as **mobile middleware,** sometimes also referred to as wireless middleware. Although specific products within this software category can vary significantly, the ultimate goal of mobile middleware is to offer mobile users transparent client/server access independent of the following variables:

- Client or server platform (operating system, network operating system)

- Applications (client/server or client/agent/server)

- Wireless transmission services

Figure 14-15 illustrates the basic components and interactions of mobile middleware.

As can be seen in Figure 14-15, the primary purpose of mobile middleware is to consolidate client/server traffic from multiple applications for transmission over a variety of potential wireless (or wire-based) transmission services. By consolidating client requests from multiple applications into a single transmission, overall transmission time and expense can be reduced. In some cases, the mobile middleware has sufficient intelligence to inform clients or servers whether the intended destination is currently reachable, thereby saving time and transmission expense. Some mobile middleware also has the ability to evaluate among available wireless services between the mobile client and the local server and to choose an optimal wireless transmission service based on performance and/or expense.

Mobile middleware is an emerging category of software characterized by proprietary APIs and a resultant lack of interoperability. As a result, applications written to interact with one vendor's mobile middleware probably won't interact with another vendor's mobile middleware. As can be

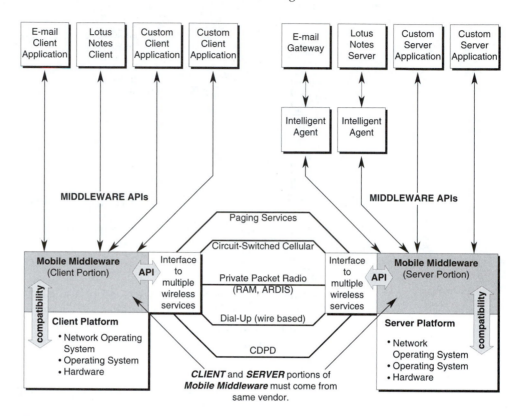

Figure 14-15   Mobile Middleware

seen in Figure 14-15, mobile middleware interacts with two sets of APIs: one between the mobile middleware and the applications, and one between the middleware and the wireless transmission services. In an effort to standardize wireless APIs for mobile middleware, two standardization efforts are currently underway:

- The Winsock 2 Forum is developing standardized Winsock 2 APIs for linking mobile middleware with Windows-based applications. This API would be able to deliver transmission-related information such as signal strength and transmission characteristics to the applications themselves. Such information could make the applications more intelligent and responsive to changing transmission quality.

- The PCCA (Portable Computer and Communications Association) is developing the standardized API for linking mobile middleware to a variety of wireless transmission services. This API will provide extensions to existing multiprotocol data-link layer device specifications such as NDIS and ODI.

MANAGEMENT AND CONFIGURATION OF REMOTE ACCESS TECHNOLOGY

Practical Advice and Information

OPTIMIZING REMOTE NODE AND REMOTE CONTROL SOFTWARE PERFORMANCE

As previously described in the section on the remote node logical topology, suitable performance of remote client applications is severely hampered by the limited transmission speed of the WAN links combined with the high-bandwidth demands of client/server applications. Besides rewriting the client/server application to minimize the amount of remote client to local server traffic, several other opportunities to improve over remote access performance are available. These optimization techniques will also improve performance of remote control applications as well:

- Use V.90 modems. This new modem specification can support transmission speeds of up to 56 Kbps over dial-up lines (in theory).

- Use ISDN (Integrated Services Digital Network) services, if available, as an alternative to asynchronous dial-up with the V.90 modem. ISDN BRI (Basic Rate Interface) delivers up to 144 Kbps (usually only 128 Kbps usable) of switched digital bandwidth. Using ISDN requires ISDN terminal adapters, the equivalent of an ISDN modem, and compatible communications software.

- Use 16550 UARTs and matching serial port drivers The UART (universal asynchronous receiver transmitter) transmits and receives data to and from a PC's serial port, which interfaces to the modem. The 16550 UART includes increased buffering capacity in order to match the performance of faster modems such as the V.90. Transmission via serial ports and UARTS is controlled by operating system software known as serial or COM drivers. Some of these COM drivers have limitations of 19.2 Kbps. More recent operating systems, such as Windows 95, and many asynchronous communications packages support serial transmission rates of at least 110.2 Kbps.

- Use data compression software/hardware and set communications software transmission speed to/from the modem to the PC (DTE rate) high enough to take full advantage of the compression software's capabilities. V.90 modems include V.42bis built-in data compression capabilities that can yield compression ratios of up to 4:1, depending on file content. Because V.90 modems have a maximum transmission speed of 56 Kbps and V.42bis supplies 4:1 data compression, maximum serial transmission rates of 224 Kbps (56×4) should be supported by PC hardware and software.

- Make sure that the remote control or remote node software being used supports **screen caching,** which allows only changes to screens, rather than entire screens to be transmitted over the limited-bandwidth WAN links. Screen caching will reduce the amount of actual traffic transmitted over the WAN link.

- Not to be confused with screen caching software, **network caching** or **LAN caching** software is able to improve overall remote node performance up to five times by caching repetitive applications commands and systems calls. These add-on packages are comprised of both client and server pieces, which work cooperatively to cache application commands and reduce network traffic over relatively low-speed WAN links. Network caching software is network operating system and protocol dependent, requiring that compatibility be assured prior to purchase.

Mobile MIB To integrate the management of mobile computing users into an overall enterprise network management system such as HP Openview or Tivoli, a specialized MIB was required to store configuration and location information specific to remote users. The Mobile Management Task Force (MMTF) has proposed a **mobile MIB** capable of feeding configuration and location information to enterprise network management systems via SNMP. A key to the design of the mobile MIB was to balance the amount of information required in order to effectively manage remote clients while considering the limited bandwidth and expense of the remote links over which the management data must be transmitted. From the enterprise network management system's side, controls will need to be installed to determine how often remote clients are to be polled via dial-up or wireless transmission in order to gather up-to-date management information. Among the fields of information included in the proposed mobile MIB are the following:

- Current user location
- Type and speed of connection device
- Type of remote client or remote control software installed on remote device
- Battery power
- Memory

■ NETWORK SERVICES

Wireless WAN Services

Although wireless LANs offer mobility to users across a local scope of coverage, a variety of wireless services is available for use across wider geographic spans. These **wireless WAN services** vary in many ways, including availability, applications, transmission speed, and cost. Among the available wireless WAN services that will be explained further are the following:

- Circuit-switched analog cellular

- CDPD—cellular digital packet data

- Private packet radio

- Enhanced paging and two-way messaging

- ESMR—enhanced specialized mobile radio

- Microcellular spread spectrum

- PCS—personal communications services

Applied Problem Solving

A TOP-DOWN APPROACH TO WIRELESS WAN SERVICES ANALYSIS

Because of the many variable factors involved in these wireless WAN services, it is important to take a top-down approach when considering their incorporation into an organization's information systems solution. Questions and issues to be considered on each layer of the top-down model for wireless WAN services are summarized in Figure 14-16.

Top-Down Layer	Issues/Implications
Business	• What is the business activity that requires wireless transmission?
	• How will payback be calculated? Has the value of this business activity been substantiated?
	• What are the anticipated expenses for the 6-month, 1-year, and 2-year horizons?
	• What is the geographic scope of this business activity? Localized? National? International?
Application	• Have applications been developed especially for wireless transmission?
	• Have existing applications been modified to account for wireless transmission characteristics?
	• Have training and help-desk support systems been developed?
Data	• What is the nature of the data to be delivered via the wireless WAN service? short bursty transactions, large two-way messages, faxes, file transfers?
	• Is the data time-sensitive or could transmissions be batched during off-peak hours for discounted rates?
	• What is the geographic scope of coverage required for wireless data delivery?

(continued)

Network	• Must the WAN service provide error correction? • Should the WAN service also provide and maintain the access devices?
Technology	• Which wireless WAN service should be employed? • What type of access device must be employed with the chosen WAN service? • Are access devices proprietary or standards-based?

Figure 14-16   Top-Down Analysis for Wireless WAN Services

As a practical example of how to use the top-down model for wireless WAN services analysis, start with the business situation that requires wireless support and examine the applications and data characteristics that support the business activity in question. For example, which of the following best describes the data to be transmitted by wireless means?

• Fax

• File transfer

• E-mail

• Paging

• Transaction processing

• Database queries

The nature of the content, geographic scope, and amount and urgency of the data to be transmitted will have a direct bearing on the particular wireless WAN service employed. Unfortunately, no single wireless WAN service fits all application and data needs. Once a wireless WAN service is chosen, compatibility with existing local area network architectures and technology must be assured. Typical uses of the currently most widely available wireless WAN services are as follows:

• Transaction processing and database queries: CDPD
  • Advantages: Fast call setup, inexpensive for short messages
  • Disadvantages: Limited availability but growing; expensive for large file transfers

• Large file transfers and faxes: Circuit-switched cellular
  • Advantages: Widely available, call duration pricing is more reasonable for longer transmissions than per kilopacket pricing
  • Disadvantages: Longer call setup time than CDPD (up to 30 sec. vs. less than 5 sec.); expensive for short messages

- Short bursty messages and e-mail: Private packet radio
  - Advantages: Wide coverage area and links to commercial e-mail systems.
  - Disadvantage: Proprietary networks, expensive for larger file transfers.

The key characteristics of these and other wireless WAN services are summarized in Figure 14-17.

Wireless WAN Service	Geographic Scope	Directionality	Data Characteristics	Billing	Access Device	Standards and Compatibility
Circuit Switched Analog Cellular	National	Full-duplex Circuit switched	14 Kbps max.	Call duration	Modems with specialized error correction for cellular circuits	MNP-10 (adverse channel enhancements) and ETC (enhanced throughput cellular)
Private Packet Radio	Nearly national, more cities than CDPD but less than circuit-switched cellular	Full duplex Packet-switched digital data	4.8 Kbps	Per character	Proprietary modem compatible with particular private packet radio service	Proprietary. Two major services: RAM Mobile Data and Ardis
CDPD	Limited to large metropolitan areas	Full-duplex Packet-switched digital data	19.2 Kbps max.	Flat monthly charge plus usage charge per kilopacket	CDPD modem	Compatible with TCP/IP for easier internetwork integration
Enhanced Paging	National	One or two-way. Relatively short messages	100 characters or less	Flat monthly charges increasing with coverage area	Pagers	
ESMR	Currently limited	One or two-way, voice, paging or messaging	4.8 Kbps	Unknown Service is under development	Proprietary integrated voice/data devices	
Microcell Spread Spectrum	Limited to those areas serviced by microcells. Good for college and corporate campuses	Full-duplex	14–45 Mbps	Monthly flat fee	Proprietary modem	Most provide access to Internet, e-mail services
PCS	Under development Should be national	Full duplex, all digital voice and data services	up to 25 Mbps		Two-way pagers personal digital assistants, PCS devices	Standards-based, should ensure device/service interoperability

Figure 14-17   Wireless WAN Services Technology Analysis

Two-Way Messaging

Two-way messaging, sometimes referred to as enhanced paging, allows short text messages to be transmitted between relatively inexpensive transmission devices such as PDAs (personal digital assistants) and alphanumeric pagers. Two distinct architectures and associated protocols have the potential to deliver these services.

One such architecture is based on **CDPD (cellular digital packet data)** and is being proposed and supported by AT&T Wireless Services, formerly known as McCaw Cellular. CDPD is a service that uses idle capacity in the circuit-switched cellular network to transmit IP-based data packets. The fact that CDPD is IP-based allows it to easily interface to IP-based private networks as well as to the Internet and other e-mail services.

By adding a protocol known as **LSM (Limited Size Messaging),** CDPD will be able to transport two-way messaging that will offer the following key services beyond simple paging:

- Guaranteed delivery to destination mobile users even if those devices are unreachable at the time the message was originally sent.

- Return receipt acknowledgments to the party that originated the message.

An alternative two-way messaging architecture is proposed by the PCIA (Personal Communicator Industry Association). Rather than building on existing IP-based networks as the CDPD/LSM architecture did, the **TDP (Telocator Data Protocol)** architecture is actually a suite of protocols defining an end-to-end system for two-way messaging to and from paging devices. Figure 14-18 illustrates the differences between the LSM and TDP two-way messaging protocols.

Analog Cellular

The current circuit-switched analog cellular network is more properly known by the transmission standard to which it adheres, known as **Advanced Mobile Phone Service (AMPS),** and operates in the 800 MHz frequency range. Transmitting data over analog cellular networks requires modems that support specialized cellular transmission protocols on both ends of the cellular transmission in order to maximize throughput. Examples of such protocols are **MNP-10 Adverse Channel Enhancements** and **Enhanced Throughput Cellular (ETC).** In some cases, cellular service providers are deploying modem pools of cellular enhanced modems at the **Mobile Telephone Switching Office (MTSO)** where all cellular traffic is converted for transmission over the wireline public switched telephone net-

LSM: Limited Size Messaging

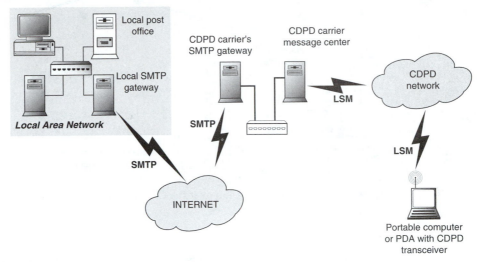

TDP: Telocator Data Protocol

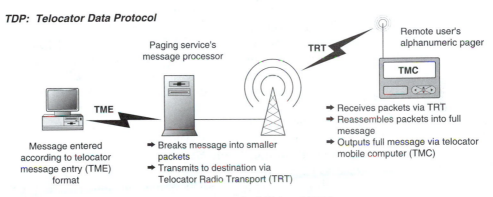

Figure 14-18   Two-Way Messaging Protocols: LSM and TDP

work (PSTN). Figure 14-19 illustrates data transmission over the circuit-switched analog cellular network.

Digital Cellular/Personal Communications Services

PCS, or **personal communications services,** is a visionary concept of an evolving all-digital network architecture that could deliver a variety of telecommunications services transparently to users at any time, regardless of their geographic location. PCS is not a totally new "from-the-bottom-up" telecommunications architecture. In fact, it is the integration of a number of existing telecommunications environments. PCS seeks to combine the capa-

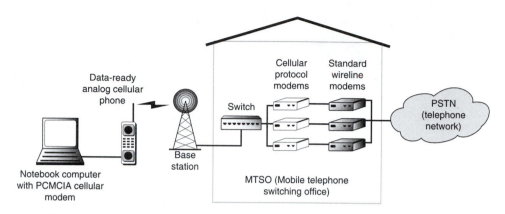

Figure 14-19   Data Transmission over the Circuit-Switched Analog Cellular Network

bilities of the PSTN, otherwise known as the **Landline Telephone Network,** with a new all-digital cellular network, together with paging networks, and satellite communications networks.

The need for seamless delivery of a combination of all of the preceding services is easily illustrated by the plight of today's mobile professional. A single person has a phone number for his or her home phone, a voice and fax number for the office, a cellular phone number for the automobile, a pager phone number for the pager, and perhaps even another phone number for a satellite service phone for use outside cellular phone areas. The premise of PCS is rather straightforward: one person, one phone number.

This **Personal Phone Number** or **PPN** would become the user's interface to PCS and the vast array of transparently available telecommunications services. This personal phone number is a key concept to PCS. It changes the entire focus of the interface to the telecommunications environment from the current orientation of a number being associated with a particular location regardless of the individual using the facility, to a number being associated with particular individual regardless of the location, even globally, of the accessed facility. Figure 14-20 illustrates the basic elements of PCS.

Digital Cellular Standards   Given the limited bandwidth (only about 140 MHz from 1.85 GHz to 1.99 GHz, referred to as the 2 GHz band) allocated to PCS and the potentially large number of subscribers needing to share that limited bandwidth, a key challenge for PCS is the ability to maximize the number of simultaneous conversations over a finite amount of bandwidth. Just as multiplexing was originally introduced in the study of wide area networks as a means of maximizing the use of wire-based circuits, two varia-

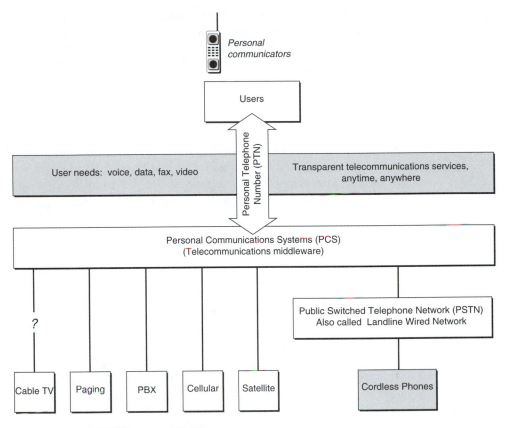

Figure 14-20   Basic Elements of PCS

tions of multiplexing are being field tested as a means of maximizing the use of the allocated bandwidth of these air-based circuits.

TDMA (Time Division Multiple Access) and **CDMA (Code Division Multiple Access)** are the two methodologies currently being used in PCS deployment. TDMA-based digital cellular may be able to support three times (some tests indicate six or seven times) the transmission capacity of analog cellular, whereas CDMA could offer as much as a tenfold increase. Note that the names of each of these techniques end in the words *multiple access* rather than *multiplexing*. The "multiple access" refers to multiple phone conversations having access to the same bandwidth and yet not interfering with each other.

TDMA achieves more than one conversation per frequency by assigning time slots to individual conversations. Ten time slots per frequency are often assigned, with a given cellular device transmitting its digitized voice only during its assigned time slot. Receiving devices must be in sync with the time slots of the sending device in order to receive the digitized voice packets and reassemble them into a natural sounding analog signal. TDMA should be able to transmit data at 9.6 Kbps. TDMA digital standards to handle call setup, maintenance, and termination have been defined by the Telecommunications Industry Association (TIA) as follows:

- IS-130: TDMA radio interface and radio link protocol 1

- IS-135: TDMA services, async data and fax

CDMA is the newest and most advanced technique for maximizing the number of calls transmitted within a limited bandwidth by using a spread spectrum transmission technique. Rather than allocate specific frequency channels within the allocated bandwidth to specific conversations as is the case with TDMA, CDMA transmits digitized voice packets from numerous calls at different frequencies spread throughout the entire allocated bandwidth spectrum.

The *code* part of CDMA lies in the fact that in order to keep track of these various digitized voice packets from various conversations spread over the entire spectrum of allocated bandwidth, a code is appended to each packet indicating to which voice conversation it belongs. This technique is not unlike the datagram connectionless service used by packet-switched networks to send packetized data over numerous switched virtual circuits within the packet-switched network. By identifying the source and sequence of each packet, the original message integrity is maintained while maximizing the overall performance of the network. CDMA should be able to transmit data at up to 14.4 Kbps. The CDMA standard defined by the TIA is IS-99: data services option for wideband spread spectrum digital cellular systems. Figure 14-21 illustrates both TDMA and CDMA.

TDMA and CDMA are being pursued and implemented primarily by cellular carriers in North America. In Europe and much of the rest of the world, **Global System for Mobile Communication (GSM)** is either currently deployed or planned for implementation, whereas **Personal Handyphone System (PHS)** is the digital cellular standard being implemented in Japan. At the present time, these various digital cellular transmission dards are not interoperable, thereby precluding the possibility of trans global access to digital cellular services.

Because digital cellular systems will be deployed on an as-needed in the most congested metropolitan areas, existing analog cellular networks will be required to coexist and interoperate with newer digital cellular networks. Transmission protocols such as TDMA and CDMA must be compatible with analog transmission protocols, and next-generation cellular phones must be able to support both analog and digital transmission.

Transmitting digital data from a notebook computer over digital cellular networks will not require modulation as was required with analog cellular networks. As a result, notebook computers should be able to interface directly to TDMA- or CDMA-based digital cellular phones via serial ports. Figure 14-22 illustrates data transmission over a digital cellular network.

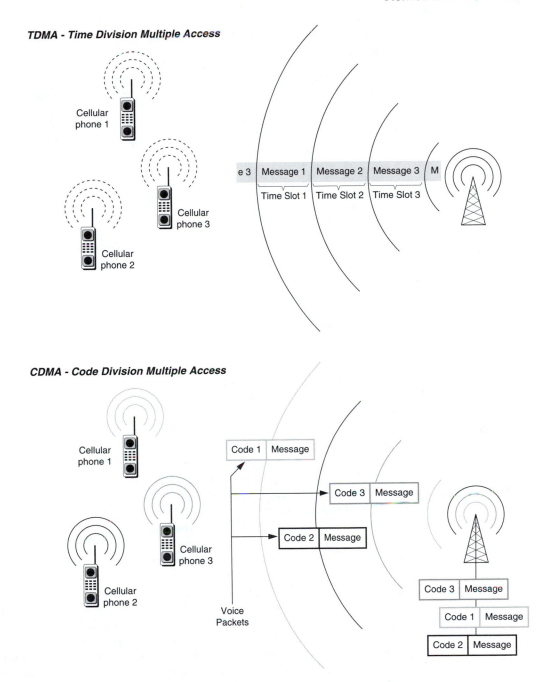

Figure 14-21   Maximizing Minimum Bandwidth: TDMA and CDMA

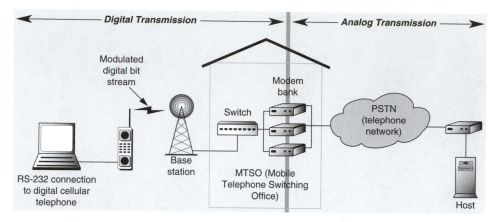

Figure 14-22 Data Transmission over a Digital Cellular Network

Managerial Perspective

THE FUTURE OF PCS

PCS faces significant challenges on its way to worldwide deployment. Required changes in thinking and behavior on the part of PCS users should not be overlooked. For instance, if a person can be called regardless of their location thanks to the PPN, who should pay for that call—the called party or the calling party? Caller ID services will now display the calling party's name or personal number rather than the number of the phone from which that person is calling. Remember, with PCS, numbers are associated with people, not with equipment and phone lines.

If the calling party is to be responsible for payment, they would probably like to know where they are calling before placing the call. However, as a potentially called party, would you want just anybody knowing your location? Vandals or your supervisor could pinpoint your location without even placing a call. Advanced call-screening services could allow only certain PPN's calls to be received on a person's personal communicator, while forwarding others to voice mail. As with any dramatically new technology, societal impact and changes will result. PCS should be no exception.

Perhaps the most significant hurdles are the individual and, at times, conflicting business missions of the various industries that must somehow achieve a metamorphosis that will produce a comprehensive, seamless, global, transparent personal communications service for subscribers. Another industry with its own distinct mission and on a possible collision course with the telecommunications industry is the cable television industry. PCS spread-spectrum communicators have been successfully demonstrated on CATV networks.

PCS vendors bid $7.7 billion for auctioned spectrum in 1995/96. It is estimated that somewhere between an additional $10 billion and $50 billion will have to be spent on PCS infrastructure before services can be deployed. The dilemma is that PCS vendors must price their services attractively enough to gain market share while maintaining enough cash flow to surrender a tremendous amount of debt.

Finally, future PCS deployment levels may be determined by simple market demand. There is always the possibility that a seamless, comprehensive, location independent communications system such as PCS is of more interest to the companies that stand to profit from it than to the buying public who are supposedly demanding it.

SUMMARY

Remote access to LANs has taken on increased importance in response to major changes in business conditions. As indicated by the top-down model, network functionality must respond to changing business conditions. Expectations of LAN remote access are significant. Remote users expect the same level of data accessibility, application services, and performances on the road as they receive at the office. Delivering this equivalent functionality is the challenge faced by today's networking professionals. The major obstacle to this lofty objective is the bandwidth, availability, and quality of the wide area network services that are expected to deliver remote connectivity to mobile users. Increasingly, wireless WAN services are at the forefront of remote access solutions.

In designing remote access solutions, it is essential to start with a thorough understanding of the needs of remote users. These needs will dictate both the logical and physical topologies of the remote access network.

There are two basic logical topologies for remote access. Remote control allows a remote PC to take over or control a local PC. Processing occurs on the local PC and only keyboard strokes and screen images are transported over the WAN link. Remote node allows the remote PC to act as a full-fledged LAN client to the local LAN server. In this case, full client/server traffic travels over the WAN link as the application executes on the remote client PC. One of these logical topologies is not preferable in all cases. Each situation must be analyzed on an individual basis.

Physical topologies include accessing a local LAN-attached PC directly via modem, accessing a shared communications server that might include PC boards for embedded shared computing power, or accessing a LAN modem that would provide access to local LAN computing resources.

Mobile computing requires specialized software including mobile-aware operating systems, mobile-aware applications, and mobile middleware to interface between multiple applications and multiple possible wireless WAN services.

Wireless WAN services vary widely in terms of availability, bandwidth, reliability, and cost. No single wireless WAN service is appropriate for all mobile computing applications. It is important to understand the application needs and data characteristics of mobile applications before choosing a wireless WAN service. Digital cellular and personal communications services may hold the promise of higher bandwidth, reliable wireless transmission. However, substantial infrastructure development remains before such services will be universally available.

KEY TERMS

access server
Advanced Mobile Phone
    Service
Advanced Power Management
Adverse Channel
    Enhancements
agent event manager
AMPS
APM
Carrier Sense Multiple Access
    with Collision Avoidance
CDMA
CDPD
Cellular Digital Packet Data
CHAP MD5
CHAP MD80
CIPX
circuit-switched cellular
client/agent/server
code division multiple access
communications server
CSMA/CA
delta file transfer
dial-in server
direct sequence spread
    spectrum
enhanced paging
Enhanced Throughput Cellular
ESMR
ETC
frequency hopping spread
    spectrum
Global System for Mobile
    Communication
GSM

IEEE 802.11
Infrared Data Association
Infrared transmission
Int14
intelligent agent
IrDA
LAN caching
LAN modem
Landline Telephone Network
Large-scale RAS
limited size messaging
LSM
message gateway
message manager
microcell spread spectrum
MNP-10
mobile computing
Mobile IP
mobile MIB
mobile middleware
Mobile Telephone Switching
    Office
mobile-aware applications
mobile-aware operating
    systems
monster RAS
MTSO
NASI
NetWare Connect
network caching
Oracle Mobile Agents
PCS
Personal Communications
    Services
Personal Handyphone System

Personal Phone Number
PHS
PPN
PPP clients
private packet radio
remote access
remote control
remote control software
remote node
remote node client software
remote node server software
remote node servers
remote node software
roaming
screen caching
Small Office Home Office
SOHO
SPAP
Spread spectrum transmission
TDMA
TDP
technical support
telecommuting
telocator data protocol
time division multiple access
time synchronous
    authentication
token authentication
token response authentication
two-way messaging
VJ
Windows NT RAS
wireless WAN services

REVIEW QUESTIONS

1. What are some of the key business trends that have led to an increased interest in LAN remote access?
2. What is the importance of needs analysis to LAN remote access design?
3. Differentiate between remote node and remote control in terms of functionality and network impact.
4. What is the major limitation in terms of delivering transparent access to remote LAN users?
5. Describe how it is possible to run remote control software via a remote node connection. What are the advantages of such a setup?
6. What are some of the security issues unique to remote access situations?
7. What added security capability can token authentication systems offer?
8. What advantages does a communications server offer over separate remote access links to multiple PCs? Disadvantages?
9. What is the common differentiation between communications servers and remote node servers?
10. Differentiate between the three major categories of remote node servers.
11. Why are dial-out solutions for remote node servers different from dial-in solutions?
12. How can dial-out solutions be implemented on LANs equipped with remote node servers?
13. Differentiate between the two-spread spectrum transmission techniques approved by the FCC in terms of functionality and application.
14. Why are wireless LAN NICs most often PCMCIA?
15. Differentiate between CSMA/CD and CSMA/CA.
16. What is roaming and why is it important to remote access users?
17. How does mobile IP work?
18. What is the relationship between the guest and host remote control software?
19. Why is remote control software not interoperable?
20. Differentiate between remote control and remote node software in terms of transport protocols and client protocol stacks.
21. Differentiate between LAN (multi-user) remote control software and point-to-point remote control software.
22. What are some of the unique functional requirements of remote control software beyond being able to control local (host) PCs?
23. What are some of the unique functional requirements of remote node server software?
24. What advantage do PPP clients offer?
25. What are some of the unique functional requirements of mobile-aware operating systems?
26. Differentiate between the client/agent/server architecture and the client/server architecture.
27. How do mobile-aware applications need to adjust to or compensate for wireless transmission services?
28. Describe the interaction between the components of Oracle Mobile Agents.
29. What two distinct interfaces do mobile middleware products transcend?
30. What are the functional objectives of mobile middleware?
31. How can the proprietary nature of mobile middleware products be overcome?
32. Describe standards development efforts that may affect mobile middleware.
33. What are some of the ways in which remote node or remote control applications can be optimized?
34. What is the difference between screen caching and network caching?
35. What unique information is required in a mobile MIB and why?
36. What are the conflicting objectives or limitations of mobile management software and the mobile MIB?
37. Why is CDPD of such interest to circuit-switched cellular vendors?
38. What standards are important to a person wishing to purchase a "cellular-ready" modem?
39. Match each of the following to the most appropriate wireless WAN service and justify your answer: transaction processing, short messages, large file transfers.

40. What are the advantages of two-way messaging systems for data transfer?
41. Differentiate between analog and digital cellular transmission systems in terms of data transfer capabilities and equipment requirements.
42. How is the notion of a personal phone number central to PCS and what changes in thinking about phone systems does it require?

43. Differentiate between TDMA and CDMA.
44. What are some of the obstacles to the vision of universal PCS?

ACTIVITIES

1. Gather articles regarding business trends that have contributed to the rise in LAN remote access. Relate these business trends to market trends for remote access technology and wireless WAN services. Use graphical presentation wherever possible.
2. Find an organization currently supporting LAN remote access. Analyze the situation from a business perspective. Which business activities are being supported? Was cost/benefit or payback period analysis performed or considered?
3. In the organization being studied, what is the physical topology employed? Links to multiple PCs? Communications server? LAN modems? Prepare a diagram of the physical topology including all software components such as network operating systems and transport protocols.
4. In the organization being studied, is remote node functionality supported? If so, which remote client software is installed? Are remote users able to access servers with multiple different network operating systems? Are PPP clients installed?
5. In the organization being studied, are dial-out capabilities supplied? If so, how?
6. In the organization being studied, have any efforts been made to optimize the performance

of remote node or remote control applications? If so, what were those adjustments, and what impact did they have?
7. What types of additional security precautions, if any, are instituted for remote users?
8. Investigate infrared wireless LANs. What is the difference between line-of-sight and diffuse infrared? Where are infrared wireless LANs being deployed? What is the percentage market share of infrared wireless LANs versus spread spectrum wireless LANs?
9. Why did the FCC choose the particular frequency bands for spread spectrum transmission?
10. What devices other than wireless LANs use the 902–928 MHz frequency range? Could this be a problem?
11. What is the difference between the CSMA/CA employed in IEEE 802.11 and that employed in Appletalk networks?
12. What is the current status of IEEE 802.11? What are the perceived shortcomings of the standard?
13. Research current PCS or digital cellular pilot tests. Compare how many use TDMA and how many use CDMA. What have been the results of these pilot tests?

CASE STUDY

Bossier City Police Have Wireless IP Net Locked Up

Bossier City says its wireless high-speed network is making the wheels of justice spin faster.

The city's police department recently completed the first phase of installing an IP wireless system that lets officers in cruisers access data directly from their IBM Thinkpads—without going through a radio dispatcher. The new system, based on IBM software and hardware, helps officers in cruisers access information, such as motor vehicle registration and criminal records, more quickly than they could using the department's old radio setup.

Faster response times mean greater safety for the officer, a primary concern for the city.

IBM's eNetwork Wireless software made the network possible. The software lets officers in cruisers download tn5250 terminal emulation screens from the police headquarters' AS/400 server.

The department decided to implement the wireless network because of the limitations imposed by the old radio dispatching system, in which officers would call headquarters, and the dispatcher would access the computer and read the information back.

Not only was the old setup slow—leaving the officer vulnerable and alone with potential suspects—but it also prevented officers from making queries in volume, says Keith Rider, the department's director of information services. He says a lot of criminals "slip through the cracks" because many police departments don't have adequate technology to catch them.

Realizing the radio dispatch method wasn't feasible to handle the number of inquiries officers wanted to make, Rider began shopping around for a way to bring the data directly into the department's 75 cruisers without another person's intervention. Rider says most of the competing systems he evaluated were proprietary and could handle only a limited number of applications.

The eNetwork Wireless package includes an eNetwork Wireless gateway; client code, called IBM Personal Communications Lite; and a server access agent called Emulator Express. The system uses an AT&T cellular digital packet data (CDPD) net for wireless transmissions.

Rider says the eNetwork Wireless software costs about $25,000; the Thinkpads were about $3,800 each and the CDPD services cost $49 per unit monthly.

Other features the Bossier City Police Department plans to add are:

- Giving officers access to city maps and building floor plans. SWAT and emergency medical teams can be better prepared when they arrive at a crime or accident scene.

- Tying city-controlled functions into the network so devices such as traffic signals can be activated via computer. An officer responding to an emergency call could trigger all traffic lights on his way to turn green.

BUSINESS CASE STUDY QUESTIONS

Activities

1. Complete a top-down model for this case by gleaning facts from the case and placing them in the proper layer of the top-down model. After completing the top-down model, analyze and detail those instances where requirements were clearly passed down from upper layers to lower layers of the model and where solutions to those requirements were passed up from lower layers to upper layers of the model.

2. Detail any questions about the case that may occur to you for which answers are not clearly stated in the article.

Business

1. What key business function does the implemented technology allow the police department to perform?

2. How does the new technology improve the ability of the department to deliver this function in comparison to the old technology?

3. What were the costs of this system?

4. How could the investment in this technology be cost-justified?

Application

1. What software is required in order to deliver the required functionality?

2. What are some features or applications that the department plans to add?

3. How could these additional applications be cost-justified?

4. How much additional bandwidth are these additional applications likely to need?

Data

1. What were the key requirements in terms of volume of inquiries?

2. How able were most applications to meet this requirement?

Network

1. Describe the wireless network used by this application?

2. What is CDPD and how does it work?

3. What are the bandwidth limitations of CDPD?

Technology

1. Describe the total technology package required to implement this solution.

LOCAL AREA NETWORK ADMINISTRATION

INTRODUCTION

At this point in the text, the reader should be comfortable designing both LANs and Internetworks. All that remains is to properly manage and secure these networks.

Chapter 15, "Local Area Network Management," exposes the reader to how each of the elements of a local area network can be managed. Although entire texts are written on network and information systems management, this chapter will provide an overview of the key issues surrounding the management of each major aspect of local area networks including standards and protocols, interoperability issues, currently available technology, key vendors, and market trends.

Chapter 16, "Local Area Network Security," explores the various processes, concepts, protocols, standards, and technology associated with network security. Although the chapter provides the reader with a methodology for developing sound LAN security solutions, it is important to remember the importance of people and their basic honesty and integrity as the underlying foundation for any successful network security implementation.

CHAPTER 15

LOCAL AREA NETWORK
MANAGEMENT

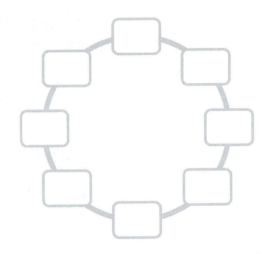

Concepts Reinforced

OSI Model	Top-Down Model
Enterprise Network Architectures	Network Development Life Cycle
Distributed Information Systems	Protocols and Interoperability

Concepts Introduced

Enterprise Network Management	Systems Administration
Server Management	Help Desk Management
Desktop Management	Consolidated Services Desk
Distributed Applications	LAN Management
Management	Internet/WWW Management
Internetwork Device Management	Network Management Technology
Distributed Network Management	

OBJECTIVES

After mastering the material in this chapter the reader should:

1. Understand the business motivations and forces at work in the current systems administration and network management arena

2. Understand the relationship between network management processes, personnel, and technology in order to produce a successful network management system

3. Understand the differences between systems administration processes and network management processes

693

4. Understand the protocols and technology associated with each area of systems administration and network management

5. Understand how systems administration and network management technology can be most effectively implemented

■ INTRODUCTION

At this point in the text, it should be clear to all readers that a local area network is a complex combination of hardware and software technologies linked by networking technologies. Once these various categories of technologies are successfully integrated, they must be properly managed. The purpose of this chapter is to expose the reader to how each of the elements of a local area network can be managed. Although entire texts are written on network and information systems management, this chapter will provide an overview of the key issues surrounding the management of each major aspect of local area networks including standards and protocols, interoperability issues, currently available technology, key vendors, and market trends. Figure 15-1 highlights some of the elements of a local area network that must be managed.

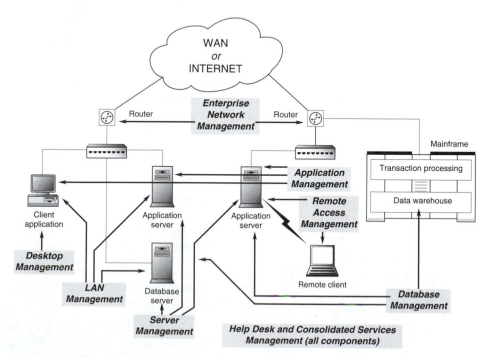

Figure 15-1   Elements of a Local Area Network That Must Be Managed

APPLICATION AND DATABASE MANAGEMENT

Distributed Application Management

Although distributed applications can be developed for local area networks that possess the power equivalent to those deployed on mainframes, client/server based applications have not yet matched mainframe applications in terms of reliability and manageability. This is primarily due to a lack of effective application management tools and underlying application management protocols that can expose an application's dependencies and measure numerous aspects of performance. This lack of application management tools can make it impossible to diagnose and correct application problems ranging from poor performance to system crashes.

Fortunately, an effort is underway to build self-diagnosing intelligence into applications during the development stage. By having these predefined events and **performance metrics** included within the application, management consoles will be able to detect problems with application performance and take corrective action. These embedded performance metrics are sometimes referred to as **instrumentation.** Two such development environments are Unify VISION and Forte Application Environment. In between the intelligent application, reporting on event conditions and performance metrics, and the management console is an autonomous piece of software known as an **agent,** which collects these performance statistics and properly formats them for transmission to the application management console. In turn, these agents are able to communicate with a variety of application management consoles or any SNMP-based administrative program. Examples of agents include AgentWorks from Computer Associates and AppMan from Unify. Eventually, it is hoped that such application management information can be consolidated into enterprise management frameworks such as CA-Unicenter and Tivoli Management Environment.

Application monitoring tools such as Application Expert and Application Insight from Optimal Networks provide real-time statistics on application behavior and network impact as well as providing the ability to perform "what-if" simulation analysis on captured applications. The two primary network-related variables that can affect distributed application performance are **bandwidth** and **latency.** It should be obvious at this point how network bandwidth can significantly impact application performance. The effect of latency on applications performance, however, is not as widely understood. Latency is simply the delay introduced by any computer or processing node that takes part in the execution of a distributed application. Downloading the client portion of an application from a server, processing SQL queries, or server-to-server queries all introduce latency to an application. The part of application optimization that is surprising to some people is that more bandwidth is not always the answer. If an application is constrained by latency, introducing more bandwidth will have little or no impact on application performance. Application monitoring and simulation tools are extremely valuable in their ability to pinpoint bandwidth and latency constraints before distributed applications are deployed throughout a global enterprise.

An alternative to developing your own applications with embedded management intelligence is to purchase a prewritten **event management tool** that has been written to monitor specific commercially available applications such as Lotus Notes, SAP R2/R3, Oracle Financials, or a variety of databases including IBM DB2, Oracle, Informix, and Sybase. PATROL from BMC Software, Inc. is an example of such an event management tool. Although effective, PATROL supports only proprietary protocols for application management data.

One of the key stumbling blocks to widespread deployment and support of distributed application management is the lack of a standard of what application performance information should be gathered and how that information should be reported. One proposal for standardizing how instrumentation should be developed within applications is known as the **applications management specification (AMS).** AMS defines a set of management objects that define distribution, dependencies, relationships, monitoring and management criteria, and performance metrics that can subsequently be processed by agents and forwarded to management consoles. These AMS agents are placed into applications through the use of the ARM software developers kit. An API that can be used by applications developers is known as **application response measurement (ARM)** and can measure several key application statistics. Agents are able to forward application performance statistics to ARM-compatible application management consoles. ARM 2.0 added the capability to track applications to multiple servers, to track business-specific transaction information, and to more effectively explain application performance problems. Vendors such as Hewlett-Packard, Tivoli, Oracle, and Compuware have committed to supporting the ARM specification. Figure 15-2 illustrates some of the key concepts involved in a distributed application management architecture.

Another possible standard for distributed application management is a proposed IETF standard known as **web-based enterprise management (WBEM)** that integrates SNMP, HTTP, and DMI (desktop management interface) into an application management architecture that can use common web browser software as its user interface. Another IETF initiative is developing a two-part applications MIB, the first part of which is known as the SysAppl MIB dealing with collection of applications performance data without the use of instrumentation and the second part of which deals with the collection of performance data that require instrumentation (performance metrics). The RMON Application MIB is explained in more detail later in this chapter. As can be seen from the previous paragraph, when it comes to application management, the standards arena is anything but decided.

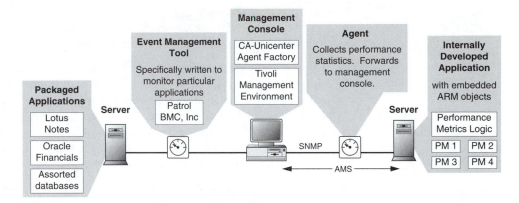

Figure 15-2   Distributed Application Management Architecture

Enterprise Database Management

Distributed database management is also important to overall enterprise information system management. Although most distributed data management platforms provide their own management system for reporting performance statistics, there is currently no way to consolidate these separate management systems into a single enterprise-wide view. Because of corporate mergers and the need to consolidate once isolated departmental databases, it is a very common phenomenon for a corporation to have data stored in a wide variety of incompatible database systems. The IETF has been working on a **Database MIB** specification that would allow any enterprise data management system to report performance statistics back to any SNMP-compliant enterprise network management system.

Enterprise database management tools that are able to manage a variety of different databases should include the following important major functional areas:

- Global user administration: User and group authorization and security management across a variety of different database are important characteristics for an enterprise-wide database management system.

- Heterogeneous data schema and content manipulation: In other words, from one console, an administrator can change the database record layout or the contents of those records, regardless of the particular database management system. In some cases, these changes can be automated across an entire enterprise's databases, scheduled to be run at a later time, or saved for future reuse. Such systems should be able to add columns to or otherwise modify database tables automatically across a variety of different databases. In some cases, databases may need to be replicated from one platform to another or one database's schema, or a portion thereof, may need to be copied to a different database platform.

- Effective troubleshooting: Enterprise database management systems must be able to monitor a variety of different databases for such critical events as inadequate free space, runaway processes, high CPU utilization, or low swap space. Events and alarms should be able to trigger e-mail, pagers, or on-screen events. In some cases, the enterprise database management system can take corrective action as defined by user-supplied script files.

- Among the databases such an enterprise database management system should support are: Oracle, Informix, SQL Server, Adaptive Server and DB2. In addition, it could run on the following computing platforms: Windows NT, OS/2, Windows 95, Windows 3.1, and Unix on such platforms as SPARC, RS/6000, Irix, Digital Alpha, and HP-UX.

CLIENT AND DESKTOP MANAGEMENT

Desktop Management

Desktop management is primarily concerned with the configuration and support of desktop workstations or client computers. In most cases, this management is more concerned with the assorted hardware and operating systems software of the desktop machines than with the applications or database software discussed in the previous section.

Desktop Management Architecture and Protocols   Desktop management systems rely upon an architecture and associated protocols proposed by the **Desktop Management Task Force (DMTF),** which is comprised of more than 50 companies including Intel, Microsoft, IBM, Digital, Hewlett-Packard, Apple, Compaq, Dell, and Sun. The overall desktop management architecture is known as the **DMI** or **Desktop Management Interface** and is illustrated in Figure 15-3.

Although differing in both strategic intent as well as governing standards-making organizations, desktop management and enterprise management systems must be able to transparently interoperate. DMI-compliant desktop management systems store performance and configuration statistics in a **MIF (Management Information Format),** and enterprise management systems employ a MIB, so a MIF-to-MIB Mapper is required in order to link desktop and enterprise management systems. The DMI architecture is comprised of four primary components:

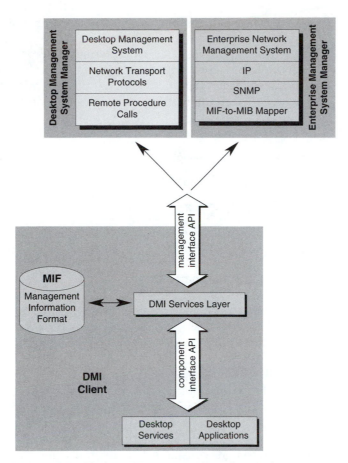

Figure 15-3   Desktop Management Interface Architecture

- **DMI Services Layer** is the DMI application that resides on each desktop device to be managed. The DMI Services Layer does the actual processing of desktop management information on the client platform and serves as an interface to two APIs.

- The **Management Interface API** is designed to interface to the desktop system management program, which will consolidate the information from this client with all other desktop information.

- The **Component Interface API** is designed to interface to the individual application programs or desktop components that are to be managed and monitored on the local client.

- Information about the local desktop components is stored locally in a MIF or Management Information Format.

Desktop Management Technology   Desktop management technology offerings from different vendors are best characterized as suites of associated desktop management applications. Current offerings differ in the variety of management modules included within a given suite as well as the extent of integration between suite modules. Among the modules that some, but not necessarily all, desktop management suites include are the following:

- Hardware and software Inventory
- Asset management
- Software distribution
- License metering
- Server monitoring
- Virus protection
- Help desk support

Key functional characteristics of desktop management systems are listed in Figure 15-4. Many of the functional areas described briefly in this figure will be explained in more detail later in the chapter.

Mobile Desktop Management   Extending desktop management functionality such as software distribution, change analysis, job scheduling, asset monitoring, and backup to mobile laptop computers linked only occasionally to corporate headquarters over relatively low bandwidth network links presents some unique challenges. The need for such management software is indeed important when one considers that laptop usage in supposed to at least double between 1998 and 2002 from 50 to 108 million users. Mobile users need to not only receive updates to their application software, but also to corporate data such as product and pricing information. It is equally important for support personnel at corporate headquarters to know exactly what is installed on each laptop computer in terms of hardware and software technology.

XcelleNet, Inc. produces a series of remote management modules known collectively as RemoteWare that are able to manage software distribution, antivirus protection, backup, and inventory management for laptop computers. RemoteWare differs from traditional desktop management software packages primarily in the fact that all files transmitted between the management software and the remote laptop computers are in a compressed format. If the transmission is interrupted midstream, the transmission is able to restart where it left off, rather than having to start over at the beginning. Once received at the remote laptop computer after disconnection from the transmission line, the installation application is executed locally on the laptop. Backup management software saves time and bandwidth by only transmitting changes to files rather than the entire file in a process known as delta file synchronization.

Functional Category	Importance/Implication
Integration	• Are all desktop management applications tied together through a single interface to a single console? • Do all desktop management applications share information with each other via a single database? • Can software modules be added individually as needed? Suites may be either modular or tightly integrated in design. • Does the system support the DMI architecture? Output data in MIF format?
Network Operating System Compatibility	• Which network operating system must the desktop management console or server run over? • Which network operating systems is the desktop management system able to monitor? Some desktop management systems can only monitor a single NOS. For example, Novell ManageWise is only able to monitor NetWare networks and Microsoft's System Management Server is only able to manage Microsoft networks although this may not always be the case. • Examples of supported network operating systems include: NetWare, Windows NT, IBM LAN Server, Banyan Vines, Artisoft LANtastic, DEC Pathworks, and AppleTalk
Desktop Compatibility	• The primary objective of this software category is to manage desktops, so it is essential that as many desktop platforms as possible are supported. • Examples of supported client platforms include: DOS, Macintosh, OS/2, Windows `95, Windows NT Workstation, Windows for Workgroups, or Windows 3.11.
Hardware and Software Inventory (Asset Management)	• Can the inventory software auto-detect client hardware and software? • Can changes in files or configuration be tracked? • Can versions of software be detected and tracked? • How many applications can be identified? Libraries of 6,000 are not uncommon. • Can CPU types and speeds be correctly identified? • Is a query utility included to identify workstations with given characteristics?
Server Monitoring	• Does the software support the setting of threshold limits for CPU activity, remaining disk space, and such? • What server attributes can be tracked? CPU activity, memory usage, free disk space, number of concurrent logins or sessions.
Network Monitoring	• Can data-link layer traffic be monitored and reported on? • Can network layer protocol traffic activity be monitored and reported on? • Can MAC layer addresses be sensed and monitored? • Can activity thresholds be established for particular data-link or network layer protocols?
Software Distribution	• Can software be distributed to local client drives as well as network servers? • Can updates be automatically installed? • Can the system track which software needs to be updated through ties with the software inventory system? • Can updates be uninstalled automatically? • Can progress and error reports be produced during and after software distribution?

(continued)

License Metering
- Where can software licenses be tracked?
  Clients
  Server
  Across multiple servers
- Can license limit thresholds be set?
- Will the manager be notified before the license limit is reached?
- Will users be notified if license limit has been reached?
- Will users be put into a queue for next available license after license limit has been reached?

Virus Protection
- Can virus protection be provided for both clients and servers?
- Can diskette drives as well as hard drives be protected?
- Can viruses embedded within application programs be detected?

Help Desk Support
- Are trouble-ticketing and call-tracking utilities included?
- Are query capabilities included to search for similar problems and solutions?
- Are reports available to spot trends and track help desk effectiveness and productivity?

Alarms
- Can managers be notified of changes to files or configuration?
- Can violations of preset thresholds be reported?
- Can alarms be sent by e-mail, pager, fax, cellular phone?

Remote Control Management
- Can managers take over remote client workstations for monitoring or troubleshooting purposes?
- Can this be done via modem as well as over the local LAN?
- Can files be transferred to/from the remote client?
- Can files on remote client be viewed without taking over complete control of the remote client?
- Can remote reboots be initiated?

Reporting Capabilities
- How many predefined reports are available?
- Can users define their own reports?
- Can information be exported to documents, spreadsheets, or databases?
- Which export file formats are supported?

Figure 15-4   Functional Categories of Desktop Management Systems

Callisto markets similar remote laptop management software known as Orbiter. A key difference between Orbiter and RemoteWare is that the Orbiter software uses a mobile agent architecture that works in conjunction with the management server at headquarters. In such a scenario, the client-based agent software executes applications and updates on a timed basis in an off-line manner as programmed by the management software. The next time that the laptop and management server are connected, the client agent updates the management server with the status of all of the jobs it was scheduled to execute in the interim.

In terms of standardized protocols for mobile desktop management, the Desktop Management Task Force has created a **Mobile MIF** as an extension to the Desktop Management Interface (DMI) 2.0. Among the types of information that management software supporting the Mobile MIF will be able to gather from compliant laptops are the following:

- Battery levels

- AC lines

- Docking status

- Infrared ports

- Video display types

- Pointing devices

- Device bays

Configuration Management

Single Sign-On   Providing single sign-on services for distributed applications deployed across multiple servers is beneficial to users as well as systems administrators. By establishing a distributed security directory housed on a central security server, single sign-on software is able to provide a single login location for multiple, different types of computing platforms. This precludes users from having to remember multiple passwords and allows systems administrators to maintain user accounts and privileges for an entire enterprise from a single location. Single sign-on software is ideally deployed as part of the consolidated service desk.

Configuration or Policy-Based Management Tools   Once hardware and software desktop configuration standards have been established and enforced, ongoing maintenance and monitoring of those standards can be ensured by configuration management tools such as electronic software distribution tools, license metering tools, and automated inventory tools. In order to more easily integrate configuration management tools with corporate policy and standards regarding desktop configurations, a new breed of **policy-based management tools** has emerged.

Policy-based management tools in their simplest form are able to automate certain tasks by using job scheduling utilities to schedule background and after-hours jobs. Another key point about these tools is that they are able to administer multiple different types of client platforms such as DOS, Windows 3.X, Windows 95, Windows NT, OS/2, HP-UX, AIX, SunOS, Solaris, to name but a few. More advanced tools not only automate administrative tasks, but also provide an interface for managing the corporate desktop configuration policies themselves. Administrators are able to set policies for an entire global enterprise, for specified domains, or for individual workstations. For example, some policy-based management software can store policies in a knowledge base that arranges the policies in a hierarchical fashion in order to identify policy conflicts. Once again, however, mere throwing technology at a problem will not provide an adequate solution. First, internal policies must be developed within the corporate environment before they can be entered into the policy-based management system. This policy development may involve a tremendous amount of work before the software can ever be implemented. Examples of the types of policies that might be enforced by policy-based management tools could be any of the following:

- User access rights to files, directories, servers, and executables

- Desktop start-up applications and background colors, or corporate approved screen savers

- Deny user access to network if desktop virus checking or metering has been disabled

- Facilitate changes when applications move or devices are added to the network

- Prevent users from trying to install and run programs their desktops cannot support

Help Desks

As processing power has moved from the centralized mainframe room to the user's desktop, the support organization required to support that processing power has undergone significant changes as well. When mission-critical business applications are shifted to client/server architectures, effective help desk operations must be in place and ready to go.

Although some help desk management technology is aimed at setting up small help desks on a single PC or workstation to provide simple trouble ticketing and tracking, the higher end of help desk technology supports such additional processes as:

- Asset management

- Change management

- Integration with event management systems

- Support of business-specific processes and procedures

The basic objective of this higher-end technology is to proactively manage system and network resources to prevent problems rather than merely reacting to system or network problems.

Because the help desk is held accountable for its level of service to end users, it is essential that help desk management technology be able to gather the statistics necessary to measure the impact of its efforts. A significant amount of the interaction with a help desk is via the phone, so it is important for help desk management software to be able to interact with call center management technology such as **automatic call distributors (ACD)** and **interactive voice response units (IVRU).** The overall integration of computer-based software and telephony equipment is known as **computer telephony integration (CTI).**

The heart of any help desk management software package is the **knowledge base,** which contains not just the resolutions or answers to problems, but the logic structure or decision tree that takes a given problem and leads the help desk staff person through a series of questions to the appropriate solution. Interestingly, the knowledge bases supplied with help desk management software may be supplied by third parties under license to the help desk management software vendor. Obviously, the knowledge base is added to by help desk personnel with corporate-specific problems and solutions, but the amount of information supplied initially by a given knowledge base can vary. The portion of the software that sifts through the knowledge base to the proper answer is sometimes referred to as the **search engine.**

Figure 15-5 summarizes some of the other key functional areas for help desk management software.

Asset Management

Asset management is a broad category of management software that has traditionally been divided into three subcategories:

- Electronic software distribution
- License metering software
- LAN inventory management software

Electronic Software Distribution   As the client/server architecture has taken hold as the dominant information systems paradigm, the increased processing power possessed by client workstations has been matched by increasing amounts of sophisticated software installed on these client workstations. The distribution of client software to multiple locally and remotely attached client workstations could be a very personnel-intensive and expensive task were it not for a new category of LAN-enabled software known as **ESD** or **Electronic Software Distribution.** ESD software can vary widely in the types of services and features offered as well as the costs for the convenience offered. For example, in addition to simply delivering software to LAN-attached clients, ESD software may also:

Help Desk Management Software Functionality	Explanation/Importance
Administration, Security, and Utilities	• What types of adds, deletes, and changes can be made with the system up and running and what types require a system shutdown? • Must all help desk personnel be logged out of the system in order to perform administrative functions? • Can major changes be done on a separate version off-line, followed by a brief system restart with the new version? • Can changes be tested in an off-line environment before committing to live installation? • Is security primarily group level or individual? Can agents belong to more than one group? • Can priorities and response times be flexibly assigned? • Can information be imported and exported in a variety of formats?
Call Logging	• How easy is it to log calls? • Can call logging link to existing databases to minimize amount of data that must be entered? • Can number of steps and keystrokes required to add a user or log a call be controlled? • Can multiple calls be logged at once? • Can one call be suspended (put on hold) while another one is logged? • Can special customers or users be flagged as such?
Call Tracking and Escalation	• How flexible are the call escalation options? • Call escalation options should be able to support internally defined problem resolution and escalation policies and processes. • Can the system support both manual and automatic escalation? • Can automatic escalation paths, priorities, and criteria be flexibly defined? • Can calls be timed as part of service level reporting? • How flexibly can calls be assigned to individual or groups of agents? • Is escalation system tied to work schedule system? • Can subject area or problem experts be identified and used as part of the escalation process?
Customizability	• Customizability is an issue at both the database level and the screen design level. • How easy is it to add knowledge and new problems/solutions to the knowledge base? • Does the software offer customizability for multinational companies? • Can entire new screens or views be designed? • Do existing screens contain undefined fields?
Integration with Other Products	• Is computer telephony integration with automatic call distributors and interactive voice response units, available? • Which other integrated modules are included: asset management, change management, scheduling, training, workstation auditing? • Does the software link to enterprise network management software such as HP OpenView or Tivoli TME?

(continued)

Performance	• Variables to consider when evaluating performance: number of simultaneous users on-line, number of calls per hour, required platform for database/knowledge base and search engine, required platform for agents.
	• Which SQL-compliant databases are supported?
	• Can searches be limited to improve performance?
Problem Resolution	• Products can differ significantly in how they search knowledge bases. This can have a major impact on performance. Decision trees, case-based retrieval, troubleshooting tools, and embedded expert systems or artificial intelligence are the most intelligent, most complicated, and most expensive options for problem resolution methodologies.
	• Many products provide more than one search engine or problem resolution method.
	• Some problem resolution products learn about your environment as more problems are entered.
	• Some problem resolution methods can use numerous different knowledge sources or problem databases.
Reporting	• How many standard reports are included?
	• How easily can customized reports be created?
	• How easily can data (especially agent performance data) be exported to spreadsheet or database programs for further analysis?

Figure 15-5   Help Desk Management Software

- Update configuration files

- Edit other files

- Capture commands entered during a manual software installation and convert the captured text into an automated script to control subsequent electronic software distribution.

Figure 15-6 summarizes some of the key functional characteristics of ESD software.

License Metering Software   Although **license metering software** was originally intended to monitor the number of executing copies of a particular software package versus the number of licenses purchased for that package, an interesting and beneficial side effect of license metering software has occurred. In recognition of this beneficial side effect, this category of software is now sometimes referred to as **license management software.** The previously mentioned beneficial side effect stems from the realization that at any time, fewer than 100% of the workstations possessing legitimate licenses for a given software product are actually executing that software product.

As a result, with the aid of license management software, fewer licenses can service an equal or greater number of users, thereby reducing the num-

ESD Software Functional Category	Description/Implication
NOS Support	• Since ESD software distributes software via the LAN, it is important to know which network operating systems are supported. Options: NetWare, LANManager, Vines, LANServer, Windows NT, Windows for Workgroups, PathWorks, LANtastic
Update Control	• Can updates be scheduled? • Can updates be selectively done based on hardware configuration? • Can updates be done only on selected machines? • Can only certain files be searched for and replaced? • Can files be edited or updated? Examples: CONFIG.SYS, AUTOEXEC.BAT, WIN.INI, SYSTEM.INI • Can files in use be replaced? • Can files be moved and renamed? • Can the update be done in the background on client workstations? • How secure is the update control? • Can updates be scripted? • Can update keystrokes be captured and converted to an automated update control file? • Can users perform their own selected updates from a distribution server? • Are unattended updates possible? • Are in-progress status screens available? • Can outside distribution lists be imported? • Can remote workstations be shut down and rebooted? • How extensive are the update reporting and logging capabilities?
Interoperability	• Is the ESD software integrated with license metering or LAN hardware/software inventory software? • Are other software packages required in order to execute the ESD software?
Licensing	• Are licensing fees based on numbers of clients or numbers of distribution servers?

Figure 15-6   Electronic Software Distribution Functionality

bers of software licenses purchased and the associated cost of software ownership. License management software is able to dynamically allocate licenses to those users wishing to execute a particular software package in a process known as **license optimization.** Three of the more popular license optimization techniques are as follows:

1. **Dynamic allocation** gives out either single user or suite licenses based on the number of suite applications used. As an example, if a user starts a word processing package within an application suite, he or she would be issued a single user license for the word processing package. However, if the user were to subsequently also execute a spreadsheet package within the same suite, he or she would be issued a suite license rather than a second single user license.

2. **Load balancing** shifts licenses between servers to meet demands for licenses put on those servers by locally attached users. Licenses are loaned between servers on an as-needed basis. In this way, every server need not have a full complement of licenses to meet all anticipated user demands. This technique is also known as **license pooling.**

3. **Global license sharing** recognizes the opportunity for license sharing presented by the widely distributed nature of today's global enterprise networks. While users on one side of the globe are sleeping, users on the other side of the globe are sharing the same pool of licenses.

License metering and management software has traditionally been supplied as add-on products written by third-party software developers. However, this trend may change abruptly. Novell and Microsoft have cooperated (an unusual circumstance in itself) on a **licensing server API (LSAPI).** This API would build license metering capability into Microsoft's and Novell's network operating systems and would eliminate the need for third-party license metering software.

LSAPI-compliant applications would communicate with a specialized **license server** that would issue **access tokens,** more formally known as **digital license certificates,** based on the license information stored in the license server database. Applications wishing to take advantage of the NOS-based license metering service would only need to include the proper commands as specified in the LSAPI.

LAN Inventory Management Software   **LAN Inventory Management Software** is often included or integrated with electronic software distribution or license-metering software. However, it has a unique and important mission of its own in a widely distributed client/server architecture in which hardware and software assets are located throughout an enterprise network. A quality LAN inventory management software system is especially important when it comes to the planning efforts for network hardware and software upgrades. An enormous amount of human energy, and associated expense, can be wasted going from workstation to workstation figuring out what the hardware and software characteristics of each workstation are when LAN inventory management software can do the job automatically and can report gathered data in useful and flexible formats. Figure 15-7 highlights some of the key functional capabilities of LAN inventory management software.

LAN Inventory Management Functional Category	Description/Functionality
Platforms	• Client platforms supported: DOS, Macintosh, Windows, OS/2 • Server platforms supported: NetWare, LANManager, LANServer, PathWorks, Vines, NetBIOS (DOS-Based), Windows NT
Data Collection	• Scheduling: How flexibly can inventory scans be scheduled? • Can inventory scans of client workstations be completed incrementally during successive logins? • Does the inventory software flag unknown software that it finds on client workstations? • How large a catalog of known software titles does the inventory software have? 6,000 titles is among the best. • Can software titles be added to the known software list? • Are fields for data collection user-definable? • Can the inventory management software audit servers as well as client workstations? • Are hardware and software inventory information stored in the same database? • What is the database format? • Can the inventory management software differentiate between and track the assets of multiple laptop computers that share a single docking bay?
Reporting	• How many predefined reports are available? • Are customized reports available? • How easy is it to produce a customized report? • Can reports be exported in numerous formats such as popular word processing, spreadsheet, and presentation graphics formats?
Query	• How user-friendly and powerful are the query tools? • Can queries be generated on unique hardware and software combinations? • Can inventory information be gathered and displayed on demand?

Figure 15-7 LAN Inventory Management Software Functionality

■ CLIENT/SERVER INFRASTRUCTURE ARCHITECTURE

Having covered the issues involved in the management of client workstations, whether mobile or desktop oriented, it is now time to look at what is involved with the management of the remainder of the client/server infrastructure. In order to delineate the processes and technology involved with the management of the infrastructure that underlies an enterprise-wide local area network, one must first define those components that comprise the infrastructure to be managed. Traditionally, a client/server infrastructure is comprised of a wide variety of servers and the various networks that connect those servers to each other and to the clients they serve. There is no single right or wrong way to divide the processes or responsibility for the management of these various components. For the purposes of this chapter, the topic of client/server infrastructure management is segmented into the following components:

- **Systems administration** focuses on the management of client and server computers and the operating systems and network operating systems that allow the client and server computers to communicate. This could also be considered as local area network administration.

- **Enterprise network management** focuses on the hardware, software, media, and network services required to seamlessly link and effectively manage distributed client and server computers across an enterprise. This could also be considered internetwork (between LANs) administration.

Both systems administration and enterprise network management are comprised of several subprocesses as illustrated in Figure 15-8.

As local area networks, internetworks, and wide area networks have combined to form enterprise networks, the management of all of these elements of the enterprise has been a key concern. LANs, internetworks, and WANs have traditionally had their own set of management tools and protocols. Once integrated into a single enterprise, these disparate tools and protocols do not necessarily meld together into an integrated cohesive system.

Figure 15-9 summarizes the key functional differences between enterprise network management and systems administration and lists some representative technologies of each category.

The Network Management Forum associated with the OSI reference model has divided the field of network management into five major categories in a document known as the **ISO Management Framework** (ISO 7498-4). This categorization is somewhat arbitrary, since standards and network management technology apply to multiple categories and even the categories themselves are interdependent. However, it is important for the network analyst to be aware of this categorization because it is often referred to when discussing network management architectures and technology. Figure 15-10 lists and explains the five OSI categories of network management.

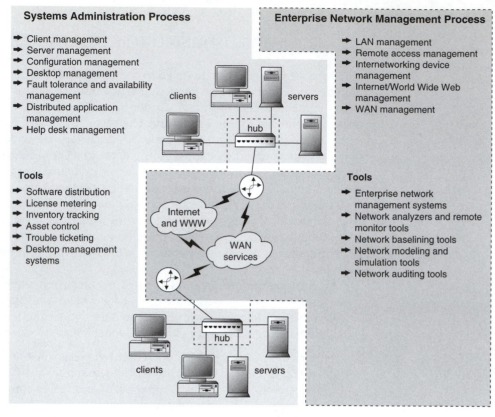

Systems Administration Process

→ Client management
→ Server management
→ Configuration management
→ Desktop management
→ Fault tolerance and availability management
→ Distributed application management
→ Help desk management

clients   servers

hub

Tools

→ Software distribution
→ License metering
→ Inventory tracking
→ Asset control
→ Trouble ticketing
→ Desktop management systems

Internet and WWW

WAN services

hub

clients   servers

Enterprise Network Management Process

→ LAN management
→ Remote access management
→ Internetworking device management
→ Internet/World Wide Web management
→ WAN management

Tools

→ Enterprise network management systems
→ Network analyzers and remote monitor tools
→ Network baselining tools
→ Network modeling and simulation tools
→ Network auditing tools

Figure 15-8   Client/Server Infrastructure Architecture: Systems Administration and Enterprise Network Management

	Functionality	Technology
Enterprise Network Management	• Monitor and manage internetwork technology— switches, routers, bridges, hubs • Monitor and manage WAN links	• HP Openview • Tivoli TME • Sun Solstice Enterprise Manager • CA Unicenter
Systems Administration Also Known as Desktop Management	• Track hardware and software inventory • Perform license metering • Monitor LAN and server activity • Software distribution • Asset management • Server monitoring	• SaberLAN Workstation - McAfee • Brightworks—McAfee • LANDesk Suite—Intel • Norton Administrator for Networks—Symantec • Frye Utilities for Desktops—Seagate • System Management Server— Microsoft • ManageWise—Novell

Figure 15-9   Systems Administration versus Enterprise Network Management

OSI Category of Network Management	Explanation/Importance
Fault Management	• Monitoring of the network or system state • Receipt and processing of alarms • Diagnosis of the causes of faults • Determination of the propagation of errors (fault isolation) • Initiation and checking of error recovery measures • Introduction of trouble ticket system • Provision of a user help desk
Configuration Management	• Compile accurate description of all network components • Control updating of configuration • Control of remote configuration • Support for network version control • Initiation of jobs and tracing of their execution
Performance Management	• Determination of quality of service parameters • Monitor network for performance bottlenecks • Measure system and network performance • Process measurement data and produce reports • Capacity planning and proactive performance planning
Security Management	• Monitor the system for intrusions • Provide authentication of users • Provide encryption in order to ensure message privacy • Implement associated security policy
Accounting Management	• Record system and network usage statistics • Maintain usage accounting system for charge-back purposes • Allocation and monitoring of system or network usage quotas • Maintain and report usage statistics

Figure 15-10   OSI Categories of Network Management

Consolidated Service Desk

Although the division of client/server infrastructure management processes into systems administration and enterprise network management is helpful in terms of distinguishing between associated function, protocols, and technology, how are these various processes actually supported or implemented in an enterprise? Reflective of the evolution of information systems in general, client/server infrastructure management has undergone an evolution of its own. The current trend in client/server infrastructure management is to offer a **consolidated service desk** (CSD) approach to end-user and infrastructure support. Such an approach offers a number of benefits:

- As a single point of contact for all network and application problem resolution, appropriate personnel processes can be matched with associated network management technologies. This match of standardized processes with technology yields more predictable service levels and accountability. CSD software should include features to support problem escalation, trouble ticketing and tracking, and productivity management reporting. Users should be able to easily check on the status of the resolution of reported problems.

- The consolidation of all problem data at a single location allows correlation between problem reports to be made, thereby enabling a more proactive than reactive management style. Incorporated remote control software will allow CSD personnel to take over end-user computers and fix problems remotely in a swift manner.

- Resolutions to known user inquiries can be incorporated into intelligent help desk support systems in order to expedite problem resolution and make the most effective use of support personnel. On-line knowledge bases allow users to solve their own problems in many cases.

- The consolidated services desk can also handle other processes not directly related to problem resolution such as inventory and asset tracking and asset optimization through the use of such technology as license metering software, and can also coordinate hardware and/or software upgrades. Software upgrades could be centrally handled by electronic software distribution technology. The management of these systems changes is referred to as change management.

- Network security policies, procedures, and technology can also be consolidated at the CSD.

- ACSD eliminates or reduces "console clutter" in which every monitored system has its own console. In large multinational corporations, this can lead to well over 100 consoles. Because all of these consoles must be monitored by people, console consolidation can obviously lead to cost containment.

Figure 15-11 conceptually illustrates how policy, procedures, personnel, and technology all merge at the consolidated service desk. It is important to note the inclusion of policy and procedures in the illustration. The formation of a CSD provides a marvelous opportunity to define or redesign processes to meet specific business and management objectives. Any technology incorporated in the CSD should be chosen based on its ability to support the previously defined corporate policies and procedures in its area of influence. It

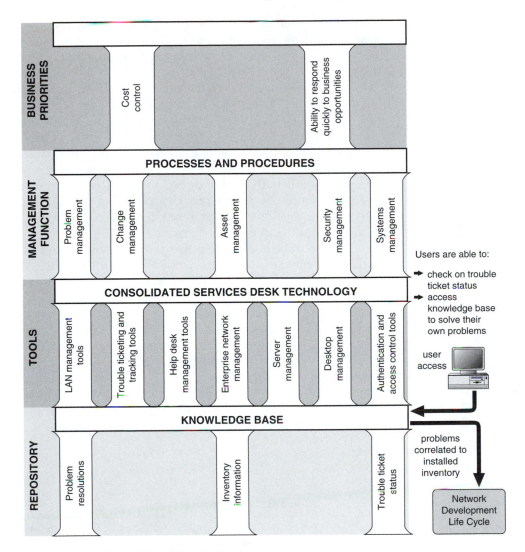

Figure 15-11   Consolidated Service Desk

is important not to first choose a CSD tool and let that tool dictate the corporate processes and procedures in that particular area of management.

■ SERVER MANAGEMENT AND SYSTEMS ADMINISTRATION

Server Management

At the heart of systems administration is the administration of the servers that are the workhorses and providers of basic system functionality. As servers continue to take on increasingly important roles to the entire enterprise, such as electronic messaging servers and enterprise directory servers, it is becoming more important to be able to effectively manage, troubleshoot, and remotely configure these critical elements of the enterprise infrastructure. Server management software seeks to ease systems administrators' chores by effectively monitoring, reporting, troubleshooting, and diagnosing server performance. Some server management software is particular to a certain brand of server, while other server management software is able to manage multiple different brands of servers. Ultimately, in order to be especially useful in meeting overall goals of systems reliability and end-user satisfaction, server management software must provide **server capacity planning** capabilities by monitoring server performance trends and making recommendations for server component upgrades in a proactive manner.

It's important to remember that server management software frequently requires a software and/or hardware module to be installed on all servers to be monitored and managed. This module will require varying amounts of system resources (CPU cycles, memory) and will have varying degrees of impact on system performance. Some server management systems perform most of the processing on the managed servers, whereas others perform most of the processing on the server management console or workstation. Similarly, some server management systems require a dedicated management workstation, while others will operate on a multifunction management workstation. Figure 15-12 summarizes some of the key potential functional areas of server management software. Figure 15-13 illustrates the implemented architecture of a server management system.

Server Management System Function	Importance/Explanation
Diagnose Server Hardware Problems	• Can alarm thresholds and status be flexibly defined? • How many alarm levels are possible? • Can RAID drive arrays be monitored and diagnosed? • Is predictive hardware failure analysis offered? • Is a diagnostic hardware module required? • Can server temperature and voltage be monitored? • Can bus configuration and utilization be reported?
Diagnose Server Software Problems	• Does the server management software track version control and correlate with currently available versions? • Can version control indicate potential impacts of version upgrades? • What diagnostics or routines are supplied to diagnose server software problems?

(continued)

Server Capacity Planning and Performance Enhancement	• Are performance enhancement and capacity planning capabilities included? • Are trend identification routines included? • Are inventory, asset management, and optimization modules included?
Share Data with Other Management Platforms	• Can data be passed to frameworks and integrated suites such as HP OpenView or Tivoli TME? • Can alerts and alarms trigger pagers, e-mail, dial-up? • Can data be exported to ODBC-compliant databases?
Remote Configuration Capability	• Can servers be remotely configured from a single console? • Is out-of-band (dial-up) management supported? • Is remote power cycling supported? • Is screen redirection/remote console control supported?
Report Generation	• Are alert logs automatically generated? • Can reports be flexibly and easily defined by users?
Protocol Issues	• Is TCP/IP required for the transport protocol? • Is IPX supported? • Is SNMP the management protocol? • Are any proprietary protocols required?
Server Platforms Managed	• Possibilities include: Windows NT, NetWare 3.X, NetWare 4.X, SCO Unix and other Unix varieties, OS2, Vines
Console Requirements	• Is a Web browser interface supported? • Is a dedicated workstation required for the console? • Operating system requirements for console? • Hardware requirements for console?
Statistics Tracked and Reported	• Logged in users • Applications running • CPU utilization • I/O bus utilization • Memory utilization • Network interface card(s) utilization • Disk(s) performance and utilization • Security management • System usage by application and by user
Mapping Capabilities	• Can the administrator map or group servers flexibly? • Can statistics be viewed across multiple server groups defined by a variety of characteristics? • How effective is the server topology map? • Can screen displays be easily printed?

Figure 15-12   Server Management Software Functionality

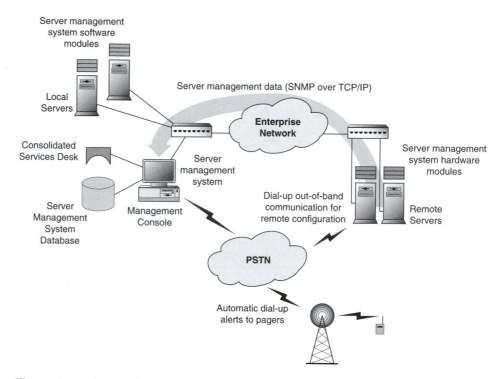

Figure 15-13 Server Management System Architecture

■ ENTERPRISE NETWORK MANAGEMENT

Enterprise Network Management Architecture and Protocols

As illustrated in Figure 15-14, today's enterprise network management architectures are comprised of relatively few elements.

Agents are software programs that run on networking devices such as servers, bridges, and routers to monitor and report the status of those devices. Agent software must be compatible with the device that it is reporting management statistics for, as well as with the protocols supported by the enterprise network management system to which those statistics are fed. Agents from the numerous individual networking devices forward this network management information to **enterprise network management systems,** which compile and report network operation statistics to the end user, most often in some type of graphical format. Enterprise network management systems are really management application programs running on a management server.

The network management information gathered must be stored in some type of database with an index and standardized field definitions so that net-

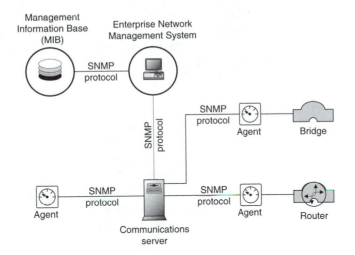

Figure 15-14   Enterprise Network Management Architecture

work management workstations can easily access this information. A **MIB,** or **Management Information Base** as these databases are known, can differ in the fields defined for different vendors' networking devices. These fields within the MIBs are known as **objects.** One fairly standard MIB is known as the **RMON MIB,** which stands for remote network monitoring MIB. Finally, a protocol is required to encapsulate the management data for delivery by network and transport layer protocols. Partly due to the dominance of TCP/IP as the internetworking protocol of choice, **SNMP (Simple Network Management Protocol)** is the de facto standard for delivering enterprise management data.

As originally conceived, the enterprise management console would collect the performance data from all of the devices, or elements, comprising an enterprise network in a single, centralized location. However, as networks grew in both complexity and size, and the numbers of devices to be managed exploded, the amount of management traffic flowing over the enterprise network has begun to reach unacceptable levels. In some cases, management traffic alone can account for 30% of network bandwidth usage, thereby reporting on the problems that it is itself creating.

An alternative to the centralized enterprise management console approach known as the **distributed device manager (DDM)** has begun to emerge. DDM takes more of an end-to-end full network view of the enterprise network as opposed to the centralized enterprise management console architecture, which takes more of an individual device or element focus. A DDM architecture relies on **distributed network probes** that are able to gather information from a variety of network devices manufactured by multiple vendors and relay that information to numerous distributed device manager consoles. Probes are strategically placed throughout the enterprise network, especially at junctions of LAN and WAN segments in order to isolate the source of network traffic problems. Management traffic is minimized and remains localized rather than monopolizing enterprise network bandwidth supplying the centralized enterprise management console. Figure 15-15 provides a conceptual view of a distributed device manager architecture.

Web-Based Management Another possible evolutionary stage in enterprise network management architectures is web-based enterprise management, first mentioned in the section on distributed application management. The WBEM logical architecture is illustrated in Figure 15-16. The overall intention of the architecture is that the network manager could manage any networked device or application from any location on the network, via any **HMMP (hypermedia management protocol)**-compliant browser. Existing network and desktop management protocols such as SNMP and DMI may either interoperate or be replaced by HMMP. Current plans call for HMMP to communicate either via Microsoft's DCOM (Distributed Component Object Model) or

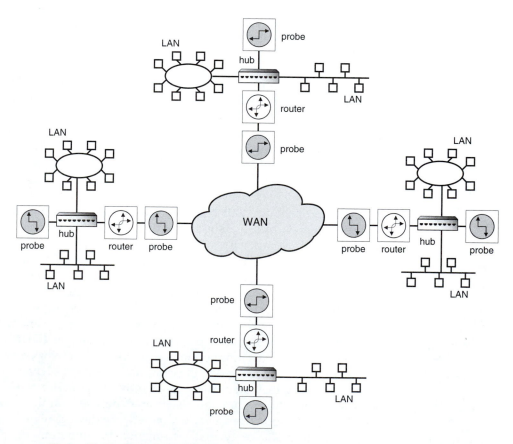

Figure 15-15 Distributed Device Manager Architecture

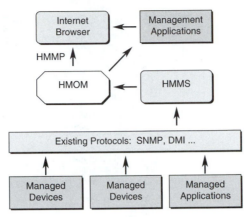

Figure 15-16   Web-Based Enterprise Management Logical Architecture

by CORBA (Common Object Request Broker Architecture). Management data from a variety of software agents would be incorporated into the web-based enterprise management architecture via the **HMMS (hypermedia management schema).** All web-based management information is stored and retrieved by the request broker formerly known as **HMOM (hypermedia object manager),** now known simply as object manager.

A proposed protocol currently under development by the DMTF (Desktop Management Task Force) that would support HMMS is known as **CIM** or **common information model.** CIM would permit management data gathered from a variety of enterprise and desktop voice and data technology all to be transported, processed, displayed, and stored by a single CIM-compliant web browser. Management data to be used by CIM would be stored in **MOF (modified object format)** as opposed to DMI's MIF format or SNMP's MIB format. Figure 15-17 illustrates the interaction of the various types of management data.

Managerial Perspective

Some would argue that CIM is the answer to finally being able to achieve transparency of enterprise management technology. Others would argue that CIM is nothing more than an added layer of complexity on top of an enterprise management system that is already overly complex. An alternative would be to make existing management protocols such as SNMP, DMI, and CMIP more interoperable without the need for additional layers of protocols. However, due to political issues and turf wars, achieving such interoperability is easier said than done, thereby creating opportunities for new all-encompassing protocols such as CIM.

From a practical standpoint, web-based management could benefit both vendors and users:

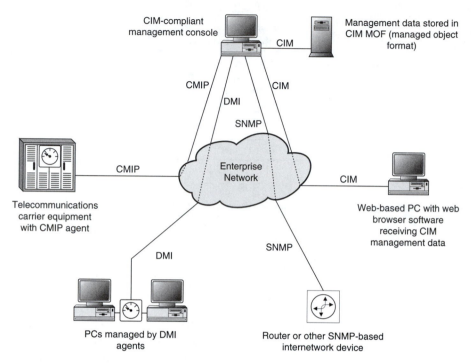

Figure 15-17 Management Data: CIM, CMIP, DMI, and SNMP

- Users would have to deal with only one common interface regardless of the enterprise network device that was to be managed.

- Vendors could save a tremendous amount of development costs by developing management applications for only a single platform.

However, the fact that a management too is web-based is not enough. It must deliver all of the functionality of the proprietary management software packages written for specific devices. Some of the most important functions for such software are listed in Figure 15-18.

Web-based network management technology is relatively new and the market is still being defined. Current technology in this category provides a web browser interface to the user in one of two ways:

- A web server application is embedded with the enterprise network management platform, and the user accesses that embedded web server via a web browser. Communications between the actual network devices being managed and the enterprise network management platform is still via SNMP, as illustrated in Figure 15-14.

- A web server application is embedded within a given network device, thereby giving a user direct access to the management data of

Functional Category	Importance/Explanation
Configuration	• Ability to remotely configure network attached devices • Ability to detect changes to remote device configurations
Polling	• Ability to poll network attached devices for performance and traffic statistics
Analysis	• Ability to consolidate and analyze statistics from multiple devices across the network • Ability to discern initial errors from cascading errors • Ability to detect trends • Ability to proactively predict potential trouble spots
Response	• Ability to respond in an appropriate manner to alarms and preset thresholds • Ability to detect false alarms • Ability to escalate problems as appropriate • Ability to notify proper personnel by a variety of means

Figure 15-18   Web-Based Management Tool Functionality

that device via any client-based web browser. Communication between the user and the network device is via HTTP.

Which SNMP Is the Real SNMP?   The original SNMP protocol required internetworking device-specific agents to be polled for SNMP encapsulated management data. Alarm conditions or exceptions to preset thresholds could not be directly reported on an as-needed basis from the agents to the enterprise network management software. The agents' inability to initiate communications with enterprise network management systems causes constant polling of agents. As a result of the constant polling, considerable network bandwidth is consumed.

Also, the original SNMP protocol did not provide for any means of manager-to-manager communication. As a result, only one enterprise network manager could be installed on a given network, forcing all internetworked devices to report directly to the single enterprise network manager. Hierarchical arrangements in which regional managers are able to filter raw management data and pass only exceptional information to enterprise managers is not possible with the original SNMP.

Another major shortcoming of the original SNMP is that it was limited to using TCP/IP as its transport protocol. It was therefore unusable on

NetWare (IPX/SPX), Macintosh (AppleTalk), or other networks. Finally, SNMP does not offer any security features that would authenticate valid polling managers or encrypt traffic between agents and managers.

The need to reduce network traffic caused by the SNMP protocol and to deal with other aforementioned SNMP shortcomings led to a proposal for a new version of SNMP known as **SNMP2, or SMP (Simple Management Protocol).**

SNMP2's major objectives can be summarized as follows:

- Reduce network traffic

- Segment large networks

- Support multiple transport protocols

- Increase security

- Allow multiple agents per device

Through a new SNMP2 procedure known as **Bulk Retrieval Mechanism,** managers can retrieve several pieces of network information at a time from a given agent. This precludes the need for a constant request and reply mechanism for each and every piece of network management information desired. Agents have also been given increased intelligence, which enables them to send error or exception conditions to managers when requests for information cannot be met. With SNMP, agents simply sent empty datagrams back to managers when requests could not be fulfilled. The receipt of the empty packet merely caused the manager to repeat the request for information, thus increasing network traffic.

SNMP2 allows the establishment of multiple manager entities within a single network. As a result, large networks that were managed by a single manager under SNMP can now be managed by multiple managers in a hierarchical arrangement in SNMP2. Overall network traffic is reduced as network management information is confined to the management domains of the individual network segment managers. Information is passed from the segment managers to the centralized network management system via manager-to-manager communication only upon request of the central manager or if certain predefined error conditions occur on a subnet. Figure 15-19 illustrates the impact of SNMP2 manager-to-manager communications.

SNMP was initially part of the Internet suite of protocols and therefore was deployed only on those networks equipped with the TCP/IP protocols. SNMP2 works transparently with AppleTalk, IPX, and OSI transport protocols.

Increased security in SNMP2 allows not just monitoring and management of remote network devices, but actual **remote configuration** of those devices as well. Furthermore, SNMP2 or a variation of SNMP known as **Secure SNMP,** will allow users to access carriers' network management information and incorporate it into the wide area component of an enter-

Before: Manager-to-Agent Communications

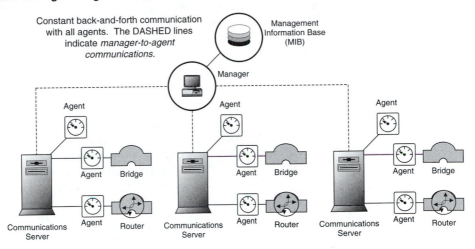

Constant back-and-forth communication with all agents. The DASHED lines indicate *manager-to-agent communications.*

After: Manager-to-Manager Communications

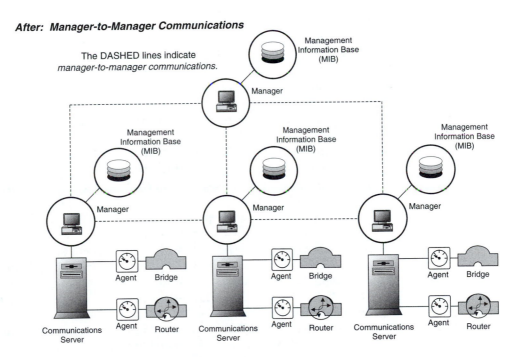

The DASHED lines indicate *manager-to-manager communications.*

Figure 15-19   SNMP2 Supports Manager-to-Manager Communications

prise network management system. This ability to actually access data from within the carrier's central office has powerful implications for users and enables many advanced users services such as SDN, or software-defined network.

Perhaps the most significant SNMP2 development in terms of implication for distributed client-server management is the ability to deploy multiple agents per device. As a practical example, on a distributed server, one agent could monitor the processing activity, a second agent could monitor the database activity, and a third could monitor the networking activity, with each reporting back to its own manager. In this way, rather than having merely distributed enterprise network management, the entire distributed information system could be managed, with each major element of the client-server architecture managed by its own management infrastructure.

Unfortunately, considerable debate over portions of the SNMP2 protocol have delayed its deployment for years. Some people feel that features of SNMP2, especially the security aspects, are too difficult to implement and use, whereas others blame the delay on concerns over marketing position and competitive advantage from technology vendors. In the interim, alternative upgrades to SNMP have been proposed by both officially sanctioned organizations such as the IETF and ad hoc forums. Figure 15-20 summarizes key points of the various SNMP2 alternatives.

MIBs   Management information bases serve as repositories for enterprise network performance information to be displayed in meaningful format by enterprise network management systems. The original RMON MIB standard, which was developed in 1991, has been updated as **RMON2.** Although the original RMON MIB required only compatible technology to be able to collect and analyze statistics on the physical and data-link layers, RMON2 requires collection and analysis of network layer protocols as well. In addition, RMON2 requires compatible technology to be able to identify from which applications a given packet was generated. RMON2 compatible agent software, which resides within internetworking devices and reports performance statistics to enterprise network management systems, is referred to as an **RMON** probe. Overall, RMON2 should enable network analysts to more effectively pinpoint the exact sources and percentages of the traffic that flows through their enterprise networks. Figure 15-21 summarizes some of the key functional areas of the RMON2 specification.

To implement RMON2-based monitoring, a network manager would purchase RMON2 probes and associated RMON2 management software.

Besides differing in the number of RMON2 options and groups implemented, probes and RMON2 management software also differ significantly in their ability to integrate transparently with enterprise network management systems such as HP Openview, Tivoli TME 10, Sunnet Manager, Solstice, and IBM Netview.

One shortcoming of RMON2 is its inability to collect and provide data regarding wide area network (WAN) performance. **RMON3** is expected to

SNMP Standard	Also Known As	Advantages	Disadvantages
SNMP		• Part of TCP/IP suite • Open standard • Works with defined MIBs	• Excessive polling • No manager-to-manager communication • Supports only TCP/IP • No security
SNMP2	SMP Secure SNMP	• Supports bulk retrieval • Supports manager-to-manager communication • Supports multiple protocols • Provides security • Remote configuration	• Never implemented due to squabbling among standards bodies
Updated SNMP2	SNMP2t SNMP2C SNMP1.5	• Supposedly easier to implement due to removal of security features	• No security features • No manager-to-manager communications • No remote configuration
Interim SNMPV2	SNMP2u SNMP2*	• Adds back some of features taken out of updated SNMP2	• SNMP2u and SNMP2* are incompatible
SNMP3	SNMP2	• Adds security features back into SNMP2 • Merges concepts and technical elements of SNMP2u and SNMP*	• Lack of support from official standards-making organization • Vendor-specific solutions are being offered as alternatives

Figure 15-20
Alternative SNMP2 Proposals

provide much-needed standards for the WAN monitoring and management technology category. RMON3 would provide a way for many of the current proprietary WAN management tools to interoperate and share data. In addition, RMON3 is supposed to offer management and statistics-gathering support for switched networks, virtual LANs, as well as the ability to measure application program response times in order to monitor distributed applications for degraded performance. Another effort to monitor distributed applications is known as the **application MIB.** Proposals for such an application MIB identify three key groups of variables for proper application tracking and management:

- **Definition variables** would store background information concerning applications such as application name, manufacturer, version, release, installation date, license number, and number of consecutive users.

RMON2 Function	Explanation/Importance
Protocol Distribution	• Tracks and reports data-link layer protocols by percentage • Tracks and reports network layer protocols by percentage • Tracks and reports application source by percentage
Address Mapping	• Maps network layer addresses to MAC layer addresses • Maps MAC layer addresses to hub or switch port
Network Layer Host Table	• Tracks and stores in table format network layer protocols and associated traffic statistics according to source host
Network Layer Matrix Table	• Tracks and stores in a matrix table format network layer protocols and associated traffic statistics according to sessions established between two given hosts
Application Host Table	• Tracks and stores in table format application-specific traffic statistics according to source host
Application Matrix Table	• Tracks and stores in a matrix table format application specific traffic statistics according to sessions established between two given hosts
Probe Configuration	• Defines standards for remotely configuring probes that are responsible for gathering and reporting network activity statistics
History	• Tracks and stores historical traffic information according to parameters determined by the user

Figure 15-21   RMON2 Specifications

- **State variables** would report on the current status of a given application. Three possible states are up, down, or degraded.

- **Relationship variables** would define all other network-attached resources on which a given distributed application depends. This would include databases, associated client applications, or other network resources.

One of the major difficulties with developing and implementing an application MIB is the vast difference that exists among distributed applications. In June 1999 the IETF approved the Switch Monitoring (SMON) MIB as a proposed standard. SMON acts as an extension to RMON, allowing switch traffic and Virtual LAN traffic to be monitored remotely. SMON offers some of the functionality proposed for RMON3.

Enterprise Network Management Technology

Technology Architectures   All of the systems administration and network management processes reviewed in this chapter can be enabled by associated technology. In most cases, network management products offer functionality across more than one category of network or systems management. One way to distinguish between different types of network management technology is to focus on the architecture of the technology. In general, network management technology can be categorized into one of three possible architectures:

- **Point products**—also known as **element managers**—are specifically written to address a particular systems administration or network management issue. The advantage of point products is that they are narrow in scope, provide the sought-after solution, and are usually relatively easy to install and understand. However, point solutions do not necessarily integrate with other systems administration and network management tools. Any necessary correlation between point products must be done by network management personnel. Backup and restoral tools, license optimization tools, or management tools specifically written for a particular vendor's equipment are examples of point solutions.

- **Frameworks**—offer an overall systems administration or network management platform with integration between modules and a shared database into which all alerts, messages, alarms, and warnings can be stored and correlated. Perhaps more important, most frameworks also offer open APIs or an entire application development environment so that third-party application developers can create additional systems administration or network management modules that will be able to plug into the existing framework and share management information with other modules. The advantage of a well-integrated framework is that it can offer the network administrator a single, correlated view of all systems and network resources. The disadvantage of frameworks is the development or integration of modules within the framework can be difficult and time consuming. In addition, not all management modules may be compatible with a given framework.

- **Integrated suites**—Although the two terms are often used interchangably, integrated suites could perhaps be looked upon as a subset of frameworks. The difference between integrated suites and frameworks is that integrated suites are filled with their own network management and systems administration applications rather than offering the user an open framework into which to place a variety of chosen applications. The advantage of integrated suites is that the applications are more tightly integrated and linked by a set of common services that tend to offer the user a more consolidated view of network resources. The disadvantage of integrated suites is that they usually do not offer the open pick-and-choose architecture of the framework. Some products in this category offer an integrated suite of applications but also support open APIs in order to accommodate third-party systems administration and network management applications.

Desired Functionality   Beyond the choices of architecture, systems administration and network management technology also differs in the level of functionality offered. For example, although most network management software can report on network activity and detect abnormal activities and report alarms, fewer packages are able to diagnose or fix problems. Among the commonly listed functions that network administrators would like to see delivered by systems administration and network management technology are the following:

- The ability to track the operational status of distributed applications

- The ability to automate reporting of system status information

- The ability to automate repetitive system management tasks

- The ability to integrate application management and systems administration information with network management information

- The ability to improve application performance by properly responding to system status messages

Currently Available Technology   Enterprise network management systems must be able to gather information from a variety of sources throughout the enterprise network and display that information in a clear and meaningful format. Furthermore, enterprise network management systems are being called on to monitor and manage additional distributed resources such as:

- Workstations and servers

- Distributed applications

- Distributed data management systems

One of the current difficulties with actually implementing enterprise network management systems is a lack of interoperability between different enterprise network management systems and third-party or vendor-specific network management systems. Popular enterprise network management systems that could be considered frameworks or integrated suites include:

- HP Openview

- Sun Soft Solstice Enterprise Manager

- Computer Associates' CA-Unicenter TNG (The Next Generation)

- TME 10 by IBM/Tivoli Systems (includes IBM System View)

- PatrolView by BMC Software Inc.

- Spectrum Enterprise Manager by Cabletron

Examples of third-party or vendor specific network management systems, sometimes known as element managers or point products, include:

- 3Com Transcend Enterprise Manager

- Cisco CiscoWorks

- Bay Networks Optivity Enterprise

- Legato Networker

- Cabletron Spectrum Element Manager

- American Power Conversion PowerNet

Among the manifestations of the lack of interoperability between third-party applications and enterprise network management systems are:

- Separate databases maintained by each third-party application and enterprise network management system.

- Redundant polling of agent software in order to gather performance statistics.

- Multiple agents installed and executed on networked devices in order to report to multiple management platforms.

The lack of interoperability between different enterprise network management systems makes it difficult if not impossible to:

- Exchange network topology information and maps

- Exchange threshold performance parameter and alarm information

The major cause of all of this lack of interoperability is the lack of common APIs both between different enterprise network management systems and between a given enterprise network management system and a variety of third-party network management systems. Figure 15-22 illustrates an architectural view of how enterprise network management systems interface to other enterprise network components. Interoperability APIs included in Figure 15-22 are either proposed or under development.

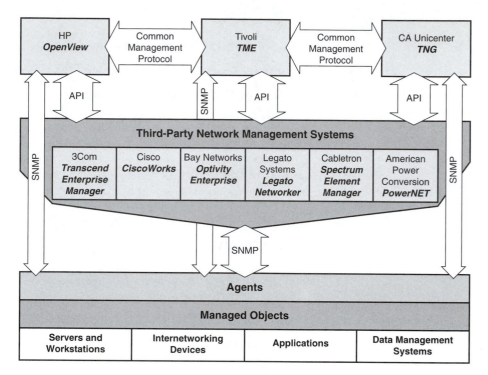

Figure 15-22   Enterprise Network Management System Architecture

In addition to interoperability issues previously discussed, key functional areas of enterprise network management software are listed in Figure 15-23.

Analysis—Network Analyzers

The only real effective way to diagnose problems with network performance is to be able to unobtrusively peer into the network transmission media and actually see the characteristics of the packets of data that are causing performance problems. LAN and WAN **network analyzers** are able to capture network traffic in real time without interrupting normal network transmission. In addition to capturing packets of data from the network, most network analyzers are able to decode those packets, monitor packet traffic statistics, and simulate network traffic through traffic generators. Filtering provided by network analyzers can isolate certain types of protocols or traffic from only particular workstations or servers. Given the multitude of protocols and the tidal wave of packets on a given network, effective filtering capabilities are enormously important to network analyzer usefulness.

Functional Category	Importance/Implication
Operating System Compatibility	• Which operating systems does the enterprise network management system run over? HP UX Sun OS Solaris SPARC IBM AIX Windows NT • How many simultaneous operators of the enterprise network management system are supported? • Can multiple operators be distributed across the enterprise network?
Database Compatibility	• Which databases can the enterprise network management system interoperate with? Oracle Ingres SyBase Informix Proprietary DB2 Flat file
Network Size and Architecture	• Is there a limit to the number of nodes supported? • Can the software map all network architectures? Ethernet, Token Ring, FDDI, Switched LANs, WANs, ATM • Can mainframes be integrated into the enterprise network management system? • Can IPX as well as IP devices be managed?
Third-Party Application Support	• How many third-party applications are guaranteed to interoperate with this enterprise network management system?
MIB and Management Protocol Support	• How many different MIBs can be both IETF sanctioned or vendor specific. Enterprise network management systems can easily support more than 200 different MIBs. • Are management protocols other than SNMP supported? CMIP (Common Management Information Protocol), Proprietary, SNMP2
Self-Configuration	• To what extent is the enterprise network management software able to self-configure or autodiscover the enterprise network topology? • Can the self-configuration process be customized or controlled?
Cascading or Effect Alarms	• Is the system able to identify and report alarms triggered by other alarms in order to more easily pinpoint the cause of problems? This capability may be known as event correlation.

Figure 15-23   Functional Categories of Enterprise Network Management Systems

Some network analyzers are software-based (you supply the PC), hardware-based (come fully installed in their own dedicated PC) or hybrid, in which an add-on hardware device with installed software is linked to your notebook PC via the parallel port. Still other analyzers, such as the Network General Sniffer, are shipped with a PCMCIA (PC Card) Ethernet adapter and software for installation on a limited number of supported notebook computers. Preconfigured sniffers are also available. Network analyzers can also differ in the number of LAN and WAN protocols that can be analyzed, the number of nodes from which traffic can be captured, and the ease of use, understanding, and flexibility of the user interface. Some network analyzers include expert systems that are able to predict oncoming problems based on observed traffic trends.

Network analyzer capabilities are most easily compared and categorized according to the 7-layer OSI model as outlined in Figure 15-24. In some

OSI Model Layer	Network Analyzer Functionality
Layer 7—Application	• Some analyzers are able to display actual text and numbers being transmitted across a medium. Because passwords and credit card numbers can be displayed by such a device, it is understandable why network analyzers are sometimes considered a security threat. Displaying protocols from layers 4 through 7 is referred to as embedded protocol decodes.
Layer 6—Presentation	• Embedded protocol decodes.
Layer 5—Session	• Embedded protocol decodes.
Layer 4—Transport	• Embedded protocol decodes.
Layer 3—Network	• Network layer protocols: X.25, ISDN Q.931, IP, IPX, Appletalk
Layer 2—DataLink	• Hardware interface modules (LAN): Ethernet, Token Ring, switched Ethernet, Fast Ethernet, FDDI • Hardware interface modules (WAN): ISDN BRI, DDS, ATM • DataLink WAN Protocols: BiSync, HDLC, SDLC, PPP, LAPB, LAPD, SLIP, frame relay, SNA
Layer 1—Physical (Also Known as Cable Scanners or Cable Testers)	• Cable scanners are able to pinpoint cable problems including locations of breaks, short circuits, miswiring, and polarity problems • Although a variety of different media types might be tested, the two most popular are Category 5 unshielded twisted pair and fiber-optic cable. • Layer 1 protocols: V.35, RS-232, RS-449, 423, 422, 530, T-1 (variety of interfaces)

(continued)

Among the key features and measurements of cable testers are the following:

- Ambient noise: level of external noise (from fluorescent lights, motors) where a cable is installed
- Attenuation: loss of signal strength over the distance traveled through media
- Attenuation-to-crosstalk: extent to which a medium resists crosstalk BERT (bit error rate tester): able to determine percent of received bits received in error.
- Capacitance: capacity of the medium to store an electrical charge
- Continuity: an uninterrupted electrical path along the medium
- Impedance: opposition to flow of a signal within a medium, measured in ohms, the lower the impedance, the better the conductor.
- Lookback device: cable tester function that sends transmitted signal out through medium and back into device for test and measurement
- Loop resistance: resistance encountered in completing a full electrical circuit
- Injector device: part of cable tester that creates signal, verifies transmission, and manages testing.
- NeXT: near-end crosstalk: signals being transmitted on one end overcoming and interfering with the weaker signals being received on the same end.
- NVP (nominal velocity of propagation): the speed of the data transmission through the tested media compared to speed of light transmission through a vacuum.
- OTDR (optical time division reflectometer): device that measures the time it takes for light to be reflected through a medium in order to detect breaks, crimps, etc.
- SNR (signal to noise ratio): comparison of signal strength to background noise. measured in dB (decibels).
- Split pair: when a wire of one pair gets spliced to the wire of an adjacent pair
- TDR (time domain reflectometer): able to measure cable lengths, distance to breaks, etc. by reflected electrical signals through a medium
- Two way NeXT: measures near-end crosstalk as well as far-end crosstalk, which is crosstalk in same direction as signal
- Wire map: verifies pin-to-pin continuity and checks for polarity reversal, short circuits, and open circuits. Displayed graphically.

Figure 15-24 Network Analyzer Functional Capabilities by OSI Model Layer

cases, devices are specific to particular layers. For example, layer 1 testers are more commonly known as **cable scanners** or cable testers, whereas devices that test layers 2 through 7 are often called **protocol analyzers.**

Monitoring—Network Baselining Tools

By combining the ability to monitor and capture SNMP, RMON, and RMON2 data from multivendor networking technology with the abilities to analyze the captured data and report on trends and exceptions, **network baselining tools** are able to track network performance over extended periods of time and report on anomalies or deviations from the accumulated baseline data. Also known as **proactive network management tools** or **network trending products,** such tools usually need several weeks of SNMP data in order to establish realistic baseline network performance averages. Network baselining tools may possess autodiscovery or auto-DNS capabilities that allow them to build graphical representations of networks by monitoring network management traffic. Such tools also exhibit characteristics such as flexible polling and event correlation that allow them to proactively seek information from network-attached devices and assimilate that information with previously collected data in order to form conclusions and make recommendations. Most network baselining tools share the results of their efforts through a wide variety of predefined and user-defined reports.

Typical reports would offer such statistics as:

- Current network volume by day, week, and month as compared with historical averages

- Network traffic volume leaders by node, actual versus expected in terms of utilization, errors, or collisions

- Nodes that are in violation of a variety of user-defined thresholds

- Predicted number of days before a node will cross a user threshold

- Nodes whose performance is degrading

Simulation—Network Modeling and Simulation Tools

Simulation software tools are also sometimes known as **performance engineering** software tools. All simulation systems share a similar trait in that the overall network performance which they are able to model is a result of the net effect of a series of mathematical formulas. These mathematical formulas represent and are derived from the actual performance of the circuits and networking equipment that comprise the final network design.

The value of a simulation system is its ability to predict the performance of various networking scenarios, otherwise known as **what-if analysis.** Simulation software uses the current network configuration as a starting point and applies what-if scenarios. The benefits of a good network simulation package include:

- Ability to spot network bottlenecks such as overworked servers, network failures, or disk capacity problems.

- Ability to test new applications and network configurations before actual deployment. New applications may run well in a controlled test environment, but may perform quite differently on the shared enterprise network.

- Ability to recreate circumstances in order to reproduce intermittent or occasional network problems.

- Ability to replicate traffic volume as well as traffic transaction type and protocol mix.

The key characteristics that distinguish simulation software are listed in Figure 15-25.

Auditing—Network Auditing Tools

Network auditing tools have not enjoyed the popularity to date of other previously described network management technology. This trend is slowly changing as network managers realize the value that network auditing tools can provide in such areas as consolidated services desks, inventory management, network management, and security. What all network auditing tools seem to have in common is the ability to provide records of which network files have been accessed by which users. The value provided by network auditing tools is sometimes provided at a performance cost. Auditing software must be installed and constantly executed on every client and server PC to be audited. The audit statistics gathered can consume significant amounts of disk space and may or may not warn of impending disk storage problems. Among the other capabilities that some, but not necessarily all, network auditing tools offer are the following:

- Keep time logs of file accesses
- Determine which users are deleting files that seem to just disappear
- Audits when users copy files to diskettes
- Ability to audit which software programs (authorized and unauthorized) are installed and/or running on any computer.

Network Simulation Software Characteristic	Importance/Explanation
Network Types	• Which different types of networks can be simulated? Circuit-switched, packet-switched, store-and-forward, packet-radio, VSAT, microwave
Network Scope	• How many of the following can the simulation software model either individually or in combination with one another? Modems and multiplexers, LANs, netware only, Internetworks, WANs, MANs
Network Services	• How many of the following advanced services can be modeled? Frame relay, ISDN (BRI and PRI), SMDS, X.25, ATM
Network Devices	• Some simulation systems have developed performance profiles of individual networking devices to the point where they can model particular networking devices (bridges, routers, muxes) made by particular manufacturers.
Network Protocols	• In addition to the network transport protocols listed in the analysis and design section, different router-to-router or WAN protocols can have a dramatic impact on network performance. Examples: RIP, OSPF, PPP
Different Data Traffic Attributes	• As studied in previous chapters, all data traffic does not have identical transmission needs or characteristics. Can the software simulate data with different traits? For example: bursty LAN data, streaming digitized voice or video, real-time transaction-oriented data, batch-oriented file transfer data.
Traffic Data Entry	• Any simulation needs traffic statistics in order to run. How these traffic statistics may be entered can make a major difference in the ease of use of the simulation system. Possibilities include manual entry by users of traffic data collected elsewhere, traffic data entered "live" through a direct interface to a protocol analyzer, a traffic generator that generates simulated traffic according to the user's parameters, or auto discovery from SNMP and RMON data generated by enterprise network management systems.
User Interface	• Many simulation software tools now offer easy-to-use graphical user interfaces with point-and-click network design capability for flexible "what-if" analysis. Some, but not all, produce graphical maps that can be output to printers or plotters. Others require users to learn a procedure-oriented programming language.
Simulation Presentation	• Some simulation tools have the ability to animate the performance of the simulated network in real time, while others perform all mathematical calculations and then play back the simulation when those calculations are complete.

Figure 15-25 Network Simulation Software Functionality

- Ability to audit only specified files and/or specified users

- Ability to integrate with security, systems management, or help desk products

- Report output format, text-based, graphical. Able to export to spreadsheet, word processing, or database products.

- Ability to track and report on configuration changes

- Ability to track logins and logouts

■ BUSINESS ISSUES

The successful implementation of a local area network management strategy requires a combination of policy, process, people, and technology. Merely throwing management technology in a vacuum at a management opportunity will not produce the desired results. What these desired results are may be a matter of perspective.

From the top-down, or business-first perspective, senior management may look to the proper management of information resources to enable a competitive advantage and to be able to deploy new network services quickly and as needed at a reasonable cost. Meanwhile, the desired result of business unit management might be that end users can successfully execute those applications that have been implemented to enable business processes and achieve business objectives. Successful execution of applications can be quantified in terms such as transactions per second, mean time between failures, average response time to database queries, and such. Such guarantees of proper execution and delivery of end-user applications are sometimes quantified in terms of a **quality of service (QOS)** guarantees. Quality of service protocol alternatives were introduced in Chapter 13. Network management personnel tend to take a more infrastructure-centric approach by concentrating on those elements of the network infrastructure that support the enterprise applications. Examples of such infrastructure components could be server performance, network traffic analysis, internetwork device performance, and WAN analysis.

How can network managers simultaneously deploy new services, control costs, provide competitive advantage, and provide guaranteed quality of service in an increasingly complicated, multi-vendor, multi-platform, multiprotocol environment? To a great extent, the answer is to combine the processes embedded in the top-down model and the network development life cycle. The top-down model forces the network manager to constantly evaluate business objectives, the nature of the applications that will meet those business objectives, the nature of the data that will support those applications, the functional requirements of the network that will deliver that data, and finally, the configuration of the technology that will provide the required network functionality. The network development life cycle forces the network manager to engage in an ongoing process of network monitoring, planning, analysis, design, modeling, and implementation based on network performance.

Network infrastructures must be flexible as well as reliable. The ability to have networks change in response to changing business conditions and opportunities is of critical importance to the successful network manager.

Cost Containment

Before a network manager can contain or reduce costs, it is first necessary to have an accurate representation of the source of those costs. Although this may sound like basic common sense, it is easier said than done, and sometimes not done at all. Figure 15-26 lists some practical suggestions for systems administration and network management cost containment.

Outsourcing

In terms of cost control, one of the key weapons in the arsenal of network managers is **outsourcing,** or the selective hiring of outside contractors to perform specific network management duties. Outsourcing is also becoming increasingly necessary for global corporations in order to cost effectively secure required systems and network support personnel throughout the world. There are several keys to outsourcing success:

- The successful identification of those processes that can be most appropriately outsourced is the first key issue. Which processes does the company really need to manage themselves and which could be more cost effectively managed by a third party? Which skills are worth investing in for the strategic needs of the corporation itself, and which skills are better hired on an as-needed basis? Which tasks can an outsourcer do more inexpensively than internal personnel? For which tasks can outsourcers supply new or on-demand expertise? Which tasks can be outsourced in order to free corporate personnel for more strategically important issues? Are there tasks that could be more effectively managed by outside experts?

- The successful management of the outsourcing process is required once network management activities have been outsourced as appropriate. It is a good idea to establish communication and evaluation mechanisms as part of the contract negotiation. Issues to be discussed include reporting requirements from the outsourcer to the customer regarding systems performance reports they are responsible for, problem resolution mechanisms, change negotiation mechanisms, performance criteria to be used for outsourcer evaluations, penalties or bonuses based on outsourcer performance.

Cost Containment Issue	Importance/Explanation
Take Inventory	• Gather accurate statistics and information as to every device including hardware and software configuration information, that is currently requiring support. • This initial inventory will produce an overall accounting of how many different platforms and standards must be supported.
Determine Support Costs	• Perform task analysis on network support personnel to determine how costly personnel are spending their time. • Are there too many fires? • Are networking personnel being managed effectively? • What is the cost of supporting multiple platforms and standards? • Are networking personnel required at all corporate sites? • Are more networking personnel required as networks become more complex?
Consolidate and Centralize	• Consolidate support personnel and deliver one-stop-support for end users. • Centralize purchasing authority. • Pool network support personnel in order to optimize use of costly personnel. • Implement centralized license metering and software distribution in order to help standardize software platforms deployed throughout the enterprise. • How can network management functions and technology be centralized in order to cap or reduce the number of network personnel required to support enterprise networks? • Centralize standardized applications on a server rather than allowing desktops to install a wide variety of applications.
Support Process Redesign	• Once task analysis has been performed on network support personnel, redesign network support processes to optimize end-user support while minimizing support costs. • Use consolidated help desk and trouble ticketing systems to organize user support efforts while minimizing fire-fighting mentality.
Standardize	• Standardize on hardware and software platforms, network architectures, network protocols, and network management platforms in order to simplify management tasks and reduce costs. • Standardized desktop platforms will lead to reduced support and maintenance costs. • Implement a software version control program so that network support people don't have to deal with multiple versions of multiple software packages.

Figure 15-26   Systems Administration and Network Management Cost Containment

- Choosing the right outsourcing provider for the right job. For example, any or all of the following areas may be outsourced, although it is unlikely that any one outsourcer could be considered as expert in all areas: application development, application maintenance, client/server systems migration, data center operation, server management, help desk operations, LAN management, end-user support, PC and workstation management, network monitoring, off-site backup and recovery, remote network access, user training and support, and WAN management. The two most common outsourcing areas are application development and data center operation, accounting for 60% of outsourcing in 1996. Among the key evaluation criteria that could be used to narrow the choices of outsourcing vendors are the following: financial stability, networking skill set, geographic coverage, customer references, pricing structure.

Flexibility

Delivering network flexibility at a reasonable cost in order to respond quickly to pending business opportunities has become a priority for many network managers. Most network managers who have achieved success in this area cite a few key underlying philosophies:

- Remove dependencies on customized or proprietary hardware and software.

- Move toward adoption of open protocols and off-the-shelf hardware and software technologies. Examples of open protocols include TCP/IP for network transport and SNMP for management information.

- Adopt network management and systems administration packages that support open APIs and can easily accommodate add-in modules.

How can such an acquisition process be managed? The top-down model provides the framework for building the technology analysis grid in which technologies to be considered are measured against requirements as dictated by the upper layers of the top-down model.

SUMMARY

Network management, like other network-related technology-based solutions, can be effectively implemented only when combined with the proper processes, people, and procedures. As information technology departments have had to become more business-oriented, network management has become more focused on cost containment. Outsourcing is one way in which costs may be contained. However, outsourcing opportunities must be properly analyzed and managed in order to ensure the delivery of quality network management.

The overall field of network management can be logically segmented into systems administration, which is most concerned with the management of clients, servers, and their installed network operating systems, whereas enterprise network management is more concerned with the elements of the enterprise network that connect these distributed systems. One solution to providing comprehensive systems administration and enterprise management services is known as the consolidated service desk.

Server management, help desk management, configuration management, desktop management, LAN management, and distributed application management are all segments of systems administration. Although each of these segments may contain unique functionality and require unique technology, there is a great deal of integration of functionality and overlap of technology.

Enterprise network management architectures and protocols can vary from one installation to the next. New architectures and protocols are under development in order to bring some order to the multi-platform, multi-vendor, multiprotocol mix of today's enterprise networks.

A variety of enterprise network management technology is available to allow network managers to be proactive rather than reactive. Besides a wide variety of enterprise network management integrated suites and element managers, other enterprise network management tools include network analyzers, network baselining tools, network modeling and simulation tools, and network auditing tools.

KEY TERMS

ACD
agent
AMS
Application MIB
application response
   measurement
applications management
   specification
ARM
automatic call distributors
bulk retrieval mechanism
cable scanners

CIM
common information model
component interface API
computer telephony integration
consolidated service desk
CTI
database MIB
DDM
definition variables
desktop management interface
desktop management task force
distributed device manager

distributed network probes
DMI
DMI services layer
DMTF
element managers
enterprise network
   management
enterprise network
   management system
event management tool
frameworks
HMMP

HMMS
HMOM
hypermedia management
  protocol
hypermedia management
  schema
Hypermedia object manger
instrumentation
integrated suites
interactive voice response unit
ISO Management Framework
IVRU
knowledge base
management information base
management information
  format
management interface API
MIB
MIF
modified object format

MOF
network analyzers
network auditing tools
network baselining tools
network modeling and
  simulation tools
network trending tool
objects
outsourcing
performance engineering
performance metrics
point products
policy-based management tools
proactive network management
  tool
protocol analyzers
QOS
quality of service
relationship variables
remote configuration

RMON MIB
RMON probe
RMON2
RMON3
search engine
secure SNMP
server capacity planning
simple management protocol
simple network management
  protocol
SMP
SNMP
SNMP2
state variables
systems administration
WBEM
web-based enterprise
  management
what-if analysis

REVIEW QUESTIONS

1. Describe some of the business-oriented pressures faced by network managers as well as some of the responses to those pressures.
2. What are some of the advantages and disadvantages to outsourcing?
3. Differentiate between systems administration and enterprise network management.
4. Differentiate between the various layers of management defined by the OSI management framework.
5. What is a consolidated service desk and what unique functionality or advantages does it offer? How does it differ from previous network management technologies?
6. What are some of the important advantages and disadvantages of server management software?
7. Why is it important for help desk software to be able to integrate with call center technology?
8. What is the difference between a knowledge base and a search engine and why are each important?
9. What are the unique features of policy-based management tools and what is the significance of such features?

10. What is the purpose and structure of the DMI?
11. How does desktop management software functionality differ from enterprise network management software functionality?
12. What are the key limitations of distributed application management and how are these limitations overcome?
13. What is the difference between distributed device management and centralized enterprise network management?
14. What disadvantage of centralized network management does distributed network management attempt to overcome?
15. Differentiate between the following terms: agent, MIB, RMON, object, SNMP.
16. What is a distributed network probe and how does it differ from an SNMP agent or an RMON probe?
17. What is CIM and what interoperability issues does it hope to overcome?
18. Describe the relationship between the various components of WBEM.
19. What are some of the shortcomings of SNMP and how are they overcome in SNMP2?

20. Why has SNMP2 not been widely accepted and implemented?
21. Differentiate between RMON and RMON2.
22. Differentiate between point products, frameworks, and integrated suites as alternate enterprise network management technology architectures.
23. What are some of the most important functional characteristics of enterprise network management systems?
24. What are some of the important functional characteristics of network analyzers?
25. What is the difference between a cable scanner and a protocol analyzer?
26. What is the overall purpose or value of a network baselining tool?
27. What is the overall purpose or value of a network modeling and simulation tool?
28. What are some of the ways in which current network configuration information can be loaded into a network modeling and simulation package?
29. What is the overall purpose of network auditing tools?
30. Why are network auditing tools becoming more popular than they once were?

ACTIVITIES

1. Investigate the current status of SNMP2. Is the IETF still working on the standard? What are businesses doing in the meantime? What are the key issues that are the cause of debate?
2. Survey businesses or organizations that have implemented enterprise network management systems? Which enterprise network management system was chosen? Why? With which third-party network management systems (if any) does the enterprise system interface? What functionality of the enterprise network management system has actually been implemented? What do the organizations feel has been the benefit of these systems? What has been the investment in terms of effort to implement and support these systems?
3. Investigate the current state of the desktop management systems market. What percentage of products support the DMI architecture? What percentage of products interface directly to enterprise network management systems? Does one product have a dominant market share? Analyze and report on your results.
4. Research the outsourcing phenomenon. Is outsourcing still increasing in popularity? What has been learned about the advantages and disadvantages of outsourcing? Which types of activities are most often outsourced? Find an organization that has hired an outsourcer and interview them. Find a company that provides outsourcing services and interview them. Do you think outsourcing is a passing phenomenon?
5. Review currently available help desk technology and report on your findings. Find a corporation using help desk software and determine how well the software fits the corporation's business processes and policies. Investigate the technology selection process to determine whether evaluation criteria were established before the purchase.
6. Review currently available policy-based management technology and report on your findings. Find a corporation using policy-based management software and determine how well the software fits the corporation's business processes and policies. Investigate the technology selection process to determine whether evaluation criteria were established before the purchase.
7. Investigate the field of distributed application management. Has the percentage of applications managed via embedded instrumentation increased? Are application developers including more embedded instrumentation within their applications? Survey corporations in your area to determine how many are using or planning to use distributed application management.
8. Investigate the current status and availability of products supporting the WBEM architecture.

9. Investigate the extent to which network simulation, network baselining, and network auditing tools are being used by corporations in your area. What common characteristics do the corporations using these tools share?

CASE STUDY

Sun Managers Improve Network Health with Concord

When applications start bogging down, everybody blames the network—regardless of whether the network deserves it.

Network managers at Sun Microsystems became tired of fending off user complaints. They wanted to prove that the slowness Sun's employees were experiencing was caused by applications and databases, not by the network.

"The user's perception is often way out of whack with what the reality is," says Curt Conrad, network consultant for Sun's Chelmsford, Mass., and Burlington, Mass., offices. To the user, "the network is always guilty until proven innocent," he says.

Several months ago, Sun installed Concord Communications' Network Health to watch its LANs and WANs. Running on Windows NT, Sun Solaris and HP-UX, Network Health software can generate reports about the performance and utilization of various parts of the network to display where prob-

lem spots are—or are not. The software can also show how well the network is meeting customer-defined service levels, how available servers are and which applications or users are driving network traffic.

Conrad says that since the installation, there have been a half-dozen cases in which he's proven the problem was else where. A user claimed that multiple 100M bit/sec links were necessary to improve response time, for example, but that wasn't really the case. Network Health showed that only 5M bit/sec was being used, Conrad says.

Still, the delays users are running into are real—they're just being caused by something else, typically the database, Conrad says. "A lot of times we're finding these databases aren't built for the wide area. They're very chatty, and they use small packets," he says.

Most of the critical applications at the Massachusetts offices are internally devel-

oped business applications for placing orders, running finances and monitoring manufacturing data. The applications are supported by Oracle and Sybase databases, and Sun's developers can often avoid the latency problems by tuning their in-house applications to run better over the wide area, Conrad says.

Last week, Sun began moving about 600 employees from its Chelmsford office to Burlington, bringing the total number of users in Burlington to 2,300 and the total number of servers to 600.

Sun plans to use the Concord software to monitor this expanded network, which uses a design the company hasn't employed in the past. Before now, Sun hasn't had a network composed exclusively of Cisco Catalyst 5500 switches, so the network managers will be watching the Burlington network carefully to ensure that it holds up under the added load. The Concord software should help the managers determine if their design is a good one, Conrad says.

The network at the Burlington site will have a high capacity. Naturally, most of the desktop systems are Sun workstations, connected via 10M bit/sec or 100M bit/sec Ethernet to the Catalyst 5500s.

In turn, these boxes are connected to a backbone over two Fast Ethernet links bound together using Cisco's proprietary Fast EtherChannel technology. Fast EtherChannel groups multiple lines together into a single logical pipe. The backbone switches are linked to each other with four Fast Ethernet lines.

Sun plans to upgrade its backbone to Catalyst 8540 switches by next summer, in order to replace the Fast EtherChannel links with Gigabit Ethernet.

FUTURE MAPPING

Conrad says the Concord software will help network managers plan for expansion. "We can begin to see where the utilization of WAN and metropolitan-area network links might creep up, and we might have to resize them," he says. Currently, the Burlington site has a T-3 (45M bit/sec) WAN connection via a Cisco 7507 router.

Network managers monitor traffic up to the edge of the WAN, says Paul Bresten, information resource manager for Sun. The Concord software replaces a hodge-podge of net management tools the firm was using, including Bay Networks' Optivity and internally developed scripts.

While Sun is pleased with Network Health as a product, its pricing structure is a different issue. Determining how much to pay for licenses was a "nightmare," Conrad says.

Concord bases pricing on the number of network elements—down to the interface level—that users wants to manage. Determining the number was difficult in a network of Sun's size and complexity, Conrad says. Ultimately, Sun paid $85,000 for 500 licenses. He says it is worth it to quell users' fears about network bandwidth. "That, to me, has no price," he says.

Source: Jeff Caruso, "Sun Managers Improve Network Health with Concord," Network World, vol. 15, no. 47 (November 23, 1998), p. 23. Copyright Network World. Reprinted by permission.

BUSINESS CASE STUDY QUESTIONS

Activities
1. Complete a top-down model for this case by gleaning facts from the case and placing them in the proper layer of the top-down model. After completing the top-down model, analyze and detail those instances where requirements were clearly passed down from upper layers to lower layers of the model and where solutions to those requirements were passed up from lower layers to upper layers of the model.
2. Detail any questions about the case that may occur to you for which answers are not clearly stated in the article.

Business
1. What was the business motivation on the part of the network managers?

2. What were the users' perceptions of the problem?
3. How can service level agreements be monitored and confirmed?
4. How is pricing for the network monitoring software determined?
5. How easily and objectively could a cost/benefit analysis be performed?

Application
1. What were the typical applications run in this environment?
2. What type of databases were these applications typically written over?
3. What is latency and what role does it play in determining application performance over a WAN?

Data

1. What are the typical causes of performance delays?
2. How can database design affect application performance over a wide area network?

Network

1. What is the Network Health software capable of providing in terms of information?
2. What network architecture(s) are employed on this network at the desktop and on the backbone?
3. What is FastEtherChannel?

Technology

1. What technology was installed?
2. On which platforms was the network management technology installed?
3. How will the network monitoring software help managers plan for expansion?

CHAPTER 16

LOCAL AREA NETWORK SECURITY

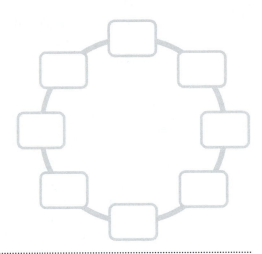

Concepts Reinforced
....

OSI Model	Internet Suite of Protocols Model
Top-Down Model	Standards and Protocols

Concepts Introduced
....

Security Policy Development	Virus Protection
Security Architecture	Security Principles
Firewalls	Authentication
Encryption	Applied Security Technology

OBJECTIVES

After mastering the material in this chapter you should:

1. Understand the many processes involved with the development of a comprehensive security policy and security architecture

2. Understand the importance of a well-developed and implemented security policy and associated people processes to effective security technology implementation

3. Understand the concepts, protocols, standards, and technology related to virus protection

4. Understand the concepts, protocols, standards, and technology related to firewalls

5. Understand the concepts, protocols, standards, and technology related to authentication

749

6. Understand the concepts, protocols, standards, and technology related to encryption

■ INTRODUCTION

As interest and activity concerning the Internet have mushroomed, and as telecommuters and remote users increasingly need access to corporate data, network security has become a dominant topic in data communications. As the various processes, concepts, protocols, standards, and technology associated with network security are reviewed in this chapter, it is important to remember the importance of people and their basic honesty and integrity as the underlying foundation for any successful network security implementation. Merely throwing network security technology at a problem without the benefit of a comprehensive, vigorously enforced network security policy including sound business processes will surely not produce desired results. As the saying goes, such action "is like putting a steel door on a grass hut."

■ BUSINESS IMPACT

What is the impact on business when network security is violated by on-line thieves? Consider these facts:

- According to federal law enforcement estimates, more than $10 billion worth of data is stolen annually in the United States.

- 60,000 credit and calling card numbers were stolen in a single incident.

- 50% of computer crimes are committed by a company's current or ex-employees.

One of the problems with gauging the true business impact of security breaches is that many companies are understandably reluctant to publicly admit that they have suffered significant losses due to failed network security. Network security is a business problem. It is not merely a network problem or an information technology problem. The development and implementation of a sound network security policy must start with strategic business assessment followed by strong management support throughout the policy development and implementation stages.

However, this management support for network security policy development and implementation cannot be assumed. For example, 71% of executives surveyed stated that they lacked confidence in the ability of their company's network security to fend off attacks from within or without. This stated lack of confidence has not translated into an infusion of support for network security efforts. From the same survey previously referenced, 73% of responding companies had three or fewer employees dedicated to network security, while 55% of respondents said that less than 5% of their information technology budgets went to network security. Enterprise network security goals must be set by corporate presidents and/or board of directors. The real leadership of the corporation must define the vision and allocate sufficient resources to send a clear message that corporate information and network resources are valuable corporate assets that must be properly protected.

■ SECURITY POLICY DEVELOPMENT

The Security Policy Development Life Cycle

One methodology for the development of a comprehensive network security policy is known as the **security policy development life cycle (SPDLC).** As illustrated in Figure 16-1, the SPDLC is aptly depicted as a cycle because evaluation processes validate the effectiveness of original analysis stages. Feedback from evaluation stages causes renewed analysis with possible ripple effects of changes in architecture or implemented technology. The feedback provided by such a cycle is ongoing, but will only work with proper training and commitment from the people responsible for the various processes depicted in the SPDLC.

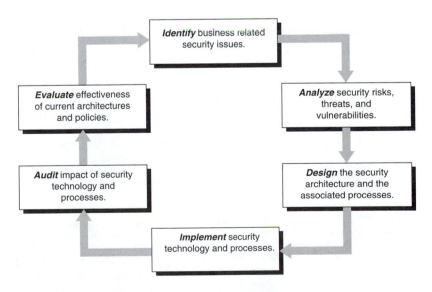

Figure 16-1   The Security Policy Development Life Cycle

Each of the processes identified in the SPDLC is explained further in Figure 16-2.

A successful network security implementation requires a marriage of technology and process. Roles and responsibilities and corporate standards for business processes and acceptable network-related behavior must be clearly defined, effectively shared, universally understood, and vigorously enforced in order for implemented network security technology to be

SPDLC Process	Explanation/Importance
Identification of Business-Related Security Issues	• Security requirements assessment • What do we have to lose? • What do we have worth stealing? • Where are the security holes in our business processes? • How much can we afford to lose? • How much can we afford to spend on network security?
Analysis of Security Risks, Threats, Vulnerabilities	• Information Asset Evaluation—what do you have that's worth protecting? • Network Architecture Documentation—What is the current state of your network? • How many unauthorized modems are dialing in? • Identify all assets, threats, and vulnerabilities. • Determine risks and create protective measures.
Architecture and Process Design	• Logical design of security architecture and associated processes. • What must be the required functionality of the implemented technology? • What business processes implemented and monitored by people must complement this security architecture?
Security Technology and Process Implementation	• Choose security technology based on logical design requirements. • Implement all security technology with complementary people processes. • Increase the overall awareness of network security, and implement training. • Design an ongoing education process for all employees, including senior management.
Audit Impact of Security Technology and Processes	• Ensure that implemented policy and technology are meeting initial goals. • Institute a method to identify exceptions to security policy standards and deal with these exceptions swiftly.
Evaluate Effectiveness of Current Architecture and Processes	• Based on results of ongoing audits, evaluate effectiveness of current policy and architecture of meeting high-level goals. • Adjust policy and architecture as required and renew the cycle.

Figure 16-2   Processes of the Security Policy Development Life Cycle

effective. Process definition and setting of corporate security standards must precede technology evaluation and implementation.

Security Requirements Assessment

Proper security requirements assessment implies that appropriate security processes and technology have been applied for any given user group's access to/from any potential corporate information resource. The proper development and application of these security processes and technology require a structured approach in order to ensure that all potential user group/information resource combinations have been considered.

To begin to define security requirements and the potential solutions to those requirements, a network analyst can create a matrix grid mapping all potential user groups against all potential corporate information resources. An example of such a security requirements assessment grid is illustrated in Figure 16-3. The user groups and corporate information resources form the row and column headings of the grid, and the intersections of these rows and columns will be the suggested security processes and policies required for each unique user group/information resource combination. These security processes refer not just to restrictions to information access imposed

User Group	Legacy Data Access	Intranet Access	Internet-Inbound Access	Internet-Outbound Access	Global E-Mail Access
Corporate HQ Employees					
Executives					
I.S. Development Staff					
Network Management					
Network Technicians					
Dept. Management					
End Users					
Remote Branch Employees					
Telecommuters					
Trading Partners					
Customers					
Vendors					
Browsers					
Casual Browsers					
Prospective Customers					
Consultants and Outsourcers					

Figure 16-3 Security Requirements Assessment Grid

upon each user group, but also to the responsibilities of each user group for security policy implementation and enforcement. Another category of information for each intersection would be the security technology to be applied to each unique user group/information resource combination in order to implement the documented security processes.

The security requirements assessment grid is meant to provide only an example of potential user groups and information resource categories. The grid should be modified to provide an accurate reflection of each different corporate security environment. Furthermore, the grid should be used as a dynamic strategic planning tool. It should be reviewed on a periodic basis and should be modified to reflect changes in either user groups or information resources. Only through ongoing auditing, monitoring, evaluation, and analysis, can a security requirements assessment plan remain accurate and reflective of a changing corporate network environment.

Scope Definition and Feasibility Studies

Before proceeding blindly with a security policy development project, it is important to properly define the scope or limitations of the project. In some cases, this scope may be defined in advance due to a management edict to develop a corporate-wide security policy perhaps in response to an incident of breached security. In other cases, feasibility studies may be performed in advance of the decision that determines the scope of the full security policy development effort.

The pilot project or feasibility study provides an opportunity to gain vital information on the difficulty of the security policy development process as well as the assets (human and financial) required to maintain such a process. In addition, vital information concerning corporate culture, especially management attitudes, and its readiness to assist in the development and implementation of corporate network security can be gathered. Only after the feasibility study has been completed can one truly assess the magnitude of the effort and assets required to complete a wider-scope policy development effort.

One of the key issues addressed during scope definition or feasibility studies is deciding on the balance between security and productivity. Security measures that are too stringent can be just as damaging to user productivity as can a total lack of enforced security measures. The optimal balance point that is sought is the proper amount of implemented security process and technology that will adequately protect corporate information resources while optimizing user productivity. Figure 16-4 attempts to graphically depict this balance.

Another issue commonly dealt with during the scope definition stage is the identification of those key values that a corporation expects an implemented security policy and associated technology to be able to deliver. By defining these key values during scope definition, policy and associated

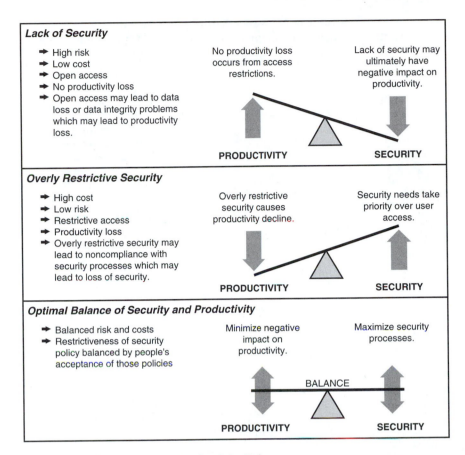

Figure 16-4   Security versus Productivity Balance

architecture can be developed to ensure that each of these values is maintained. These key values represent the objectives or intended outcomes of the security policy development effort. Figure 16-5 lists and briefly explains the five most typical fundamental values of network security policy development.

Yet another way to organize an approach to security policy and architecture development is to use a model or framework such as **ISO 7498/2,** the **OSI security architecture.** This framework maps 14 different security services to specific layers of the OSI 7-layer reference model. The OSI model security architecture can be used as an open framework in which to categorize security technology and protocols, just as the OSI 7-layer model can be used to categorize internetworking technology and protocols. Although more specific and varying slightly in terminology from the five fundamental values listed in Figure 16-5, the OSI security architecture is consistent with and includes all of these fundamental values. As illustrated in Figure 16-6, the ISO 7498/2 security architecture could be used as a grid or checklist to

Value of Network Security Policy Development	Explanation/Implication
Identification/Authentication	Want to be assured that users can be accurately identified and that only authenticated users are allowed access to corporate resources
Access Control/Authorization	Want to be assured that even authenticated users are only allowed access to those information and network resources they are supposed to access
Privacy/Confidentiality	Want to be assured that network-based communication is private and not subject to eaves-dropping
Data Integrity	Want to be assured that data are genuine and cannot be changed without proper controls
Non-Repudiation	Want to be assured that users cannot deny the occurrence of given events or transactions

Figure 16-5   Fundamental Values of Network Security Policy Development

assess whether the listed security service has been provided for each associated OSI model layer protocols and by what technologies each service is to be provided. Not all services will necessarily be provided to all suggested layers in all corporate settings. This does not diminish the values of the OSI security architecture as a planning framework, however.

Assets, Threats, Vulnerabilities, and Risks

Although Figure 16-4 graphically illustrates the theoretical goal of the security policy development process—balance between productivity and security—how can such a balance actually be delineated within the context of a structured methodology such as the security requirements assessment grid? Most security policy development methodologies boil down to the following six major steps:

1. Identify assets

2. Identify threats

3. Identify vulnerabilities

4. Consider the risks

5. Identify risk domains

6. Take protective measures

ISO 7498/2 Security Architecture	Associated OSI Model Layer(s)
Peer Entity Authentication: Verifies that a peer entity in an association is the one claimed. Verification is provided to the next layer.	Application, Transport Network
Data Origin Authentication: Verifies that the source of the data is as claimed. Verification is provided to the next layer.	Application, Transport Network
Access Control Service: This service protects against unauthorized access of network resources, including by authenticated users.	Application, Transport Network
Connection Confidentiality: Provides for the confidentiality of all data at a given layer for their connection to a peer layer elsewhere, provided primarily by encryption technology.	Application, Transport Network, Data Link
Connectionless Confidentiality: Same security as above applied to connectionless communication environment.	Application, Transport Network, DataLink
Selective Field Confidentiality: Provides for the confidentiality of selected fields of application level information on a connection; for example, a customer's PIN (Personal ID Number) on an ATM transaction.	Application, Transport Network, Data Link
Traffic Flow Confidentiality: Protects against unauthorized traffic analysis such as capture of source and destination addresses.	Application, Network Physical
Connection Integrity with Recovery: Provides for data integrity for data on a connection at a given time and detects any modifications with recovery attempted.	Application, Transport
Connection Integrity without Recovery: Same as above except no recovery attempted.	Application, Transport Network
Selective Field Connection Integrity: Provides for the integrity of selected fields transferred over a connection and determines whether the fields have been modified in any manner.	Application
Connectionless Integrity: Provides integrity assurances to the layer above it, and may also determine if any modifications have been performed. Network may also determine if any modifications have been performed.	Application, Transport Network
Selective Field Connectionless Integrity: Provides for the integrity of selected fields and may also determine if any modifications have been performed.	Application
Nonrepudiation, Origin: The recipient of the data is provided with proof of the origin of the data. Provides protection against the sender denying the transmission of the data.	Application
Nonrepudiation, Delivery: The sender is provided with proof that the data were delivered. Protects against attempts by the recipient to falsify the data or deny receipt of the data.	Application

Figure 16-6   OSI 7498/2 Security Architecture

The terms used within these six major steps are related in a process-oriented manner.

Assets are corporate property of some value that require varying degrees of protection. In the case of network security, assets most often include corporate data and the network hardware, software, and media used to transport and store that data.

Data or Information Classification   The most common asset to be protected in an information systems environment is the information or data itself, so it is important that an organization adopt an information classification scheme that is easily understood and globally implemented. As will be seen in the discussion of security architectures, properly classified data are an input assumption for a security architecture. If information is not properly classified, the security architecture will be unable to protect it appropriately. Most information classification schemes are based on some variation of the classification scheme used by the Department of Defense:

- Unclassified or Public—Information that is readily available to the public. No restrictions as to storage, transmission, or distribution.

- Sensitive—Information whose release could not damage the corporation but could cause potential embarrassment or measurable harm to individuals. Salary and benefits data would be examples of sensitive data.

- Confidential—Information whose release could cause measurable damage to the corporation. Corporate strategic plans and contracts would be considered confidential.

- Secret—Information whose release could cause serious damage to a corporation. Trade secrets or engineering diagrams would be examples of secret information.

- Top Secret—Information whose release could cause grave or permanent damage. Release of such information could literally put a company out of business. Secret formulas for key products would be considered top secret.

Threats are processes or people that pose a potential danger to identified assets. A given asset can be potentially threatened by numerous threats. Threats can be intentional or unintentional, natural or man-made. Network-related threats include hackers, line outages, fires, floods, power failures, equipment failures, and dishonest or incompetent employees.

Vulnerabilities are the manner or path by which threats are able to attack assets. Vulnerabilities can be thought of as weak links in the overall security architecture and should be identified for every potential threat/asset combination. Vulnerabilities that have been identified can be blocked.

Once vulnerabilities have been identified, how should a network analyst proceed in developing defenses to these vulnerabilities? Which vulnerabilities should be dealt with first? How can a network analyst determine an objective means to prioritize vulnerabilities? By considering the **risk,** or probability of a particular threat successfully attacking a particular asset in a given amount of time via a particular vulnerability, network analysts are able to quantify the relative importance of threats and vulnerabilities. A word of caution, however; risk analysis is a specialized field of study, and quantification of risks should not be viewed as an exact science. In identifying the proper prioritization of threats and vulnerabilities to be dealt with, network analysts should combine subjective instincts and judgment with objective risk analysis data.

A **risk domain** consists of a unique group of networked systems sharing both common business function and common elements of exposure. These common business functions and risk are identified during initial risk analysis or assessment. Risk domains are differentiated or isolated from each other based on the differences in risks associated with each risk domain. Because each risk domain has unique business functions and risks, it would stand to reason that each should have a uniquely designed set of technology control processes and technology to offer the required level of security for that particular risk domain. The column headings in Figure 16-3 could be considered potential risk domains. Risk domains are important to security analysts because of their use in organizing security strategies and technology.

Once the order in which threats and vulnerabilities will be attacked has been determined, **protective measures** are designed that effectively block the vulnerability in order to prevent threats from attacking assets. Recalling that multiple vulnerabilities (paths) may exist between a given asset and a given threat, it should be obvious that multiple protective measures may need to be established between given threat/asset combinations. Among the major categories of potential protective measures are:

- Virus protection

- Firewalls

- Authentication

- Encryption

An explanation of each of these categories of protective measures, as well as examples and applications of each category, are supplied in the remainder of this chapter. Figure 16-7 illustrates the relationships between assets, threats, vulnerabilities, risks, and protective measures.

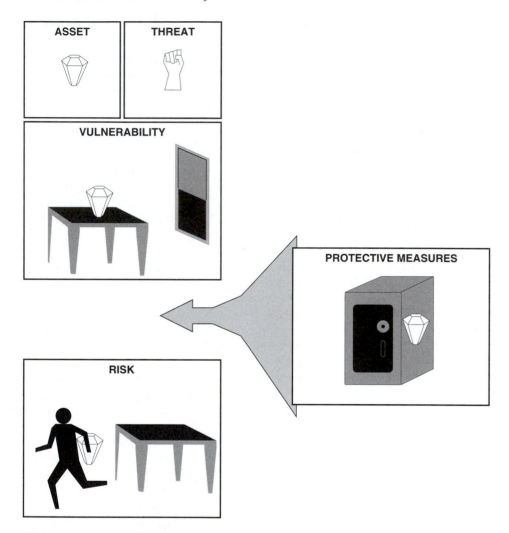

Figure 16-7   Assets, Threats, Vulnerabilities, Risks, and Protective Measures

Attack Strategies

Attack strategies often concentrate on vulnerabilities of specific network operating systems. For example, attack strategies for NetWare servers differ from those intended for Windows NT or Unix servers. Often, such attack strategies are shared openly on the Internet. In order to understand how to properly protect servers, it is important to use all possible means to discover the server's vulnerabilities. Paying attention to hackers' forums on the Internet is one way to stay on top of these issues.

Figure 16-8 lists some of the more common attack strategies as well as potential protective measures.

Network/Information System Attack Strategies	Protective Measure
Masquerading	Authentication
Eavesdropping	Encryption
Man-in-the-Middle-Attack	Digital certificates, digital signatures
Address Spoofing	Firewalls
Data Diddling	Encrypted message digest
Dictionary Attack	Strong passwords, intruder detection
Replay Attack	Time stamping or sequence numbering
Virus Attack	Virus management policy
Trojan Horse Attack	Firewalls
Denial of Service Attack	Authentication, service filtering

Figure 16-8   Network/Information System Vulnerabilities and Protective Measures

Rather than attacking a specific network operating system, some hackers choose to attack the underlying transport protocols used to communicate between servers. The most common transport protocol is **TCP** or **transmission control protocol.** When two servers that are communicating via TCP wish to set up a connection to each other, they engage in a three-step exchange of addresses and confirmations known as a **three-way handshake.** The following two attack strategies take advantage of this three-way handshake in slightly different ways:

- **Denial of service attack:** In the denial of service attack, the hacker floods the server with requests to connect to other servers that do not exist. The server tries to establish connections with the nonexistent servers and wait for a response while being flooded with thousands of other bogus connection requests. This causes the server to deny service to legitimate users because it is overwhelmed trying to handle the bogus requests.

- **Land attack:** The land attack is a variation on the denial of service attack in which the hacker substitutes the targeted server's own address as the address of the server requesting a connection. This causes the attacked server to constantly try to establish connections to itself, thereby often crashing the server.

Web Specific Attack Strategies   All web servers employ some type of operating or network operating system and are subject to any of the previously mentioned attack strategies. In addition, there are other web-specific vulnerabilities and associated attack strategies. In order to minimize the possibility of attack the following techniques should be considered:

- Eliminate all unused user accounts, especially default accounts such as GUEST.

- Remove or disable all unused services such as FTP, Telnet, and Gopher. If such services must be enabled, consider installing a Proxy server or application layer firewall.

- Remove unused Unix command shells and interpreters so that hackers can't access the web server's operating system directly.

- Be sure that permission levels on files and directories are properly set. Default permissions often grant access to too many user groups or individual user accounts.

- Consult WWW Security Frequently Asked Questions (FAQ) sites on an ongoing basis to stay up-to-date with current attack strategies and defenses.

- Common Gateway Interface (CGI) programs are capable of extracting a Unix-based web server's password file.

- Server Side Includes (SSIs) can be embedded in web pages such as guest books and can instruct a web server to remove an entire directory's contents.

Management Role and Responsibilities

Once the scope of the security policy development effort has been determined and assets, threats, vulnerabilities, risks, and protective measures have been identified, it is time to secure management buy-in for the security policy development process before proceeding any further. Results of the feasibility study will form the basis of the presentation for management.

Be certain that this presentation for management is objective and that any estimates of financial losses owing to security threats can be substantiated. You will be asking for financial and moral support from management. Your success at securing this support will be a simple matter of management's perception of the cost/benefit analysis of your threat/asset/protective measure scenarios. In other words, have you clearly proven that the costs involved to provide protective measures for corporate assets are outweighed by the benefits of ensuring proper protection of those assets?

Having substantiated the existence of security threats and vulnerabilities, you can propose your plan of action to develop and implement a solution. It is important not to underestimate the labor resources and time requirements necessary to scale up your security analysis from a limited scope feasibility study to a full-fledged enterprise-wide security policy development and implementation process.

But what are the responsibilities of executives and managers beyond merely approving budgets and providing policy enforcement? Figure 16-9 provides a brief list of key executive responsibilities, whereas Figure 16-10 provides a brief list of management responsibilities. Each list was summarized from publications available from the National Institute of Standards and Technology. The NIST publishes a series of Federal Information Processing Standards (FIPS) as well as a series of special publications on a variety of computer and network security-related topics.

Policy Development Process

It is important to reiterate that although technology may well be implemented as part of the protective measures to eliminate vulnerabilities and protect assets from their associated threats, it is the processes and policies associated with each of those protective measures that determine the success or failure of a network security policy implementation.

Executive's Responsibilities for Protection of Information Resources

1. Set the security policy (acceptable use policy) of the entire organization.

2. Allocate sufficient staff, funding, and positive incentives to successfully implement policy.

3. State the value of information as a corporate resource to your organization.

4. Demonstrate your organization's commitment to the protection of its information resources.

5. Make it clear that the protection of the corporate information resources is everyone's responsibility.

6. Assign ultimate responsibility for information and network security to specific individuals.

7. Require computer and network security and awareness training.

8. Hold employees personally responsible for the resources in their care, including network access and corporate information.

9. Monitor and assess security through external and internal audits (over and covert).

10. State and follow through on penalties for nonadherence to network security policies.

11. Lead by example.

Figure 16-9   Executive's Responsibilities for Protection of Information Resources. Excerpted from NIST Special Publication SP 500-169: *Executive Guide to the Protection of Information Resources.*

Management's Responsibilities for Protection of Information Resources

1. Assess the consequences of a security breach in the area for which you are responsible. Risks include: inability or impairment to perform necessary duties; waste, misuse, or theft of funds or resources; and internal or external loss of credibility.

2. Find the optimal balance between security needs and productivity needs.

3. Assess vulnerabilities. How long can each information resource be unavailable before business processes become threatened?

4. Ensure data integrity within the systems for which you are responsible.

5. Maintain required confidentiality and data privacy.

6. Ensure that nonrepudiation and auditing are present in the systems for which you are responsible.

7. Adhere by and enforce corporate acceptable use policies.

Figure 16-10   Management's Responsibilities for the Protection of Information Resources. Excerpted from NIST Special Publication SP 500-170: *Management Guide to the Protection of Information Resources.*

Be sure that all affected user groups are represented on the policy development task force. Start from a business perspective with a positive philosophy and a universally supportable goal (e.g., "The purpose of this policy is to protect our vital corporate resources in order to ensure that we can all keep our jobs. This is in our collective best interests."). The emphasis should be on corporate-wide awareness and shared values of the importance of protecting corporate resources such as information and network access. The policy should not be portrayed as administrative edicts to be obeyed under consequence of termination.

Areas that may be considered for development of acceptable use policies are listed in Figure 16-11.

The list of suggested areas for policy development in Figure 16-11 is not meant to be exhaustive or all-inclusive. Each corporation should amend such a list to include those areas of policy development most appropriate to their corporation. Once policies have been developed for those agreed-upon areas, those policies should be measured against the user group/information resource matrix produced in the security requirements assessment grid (Figure 16-3) to be sure that all potential needs for acceptable use policies have been met.

Policy Implementation Process

Once policies have been developed, it is up to all employees to support those policies in their own way. The required types of support of executives and

Potential Areas for Development of Acceptable Use Policies

1. Password protection and management (i.e., it is against corporate policy to write your password on a Post-it note and paste it to your monitor; it is against corporate policy to allow anyone else to use your userid or password)

2. Software license policy (policies on using illegal or pirated software on corporate machines, policy on use of shareware on corporate machines, policy regarding who is allowed to install any type of software on corporate machines)

3. Virus protection policy (policies re: use of diskettes on network attached PCs, use of corporate computing resources by consultants and outsource personnel, related to Internet access policies)

4. Internet access policy (policies re: acceptable use of Internet for corporate business)

5. Remote access policy (policies re: use of single use passwords, Smart Cards, secure transfer of corporate data)

6. E-mail policy (policies re: enrollment in e-mail news groups, personal use of e-mail systems)

7. Policies regarding penalties, warnings, and enforcements for violation of corporate acceptable use policies

8. Physical access policies (policies re: access to locked areas, offices, computer and telecom rooms, combinations for limited access areas, visitor policies, logging out or locking keyboard when leaving office)

Figure 16-11   Potential Areas for Development of Acceptable Use Policies

managers were listed in Figures 16-9 and 16-10, respectively. Having been included in the policy development process, users should also be expected to actively support the implemented acceptable use policies. Users' responsibilities for the protection of information resources are included in Figure 16-12.

Organizing Policy Implementation: The Security Architecture   Once security policy has been determined, appropriate technology and associated processes must be implemented in order to execute that policy. It is difficult to organize all security technologies and processes and map them to security policies without overlooking something. What is a required is an overall security model or architecture that starts with business drivers and ends with a combination of available security tools, mapping policy to processes and technology controls.

A security architecture implies an open framework into which business-driven security processes and requirements can be quickly and easily organized, now or in the future. Security architectures map clearly justified security functional requirements to currently available security technical solutions. Security architectures imply that standardized security solutions have been predefined for a given corporation's variety of computing and

Users' Responsibilities for Protection of Information Resources

1. You are ultimately responsible for protecting the data to which you have access.

2. Know which information is especially sensitive or confidential. When in doubt, ask.

3. Information is a valuable, shared corporate asset—as valuable as buildings, stock price, sales, or financial reserves.

4. The computing resources that the company provides for you are the property of the company and should be used only for purposes that benefit the company directly.

5. Familiarize yourself with and abide by the acceptable use policies of your company.

6. Understand that you will be held accountable for whatever actions you take with corporate computing or networking resources.

7. If you ever observe anything or anyone unusual or suspicious, inform your supervisor immediately.

8. Never share your password or userID with anyone.

9. If you are allowed to choose a password, choose one that could not be easily guessed.

10. Always log off before leaving your computer or terminal.

11. Keep sensitive information, whether on diskettes or on paper, under lock and key.

12. Don't allow others to look over your shoulder if you are working on something confidential.

13. Don't smoke, eat, or drink near computer equipment.

14. Know the location of the nearest fire extinguisher.

15. Backup your data onto diskettes early and often.

Figure 16-12 Users' Responsibilities for the Protection of Information Resources. Excerpted from NIST Special Publication SP 500-171: *Computer Users' Guide to the Protection of Information Resources.*

network platforms. In this manner, security solutions are implemented consistently across an enterprise without the need for security personnel to become personally involved in every implementation. The use of a well-designed security architecture should provide a more secure and cost-effective information systems environment.

Information systems architectures in general, and information security architectures in particular, separate business needs from the logical requirements that meet those business needs and the physically implemented technology that meets those logical requirements. In doing so, the architecture enables security analysts to separately analyze these major elements of the security architecture while understanding the relationship between the various layers of the architecture. This allows the architecture to stand the test of time by allowing changing business drivers to be mapped to changing logical requirements to be mapped to changing security technology without having to change the overall architecture into which all of these changing elements are organized. As new threats or vulnerabilities are discovered, a well-designed security architecture should provide some structure to the manner in which protective measures are designed to counteract these new threats and vulnerabilities.

Information security architectures could, and perhaps should, vary from one organization to the next. Figure 16-13 is a representative example of a security architecture that clearly maps business and technical drivers through security policy and processes to implemented security technology. One or more of the layers of the security architecture could be subsequently expanded into more detailed multi-layer models. Figure 16-14 explains each layer of the representative architecture in terms of the significance of each layer as well as the relationships or impacts between layers.

At this point, an effective security policy, including associated technology and processes, should have been developed and be ready for implementation. If user involvement was substantial during the policy development stage and if buy-in was ensured at each stage of the policy development,

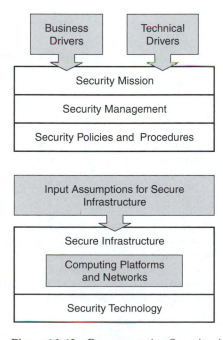

Figure 16-13   Representative Security Architecture

Security Architecture Layer	Importance/Implication/Examples
Business and Technical Drivers	Business drivers are inherited from the corporation's overall strategic business plan. The security architecture must play its part in the achievement of the corporation's overall business mission. Technical drivers are enablers or limiting factors that determine the extent to which technology can contribute to the security architecture's achievement of the overall corporate business mission.
Security Mission	The security mission is the definition of the role of the security architecture as driven by the business and technical drivers. An example would be: "To enable secure information sharing and protect information resources throughout the corporate enterprise."
Security Management	Security management bridges the gap between the high-level security mission statement and the policies and procedures that actually implement and achieve the security mission. These are the parts of the security architecture that do not change, even though security policies and procedures may change. Examples include: communications mechanisms, educational programs, and other efforts that ensure that security policies and procedures are well understood, widely observed, and strictly enforced.
Security Policies and Procedures	Security policies and procedures are meant to protect identified assets from identified threats by neutralizing identified vulnerabilities through the implementation of appropriate protective measures.
Input Assumptions for Secure Infrastructure	Examples of input assumptions might be the following: • All information will be properly classified prior to entering the secure infrastructure so that the secure infrastructure is able to handle each type of information classification accordingly. • All users will be properly categorized in terms of what resources they have a right to access, so that if the secure infrastructure properly authenticates an individual, it will know what resources that individual can access.
Secure Infrastructure	The secure infrastructure is a combination of technology and associated procedures applied to a corporation's computing platforms and networks.
Computing Platforms and Networks	Since vulnerabilities are specific to different computing platforms and networks, proper technology controls must be applied to specific computing platforms and networks. Similarly, security analysts must be constantly vigilant, looking for new vulnerabilities on any installed computing platform or network.
Security Technology	Security technology, sometimes known as the security tool kit, is the constantly changing combination of potential solutions that can be implemented in order to achieve a secure infrastructure. As vulnerabilities change, security technology constantly changes to keep pace. It is essential for security analysts to be students of security technology, constantly seeking the best and most effective security solutions for their corporations.

Figure 16-14   Layers of the Security Architecture

then implementation stands a better chance of succeeding. However, policy implementation will inevitably force changes in people's behaviors, which can cause resistance. Resistance to change is both natural and to be expected. Handled properly, resistance to change can be just a temporary implementation hurdle. Handled improperly, it can spell disaster for an otherwise effective network security policy. Figure 16-15 summarizes some of the key behaviors and attitudes that can help ensure a successful network security policy implementation.

Auditing

Manual Audits In order to judge whether a corporate security policy is successful, it must be audited and monitored on a continual basis. Auditing as it

Critical Success Factors for Network Security Policy Implementation

1. The policy must have been developed in a team effort with all affected parties feeling that they had input to the process. Policy development must be a bottom-up, grass-roots effort rather than a top-down, administration-imposed effort.

2. The security policy must be coordinated with and in compliance with other corporate policies (re: disaster recovery, employee rights, personnel policies).

3. It is important to ensure that no part of the security policy is illegal. This is particularly important for corporations that do business in multiple states or countries. For example, in some localities it is illegal to monitor phone conversations of employees.

4. Technology must not be promoted as a security solution. Dedicated people, implementing well-designed processes on a consistent basis, combined with the effective use of technology, is the only means to a true security solution.

5. The network security policy must not be put on a shelf and forgotten. Security awareness must be a priority, and ongoing auditing and monitoring should ensure that security remains at the forefront of people's thoughts.

6. An attitude must be fostered that security threats are indeed real, and that they can, and will, occur in your company if people do not follow corporate security procedures.

7. Management must be ready to impose prescribed penalties on employees who fail to follow corporate security policy. To do otherwise will quickly send the message that the security policy is a farce.

8. Corporate culture may indeed need to change. This is especially true for growing companies that started out as very open, entrepreneurial cultures. Such companies often have difficulty adjusting to structure and controlled access to corporate resources imposed by corporate security policies.

Figure 16-15 Critical Success Factors for Network Security Policy Implementation

relates to network security policy may be either automated or manual. Manual audits can be done by either internal or external personnel. Manual audits serve to verify the effectiveness of policy development and implementation, especially the extent to which people understand and effectively execute their assigned processes in the overall corporate security policy. Manual audits are also referred to as **policy audits** or **off-line** audits. Consulting firms that specialize in network security have generated some rather startling results during security audits when they were able to gain entry to a corporate president's office, access his e-mail account, and send e-mail to the Chief Information Officer informing he was fired for his lack of effective security policy. As it turns out, the CIO was not really fired. In fact, it was poorly designed and poorly executed people processes that allowed this incident to occur. A receptionist was solely responsible for physical access security to the executive offices and the president left his PC logged in.

Automated Audits Automated audits, otherwise known as **event detection** or **real-time audits,** depend on software that is able to assess the weaknesses of your network security and security standards. Most audit software depends on capturing large amounts of event data and then filtering that data for exceptional or unusual events. Captured events can be telephone calls, login attempts, network server directory access attempts, access to Internet news groups or web sites, or remote access attempts via dial-up lines. In order to generate meaningful exception reports, audit software allows users to create filters that will allow only those events deemed exceptional by the users to appear on reports.

Some automated audit tools are able to analyze the network for potential vulnerabilities and make recommendations for corrective action, while others merely capture events so that you can figure out who did what and when after a security breach has occurred. Other automated tools are able to benchmark or compare events and security-related parameters with a set of government issued security standards known as C2 or Orange Book standards (officially known as the Trusted Computer System Evaluation Criteria or TCSEC) and issue a report card or "Top 10 Risks" list about how well a given network measures up. The C2 standards and other security standards will be explained later in the chapter. Some audit tools are able to save previous audit data as baseline information so that network analysts and security specialists can measure improvement in network security, including the impact of any security improvements that may have been implemented.

Security Probes and Intrusion Detection Systems Rather than passively gathering network statistics like auditing tools, security probes actively test various aspects of enterprise network security and report results and suggest improvements. **Intrusion detection systems** test the perimeter of the enterprise network through dial modems, remote access servers, web servers, or Internet access. In addition to merely detecting intrusions, such as unsuccessful login attempts over a preset limit, some tools are also able to provide automated responses to these intrusion attempts. Also, some of the more sophisticated intrusion detection systems are dynamic or self-learning and are able to become better at detecting intrusions or to adjust exception parameters as they gain experience in a given enterprise network environment.

Another security probe known as **Security Analyzer Tool for Analyzing Networks (SATAN)** is able to probe networks for security weak spots. The SATAN probe is especially written to analyze Unix and TCP/IP-based systems, and once it has found a way to get inside an enterprise network, it continues to probe all TCP/IP machines within that enterprise network. Once all vulnerabilities have been found, SATAN generates a report that not only details the vulnerabilities found, but also suggests methods for eliminating the vulnerabilities. SATAN tries to start TCP/IP sessions with target computers by launching applications such as Telnet, FTP, DNS, NFS, and TFTP. It is able to target specific computers because all TCP/IP-based machines use the same 16-bit address or port number for each of these previously mentioned applications. This application specific port address plus the 32-bit IP address is known as a socket. Although SATAN was developed as a tool for network managers to detect weaknesses in their own networks, it is widely available on the Internet and can easily be employed by hackers seeking to attack weaknesses in target networks of their choice. Because of the potential for unscrupulous use of SATAN, tools such as Courtney, from the Department of Energy's Computer Incident Advisory Capability and Gabriel from Los Altos Technologies are able to detect the use of SATAN against a network and are able to trigger alarms.

Internet Security Systems has developed a security probe known as RealSecure that looks for more than 200 known security weaknesses on firewalls, routers, Unix machines, Windows machines, or Windows NT machines or any other device that uses TCP/IP as its transport protocol stack. RealSecure combines network-analyzer, attack signature recognition, and attack response in a single unit. If an attack is detected, RealSecure is able to terminate the connection by spoofing both hosts involved in the communication.

En Garde Systems has developed two products that could be used legitimately for network monitoring and management but that have been used by hackers to hijack network connections after gaining access to the root directory of a computer, to masquerade as legitimate users, and to watch and capture FTP, Telnet, and HTTP sessions. TTY-Watcher allows users take over one machine, while IP watcher allows users to monitor all sessions on an IP-based network.

■ VIRUS PROTECTION

Virus protection is often the first area of network security addressed by individuals or corporations. A comprehensive virus protection plan must combine policy, people, processes, and technology in order to be effective. Too often, virus protection is thought to be a technology-based quick fix. Nothing could be farther from the truth. A 1996 survey conducted by the National Computer Security Association revealed the following:

- Computer viruses are the most common microcomputer security breach.

- 90% of the organizations surveyed with 500 or more PCs experience at least one virus incident per month.

- Complete recovery from a virus infection costs an average of $8,300 and 44 hours over a period of 22 working days.

- In January 1998 there were more than 16,000 known viruses with as many as 200 new viruses appearing per month. There were more than 2,000 macro viruses with this category experiencing exponential growth.

- A 1999 study found virus attacks to be the most common security breach, attacking 64% of all companies surveyed and causing downtime in 36% of these cases.

Virus Categories

Although definitions and parameters may vary, the term *computer virus* is generally used to describe any computer program or group of programs that gains access to a computer system or network with the potential to disrupt the normal activity of that system or network. Virus symptoms, methods of infection, and outbreak mechanisms can vary widely, but all viruses share a few common characteristics or behaviors:

- Most viruses work by infecting other legitimate programs and causing them to become destructive or disrupt the system in some other manner.

- Most viruses use some type of replication method in order to get the virus to spread and infect other programs, systems, or networks.

- Most viruses need some sort of trigger or activation mechanism to set them off. Viruses may remain dormant and undetected for long periods of time.

Viruses that are triggered by the passing of a certain date or time are referred to as **time bombs,** while viruses that require a certain event to transpire are known as **logic bombs.** Logic bombs in event-driven or visual programs may appear as a button supposedly providing search or some other function. When the button is pushed, however, the virus is executed causing a wide ranger of possibilities from capturing passwords to wiping out the disk drive. One of the ways in which viruses are able to infect systems in the first place is by a mechanism known as a **trojan horse.** In such a scenario, the actual virus is hidden inside an otherwise benign program and delivered to the target system or network to be infected. The Microsoft Word Macro (or Concept) Virus is an example of a trojan horse virus because the virus itself is innocently embedded within otherwise legitimate Word documents and templates. **Macro viruses** can infect Macintosh as well as Windows-based computers and are not limited to Word, but can also infect files through such programs as Corel WordPerfect, Lotus Word-Pro, and Microsoft Excel.

Although new types of viruses will continue to appear, Figure 16-16 lists the major virus categories and gives a brief explanation of each.

Antivirus Strategies

An effective antivirus strategy must include policy, procedures, and technology. Policy and procedures must be tied to those vulnerabilities that are specific to virus infection. Viruses can attack systems at the client PC, the server PC, or the network's connection to the Internet. By far, the most common physical transport mechanism for the spread of viruses is the diskette. Effective antivirus policies and procedures must first focus on the use and checking of all diskettes before pursuing technology-based solutions. In fact, 61% of all viral infections are caused by infected diskettes. However, the macro viruses that infect Word documents and Excel spreadsheets are becoming a predominant virus transport mechanism owing to the frequency with which such documents are shared between coworkers and across networks as e-mail attachments. Figure 16-17 lists some example of antivirus strategies, although this list should be tailored for each situation and reviewed and updated on a regular basis.

As collaborative applications such as groupware have become more commonplace in corporations, a new method of virus infection and virus reinfection has emerged. Because groupware messages and data are stored in a shared database, and because documents can be distributed throughout the network for document conferencing or workflow automation, the virus is spread throughout the network. Moreover, groupware servers usually replicate their databases in order to ensure that all servers on the network are providing consistent information, so the virus will continue to spread. Even if the virus is eliminated from the originating server, responses from still-infected replicated servers will reinfect the original server as the infection/reinfection cycle continues. Virus scanning software specially designed for groupware databases has been designed to combat this problem. Norton AntiVirus for Lotus Notes is an example of such a specialized antivirus tool. Figure 16-18 illustrates the collaboration software infection/reinfection cycle.

Virus Category	Explanation/Implication

File Infectors	• Attach themselves to a variety of types of executable files.
	• Subcategories of file infectors include
	  • Direct action file infectors infect a program each time it is executed.
	  • Resident infectors use the infected program to become resident in memory from where they attack other programs as they are loaded into memory.
	  • Slow infectors infect files as they are changed or created, thus assuring that the infection is saved.
	  • Sparse infectors seek to avoid detection by striking only certain programs on an occasional basis.
	  • Companion viruses create new infected programs that are identical to the original uninfected programs.
	  • Armored viruses are equipped with defense mechanisms to avoid detection and antivirus technology. **Polymorphic viruses** change their appearance each time an infected program is run in order to avoid detection.

System/Boot Infectors	• Attack the files of the operating system or boot sector rather than application programs. • System/Boot Sector viruses are memory resident.
Multipartite Viruses	• Also known as boot-and-file viruses, attack both application files as well as system and boot sectors.
Hostile Applets	• Although specific to web technology and Java embedded programs, hostile applets could still be considered viruses. **Attack applets** are intent on serious security breaches, while **malicious applets** tend to be annoying rather than destructive. Hostile applets are unknowingly downloaded while web surfing. Hostile ActiveX components present a similar threat. Some people would argue that such malicious code is not technically a virus. However, there is little doubt as to the potential destructiveness of the code.
E-Mail Viruses	• Some sites report that 98% of viruses are introduced through e-mail attachments. • Antivirus software must be version specific to the e-mail messaging system (i.e., Exchange Server 5.5). • Such software scans files after decryption before releasing the files to the users, while questionable files are quarantined.
Cluster/File System Viruses	• Attack the file systems, directories, or file allocation tables so that viruses can be loaded in to memory before requested files.

Figure 16-16 Virus Categories

Antivirus Strategies

1. Identify virus infection vulnerabilities and design protective measures.

2. Install virus scanning software at all points of attack. Ensure that network-attached client PCs with detected viruses can be quarantined in order to prevent the spread of the virus over the network.

3. All diskettes must be scanned at a stand-alone scanning PC before being loaded onto network attached clients or servers.

4. All consultants and third-party contractors are prohibited from attaching notebook computers to the corporate network until the computer has been scanned in accordance with security policy.

5. All vendors must run demonstrations on their own equipment.

6. Shareware or downloaded software should be prohibited or controlled and scanned.

7. All diagnostic and reference diskettes must be scanned before use.

8. Write protect all diskettes with .exe, .com files.

9. Create a master boot record that disables writes to the hard drive when booting from a floppy or disable booting from a floppy, depending on operating system.

Figure 16-17   Antivirus Strategies

Managerial Perspective

Antivirus awareness and a mechanism for quickly sharing information regarding new virus outbreaks must accompany the deployment of any antivirus technology. These antivirus awareness and communications mechanisms must be enterprise wide in scope rather than being confined to a relatively few virus aware departments. Procedures and policies on how and when antivirus technology is to be employed must be universally understood and implemented. Never were enterprise-wide procedures more important than on March 20, 1999, when the Melissa virus struck, propagating itself throughout enterprise e-mail systems and crippling entire enterprise networks.

Antivirus Technology

Because viruses can attack locally or remotely attached client platforms, server platforms, and/or the entrance to the corporate network via the Internet, all four points of attack must be protected. Viruses must be detected and removed at each point of attack. **Virus scanning** is the primary method for successful detection and removal. However, virus scanning software most often works from a library of known viruses, or more specifically the unique digital signatures of these viruses, while new viruses appear at the rate of

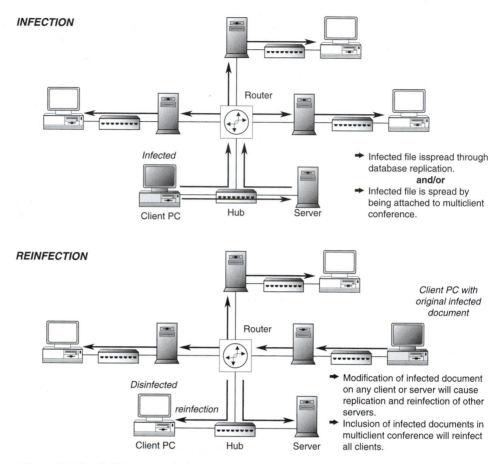

Figure 16-18 Collaborative Software Infection/Reinfection Cycle

nearly 200 per month. Because of this, it is important to buy virus scanning software whose vendor supplies updates of virus signatures at least once a .month. As virus introduction accelerates, it is likely that virus signature updates to virus scanning software will become more frequent as well. Vendors are currently updating virus signatures files every four hours, with hourly updates expected in the near future. Also, some virus scanners can remove a virus from an infected file, while others merely destroy the infected file as a remedy. Because virus scanners are really scanning for known digital signatures or viruses, they are sometimes referred to as **signature scanners.**

In an effort to be more proactive than reactive, **emulation technology** attempts to detect as-yet unknown viruses by running programs with a software emulation program known as a **virtual PC.** In so doing, the executing program can be examined in a safe environment for any unusual behavior or other tell-tale symptoms of resident viruses. The advantage of such programs is that they identify potentially unknown viruses based on their behavior rather than by relying on identifiable signatures of known viruses. Because of their ability to monitor behavior of programs, this category of antivirus technology is also sometimes known as **activity monitors** or **heuristic analysis.** Such programs are also capable of trapping encrypted or polymorphic viruses that are capable of constantly changing their identities or signatures. In addition, some of these programs are self-learning, thereby increasing their knowledge of viruslike activity with experience. Obviously, the key operational advantage is that potentially infected programs are run in the safe, emulated test environment before they are run on actual PCs and corporate networks.

A third category of antivirus technology known as **CRC checkers** or **hashing checkers** creates and saves a unique cyclical redundancy check character or hashing number for each file to be monitored. Each time that file is subsequently saved, the new CRC is checked against the reference CRC. If the CRCs do not match, then the file has been changed. These changes are then evaluated by the program in order to determine the likelihood that the change was caused by a viral infection. The shortcoming of such technology is that it is only able to detect viruses after infection, which may already be too late. Perhaps as a solution to this problem, **decoys** are files that are allowed to become infected in order to detect and report on virus activity.

Antivirus software is now available for clients, servers, e-mail gateways, web browsers, firewalls, and groupware. It is even being installed in the firmware on network interface cards. Overall, the trend is to catch Internet-borne viruses before they reach servers and clients' computers by installing virus protection technology at the Internet gateways capable of scanning FTP, HTTP, and SMTP traffic. Antivirus products are now certified by the **National Computer Security Association (NCSA),** which also maintains a list of known or sighted viruses. Figure 16-19 illustrates the typical points of attack for virus infection as well as potential protective measures to combat those attacks.

◼ FIREWALLS

When a company links to the Internet, a two-way access point out of as well as *into* that company's confidential information systems is created. In order to prevent unauthorized access from the Internet into a company's confidential data, specialized software known as a **firewall** is often deployed. Firewall software usually runs on a dedicated server that is connected to, but outside of, the corporate network. All network packets entering the firewall are filtered, or examined, to determine whether those users have authority to access requested files or services and whether the information contained within the message meets corporate criteria for forwarding over the internal network. Firewalls provide a layer of isolation between the inside network and the outside network. The underlying assumption in such a design sce-

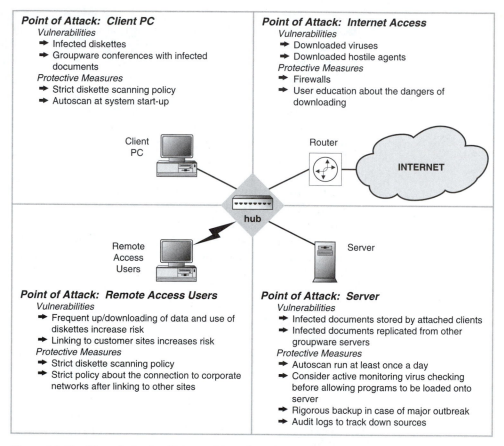

Point of Attack: Client PC
Vulnerabilities
➡ Infected diskettes
➡ Groupware conferences with infected documents
Protective Measures
➡ Strict diskette scanning policy
➡ Autoscan at system start-up

Point of Attack: Internet Access
Vulnerabilities
➡ Downloaded viruses
➡ Downloaded hostile agents
Protective Measures
➡ Firewalls
➡ User education about the dangers of downloading

Client PC

Router

INTERNET

hub

Remote Access Users

Server

Point of Attack: Remote Access Users
Vulnerabilities
➡ Frequent up/downloading of data and use of diskettes increase risk
➡ Linking to customer sites increases risk
Protective Measures
➡ Strict diskette scanning policy
➡ Strict policy about the connection to corporate networks after linking to other sites

Point of Attack: Server
Vulnerabilities
➡ Infected documents stored by attached clients
➡ Infected documents replicated from other groupware servers
Protective Measures
➡ Autoscan run at least once a day
➡ Consider active monitoring virus checking before allowing programs to be loaded onto server
➡ Rigorous backup in case of major outbreak
➡ Audit logs to track down sources

Figure 16-19 Virus Infection Points of Attack and Protective Measures

nario is that all of the threats come from the outside network. As evidenced by the statistic cited earlier, this is often not the case. In addition, outside threats may be able to circumvent the firewall entirely if dial-up modem access remains uncontrolled or unmonitored. In addition, incorrectly implemented firewalls can actually exacerbate the situation by creating new, and sometimes undetected, security holes.

Firewall Architectures

Another difficulty with firewalls is that there are no standards for firewall functionality, architectures, or interoperability. As a result users must be especially aware of how firewalls work in order to evaluate potential firewall technology purchases. Firewall functionality and architectures are explained in the next few sections.

Packet Filtering   Every packet of data on the Internet is uniquely identified by the source address of the computer that issued the message and the destination address of the Internet server to which the message is bound. These addresses are included in a portion of the packet called the header.

A **filter** is a program that examines the source address and destination address of every incoming packet to the firewall server. Network access devices known as routers are also capable of filtering data packets. **Filter tables** are lists of addresses whose data packets and embedded messages are either allowed or prohibited from proceeding through the firewall server and into the corporate network. Filter tables can also limit the access of certain IP addresses to certain directories. This is how anonymous FTP users are restricted only to certain information resources. It obviously takes time for a firewall server to examine the addresses of each packet and compare those addresses with filter table entries. This filtering time introduces **latency** to the overall transmission time. A filtering program that only examines source and destination addresses and determines access based on the entries in a filter table is known as a **port level filter** or **network level filter** or **packet filter.**

Packet filter gateways can be implemented on routers. This means that an existing piece of technology can be used for dual purposes. However, maintaining filter tables and access rules on multiple routers is not a simple task, and packet filtering does have its limitations in terms of the level of security it is able to provide. Dedicated packet-filtering firewalls are usually easier to configure and require less in-depth knowledge of protocols to be filtered or examined. Packet filters can be breached by hackers in a technique known as **IP spoofing.** Packet filters make all filtering decisions based on IP source and destination addresses, so if a hacker can make a packet appear to come from an authorized or trusted IP address, it can pass through the firewall.

Application Gateways   **Application-level filters,** otherwise known as **assured pipelines, application gateways,** or **proxies,** go beyond port-level filters in their attempts to prevent unauthorized access to corporate data. While port-level filters determine the legitimacy of the party asking for information, application-level filters ensure the validity of what they are asking for. Application-level filters examine the entire request for data rather than just the source and destination addresses. Secure files can be marked as such and application-level filters will not allow those files to be transferred, even to users authorized by port-level filters.

Certain application-level protocols commands that are typically used for probing or hacking into systems can be identified, trapped, and removed. For example, SMTP (simple mail transfer protocol) is an e-mail interoperability protocol that is a member of the TCP/IP family and used widely over the Internet. It is often used to mask attacks or intrusions. MIME (multipurpose Internet mail extension) is also often used to hide or encapsulate malicious code such as Java applets or ActiveX components. Other application protocols that may require monitoring include World Wide Web protocols such as HTTP, as well as Telnet, FTP, Gopher, and Real Audio. Each of these application protocols requires its own proxy, and each application-specific proxy must be intimately familiar with the commands within each application that will need to be trapped and examined. For example, an SMTP proxy should be able to filter SMTP packets according to e-mail content, message length, and type of attachments. A given application gateway may not include proxies for all potential application-layer protocols.

Circuit-level proxies provide proxy services for transport layer protocols such as TCP. **Socks** creates a proxy data channel to the application server on behalf of the application client. Because all data go through Socks, it can audit, screen, and filter all traffic in between the application client and server. Socks can control traffic by disabling or enabling communication according to TCP port numbers. Socks4 allowed outgoing firewall applications, while Socks5 supports both incoming and outgoing firewall applications. In Socks5 authentication is also supported. The key negative characteristic is that applications must be "socksified" in order to communicate with the Socks protocol and server. In the case of Socks4 this meant that local applications had to be literally recompiled. However, with Socks5, a launcher is employed that avoids "socksification" and recompilation of client programs that don't natively support Socks in most cases. Socks5 uses a private routing table and hides internal network addresses from outside networks. Winsock Proxy, available in such products as Microsoft Proxy Server, provides similar functionality for Windows-based programs adhering to the Winsock API. In such cases, a Winsock Proxy client piece of software must be installed on the client workstation.

Application gateways are concerned with what services or applications a message is requesting in addition to who is making that request. Connections between requesting clients and service-providing servers are only created after the application gateway is satisfied as to the legitimacy of the request. Even once the legitimacy of the request has been established, only proxy clients and servers actually communicate with each other. A gateway firewall does not allow actual internal IP addresses or names to be transported to the external nonsecure network. To the external network, the proxy application on the firewall appears to be the actual source or destination, as the case may be.

An architectural variation of an application gateway that offers increased security is known as a **dual-homed gateway.** In this scenario, the application gateway is physically connected to the private secure network and the packet-filtering router is connected to the nonsecure network or the Internet. Between the application gateway and the packet filter router is an area known as the screened subnet, occasionaly referred to as a DMZ. Also attached to this screened subnet are information servers, WWW servers, or other servers that the company may wish to make available to outside users. However, all outside traffic still goes through the application gateway first, and then to the information servers. TCP/IP forwarding is disabled, and access to the private network is available only through one of the installed proxies. Remote logins are allowed only to the gateway host.

An alternative to the dual-homed gateway that seeks to relieve all the reliance on the application gateway for all communication, both inbound and outbound, is known as a **trusted gateway** or trusted application gateway. In a trusted gateway, certain applications are identified as trusted and are able to bypass the application gateway entirely and are able to establish connections directly rather than be executed by proxy. In this way, outside users can access information servers and WWW servers without tying up the proxy applications on the application gateway. Figure 16-20 differentiates between packet filters, application gateways, proxies, trusted gateways, and dual-homed gateways.

Proxies are also capable of approving or denying connections based on directionality. Users may be allowed to upload files but not download. Some application-level gateways have the ability to encrypt communications over these established connections. The level of difficulty associated with configuring application-level gateways versus router-based packet filters is debatable. Router-based gateways tend to require a more intimate knowledge of protocol behavior, whereas application-level gateways deal with more upper-level, application-layer, protocols. Proxies introduce increased latency as compared with port-level filtering. The key weakness of an application-level gateway is its inability to detect embedded malicious code such as trojan horse programs or macro viruses.

Internal Firewalls   Not all threats to a corporation's network are perpetrated from the Internet by anonymous hackers, and firewalls are not a stand-alone, technology-based quick fix for network security as evidenced by the following facts:

- 60% of network attacks are made by internal users, people inside the firewall

- 568 out of 600 incidents of network hacking were conducted by disgruntled employees, former employees, or friends of employees

- 30% of Internet sites that reported breaches had firewalls in place

In response to the reality that most episodes of computer crime are inside jobs, a new category of software known as **internal firewalls** has begun to emerge. Internal firewalls include filters that work on the data-link, network, and application layers to examine communications that occur only on a corporation's internal network, inside the reach of traditional firewalls. Internal firewalls also act as access control mechanisms, denying access to any application for which a user does not have specific access approval. In order to ensure the security of confidential or private files, encryption may also be used, even during internal communication of such files.

Enterprise Firewall Architectures   Although the previous section described different approaches to firewall architecture on an individual basis, key

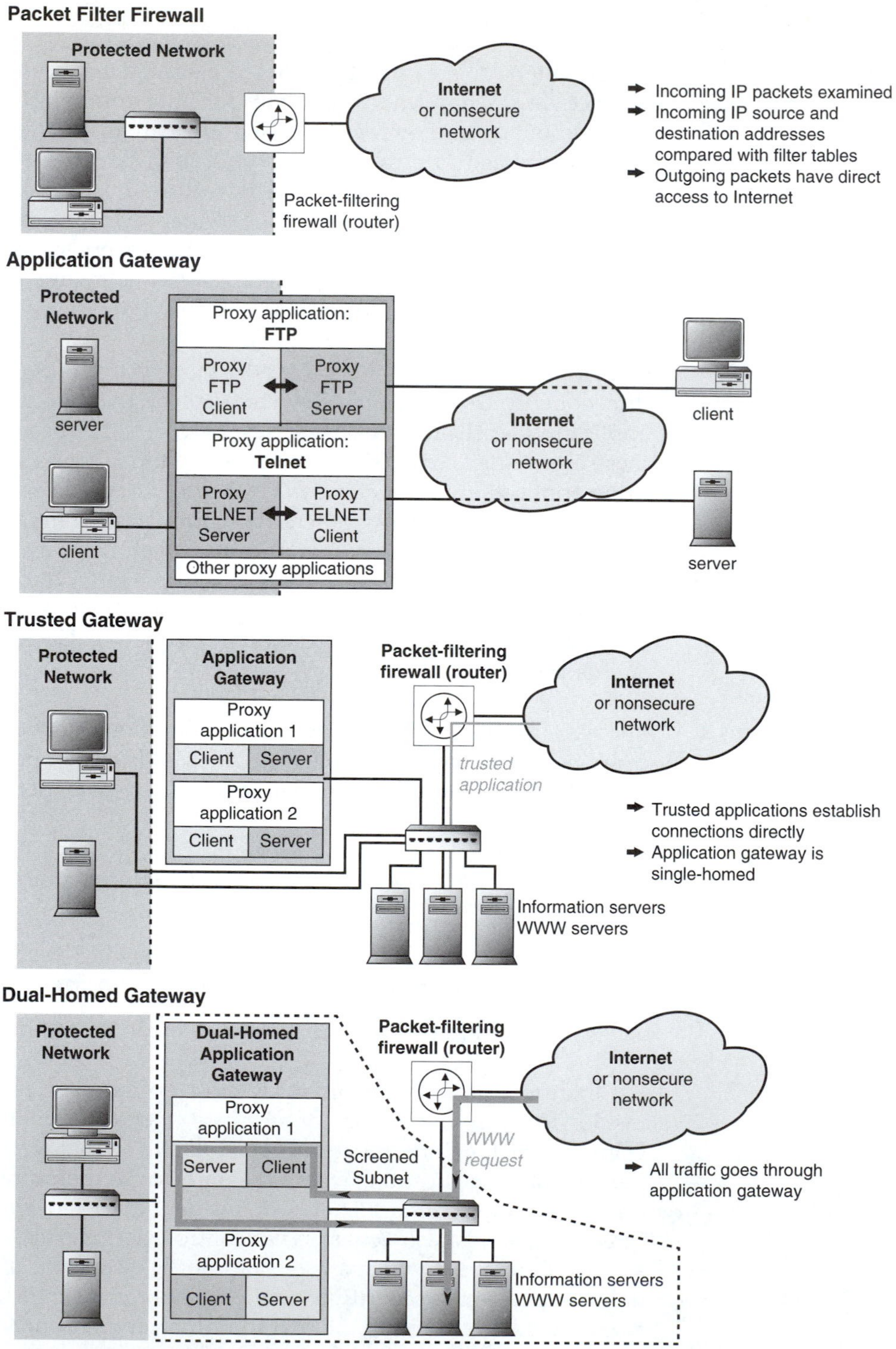

Packet Filter Firewall

Protected Network

Packet-filtering
firewall (router)

Internet
or nonsecure
network

→ Incoming IP packets examined
→ Incoming IP source and
  destination addresses
  compared with filter tables
→ Outgoing packets have direct
  access to Internet

Application Gateway

Protected
Network

server

client

Proxy application:
FTP

| Proxy
FTP
Client | Proxy
FTP
Server |

Proxy application:
Telnet

| Proxy
TELNET
Server | Proxy
TELNET
Client |

Other proxy applications

Internet
or nonsecure
network

client

server

Trusted Gateway

Protected
Network

| **Application**
Gateway |
| Proxy
application 1 |
| Client | Server |
| Proxy
application 2 |
| Client | Server |

Packet-filtering
firewall (router)

Internet
or nonsecure
network

trusted
application

Information servers
WWW servers

→ Trusted applications establish
  connections directly
→ Application gateway is
  single-homed

Dual-Homed Gateway

Protected
Network

| **Dual-Homed**
Application
Gateway |
| Proxy
application 1 |
| Server | Client |
| Proxy
application 2 |
| Client | Server |

Screened
Subnet

Packet-filtering
firewall (router)

Internet
or nonsecure
network

WWW
request

Information servers
WWW servers

→ All traffic goes through
  application gateway

Figure 16-20   Packet Filters, Application Gateways, Proxies, Trusted Gateways, and
Dual-Homed Gateways

decisions must be made regarding the number and location of these firewalls in relation to the Internet and a corporation's public and private information resources. Each of the alternative enterprise firewall architectures explored below are attempting to segregate the following three distinct networks or risk domains:

- The Internet contains both legitimate customers and business partners as well as hackers.

- The demilitarized zone, DMZ, otherwise known as the external private network or screened sub-net, contains web servers and mail servers.

- The internal private network, otherwise known as the secure network, contains valuable corporate information.

Figure 16-21 illustrates the various ways in which one or two firewalls can be arranged in an enterprise firewall architecture; Figure 16-22 describes the functionality of each alternative.

Firewall Functionality and Technology Analysis

Commercially available firewalls usually employ either packet filtering or proxies as a firewall architecture and add an easy-to-use graphical user interface in order to ease the configuration and implementation tasks. Some firewalls even use industry standard web browsers as their GUIs. Firewall technology is now certified by the **National Computer Security Association.** The NCSA certifies the following:

- That firewalls meet the minimum requirements for reliable protection

- That firewalls perform as advertised

- That Internet applications perform as expected through the firewall

Figure 16-23 summarizes some of the key functional characteristics of firewall technology.

Small Office Home Office (SOHO) Firewalls   As telecommuting has boomed and independent consultants have set up shop in home offices, the need for firewalls for the SOHO market has grown as well. These devices are most often integrated with ISDN-based multiprotocol routers that supply bandwidth on demand capabilities for Internet access. Some of these SOHO firewalls offer sophisticated features such as support for virtual private networks and NCSA certification.

Single Firewall, Behind DMZ

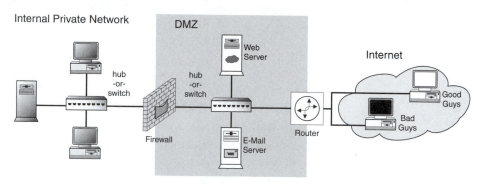

Single Firewall, In Front of DMZ

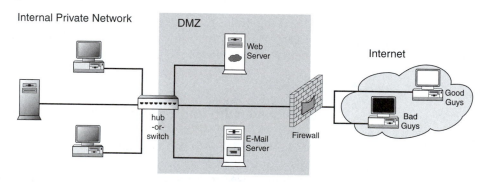

Dual or Multi-Tier Firewall

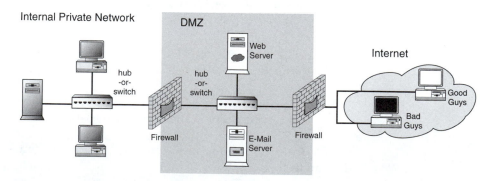

Figure 16-21   Enterprise Firewall Architectures

Enterprise Firewall Architecture	Key Functional characteristics
Single Firewall, Behind DMZ	• Exposes web servers and mail servers to Internet without protection
Single FireWall, in Front of DMZ	• Must open paths through single firewall to allow public access to web server and mail server • No firewall protection to Internal Private Network because it is on the same physical network as the DMZ
Dual or Multi-tier Firewall	• Allows controlled access to DMZ while blocking unauthorized access to secure network • Same functionality may be offered in a single product known as a tri-homed firewall

Figure 16-22   Comparative Functionality of Enterprise Firewall Architectures

Firewall Functional Characteristic	Explanation/Importance
Encryption	• Allows secure communication through firewall • Encryption schemes supported: DES • Encryption key length supported: 40, 56, 128 bits
Virtual Private Network Support	• Allows secure communication over the Internet in a virtual private network topology • VPN Security protocols supported: IPsec
Application Proxies Supported	• How many different application proxies are supported? Internet application protocols? (HTTP, SMTP, FTP, Telnet, NNTP, WAIS, SNMP, rlogin, ping traceroute) Real Audio? • How many controls or commands are supported for each application?
Proxy Isolation	• In some cases, proxies are executed in their own protected domains in order to prevent penetration of other proxies or the firewall operating system should a given proxy be breached
Operating Systems Supported	• Unix and Varieties, Windows NT, UnixWare
Virus Scanning Included	• Since many viruses enter through Internet connections, it would stand to reason that the firewall would be a logical place to scan for viruses
Web Tracking	• In order to ensure compliance with corporate policy regarding use of the World Wide Web, some firewalls provide web tracking software. The placement of the web tracking software in the firewall makes sense because all Web access must pass through the firewall. Access to certain URLs can be filtered.

(continued)

Violation Notification	• How does the firewall react when access violations are detected? Options include: SNMP traps, e-mail, pop-up windows, pagers, reports
Authentication Supported	• As a major network access point, the firewall must support popular authentication protocols and technology. Options include: SecureID, Cryptocard, Enigma Logic, DES Gold, DES Silver, Safeword, Radius, ASSUREnet, FW-1, Digital Pathways, S/Key, OS Login
Network Interfaces Supported	• Which network interfaces and associated data-link layer protocols are supported? Options include: Ethernet, Fast Ethernet, FDDI, Token Ring, High-speed serial for CSU/DSUs, ATM, ISDN, T-1, T-3, HDLC, PPP
System Monitoring	• Are graphical systems monitoring utilities available to display such statistics as disk usage or network activity by interface?
Auditing and Logging	• Is auditing and logging supporting? • How many different types of events can be logged? • Are user-defined events supported? • Can logged events be sent to SNMP managers?
Attack Protection	• Following is just a sample of the types of attacks that a firewall should be able to guard against: TCP denial-of-service attack, TCP sequence number prediction, source routing and routing information protocol (RIP) attacks, exterior gateway protocol infiltration and Internet control message protocol (ICMP) attacks, authentication server attacks, finger access, PCMAIL access, domain name server (DNS) access, FTP authentication attacks, anonymous FTP access, SNMP access, remote booting from outside networks, IP media access control (MAC) and address resolution protocol (ARP) spoofing and broadcast storms, trivial FTP and filter to/from the firewall, reserved port attacks, TCP wrappers, Gopher spoofing, and MIME spoofing.
Administration Interface	• Is the administration interface graphical in nature? Forms-based? • Is a mastery of Unix required to administer the firewall?

Figure 16-23   Functional Characteristics of Firewall Technology

■ AUTHENTICATION AND ACCESS CONTROL

The overall purpose of **authentication** is to ensure that users attempting to gain access to networks are really who they claim to be. Although password protection was the traditional means to ensure authentication, password protection by itself is no longer sufficient to ensure authentication. As a result, a wide variety of technology has been developed to ensure that users really are who they say they are. Authentication products break down into three overall categories:

- *What you know.* Authentication technology that can deliver **single sign-on (SSO)** access to multiple network attached servers and resources via passwords.

- *What you have.* Authentication technology that uses one-time or session passwords or other techniques to authenticate users and validate the authenticity of messages or files. This category of technology requires the user to possess some type of Smart Card or other token authentication device in order to generate these single-use passwords.

- *What you are.* Authentication technology that validates users based on some physical characteristic such as fingerprints, hand geometry, or retinal scans.

Token Authentication—Smart Cards

Token authentication technology provides one-time-use-session passwords that are authenticated by associated server software. This token authentication technology may take multiple forms:

- Hardware-based **Smart Cards** or smart IDs that are about the size of a credit card with a numeric keypad.

- In-line token authentication devices that connect to the serial port of a computer for dial-in authentication through a modem.

- Software tokens that are installed on the client PC and authenticate with the server portion of the token authentication product transparently to the end user. The user must only enter a personal ID number (PIN) to activate the authentication process.

Token authentication technology is really a system of interacting components that could include any or all of the following:

- A Smart Card to generate the session password

- Client software to enter session passwords and communicate with the token authentication server software

- Server software to validate entries for session passwords and keep track of which Smart Cards are issued to which users

- Application development software to integrate the token authentication technology with existing information systems

There are two overall approaches to the token authentication process.

- **Challenge-response token authentication**

- **Time-synchronous token authentication**

Challenge-response token authentication involves the following steps:

1. The user enters an assigned user ID and password at the client workstation.

2. The token authentication server software returns a numeric string known as a challenge.

3. The challenge number and a personal ID number are entered on the hand-held Smart Card.

4. The Smart Card displays a response number on the LCD screen.

5. This response number is entered on the client workstation and transmitted back to the token authentication server.

6. The token authentication server validates the response against the expected response from this particular user and this particular Smart Card. If the two match, the user is deemed authentic and the login session is enabled.

Time synchronous token authentication uses slightly more sophisticated technology to simplify the challenge-response procedure somewhat. The result is that in time synchronous token authentication, there is no server-to-client challenge step. SecurID tokens from Security Dynamics are examples of time synchronous token authentication using a protocol known as SecurID ACE (access control encryption).

1. Every 60 seconds, the time-synchronous Smart Card and the server-based software generate a new access code.

2. The user enters their userID, a personal ID number, and the access code currently displayed on the Smart Card.

3. The server receives the access code and authenticates the user by comparing the received access code with the expected access code unique to that Smart Card which was generated at the server in time synchronous fashion.

Figure 16-24 differentiates between challenge-response token authentication and time synchronous token authentication.

Biometric Authentication

If the security offered by token authentication is insufficient, **biometric authentication** can authenticate users based on fingerprints, palm prints, retinal patterns, hand geometry, facial geometry, voice recognition, or other physical characteristics. Passwords can be stolen, Smart Cards can be stolen,

Challenge - Response

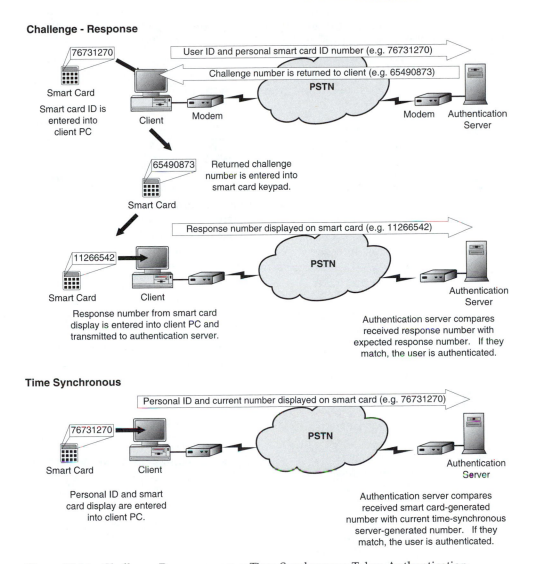

Figure 16-24   Challenge Response versus Time-Synchronous Token Authentication

but fingerprints and retinal patterns cannot. All biometric authentication devices require that valid users register by storing copies of their fingerprints, voice, or retinal patterns in a validation database. This gives the biometric device something to reference each time an intended user logs in.

Biometric authentication devices are not yet perfect or foolproof. Most biometric authentication devices must be calibrated for sensitivity. If the biometric device comparison algorithm is set too sensitively, **false rejects,** or Type I error, will occur when valid users are denied access because of slight variations detected between the reference biometric characteristic and the current one. If the biometric device comparison algorithm is not set sensitively enough, **false accepts,** or Type II error, will occur when impostors are allowed access because the comparison was not detailed enough. Users of biometric authentication equipment must calibrate the sensitivity of the equipment in order to produce acceptable levels of false rejects and false accepts.

Authorization

Sometimes perceived as a subset of authentication, authorization is concerned with ensuring that only properly authorized users are able to access particular network resources or corporate information resources. In other words, although authentication ensures that only legitimate users are able to log into the network, authorization ensures that these properly authenticated users access only the network resources for which they are properly authorized. This assurance that users are able to log into a network, rather than each individual server and application, and be able to access only those resources for which they are properly authorized, is known as **secure single login.**

The authorization security software can be either server-based, also known as **brokered authorization,** or workstation-based, also referred to as **trusted node.**

Kerberos

Perhaps the most well-known combination authentication/authorization software is **Kerberos,** developed originally at Massachusetts Institute of Technology and marketed commercially by a variety of firms. The Kerberos architecture is illustrated in Figure 16-25.

As illustrated in Figure 16-25, a Kerberos architecture consists of three key components:

- Kerberos client software

- Kerberos authentication server software

- Kerberos application server software

To ensure that only authorized users are able to access a particular application, Kerberos must be able to communicate directly with that application. As a result, the source code of the application must be "Kerberized," or modified to be compatible with Kerberos. If source code is not available, perhaps the software vendor sells Kerberized versions of their software. Kerberos is unable to offer authorization protection to applications with which it cannot communicate. Kerberos enforces authentication and authorization through

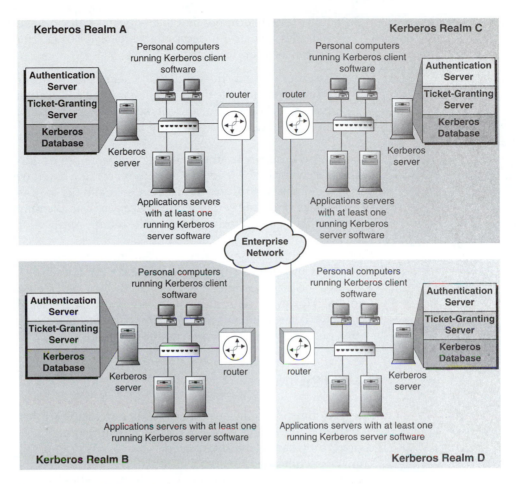

Figure 16-25   Kerberos Architecture

the use of a ticket-based system. An encrypted **ticket** is issued for each server-to-client session and is valid only for a preset amount of time. The ticket is valid only for connections between a designated client and server, thus precluding users from accessing servers or applications for which they are not properly authorized.

Logically, Kerberos works as follows:

1. Users are first authenticated by the Kerberos authentication server, which consults its database and grants a ticket for the valid user to communicate with the ticket granting server (TGS). This ticket is known as a **ticket-granting ticket.**

2. Using this ticket, the user sends an encrypted request to the TGS requesting a ticket for access to a particular applications server.

3. If the TGS determines that the request is valid, a ticket is issued that will allow the user to access the requested server. This ticket is known as a **service-granting ticket.**

4. The user presents the validated ticket to the application server, which evaluates the ticket's validity. If the application determines that the ticket is valid, a client/server session is established. This session can optionally be encrypted.

Enterprise networks implementing Kerberos are divided into Kerberos **realms,** each served by its own Kerberos server. If a client wishes to access a server in another realm, it requests an **inter-realm** ticket-granting ticket from its local ticket-granting server to authorize access to the remote ticket-granting server that can authorize access to the remote applications server.

Managerial Perspective

From a network analyst's perspective, concern should be centered on the amount of overhead or network bandwidth consumed by the addition of Kerberos security. Research has indicated that, in fact, the network impact is minimal. However, the additional administrative responsibility of maintaining the Kerberos databases that indicate which users are authorized to access which network resources should not be ignored.

■ ENCRYPTION

Encryption involves the changing of data into an indecipherable form prior to transmission. In this way, even if the transmitted data are somehow intercepted, they cannot be interpreted. The changed, unmeaningful data are known as **ciphertext.** Encryption must be accompanied by decryption, or changing the unreadable text back into its original form.

DES—Private Key Encryption

The decrypting device must use the same algorithm or method to decode or decrypt the data as the encrypting device used to encrypt the data, which is why **private key encryption** is sometimes known as symmetric encryption. Although proprietary standards do exist, a standard known as **DES (Data Encryption Standard),** originally approved by the National Institute of Standards and Technology (NIST) in 1977, is often used, allowing encryption devices manufactured by different manufacturers to interoperate successfully. The DES encryption standard actually has two parts that serve to offer greater overall security. In addition to the standard algorithm or method of encrypting data 64 bits at a time, the DES standard also uses a 64-bit key.

The encryption key customizes the commonly known algorithm to prevent anyone without this private key from possibly decrypting the document. This private key must be known by both the sending and receiving encryption devices and allows so many unique combinations (nearly 2 to the 64th power), that unauthorized decryption is nearly impossible. The safe and reliable distribution of these private keys among numerous encryption devices can be difficult. If this private key is somehow intercepted, the integrity of the encryption system is compromised.

RSA—Public Key Encryption

As an alternative to the DES private key standard, **Public Key Encryption** can be utilized. The current standard for public key encryption is known as **RSA,** named after the three founders of the protocol (Rivest-Shamir-Adelman). Public key encryption could perhaps more accurately be named Public/Private Key Encryption, since the process actually combines usage of both public and private keys. In public key encryption, the sending encryption device encrypts a document using the intended recipient's public key and the originating party's private key. This public key is readily available in a public directory or is sent by the intended recipient to the message sender. In order to decrypt the document, however, the receiving encryption/decryption device must be programmed with the recipient's own private key and the sending party's public key. In this method, the need for transmission of private keys between sending and receiving parties is eliminated.

Digital Signature Encryption

As an added security measure, **Digital Signature Encryption** uses this public key encryption methodology in reverse as an electronic means of guaranteeing authenticity of the sending party and assurance that encrypted documents have not been altered during transmission.

With Digital Signature encryption, a document's digital signature is created by the sender using a private key and the original document. The original document is processed by a one-way hashing program such as Secure Hash Algorithm, Message Digest 2, or Message Digest 5, to produce a mathematical string that is unique to the exact content of the original document. This unique mathematical string is then encrypted using the originator's private key. The encrypted digital signature is then appended to and transmitted with the encrypted original document.

To validate the authenticity of the received document, the recipient uses a public key associated with the apparent sender to regenerate a digital signature from the received encrypted document. The recipient then compares the transmitted digital signature with the regenerated digital signature produced by using the public key and the received document. If the two digital signatures match, the document is authentic (actually produced by alleged originator) and has not been altered. Figure 16-26 illustrates the differences

Private Key or Symmetric

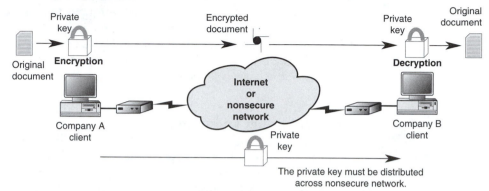

The private key must be distributed across nonsecure network.

Public Key

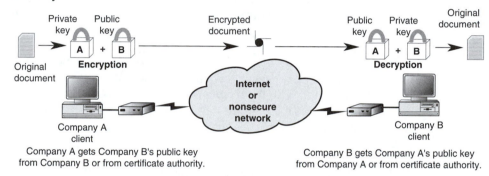

Company A gets Company B's public key from Company B or from certificate authority.

Company B gets Company A's public key from Company A or from certificate authority.

Digital Signature

Locally regenerated digital signature is compared with original transmitted digital signature.

Figure 16-26 Private Key Encryption, Public Key Encryption, and Digital Signature Encryption

between private key encryption, public key encryption, and digital signature encryption, whereas Figure 16-27 summarizes some key facts about currently popular encryption standards.

Key Management Alternatives

Before two computers can communicate in a secure manner, they must be able to agree on encryption and authentication algorithms and establish keys in a process known as key management. Two standards for key management are:

- **ISAKMP (Internet Security Association and Key Management Protocol)** from the IETF

- **SKIP (Simple Key Management for IP)** from Sun

Public key dissemination must be managed so that users can be assured that public keys received are actually the public keys of the companies or organizations they are alleged to be. This added level of assurance is provided by **public key certificates.** The organization required to manage digital keys is generally described as the public key infrastructure (PKI). **PKIX (Public Key Infrastructure X.509)** is an international ISO standard for public key certificates. The IETF has been working on an alternative public key

Standard	Type	Key Size	Explanation
3DES	Private	40, 56 bits	Triple DES, uses 2 or 3 keys and multiple encryption/decryption passes
DES	Private	40,56 bits	Digital encryption standard, widely used for private key encryption
DSA	Digital Signature	1024	Digital signature algorithm generates appended digital signatures based on original document to ensure document has not been altered
ECC	Public	160	Elliptical curve cryptography, claims to produce equivalent security of 1024-bit RSA key in only 160 bits
IDEA	Private	128 bit	International data encryption algorithm, generates one-time use session keys, used in PGP (pretty good privacy)
MD5	Digest		Produces 128-bit hash number based on original document. Can then be incorporated into digital signature . Replaced MD4 and MD2.
RSA	Public	512 to 2048 bits	Rivest-Shamir-Adelman, popular public key encryption standard, minimum key length of 1024 recommended.
Skipjack	Private	80	Used for Clipper and Capstone encryption chips and Defense Messaging System (DMS)

Figure 16-27   Encryption Standards

infrastructure standard that is oriented toward varying authorization levels rather than personal identities, by using what are known as privilege-based certificates. This draft standard, known as **SPKI/SDSI (Simple Public Key Infrastructure/Simple Distributed Security Infrastructure),** specifies a distributed client/server model in which humanly readable certificates and the authorization levels they represent can be delegated and processed according to user-defined rules.

Public key infrastructures that link a particular user to a particular public key are implemented through the use of server-based software known as **certificate servers.** Certificate server software also supports encryption and digital signatures while flexibly supporting directory integration, multiple certificate types, and a variety of request fulfillment options. Third-party key certification services, or **certificate authorities (CA),** issue the public keys along with a certificate assuring the authenticity of the key. Such certification authorities issue public keys of other organizations, together with certificates of authenticity, assured by their own digital signature. VeriSign is one example of a trusted third-party issuer of X.509 public-key certificates. The U.S. Postal Service has also announced plans to begin issuing public key certificates.

Digital certificates, or **Digital IDs** issued from CAs such as VeriSign, contain an organization's encrypted public key along with a minimal amount of information about the organization such as e-mail address, department, company, state or province, and country. Once a certificate has been issued by a CA, an organization can post its Digital ID on a web page and be assured that the CA will stand behind the Digital ID's authenticity.

Digital IDs may eventually replace passwords for Internet-based communications. Recognizing the potential for electronic commerce vendors to quickly gather demographic data about their customers, VeriSign has enhanced their Class 1 Digital ID format to include additional fields in which to store demographic data such as gender, age, address, zip code, or other personal data. Information stored in the encrypted Class 2 Digital ID could allow customized web pages to be built based on the information contained therein. The Digital ID service from VeriSign costs $6.00 per year for a Class 1 Digital ID and $12.00 per year for a Class 2 Digital ID.

■ APPLIED SECURITY SCENARIOS

Overall Design Strategies

Although it is impossible to prescribe a network security design that would be appropriate for any given situation, some general guidelines that would apply to most situations are as follows:

- Install only software and hardware that you really need on your network. Every time that hardware or software is installed on a network, potential security vulnerabilities due to misconfiguration or design flaws are introduced.

- Allow only essential traffic into and out of the corporate network and eliminate all other types by blocking with routers or firewalls. E-mail and domain name service (DNS) queries are a good place to start.

- Investigate the business case for outsourcing web-hosting services so that the corporate web server is not physically on the same network as the rest of the corporate information assets.

- Use routers to filter traffic by IP address. Allow only known authorized users to have access through the router and into the corporate information network.

- Make sure that router operating system software has been patched to prevent denial of service and land attacks by exploiting TCP vulnerabilities, or better still, block all incoming TCP traffic.

- Identify those information assets that are most critical to the corporation, and protect those servers first. It is better to have the most important assets well protected than to have all of the information assets somewhat protected.

- Implement physical security constraints to hinder physical access to critical resources such as servers.

- Monitor system activity logs carefully, paying close attention to failed login attempts and file transfers.

- Develop a simple, effective, and enforceable security policy and monitor its implementation and effectiveness.

- Consider installing a proxy server or applications layer firewall.

- Block incoming DNS queries and requests for zone transfers. This is how hackers are able to map a corporation's internal network resources.

- Don't publish the corporation's complete DNS map on DNS servers that are outside the corporate firewall. Publish only those few servers that the Internet needs to know: e-mail gateway, DNS server, web site.

- Disable all TCP ports and services that are not essential so that hackers are not able to exploit and use these services.

Integration with Information Systems and Application Development

Authentication products must be integrated with existing information systems and applications development efforts. APIs (application program interfaces) are the means by which authentication products are able to integrate with client/server applications. Beyond APIs are application development environments or software development kits that combine an application development language with the supported APIs. APIs or application development environments must be compatible with the programming language in which applications are to be developed.

AT&T provides a software development kit that includes a library of C language security APIs and software modules for integrating digital signature and other security functionality into Windows NT and Windows 95 applications.

Security Dynamics, which markets SecurID time-synchronous token authentication products, also provides software development kits known as BSAFE 3.0 and Toolkit for Interoperable Privacy Enhanced Massaging.

Microsoft's CryptoAPI (CAPI) allows security services such as authentication, encryption, certificate management services, and digital signatures to be integrated with applications. Obviously, these applications must then be executed over Microsoft platforms.

Intel, IBM, and Netscape have collaborated on a multi-API security framework for encryption and authentication known as common data security architecture (CDSA) that can be integrated with Java-based objects. Other security APIs may be forthcoming from Sun and Novell also.

An open API that would allow applications to communicate with a variety of security authorization programs is known as **GSS-API (Generic Security Service-Applications Program Interface)** and is documented in RFCs (requests for comments) 1508 and 1509. Security products companies such as Nortel, producers of the Entrust file signing and encryption package, and Cybersafe Corporation support the GSS-API. GSS-API is described as open because it interfaces between user applications and a variety of security services such as Kerberos, secure FTP, or encryption services. The applications developer does not need to understand the intricacies of these security services and is able to flexibly choose those security services that best meet the needs of the application under development. The GSS-API can also be integrated with Intel's CDSA.

Remote Access Security

The biggest challenge facing remote access security is how to manage the activity of all of the remote access users that have logged in via a variety of multi-vendor equipment and authentication technology. A protocol and associated architecture known as **remote authentication dial-in user service (RADIUS)** (RFC 2058) is supported by a wide variety of remote access technology and offers the potential to enable centralized management of remote access users and technology. The RADIUS architecture is illustrated in Figure 16-28. This architecture is referred to as three-tiered because it enables communication between the following three tiers of technology:

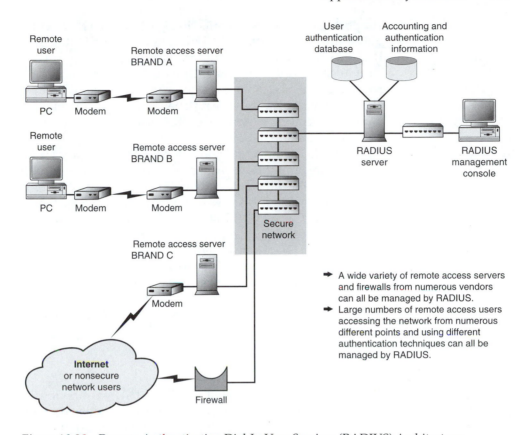

Figure 16-28   Remote Authentication Dial-In User Services (RADIUS) Architecture

- Remote access devices such as remote access servers and token authentication technology from a variety of vendors, otherwise known as network access servers (NAS)

- Enterprise database that contains authentication and access control information

- RADIUS authentication server

In this architecture, users request connections and provide useRIDs and passwords to the network access servers which, in turn, pass the information along to the RADIUS authentication server for authentication approval or denial.

RADIUS allows network managers to centrally manage remote access users, access methods, and logon restrictions. It allows centralized auditing capabilities such as keeping track of volume of traffic sent and amount of time on-line. RADIUS also enforces remote access limitations such as server access restrictions or on-line time limitations. For authentication, it supports **password authentication protocol (PAP), challenge handshake authentication protocol (CHAP),** and SecurID token authentication. RADIUS transmits passwords in encrypted format only. Some RADIUS-based centralized management products may require that a new centralized database of remote access user information be built, whereas others, such as Funk Software's Steel Belted RADIUS, are able to use an existing network operating system's directory services, such as NetWare's NDS, as the management database.

RADIUS is not the only open protocol for communication between centralized remote access management technology and multi-vendor remote access technology. **Extended terminal access controller access-control system (XTACACS),** also known simply as TACACS or the updated version known as TACACS+ (RFC 1492), is another example of remote access management protocol that supports three-tiered remote access management architectures. The most widely known implementation of TACACS is as Cisco System's server-based security protocol. TACACS transmits authentication information in cleartext format, whereas TACACS+ employs MD hashing and encrypts the entire packet. TACACS+ can also handle multiprotocol logins (IP and IPX) and incorporate PAP/CHAP as well.

PAP/CHAP

PAP and CHAP, incorporated within RADIUS as previously described, are two other protocols that can be used on a stand-alone basis for remote access authentication. **Password authentication protocol** (RFC 1334) is the simpler of the two authentication protocols designed for dial-in communication. PAP repeatedly sends the user ID and password to the authenticating system in clear text pairs until it is either acknowledged or the connection is dropped. Otherwise known as a two-way handshaking protocol, there is no encryption performed with PAP.

Challenge handshake authentication protocol (RFC 1994) provides a more secure means for establishing dial-in communication. It uses a three-way challenge or handshake that includes the user ID, password, and a key that encrypts the ID and password. The process of sending the pair to the authentication system is the same as with PAP, but the encryption reduces the chance that someone will be able to pick up the ID and password and use it to access a system. CHAP is initiated by the server by issuing a challenge to the client that wishes to log in. The client must calculate a value using a one-time key and the challenge that it just received from the server. The server would then verify the calculated value based on the challenge it had initially sent the client. The problem with this, and any single key system for that matter, is that some mechanism must be in place for both the receiver and sender to know and have access to the key. To address this problem, a public key technique may be used to encrypt the single private key for transmission. In addition, CHAP repeats the authentication procedure after the link is initially established to ensure that the session or link has not been compromised or taken over by an unauthorized party.

E-Mail, Web, and Internet/Intranet Security

Two primary standards exist for encrypting traffic on the World Wide Web:

- **S-HTTP: Secure Hypertext Transport Protocol**
- **SSL Secure Sockets Layer**

S-HTTP   Secure HTTP is a secure version of HTTP that requires both client and server S-HTTP versions to be installed for secure end-to-end encrypted transmission. S-HTTP, based on public key encryption, is described as providing security at the document or application level because it works with the actual HTTP applications to secure documents and messages. S-HTTP uses digital signature encryption to ensure that the document possesses both authenticity and message integrity. The use of S-HTTP has diminished with the growing popularity of Netscape's secure browser and server as well as other alternatives for secure web-based transmissions.

SSL   SSL is described as wrapping an encrypted envelope around HTTP transmissions. Whereas S-HTTP encrypts only web documents, SSL can be wrapped around other Internet service transmissions such as FTP, Telnet, and Gopher, as well as HTTP. SSL is a connection level encryption method, providing security to the network link itself. SSL Version 3 (SSL3) added support for more key exchange and encryption algorithms as well as separate keys for authentication and encryption.

SSL and S-HTTP are not competing or conflicting standards, although they are sometimes viewed that way. In an analogy to a Postal Service scenario, SSL provides the locked postal delivery vehicle, while S-HTTP provides the sealed, tamper-evident envelope that allows only the intended recipient to view the confidential document contained within.

Another Internet security protocol directed specifically toward securing and authenticating commercial financial transactions is known as **Secure Courier** and is offered by Netscape. Secure Courier is based on SSL and allows users to create a secure digital envelope for transmission of financial transactions over the Internet. Secure Courier also provides consumer authentication for the cybermerchants inhabiting the commercial Internet.

PCT   Microsoft's version of SSL is known as **PCT** or **Private Communications Technology.** The key difference between SSL and PCT is that PCT supports secure transmissions across unreliable (UDP rather TCP based) connections by allowing decryption of transmitted records independently from each other, as transmitted in the individual datagrams. PCT is targeted primarily toward on-line commerce and financial transactions, whereas SSL is more flexibly targeted toward web and Internet applications in general.

PEM   Privacy enhanced mail was the application standard encryption technique for e-mail use on the Internet, and was used with SMTP, simple mail transport protocol. It was designed to use both DES and RSA encryption techniques, but it would work with other encryption algorithms as well. PEM did not receive much support, however, and has been placed in "historical status" by the IETF, meaning that it is no longer being implemented. The reason for this is that PEM did not gain support from either the vendor or user populations. The vendors had their own products they supported, and the user population preferred using other e-mail programs and protocols such as PGP and S/MIME.

PGP   An Internet e-mail specific encryption standard that also uses digital signature encryption to guarantee the authenticity, security, and message integrity of received e-mail is known as **PGP,** which stands for **pretty good privacy** (RFC 1991). PGP overcomes inherent security loopholes with public/private key security schemes by implementing a web of trust in which e-mail users electronically sign each other's public keys to create an interconnected group of public key users. Digital signature encryption is provided using a combination of RSA and **MD5** (Message Direct Version 5) encryption techniques. Combined documents and digital signatures are then encrypted using **IDEA (International Data Encryption Algorithm),** which makes use of one-time 128-bit keys known as **session keys.** PGP is also able to compress data transmissions as well. PGP/MIME overcomes PGP's inability to encrypt multimedia (MIME) objects.

SET   Secure electronic transactions (SET) are a series of standards to ensure the confidentiality of electronic commerce transactions. These standards are being largely promoted by credit card giants VISA and Master-Card. SET standards are specifically aimed at defining how bank-card transactions can be conducted in a secure manner over the Internet. However, the assurance of e-commerce confidentiality is not without costs in terms of processing overhead. A single SET-compliant electronic transaction could require as many as six cryptographic functions, taking from one-third to one-half a second on a high-powered Unix workstation. The impact of thousands or millions of transactions per second could be enormous.

A large part of ensuring the authenticity of e-commerce will depend on trusting the e-customers and e-vendors who are really who they say they are. An important aspect of the SET standards is the incorporation of digital certificates or digital IDs, more specifically known as SET Digital IDs that are issued by such companies as VeriSign.

S/MIME   Secure multipurpose Internet mail extension secures e-mail traffic in e-mail applications that have been S/MIME enabled. S/MIME encrypts and authenticates e-mail messages for transmission over SMTP-based e-mail networks. S/MIME will enable different e-mail systems to exchange encrypted messages and is able to encrypt multimedia as well as text-based e-mail.

Virtual Private Network Security

In order to provide virtual private networking capabilities using the Internet as an enterprise network backbone, specialized **tunneling protocols** needed to be developed that could establish private, secure channels between connected systems. Two rival standards are examples of such tunneling protocols:

- Microsoft's **Point-to-Point Tunneling Protocol (PPTP)**
- Cisco's **Layer Two Forwarding (L2F)**

An effort is underway to have the Internet Engineering Task Force (IETF) propose a unification of the two rival standards known as **Layer 2 Tunneling Protocol (L2TP).** One shortcoming of the proposed specification is that it does not deal with security issues such as encryption and authentication. Figure 16-29 illustrates the use of tunneling protocols to build virtual private networks using the Internet as an enterprise network backbone.

Two rival specifications currently exist for establishing security over VPN tunnels:

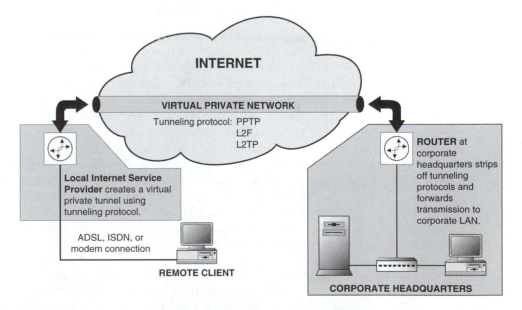

Figure 16-29 Tunneling Protocols Enable Virtual Private Networks

- **IPsec** is largely supported by the firewall vendor community and is intended to provide interoperability between VPN firewalls from different vendors.

- PPTP is Microsoft's tunneling protocol that is specific to Windows NT Servers and remote access servers. It has the backing of several remote access server vendors.

IPSec—Secure IP   IPsec is a protocol that ensures encrypted (56-bit key DES) communications across the Internet via virtual private networks through the use of manual key exchange. IPsec supports only IP-based communications. IPsec is a standard that, in theory at least, should enable interoperability between firewalls supporting the protocol. Although firewalls of the same brand seem to interoperate sufficiently via IPsec, that does not seem to be the case between different brands of firewall technology.

IPsec is also proposed to be able to support both authentication and encryption. These capabilities are optional for IPv4 and mandatory for **IPv6** and are outlined in IETF RFCs 1825 through 1829. In addition to encryption and authentication, IPsec also includes the ISAKMP (Internet Security Association key management protocol). In order to deliver these functions, two new headers are added to the existing IP header:

- The **authentication header** (RFC 1826) provides data integrity and allows for the authentication of IP packets. It can specify the security association to provide authentication between the source and destination parties, and it can also supply data to be used by the agreed-upon particular authentication algorithm.

- The **encapsulating security payload header (ESP)** (RFC 1827) ensures the privacy of the transmission. The ESP header can be used in two different modes depending on the user's privacy needs:
  - **Transport mode ESP** is used to encrypt the data carried by the IP packet. The contents of the data field of an IP (network layer) packet are the upper layer or transport layer protocols TCP (connection-oriented) or UDP (connectionless). These transport layer envelopes encapsulate upper layer data.
  - **Tunnel mode ESP** encrypts the entire IP packet, including its own header. This mode is effective at countering network analyzers or sniffers from capturing IP address information. Tunnel mode is most often used in a network topology that includes a firewall that separates a protected network from an external nonsecure network.

It is important to note that the mere inclusion of fields in a protocol does not ensure implementation. Applications, authentication products, and trusted security associations would all have to modify hardware and/or software technology to avail themselves of the protocol's new functionality. Figure 16-30 illustrates an IPsec packet with authentication and encryption headers added.

PPTP—Point-to-Point Tunneling Protocol   PPTP is essentially a tunneling protocol that allows managers to choose whatever encryption or authentication technology they wish to hang off either end of the established tunnel. PPTP supports multiple network protocols including IPX, NetBEUI, and IP. PPTP is primarily concerned with secure remote access in that PPP-enabled clients would be able to dial in to a corporate network via the Internet.

Enterprise Network Security

In order to maintain proper security over a widely distributed enterprise network, it is essential to be able to conduct certain security-related processes from a single, centralized, security management location. Among these processes or functions are the following:

- **Single point of registration (SPR)** allows a network security manager to enter a new user (or delete a terminated user) from a single centralized location and assign all associated rights, privileges, and access control to enterprise resources from this single point rather

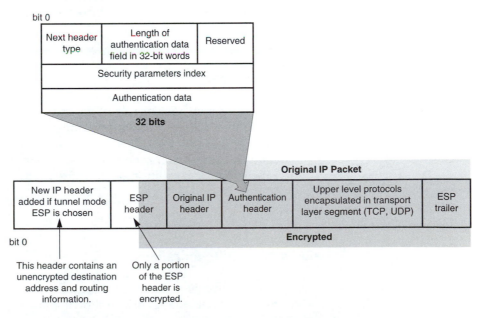

Figure 16-30   IP Packet Plus Authentication and Encryption Headers

than having to enter this new user's information on multiple resources distributed throughout the enterprise.

- **Single sign-on (SSO),** also sometimes known as secure single sign-on (SSSO), allows the user to login to the enterprise network and to be authenticated from their client PC location. It is not necessary for the user to remember a variety of different userIDs and passwords to the numerous different enterprise servers from which they may request services. Because this is the single entry point onto the enterprise network for this user, auditing software can be used to keep non-repudiation records of all activities and transactions. Any of the variety of authentication technologies discussed earlier can be used in support of single sign-on.

- **Single access control view** allows the user's access from their client workstation to only display those resources that the user actually has access to. Any differences between server platforms should be shielded from the user. The user should not need to memorize different commands or control interfaces for the variety of enterprise servers that a user may need to access.

- **Security auditing and intrusion detection** is able to track and identify suspicious behaviors from both internal employees and potential intruders. In addition to detecting and reporting these instances, it is essential to be able to respond in an appropriate and automated fashion to these events. Although the intrusions may take place anywhere on the widely distributed network, the detection and response to such events must be controlled from a centralized security management location.

◼ GOVERNMENT IMPACT

Government agencies play a major role in the area of network security. The two primary functions of these various government agencies are:

- Standards-making organizations that set standards for the design, implementation, and certification of security technology and systems

- Regulatory agencies that control the export of security technology to a company's international locations

Standards-Making Organizations

Although many standards-making organizations are involved to varying degrees in the field of network security, following are some of the most significant ones.

ANSI   The American National Standards Institute, or ANSI, is the U.S. representative to the International Standards Organization, or ISO. Any submissions to the ISO from other U.S. standards organizations must first be submitted to ANSI.

NIST   The National Institute of Standards and Technology, or the NIST, was formed in 1987, but it was formerly known as the National Bureau of Standards. This organization issues publications called the Federal Information Processing Standards, or FIPS publications. Category 5 FIPS publications deal with computer security standards and guidelines and include subcategories of access control, cryptography, general computer security, risk analysis and contingency planning, and security labels. The NIST also publishes a series of special publications related to computer security included in the SP 500 and SP 800 series. The NIST also operates a very useful computer security resource clearinghouse on the World Wide Web at http://csrc.ncsl.nist.gov/

IAB   The Internet Architecture Board is the policy setting and decision review board for the Internet. The IETF, or Internet Engineering Task Force, is a subgroup of the IAB that is responsible for setting the technical standards that run the Internet. This is the group responsible for issuing and gathering the responses RFC (requests for comments).

ISO   The International Standards Organization is a voluntary organization sanctioned by the United Nations. It is responsible for international standards in a variety of fields, not just data communications. Besides the OSI 7-layer reference model, the ISO is also responsible for the security-related addendum to the OSI model known as ISO 7498/2, the OSI security architecture.

NSA   The National Security Agency is a secretive governmental organization that works closely with the NIST and is responsible for the design and use of nonmilitary encryption technology. The NSA also runs the NCSC, or the National Computer Security Center.

NCSC   The purpose of this organization is to work with members of the computer industry to provide guidelines to help them develop trusted systems and computer products. This organization is also known for a security certification program called the Trusted Computer System Evaluation Criteria (TCSEC). It is commonly known as the Orange Book because of the color of the jacket. There is also a Red Book from the NCSC, which was developed in 1987 as a supplement to the Orange Book. These "colored book" security guidelines have been criticized for focusing primarily on computer security rather than network security.

Orange Book Certification   The primary focus of the Orange Book is to provide confidential protection of sensitive information based on six fundamental requirements:

- Security policy: An explicit and well-defined security policy must be enforced by the system

- Marking: Access control labels must be associated with all objects.

- Identification: Individual users must be identified.

- Accountability: Audit information must be kept and protected so that actions affecting security can be traced to the responsible party.

- Assurance: The system must contain hardware and/or software components that can be evaluated independently to provide sufficient assurance that the security policy and accountability criteria can be enforced.

- Continuous protection: The preceding components that enforce these basic requirements must be continuously protected against tampering and/or unauthorized changes.

The Orange Book is broken into two primary parts; the first is illustrated in Figure 16-31. It specifies the criteria that must be met in order to achieve a specific rating. The criteria are defined in hierarchical fashion, with four different ratings possible. The *A* rating is the most secure possible and the *D* rating corresponds to the least secure rating possible.

The second portion of the Orange Book contains information about the basic objectives, rationale, and government policy behind the development of each of the criteria. It is also intended to provide guidelines for product developers to aid them in achieving a specific criterion.

The Orange Book certification process is both costly and lengthy. Typically, the certification process is projected to take two years to complete at a cost of $17 million. To date, both NetWare and NT Server have achieved the C2 certification. It's important to remember that many products may advertise a certification compliance with an Orange Book level, but compliance and certification are two very different terms. Any vendor can claim compliance, but only vendors that have spent the time and money to pursue the certification process can claim that their products are C2 certified.

Encryption Export Policy and Key Recovery

Many corporations and organizations depend on the ability to have private and confidential communication on an international basis. In the United States, however, export of encryption software is tightly controlled. The traditional limit on exportable encryption technology was a 40-bit key. However, 40-bit keys can be cracked in a matter of minutes and do not offer much protection. Businesses conducting operations internationally obviously want to be able to use stronger encryption technology. The government, on

Division	Protection	Class	Protection	Description
D	Minimal	D	Minimal	Evaluated but does not meet any higher class requirements
C	Discretionary	C1	Discretionary security	Confidence in hardware and software controls
		C2	Controlled access	Isolates and authenticates users and data Encapsulates resources; login and explicit auditing
B	Mandatory	B1	Labeled security	Explicit protection model; execution domains, file labels, system security officer, and documentation required
		B2	Structured	Formal security model; kernelized, covert channel ID, mandatory controls including communication lines required
		B3	Security domains	Central encapsulation, reference monitor, tamper proof, recovery procedures, protected against authentication attacks
A	Verified	A1	Verified design	Extensive security considerations during all developmental phases. Math tools, formal models with explicit math theorems, formal top-level specifications, trusted software distribution required
		Beyond A1		Developmental; source verification required

Figure 16-31   Orange Book Certification Criteria

the other hand, wishes to gain greater control over international encrypted communication as evidenced by its **clipper chip** initiative.

The clipper chip initiative proposed that every phone and data communications device in the United States would be equipped with a clipper chip to support encryption. The part of the proposal that had businesses and individuals concerned was that the government would hold a spare set of keys that could decrypt any messaged encrypted by a clipper chip device. The notion of trusting the government with a spare set of keys caused quite an uproar and the proposal was not pursued. However, the initiative clearly showed the government's intention to seek greater control of international encrypted communications.

The current proposal, which some might consider a compromise, is that U.S. companies with international subsidiaries may now export 56-bit key-based encryption technology provided that they establish within two years a **key recovery mechanism** that will offer a back door into encrypted data for the government. Once the key recovery mechanism is in place, the companies are allowed to export keys of any length. All banks, whether U.S. based or not, are also allowed to export 56-bit encryption technology. However, even 56-bit keys can be cracked. Experts estimate that 56-bit keys can be cracked in 19 days at a cost of $500,000. The new regulation also moved responsibility for encryption product export from the U.S. State Department to the U.S. Commerce Department, thereby no longer classifying encryption technology as munitions and speeding the export permit approval process. In September 1999, the White House proposed that encryption hardware with up to 56-bit keys and encryption software with up to 64-bit keys would no longer require export license.

Key recovery schemes basically ensure that a spare set of encryption keys are always available. With key recovery, the actual information used to reconstruct a key travels with the message header. However, someone with the key decryption codes (the spare set of keys) must combine the decryption codes with the key information in the message header in order to decrypt the message. The big question seems to be, "Who will hold the keys?" Key escrow agencies, otherwise known as trusted third parties, are the most commonly proposed solution. Other proposals say that large multinational corporations should be able to act as their own key escrow agents. At present there are about 13 different key recovery mechanisms, and no single standard has been proposed, although an IBM-led key-recovery alliance with 40 corporate members has been formed. If key recovery were to be extended to a domestic basis, the implications could be phenomenal. Everyone who uses the Internet for communication would need a key and a key escrow agent. This could mean tens of millions of keys unless some type of key sharing was initiated.

SUMMARY

Without question, the overriding theme in this chapter has been that the implementation of security technology in the absence of a comprehensive security policy including senior management support is a waste of time and money. Security policy must be developed as part of an overall increase in security awareness on the part of all users. It must be accompanied by a clear understanding of business processes and personal responsibilities as they relate to security policy implementation. Only in the context of a dynamic, constantly audited security policy can security technology implementation be successful.

The first security process that is generally addressed is virus protection, most often in response to a virus incident. Virus-scanning technology is of little use without comprehensive, enforced policies regarding use and handling of diskettes and downloaded files. Activity monitors and signature scanners are two major types of virus scanning software.

The next security process that is generally addressed is authentication, ensuring that users attempting to log into network resources are really who they claim to be. Authentication technology includes challenge-response and time-synchronous token authentication systems.

Authorization and access control ensures that authenticated users are able to access only those files, directories, and applications to which they are entitled. Kerberos is the best example of a comprehensive authentication/authorization system.

Firewalls are an effective means of shielding private, secure, internal networks from nonsecure external networks. Like other security technology, they must be implemented correctly and in accordance with the overall security policy. Two major categories of firewalls are packet filters, which discriminate between traffic based on source and destination addresses, and application gateways of proxies, which examine individual commands within applications.

Privacy of network communications is ensured by encryption. Private key encryption, public key encryption, and digital signature encryption are the major categories of encryption technology. Encryption sessions are customized through the use of keys. The longer the key, in bits, the more secure the transmission.

Encryption technology is regulated as to the key length that can be exported from the United States. Key recovery mechanisms are plans through which the government would be able to decipher encrypted communications. In order for organizations to be able to encrypt communication internationally, they must be willing to submit a key recovery mechanism to the U.S. government.

KEY TERMS

activity monitors
application gateways
Application-level filters
assets
assured pipelines
Attack applets
authentication
Authentication Header
biometric authentication
brokered authorization
C2 certification
CA
certificate authorities
certificate servers
Challenge Handshake
    Authentication Protocol
Challenge Response Token
    Authentication
CHAP
Ciphertext

Circuit-level proxy
Clipper Chip
CRC Checkers
Data Encryption Standard
Denial of service attack DES
Digital IDs
Digital Signature Encryption
DMZ
Dual firewalls
dual-homed gateway
emulation technology
Encapsulating Security Payload
    Header
ESP
event detection
Extended Terminal Access
    Control Access System
false accepts
false rejects
filter

Filter tables
firewall
Generic Security Service-
    Applications Program
    Interface
GSS-API
Hashing Checkers
Heuristic analysis
IDEA
inter-realm
internal firewalls
International Data Encryption
    Algorithm
Internet Security Association
    and Key Management
    Protocol
Intrusion detection systems
IP spoofing
IPsec
IPv6

ISAKMP
ISO 7498/2
Kerberos
Key Escrow agencies
key recovery mechanism
L2F
L2TP
Land attack
latency
Layer-Two Tunneling Protocol
Layer-Two Forwarding
logic bombs
malicious applets
MD5
Multi-tiered firewall
National Computer Security
   Association
NCSA
network level filter
OSI Security Architecture
packet filter
PAP
Password Authentication
Protocol
PCT
PEM
PGP
PKIX
Point-to-Point Tunneling
Protocol
policy audits
Polymorphic viruses
port level filter
PPTP
Pretty Good Privacy

Privacy Enhanced Mail
Private Communications
   Technology
private key encryption
protective measures
proxies
public key certificates
Public Key Encryption
RADIUS
real-time audits
realms
Remote Authentication Dial-In
   User Service
risks
RSA
S-HTTP
S/MIME
SATAN
Secure Electronic Transactions
Secure Hypertext Transport
   Protocol
Secure Multipurpose Internet
   Mail Extension
secure single login
Secure Sockets Layer
Security Analyzer Tool for
   Analyzing Networks
Security Auditing and Intrusion
   Detection
security policy development
   life cycle
security probes
service-granting ticket
session keys
SET

signature scanners
Simple Key Management for IP
Single Access Control View
Single Point of Registration
single sign-on
SKIP
Smart Cards
SOCKS
SPDLC
SPR
SSL
SSO
TCP
Threats
Three-way handshake
ticket
ticket-granting ticket
time bombs
Time Synchronous Token
   Authentication
Token authentication
Transmission Control Protocol
Transport Mode ESP
trojan horse
trusted gateway
trusted node
Tunnel Mode ESP
tunneling protocols
virtual PC
Virus scanning
vulnerabilities
X.509
XTACACS

REVIEW QUESTIONS

1. What are some recent changes in the business and networking worlds that have brought network security to the forefront?
2. What is the importance of the cyclical nature of the security policy development life cycle?
3. What is the purpose of the security requirements assessment grid?
4. What is the dilemma involved with the security/productivity balance?

5. How do the critical success factors introduced with the network development life cycle apply to security policy development?
6. What is the purpose of the OSI Security Architecture and how does it relate to the OSI 7-layer reference model?
7. Differentiate among and give an example, in a network security context, of each of the

following: asset, threat, vulnerability, risk, protective measures.

8. Are all of the entities listed in the previous question related by one-to-one relationships? Give an example to defend your answer.

9. Briefly summarize the roles of executives, management, and users in the successful development and implementation of security policy.

10. What is the difference between off-line audits and real-time audits?

11. What is the difference between event detection technology and intrusion detection technology?

12. What is the difference between security audit tools and security probes?

13. What is a virus?

14. What is the difference between a logic bomb and a time bomb?

15. What is a trojan horse?

16. What is a polymorphic virus?

17. What are hostile applets and in which environment do they exist?

18. Why are collaborative applications such as groupware an especially friendly environment for viruses?

19. Differentiate between virus scanning and activity monitors as antivirus technology.

20. What is the shortcoming of CRC and hashing checkers as antivirus solutions?

21. What is a firewall?

22. Differentiate between packet filtering firewalls and application gateway firewalls.

23. Describe the advantages and disadvantages of proxies.

24. What is a dual-homed gateway?

25. What is a trusted gateway?

26. How does a trusted gateway differ from a dual-homed gateway?

27. What is an internal firewall and what is the motivation for such a device?

28. What is authentication?

29. Differentiate between challenge response authentication and time-synchronous authentication.

30. What is biometric authentication? Give some examples of biometric authentication technology.

31. What is Kerberos?

32. How does Kerberos ensure both authentication and authorization?

33. Differentiate between private key encryption, public key encryption, and digital signature encryption.

34. Why are public key certificates and certificate authorities necessary?

35. Why are APIs and application development environments required in order to integrate security services with information systems? What would be the alternative?

36. What is RADIUS and what added functionality does it offer over an environment without a three-tiered approach?

37. Differentiate between S-HTTP and SSL.

38. Differentiate between PAP and CHAP.

39. What is PGP? What are its advantages and disadvantages?

40. What is SET and what industry is it targeted toward?

41. What is a tunneling protocol and why is it necessary?

42. What is Secure IP (IPv6) and what services can it offer?

43. What is the difference between transport mode ESP and tunnel mode ESP?

44. What is the difference between single sign-on, single point of registration, and single access control view? What do they all have in common?

45. What is Orange Book or C-2 certification?

46. What is the clipper chip?

47. What is the purpose of a key recovery mechanism and how does it work?

48. What is the role of key escrow agencies in enabling a key recovery mechanism?

49. What are the potential implications if all Internet users were required to use key recovery mechanisms?

50. Discuss the advantages and disadvantages of the alternative enterprise firewall architectures discussed in the text. Are there other viable alternatives that were not mentioned?

ACTIVITIES

1. Research topics such as network security losses or computer crime and report on your results. What is the trend of the statistics over the last five years? How valid are the statistics in terms of being an accurate reflection of the entire extent of the problem?

2. Find an organization or business that will let you prepare a security policy document. Run the entire process as a well-organized plan, using project management software if possible. Start with a small feasibility and report your results before defining the full project scope. Use the planning tools supplied in the chapter and adapt them to your own situation as needed.

3. Choose any network security-related topic of interest and research it using only Internet resources. Two good sites to start with: http://www.ncsa.com and http://csrc.ncsl.nist.gov/.

4. Consider the statement: "The implementation of security technology in the absence of a comprehensive security policy is like putting a steel door on a grass hut." Find actual examples of network security implementations to either support or refute the statement.

5. Download a copy of Security Analyzer Tool for Analyzing Networks from ftp://ftp.win.tue.nl/pub/security/index.html. After obtaining proper permissions, run the analysis tool and report on your results.

6. Log into Internet Security Systems web site at www.iss.net and review information regarding their RealSecure network-based attack analyzer. Compare its features with those of SATAN. What would be the most appropriate use for each technology?

7. Create a virus clearinghouse and information center for your school, business, or organization if one does not already exist. Does your organization have a published antivirus strategy? If not, create one. Report on your results.

8. Research the problem of hostile applets and components. What are the potential solutions to the problem? Is this a problem with the development languages?

9. What is Word Macro Concept virus? Find out exactly how it works and figure out how it can be eradicated and kept from spreading. How much of the solution is technology versus procedures?

10. Design and prepare a budget for a safe remote access network including remote access server, firewall, authentication technology, and modems. Prepare alternative budget proposals for challenge response versus time synchronous token authentication technology. Was the price difference significant? If so, how could the price difference be justified?

11. Resarch the field of biometric authentication technology. What are the most stable and dependable products? What are the latest products? Can you find data on false accept and false reject rates of biometric authentication technology?

12. What is the current rate of acceptance and implementation of Kerberos in industry? What are the strengths and limitations of the architecture?

13. Research the issue of privacy in the age of electronic commerce. What impact might Digital IDs and key recovery schemes have on an individual's right to privacy? Consider debating the issue in class. What are the conflicting motivations or goals behind the issue?

14. Research virtual private networks. What is the extent of actual implementation of virtual private networks as opposed to the amount of press coverage and technology development? Explain your results.

15. Research and prepare a presentation, timeline, or bulletin board on the government's role in encryption technology control, especially in terms of export control. Begin with the clipper chip initiative and follow it through the present day.

CASE STUDY

Motley Fooling Around with Electronic Commerce

Walk into the headquarters of a company that's building one of the World Wide Web's most state-of-the-art electronic commerce sites and you'll be confronted with techies playing pool, screams from someone losing his Sega Genesis game and an array of workers sporting jester hats.

This is The Motley Fool, the country's nouveau online financial advisory firm. While most think of Wall Street pundits as a bunch of buttoned-down suits, employees at this one-time America Online venture are more comfortable in South Park T-shirts and jeans. After all, this is the company that has made its name from being, well … Foolish.

Start talking about the future of the company's Fool-Mart online store and Chief Technical Fool Dwight Gibbs draws you into the company's radio studio/board-room. In walks Jill Kianka, an MBA from Georgetown University who dodged the traditional world of high finance to create FoolMart, which Gibbs hopes will become one of the company's most profitable endeavors. In fact, Gibbs says that FoolMart sales will account for half of the company's revenue within a couple of years, complementing the revenue pulled in by the company through consulting and other services.

But he knows that just selling jester hats, the company's staple promotional item, will not help The Motley Fool reach its financial goals.

The real money is in selling more daily e-mail subscriptions, portfolio tracking software and reports. In order to deliver these products reliably and bill customers efficiently, The Motley Fool has had to embark on a $35,000 Web site hardware, software and bandwidth upgrade. And the company no longer can rely on AOL's electronic commerce infrastructure, given that The Motley Fool created FoolMart after spinning off its own Web site last year.

TAKING ON A "FOOL" LOAD

FoolMart has been operating on a single Pentium Pro 200 Dell Server that boasts 120M bytes of RAM and runs Microsoft's Site Server Commerce Edition 2.0. The server has been connected to a similar machine running Microsoft's SQL Server database that is shared by departments across the company.

"Other applications within Fool headquarters, such as application development, were taking up resources on the SQL box," Gibbs says. "This would leave FoolMart begging for resources."

And customers were left waiting to place orders, he adds.

The new system, which is still in the process of being installed, is anchored by a pair of Compaq 3000 servers. One machine powered by a single 333-MHz Pentium II processor and outfitted with 256M bytes of RAM will host Version 3.0 of Microsoft's Site Server electronic commerce software. The machine is linked through a firewall to a dual Pentium II processor box running SQL Server 6.5. The database server is dedicated to housing FoolMart's customer and order databases.

The upgrade to Site Server 3.0 provides the site with better security features, including support for Secure Sockets Layer 2.0 and 3.0.

Also getting a lift is the company's total bandwidth. In order to accommodate the increased traffic on FoolMart and the main site at www.

motleyfool.com, Gibbs is boosting the company's pipeline from three T-1s to a fractional T-3, offering between 9M bit/sec and 12M bit/sec throughput. Gibbs says that should be enough to handle the more than one million page requests a day made to The Motley Fool site.

THE WISDOM OF A FOOL

No matter what technology a company is using, Kianka says, the key for a company to be successful in electronic commerce is knowing what types of products it is going to be offering and optimiz-

ing its infrastructure accordingly.

For instance, if the company is going to sell online products such as e-mail subscriptions and software downloads, the company needs to make sure it has the hardware, software and bandwidth to support them.

The Motley Fool uses a homemade Pentium II machine with 64M bytes of RAM running Linux to generate its more than 60,000 e-mail newsletters, which are created in-house.

"The Linux machine is not even breaking a sweat," Gibbs says. "It's a shame right

now we can't put out enough e-mail to push it to capacity."

The Motley Fool used to rely on a third party to do its credit card transaction processing, but Kianka says it was easier and less expensive to bring this task in-house.

What has Gibbs learned from the whole experience so far?

"You have to have multiple disciplines to put together a store," he says. "You need someone who's tech-savvy, but you also need someone who's product-savvy. Trying it any other way would be foolish."

Source: Sandra Gittlen, "Motley Fooling Around with Electronic Commerce," *Network World,* vol. 15, no. 37 (September 14, 1998), p. 37. Copyright Network World. Reprinted with permission.

BUSINESS CASE STUDY QUESTIONS

Activities

1. Complete a top-down model for this case by gleaning facts from the case and placing them in the proper layer of the top-down model. After completing the top-down model, analyze and detail those instances where requirements were clearly passed down from upper layers to lower layers of the model and where solutions to those requirements were passed up from lower layers to upper layers of the model.
2. Detail any questions about the case that may occur to you for which answers are not clearly stated in the article.

Business

1. In what business is the organization profiled in this article?
2. What did the hardware upgrade cost?
3. Do you think this investment can be cost justified? Defend your answer.

4. What do the people interviewed for this article feel is the key for success in e-commerce?
5. Has this company followed its own advice in this regard? Defend your answer.
6. Were any activities outsourced? Explain.

Application

1. What applications needed to be developed or purchased to support this business initiative?
2. How many requests per day are made to this company's site?

Data

1. What database technology is required to support applications?

Network

1. How much network bandwidth is required to support the application?
2. Is a bandwidth upgrade required? Why or why not?

3. What types of security, if any, are provided on this network?

Technology

1. What type of technology was used initially?
2. What type of technology is the company migrating to?

3. List which different computing platforms and operating systems are used for which applications.

GLOSSARY

1Base5 A 1Mbps Ethernet standard for unshielded twisted pair

4 conductor station wire The type of phone wire installed in most homes consists of a tan plastic jacket containing four untwisted wires: red, yellow, green, and black and is also known as 4 conductor station wire or RYGB

7 Hop limit One very important limitation of source routing bridges as applied to large internetworks is known as the 7 Hop Limit. Because of the limited space in the RIF (Router Information Field) of the explorer packet, only 7 hop locations can be included in the path to any remote destination

10Base2 A 10Mbps Ethernet standard for thin coaxial cable media

10Base5 A 10Mbps Ethernet standard for thick coaxial cable media

10BaseF A 10Mbps Ethernet standard for fiber optic cable media

10BaseT A 10Mbps Ethernet standard for unshielded twisted pair media

10/100 NICs Most of the 100BaseT NICs are called 10/100 NICs, which means that they are able to support either 10BaseT or 100BaseT, but not simultaneously

16-bit sub-system A shared memory address space, sometimes referred to as a 16-bit sub-system, allows 16-bit applications to execute in a 32-bit operating environment

100BaseFX Physical layer standard for 100Mbps transmission over fiber optic cable

100BaseT4 Physical layer standard for 100Mbps transmission over 4 pair of Category 3, 4, or 5 UTP

100BaseTX The most common of the three 100BaseX standards and the one for which the most technology is available. It specifies 100Mbps performance over 2 pair of Category 5 UTP (Unshielded Twisted Pair) or 2 pair of type 1 STP (Shielded Twisted Pair

100VG-AnyLAN 100VG-AnyLAN is a 100Mbps alternative to 100BaseT, which replaces the CSMA/CD access methodology with Demand Priority Access or DPA, otherwise known as Demand Priority Protocol or DPP

1000BaseCX Uses copper twinaxial cable and transceivers for distances of only 25 meters. Used primarily to link servers within a data center or high speed network devices within a wiring closet

1000BaseLX Uses long wavelength (1300 nanometers) laser fiber optic media. Primarily used for high speed campus backbone applications

1000BaseSX Uses short wavelength (850 nanometers) laser fiber optic media. Primarily used for horizontal building cabling on a given floor

1000BaseTX Expected to be ratified in 1999, this standard would allow gigabit Ethernet to travel over 4 pair of Category 5 unshielded twisted pair at a distance of 100 meters

3270 protocol conversion card Inserted into an open expansion slot of a PC. Additional protocol conversion software, which may or may not be included with the protocol conversion card, must be loaded onto the PC to make the PC keyboard behave like a 3270 terminal keyboard

absolute path names In Unix, absolute path names start at the root directory in the listing of the path to the destination directory while relative path names start at the current directory

Access Control List See ACL

access methodologies Since the LAN media is to be shared by numerous PC users, there must be some way to control access by multiple users to that media. These media sharing methods are properly known as access methodologies

access server See Communications server

access tokens See digital license certificates

ACD it is important for help desk management software to be able to interact with call center management technology such as automatic call distributors (ACD) and interactive voice response units (IVRU). The overall integration of computer-based software and telephony equipment in known as computer telephony integration (CTI)

ACID test   A set of rules that describe the capabilities of a transaction process monitoring system

acknowledgment and polling traffic   The first characteristic of SNA that can cause trouble on a LAN is the great amount of acknowledgment and polling traffic between SNA processors and SNA end-user devices. This constant chatter could quickly monopolize the better part of the LAN bandwidth

ACL   A list of users that are authorized to access a given resource. An ACL is located on the server containing the resource and includes the effective rights or permissions that the user has to the resource

ACL   NT's security reference monitor compares the requested object's security description as documented in access control lists (ACL), with the requesting user's security information as documented on their security access token

ACR   Attenuation to Crosstalk Ratio is measured in dB or decibels. A decibel is a logarithmic rather than linear measurement of the ratio between two powers, often a data signal and some type of noise or interference

active data objects   See ADO

Active Directory   See AD

active management MAUs   Able to send alerts to management consoles regarding malfunctioning Token Ring adapters and can also forcibly remove these misbehaving adapters from the ring

active monitor   In a token passing access methodology, the token is generated in the first place by a designated PC known as the active monitor and passed among PCs until one PC would like to access the network

ActiveX   An object based technology from Microsoft used to build and distribute software components. While the term ActiveX can refer to the entire DCOM architecture, it is most commonly used to refer to specific software components

activity monitors   Because of their ability to monitor behavior of programs, this category of anti-virus technology is also sometimes known as activity monitors

AD   A distributed database containing information about Windows 2000 network resources similar in function to the NetWare NDS service

ad hoc workflow   This category of workflow software automates more open-ended, creative, or flexible business processes that are done occasionally or in an unscheduled manner

address bit order reversal   In the case of IEEE 802.3, the least significant bit is the right-most bit of the byte and in the case of IEEE 802.5, the least significant bit is the left-most bit of the byte. This bit order reversal is especially troublesome for translating bridges that must translate between token ring and Ethernet frames

address caching   To avoid constantly flooding the network with explorer packets seeking destinations, source routing bridges may employ some type of address caching or RIF caching, so that previously determined routes to known destinations are saved and reused

address classes   IP addresses are categorized into address classes A, B, C, D, or E

address resolution   The process of resolving a hardware (MAC) address from a layer three network layer address

address resolution protocol   See ARP

address resolution server   LAN emulation is most often implemented by the ATM vendor by the installation of an address resolution server that provides translation between the ATM addressing scheme and the addressing scheme, which is native to a particular emulated LAN

administrative workflow   This category of workflow software automates routine business processes that nearly all businesses have in common. Examples include purchase order requisition and approval, accounts payable approval, review of job applicants' files, or expense report approval

ADO   Active Data Objects are part of the OLE DB API. Active Data Objects replace the RDO and DAO interfaces from the initial ODBC standard

ADSP   A connectionless session layer protocol used in the AppleTalk protocol suite

Advanced mobile phone service   See AMPS

advanced peer to peer networking   See APPN

Advanced Power Management   See APM

advanced server for UNIX   A commercial package for UNIX that emulates a Windows NT 4.0 server

Adverse Channel enchancements   Transmitting

data over analog cellular networks requires modems that support specialized cellular transmission protocols on both ends of the cellular transmission in order to maximize throughput. Examples of such protocols are MNP-10 Adverse Channel Enhancements and Enhanced Throughput Cellular (ETC)

advisory agents   Advisory agents or wizards assist users as they learn their way around new software packages, thereby easing frustration and shortening the learning curve. Advisory agents can sense when a user is performing a repetitive task that could perhaps be automated or done more efficiently

AEP   A protocol used to test network connectivity on AppleTalk networks through echo-reply packets

AFP   The file sharing application layer protocol used in the AppleTalk protocol suite

agent   Each network-attached device that is to be SNMP-compliant must be equipped with software capable of reporting required performance statistics in standardized SNMP format. This embedded SNMP reporting software is known as a software agent, SNMP agent, or management agent

agent   In between the intelligent application, reporting on event conditions and performance metrics, and the management console is an autonomous piece of software known as an agent, that collects these performance statistics and properly formats them for transmission to the application management console

agent event manager   One of three cooperating components of the agent portion of the client/agent/server architecture. The agent event manager is combined with a customer written transaction handler to form an entity known as the intelligent agent that resides on the local server. Once the agent event manager receives a request from a mobile client, it acts on behalf of that client in all communications with the local server until the original client request is totally fulfilled

agents   Intelligent software, also known as smart software, utilizes agents, which assist end-users in their quest for increased productivity

agents   Network statistics and information are gathered in the first place and packetized in SNMP format by specialized software known as agents,

which reside within the monitored network device and are supplied by the network device's manufacturer

Aggregation   Used to more generally describe any circumstance when a subnet's entire address space can be represented by only the common portion of those addresses in a routing advertisement

AMPS   The current circuit switched analog cellular network is more properly known by the transmission standard to which it adheres known as Advanced Mobile Phone Service (AMPS) and operates in the 800MHz frequency range

AMS   One proposal for standardizing how instrumentation should be developed within applications is known as the applications management specification (AMS

API   Application programming interface provides a means of accessing the functionality of an application. External software is written to conform to the API

API wrapping   The process of converting a mainframe application to a support client/server computing. The clients access data on the server via a specialized piece of middleware that communicated with the server application via the server application's APIs

APM   Power management features offered by operating systems have been standardized as the Advanced Power Management (APM) specification

applet   An application that runs inside of another application. Most commonly used to describe JAVA applications that run inside of a web browser

AppleTalk   AppleTalk is included as a communications protocol in order to support NT's Services for Macintosh (SFM)

AppleTalk Data Stream Protocol   See ADSP

AppleTalk Echo Protocol   See AEP

AppleTalk Filing Protocol   See AFP

AppleTalk Session Protocol   See ASP

AppleTalk Transaction Protocol   See ATP

application gateways   Concerned with what services or applications a message is requesting in addition to who is making that request. Connections between requesting clients and service providing servers are only created after the application gateway is satisfied as to the legitimacy of the request.

Even once the legitimacy of the request has been established, only proxy clients and servers actually communicate with each other

Application Installation Service   A Windows 2000 service designed to provide a consistent set of applications to be available to a user. Applications are assigned to users or groups of users. Whenever a user logs into a network station, the application installation service will ensure that the required applications are installed on the station. If not, the service will install the applications as part of the login sequence

application level filters   Examine the entire request for data rather than just the source and destination addresses. Secure files can be marked as such and application level filters will not allow those files to be transferred, even to users authorized by port level filters

Application MIB   Identifies three key groups of variables for proper application tracking and management:

application program interface   Whether or not an application is executable over a particular network operating system is dependent upon whether or not that application issues commands and requests for network-based services in a pre-determined format defined by the network operating system's application program interface. See API

application response measurement   See ARM

application services   The server network operating system that is responsible for application services which includes not only executing the back-end engine portion of the application, but also supplying the messaging and communications services to enable interoperability between distributed clients and servers

applications layer   The application layer, layer 7 of the OSI Model, is also open to misinterpretation. Application layer protocols do not include end-user application programs. Rather, they include utilities that support end-user application programs. Some people include network operating systems in this category. Strictly speaking, the best examples of application layer protocols are the OSI protocols X.400 and X.500

applications management specification   See AMS

applications software   Applications software on a

LAN is divided into client front-ends and server back-ends or engines and is concerned with accomplishment of a specific type of task or transaction. LAN applications software can be divided into two major sub-categories: LAN productivity software and LAN resource management software

APPN   Advanced Peer to Peer Networking is an IBM multi-protocol solution that allows computers to talk directly on an SNA network

APPN   APPN, Advanced Peer to Peer Network, is IBM's answer to multiprotocol networking on a peer to peer basis using the SNA architecture, rather than a LAN-based network architecture

Area 0   All OSPF networks have at least one area, known as Area 0 or the backbone area, configured

ARM   An API that can be used by applications developers is known as application response measurement (ARM) and can measure several key application statistics

ARP   ARP or Address Resolution Protocol (RFC 826) is used if an IP address of workstation is known but a datalink layer address for the same workstation is required

ASP   The session layer protocol used in the AppleTalk protocol suite

assembly language   A low level programming language that uses pneumonic instructions rather than numeric machine instructions. Also known as assembler

assets   Corporate property of some value that require varying degrees of protection

assistant agents   Act much like a human administrative assistant by performing specific tasks on behalf of, but out of the direct control of, the end-user. Examples of assistant agents' tasks might be to screen, manage, and reformat electronic received e-mail and faxes and to surf the Internet in search of articles or research on a given topic

assured pipelines   See Application gateways

asynchronous application communications   A communications model where an application does not have to wait for a reply before continuing processing. The opposite of synchronous communications

asynchronous frames   In FDDI, while synchronous frames are being transmitted, any unused network capacity can still be used by other workstations transmitting asynchronous frames

asynchronous I/O   A situation in which a client application spawns a thread for information or processing and proceeds with the execution of the client application without waiting for the results of the spawned thread

asynchronous transfer mode   See ATM

ATM   Asynchronous Transfer Mode, a type of switching that allows not only LAN network architectures to be switched extremely quickly but can also switch voice, video, and image traffic equally well. In fact ATM can switch any type of digital information over LANs or WANs with equal ease and speeds currently in the 622Mbps range and rapidly approaching the gigabit/second range

ATP   The transport layer protocol used in the AppleTalk protocol suite

Attachment Units   See AU

Attack applets   Java applets downloaded from the web that are intent on serious security breaches

attenuation   The decrease in the power of signal over a distance in a particular type of wire or media

Attenuation to crosstalk ratio   See ACR

AU   Iso-Ethernet hubs are known as Attachment Units (AU) and cost between $400 and $500 per port

audiotex   These systems deliver audio information to callers based on responses on the touch-tone keypad to pre-recorded questions. Primarily used for information hot-lines

auditing system   In NetWare 4.1, an extensive auditing system monitors and reports on what valid users are doing. The auditor acts independently of the supervisor and separately monitors activity on both the file system and the NetWare Directory Services database

authentication   The process of proving that users are who they say they are. Authentication is a two step process: identification and proof of identification

authentication   Authentication in NetWare 4.1 uses a combination of private encryption keys and passwords, while the VLM requester security

agent on the client workstation and NDS file server combine to ensure that users are properly authenticated before being logged in

authentication   The overall purpose of authentication is to ensure that users attempting to gain access to networks are really whom they claim to be

authentication credentials   The means used to authenticate a user. Most commonly a user ID and a password

Authentication Header   In Secure IP, The Authentication Header provides data integrity and allows for the authentication of IP packets

authorization   The process of determining the access rights a user should have for resources. Authorization is usually accomplished through the use of Access Control Lists

auto-detection and configuration   Auto-detection and configuration of installed controllers, interface cards and peripherals by network operating systems is dependent on the network operating system possessing a compatible driver for that device

automated attendant   Allows callers to direct calls to a desired individual at a given business without necessarily knowing their extension number

automated call distribution   Used primarily in call centers staffed by large numbers of customer service agents. Incoming calls are automatically distributed to the first available rep, or in some cases, the rep who serves a given geographic region as automatically determined by the computer based on the incoming phone number

automatic call distributors   See ACD

Autonomous systems   A network under the authority of a single entity whose interior routing policies or interior gateway protocols (IGP) are independent of those of any other autonomous system

AWG   Wire thickness is measured by gauge and represented with the unit AWG (American Wire Gauge)

B channel   In Isochronous Ethernet, The 6.144 Mbps C channel is in fact further subdivided into 96 64Kbps ISDN B channels, which carry the actual multimedia traffic. Applications are able to aggregate these B channels as needed up to the 6.144Mbps limit

Back Office   A collection of server products that

support the development of enterprise applications on the Windows NT platform

backbone network In a hierarchical enterprise network design, the high speed inter-LAN portion of the network is often referred to as the backbone network

backbone/data center switch Offers high capacity, fault tolerant, switching capacity with traffic management capabilities. These high-end switches are really a self-contained backbone network sometimes referred to as a collapsed backbone network

backbone-attached LAN switch Offers all of the local switching capabilities of the stand-alone workgroup/departmental LAN switch plus switched access to higher speed backbone networks

backpressure In the case of Ethernet switches, backpressure prevents lost frames during overload conditions by sending out false collision detection signals in order to get transmitting clients and servers to time-out long enough to give the switch a chance to forward buffered data

backward compatibility A very important aspect of any migration plan to a new client network operating system is the extent of support for backward compatibility in terms of application support, also known as legacy application support. In other words, will current applications run without modification on the new network operating system?

Base I/O address Defines a memory location through which the data will flow between the network interface card and the CPU

Base memory address Not to be confused with Base I/O address, some NICs require a base memory address to indicate the starting location in the computer's memory that can be used by the NIC as a buffer memory

baseband transmission The entire bandwidth of the media is devoted to one data channel

BASIC An English like programming language that is easy for beginning programmers to learn. However, it is a powerful programming language that is often used to develop client applications in the Microsoft Windows environment

BGP Border Gateway Protocol, an exterior gate-

way protocol used to exchange routing information between autonomous systems

BGP4 BGP (Border Gateway Protocol) is an exterior gateway protocol that performs routing between multiple autonomous systems or domains and exchanges routing and reachability information with other BGP systems

bindery Network operating systems have always depended on some sort of naming service or directory in which to store information about users as well as systems resources such as disks, servers, and printers. NetWare 3.x servers stored this type of information in a bindery

bindery emulation Bindery emulation allows newly migrated NetWare 4.1 servers to enjoy most of the benefits of NetWare 4.1 without having to fully convert NetWare 3.12 bindery objects into a NetWare 4.1 NDS database. Bindery emulation allows the use of NetWare 2.x or NetWare 3.x software, NLMs, and Netx Shells but still offers many NetWare 4.1 benefits

bindery files In a NetWare 3.12 environment, this type of security and network resource information is stored in bindery files

bindery synchronization Allows a single NetWare 4.1 server to be automatically and transparently synchronized with up to 12 NetWare 2.x or 3.x servers

binding NDIS specifies a binding operation that is managed by a separate program known as the Protocol Manager that combines separate NDIS compliant driver software supplied by NIC and NOS vendors

biometric authentication Can authenticate users based on fingerprints, palm prints, retinal patterns, voice recognition, or other physical characteristics

blocking Process of forcing an application to wait on a response from another application before it can continue. Blocking is directly associated with synchronous application communication

BootP Originally designed to configure local diskless workstations that were not able to store IP configuration information locally. In the case of BootP, the MAC address of the BootP client had to be known beforehand, entered into a database in the BootP server, and permanently associated with an IP address

Border gateway protocol version 4   See BGP4

BorderManager   NetWare's add-on solution for managing access to remote networks. BorderManager is designed to protect the private network from threats from external networks (such as the Internet) and to provide a means to manage how internal users access external networks

boundary router   In the case of boundary or branch office routers, all routing information is kept at the central site router. This allows the boundary router to require less technical configuration and to be available for a lower cost than central site routers

bridge   A bridge uses MAC layer addressing to logically segment traffic between attached LANs

broadcast   In a broadcast logical topology, a data message is sent simultaneously to all nodes on the network. Each node decides individually if the data message was directed toward it. If not, the message is simply ignored

broadcast address   A special network address that identifies all nodes on a network segment rather than a single node

broadcast filtering   The process of removing SNA broadcast messages at a router to prevent them from proliferating across an inter-network

broadcast filtering   Instead of allowing explorer packets onto the internetwork, routers can filter these broadcast packets out of the traffic, read the destination address to which the PC is seeking a route, and supply the PC directly with that information after consulting its own routing tables

broadcast storm   In the case of improperly addressed frames or frames destined for non-existent addresses, frames can be infinitely perpetuated or flooded onto all bridged LANs in a condition known as a broadcast storm

brokered authorization   Authorization security software can be either server-based, also known as brokered authorization, or workstation-based, also referred to as trusted node

brouters   At one time, specialized devices that could either bridge or route were referred to as brouters; however, today most advanced routers include bridging functionality

bulk retrieval mechanism   Through a new SNMP2

procedure known as bulk retrieval mechanism, managers can retrieve several pieces of network information at a time from a given agent

burst mode IPX   NetWare 4.1 introduced packet bursts otherwise known as Burst Mode IPX. This capability is built into the NetWare kernel and allows the NetWare 4.1 VLM requester on the clients and the NetWare 4.1 kernel on the servers to negotiate how many packets can be transmitted before an acknowledgment is required; 10 to 20 packets prior to acknowledgment is not uncommon

bus   The bus topology is a linear arrangement with terminators on either end and devices connected to the "bus" via connectors and/or transceivers

bus and tag   A standard for high speed data channels between FEPs and IBM mainframes, bus and tag has a transmission rate of 4.5 Mbps and has been available since 1967

bus mastering DMA   In bus mastering DMA, the CPU on the network adapter card manages the movement of data directly into the PC's RAM memory without interruption of the system CPU by taking control of the PC's expansion bus

business process reengineering   An analysis methodology that provides an opportunity to critically re-examine business processes

bytecode   An intermediate file format that is supported on multiple operating platforms. Java applications are compiled into bytecode, which can then be executed by a Java virtual machine regardless of the base hardware and operating system

C   A high level programming language commonly used to develop operating systems and application programs

C channel   In Isochronous Ethernet, A 6.144 Mbps ISDN C channel is reserved for streaming time-sensitive traffic such as multimedia applications

C++   A version of the C programming language that supports object-oriented programming

C-2 certification   The Orange Book certification process is both costly and lengthy. Typically, the certification process is projected to take two years to complete and cost of $17 million dollars. To date, both NetWare and NT Server have achieved the C-2 certification

C2 level security   A standard security level required by the US government for stand-alone systems

CA Third party key certification services, or certificate authorities (CA), issue the public keys along with a certificate ensuring the authenticity of the key

cable scanners Layer 1 testers are more commonly known as cable scanners or cable testers

cache manager Works closely with the file systems supported by NT to optimize the file services offered to applications. By effectively managing cache memory, the cache manager can minimize the number of physical read/writes to disks, thereby optimizing the performance of applications programs

calendaring The placement and manipulation of data onto a calendar

call control Using computer-based applications users are more easily able to use all of the features of their phone system or PBX, especially the more complicated but seldom used features. Includes use of features like on-line phone books, auto-dialing, click-and-point conference calls, on-line display and processing of voice mail messages

card and socket services See CSS

card services The card services sub-layer of PCM-CIA Card and Socket Services is hardware independent and interfaces to the client operating system or network operating system driver software

Carrier Sense Multiple Access with Collision Detection See CSMA/CD

CAS Communications Applications Specification is a FAX API that was developed by Intel and DCA. This API allows software vendors to integrate FAX capabilities into their application software by allowing the software to include standardized, embedded commands which are understood by FAX boards and FAX modems

cascading ports Hubs may also be cascadable or stackable via cascading ports, which may be specialized ports on the hub or switch configurable "normal" ports, allowing repeated data to flow out of a cascading port to the next hub rather than the normal inbound-only port traffic flow

CASE See Computer Assisted Systems Engineering

CAT 5 Category 5 UTP -22 or 24 AWG. Tested for attenuation and near-end crosstalk to 100MHz. Capable of transmitting up to 100Mbps when strictly installed to EIA/TIA 568 specifications. Currently the most commonly installed category of UTP

CDDI Copper Distributed Data Interface employs FDDI over twisted pair media. The official ANSI standard for CDDI is known as TP-PMD (Twisted Pair-Physical Media Dependent)

CDE Common Desktop Environment (CDE) is an effort by a consortium of Unix vendors to establish standards for a unified graphical user interface that allows those Unix varieties that support the CDE to present an identical interface to users

CDFS CDFS (CD File System)

CDMA Code division multiple access - CDMA transmits digitized voice packets from numerous calls at different frequencies spread all over the entire allocated bandwidth spectrum

CDPD Cellular Digital Packet Data (CDPD) is a service that uses idle capacity in the circuit-switched cellular network to transmit IP-based data packets. The fact that CDPD is IP-based allows it to easily interface to IP-based private networks as well as to the Internet and other e-mail services

Cellular Digital Packet Data See CDPD

Central Directory Server In APPN, the central directory server can save time as well as network traffic for the network nodes. Instead of each network node on an internetwork doing its own information gathering and internetwork exploration and inquiry, it can simply consult the central directory server

central site router Central site routers, otherwise known as enterprise or backbone routers, are employed at large corporate sites, while boundary or branch office routers are employed at remote corporate locations with less routing requirements and fewer technical support personnel

certificate authorities See CA

certificate servers Public key infrastructures that link a particular user to a particular public key are implemented through the use of server-based software known as certificate servers. Certificate server software also supports encryption and digital signatures while flexibly supporting directory integration, multiple certificate types, and a variety of request fulfillment options

CGI A method of developing scripts that run on a web server. Through the use of Common Gateway Interface scripts, a web browser can access server based data

Challenge Handshake Authentication Protocol See CHAP

Challenge Response Token Authentication A token authentication protocol in which a user uses a Smart Card to generate a one-time session key response to a server-initiated challenge

channel-attached gateways As an alternative to LAN-based gateways, channel-attached gateways are able to interface directly to the mainframe's high speed data channel, thereby bypassing the FEP entirely. Physically, the channel attached gateways are often modules that are added to enterprise routers

CHAP An encryption protocol used for user IDs and passwords

CHAP Challenge Handshake Authentication Protocol provides a more secure means for establishing dial-in communication. It uses a three-way challenge that includes the user ID, password and also a key that encrypts the ID and password

CHAP MD5 A protocol for PPP encrypted authentication included with most PPP clients

CHAP MD80 A protocol for authentication for Windows NT RAS included with most PPP clients

child processes Processes in Unix are controlled by the fork system call as initiated through the shell interface, which allows parent processes to spawn multiple sub-processes known as child processes

CIDR Classless interdomain routing eliminates the traditional concept of Class A, B, and C addresses entirely. The only factor that determines the capacity of a CIDR block is the network prefix assigned by the Internet authorities when the CIDR block is issued

CIDR block CIDR addresses are issued in blocks known as CIDR blocks

CIM A proposed protocol currently under development by the DMTF (Desktop Management Task Force) that would support HMMS is known as CIM or Common Information Model. CIM would

permit management data gathered from a variety of enterprise and desktop voice and data technology to be transported, processed , displayed, and stored by a single CIM-compliant web browser

ciphertext In encryption, the changed, unmeaningful data is known as ciphertext

CIPX A protocol for compression of IPX headers included with most PPP clients

Circuit level proxy Provides proxy services for transport layer protocols such as TCP

circuit-switched cellular Analog cellular service capable of supporting 14.4Kbps max

class of service A method of prioritizing traffic to ensure that important packets are not delayed at routers or switches

classfull address An IP address that is broken into network segment and node portions at octet boundaries

Classfull IP addressing Classfull addresses are broken apart on octet boundaries. Therefore, there are three basic classes of addresses. These classes are known as class A, B, and C networks

classical IP See IP over ATM

classless address An IP address that is broken into network segment and node portions at locations other than octet boundaries

Classless Inter Domain Routing See CIDR

client In X Windows the application itself is known as the client

client A computer that a user logs into to access LAN-attached resources and services

client network operating systems Integrate traditional operating system functionality with advanced network operating system features to enable communication with a variety of different types of network operating system servers

client/server network operating systems Offer the ability to support hundreds of users and to interact with other network operating systems via gateways. These systems are both considerably more expensive and considerably more complicated to install and administer than peer-to-peer network operating systems

Client32 Requester An upgrade to the NetWare DOS Requester that is able to offer a wider variety of VLM-based services while using client memory resources more efficiently

client-agent-server The overall objective of a client-agent-server architecture, as opposed to the more common LAN-based client/server architecture, is to reduce the amount of mobile client to server network traffic by building as much intelligence as possible into the server-based agent so that it can act on behalf of the mobile client application

client-side caching Transparently synchronizes data between the notebook and the network. Whenever the user logs into the network, the system will analyze the cached data and automatically synchronize with the network copy of the data, ensuring that an updated copy of the user's data is always available regardless of whether the user is connected to the network

Clipper Chip The Clipper Chip initiative proposed that every phone and data communications device in the United States would be equipped with a Clipper Chip to support encryption

cluster controller A device that allows connection of both 3270 terminals as well as LANs with possible wide area links to packet switched networks (X.25) or high speed leased lines. A cluster controller concentrates the transmissions of its numerous input devices and directs this concentrated data stream to the FEP either locally or remotely

COBOL A high level programming language traditionally used to develop applications that run in a mainframe environment

Code division multiple access See CDMA

CODEC At the heart of the videoconferencing system is the video CODEC (COder-DECoder), which digitizes not only analog video signals but also analog voice signals

collaborative work sessions Allow users connected via networks to participate in joint work sessions as if they were all in the same room working at the same whiteboard or conference table

collapsed backbone network A switched network architecture that employs backbone/data center switches to offer high capacity, fault tolerant, switching capacity with traffic management capabilities

COM A method of developing object-oriented systems developed by Microsoft. Commonly distributed across multiple computers as part of DCOM

Common Desktop Environment See CDE

common gateway interface See CGI

common information model See CIM

common object model See COM

common object request broker See CORBA

Communications Applications Specification See CAS

communications server Remote users could attach to a dedicated multi-user server, known as an access server or communications server through one or more modems. Depending on the software loaded on the communications server, it may deliver remote node functionality, remote control functionality, or both

communications-based groupware Deals with establishing, maintaining, and managing a variety of types of ad-hoc communications between networked group members

compatibility Can be thought of as successfully bridging the gap or communicating between two or more technology components, whether hardware or software

compiler A software tool that converts high level programs into machine language executable programs

component interface API Designed to interface to the individual application programs or desktop components that are to be managed and monitored on the local client

computer assisted systems engineering Any software tool that aids in the development of application programs. Computer assisted systems engineering components vary from planning and project management tools to code generation tools

computer telephony integration See CTI

conditional branch routing In workflow automation software, conditional branch routing introduces multiple possible routes to a process dependent on results or outcomes at a particular step in the process. Exception handling and sophisticated rules-based or expert systems can all be supported or integrated into conditional branch routing workflow automation software

configuration bridge protocol data unit Spanning

tree algorithm bridges accomplish path management by communicating with each other via configuration bridge protocol data units (configuration BPDU)

connectionless IP allows each packet to be processed individually within the network and does not provide any guarantees as to whether packets will arrive at their intended destination in sequence, if at all. As such, IP is described as a connectionless, unreliable protocol

connectionless Implying individual, fully addressed packets, or datagrams, are free to negotiate their way through the network in search of their final destination

connection-oriented implying that specific paths known as virtual circuits are explored and determined before the first packet is sent. Once the virtual circuit is established directly from the source host or node to destination node, then all packets bound for that address follow each other in sequence down the same physical path

ConsoleOne A Java based graphical administration utility designed to replace nwadmin. Similar to nwadmin in look and feel, ConsoleOne can be run on the server or any Java enabled client

consolidated service desk A single point of contact for all network and application problem resolution. Appropriate personnel processes can be matched with associated network management technologies

container objects In NDS, organizational units such as companies, divisions, and departments are referred to as container objects. Container objects can be cascaded and can contain leaf objects. Leaf objects cannot be cascaded

cooked interfaces Both block-oriented and character-oriented I/O may use buffers and queues to organize the transfer of data from the operating system to the hardware device in question through their respective cooked interfaces

Copper Distributed Data Interface See CDDI

CORBA A set of object-oriented middleware specifications published by the Object Management Group (OMG). The CORBA specifications define the way objects are defined, created, dispatched, invoked, and how they communicate with one another

CRC A 32 bit cyclical redundancy check (CRC) is generated over the address, type, and data fields as a frame check sequence in Ethernet networks

CRC Checkers Category of anti-virus technology known as CRC Checkers or Hashing Checkers, creates and saves a unique cyclical redundancy check character or hashing number for each file to be monitored

CSMA/CA Part of the IEEE 802.11 standard, CSMA/CA (Carrier Sense Multiple Access with Collision Avoidance) is similar to CSMA/CD except that collisions cannot be detected in wireless environments as they can in wire-based environments. Before transmitting, workstations wait a predetermined amount of time to avoid collisions, and set up a point-to-point wireless circuit to the destination workstation

CSMA/CD Carrier Sense Multiple Access with Collision Detection or CSMA/CD is the access methodology used by Ethernet media sharing LANs

CSS Card and Socket Services is the driver specification for PCMCIA devices that enables the following capabilities and is supposed to relatively self-configuring: hot swappable devices allowing PCMCIA cards to be removed and inserted while the notebook computer is powered up, automatic PCMCIA card configuration, multiple PCMCIA card management, standby mode, I/O conflict management

CTI CTI or Computer Telephony Integration seeks to integrate the two most common productivity devices, the computer and the telephone, to enable increased productivity not otherwise possible by using the two devices in a non-integrated fashion. CTI is not a single application, but an ever-widening array of possibilities spawned by the integration of telephony and computing

CTI it is important for help desk management software to be able to interact with call center management technology such as automatic call distributors (ACD) and interactive voice response units (IVRU). The overall integration of computer-based software and telephony equipment in known as computer telephony integration (CTI)

cut-through switches Read only the address information in the MAC layer header before beginning processing. Cut-through switching is very fast.

However, because the frame check sequence on the forwarded frame was not checked, bad frames are forwarded

cyclical redundancy check   See CRC

D channel   In Isochronous Ethernet, 1 64Kbps ISDN D channel is used for management tasks such as call control and signaling

daemon   The server piece of a TCP/IP utility is usually referred to as a daemon, and is named with a "d" suffix. For example, the client piece of the FTP utility is known as FTP, while the server piece is known as ftpd

DAO   A high level API for Microsoft ODBC programming environments. Data Access Objects are commonly used to address data in the Microsoft Jet database engine

DARPA   TCP/IP was developed during the 1970s and widely deployed during the 1980s under the auspices of DARPA or Defense Advanced Research Projects Agency

DAS   Dual Attachment Station devices attach to both of FDDI's rings

data access objects   See DAI

data display channel   See DDC

Data Encryption Standard   See DES

Data Link Control   See DLC

data link switching   IBM's version of encapsulating SNA traffic in TCP/IP. See DLSw

data migration   Data migration utilities manage the migration of data among different types of storage devices as part of a comprehensive hierarchical storage management (HSM) program

data migration   Data migration features have been added to NetWare 4.1, which allow files to be automatically migrated and archived in a structured fashion to the archival storage media of choice such as optical drives. Which files get migrated and when are totally controlled by parameters set by the system manager

database MIB   The IETF has been working on a Database MIB specification, which would allow any enterprise data management system to report performance statistics back to any SNMP-compliant enterprise network management system

database wrapping   The process of developing a new client application that integrates with the legacy system directly through the legacy application's data store

Datagram Delivery Protocol   See DDP

data-link layer   Layer 2 of the OSI model. Responsible for providing protocols that deliver reliability to upper layers for the point-to-point connections established by the physical layer protocols. The data-link layer is of particular interest to the study of local area networks, as this is the layer in which network architecture standards are defined

DCE   The Open Software Foundation (OSF) has developed an entire architecture for the development of distributed applications known as the Distributed Computing Environment (DCE). See Distributed Computing Environment

DCOM   The Distributed Common Object Model (DCOM) is a Microsoft proprietary solution for building distributed object-oriented applications. DCOM allows objects to be defined, created, dispatched, invoked, and communicated with one another

DDM   Distributed device manager. A DDM architecture relies on distributed network probes that are able to gather information from a variety of network devices manufactured by multiple vendors and relay that information to numerous distributed device manager consoles

DDP   The network layer protocol associated with the AppleTalk protocol suite

decision support room   In electronic meeting support software, meetings may be held in specially equipped decision support rooms in which all forum participants gather in what is known as a same-place, same-time meeting or may convene via a local or wide area network according to participants' availability in what is known as a different-place, different-time meeting

dedicated backup server   A network backup architecture, dedicated backup server architectures allow multiple servers to be backed up across the network backbone onto a dedicated backup server linked to multiple backup devices

de-encapsulation   The process of extracting higher layer protocols from the data section of the underlying lower layer protocols. The opposite of encapsulation

de-encapsulation   Each successive layer of the OSI

model removes headers and/or trailers and processes the data which was passed to it from the corresponding layer protocol on the source client

definition variables   In Application MIB, definition variables would store background information concerning applications such as application name, manufacturer, version, release, installation date, license number, number of consecutive users, etc

delphi   An event driven programming environment developed by Borland that uses the Pascal structured programming language

delta file synchronization   Perhaps the most significant file synchronization option in terms of its potential impact on reducing required bandwidth and file transfer time to accomplish the synchronization. Rather than sending entire files across the dial-up or LAN link, delta file synchronization transfers only the changes to those files

delta file transfer   Allows only changes to files to be transferred

demand paged virtual memory system   See paging

demand paging   A process in which the virtual memory manager moves program code and data between assigned physical RAM and the disk-based paging or swap file unbeknownst to the unsuspecting process

Demand Priority Access   See DPP

Demand Priority Protocol   See DPP

Denial of service attack   In the denial of service attack, the hacker flooded the server with requests to connect to other servers that did not exist. The server would try to establish connections with the non-existent servers and wait for a response while being flooded with thousands of other bogus connection requests. This caused the server to deny service to legitimate users because it was overwhelmed trying to handle the bogus requests

departmental image management   See document managment and imaging

DES   a private key encryption standard (Data Encryption Standard) originally approved by the National Institute of Standards and Technology (NIST) in 1977

desktop management interface   See DMI

desktop management task force   See DMTF

destination address   Rather than merely transferring all data between LANs or LAN segments, a bridge reads the destination address (MAC layer address of destination NIC) of each data frame on a LAN, decides whether the destination is local or remote (on the other side of the bridge), and only allows those data frames with non-local destination addresses to cross the bridge to the remote LAN

device driver   Also known as hardware device drivers. Specifically written to support a particular hardware device such as a printer, keyboard, or mouse. Windows NT provides a standardized environment within the I/O manager in which these device drivers can execute

DFS   A Windows 2000 network storage service that allows resources on multiple servers to be combined into a virtual directory tree

DHCP   Dynamic Host Control Protocol dynamically assigns IP upon requests from clients. With DHCP, IP addresses are leased for a fixed length of time rather than being permanently assigned

DHCP   Dynamic Host Configuration Protocol allows NT servers using TCP/IP to dynamically assign TCP/IP addresses to NT workstations, Windows for Workgroups clients, Win'95 clients, or DOS clients running the TCP/IP-32 protocol stack

dial-in server   See LAN modem

dial-up router   In those cases where the amount of inter-LAN traffic from a remote site does not justify the cost of a leased line, dial-up routers may be the appropriate choice of internetworking equipment

dial-up server   See remote node server

different-place different-time meeting   In electronic meeting support software, meetings may be held in specially equipped decision support rooms in which all forum participants gather in what is known as a same-place, same-time meeting or may convene via a local or wide area network according to participants' availability in what is known as a different-place, different-time meeting

Diff-Serv   Provides the following functionality: uses the type of service (ToS) bits already in the IP header to differentiate between different levels of service required by different applications, allows service level agreements between users and service providers to be supported

Digital IDs   Digital certificates or Digital IDs issued from CAs such as VeriSign contain an organization's encrypted public key along with a minimal amount of information about the organization such as e-mail address, department, company, state or province, and country

Digital Signature Encryption   Provides an electronic means of guaranteeing authenticity of the sending party and assurance that encrypted documents have not been altered during transmission

DII   A CORBA object interface that allows for dynamic binding between CORBA compliant objects

direct enablers   If compatible CSS drivers are not available for a particular PC Card/Controller combination, or if the amount of memory CSS drivers require is unacceptable, then lower-level drivers known as direct enablers must be configured and installed

direct sequence spread spectrum   Direct sequence spread spectrum (DSSS) transmits at a particular frequency within the allowable range. To distinguish between transmissions from multiple wireless workstations, DSSS adds at least 10 bits to the data message in order to uniquely identify a particular transmission. DSSS receivers must be able to differentiate between these bits, known as chips, in order to properly distinguish transmissions

directory services   Network operating systems have always depended on some sort of directory or naming service in which to store information about users as well as systems resources such as disks, servers, and printers

directory synchronization software   See file synchronization

discussion categories   See sections

disk allocation blocks   Disks in a NetWare environment are divided into disk allocation blocks that can range in size from 4KB to 64KB. In the past, when a file needed a portion of a disk allocation block to complete file storage, the remainder of the partially occupied disk allocation block could not be used by other files and was effectively wasted

disk block sub-allocation   A process aimed at optimizing the use of disk space for file storage. By dividing all disk allocation blocks into 512 byte

(.5KB) suballocation blocks, multiple files are allowed to occupy single disk allocation blocks and disk storage efficiency is maximized

display   In X Windows that combination of keyboard, mouse, and monitor upon which the output of an application is displayed

display server   In X Windows the code running on the computer that is displaying the output of the application

distance vector   RIP uses a distance vector algorithm only measures the number of hops to a distant router, to a maximum of 16

distance vector protocols   Router to router protocols, such as RIP, which only consider the distance between networks in hops as a determination of the best inter-network path

distinct layer 2 switching and layer 3 routing   An internetwork evolutionary design scenario in which separate Layer 2 switches and Layer 3 routers cooperatively contribute what each does best to deliver internetwork traffic as efficiently as possible

distributed   A database application that consists of a central data repository with separate clients connecting to it

distributed component object model   See DCOM

distributed computing environment   An open standard middleware architecture. The Distributed Computing Environment is represented by a single source code currently owned and maintained by The Open Group (formerly the Open Software Foundation). See DCE

distributed device manager   See DDM

Distributed File System   See DFS

distributed network probes   A DDM architecture relies on distributed network probes that are able to gather information from a variety of network devices manufactured by multiple vendors and relay that information to numerous distributed device manager consoles

distributed routing   An internetwork evolutionary design scenario in which layer 2 switching and layer 3 routing functionality are combined into a single device sometimes referred to as a multi-layer switch

distributed transaction processing   With the advent of client/server information systems, multiple geographically dispersed computers are linked, allowing transactions to be posted across multiple, distributed computers. This process is known as Distributed Transaction Processing (DTP) and requires a distributed TP Monitor. DTP is sometimes also known as Enterprise Transaction Processing or ETP

DLC DLC or Data Link Control is a Windows NT communication protocol that has been traditionally reserved for communication with IBM mainframe computers. Recently, this same communication protocol has been used to communicate between Windows NT servers and printers that are attached directly to the network by network interface cards such as the Hewlett-Packard LaserJet 4Si equipped with a JetDirect card

DLSw IBM's version of TCP/IP encapsulation is known as Data Link Switching or DLSw and has been proposed as a standard to the IETF (Internet Engineering Task Force) as RFC (Request for Comment) 1434. DLSw does not propose anything radically new but incorporates many vendor-specific TCP/IP encapsulation features into a single standard, which will hopefully be widely supported

DLUR/S The protocol that implements SNA integration into the IBM APPN architecture

DMA Interoperability standards among document management packages are contained in a specification known as DMA, or Document Management Alliance

DMI Desktop management systems rely upon an architecture and associated protocols proposed by the Desktop Management Task Force (DMTF), which is comprised of over 50 companies including Intel, Microsoft, IBM, Digital, Hewlett-Packard, Apple, Compaq, Dell, and Sun. The overall desktop management architecture is known as the DMI or Desktop Management Interface. See DMTF

DMI services layer The DMI application that resides on each desktop device to be managed

DMTF The DMTF or Desktop Management Task Force has developed a common management environment for the management of desktop devices known as the DMI (Desktop Management Interface). Specific aspects of the DMI are contained in MIF (Management Information File) definitions

DMTF Desktop management systems rely upon an architecture and associated protocols proposed by the Desktop Management Task Force (DMTF), which is comprised of over 50 companies including Intel, Microsoft, IBM, Digital, Hewlett-Packard, Apple, Compaq, Dell, and Sun. The overall desktop management architecture is known as the DMI or Desktop Management Interface

DMZ The De-militarized zone, DMZ, otherwise known as the external private network, contains web servers and mail servers

DNS The Domain Name System or DNS has been created to provide the following key services: Uniquely identify all hosts connected to the Internet by name; Resolve, or translate, host names into IP addresses (and vice versa); Identify which services are offered by each host such as gateway or mail transfer, and to which networks these services are offered

DNS The Internet uses a naming service known as DNS or Domain Name System to translate between host names and IP addresses

DNS server DNS is physically implemented in a client/server architecture in which client-based DNS software known as the DNS or name resolver, sends requests for DNS name resolution to a DNS (or name) Server

document conferencing software When electronic whiteboard software sessions involve collaborative development or review of documents by multiple users linked via LAN or WAN links, the software category is occasionally referred to as document conferencing software

document management and imaging When workflow automation involves a great deal of handling, storage, indexing, and retrieval of documents, an ancillary document management and imaging software package may be required

Document Management Alliance See DMA

document-based groupware Document-based Groupware deals with the management, storage, retrieval, and transport of structured documents among participating networked co-workers

domain A grouping unit that consists of a group of closely related network objects for administrative purposes

domain directory services Network operating systems have always depended on some sort of naming service or directory in which to store information about users as well as systems resources such as disks, servers, and printers. Windows NT uses a domain directory service

Domain Name Service See DNS

domain name system See DNS

Domain Object Wizard Merges all existing NT data in to an NDS tree when NDS for NT is installed

domain OS In NetWare 4.1's ring memory protection scheme, the area reserved for the operating system is known as Ring 0, otherwise known as domain OS (operating system)

domain OSP In NetWare 4.1's ring memory protection scheme, the area reserved for NLMs is known as Ring 3 or domain OSP (operating system protected)

Domain SAP/RIP Server See DSS Server

domains Domain directory services see the network as a series of linked sub-divisions known as domains

domains Windows NT networks are organized around the concept of domains. A domain is a collection of Windows NT servers that share a single security sub-system that controls access to all resources in that domain

DOS Partition To install the NetWare server software in the first place, the native operating system of the server must be present in its own disk partition. This might be referred to as a DOS partition, but the native operating system could have just as easily been UNIX or Windows NT

DPA See DPP

DPP Demand Priority Protocol (Demand Priority Access) is the access methodology of 100VG-AnyLAN. Ports can be designated as high priority, thereby giving priority delivery status to time-sensitive types of traffic such as video or voice, which require guaranteed delivery times for smooth presentation. This makes 100VG-AnyLAN especially well suited for multimedia traffic

DSS Server A server that provides SAP support for NetWare 4 installations running NetWare/IP

Dual Attachment Station See DAS

dual firewalls An enterprise firewall architecture that allows controlled access to DMZ while blocking unauthorized access to secure network Same functionality may be offered in a single product known as a tri-homed firewall

dual homing In FDDI, a given server may be connected to more than one FDDI concentrator to provide redundant connections and increased fault tolerance. Dual connecting servers in this manner is known as dual homing

dual ring of trees Multiple concentrators attaching multiple devices to the FDDI rings known as a dual ring of trees

dual-homed gateway The application gateway is physically connected to the private secure network, and the packet filtering router is connected to the nonsecure network or the Internet. Between the application gateway and the packet filter router is an area known as the screened subnet

Dynamic Host Configuration Protocol See DHCP

dynamic invocation interface See DII

dynamic link library A DLL or dynamic link library file is loaded into memory as needed at run time by Windows NT rather than having to be compiled into, and permanently added to the applications programs themselves

dynamic reconfiguration PnP standards include support for dynamic reconfiguration that will enable such things as PCMCIA cards being inserted into and removed from computers without a need to reboot, hot docking (powered up) of laptop computers into docking bays or stations, dynamic reconfiguration-aware applications software which could automatically respond to changes in system configuration

dynamic routing Achieved when routers are allowed to build their own routing tables based on route advertisements received from other routers

DynaText on-line help The transparent integration of CD-ROMs into the NetWare 4.1 file system has enabled the use of the DynaText On-Line Help system as the means of accessing all of the NetWare 4.1 manuals

early token release mechanism 16Mbps Token Ring network architectures use a modified form of token passing access methodology known as early token release mechanism in which the token is set to free and release as soon as the transmission of the data frame is completed rather than waiting for the transmitted data frame to return to the source workstation

edge switches   Deployed within the LANs will be programmed with minimal routing information. Edge switches will consult distributed route servers for "directory assistance" when they encounter routing situations that they are not equipped to handle

EGP   Autonomous systems talk to each other via mutually agreed upon exterior gateway protocols (EGP)

EIA/TIA 568   Electronics Industry Association/Telecommunications Industry Association. In addition to specifying UTP specifications, EIA/TIA 568 also specifies the topology, cable types, and connector types to be used in EIA/TIA 568-compliant wiring schemes the minimum performance specifications for cabling, connectors and components such as wall plates, punch down blocks, and patch panels to be used in an EIA/TIA 568 compliant installation

electronic conferencing and meeting support   Electronic conferencing and meeting support software offers opportunities for workers to interact electronically. Brainstorming or idea generation sessions are conducted via the network and managed by the workgroup conferencing software package

electronic mail   Electronic mail (e-mail) is by far the most popular and most widely used component of groupware. When people hear the term groupware or collaborative computing the majority of people immediately think of e-mail. It is the easiest of the components to learn how to use. This ease of use has led to some people being hit with "information overload."

electronic whiteboard software   A hybrid category of groupware software combining elements of electronic meeting support, document conferencing, and videoconferencing. As a result, many electronic whiteboard software packages are incorporated into a variety of different types of software packages

element managers   Point products also known as element managers are specifically written to ad-

dress a particular systems administration or network management issue

e-mail   See electronic mail

e-mail gateways   E-mail system-to-e-mail system translation is accomplished by specially written software known as e-mail gateways. E-mail systems vary in the number of e-mail gateways supported and whether or not the gateway software must be run on a dedicated server

EMI   Electro magnetic Interference

emulation technology   Attempts to detect as yet unknown viruses by running programs with a software emulation program known as a virtual PC

encapsulating bridges   Takes the entire Ethernet data link layer frame and stuffs it in an "envelope" (data frame), which conforms to the FDDI data link layer protocol

Encapsulating Security Payload Header   See ESP

encapsulation   In a network system, higher layer packets are placed into lower layer protocol payload sections. This process is known as encryption

encapsulation   The process of placing one protocol into another protocol for processing

encapsulation   A data message emerges from a client front end program and proceeds down the protocol stack of the network operating system installed in the client PC in a process known as encapsulation. Each successive layer of the OSI model adds a header according to the syntax of the protocol that occupies that layer

enclosures   In electronic meeting support software, user comments on topics are made up of a series of messages that may contain supporting material or documents known as enclosures

encryption   The process of "scrambling" a message for transmission to ensure that it is not intercepted along the way

end nodes   End user processing nodes, either clients or servers without any information on the overall network, available internetwork links, or routing tables

end nodes   In APPN, end nodes are end user processing nodes, either clients or servers without any information on the overall network, available internetwork links, or routing tables

end-to-end network links The network layer protocols are responsible for the establishment, maintenance, and termination of end-to-end network links. Network layer protocols are required when computers that are not physically connected to the same LAN must communicate

Enhanced CAT 5 Enhanced Category 5 UTP (EC5), otherwise known as Category 5+ or CAT5e, offers enhanced performance over CAT5 UTP due to the following improvements in electrical specifications: attenuation to crosstalk ratio of 10dB at 155MHz, a minimum 400% improvement in capacitance or ability of a wire to store an electrical charge, a 250% improvement in frequency, a 35% improvement in resistance, an average of 5% improvement in attenuation, an average of a 6dB improvement in NEXT

enhanced paging A pager based wireless service capable of delivering one or two way messages of 100 characters or less

Enhanced throughput cellular See ETC

ENS Sends customizable messages to users about printer status and events on a NetWare 5 network

enterprise hubs Modular by design, offering a chassis-based architecture to which a variety of different modules can be inserted. In some cases, these modules can be inserted and/or removed while the hub remains powered-up, a capability known as hot-swappable

enterprise network management Focuses on the hardware, software, media, and network services required to seamlessly link and effectively manage distributed client and server computers across an enterprise

enterprise network management systems Compile and report network operation statistics to the end user, most often in some type of graphical format. Enterprise network management systems are really management application programs running on a management server

enterprise network management systems Enterprise network management systems such as HP OpenView, IBM NetView, Sun SunNet Manager, are able to manage a variety of multi-vendor network attached devices distributed throughout an enterprise network

error-free cut-through switches Read both the ad-dresses and frame check sequences for every frame. Frames are forwarded immediately to destinations nodes in an identical fashion to cut-through switches. However, should bad frames be forwarded, the error-free cut-through switch is able to reconfigure those individual ports producing the bad frames to use store-and-forward switching

ESCON A standard for high speed data channels between FEPs and IBM mainframes, ESCON II (Enterprise System CONnection) has a maximum transmission rate of 70Mbps, has been available since 1990, and is able to transmit up to 30 miles over fiber optic cable

ESMR Enhanced specialized mobile radio. Currently under development, this wireless WAN service offers one or two way voice, paging, or messaging at speeds up to 4.8Kbps over proprietary integrated voice/data devices

ESP In Secure IP, The Encapsulating Security Payload Header (ESP) ensures the privacy of the transmission

ETC Transmitting data over analog cellular networks requires modems that support specialized cellular transmission protocols on both ends of the cellular transmission in order to maximize throughput. Examples of such protocols are MNP-10 Adverse Channel Enhancements and Enhanced Throughput Cellular (ETC)

Ethernet Although strictly speaking, Ethernet and IEEE 802.3 are conflicting standards, the term Ethernet is commonly used to refer to any IEEE 802.3 compliant network

Ethernet II The first Ethernet standard was developed by Digital, Intel and Xerox corporation in 1981 and was known as DIX 1.0, sometimes referred to as Ethernet I. This standard was superseded in 1982 by DIX 2.0, the current Ethernet standard, also known as Ethernet II

event Circumstance that causes processing to be performed in an event-driven programming environment. Examples of events include mouse clicks, key presses, or incoming data

event detection Most audit software depends on capturing large amounts of event data and then filtering that data for exceptional or unusual events

event handler   The procedure that executes as the result of an event's occurrence

event management tool   An alternative to developing your own applications with embedded management intelligence is to purchase a pre-written event management tool that has been written to monitor specific commercially available applications

Event Notification Service   See ENS

explorer packet   In an internetwork connected via source routing bridges, the PC sends out a special explorer packet that determines the best path to the intended destination of its data message. The explorer packets are continually propagated through all source routing bridges until the destination workstation is finally reached

Extended network prefix   The classfull network prefix (/16 in the case of a Class B address) plus the number of bits borrowed from the host ID is called the extended network prefix

Extended Terminal Access Control Access System   See XTACACS

Exterior gateway protocols   See EGP

External data representation   See XDR

false accepts   In biometric authentication, false accepts will occur when impostors are allowed access because the comparison was not detailed enough

false rejects   In biometric authentication, false rejects will occur when valid users are denied access because of slight variations detected between the reference biometric characteristic and the current one

fast packet forwarding   See packet overlapping

Fast Track   A web server for NetWare 5 servers

FAT   File Allocation Table is as DOS operating system—only file system for diskettes

FAX APIs   Standards for FAX software APIs that define interfaces between FAX software and hardware components

FaxBIOS   A FAX API developed and supported by the FaxBIOS Association, which is comprised of FAX circuit board vendors

fax-on-demand   By combining computer-based faxing with interactive voice response, users can dial in and request that specific information be faxed to their fax machine

FDDI   Fiber Distributed Data Interface is a 100Mbps network architecture that was first specified in 1984 by the ANSI (American National Standards Institute) subcommittee entitled X3T9.5

FEP   A front end processor is a computer that offloads the communications processing from the mainframe, allowing the mainframe to be dedicated to processing activities. A high speed data channel connects the FEP to the mainframe locally, although FEPs can be deployed remotely as well

Fiber Distributed Data Interface   See FDDI

file compression   File compression is incorporated into NetWare 4.1 and is controllable on a file-by-file basis. The file compression process is highly customizable with adjustable settings for how often compression takes place as well as minimum acceptable disk space gained by compression

file synchronization software   Able to synchronize versions of files on laptops and desktop workstations and is now often included as a standard or optional feature in client network operating systems. Also known as version control software or directory synchronization software

file system drivers   In order for NT to communicate with multiple different file systems (NTFS, FAT, HPFS), an intermediate layer of software known as file system drivers that can interact with both NT and the particular file system must be written

file transfer protocol   See FTP

filesystem   The term filesystem has two meanings in UNIX: the overall filesystem and any subdirectory structure housed in a separate disk partition

filter   A program that examines the source address and destination address of every incoming packet to the firewall server

Filter tables   Lists of addresses whose data packets and embedded messages are either allowed or prohibited from proceeding through the firewall server and into the corporate network

filtering   Occurs when a bridge reads the destination address on an Ethernet frame or Token Ring packet and decides whether or not that packet should be allowed access to the internetwork through the bridge

filtering rate   Measured in packets/sec or frames/sec, a measure of the filtering performance of a given bridge

firewall   To prevent unauthorized access from the Internet into a company's confidential data, specialized software known as a firewall is often deployed. All network packets entering the firewall are filtered, or examined, to determine whether or not those users have authority to access requested files or services and whether or not the information contained within the message meets corporate criteria for forwarding over the internal network

flat gray modular   Flat gray modular wiring, also known as gray satin or silver satin, contains either 4, 6 or 8 wires that get crimped into either RJ-11 (4 wire), RJ-12 (6 wire), or RJ-45 plugs (8 wire) using a specialized crimping tool

forest   For very large enterprises, multiple active directory trees can be combined into an active directory forest

fork   Processes in Unix are controlled by the fork system call as initiated through the shell interface, which allows parent processes to spawn multiple sub-processes known as child processes

format converter   A special type of bridge that includes a format converter can bridge between Ethernet and Token Ring. These special bridges may also be called multi-protocol bridges or translating bridges

forums   In electronic meeting support software discussion groups are called forums

forward if not local   Since only frames with destination addresses not found in the known local nodes table are forwarded across the bridge, bridges are sometimes known as a "forward-if-not-local" devices

forward if proven remote   Once the router is satisfied with both the viability of the destination address as well as with the quality of the intended path, it will release the carefully packaged data packet via processing known as forward-if-proven-remote logic

forwarding   The bridge process necessary to load the packet onto the internetwork media whether local or remote

forwarding rate   Measured in packets/sec or frames/sec, a measure of the forwarding performance of a given bridge

FRAD   The access device to the frame relay network, known as a frame relay access device or FRAD must be able to respond to requests from the frame relay network to "throttle back" or slow down the input to the network or risk losing transmitted packets due to network overload

fragmentation   As contiguous blocks of memory of varying sizes are continuously cut out of a finite amount of primary memory, that primary memory suffers from fragmentation where numerous, small leftover pieces of contiguous memory remain unused

frame check sequence   (FCS) An error detection mechanism generated by the transmitting Ethernet network interface card

Frame relay   A WAN packet switched network service known as frame relay has become a popular alternative SNA/LAN integration WAN service. The key positive attribute of frame relay is that charges are based on actual amounts of traffic transmitted rather than fixed monthly rates

frame relay access device   See FRAD

frame status flags   In a token passing access methodology, successful delivery of the data frame is confirmed by the destination workstation setting frame status flags to indicate successful receipt of the frame and continuing to forward the original frame around the ring to the sending PC

frames   The data-link layer provides the required reliability to the physical layer transmission by organizing the bit stream into structured frames, which add addressing and error checking information

frameworks   Offer an overall systems administration or network management platform with integration between modules and a shared database into which all alerts, messages, alarms, and warnings can be stored and correlated

frequency hopping spread spectrum   FHSS hops from one frequency to another throughout the allowable frequency range. The pattern of frequency hopping must be known by the wireless receiver so that the message can be reconstructed correctly

front end processor   See FEP

FTP   File Transfer Protocol provides a common

mechanism for transferring files between a variety of different types of networked computers. Strictly speaking, FTP does not provide a user interface but rather an API for FTP services

Full duplex Ethernet   Requires specialized full duplex Ethernet NICs, NIC drivers, and full duplex Ethernet switches. Should allow twice the normal Ethernet performance speed by offering a dedicated 10Mpbs communication channel in each direction for a total available bandwidth of 20Mbps

full-duplex Ethernet   This switch-dependent capability requires specialized full duplex Ethernet NICs and supports full-duplex communication between the two computers that serve as the endpoints of a switched dedicated connection, thereby allowing them to both send and receive data simultaneously

functions   Software modules that return a single result based on the parameters passed to them

gateway   A machine that converts between one protocol or segment to another

gateway   A hardware/software solution that allows for the translation between different physical signals and/or protocols

gateway   A LAN server-based, shared protocol converted access to a mainframe

gateway of last resort   If a router cannot find a match in a routing table for a destination packet, then it will forward that packet to the address of the gateway of last resort under the assumption that the gateway of last resort may know of additional networks that were unknown to the original router

Gateway Services for NetWare   An optional component of Windows NT Server that allows transparent access to NetWare resources from NT clients

Generic Security Service-Applications Program Interface   See GSS-API

Gigabit Ethernet   Also known as 1000Base-X. An upgrade to Fast Ethernet that was standardized as the IEEE 802.3z standard by the IEEE on June 25, 1998

global directory service   NDS is a global directory service, organizing and managing all networked resources over an entire distributed enterprise. See NDS

global system for mobile communication   See GSM

grafted   Entire branches of the tree, designated as partitions, and including all subordinate container objects and leaf objects, can be pruned (removed) from one point in the NDS structure and grafted to another branch. In fact two entire trees can be merged together into a single tree

granularity   How finely access can be controlled by disk, directory, or file level) is sometimes referred to as the granularity of the access control scheme

group scheduling software   Group scheduling software or calendar packages can be a very efficient way to schedule electronic or face-to-face meetings or conferences and is often integrated with e-mail systems so that requests for meetings can be automatically sent and replied to via e-mail

groupware   The name of a category of software that seeks to take advantage of the fact that workers are networked together electronically in order to increase communication and maximize worker productivity

GSM   In Europe and much of the rest of the world, Global System for Mobile Communication (GSM) is either currently deployed or planned for implementation as the digital cellular standard

GSS-API   An open API that would allow applications to communicate with a variety of security authorization programs

guest   The terms remote and local are often replaced by guest (remote) and host (local), when referring to Remote Control Software

H.221   Framing and synchronization specification that standardizes the CODEC's handshaking and interface to WAN services such as ISDN used for videoconference transmission

H.230   Multiplexing specification that describes how audio and video information should be transmitted over the same digital WAN link

H.231   Multipoint control unit (MCU) specification that defines standards for a device to bridge three or more H.320 compliant codecs together on a single multipoint videoconference

H.233   Specification for encryption of video and audio information transmitted through H.320 compliant codecs. Also known as H.KEY

H.242 Specification for call set-up and tear-down for videoconference calls

H.261 Also known as Px64, describes compression and decompression algorithms used for videoconferencing. Also defines two screen formats, CIF (Common Intermediate Format) 288 lines x 352 pixels/line and QCIF (Quarter Common Intermediate Format) 144 lines x 176 pixels/line

H.320 The International Telecommunications Union (ITU) has overseen the development of a family of videoconferencing standards known collectively as H.320

HAL Most of the hardware specific portions of Windows NT are isolated in a sub-section known as the hardware abstraction layer, or HAL. The hardware abstraction layer in Windows NT provides similar functionally to the BIOS in DOS. It is the hardware (CPU) specific HAL that affords Windows NT its portability

hardware abstraction layer See HAL

hardware/software solutions A network faxing architecture in which the user supplies the PC to which vendor-supplied FAX boards and bundled software are loaded

Hashing Checkers Category of anti-virus technology known as CRC Checkers or Hashing Checkers, creates and saves a unique cyclical redundancy check character or hashing number for each file to be monitored

header Additional information added to the front of data

heuristic analysis Because of its ability to monitor behavior of programs, this category of anti-virus technology is also sometimes known as activity monitors or heuristic analysis. Such programs are also capable of trapping encrypted or polymorphic viruses that are capable of constantly changing their identities or signatures

hierarchical The NDS database is organized in a hierarchical fashion, which can be logically thought of as a tree. The hierarchical design of the NDS database can be roughly equivalent to the hierarchical and geographical organization of the corporation being modeled

hierarchical networking An internetworking design strategy known as hierarchical networking isolates local LAN traffic on a local network architecture such as Ethernet or Token Ring while transmitting internetwork traffic over a higher speed network architecture such as FDDI or Fast Ethernet. Servers are often directly connected to the backbone network, while individual workstations access the backbone network only as needed through routers

Hierarchical Storage Management See HSM

high level languages Text-based programming languages that resemble standard language. The high level language code is then compiled into machine language for execution by the processor

high speed token ring See HSTR

HMMP The overall intention of the WBEM architecture is that the network manager could manage any networked device or application from any location on the network, via any HMMP (hypermedia management protocol)-compliant browser

HMMS Management data from a variety of software agents would be incorporated into the web based enterprise management architecture via the HMMS (hypermedia management schema)

HMOM All web-based management information is stored and retrieved by the request broker known as HMOM (hypermedia object manager)

horizontal integration The integration between middleware layers on two different computers. For horizontal integration to occur, both computers must be running compatible middleware solutions

host In X Windows the computer running the application

host The terms remote and local are often replaced by guest (remote) and host (local), when referring to Remote Control Software

hot swappable In some cases, enterprise hub modules can be inserted and/or removed while the hub remains powered-up, a capability known as hot-swappable

HPFS High Performance File System—OS/2 operating system

HPR/AnyNET Recent enhancements to APPN known as HPR (High Performance Routing)/AnyNET allow multiple transport protocols such as IP and IPX to travel over the APPN network simultaneously with SNA traffic. In such an implementation, APPN rather than TCP/IP serves as the single backbone protocol able to transport multiple LAN protocols and SNA traffic simultaneously

HSM   A service that automatically moves data that have not been accessed recently to remote media when the level of free space on a disk falls below a set level. By moving infrequently used data to slower, less expensive media such as optical disk or magnetic tape, HSM frees local disk space for newer, more commonly accessed files

HSTR   A 100Mbps Token Ring network architecture, otherwise known as high speed token ring (HSTR) has been approved by an organization known as the High Speed Token Ring Alliance that is also supposedly working on a Gigabit Token Ring standard, due sometime in 1999

HTML   The presentation language used to format data for World Wide Web browsers. HTML provides a means of both entering content and formatting the content for presentation

hub   Provides a connecting point through which all attached devices are able to converse with one another. Hubs must be compatible with both the attached media and the NICs installed in client PCs

hubs   Wiring centers for network architectures other than token ring are known as hubs

hypermedia management protocol   See HMMP

hypermedia management schema   See HMMS

Hypermedia object manager   See HMOM

hypertext markup language   See HTML

I/O manager   In charge of managing all input and output for the Windows NT operating system and is particularly concerned with managing the communications between: Device drivers, Network drivers, Cache Manager , File Systems Drivers

I/O request packets   The I/O manager oversees the interaction among the various categories of drivers to ensure that applications programs are delivered requested services in a timely fashion. Communication among these various drivers is standardized by the I/O manager through the use of I/O request packets

IBM 3270   A screen-at-a-time terminal solution associated with IBM mainframe computers. The first terminal that implemented this functionality was the model 3270

IBM 3270   In micro-mainframe connectivity, the micro (Standalone or LAN-attached PC) pretends to be or "emulates" a mainframe terminal such as an IBM 3270 attached and logged into the mainframe

ICMP   Although IP is by definition an unreliable transport mechanism, ICMP or Internet Control Message Protocol does deliver a variety of error status and control messages related to the ability of IP to deliver its encapsulated payloads

IDEA   International Data Encryption Algorithm makes use of one-time 128-bit keys known as session keys

idea generation   The second of three major functional categories of workgroup conferencing software. The major purpose of an electronically supported meeting is to generate ideas in a non-threatening, politically neutral environment

IDL   A high level universal notation language used to define the interfaces of an RPC interface. IDL derivatives are also used to define interfaces for dynamic binding in CORBA and DCOM solutions

IEEE 802   Local area network architecture standards are defined, debated and established by the IEEE (Institute of Electrical and Electronic Engineers) 802 committee

IEEE 802.1   See Spanning Tree Algorithm

IEEE 802.11   A lack of interoperability among the wireless LAN offerings of different vendors is a shortcoming being addressed by a proposal for a new wireless LAN standard known as IEEE 802.11

IEEE 802.12   Details of the 100VG-AnyLAN network architecture are contained in the proposed IEEE 802.12 standard

IEEE 802.2   The upper sub-layer of the data-link layer which interfaces to the network layer is known as the logical link control or LLC sub-layer and is represented by a single IEEE 802 protocol (IEEE 802.2)

IEEE 802.3   Although strictly speaking , Ethernet and IEEE 802.3 are conflicting standards, the term Ethernet is commonly used to refer to any IEEE 802.3-compliant network

IEEE 802.3u   The details of the operation of 100BaseT are in the IEEE 802.3u proposed standard

IEEE 802.3x   Full duplex Ethernet has gathered sufficient interest from the networking technology vendor and user communities to warrant the formation of the IEEE 802.3x committee to propose standards for full duplex Ethernet

IEEE 802.3z See Gigabit Ethernet

IEEE 802.5 IBM has been the driving force behind the standardization and adoption of Token Ring with a prototype in IBM's lab in Zurich, Switzerland serving as a model for the eventual IEEE 802.5 standard

IEEE 802.9a Details of the Iso-Ethernet network architecture are contained in the IEEE 802.9a standard, which is officially known as Isochronous Ethernet Integrated Services

IETF The IETF (Internet Engineering Task Force) is the group in charge of seeking approval for a printer management MIB (management information base), which would transport printer management information over TCP/IP networks in SNMP (Simple Network Management Protocol) format

IGP An autonomous system is rather arbitrarily defined as a network under the authority of a single entity whose interior routing policies or interior gateway protocols (IGP) are independent of those of any other autonomous system

IGRP Interior Gateway Routing Protocol, Cisco's proprietary distance vector protocol

IIOP A standard protocol implemented in all CORBA based ORBs that provides for inter-orb communications via TCP/IP

IIS A full feature Internet server. IIS provides web, FTP, and Gopher server capabilities natively and is written in a modular format to allow other Internet services (such as a proxy server) to be added

indexed sequential access method See ISAM

Infrared Data Association To ensure multi-vendor interoperability between laptops and mobile aware operating systems, the infra-red transmission should conform to the IrDA (Infrared Data Association) standards

Infrared transmission A wireless LAN transmission methodology limited by its line-of-sight requirement

inheritance interface An interface on a class object that allows instances of the class to gain information about changes in the class structure

instances An object in an object-oriented programming environment that is based on a class model. An instance can be thought of as an entity created from a class mold

instantiation The process of creating instances from classes in an object-oriented environment

Institute of Electrical and Electronic Engineers 802 Committee See IEEE 802

instrumentation Embedded performance metrics are sometimes referred to as instrumentation

Int14 Int14, or Interrupt 14, is one of the supported dial-out software re-directors and is most often employed by Microsoft network operating systems. Int14 is actually an IBM BIOS serial port interrupt used for the purpose of redirecting output from the local serial port

integrated messaging services Application programs such as e-mail are also able to use the NDS databases for network resource information such as UserIDs, passwords, and security restrictions. These integrated messaging services offered by NDS allow network managers to maintain a single database of user information for both network services and e-mail services

Integrated Services Digital Network See ISDN

Integrated Services Terminal Equipment See ISTE

integrated suites The difference between integrated suites and frameworks is that integrated suites are filled with their own network management and systems administration applications rather than offering the user an open framework into which to place a variety of chosen applications

integration Transitionary period of time in the migration process when both network operating systems must be running simultaneously and interacting to some degree

integration/migration services Integration refers to that transitionary period of time in the migration process when both network operating systems must be running simultaneously and interacting to some degree Migration features are aimed at easing the transition from NetWare 3.12 to either NetWare 4.1 or Windows NT

intelligent agent See agent event manager

intelligent software Intelligent software, also known as smart software, utilizes agents that assist end-users in their quest for increased productivity

Intellimirror A next generation roaming profile that ensures a user's desktop, data, and applications are available wherever they log into the network

interactive voice response Interactive voice response systems differ from audiotex systems in that IVR systems support on-line transaction processing rather than just information hot-line applications. As an example, banks use IVR systems to allow users to transfer funds between accounts by using only a touch tone phone

interactive work session See collaborative work sessions

Interdomain Trust In the case of a domain directory service such as Windows NT 3.51, the remote or foreign server receives the user authentication from the user's primary domain controller (local server) in a process known as Interdomain Trust (IT)

interdomain trust accounts Allow NT server domain controllers to perform passthrough authentication to other domains

interface The logical gap between hardware and software components

interface definition language See IDL

interfaces The means through which software and hardware objects communicate

Interior gateway protocols See IGP

internal firewalls Include filters that work on the datalink, network, and application layers to examine communications that occur only on a corporation's internal network, inside the reach of traditional firewalls

International Data Encryption Algorithm See IDEA

internet control message protocol See ICMP

internet inter-orb protocol See IIOP

Internet Packet Exchange See IPX

Internet Protocol See IP

Internet Security Association and Key Management Protocol See ISAKMP

Internet Suite of Protocols TCP/IP (Transmission Control Protocol/Internet Protocol) is the term generally used to refer to an entire suite of protocols used to provide communication on a variety of layers between widely distributed different types of computers. Strictly speaking, TCP and IP are just two of the protocols contained within the family of protocols more properly known as the Internet Suite of Protocols

Internet Suite of Protocols A suite or collection of protocols associated with TCP/IP that supports open systems internetworking

internetworking Linking multiple LANs together in such as way as to deliver information more efficiently from cost, business, and performance perspectives

interpreter Converts a high level language to machine language for execution in real time

inter-realm In Kerberos, If a client wishes to access a server in another realm, it requests an inter-realm ticket granting ticket from its local ticket granting server to authorize access to the remote ticket granting server, which can authorize access to the remote applications server

inter-ring gate calls NLMs executing in Ring 3 access operating systems services in Ring 0 by issuing structured inter-ring gate calls, thereby protecting the operating system from mis-behaving NLMs overwriting its memory space

inter-ring gate calls NLMs executing in Ring 3 access operating systems services in Ring 0 by issuing structured inter-ring gate calls, thereby protecting the operating system from mis-behaving NLMs overwriting its memory space

Interrupt request See IRQ

IntraNetWare A special version of NetWare 4 that includes web server software with built-in TCP/IP support

Intrusion detection systems Test the perimeter of the enterprise network through dial modems, remote access servers, web servers, or internet access

inverse multiplexing MLPPP compliant devices are able to deliver "bandwidth on demand" in a process referred to as inverse multiplexing

IP IP (Internet Protocol) is the network layer protocol of the TCP/IP suite of protocols. As such, it is primarily responsible for providing the addressing functionality necessary to ensure that all reachable network destinations can be uniquely and correctly identified

IP over ATM Otherwise known as Classical IP, adapts the TCP/IP protocol stack to employ ATM services as a native transport protocol directly. This is an IP-specific proposal and is not an option for LANs using other protocol stacks such as Net-Ware's IPX/SPX

IP spoofing Packet filters can be breached by hackers in a technique known as IP spoofing. Since packet filters make all filtering decisions based on IP source and destination addresses, if a hacker can make a packet appear to come from an authorized or trusted IP address, then it can pass through the firewall

IP switching IP switching technology distinguishes between the length of data streams and switches or routes accordingly on a case by case basis

IPng IPng (IP next generation), otherwise known as IPv6 (IP version 6), offers significant increases in functionality as well as increased address space in comparison to IPv4 (current version, IP version 4)

I-P-O Model Provides a framework in which to focus on the difference between the data that came into a particular networked device (I) and the data that came out of that same device(O). By defining this difference, the processing (P) performed by the device is documented

IPsec For establishing security over VPN tunnels. IPsec is largely supported by the firewall vendor community and is intended to provide interoperability between VPN firewalls from different vendors

IPv4 IPv4 (current version, IP version 4)

IPv6 See IPng

Ipv6 IPsec is also proposed to be able to support both authentication and encryption. These capabilities are optional for IPv4 and mandatory for IPv6 and are outlined in IETF RFCs 1825 through 1829

IPX Internet Packet Exchange (IPX), like most OSI network layer protocols, serves as a basic delivery mechanism for upper layer protocols such as SPX, RIP, SAP, and NCP. It is connectionless and unreliable

IrDA See Infrared Data Association

IRQ Interrupt request - The network interface card,

like every other hardware device in the computer, must interrupt and request resources such as CPU cycles and memory from the CPU itself. It must be assigned an IRQ or interrupt request number so that the CPU knows that it is the NIC requesting these services

ISAKMP ISAKMP (Internet Security Association and Key Management Protocol) ,a key management protocol from the IETF

ISAM A method for managing how a computer accesses records and files stored on a hard disk

ISDN Integrated Services Digital Network is a circuit-switched digital WAN service that is the support network transport service for Isochronous Ethernet

ISO 7498/2 This framework maps fourteen different security services to specific layers of the OSI 7 Layer Reference Model

ISO Management Framework The Network Management Forum associated with the OSI Reference Model has divided the field of network management into five major categories in a document known as the ISO Management Framework (ISO 7498-4)

isochronous Refers to any signaling system in which all connections or circuits are synchronized using a single common clocking reference. This common clocking mechanism allows such systems to offer guaranteed delivery times that are very important to streaming or time-sensitive traffic such as voice and video

Isochronous Ethernet See Iso-Ethernet

Iso-Ethernet Also known as Isochronous Ethernet offers a combination of services by dividing the overall 16.144 Mbps bandwidth delivered to each workstation into several service-specific channels

ISTE A workstation with an Iso-Ethernet NIC installed is properly referred to as Integrated Services Terminal Equipment

IT See Interdomain Trust

IVRU It is important for help desk management software to be able to interact with call center management technology such as automatic call distributors (ACD) and interactive voice response units (IVRU). The overall integration of computer-based software and telephony equipment in known as computer telephony integration (CTI)

Java A programming environment originally developed by Sun Microsystems that allows a programmer to write a single program that can execute on any platform that contains a Java virtual machine

Kerberos A three stage client/server security system

Kerberos Perhaps the most well-known combination authentication/authorization software is Kerberos, developed originally at Massachusetts Institute of Technology and marketed commercially by a variety of firms

kernel mode To access the I/O manager portion of the NT executive, applications must enter Ring 0, or kernel mode execution

Key Escrow agencies Otherwise known as Trusted Third Parties. Hold the keys necessary to decrypt key recovery documents

key recovery mechanism U.S. companies with international subsidiaries may now export 56 bit key-based encryption technology provided that they establish within two years a key recovery mechanism that will offer a back door into encrypted data for the government

knowledge base Contains not just the resolutions or answers to problems, but the logic structure or decision tree that takes a given problem and leads the help desk staff person through a series of questions to the appropriate solution

known local nodes Data-Link protocols such as Ethernet contain source addresses as well as the destination addresses within the predefined Ethernet Frame layout. A bridge checks the source address of each frame it receives and adds that source address to a table of known local nodes

L2F Cisco's Layer Two Forwarding (L2F) tunneling protocol for virtual private networks

L2TP An effort is underway to have the Internet Engineering Task Force (IETF) propose a unification of the two rival virtual private network tunneling standards known as Layer 2 Tunneling Protocol (L2TP)

LAN A Local Area Network is a combination of hardware and software technology that allows computers to share a variety of resources such as printers and other peripheral devices, data, application programs, and storage devices

LAN caching See network caching

LAN emulation LAN Emulation provides a translation layer which allows ATM to emulate existing Ethernet and token ring LANs and allows all current upper-layer LAN protocols to be transported by the ATM services in an unmodified fashion

LAN inventory management software

LAN modem Also known as a Dial-In Server. Offers shared remote access to LAN resources. LAN modems come with all necessary software pre-installed and therefore do not require additional remote control or remote node software. LAN modems are often limited to a single network architecture such as Ethernet or Token Ring, and/or to a single network operating system protocol such as IP, IPX (NetWare), NetBIOS, NetBEUI, or AppleTalk

LAN productivity software Application software that contributes directly to the productivity of its users. In other words, this is the software that people use not only to get their work done, but more importantly, to get their work done more quickly, effectively, accurately, or at a lower cost than if they did not have the benefit of this software

LAN resource management software Concerned with providing access to shared network resources and services. Examples of such shared network-attached resources include printers, fax machines, CD-ROMs, modems and a variety of other devices and services

LAN software architecture To organize and illustrate the inter-relationships between the various categories of LAN software, a LAN software architecture can be constructed divided into two major categories: network operating systems and applicaitons software. Also included are security software and management software

LAN switch See switching hub

land attack A variation on the denial of service attack in which the hacker substituted the targeted server's own address as the address of the server requesting a connection. This caused the attacked server to constantly try to establish connections to itself, thereby often crashing the server

Landline telephone network PSTN, otherwise known as the Landline Telephone Network

Large Internet Packets See LIP

Large Packet IPX See LIP

Large scale RAS Large Scale Remote Access Servers (RAS), also known as Monster RAS, is differentiated from previously mentioned RAS hardware by their scalability (number of modem ports), manageability, and security. These are enterprise class machines boasting modem port counts up to 1,344 per chassis, fast ethernet LAN interfaces, and ATM DS3 (45Mbps) or OC3 (155Mbps) WAN connections

latency Filtering time introduces latency to the overall transmission time

Layer 2 switch A LAN switch that supports a layer 2 virtual LAN distinguishes only between the MAC addresses of connected workstations

Layer 2 Tunneling Protocol See L2TP

Layer 3 switch These devices are able to perform filtering based on network layer protocols and addresses. They are able to support multiple virtual LANs using different network layer protocols

Layer 4 switch Process TCP port numbers and can distribute multiple requests for a given service to multiple different physical servers, thus providing load balancing

Layer Two Forwarding See L2F

LDAP A subset of the X.500 directory service standardized by the IETF for use on TCP/IP networks

leaf objects In NDS, network resources are considered leaf objects

lease duration IP addresses issued by DHCP are leased, rather than being permanently assigned, and the length of time that IP addresses can be kept by DHCP clients is known as the lease duration

least significant bit Both Ethernet and Token Ring believe that bit 0 on byte 0, referred to as the least significant bit, should be transmitted first

legacy applications Existing non-client/server applications, commonly implemented on mainframe computers that contain important data and information. See backward compatibility

library services Part of the DMA document management interoperability standards, library services will include interoperable version control and access control

Lightweight Directory Access Protocol See LDAP

limited size messaging See LSM

line printer services LPS or Line Printer Services are available in client (requests) and server (responses) versions. The client portion runs on the client PC requesting services and the server portion runs on the print server. LPS supplies the printer services typically supplied by network operating systems such as NetWare, Windows for Workgroups, or Windows NT

link state OSPF protocol uses a more comprehensive link state algorithm that can decide between multiple paths to a given router based upon variables other than number of hops such as delay, capacity, throughput, and reliability of the circuits connecting the routers

link state packets See LSP

link state protocols Routing protocols that take into account other factors regarding internetwork paths such as link capacity, delay, throughput, reliability, or cost

link support layer A layer of the ODI architecture. LSL.COM is the program that orchestrates the operation of ODI drivers

LIP LIP or Large Internet Packets applies only to NetWare 4.1 LANs that are linked to each other via a wide area network through routers. LIP, also known as Large Packet IPX, allows NetWare clients to negotiate with the routers as to the size of the IPX frame. From the NetWare client's perspective, the larger the IPX frame, the larger the IPX frame's data field, and the greater the amount of data that the client can cram into a single IPX frame

LLC For an IEEE 802.3-compliant network interface card to be able to determine the type of protocols embedded within the data field of an IEEE 802.3 frame, it refers to the header of the IEEE 802.2 Logical Link Control (LLC) data unit

LLC sub-layer The upper sub-layer of the data-link layer that interfaces to the network layer is known as the logical link control or LLC sub-layer and is represented by a single IEEE 802 protocol (IEEE 802.2)

load balancing The effective use of a network's redundant paths allows routers to perform load balancing of total network traffic across two or more links between two given locations

local area network See LAN

local hub management software Usually supplied by the hub vendor and runs over either DOS or Windows. This software allows monitoring and management of the hub from a locally attached management console

local procedure call facility A message passing environment that controls the internal communication within Windows NT between internal client requests and server responses is controlled

local security authority In Windows NT, the platform-specific login process interacts with the local security authority that actually provides the user authentication services

local session number A NetBIOS varaible that typically limits NetBIOS and NetBEUI clients and servers to a 254 session limit

locally attached multiple tape drives A network backup architecture in which locally attached multiple tape drives are attached directly to each server. The multiple tape drives provide both faster backup performance and fault tolerance

log file service File system activity is looked upon as a series of transactions that are documented by the log file service of NTFS

logic bombs Viruses that require a certain event to transpire are known as logic bombs

logical link control See LLC

logical network design The network performance criteria that could be referred to as what the implemented network must do to meet the business objectives outlined at the outset of the top-down analysis are also sometimes referred to as the logical network design

logical ring physical star IBM's Token Ring network architecture, adhering to the IEEE 802.5 standard, utilizes a star configuration, sequential message delivery, and a token passing access methodology scheme. Since the sequential logical topology is equivalent to passing messages from neighbor to neighbor around a ring, the token ring network architecture is sometimes referred to as: logical ring, physical star

logical topology The particular message passing methodology, or how a message will be passed from workstation to workstation until the message ultimately reaches its intended destination workstation. is more properly known as a network architecture's logical topology

logon process Process responsible for the interaction with users on whatever computer platform they may wish to log in on

Longest match algorithm Whenever a router consults its routing table to find the proper route on which to forward a given packet, it chooses that route via a method known as the longest match algorithm. Simply stated, this means that the more specific the direction, the better

low level languages Programming languages that represent the actual processor instructions. The two classes of low level languages are machine language and assembly language

LPS See Line printer services

LSL See link support layer

LSM By adding a protocol known as LSM (Limited Size Messaging), CDPD will be able to transport two-way messaging that will offer the following key services beyond simple paging: Guaranteed delivery to destination mobile users even if those devices are unreachable at the time the message was originally sent, return receipt acknowledgments to the party that originated the message

MAC sub-layer The media access control or MAC sub-layer is a sub-layer of the data-link layer that interfaces with the physical layer and is represented by protocols that define how the shared local area network media is to be accessed by the many connected computers

machine language The actual series of instructions executed by the computer processor. Machine language consists entirely of binary numbers. High level language programs are converted to machine language through the use of interpreters and compilers

mailslot An interprocess communication mechanism used by the OS/2 LAN Manager network operating system

mainframe A large multi-user, multi-processing computer. A mainframe can support thousands of users concurrently and was the main technology used for data processing prior to the advent of client/server computing

Major network ID That portion of the network ID assigned by the internet authorities

malicious applets   Java applets downloaded from the web that tend to be annoying rather than destructive

management information base   See MIB

management information format   See MIF

management interface API   Designed to interface to the desktop system management program that will consolidate the information from this client with all other desktop information

management software   Software that is incorporated into the network to provide a single, consolidated view of all networked resources, both hardware and software. From a single location, all of the distributed elements that comprise today's client/server information systems must be able to be effectively monitored and managed

MAPI   Most popular of the messaging APIs. It was developed by Microsoft and is supported by almost every vendor. MAPI provides a way for applications to access different types of messaging systems

mars_nwe   A daemon set for UNIX that emulates a bindery-based NetWare server (i.e., NetWare 3)

master domain architecture   A hierarchical architecture in which a single master domain is established into which all users are defined. Multiple sub-domains all offer inter-domain trust accounts to the single master domain, but the master domain does not allow trusted access from the sub-domains

Master File Table   See MFT

MAU   Token Ring wiring centers (Multistation Access Unit)

Maximum Transmission Unit   See MTU

MD5   Produces 128 bit hash number based on original document. Can then be incorporated into digital signature. Replaced MD4 and MD2

MDAC   Collectively, the latest versions of ODBC, OLE DB, and ADO

media access control   See MAC

media sharing LANs   Local area networks that use access methodologies to control the access of multiple users to a shared media are known as media sharing LANs

meeting creation   The first of three major functional categories for workgroup conferencing software. Meetings must first be created or established

meeting results reporting   The third of three major functional categories of workgroup conferencing software. To benefit fully from the ideas generated at the meeting, results must be easily, accurately, and flexibly reported

message   Transport layer protocols also provide mechanisms for sequentially organizing multiple network layer packets into a coherent message

message gateway   One of three cooperating components of the agent portion of the client/agent/server architecture. The message gateway can execute on the local server or on a dedicated Unix or Windows workstation, and acts as an interface between the client's message manager and the intelligent agent on the local server. The gateway also acts as a holding station for messages to and from mobile clients that are temporarily unreachable

message manager   One of three cooperating components of the agent portion of the client/agent/server architecture. The message manager executes on the mobile client and acts as an interface between client applications requesting services and the wireless link over which the requests must be forwarded

message queuing   A middleware communication solution through which applications exchange messages through buffered queues. Message queuing middleware is asynchronous in nature, allowing each application to continue to process data rather than waiting for a response from other application

message transfer agents   See MTA

messages   In electronic meeting support software, user comments on topics are made up of a series of messages that may contain supporting material or documents known as enclosures

Messaging Application Programming Interface   See MAPI

messaging middleware   A category of middleware that operates through the passing of independent messages between applications

methods   The defined set of commands for a software object. Other objects can invoke an object's methods

MFT An NTFS feature that attempts to accomplish two key objectives that are often contradictory: fast performance and lookups, especially on small files and directories, and reliable performance thanks to numerous redundant features

MIB Performance statistics are often gathered and stored in databases known as MIBs (Management Information Base)

MIB The decision as to which information should be requested, transported, and stored for a variety of different devices is defined by a protocol related to SNMP known as MIB or Management Information Base. These defined fields and quantities, which are encapsulated by SNMP and delivered via UDP, are known as MIB objects

MIB The network management information gathered must be stored in some type of database with an index and standardized field definitions so that network management workstations can easily access this data. A MIB, or Management Information Base, as these databases are known, can differ in the fields defined for different vendors' networking devices

MIB The types of information to be gathered and stored for enterprise network management systems have been defined as MIBs or Management Information Bases

microcell spread spectrum Limited to those areas such as college and corporate campuses that are served by microcells, this wireless WAN service offers full-duplex transmission at rates up to 104.5Mbps via proprieatary modems

micro-mainframe connectivity In micro-mainframe connectivity, the micro (Stand-alone or LAN-attached PC) pretends to be or "emulates" a mainframe terminal such as an IBM 3270 attached and logged into the mainframe

micro-segmentation When segmentation is taken to the extreme of limiting each LAN segment to only a single workstation, the internetworking design strategy is known as micro-segmentation. A micro-segmented internetwork requires a LAN switch that is compatible with the NICs installed in the attached workstations

Microsoft Clustering Services See MSCS

microsoft data access components See MDAC

middleware Middleware is an enabling software layer that provides a transparent means of accessing information between clients and servers

MIF The DMTF or Desktop Management Task Force has developed a common management environment for the management of desktop devices known as the DMI (Desktop Management Interface). Specific aspects of the DMI are contained in MIF (Management Information File) definitions

MIF DMI-compliant desktop management systems store performance and configuration statistics in a MIF (Management Information Format)

migration Migration features are aimed at easing the transition from NetWare 3.12 to either NetWare 4.1 or Windows NT

migration agent A network protocol gateway running on a NetWare 5 server that automatically converts between IPX, NetWare/IP, and Pure IP packets

MIME Multipurpose Internet Mail Extension allows binary files to be attached to SMTP delivered e-mail messages

MIME This standard is an extension of SMTP. MIME provides each attachment of an e-mail message with its own header

Mirrored Server Link See MSL

MLID Network interface card drivers are referred to as Multi-Link Interface Drivers or MLID in an ODI-compliant environment

MLPPP Multilink Point-to-Point Protocol or MLPPP (RFC 1717) is able to support multiple simultaneous physical WAN links and is also able to combine multiple channels from a variety of WAN services into a single logical link

MNP- 10 Transmitting data over analog cellular networks requires modems that support specialized cellular transmission protocols on both ends of the cellular transmission in order to maximize throughput. Examples of such protocols are MNP-10 Adverse Channel Enhancements and Enhanced Throughput Cellular (ETC)

mobile computing Addresses the need for field representatives to be able to access corporate information resources to offer superior customer service while working on the road. These field reps may or may not have a corporate office PC into which to dial

Mobile IP Mobile IP, under consideration by the

IETF, may be the roaming standard that wireless LANs require. Mobile IP, limited to TCP/IP networks, employs two pieces of software in order to support roaming: A mobile IP client is installed on the roaming wireless client workstation, A mobile IP home agent is installed on a server or router on the roaming user's home network

mobile MIB   The Mobile Management Task Force (MMTF) has proposed a mobile MIB capable of feeding configuration and location information to enterprise network management systems via SNMP. A key to the design of the mobile MIB was to balance the amount of information required to effectively manage remote clients while taking into account the limited bandwidth and expense of the remote links over which the management data must be transmitted

mobile middleware   The ultimate goal of mobile middleware is to offer mobile users transparent client/server access independent of the following variables: client or server platform (operating system, network operating system), applications (client/server or client/agent/server), wireless transmission services

Mobile telephone switching office   See MTSO

mobile-aware applications   The overall objective of mobile-aware applications is to reduce the amount of mobile client to server network traffic by building as much intelligence as possible into the server-based agent so that it can act on behalf of the mobile client application

mobile-aware operating systems   Operating systems that are able to easily adapt to these different computing modes with a variety of included supporting accessory programs and utilities are sometimes referred to as mobile-aware operating systems

modified object format   See MOF

modular concentrators   See enterprise hubs

modularity of design   The NT architecture with structured communications between sub-systems affords NT an architectural characteristic known as modularity of design, which allows entire subsystems to be easily added or replaced. For example, the replacement of the current Windows NT security sub-system with the Kerberos authentication system would be a relatively straight forward modification

MOF   Management data to be used by CIM would be stored in MOF (Modified Object Format) as opposed to DMI's MIF format or SNMP's MIB format

monolithic drivers   Network interface card drivers written for specific adapter card/network operating system combinations

Monster RAS   See Large Scale RAS

MPLS   Cisco's tag switching protocol became known as MPLS (Multi-protocol label switching) when it began deliberation by the IETF. Although MPLS was originally intended for use within a switched internetwork environment, the scope of its application has broadened to include the Internet. MPLS uses labels to provide shortcuts to specific circuits for fast routing of IP packets without the typical packet-by-packet routing table lookups

MPR   Novell's software-only router

MPR   Windows NT can also support simultaneous access to NetWare files stored on NetWare servers thanks to a layer of software that acts as a sort of redirector for file system requests known as the multiple provider router (MPR). The MPR is an open interface that accepts requests to any supported file system from application programs adhering to the Win32 API

MSCS   Provides support for fail-over clustering in Windows 2000

MSL   In NetWare 4.1 SFT III, synchronization of the servers is accomplished through a dedicated link known as the Mirrored Server Link (MSL). The use of the dedicated MSL link and dedicated MSL adapters prevents the server duplexing from adversely effecting LAN traffic

MTA   Mail messages are just files that are transferred to the proper destination postoffice, or file server, by message transfer agent (MTA) software, which is usually executed on a dedicated workstation

MTSO   Cellular service providers are deploying modem pools of cellular enhanced modems at the Mobile Telephone Switching Office (MTSO) where all cellular traffic is converted for transmission over the wireline public switched telephone network (PSTN)

MTU   The maximum capacity of a layer-two data frame

multi-casting   The process of sending a single

packet to multiple nodes on one or more network segments

multi-homed   A node that has NICs on more than one network segment

multi-layer switch   A single device in which layer 2 switching and layer 3 routing functionality are combined

multilevel security services   Part of the DMA document management interoperability standards, Multilevel security services provide a variety of security levels for individual documents regardless of which DMA compliant document management system they are stored in

multi-link interface drivers   See MLID

Multilink Point-to-Point Protocol   See MLPPP

multimode   In a multimode or multimode step index fiber optic cable, the rays of light bounce off of the cladding at different angles and continue down the core while others are absorbed in the cladding. These multiple rays at varying angles cause distortion and limit the overall transmission capabilities of the fiber

multimode graded index   By gradually decreasing a characteristic of the core known as the refractive index from the center to the outer edge, reflected rays are focused along the core more efficiently yielding higher bandwidth (3 GBps) over several kilometers in a type of fiber optic cable known as multimode graded index fiber

multimode step index   See multimode

multi-platform e-mail client software   Multi-platform e-mail client software varies by the number of different computing platforms for which client e-mail software is available

multiple master domains architecture   Two-tiered architecture that supports multiple master domains, with up to 10,000 users each. All sub-domains offer inter-domain trust accounts to all master domains

multiple non-trusting domains architecture   If multiple divisions or departments within a given organization do not need access to each other's data or network resources, then multiple independently managed domains can be established without defining any trust relationships between the domains

multiple provider router   See MPR

multiple trust architecture   In this idealistic, flat architecture, all domains offer inter-domain trust accounts to all other domains. The difficulty with this architecture is that all domains are independently administered and trust relationships must be established for every possible domain-domain combination

multiprotocol bridges   See translating bridge

multiprotocol network printing   When shared printing services are required across multiple, different network operating systems, using multiple different types of printers, then specialized multiprotocol network printing hardware and software is required

multiprotocol routers   Have the capability to interpret, process and forward data packets of multiple routable and non-routable protocols. See MPR

Multiprotocol routing   Multiprotocol routing provides the functionality necessary to actually process and understand multiple network protocols as well as translate between them. Without multiprotocol routing software, clients speaking multiple different network protocols cannot be supported

Multiprotocol Transport Networking Layer   See MPTN

multipurpose internet mail extension   See MIME

multistation access unit   See MAU

Multi-tier firewall   Allows controlled access to DMZ while blocking unauthorized access to secure network. Same functionality may be offered in a single product known as a tri-homed firewall

NAIS   A software-only remote access server solution providing both dial-in and dial-out access for NetWare 5

named pipes   Included in NT as an interprocess communication mechanism used by the OS/2 operating system

NASI   NetWare Asynchronous Services Interface. A software interrupt that links to the NetWare shell on NetWare clients. As with the Int14 implementation, a TSR intercepts all of the information passed to the NASI interrupt and forwards it across the network to the dial-out modem pool

National Computer Security Association   Firewall technology is now certified by the National Computer Security Association

NBF   NetBEUI Frame (NBF) is the Windows NT version of the NetBEUI protocol stack included for backward compatibility purposes with such Net-BEUI-based network operating systems as Microsoft LAN Manager and OS/2 LAN Server

NC   Client computer platforms that have minimal memory, no disk storage, and an operating system specifically designed to run software downloaded at application run time. Most NCs are designed to run Java applications

NCP   NetWare Core Protocols (NCP) provide a standardized set of commands or messages that can be used to communicate requests and responses for services between clients and servers

NDIS   Network Driver Interface Specification is a driver specification that offers standard commands for communications between NDIS-compliant network operating system protocol stacks (NDIS Protocol Driver) and NDIS-compliant network adapter card drivers (NDIS MAC Drivers). In addition NDIS specifies a binding operation that is managed by a separate program known as the Protocol Manager

NDPS   A new printing subsystem introduced in NetWare 5 that enhances NetWare's printing capabilities while reducing associated administrative tasks

NDPS Broker   Controls the NDPS servers running on a NetWare 5 server

NDPS Gateway   A NetWare 5 NDPS Gateway provides a means of translating information between the NDPS manager and the printer's native interface

NDPS Manager   NDPS Managers manage the communication between the broker and the printer on NetWare 5 networks. At least one manager must be present on the network to support printing. A single NDPS Manager can manage multiple printers, but only one manager can be installed per server

NDS   Network operating systems have always depended on some sort of naming service or directory in which to store information about users as well as systems resources such as disks, servers, and printers. NetWare 4.1 employs a global directory service known as NDS or NetWare Directory Services

NDS   NDS is a single logical database containing information about all network-attached resources that replaces the independently maintained, server-specific bindery files. The term "single logical database" is used because portions of the NDS database may be physically distributed on different servers throughout the network

NDS Catalog Services   Provides a means of storing information from a distributed NDS database into a flat (ASCII) file that can be quickly searched

NDS for NT   Integrates the Windows NT domain system directly into NDS. By extending the NDS schema to include NT domain information, NDS for NT allows for a single, unified directory. In this manner, NDS for NT is acting as a gateway between the two directory systems

NDS for NT Client   The network client portion of NDS for NT

NDS for Solaris   Allows servers running the Sun Microsystems Solaris UNIX style operating system to be tightly integrated into an NDS directory

near-end crosstalk   See NExT

net PC   Low end personal computers optimized to run applications from a network file server. Similar in concept to diskless workstations, these platforms are designed to run existing Windows applications directly on the distributed platform

NetBEUI Frame   See NBF

NetSync cluster   By running NETSYNC NLMs on both the NetWare 4.1 and NetWare 3.12 servers, all administration of the NetWare 3.12 servers, or NetSync Cluster, is done through NDS on the NetWare 4.1 server, with changes automatically replicated to the binderies on the NetWare 3.12 servers

NetWare 4 SFT III   A special version of NetWare 4 that includes server clustering capabilities

NetWare 4 SMP   A special version of NetWare 4 that includes a symmetrical multi-processing kernel

NetWare Connect   NetWare's software-only remote access server solution providing both dial-in and dial-out access capabilities for up to 128 simultaneous users

NetWare Connect   Novell's remote node server software

NetWare Core Protocol   See NCP

NetWare Directory Services   See NDS

NetWare Distributed Print System   See NDPS

NetWare DOS Requester   The NetWare DOS Requester actually works through DOS by having a VLM management program known as VLM.EXE interrupt DOS as appropriate and request services

NetWare for Macintosh   An add-in product from Pro Soft Engineering that tightly integrates Macintoshes into the NetWare environment

NetWare I/O Subsystem   See NIOS

NetWare Internet Access Server   See NAIS

NetWare Licensing Services   See NLS

NetWare Link Services Protocol   See NLSP

NetWare Loadable Module   See NLM

NetWare NFS   Allows UNIX systems to access NetWare file servers as if they were native NFS servers. NetWare NFS is actually a group of NLMs that runs on a NetWare server

NetWare NFS Gateway   Allows NetWare users to access NFS file systems on UNIX servers as if they were NetWare file servers. The gateway software is available for DOS, OS/2 or Macintosh computers

NetWare Partition   The NetWare kernel resides in a section of the server's disk drive known as the NetWare partition. This is the only portion of the disk that the NetWare kernel is physically able to access

NetWare Storage System   A disk sub-system available for NetWare 5 that supports large disks and ensures disk integrity in the event of unexpected system shutdown

NetWare/IP   NetWare/IP Version 2.1 is currently included with NetWare 4.1 and layers NCP (NetWare Core Protocols) over TCP/IP

network address translation   Computers on a network using the Private IP address space can still send and receive traffic to/from the Internet by using network address translation

network analyzers   LAN and WAN network analyzers are able to capture network traffic in real time without interrupting normal network transmission. In addition to capturing packets of data from the network, most network analyzers are able to decode those packets, monitor packet traffic sta-

tistics, and simulate network traffic through traffic generators

network auditing tools   What network auditing tools all seem to have in common is the ability to provide records of which network files have been accessed by which users

network baselining tools   By combining the ability to monitor and capture SNMP and RMON data with the abilities to analyze the captured data and report on trends and exceptions, network baselining tools are able to track network performance over extended periods of time and report on anomalies or deviations from the accumulated baseline data

network byte order   The IP header can be either 20 or 24 bytes long, with the bits actually being transmitted in network byte order or from left to right

network caching   Network caching or LAN caching software is able to improve overall remote node performance up to five times by caching repetitive applications commands and systems calls. These add-on packages are comprised of both client and server pieces that work cooperatively to cache application commands and reduce network traffic over relatively low-speed WAN links. Network caching software is network operating system and protocol dependent, requiring that compatibility be ensured prior to purchase

network computing   Client/server based systems that use low powered clients connected to high powered servers to deliver distributed applications. Network computing solutions can be categorized as NCs, Net PCs, or Windows Terminals. See NC

network device interface specification   See NDIS

network driver   Network drivers provide support for multi-layer communications over a network. Examples include NetBIOS, Redirector, and the SMB server interface to applications and file systems. Communication protocols such as TCP/IP, NetBEUI, and IPX/SPX provide transport services, NDIS provides the ability for a network interface card to support multiple protocols as well as the ability for a network operating system to communicate with more than one NIC in a single computer

Network File System   See NFS

Network Information System   See NIS

network interface card   The network interface card (or adapter) provides a transparent interface between the shared media of the LAN and the computer into which it is physically installed. The NIC takes messages that the computer directs it to send to other LAN attached computers or devices and formats those messages in a manner appropriate for transport over the LAN

network interface card   The data-link layer frames are built within the network interface card installed in a computer according to the pre-determined frame layout particular to the network architecture of the installed network interface card. Network interface cards are given a unique address in a format determined by their network architecture

network interface card drivers   Small software programs responsible for delivering full interoperability and compatibility between the NIC and the network operating system installed in a given computer

network layer   The network layer protocols are responsible for the establishment, maintenance, and termination of end-to-end network links. Network layer protocols are required when computers that are not physically connected to the same LAN must communicate

network level filter   A filtering program that only examines source and destination addresses and determines access based on the entries in a filter table is known as a port level filter or network level filter or packet filter

network message concentration   The process of combining multiple messages together into a single session between clients and servers rather than maintaining multiple sessions

network modeling and simulation tools   Simulation software uses the current network configuration as a starting point and applies what-if scenarios

network nodes   Any device that connects to a data network

network nodes   In APPN, network nodes are processing nodes with routing capabilities. They have the ability to locate network resources, maintain tables of information regarding internetwork

links, and establish a session between the requesting end-node and the internetwork service requested

network objects   In some cases, directory services may view all users and network resources as network objects, with information concerning them stored in a single database, arranged by object type. Object attributes can be modified and new network objects can be defined

network operating system   The software that runs on personal computers and allows them to log into a LAN and converse with other LAN-attached devices. Examples of popular network operating systems are NetWare, Vines, and Windows NT (not to be confused with Windows)

network operating systems   Concerned with providing an interface between LAN hardware, such as network interface cards, and the application software installed on a particular client or server. The network operating system's job is to provide transparent interoperability between client and server portions of a given application program

network segment address   The portion of a network layer address that determines the network segment upon which the node resides

network trending tools   Network baselining tools are able to track network performance over extended periods of time and report on anomalies or deviations from the accumulated baseline data. Also known as proactive network management tools or network trending products, such tools usually need several weeks of SNMP data to establish realistic baseline network performance averages

network virtual terminal   See Telnet negotiation

networked group presentations   Allow one individual to present a graphically oriented presentation to multiple network-attached group members as if all seminar participants were seated in a single room

network-network interface   See NNI

NExT   Near-End Crosstalk (NExT) is signal interference caused by a strong signal on one-pair (transmitting) overpowering a weaker signal on an adjacent pair (receiving)

NFS   NFS or Network File System is the file system most often associated with UNIX

NFS NFS or Network File System was originally developed by Sun Microsystems as part of their Open Network Computing (ONC) environment. NFS allows multiple, different computing platforms to share files

NICs Network Interface Cards are installed either internally or externally to client and server computers in order to provide a connection to the local area network of choice

NIOS DOS, Windows, and Windows '95 versions of the NetWare client software are based on a new 32-bit architecture known as NetWare I/O Subsystem or NIOS

NIS Provides a facility to synchronize the user authentication and authorization functions of UNIX systems

NLMs Additional functionality can be added to the basic NetWare kernel through the use of NetWare Loadable Modules or NLMs. NLMs are programs specially written to interact with and add functionality to the NetWare kernel

NLS A distributed, enterprise network service for NetWare 5 that allows the use of licensed applications to be monitored and controlled

NLSP NLSP or NetWare Link Services Protocol is introduced in NetWare 4.1 in an effort to overcome the inefficiencies introduced by RIP NLSP only broadcasts as changes occur, or every 2 hours at a minimum. Real world implementations of NLSP have reported 15 to 20 times (not %) reduction in WAN traffic with Novell claiming up to 40-fold decreases in router-to-router traffic as possible

NNI Network-Network Interface defines interoperability standards between various vendors' ATM equipment and network services. These standards are not as well defined as UNI

node address The portion of a network layer address that determines which NIC the network layer address correlates

non-persistent queues A message queue that does not maintain its contents when restarted

non-routable Protocols processed by some routers are actually data link layer protocols without network layer addressing schemes. These protocols are considered non-routable

non-routable protocol Can be processed by routers by either having the routers act as bridges or by encapsulating the non-routable data link layer frame's upper layer protocols in a routable network layer protocol such as IP

Novonyx A joint venture between Novell and Netscape

NT Executive Application programs and APIs are prohibited from interacting directly with hardware resources in Windows NT. Instead, applications and APIs must access hardware resources by requesting services through the collection of system services known as the NT Executive

NT Kernel Communications between the various NT Executive sub-systems and the I/O manager are controlled by the NT Kernel, sometimes referred to as a microkernel

NTFS NT File System—Windows NT

Null interface routers can be configured with a null interface, sometimes referred to as a bit bucket, so that undesirable traffic can be discarded rather than endlessly forwarded

nwadmin The application used to administer NetWare servers. Nwadmin is run on client computers

NWLink IPX/SPX is supported in the Windows NT environment through a protocol stack known as NWLink that allows IPX/SPX to serve as the native communications protocol for all communications between NT clients and NT servers

object layering and embedding See OLE

object layering and embedding custom controls See OCX

object manager Responsible for overall management of all Windows NT objects including enforcement of naming conventions and authorization for accessing and manipulating any object. In a very real sense, the object manager is responsible for object security

object oriented A programming paradigm designed around the concept of self-contained, reusable software components known as objects

object oriented user interfaces Present the user with a graphical desktop on which objects such as files, directories, folders, disk drives, programs, or devices can be arranged according to the user's whim

object request broker See ORB

objects Objects can be thought of as the system resources that are to be controlled or managed. User groups, users, printers, print servers, print queues, and disk volumes can all be considered objects by bindery services

objects Fields within the MIBs

octet An eight bit section of an IPv4 network layer address

octet A unit of data 8 bits long. The term byte is often used to refer to an 8 bit character or number. Since today's networks are likely to carry digitized voice, video, and images as well as data, the term octet is more often used to refer to these 8 bit packets of digital network traffic

OCX A software object that conforms to Microsoft's Object Layering and embedding specification

ODBC A Microsoft solution that allows a client to seamlessly communicate with any relational database server as long as the data structures are consistent

ODI Open DataLink Interface operates in a manner similar to the basic functionality of NDIS and is orchestrated by a program known as LSL.COM where LSL stands for Link Support Layer

OLE A compound document standard from Microsoft. OLE allows an object from one application to be embedded into another application

open database connectivity See ODBC

open data-link interface See ODI

Open Group The UNIX standards organization resulting from the merger of X/Open and OSF

open shortest path first See OSPF

Open Software Foundation See OSF

open source Software distributed under the GNU public license that ensures that the software's source code must remain freely available to the public

Oracle Mobile Agents Formerly known as Oracle-in-Motion. Perhaps the best example of the overall architecture and components required to produce mobile-aware applications. The Oracle Mobile Agents architecture adheres to an overall client-agent-server architecture, as opposed to the more common LAN-based client/server architecture

ORB A distributed software component that provides an interface through which objects make requests and receive responses

OSF UNIX vendors other than AT&T and Sun Microsystems banded together under the guise of The Open Software Foundation (OSF)to work on merging BSD and System V into a single UNIX version known as OSF/1. Later merged into the Open Group

OSI Model A framework for organizing networking technology and protocol solutions has been developed by the International Standards Organization (ISO) and is known as the Open Systems Interconnection (OSI) model

OSI Model Consists of a hierarchy of 7 layers that loosely group the functional requirements for communication between two computing devices. The power of the OSI Model lies in its openness and flexibility. It can be used to organize and define protocols involved in communicating between two computing devices in the same room as effectively as two devices across the world from each other

OSI Security Architecture This framework maps fourteen different security services to specific layers of the OSI 7 Layer Reference Model

OSPF OSPF or Open Shortest Path First (RFC 1247) is an example of a link state protocol that developed to overcome some of RIP's shortcomings such as the 15 hop limit and full routing table broadcasts every 30 seconds. OSPF uses IP for connectionless transport

OSPF Open Shortest Path First, a link state routing protocol

OSPF area If the interior gateway protocol in a given network is OSPF, then an additional layer of network hierarchy known as the OSPF area is introduced. All OSPF networks have at least one area, known as Area 0 or the backbone area, configured

outsourcing The selective hiring of outside contractors to perform specific network management duties

P channel In Isochronous Ethernet, A 10 Mbps ISDN P channel is reserved for Ethernet traffic and is completely compatible with 10BaseT Ethernet

packet bursts See Burst Mode IPX

packet filter A filtering program that only examines source and destination addresses and determines access based on the entries in a filter table is known as a port level filter or network level filter or packet filter

packet overlapping With packet overlapping technology, the next packet of information is immediately forwarded as soon as its start of frame is detected rather than waiting for the previous frame to be totally onto the network media before beginning transmission of the next packet

packet signing In NetWare 4.1, every packet transmitted from a particular client workstation can have a unique, encrypted digital signature attached to it, which can be authenticated only by the server in a process known as packet signing. However, a performance price of 5-7% is paid for the increased security as valuable CPU cycles are spent encrypting and decrypting digital signatures

packets Network layer protocols are responsible for providing network layer (end-to-end) addressing schemes and for enabling inter-network routing of network layer data packets. The term packets is usually associated with network layer protocols, while the term frames is usually associated with data link layer protocols

pages Fixed size portions of the process that are loaded into primary memory on demand

paging Seeks to eliminate, or at least minimize, fragmentation, by allowing processes to execute with only portions, rather than the entire process physically present in primary memory

PAP The remote network printing protocol used in the AppleTalk protocol suite

PAP An encryption protocol used for user IDs and passwords

PAP Password Authentication Protocol, repeatedly sends the user ID and password to the authenticating system in clear text pairs until it is either acknowledged or the connection is dropped. There is no encryption performed with PAP

parallel networks model A network design in which separate networks for SNA and LAN traffic had to be established between the same corporate locations

parallel routing Adds a layer of sophistication to workflow automation software by allowing sub-processes to be completed by multiple users simultaneously. Parallel routing may be combined with conditional branch routing

parent processes Processes in Unix are controlled by the fork system call as initiated through the shell interface, which allows parent processes to spawn multiple sub-processes known as child processes

partitions Entire branches of the tree, designated as partitions, and including all subordinate container objects and leaf objects, can be pruned (removed) from one point in the NDS structure and grafted to another branch. In fact two entire trees can be merged together into a single tree

Pascal A high level procedural programming language named after Blaise Pascal. Used in Borland's Delphi event-driven programming environment

passthrough authentication Users allowed into domains based on the trust relationships established by domain controllers are considered to be authorized by passthrough authentication

Password Authentication Protocol See PAP

path names Used in Unix to identify the specific path through the hierarchical file structure to a particular destination file

path vector protocol BGP routers exchange path information, which is a series of AS numbers, to indicate paths between autonomous systems

PCS Personal Communications Services will provide national full duplex digital voice and data at up to 25Mbps via 2-way pagers, PDAs, and PCS devices

PCT Microsoft's version of SSL is known as PCT or Private Communications Technology. The key difference between SSL and PCT is that PCT supports secure transmissions across unreliable (UDP rather TCP based) connections by allowing decryption of transmitted records independently from each other, as transmitted in the individual datagrams

PDC Domain directory services associate network users and resources with a primary server known as a PDC or Primary Domain Controller

peer-to-peer internetworking With full peer-to-peer internetworking, the PC can exchange data with any mainframe or any other PC on a host-to-host level rather than acting like a "dumb" terminal as in the case of micro-mainframe connectivity

peer-to-peer network operating systems Also known as DOS-based LANs or Low-cost LANs. Offered easy-to-install-and-use file and print services for workgroup and departmental networking needs

PEM Privacy Enhanced Mail was the application standard encryption technique for e-mail use on the Internet and with SMTP, Simple Mail Transport Protocol. It was designed to use both DES and RSA encryption techniques, but it would work with other encryption algorithms as well

performance engineering Simulation software tools are also sometimes known as performance engineering software tools

performance metrics By having these predefined events and performance metrics included within the application, management consoles will be able to detect problems with application performance and take corrective action

performance monitoring Performance monitoring software should offer the ability to set thresholds for multiple system performance parameters. If these thresholds are exceeded, alerts or alarms should notify network management personnel of the problem and offer advice as to possible diagnoses or solutions. Event logging and audit trails are often included as part of the performance monitoring package

Perl language Practical Extraction and Reporting Language adds the following functionality to that offered by the Korn and Bourne shells: list processing, associative arrays, modern subroutines and functions, more control statements, better I/O, full function library

persistent queues A message queue that maintains its contents when restarted

Personal Communications Services See PCS

Personal Handyphone System See PHS

PGP An Internet e-mail specific encryption standard that also uses digital signature encryption to guarantee the authenticity, security, and message integrity of received e-mail is known as PGP, which stands for Pretty Good Privacy

PHS Personal Handyphone System (PHS) is the digital cellular standard being implemented in Japan

physical layer Also known as layer 1 of the OSI model, is responsible for the establishment, maintenance and termination of physical connections between communicating devices. These connections are sometimes referred to as point-to-point data links

physical network design The technology layer analysis will determine how various hardware and software components will be combined to build a functional network that will meet pre-determined business objectives. The delineation of required technology is often referred to as the physical network design

physical topology Clients and servers must be physically connected to each other according to some configuration and be linked by the shared media of choice. The physical layout of this configuration can have a significant impact on LAN performance and reliability and is known as a network architecture's physical topology

piggyback updates A dial-up router update mechanism in which updates are performed only when the dial-up link has already been established for the purposes of exchanging user data

pipes In Unix, an interprocess communication mechanism that allows the output of one process to be used as the input for another process. Pipes is limited to communication between two processes executing on the same local computer and is initiated by a pipes system call

PKIS A set of services that enable a NetWare system to use RSA public-key encryption and digital certificates to verify data sources and ensure secure transmission. The certificate authority features of PKIS allow a NetWare server to manage digital certificates and public keys, thus enabling certificate-based services such as SSL security for LDAP servers

PKIX PKIX (Public Key Infrastructure X.509) is an international ISO standard for public key certificates

Plug-n-play See PnP

PnP The goal of plug-n-play is to free users from having to understand and worry about such things as IRQs (Interrupt Requests) , DMA (Direct Memory Access) channels, memory addresses, COM ports, and editing CONFIG.SYS whenever they want to add a device to their computer

PnP BIOS A PnP BIOS (Basic Input Output System) is required to interface directly to both PnP and non-PnP compliant hardware

point products   Also known as element managers. Specifically written to address a particular systems administration or network management issue

point-to-point data links   The physical layer, also known as layer 1 of the OSI model, is responsible for the establishment, maintenance and termination of physical connections between communicating devices. These connections are sometimes referred to as point-to-point data links

Point-to-Point Protocol   See PPP

Point-to-Point Tunneling Protocol   See PPTP

policy audits   Manual audits verify the effectiveness of policy development and implementation, especially the extent to which people understand and effectively execute their assigned processes in the overall corporate security policy

policy-based management tools   To more easily integrate configuration management tools with corporate policy and standards regarding desktop configurations, a new breed of policy-based management tools has emerged

poll spoofing   The ability of an internetworking device, such as an SDLC converter or router, to respond directly to, or acknowledge, the FEP's constant polling messages to the remote cluster controller. By answering these status check messages locally, the inquiry and its answer never enter the wide area link portion of the internetwork

Polymorphic viruses   Change their appearance each time an infected program is run in order to avoid detection

port level filter   A filtering program that only examines source and destination addresses and determines access based on the entries in a filter table is known as a port level filter or network level filter or packet filter

port mirroring   Copies information from a particular switch port to an attached LAN analyzer. The difficulty with this approach is that it allows only one port to be monitored at a time

portability   Evidenced by Windows NT's unique ability to execute over multiple different CPUs such as Intel x86, MIPs RISC, DEC Alpha, and PowerPC

ports   Specific addresses uniquely related to particular applications

POTS   Dial-up phone service is sometimes referred to as POTS (Plain Old Telephone Service)

Powersum crosstalk   Taking into account the crosstalk influence from all pairs in the cable, whether four-pair or 25-pair rather than just crosstalk between adjacent pairs, or pair-to-pair

PPN   Personal Phone Number or PPN would become the user's interface to PCS, a number associated with a particular individual regardless of the location, even globally, of the accessed facility

PPP   A WAN data-link layer protocol that is able to support multiple network layer protocols simultaneously over a single WAN connection. In addition, PPP is able to establish connections over a variety of WAN services including ISDN, Frame Relay, SONET, X.25, as well as synchronous and asynchronous serial links

PPP   Point-to-Point protocol is a data-link layer WAN protocol that is supported by NetWare Connect

PPP clients   Standardized remote clients with the ability to link to servers running a variety of different network operating systems are sometimes referred to as PPP clients. In general, they can link to network operating systems that support IP, IPX, NetBEUI, or XNS as transport protocols

PPTP   Microsoft's tunneling protocol that is specific to Windows NT Servers and remote access servers. It has the backing of several remote access server vendors

presentation layer   The presentation layer protocols provide an interface between user applications and various presentation-related services required by those applications. For example, data encryption/decryption protocols are considered presentation layer protocols as are protocols that translate between encoding schemes such as ASCII to EBCDIC

Pretty Good Privacy   See PGP

primary domain controller   Information concerning the network resources in a domain and the users that are allowed access to those resources are housed in a Windows NT server designated as the primary domain controller. See PDC

Printer Access Protocol   See PAP

Printer Agents   Represent the printer on a NetWare 5 network. Combining the role of print server, queue, and spooler, Print Managers interface the printer with the print manager

Privacy Enhanced Mail   See PEM

private addressing   Traffic that remains only on an organization's private network does not need to be globally unique. It only needs to be unique across that organization's private network. In support of this the Internet Assigned Numbers Authority (IANA) has set aside three ranges of private IP addresses

Private Communications Technology   See PCT

private key encryption   The decrypting device must use the same algorithm or method to decode or decrypt the data as the encrypting device used to encrypt the data. For this reason private key encryption is sometimes also known as symmetric encryption

private packet radio   Proprietary wireless WAN service offered by RAM and Ardis in most major US cities. Offers full duplex packet switched data at speeds of up to 4.8Kbps via proprietary modems

privileged mode   The NT kernel runs in privileged mode and is therefore never paged out of memory

proactive network management tool   Network baselining tools are able to track network performance over extended periods of time and report on anomalies or deviations from the accumulated baseline data. Also known as proactive network management tools or network trending products, such tools usually need several weeks of SNMP data to establish realistic baseline network performance averages

procedural language   Procedural languages (also known as imperative languages) were the first application development environments to be developed. These languages allow the programmer to maintain total control over the execution of the code. As the name would imply, procedural languages follow a specific set of instructions exactly in order

process group   In Unix, processes may be organized into a process group for the purpose of more easily or effectively accomplishing a common goal, and may communicate with each other via an interprocess communication mechanism known as pipes

process manager   Ultimately responsible for the creation, maintenance, and termination of processes within Windows NT and communicates with the object manager and virtual memory manager to provide required resources and protection for the process in question

production workflow   This category of workflow software automates complicated business processes, which are performed on a regular basis, perhaps daily

productivity paradox   In the past decade, over $1 trillion dollars was invested by business in information technology. Despite this massive investment, carefully conducted research indicates that there has been little if any increase in productivity as a direct result of this investment. This dilemma is known as the productivity paradox

promiscuous listen   Means that transparent bridges receive all data packets transmitted on the LANs to which they are connected

propagation   Forwarding messages by bridges to all workstations on all intermittent LANs

propagation delay   The time it takes a signal from a source PC to reach a destination PC. Because of this propagation delay, it is possible for a workstation to sense that there is no signal on the shared media, when in fact another distant workstation has transmitted a signal that has not yet reached the carrier sensing PC

properties   Properties are associated with objects and those aspects of objects that can or must be controlled. Examples of properties include such things as login time restrictions, network address restrictions, e-mail address, print job configuration, file and directory access rights, and user group membership

protected address space   The memory given to an application in a pre-emptive multi-tasking operating system. Each application's protected memory is protected from all other applications

protected memory mode   Client network operating systems may execute 32-bit applications in their own address space, otherwise known as protected memory mode

protective measures   Measures that are designed and taken that effectively block the vulnerability in order to prevent threats from attacking assets

protocol A set of rules that govern communication between hardware and/or software components

protocol analyzers devices that test layers 2 through 7

protocol conversion Must take place to allow the PC to appear to be a 3270 terminal in the eyes of the mainframe

protocol conversion Translation between protocols that may be necessary to get any two network nodes to communicate successfully

protocol discriminator To differentiate which particular noncompliant protocol is embedded, any packet with AA in the DSAP and SSAP fields also has a 5 octet SNAP header known as a protocol discriminator following the control field

protocol manager The NDIS program that controls the binding operation that combines separate NDIS-compliant software from NOS and NIC vendors into a single compatible driver

protocol stack The sum of all of the protocols employed in a particular computer

proxies See application gateways

proxy polling Emulates the FEP's polling messages on the remote side of the network, thereby assuring the remote cluster controller that it is still in touch with an FEP

pruned Entire branches of the tree, designated as partitions, and including all subordinate container objects and leaf objects, can be pruned (removed) from one point in the NDS structure and grafted to another branch. In fact two entire trees can be merged together into a single tree

public key certificates A certificate ensuring the authenticity of the public encryption key

Public Key Encryption Could perhaps more accurately be named Public/Private Key Encryption, as the process actually combines usage of both public and private keys

Public Key Infrastructure Services See PKIS

Pure IP The ability of NetWare 5 to place NCP directly in IP packets rather than encapsulating IPX in IP for transmission across IP based networks

QoS Quality of Service. General term for being able to differentiate between the level of network performance and reliability required by different applications

QOS Guarantees of proper execution and delivery of end-user applications are sometimes quantified in terms of a quality of service (QOS) guarantees

quality of service The acceptable level of network latency for a particular message. Quality of service can be thought of as a message prioritization scheme whereby time critical messages are processed prior to non-time critical messages

query services Part of the DMA document management interoperability standards

queue management This software manages and monitors the distribution of print jobs to various printers. It also allows printers to be enabled or disabled, or assigned to different personal computers

queue manager A special process that manages message queues and handles delivery of messages in message queuing middleware solutions

R commands A group of application layer service commands that can be executed remotely. For example, rlogin allows a user to remotely login to another computer and rexec allows the same user to execute a program on that remote computer

RADIUS A protocol and associated architecture known as Remote Authentication Dial-In User Service (RADIUS) is supported by a wide variety of remote access technology and offers the potential to enable centralized management of remote access users and technology

RARP RARP or Reverse Address Resolution Protocol is used if the datalink layer address of the workstation is known, but the IP address of the same workstation is required

RAS Windows NT offers a service known as RAS or Remote Access Service, which consists of both client and server software

raw interfaces Both block-oriented and character-oriented I/O may also bypass all buffers and queues and interact directly with hardware devices through their respective raw interfaces

RDO A high level API used in Microsoft Windows programming languages such as Visual BASIC and Delphi to access relational database data via ODBC

read ahead cache buffering A NetWare 4.1 feature that improves performance by reading ahead in the sequentially accessed file and caching that information in anticipation of the next request for information from the user

real-mode device drivers Programs or sub-routines that write directly to computer hardware

realms Enterprise networks implementing Kerberos are divided into Kerberos realms, each served by its own Kerberos server

real-time audits Most audit software depends on capturing large amounts of event data and then filtering that data for exceptional or unusual events

recursion If the local DNS cannot resolve an address itself, it may contact the higher authority DNS server, thereby increasing its own knowledge while meeting the client request in a process known as recursion

recursion Addresses that are contained within any lower level subnet can be rolled up, or aggregated into a single address at the next higher level of addressing

redistribution Routers running more than one routing protocol simultaneously and sharing or translating routing information between those routing protocols are able to do so through a process known as redistribution

relationship variables In Application MIB, relationship variables would define all other network attached resources on which a given distributed application depends. This would include databases, associated client applications, or other network resources

relative path names In Unix, absolute path names start at the root directory in the listing of the path to the destination directory, while relative path names start at the current directory

reliable Reliable transmission for upper layer application programs or utilities is assured through the additional fields contained within the TCP header, which offer the following functionality: flow control , acknowledgments of successful receipt of packets after error checking, retransmission of packets as required, proper sequencing of packets

remote access The term remote access is most often used to generally describe the process of linking remote PCs to local LANs without implying the particular functionality of that link (remote node vs. remote control). Unfortunately, the term re-

mote access is also sometimes more specifically used as a synonym for remote node

Remote Access Service See RAS

Remote Authentication Dial-In User Service See RADIUS

remote configuration Increased security in SNMP2 allows not just monitoring and management of remote network devices, but actual remote configuration of those devices as well

remote control In remote control mode, the remote PC is merely supplying input and output devices for the local client that interacts as normal with the local server and other locally attached LAN resources

remote control software Especially designed to allow remote PCs to "take-over" control of local PCs, should not be confused with the asynchronous communications software used for dial-up connections to asynchronous hosts via modems

remote e-mail client software Must strike a balance between the need to offer users the same services as locally connected users while delivering those services over the comparatively limited bandwidth offered by dial-up telecommunications services as compared to local area network bandwidth

remote monitoring See RMON

remote node Remote node or remote client computing implies that, in theory, the remote client PC should be able to operate as if it were locally attached to network resources. In other words, the geographic separation between the remote client and the local LAN resources should be transparent

remote node client software Most of the remote node server software packages also include compatible remote node client software. A problem arises, however, when a single remote node client needs to login to a variety of different servers running a variety of different network operating systems or remote node server packages

remote node server An alternative to server-based remote access software is a standalone device alternatively known as a dial-up server or remote node server. Such a self-contained unit includes modems, communications software, and NOS-specific remote access server software in a turnkey system

remote node server software   Traditionally remote node client and server software were supplied by the vendor of the network operating system on the server to be remotely accessed. Windows NT RAS (Remote Access Service) and NetWare Connect are two examples of such NOS-specific remote node server software

remote node servers   Strictly concerned with controlling remote access to LAN attached resources and acting as a gateway to those resources. Applications services are supplied by the same LAN-attached applications servers that are accessed by locally attached clients

remote node software   Requires both remote node server and compatible remote node client software in order to successfully initiate remote node sessions

remote procedure call   See RPC

Remote Storage Services   See RSS

Removable Storage Manager   See RSM

repeater   A repeater's job is to repeat the digital signal by regenerating and retiming the incoming signal, pass all signals between all attached segments, do not read destination addresses of data packets, allow for the connection of and translation between different types of media, effectively extend overall LAN distance by repeating signals between

replicate   The process of automatically copying a database from one server to another

replicated   One of the key characteristics of the NDS database is its ability to have partitions be replicated, or physically stored on multiple file servers. Replication implies that these multiple copies of the same NDS partition are kept synchronized

requester   Unlike the DOS client software of previous NetWare versions known as the NETx shell that acted as a replacement redirector, the DOS client software for NetWare 4.1 is referred to as the requester

resolver   DNS is physically implemented in a client/server architecture in which client-based DNS software known as the DNS or name resolver, sends requests for DNS name resolution to a DNS (or name) Server

Resource Management Service   See RMS

reverse address resolution protocol   See RARP

reverse poison   reverse poison allows a router to immediately set a hop count on a given route to 16 (unreachable) as soon as it senses that it and a neighboring router are incrementing hop counts by 1 to a given network on successive routing table exchanges. See split horizon

Rexx   The Rexx scripting language offers an easier to learn and use alternative to Perl, which supports structured programming techniques such as modularity while still offering access to shell commands

RFI   Radio Frequency Interference

RIF   One very important limitation of source routing bridges as applied to large internetworks is known as the 7 Hop Limit. Because of the limited space in the RIF (Router Information Field) of the explorer packet, only 7 hop locations can be included in the path to any remote destination

Ring 0   In NetWare 4.1's ring memory protection scheme, the area reserved for the operating system is known as Ring 0, otherwise known as domain OS (operating system)

Ring 3   In NetWare 4.1's ring memory protection scheme, the area reserved for NLMs is known as Ring 3 or domain OSP (operating system protected). NLMs executing in Ring 3 access operating systems services in Ring 0 by issuing structured inter-ring gate calls, thereby protecting the operating system from mis-behaving NLMs overwriting its memory space

ring logical topology   See sequential

ring memory protection   NetWare 4.1 introduces ring memory protection that seeks to isolate and protect the operating system from potentially dangerous NLMs that were able to crash the entire system in previous versions of NetWare

ring physical topology   In a ring physical topology, each PC is actually an active part of the ring, passing data packets in a sequential pattern around the ring. If one of the PCs dies, or a network adapter card malfunctions, the "sequence" is broken, the token is lost, and the network is down

RIP   A router-to-router protocol used to keep routers synchronized and up-to-date via broadcasts every 30 seconds

RIP   Routing Information Protocol, a distance vector routing protocols

risk   Probability of a particular threat successfully attacking a particular asset in a given amount of time via a particular vulnerability

RMON   The most commonly used MIB for network monitoring and management is known as the RMON (Remote Monitoring) MIB

RMON MIB   Remote Network Monitoring MIB

RMON probe   RMON2-compatible agent software which resides within internetworking devices and reports performance statistics to enterprise network management systems is referred to as an RMON probe

RMON2   While the original RMON MIB only required compatible technology to be able to collect and analyze statistics on the physical and data link layers, RMON2 requires collection and analysis of network layer protocols as well

RMS   Provides a centralized storage location for printer resources such as fonts, banner pages, client printer drivers, and printer definition files on a NetWare 5 network

roaming   One important issue not included in the IEEE 802.11 standard is roaming capability, which allows a user to transparently move between the transmission ranges of wireless LANs without interruption. Proprietary roaming capabilities are currently offered by many wireless LAN vendors

role based administration   In NetWare 5, role based administration allows for tighter security by assigning only those rights to individual system administrators their position requires. Administration capabilities can be divided into various roles and spread among users

root   A special account that has ultimate rights over a UNIX system

root object   In NDS, the tree hierarchy starts at the top with the root object. There is only one root object in an entire global NDS database. Branches off the root object are represented by container objects

round robin polling scheme   In 100VG-AnyLAN, the Demand Priority Protocol access methodology uses a round robin polling scheme in which the hubs scan each port in sequence to see if the attached workstations have any traffic to transmit. The round robin polling scheme is distributed

through a hierarchical arrangement of cascaded hubs

router   A device that forwards packets between layer three segments based on the layer three network address

router servers   An internetwork evolutionary design scenario in which route servers will provide a centralized repository of routing information while edge switches deployed within the LANs will be programmed with minimal routing information

Routing Information Field   See RIF

Routing Information Protocol   See RIP

Routing loop   Two routers continue to trade routing table updates for a route that is in fact no longer reachable

Routing Table Maintenance Protocol   See RTMP

routing tables   Routers consult routing tables to determine the best path on which to forward a particular data packet

roving port mirroring   Creates a roving RMON (Remote Monitoring) probe that gathers statistics at regular intervals on multiple switch ports. The shortcoming with this approach remains that at any single point in time, only one port is being monitored

RPC   The interprocess communication service defined within DCE is known as RPC or Remote Procedure Call. Windows NT, along with many other operating systems, supports RPC. Remote Procedure Calls is more like a "super" interprocess communication mechanism in that it has the ability to use other interprocess mechanisms such as named pipes, NetBIOS, or WinSock, should that be what a particular application requires

RPC   RPC (Remote Procedure Call) is a session layer protocol responsible for establishing, maintaining, and terminating communications sessions between distributed applications in an NFS environment

RPC   RPCs can be thought of as remote sub-routines. The application programmer calls a link to a sub-routine or procedure located on a remote server. The local link to the remote procedure is known as a stub function. The stub function transfers the calling parameters to the RPC based middleware on the server and waits until the server responds

RSA The current standard for public key encryption

RSM Provides a standard interface to multiple tape autoloaders and robotic tape and optical disk changers for Windows 2000

RSS A hierarchical storage management (HSM) application. RSS provides an inexpensive method to increase storage capacity by constantly monitoring file usage and the level of free disk space on an NTFS partition

RTMP A routing protocol used in the AppleTalk protocol suite

RYGB The type of phone wire installed in most homes consists of a tan plastic jacket containing four untwisted wires: red, yellow, green, and black and is also known as 4 conductor station wire or RYGB

S/MIME Secure Multipurpose Internet Mail Extension secures e-mail traffic in e-mail applications that have been S/MIME enabled. S/MIME encrypts and authenticates e-mail messages for transmission over SMTP-based e-mail networks

samba A freely available daemon set for UNIX that emulates a Windows NT 4.0 server

same-place same-time meeting In electronic meeting support software, meetings may be held in specially equipped decision support rooms in which all forum participants gather in what is known as a same-place, same-time meeting or may convene via a local or wide area network according to participants' availability in what is known as a different-place, different-time meeting

SAMSRV.DLL The Windows NT security DLL used to authenticate and authorize users

sandbox A security mechanism used with Java applets. A limited environment called the sandbox is created for the exclusive use of the applet. The applet cannot access any resources beyond the sandbox

SAP SAP, or Service Advertising Protocol, is used by all network servers to advertise the services they provide to all other reachable networked servers. SAP uses IPX packets as its means of delivering its service advertising requests or responses throughout the network

SAP filtering To eliminate the every 60 second broadcast of SAP packets, an associated feature of advanced IPX known as SAP filtering, ensures that SAP broadcasts are synchronized to take place only with NLSP updates

SAS A new authentication API for Novell NetWare 5. SAS currently supports the Secure Sockets Layer (SSL), the Internet standard for encrypted authentication. The modular design of SAS allows for new authentication standards (such as biometrics) to be added to NetWare as they are developed and standardized

SAS Single Attachment Stations attach to only one of FDDI's two rings

SATAN The SATAN probe is especially written to analyze Unix and TCP/IP based systems, and once it has found a way to get inside an enterprise network, it continues to probe all TCP/IP machines within that enterprise network

SBA In FDDI, frames transmitted in a continuous stream are known as synchronous frames and are prioritized according to a methodology known as synchronous bandwidth allocation or SBA, which assigns fixed amounts of bandwidth to given stations

scheduler When multiple processes are all contending for the same limited amount of primary memory not occupied by the non-swappable Unix kernel, the scheduler process, also known as the swapper, decides which processes should be removed from primary memory to the swap partition and which should be moved from the swap partition into main memory

screen In X Windows one of multiple virtual "desktops" upon which an application's output can be displayed

screen caching Allows only changes to screens, rather than entire screens to be transmitted over the limited bandwidth WAN links. Screen caching will reduce the amount of actual traffic transmitted over the WAN link

screen scraper A piece of software used to provide interaction between a legacy application and a client through the terminal screen interface originally designed for human use of the legacy system. The screen scraper presents an API to the application programmer and emulates a user terminal session to the business application. From the perspective of the mainframe application, the screen scraper appears as a human operator

script wrapper   Used to integrate legacy applications that support command line switches rather than an API. The script wrapper executes the legacy application for each potential command line flag

SDLC   IBM SNA's data link layer protocol. SDLC frames do not contain anything equivalent to the OSI network layer addressing information for use by routers, which makes SDLC a non-routable protocol

SDLC conversion   SDLC frames are converted to Token Ring Frames by a specialized internetworking device known as a SDLC Converter

SDLC converter   See SDLC conversion

search engine   The portion of the software that sifts through the knowledge base to the proper answer

sections   In electronic meeting support software, each forum would probably contain multiple topics for discussion known alternatively as discussion categories or sections

Secure Authentication Services   See SAS

Secure Courier   Based on SSL and allows users to create a secure digital envelope for transmission of financial transactions over the Internet

Secure Electronic Transactions   See SET

Secure Hypertext Transport Protocol   See S-HTTP

Secure Multipurpose Internet Mail Extension   See S/MIME

secure single login   Assurance that users are able to log into a network, rather than each individual server and application, and be able to access only resources for which they are properly authorized is known as secure single login

secure SNMP   SNMP2, or a variation of SNMP known as secure SNMP, will allow users to access carriers' network management information and incorporate it into the wide area component of an enterprise network management system

Secure Sockets Layer   See SSL

security   Especially important in networked, LAN software environments as logged-in users can be physically dispersed over large areas. Increased deployment of remote workers has led to increased need for remote access to corporate information resources. As important corporate data are transferred over network links, precautions must be taken to prevent unauthorized access to transmitted data, as well as to corporate networks and computer systems

security access tokens   In Windows NT, the local security authority generates a security access token for authorized users, which contains security IDs (SID) for this user and all of the user groups to which this user belongs

security account manager   In Windows NT, all of the user and user group ID and permission level information is stored in and maintained by the security account manager, which interacts with the local security authority to verify user IDs and permission levels

Security Analyzer Tool for Analyzing Networks   See SATAN

Security Auditing and Intrusion Detection   Able to track and identify suspicious behaviors from both internal employees and potential intruders

security IDs   See security access tokens

security policy development life cycle   See SPDLC

security probes   Actively test various aspects of enterprise network security and report results and suggest improvements

security reference monitor   Concerned primarily with authorization or authentication for processes that wish to access objects and users that wish to access the system via the logon process. It is the only kernel mode portion of the NT security system

segmentation   Usually the first internetworking approach employed to reduce shared media congestion. By having fewer workstations per segment, there is less contention for the shared bandwidth

send window   With an adaptive sliding window protocol, the number of packets allowed to be sent before the receipt of an acknowledgment determines the size of the send window

Sequenced Packet Exchange   See SPX

sequential   In a sequential logical topology, also known as a ring logical topology, data are passed from one PC (or node) to another. Each node examines the destination address of the data packet to determine if this particular packet is meant for it. If the data were not meant to be delivered at this node, they are passed along to the next node in the logical ring

sequential routing   In workflow automation software, the simplest of the routing schemes in which business processes follow predictable paths with individual steps following each other in a linear fashion

Serial Line Internet Protocol   See SLIP

server capacity planning   Server management software must provide server capacity planning capabilities by monitoring server performance trends and making recommendations for server component upgrades in a proactive manner

server duplexing   NetWare 4.1 SFT III offers a unique fault tolerant feature known as server duplexing. In such a case, the contents of not only the disks but also the servers' memory and CPUs are synchronized. In case of the failure of the primary server, the duplexed server takes over transparently

server front-end LAN switch   A switched network architecture in which dedicated LAN switch ports are necessary only for servers, while client workstations share a switch port via a cascaded media-sharing hub

server isolation   Instead of assigning all workstations to their own LAN segment as in micro-segmentation, only selected high-performance devices such as servers can be assigned to their own segment in an internetworking design strategy known as server isolation. By isolating servers on their own segments, guaranteed access to network bandwidth is ensured

server network operating systems   Server network operating systems are able to be chosen and installed based on their performance characteristics for a given required functionality. For example, NetWare servers are often employed as file and print servers, whereas Windows NT, OS/2, or UNIX servers are more likely to be employed as application servers

server trust accounts   Allow NT servers to download copies of the master domain database from a domain controller. This trust relationship is what enables backup domain controllers

servers   Servers such as application servers and print servers are usually dedicated computers ac-

cessed only through LAN connections. Whereas a client could be considered a service requester, servers are characterized as service providers

Service Advertising Protocol   See SAP

Service Location Protocol   See SLP

Service Registry Service   See SRS

service-granting ticket   In Kerberos, if the ticket granting server determines that the request is valid, a ticket is issued that will allow the user to access the requested server. This ticket is known as a service-granting ticket

Services for Macintosh   See SFM

session keys   Unique, one-time use keys used for encryption

session layer   The session layer protocols are responsible for establishing, maintaining, and terminating sessions between user application programs. Sessions are interactive dialogues between networked computers and are of particular importance to distributed computing applications in a client/server environment

session limits   The second major improvement of NBF over NetBEUI has to do with session limits. Since NetBEUI is NetBIOS-based, it was forced to support the 254 session limit of NetBIOS. With NBF, each client-to-server connection can support 254 sessions, rather than a grand total for all connections of 254 sessions

SET   Secure Electronic Transactions are a series of standards to ensure the confidentiality of electronic commerce transactions. These standards are being largely promoted by credit card giants VISA and MasterCard

SFM   Services for Macintosh. These independently controlled services, which include File Server for Macintosh and Print Server for Macintosh, allow an NT server to act as an Appleshare server for Macintosh clients

shared media LANs   The various connected computers and peripheral devices all share some type of media to converse with each other. As a result, LANs are sometimes more specifically referred to as shared media LANs or media-sharing LANs

shared media network architecture   Employs media-sharing network wiring centers such as hubs that offer all attached workstations shared access to a single LAN segment

shell   In Unix, the command interpreter that is the user's interface to the system is a specialized user process known as a shell

shielding   May be a metallic foil or copper braid. The function of the shield is rather simple. It "shields" the individual twisted pairs as well as the entire cable from either EMI (electromagnetic interference) or RFI (radio frequency interference)

S-HTTP   Secure HTTP is a secure version of HTTP that requires both client and server S-HTTP versions to be installed for secure end-to-end encrypted transmission

signals   The exception and interrupt handling facility in Unix

signature scanners   Because virus scanners are really scanning for known digital signatures or viruses, they are sometimes referred to as signature scanners

SII   An interface used by CORBA objects to interface in a static manner. Static interfacing implies that the object's interfaces do not change over time. The interface characteristics for an object are defined using IDL

Simple key management for IP   See SKIP

simple mail transfer protocol   See SMTP

simple management protocol   See SMP

simple network management protocol   See SNMP

simultaneous RMON view   Allows all network traffic to be monitored simultaneously. Such a monitoring scheme is possible only on those switches that incorporate a shared memory multigigabit bus as opposed to a switching matrix internal architecture. Furthermore, unless this monitoring software is executed on a separate CPU, switch performance is likely to degrade

Single Access Control View   Allows the user's access from their client workstation to display only those resources that the user actually has access to

Single Attachment Station   See SAS

single domain architecture   All users and network resources are organized into a single domain of up to 10,000 users. This is a flat architecture with no inter-domain trust relationships involved

single mode   Fiber optic cable that is able to focus the rays of light so that only a single wavelength can pass through at a time. Without numerous re-

flections of rays at multiple angles, distortion is eliminated and bandwidth is maximized

single point of failure   Any network attached device or piece of technology whose failure would cause the failure of the entire network

Single Point of Registration   See SPR

single sign-on   See SSO

Single Unix Specification   See Spec 1170 APIs

SKIP   Simple Key Management for IP, a proposed key management protocol from Sun

slices   Each disk in Unix is divided into multiple slices each of which can be used to accommodate either a file system, a swap area, or a raw data area. A Unix slice is equivalent to a partition in DOS

SLIP   Serial Line Interface Protocol is able to establish asynchronous serial links between two computers that support both SLIP and TCP/IP over any of the following connections: via modems and a dial-up line, via modems and a point-to-point private or leased line, via hard-wired or direct connections

SLIP   Serial Line Internet Protocol is a dara-link WAN protocol that is supported by NetWare Connect

slot time   In Ethernet networks, the time required for a given workstation to detect a collision is known as slot time and is measured in bits

slow convergence   Delay that occurs while all of the routers are propagating their routing tables using RIP, known as slow convergence, could allow certain routers to think that failed links to certain networks are still viable

slow convergence   Delay that occurs while all of the routers are propagating their routing tables

SLP   An IETF standard that replaces SAP in NetWare 5 networks. SLP registers service information in a database that is queried by clients looking for a specific service. Services register with SLP when they are initially started. The use of SLP greatly decreases network broadcast traffic compared to the SAP paradigm where every service announced itself every 60 seconds

Small Office Home Office   See SOHO

Smalltalk   The first object-oriented programming language. Developed by Xerox in the lat 1960s.

Smalltalk provides the most complete object implementation of any object-oriented programming language

smart cards   Used in token authentication systems, Hardware-based smart cards or Smart IDs that are about the size of a credit card with or without a numeric keypad

smart software   See intelligent software

SMP   High powered application servers require network operating systems that can support multiple CPUs, otherwise known as symmetrical multiprocessing or SMP

SMP   The need to reduce network traffic caused by the SNMP protocol, as well as to deal with other aforementioned SNMP shortcomings, led to a proposal for a new version of SNMP known as SNMP2, or SMP (Simple Management Protocol)

SMP kernel   Since the original NetWare 4.1 did not have SMP capability, some way needed to be found to support SMP while still ensuring backward compatibility with all existing NLMs. This was done by having NetWare 4.1 SMP load a second operating system kernel, known as the SMP kernel, which works cooperatively with the first or native operating system kernel

SMP scalability   The percentage of increased performance achieved for each additional CPU

SMTP   Simple Mail Transfer Protocol allows different computers that support the TCP/IP protocol stack to exchange e-mail messages. SMTP is able to establish connections, provide reliable transport of e-mail messages via TCP, notify users of newly received e-mail, and terminate connections

SNA   Systems Network Architecture, IBM's proprietary network architecture, was originally designed to link mainframes

SNAP   To ease the transition to IEEE 802 compliance, an alternative method of identifying the embedded upper layer protocols was developed, known as SNAP or Sub-Network Access Protocol. Any protocol can use SNAP with IEEE 802.2 and appear to be an IEEE 802-compliant protocol

SNMP   Performance management information can be communicated to Enterprise Management Systems such as HP OpenView or IBM SystemView in the proper SNMP (Simple Network Management Protocol) format

SNMP   SNMP offers a standardized protocol for the transport of management information such as device status, device activity, and alarm conditions

SNMP   Partly due to the dominance of TCP/IP as the internetworking protocol of choice, SNMP (Simple Network Management Protocol) is the defacto standard for delivering enterprise management data

SNMP   Network management information is formatted according to the SNMP or Simple Network Management Protocol, which is a member of the Internet Suite of Protocols (TCP/IP)

SNMP manager   Collect and parse data from the various agents. Managers are specialized software applications that run as applications on computer platforms

SNMP2   The need to reduce network traffic caused by the SNMP protocol, as well as to deal with other aforementioned SNMP shortcomings, led to a proposal for a new version of SNMP known as SNMP2, or SMP (Simple Management Protocol)

socket   The unique port address of an application combined with the unique 32 bit IP address of the computer on which the application is executing

socket services   The socket services sub-layer of the PCMCIA Card and Socket Services driver specification is written specifically for the type of PCMCIA controller included in a notebook computer

sockets   In Unix, Sockets is a more powerful and flexible interprocess communications mechanism than Pipes and is able to provide interprocess communications across network interfaces to processes running on widely distributed computers

SOCKS   Used by circuit level proxy programs, SOCKS creates a proxy data channel to the application server on behalf of the application client. Since all data goes through SOCKS, it can audit, screen and filter all traffic in between the application client and server

software-only solutions   A network faxing architecture in which the user supplies both the PC to execute the FAX software and compatible FAX boards or modems

SOHO   See telecommuting

source address   Data-Link protocols such as Ethernet contain source addresses as well as the destination addresses within the predefined Ethernet

Frame layout. A bridge checks the source address of each frame it receives and adds that source address to a table of known local nodes

source routing bridge   Used to connect two source-routing enabled Token Ring LANs. Data messages arrive at a source routing bridge with a detailed map of how they plan to reach their destination

source routing transparent bridge   Bridges that can support links between source routing Token Ring LANs or transparent LANs, are known as Source Routing Transparent (SRT) bridges

Spanning Tree Algorithm   The Spanning Tree Algorithm (STA) has been standardized as IEEE 802.1 for the purposes of controlling redundant paths in bridged networks and thereby reducing the possibility of broadcast storms

SPAP   Shiva's proprietary authentication protocol that includes password encryption and callback capability

SPDLC   Security Policy Development Life Cycle - One methodology for the development of a comprehensive network security policy

Spec 1170 APIs   In attempting to standardize the operating system elements of Unix, a consortium of vendors has been working on the single Unix specification, otherwise known as the Spec 1170 APIs. This is a collection of more than 1,000 APIs which, hopefully, all versions of Unix will support

split horizon   To reduce slow convergence in RIP based router networks, split horizon and reverse poison prevent routers from wasting time broadcasting routing table changes back to the routers that just supplied them with the same changes in the first place

spoofing   A method of filtering chatty or unwanted protocols from the WAN link while ensuring that remote programs that require on-going communication from these filtered protocols are still reassured via emulation of these protocols by the local dial-up router

SPR   Single Point of Registration allows a network security manager to enter a new user (or delete a terminated user) from a single centralized location and assign all associated rights, privileges, and access control to enterprise resources from this single point rather than having to enter this new user's

information on multiple resources distributed throughout the enterprise

Spread spectrum transmission   Spread spectrum transmission, as its name implies, spreads a data message across a wide range or spectrum of frequencies. This technique was originally employed as a security measure since a receiver would need to know exactly how the message was spread across the frequency spectrum in order to intercept the message in meaningful form

SPX   NetWare's connection-oriented, reliable transport layer protocol

SQL   A standard language developed to facilitate querying relational database servers. SQL is a comprehensive relational database language providing a means of performing common database operations such as record additions, updates, and database design modifications in addition to query capabilities. The American National Standards Institute (ANSI) has standardized the SQL language

SRM   See Security Reference Monitor

SRS   Stores information about public access printers available on a NetWare 5 network. This information includes manufacturer, model, and printer type

SSL   A connection level encryption method providing security to the network link itself. SSL Version 3 (SSL3) added support for more key exchange and encryption algorithms as well as separate keys for authentication and encryption

SSO   Authentication technology that delivers single sign-on (SSO) access to multiple network attached servers and resources via passwords

stackable hubs   Add expandability and manageability to the basic capabilities of the stand-alone hub. Stackable hubs can be linked together, or cascaded, to form one larger virtual hub of a single type of network architecture and media

stand-alone hubs   Stand-alone hubs are fully configured hubs offering a limited number (12 or fewer) ports of a particular type of network architecture (Ethernet, Token Ring) and media

stand-alone LAN switches   Stand-alone Workgroup/Departmental LAN switches offer dedicated connections to all attached client and server computers via individual switch ports

star   The star physical topology employs some type

of central management device. Depending on the network architecture and sophistication of the device, it may be called a hub, a wiring center, a concentrator, a MAU (Multiple Access Unit), a repeater or a switching hub

state variables   In application MIB, state variables would report on the current status of a given application. Three possible states are up, down, and degraded

Static routes   Can be manually entered by a network administrator into a router's routing table

STDL   A vendor independent transaction definition language used in transaction processing. A client access the transaction processing monitor via STDL

store-and-forward messaging   Technology in which messages are sent, received, replied to, and delivered in discrete steps performed in a disjointed fashion over a period of time. This series of events is sometimes also described as an asynchronous messaging system

store-and-forward switches   Read the entire frame into a shared memory area in the switch. The contents of the transmitted frame check sequence field is read and compared to the locally recalculated frame check sequence. Store-and-forward switching is slower than cut-through switching but does not forward bad frames

structured programming   A method of organizing a computer program as a series of hierarchical modules, each having a single entry and exit point. Processing within a module takes place in a step by step manner without unconditional branches (such as GOTO statements) to higher levels within the module

structured query language   See SQL

stub function   The local link to the remote procedure in a remote procedure call environment

stubs   Client and server programs that wish to use the RPC service simply issue program calls for that service via specialized calls to the RPC mechanism known as stubs

suballocation blocks   Disk block suballocation is a process aimed at optimizing the use of disk space for file storage. By dividing all disk allocation blocks into 512 byte (.5KB) suballocation blocks, multiple files are allowed to occupy single disk al-

location blocks, and disk storage efficiency is maximized

Subnet   Provides a third layer of organization or hierarchy between the existing network ID and the existing host ID

Subnet mask   By applying a 32 bit subnet mask to a Class B IP address, a portion of the bits that comprise the host ID can be reserved for denoting subnetworks, with the remaining bits being reserved for host IDs per sub-network

sub-network access protocol   See SNAP

sub-networking   Allows organizations issued an IP address with a single network ID to use a portion of their host ID address field to provide multiple sub-network IDs to implement internetworking

subroutines   Code modules that perform general processing. Subroutines can be nested so that one subroutine calls another subroutine. By dividing frequently used code segments into subroutines, a programmer can greatly reduce code repetition within a structured program

summarization   Reserved to describe those circumstances in which subnet addresses have been rolled up all the way to the major network prefix as assigned by the Internet authorities

supernetting   CIDR is also sometimes referred to as supernetting

superuser account   See root

swapper   See Scheduler

swapping   Swapping implies that entire processes are swapped in and out of physical memory and onto the swap space partition of one or more disk drives

switched LAN network architectures   Depend on wiring centers called LAN switches or switching hubs that offer all attached workstations access to a switching matrix that provides point-to-point, rather than shared, connections between any two ports

switching hub   Able to create connections, or switch, between any two attached Ethernet devices on a packet by packet basis in as little as 40 milliseconds. The "one-at-a-time" broadcast limitation previously associated with shared media Ethernet is overcome with an Ethernet switch

symmetrical multiprocessing   See SMP

synchronous bandwidth allocation   See SBA

synchronous communication   The most common approach taken in middleware solutions. In this scenario, the client application issues a request to the server application. While waiting on a reply to the request, the client is prevented from performing other application tasks

Synchronous Data Link Control   See SDLC

synchronous frames   In FDDI, frames transmitted in a continuous stream are known as synchronous frames and are prioritized according to a methodology known as synchronous bandwidth allocation or SBA, which assigns fixed amounts of bandwidth to given stations

synchronous I/O   Synchronous I/O or inter-process communication refers to the situation when a client application spawns a thread for information or processing and waits for the results of that thread before continuing with the execution of the client application. Sometimes also referred to as connection-oriented communication

systems administration   Focuses on the management of client and server computers and the operating systems and network operating systems that allow the client and server computers to communicate

Systems Network Architecture   See SNA

tape changers   Required in order to swap tapes into/out of backup devices for multi-Gigabyte backup sessions

TAPI   TAPI or Telephony API is a computer telephony integration API that was jointly developed and sponsored by Intel and Microsoft

TCP   TCP or Transmission Control Protocol is a transport layer protocol that provides connection-oriented, reliable transmission for upper layer application programs or utilities

TCP   Transmission control protocol. Connection oriented transport layer protocol whose 3 way handshake for connection setup is vulnerable to attack

TCP/IP   TCP/IP (Transmission Control Protocol/Internet Protocol) is the term generally used to refer to an entire suite of protocols used to provide communication on a variety of layers between widely distributed different types of computers. Strictly speaking, TCP and IP are just two

of the protocols contained within the family of protocols more properly known as the Internet Suite of Protocols

TCP/IP   TCP/IP (Transmission Control Protocol/Internet Protocol) just two of many of the protocols included in the Internet Suite of Protocols. Also used as a name for the entire suite of associated protocols and utilities

TCP/IP encapsulation   Each non-routable SNA SDLC frame is "stuffed" into an IP "envelope" for transport across the network and processing by routers supporting TCP/IP internetworking protocol

TDMA   Time Division Multiple Access - TDMA achieves more than one conversation per frequency by assigning timeslots to individual conversations. Ten timeslots per frequency are often assigned, with a given cellular device transmitting its digitized voice only during its assigned timeslot

TDP   An alternative two-way messaging architecture is proposed by the PCIA (Personal Communicator Industry Association). Rather than building on existing IP-based networks as the CDPD/LSM architecture did, the TDP (Telocator Data Protocol) architecture is actually a suite of protocols defining an end-to-end system for two-way messaging to and from paging devices

technical support   The third major usage of remote computing is for technical support organizations which must be able to dial-in to client systems with the ability to appear as a local workstation, or take control of those workstations, in order to diagnose and correct problems remotely

telecommuting   Telecommuting, or more simply, working from home with all the information resources of the office LAN at one's fingertips, is often referred to as SOHO, or Small Office Home Office

telephony API   See TAPI

telephony services API   See TSAPI

Telnet   A terminal access API that allows remote terminals to connect to hosts running Telnetd (the Telnet server program). If the remote terminal accessing the Telnet server is not truly a "dumb" terminal, then terminal emulation software must be executed to make it appear to be just a "dumb" terminal to the Telnet server host

Telnet negotiation   Because Telnet must be able to operate with a variety of terminal types, it contains an adaptive negotiation mechanism known as Telnet negotiation, which allows Telnet to establish sessions assuming very basic functionality known as the Network Virtual Terminal, and progressively negotiate those more advanced terminal features that must be supported for the particular terminal and application in question

telocator data protocol   See TDP

TFTP   TFTP, or Trivial File Transfer Protocol, was designed to be a simpler and less memory intensive alternative to FTP. TFTP uses UDP rather than TCP as its transport layer protocol

threads   In electronic meeting support software, specific discussion topics on which participants are welcome to comment are generally referred to as threads

threats   Processes or people that pose a potential danger to identified assets

Three way handshake   TCP vulnerability that can be exploited for denial of service or land attacks

ticket   In Kerberos, an encrypted ticket is issued for each server to client session and is valid only for a pre-set amount of time

ticket-granting ticket   Users are first authenticated by the Kerberos Authentication server that consults its database and grants a ticket for the valid user to communicate with the ticket granting server (TGS). This ticket is known as a ticket-granting ticket

time bombs   Viruses that are triggered by the passing of a certain date or time

Time division multiple access   See TDMA

time synchronous authentication   With time synchronous authentication, due to the time synchronization, the server authentication unit should have the same current random authentication number as the one transmitted from the remote client

Time Synchronous Token Authentication   A token authentication process in which no challenge is sent since both the SecureID card and the server are time synchronized, so only the displayed one-time session key is transmitted

timed updates   A dial-up router update mechanism in which updates are performed at regular predetermined intervals

timing limitation   The second SNA characteristic that can cause problems when run over a shared LAN backbone is that SNA has timing limitations for transmission duration between SNA hosts and end-user devices. Thus on wide area, internetworked LANs over shared network media, SNA sessions can "time-out", effectively terminating the session

token   In a token passing access methodology, a specific packet (24 bits) of data is known as a token

token authentication   All token authentication systems include server components linked to the communications server, and client components which are used with the remote access clients. Physically, the token authentication device employed at the remote client location may be a hand-held device resembling a calculator, a floppy disk, or an in-line device linked to either the remote client's serial or parallel port

Token authentication   Provides one-time-use session passwords that are authenticated by associated server software

token passing   An access methodology that ensures that each PC User has 100% of the network channel available for data requests and transfers by insisting that no PC accesses the network without first possessing a specific packet (24 bits) of data known as a token

token response authentication   Begins when the transmitted challenge response is received by the authentication server and compared to the expected challenge response number generated at the server. If they match, the user is authenticated and allowed access to network attached resources

top down model   A graphical representation of the top down approach Insisting that a top-down approach to network analysis and design is undertaken should ensure that the network design implemented will meet the business needs and objectives that motivated the design in the first place

total cost of ownership   There are three major expense categories associated with the deployment of distributed client applications platforms: initial implementation costs, user training costs, and administration and maintenance costs. Collectively these costs are referred to as total cost of ownership

TPM   Transaction processing requires careful monitoring to ensure that all, and not just some, postings related to a particular business transaction are successfully completed. This monitoring of transaction posting is done by a specialized type of software known as TP(Transaction Posting) Monitors

TP-PMD   The official ANSI standard for CDDI is known as TP-PMD (Twisted Pair-Physical Media Dependent)

trailer   Information added to the back of data

transaction process monitor   See TPM

translating bridges   A special type of bridge which includes a format converter can bridge between Ethernet and Token Ring. These special bridges may also be called multi-protocol bridges or translating bridges

Transmission Control Protocol   TCP or Transmission Control Protocol is a transport layer protocol that provides connection-oriented, reliable transmission for upper layer application programs or utilities. This reliability is assured through the additional fields contained within the TCP header

Transmission Control Protocol/Internet Protocol   See TCP/IP

transparent   Bridges are passive or transparent devices, receiving every frame broadcast on a given LAN. Bridges are known as transparent due to their ability to only process data link layer addresses while transparently forwarding any variety of upper layer protocols safely embedded within the data field of the datalink layer frame

transparent bridge   Bridges that connect LANs of similar data link format are known as transparent bridges

transport driver interface   A protocol specification that provides a layer of transparency between session layer redirectors and transport layer protocols. This allows session layer redirector software to be written independently of the particular transport layer software with which the redirector software will need to communicate

transport layer   The transport layer protocols are responsible for providing reliability for the end-to-end network layer connections. Transport layer protocols provide end-to-end error recovery and

flow control and mechanisms for sequentially organizing multiple network layer packets into a coherent message

Transport Mode ESP   In Secure IP, transport mode ESP is used to encrypt the data carried by the IP packet

tree   An active directory tree consists of multiple domains arranged in a hierarchical manner referred to as a tree

triggered updates   To reduce slow convergence in RIP based router networks, triggered updates allow routers to immediately broadcast routing table updates regarding failed links rather than having to wait for the next 30-sec.periodic update

triggered updates   A dial-up router update mechanism in which updates are performed whenever a certain programmable event, such as a change in available services, occurs

trivial file transfer protocol   See TFTP

trojan horse   The actual virus is hidden inside an otherwise benign program and delivered to the target system or network to be infected

trust   To accomplish access to network resources beyond local domains without the need to have all user account and security information for every domain on all domain controllers, domains interact in a relationship known as trust

trust relationship   As long as trust relationships have been established between the Windows NT primary domain controllers in a multi-domain environment, then authorized users within those domains can access the resources on the multiple domains without the need to have user accounts previously established on all domains

trusted gateway   In a trusted gateway, certain applications are identified as trusted and are able to bypass the application gateway entirely and are able to establish connections directly rather than be executed by proxy

trusted node   Authorization security software can be either server-based, also known as brokered authorization, or workstation-based, also referred to as trusted node

TSAPI   TSAPI or Telephony Services API is a computer telephony integration API that was jointly developed and sponsored by Novell and AT&T

TTY   The acronym TTY refers to terminals in general but actually stands for teletypewriter and is a holdover from the days before terminals had video monitors

Tunnel Mode ESP In Secure IP, Tunnel Mode ESP encrypts the entire IP packet including its own header. This mode is effective at countering network analyzers or sniffers from capturing IP address information

tunneling protocols To provide virtual private networking capabilities using the Internet as an enterprise network backbone, specialized tunneling protocols needed to be developed that could establish private, secure channels between connected systems

turnkey solutions A network faxing architecture in that specially made LAN-attached devices which are preconfigured with both software and all necessary FAX hardware are employed

two-way messaging Sometimes referred to as enhanced paging. Allows short text messages to be transmitted between relatively inexpensive transmission devices such as PDAs (Personal Digital Assistants) and alphanumeric pagers

UDP User Datagram Protocol is used to provide unreliable, connectionless messaging services for applications

UNI UNI or User-Network Interface defines standards for interoperability between end-user equipment and ATM equipment and networks. These standards are well defined and equipment is fairly widely available

unified messaging Perhaps the most interesting for the LAN-based user, unified messaging, also known as the Universal In-Box will allow voice mail, e-mail, faxes, and pager messages all to be displayed on a single graphical screen. Messages can then be forwarded, deleted, or replied to easily in point and click fashion. Waiting calls can also be displayed in the same Universal In-Box

universal client A client workstation's ability to interoperate transparently with a number of different network operating system servers without the need for additional products or configurations

universal data access An umbrella term covering Object Layering and Embedding Database services (OLE DB) and Active Data Objects (ADO)

universal inbox Universal inbox implies that users can get all of their e-mails, faxes, and voice messages in a single interface. From the universal inbox the users can read, respond, file and delete all of their messages

UNIX A large family of related operating systems that all descended from work initially done by Ken Thompson and Dennis Ritchie at Bell Laboratories in the late 1960s and early 1970s

UNIX International Created by AT&T, the owner of Bell Labs and UNIX System V, and Sun Microsystems, the leading proponent of BSD UNIX to integrate BDS functionality into System V

UNIX system kernel Fulfills requests for services from UNIX systems programs by interacting with the hardware layer and returning requested functionality to the systems programs and utilities

UNIX systems programs UNIX systems programs and utilities deliver requested functionality to users by issuing system calls to the UNIX system kernel

UnixWare UNIXWare is a full implementation of NetWare that runs over UNIX. The advantage of such an implementation is that the inherent capabilities of UNIX such as symmetrical multiprocessing are immediately available

unreliable An unreliable protocol does not require error checking and acknowledgment of error-free receipt by the destination host

unshielded twisted pair See UTP

user accounts database In Windows NT, the user accounts database is physically stored on the primary domain controller except in those cases when an individual workstation may have a need to verify specific User IDs for remote access to that workstation

User Datagram Protocol See UDP

user mode Windows NT applications are normally executed in Ring 3, known as user mode, in which they are limited to their own protected memory area. This prevents applications from writing into each other's memory space and thereby causing general protection faults and system crashes

user-network interface See UNI

UTP Twisted pair wiring consists of one or more pairs of insulated copper wire that are twisted at varying lengths, from two to twelve twists per foot, to reduce interference both between pairs and from outside sources such as electric motors and fluorescent lights. No additional shielding is added before the pairs are wrapped in the plastic covering

values Values are associated with properties and, in turn, with objects. For example, a value of Monday through Friday, 8:00 A.M. to 5:00 P.M. would be a value associated with the login time restriction property associated with a particular user or user group object

variable length subnet masking See VLSM

vector Once a NDIS driver is bound and operating, packets of a particular protocol are forwarded from the adapter card to the proper protocol stack by a layer of software known as the vector

version control software See file synchronization

vertical integration Integration of components within a single computer. The interface to the network operating system and the interface with the business application represent vertical integration

virtual device drivers See VxDs

virtual loadable modules See VLM

virtual machine A Java interpreter that allows Java bytecode to run on the system

virtual machines Some client network operating systems, such as Windows NT, have the ability to support multiple APIs and multiple different operating system sub-systems, sometimes known as virtual machines

virtual memory An operating system can often swap the content of physical memory to a special area of a hard drive. The memory content on the hard drive is known as virtual memory

virtual memory manager To allow application programs easy access to large amounts of memory despite limited physically installed memory, Windows NT uses portions of the disk drive as a swap file in order to offer up to 4GB (gigabytes) of memory to every process. That some of a process' allocated memory is physically located on a disk drive rather than in RAM is kept transparent to the process by the virtual memory manager

virtual PC Emulation technology attempts to detect as yet unknown viruses by running programs with a software emulation program known as a virtual PC

virus scanning The primary method for successful detection and removal

visual BASIC One of the most popular event-driven languages for the development of business applications. Designed for the Microsoft Windows family of operating environments, Visual BASIC provides a powerful development platform, yet is easy to program. As the name would suggest, Visual BASIC utilizes the BASIC language for the development of event handlers

VJ A protocol for compression of IP headers included with most PPP clients

VLMs Rather than remaining as a monolithic, stand-alone operating system, the requester has taken on a more flexible modular appearance. NetWare client functionality can be added or updated on an incremental basis thanks to the introduction of Virtual Loadable Modules or VLMs

VLSM Variable Length Subnet Masks, defined in 1987 as RFP1009, specified how a single network ID could have different subnet masks among its subnets

voice digitization A process by which a sample of a video signal is digitized into an 8 bit binary code

VSAM A file management system used on IBM mainframes. VSAM speeds up addess to data in files through the use of an inverted index known as a B+tree

vulnerabilities The manner or path by which threats are able to attack assets

VxDs More secure 32-bit operating systems control access to hardware and certain system services via virtual device drivers, otherwise known as VxDs

WAN Traffic Manager Services A NetWare 5 service set that controls traffic based on a WAN policy. Although WAN policies can be manually defined, NetWare 5 ships with several policies that can simply be activated. WAN policies can either be attached directly to a server or servers can be grouped into LAN areas with a WAN policy assigned to the area. In this manner all servers in the LAN area are automatically assigned the same WAN policy

WBEM Another possible standard for distributed application management is a proposed IETF standard known as web-based enterprise management (WBEM) that integrates SNMP, HTTP, and DMI (desktop management interface) into an application management architecture that can use common web browser software as its user interface

web-based enterprise management   See WBEM

what-if analysis   The value of a simulation system is its ability to predict the performance of various networking scenarios otherwise known as what-if analysis

window manager   The window manager, part of the GUI operating system, monitors the application for events. When an event occurs, the event manager starts a process to complete the code associated with the event handler for the triggered event

Windows Internet Naming Service   See WINS

Windows NT RAS   Microsoft's remote node server software for Windows NT

Windows Sockets   The Windows Sockets interprocess communications mechanism, more commonly known as WinSock is the most flexible of all of the interprocess mechanisms currently supported by Windows NT. It allows programs written to support this protocol to operate transparently over a variety of different vendors' TCP/IP protocol stacks

windows terminal   Acts as a graphical terminal for Windows applications running on a remote host. This approach is conceptually very similar to mainframe style processing. Terminals display the output of client applications running on a remote host and serve as input devices to the remote client application

WINS   Because users and their workstations are easier to remember and access by name rather than address, NT keeps track of user names and associated IP addresses with a service known as WINS (Windows Internet Name Service)

WinSock   The most flexible of all of the interprocess mechanisms currently supported by Windows NT

WinSock 2   Added to WinSock's TCP/IP functionality by allowing WinSock-compliant applications to operate transparently over IPX/SPX, Appletalk, DECnet, and OSI transport protocols

wireless bridge   Wireless bridges use spread spectrum radio transmission between LAN sites (up to 3 miles) and are primarily limited to Ethernet networks at this time

wireless WAN services   A variety of wireless services are available for use across wider geographic spans. These wireless WAN services vary in many ways including availability, applications, transmission speed, and cost

wizards   See advisory agents

workflow automation software   Allows geographically dispersed co-workers to work together on project teams as documents and information are automatically routed according to pre-programmed rules or workflow directives

workgroup   Windows NT computers, especially Windows NT Workstation clients, can alternatively belong to workgroups, rather than domains. The key difference between workgroups and domains is that in a workgroup, there is no domain controller, and therefore, each workgroup computer must maintain its own security sub-system. In a workgroup, users log into a particular computer, whereas in domains, users log into a domain

workgroup conferencing software   See electronic conferencing and meeting support

workstation trust accounts   Allow the workstation to connect to a domain by providing passthrough authentication for a Windows NT server in the domain

wrapping   The process of taking a legacy application and making its functionality and data accessible in a client/server. A new software envelope that hides the actual implementation details from the end user is developed to surround the legacy application. Wrapping can be considered the process of developing new user interfaces for existing legacy applications

X.500   As enterprise networks become more heterogeneous, comprised of network operating systems from a variety of different vendors, the need will arise for different network operating systems to share each other's directory services information. A directory services specification known as X.500 offers the potential for this directory services interoperability

X.509   An international standard for public key certificates

XDR   XDR (External Data Representation) is a presentation layer protocol responsible for formatting data in a consistent manner so that all NFS clients and servers can process it, regardless of the computing platform or operating system on which the NFS suite may be executing

XML An advanced markup language that may replace HTML as the standard for document formatting on the World Wide Web

XTACACS Extended Terminal Access Control Access System is another example of a remote access management protocol that supports three-tiered remote access management architectures

X-Windows A software solution that provides a standard graphical console for UNIX applications

Z.E.N. Works A NetWare 5 client package that allows system policies to be set that limit the administrative tasks a user can perform

zero slot LANs Refers to the fact that by using existing serial or parallel ports for network communications, zero expansion slots are occupied by network interface cards

zone The scope of coverage, or collection of domains, for which a given DNS server can resolve names is known as a DNS zone.

INDEX

880   Index